GLOBAL POLITICAL ECONOMY

GLOBAL POLITICAL ECONOMY

1ST EDITION

Edited by

NICOLA PHILLIPS

OXFORD

UNIVERSITY PRESS

Great Clarendon Street, Oxford, OX2 6DP,
United Kingdom

Oxford University Press is a department of the University of Oxford.
It furthers the University's objective of excellence in research, scholarship,
and education by publishing worldwide. Oxford is a registered trade mark of
Oxford University Press in the UK and in certain other countries

Published in the United States of America by Oxford University Press
198 Madison Avenue, New York, NY 10016, United States of America

British Library Cataloguing in Publication Data
Data available

Library of Congress Control Number: 2022950250

ISBN 978–0–19–885322–0

Printed in the UK by
Bell & Bain Ltd., Glasgow

Dedicated to Steve, with love

Preface

Praise for *Global Political Economy*

'Provoking and highly readable: this book is just what every student and teacher of Global Political Economy needs. *Global Political Economy* offers a detailed and accessible understanding of the theoretical and empirical foundations of the field, while also showing the reader how such foundations can be ripped up, debated, and revisited. I wish I had this book when I was a student.'

Sophie Harman, Professor of International Politics, Queen Mary University of London

'We have here a fresh and innovative approach to the subject of Global Political Economy. The chapters reflect the field in its full scale and complexity, but do so with admirable clarity and exuberant writing. Phillips has brought together a genuinely diverse group of scholars who have taken to heart the goals of their editor to bring a fascinating subject to life in a compelling and authoritative manner. This volume is the new benchmark.'

Professor Randall Germain, Professor, Department of Political Science, Carleton University, Ottawa, Canada

'*Global Political Economy* edited by Nicola Phillips is an impressive study and fills an important gap in the literature. The thematic approach based on the contributions of well-known scholars of political economy will be particularly useful to students. I certainly plan to use it as the principal text in my core course on Global Political Economy and would strongly recommend it to colleagues who teach similar courses.'

Ziya Öniş, Professor of International Political Economy, Koç University, Istanbul, Turkey

'Innovative, inspiring, and informative in equal measure, this carefully crafted and thought-provoking textbook provides a wonderful introduction—and warm welcome—to the fascinating field of Global Political Economy. Highly engaging and accessible, it stands as an invaluable resource for students and educators alike.'

Elizabeth Thurbon, Scientia Associate Professor of International Political Economy, UNSW Sydney

'This volume provides a great multi-disciplinary approach to the study of global political economy. The various viewpoints will help students navigate the most pressing issues in today's world.'

Dr Patrick Shea, Senior Lecturer in International Relations and Global Governance, University of Glasgow, UK

'With an accessible dissection of pertinent debates in Global Political Economy, this book successfully manages to bridge diverse GPE traditions, including both traditional frameworks and critical-reflective perspectives. Through case studies and Roundtable debates, the book inspires theoretically informed discussions while providing insight into concrete policy problems.'

Dr Matthew Eagleton-Pierce, Reader (Associate Professor) in International Political Economy, SOAS University of London, UK

Brief Contents

Part 1: The Foundations

Part 2: Debating GPE

Detailed Contents

Part 1: The Foundations

Part 2: Debating GPE

Acknowledgements

I'll say this without any trace of exaggeration: this textbook would simply never have seen the light of day were it not for the quite remarkable editorial and project management skills of Dr Danielle Cohen.

Danielle and I became acquainted when she worked as the editorial assistant on a different textbook, also published by OUP and to which I contributed a chapter. On the basis of that experience, right at the start of conversations with OUP about this book I had no hesitation in indicating to my commissioning editor that Danielle was the person I wanted to work with, and I was over the moon when she agreed.

A brilliant teacher and scholar, and a wonderful person, Danielle has brought to this project rigour, patience, humour and fun, quite frightening levels of organizational discipline, professionalism, friendship and solidarity, pragmatism, a keen eye for detail, acute insight, inspiring feedback, enthusiasm and optimism, and impressive editorial skill.

I offer her my deep professional admiration and sincere personal thanks for all these things, and for the companionship she has offered over the several Covid-stricken years that this project has taken to bring to fruition.

I have also been privileged to work with the very best of commissioning editors—Sarah Iles and, for a time while Sarah was on leave, Katie Staal. I thank Sarah for approaching me in the first place with that timeless 'I've got an idea I'd like to discuss with you' line, and for her astute advice and her infectious enthusiasm as the thinking and planning took shape about what this volume could look like, what it could do for students and for the field, and who might be involved in it. Her observations, input, and suggestions throughout the process have been marked by a real generosity and have been uniformly spot-on. I'm deeply grateful.

Finally, I would like to acknowledge all the colleagues who have contributed to this book as authors. I have known some of them for many years; others I contacted out of the blue on the basis of what I had heard about them or the work I read as I considered who would be the best people to ask to contribute. I have enjoyed the pleasure of collaborating with everyone involved. I also thank them all for their patience and ongoing commitment as this project unfolded, especially through the Covid years.

Nicola Phillips

The authors of Chapter 10 are very grateful for research assistance from L. Guillermo Woo-Mora and Salome Ecker.

Guide to Using This Book

Outlined here are the key features and online resources included in the book to ensure that you understand the topics, big questions, debates, theories, and methods that animate GPE. Access the online resources at **www.oup.com/he/phillips-gpe1e**.

Consolidate Your Understanding

Multiple choice questions at the end of each section test your knowledge and understanding as you progress through the chapters. Each chapter's **Flashcard Glossary** available on the online resources offers further ways to test your knowledge of both the specific and the broader issues associated with the topic.

Explore Key Debates and Arguments

Each chapter in Part II ends with a Roundtable where you can gain an insight into how scholars in the field engage with one another, how they debate with one another over the big questions, and how different perspectives can be brought to bear on the issues that interest us.

Apply Theory to Practice

Case studies drawn from around the world, representing a wide range of issues, help you understand how the global political economy works, and the impact of key processes and dynamics. Broadcast quality **videos** curated from news clips of real-world events help demonstrate global political economy in action.

Resources for Lecturers

 The online resources for lecturers are available at: **www.oup.com/he/phillips-gpe1e**

Global Political Economy offers a complete package of information and resources to support your teaching of international political economy.

Adopting lecturers can access the following online resources:

- Lecturer Multiple-Choice Questions to be used in assessment;
- Seminar activities to help embed the Roundtable discussions in your teaching;
- Customizable PowerPoint® slides, arranged by chapter, for use in lectures or as hand-outs to support efficient, effective teaching preparation.

About the Contributors

Seye Abimbola is an Associate Professor in the School of Public Health at the University of Sydney (Australia) and the 2020–22 Prince Claus Chair on Justice in Global Health Research at Utrecht University (Netherlands).

Matthew Alford is Senior Lecturer at Alliance Manchester Business School, University of Manchester (UK).

Mark Anner is Professor of Labor and Employment Relations, and Political Science at the Pennsylvania State University (USA).

Oliver Bakewell is Reader in Migration Studies at the Global Development Institute, University of Manchester (UK).

Tim Bartley is Professor of Sociology at Washington University in St. Louis (USA).

Jacqueline Best is a Full Professor in the School of Political Studies at the University of Ottawa (Canada).

Benjamin J. Cohen is Distinguished Professor Emeritus and was previously Louis G. Lancaster Professor of International Political Economy at the University of California, Santa Barbara (USA).

Scarlett Cornelissen is Professor of Political Science at Stellenbosch University (South Africa).

Giselle Datz is an Associate Professor in the Government and International Affairs Program at the School of Public and International Affairs, Virginia Tech (USA).

Surya Deva is a Professor at the Macquarie Law School (Australia) and Director of the Centre for Environmental Law.

Asif Efrat is an Associate Professor at the Lauder School of Government, Diplomacy and Strategy, Reichman University (Israel).

Juanita Elias is Professor in International Political Economy at the University of Warwick (UK).

Lorraine Elliott is Professor Emerita in the Department of International Relations, College of Asia and the Pacific, at the Australian National University.

Ariadna Estévez is a Professor at the Centre for Research on North America at the National Autonomous University of Mexico.

Peter Ferguson is Senior Lecturer in Politics and International Relations at Deakin University (Australia).

Adam J. Ferhani is an ESRC Postdoctoral Fellow in the Department of Politics and International Relations at the University of Sheffield (UK).

H. Richard Friman is the Eliot Fitch Professor for International Studies at Marquette University (USA).

Shane Godfrey is an Honorary Research Associate with the Labour, Development and Governance Research Institute, University of Cape Town (South Africa).

Samanthi J. Gunawardana is Senior Lecturer in Gender and Development in the School of Social Science at Monash University and a member of the Monash Gender, Peace, and Security Centre (Australia).

Erin Hannah is Associate Professor and Chair of the Department of Political Science at King's University College at the University of Western Ontario (Canada).

Andrew Hurrell is Montague Burton Emeritus Professor of International Relations at Oxford University (UK) and an Einstein Visiting Fellow in Berlin (Germany).

Eka Ikpe is a Reader in Development Economics in Africa and Director of the African Leadership Centre, King's College London (UK).

Anja P. Jakobi is Head of the Institute of International Relations at the TU Braunschweig (Germany).

Xianbai Ji is an Associate Professor in the School of International Studies, Renmin University (China).

Tana Johnson is Associate Professor of Public Affairs and Political Science at the University of Wisconsin-Madison (USA).

Richard Jolly is Honorary Professor and Research Associate of the Institute of Development Studies, University of Sussex (UK).

Gabriele Koehler is UNRISD Senior Research Associate (Germany).

Mustafa Kutlay is Lecturer in Comparative Politics at City, University of London (UK).

Jane Lister is Research Associate at the Sauder School of Business, University of British Columbia (Canada).

Kate Macdonald is Associate Professor of Political Science at the University of Melbourne (Australia).

Ana Carolina Evangelista Mauad is an Assistant Professor of International Relations at Pontificia Universidad Javeriana Bogotá (Colombia).

Manuela Moschella is Associate Professor of International Political Economy, Scuola Superiore Normale (Italy).

Craig N. Murphy is the Betty Freyhof Johnson '44 Professor of Political Science at Wellesley College (USA).

Eduardo Ortiz-Juarez is a Lecturer in Development Economics in the Department of International Development at King's College London (UK).

Lena Partzsch is Professor of Comparative Politics with a focus on Environmental and Climate Politics at Otto Suhr Institute, Freie Universitaet Berlin (Germany).

Nicola Phillips is a Professor of Political Economy and the Provost at the University of Melbourne (Australia).

Nicola Piper is British Academy Global Professor Fellow at Queen Mary University of London's School of Law (UK) and Professor of International Migration at the University of Sydney (Australia).

Evgeny Postnikov is Senior Lecturer in International Relations at the School of Social and Political Sciences, University of Melbourne (Australia).

John Ravenhill is Chair of the Department of Political Science at the University of Waterloo (Canada).

Lena Rethel is Professor of International Political Economy at the University of Warwick (UK).

Stuart Rosewarne is an Associate Professor in the Department of Political Economy, University of Sydney (Australia).

Simon Rushton is Professor of International Politics at The University of Sheffield (UK).

James Scott is Senior Lecturer in International Politics in the Department of Political Economy at King's College London (UK).

Leonard Seabrooke is Professor of International Political Economy and Economic Sociology in the Department of Organization at the Copenhagen Business School (Denmark).

Susan K. Sell is a Professor in the School of Regulation and Global Governance, College of Asia and the Pacific, at the Australian National University.

Quinn Slobodian is Marion Butler McLean Professor of the History of Ideas at Wellesley College (USA).

Hayley Stevenson is Associate Professor of International Relations at Universidad Torcuato Di Tella (Argentina).

Andy Sumner is Professor of International Development in the Department of International Development at King's College London (UK).

Hiroko TAKEDA is Professor of Political Analysis, Graduate School of Law, Nagoya University (Japan).

Cemal Burak Tansel is Senior Lecturer in International Political Economy and Politics of Global Development at Newcastle University (UK).

Jorge Tigno is Professor of Political Science at the University of the Philippines.

Hongying Wang is Associate Professor of Political Science at the University of Waterloo and the Balsillie School of International Affairs (Canada).

Jue Wang is Assistant Professor of Chinese Economy and International Political Economy at Leiden University (Netherlands).

Thomas G. Weiss is Presidential Professor of Political Science and Director Emeritus of the Ralph Bunche Institute for International Studies at the CUNY Graduate Center (USA).

Lay Hwee Yeo is Adjunct Senior Fellow in the S. Rajaratnam School of International Studies, Nanyang Technological University (Singapore).

Kevin L. Young is Associate Professor in the Department of Economics at the University of Massachusetts Amherst (USA).

Arief Yusuf is Professor of Economics at Padjadjaran University (Indonesia).

GLOBAL POLITICAL ECONOMY

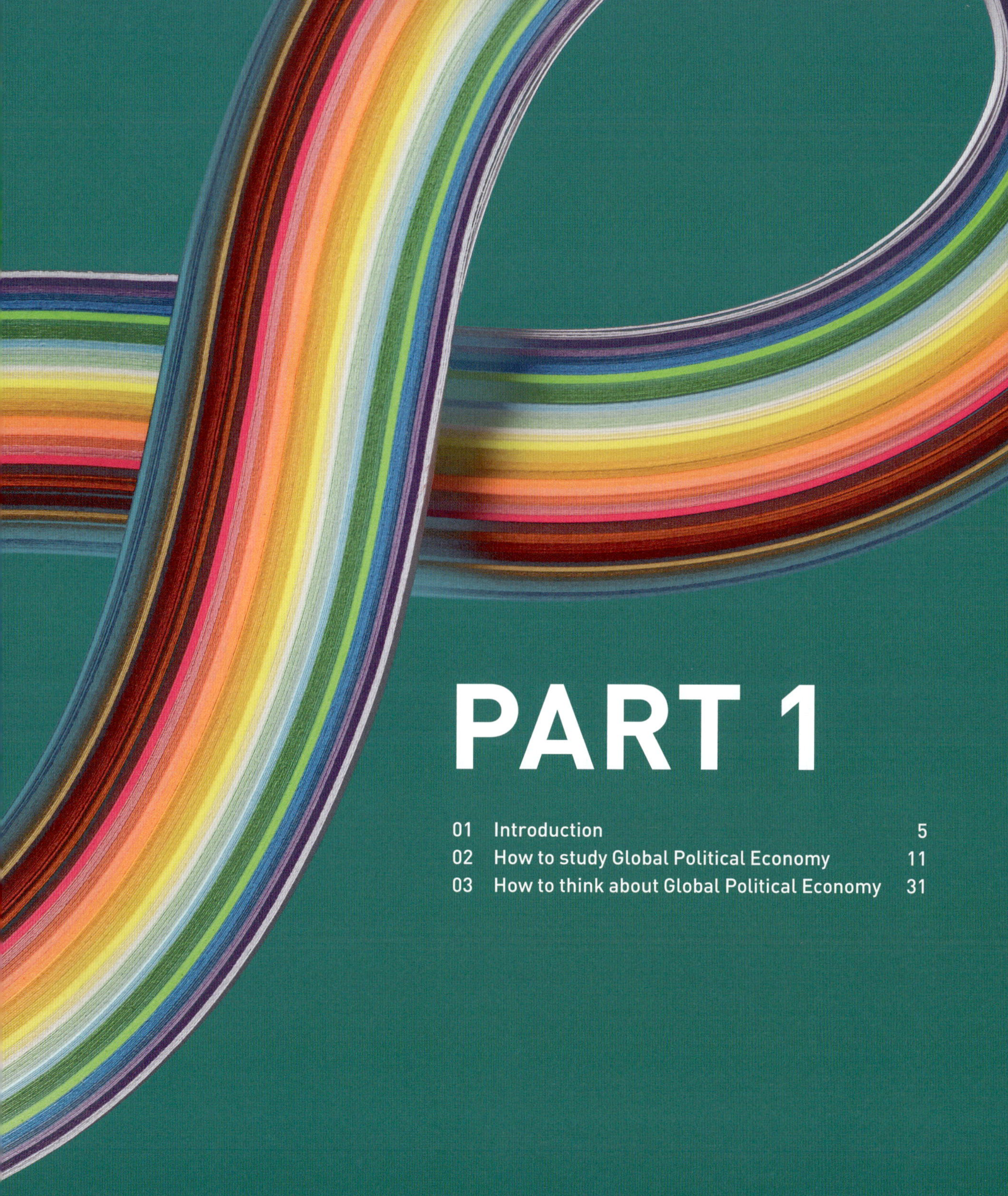

PART 1

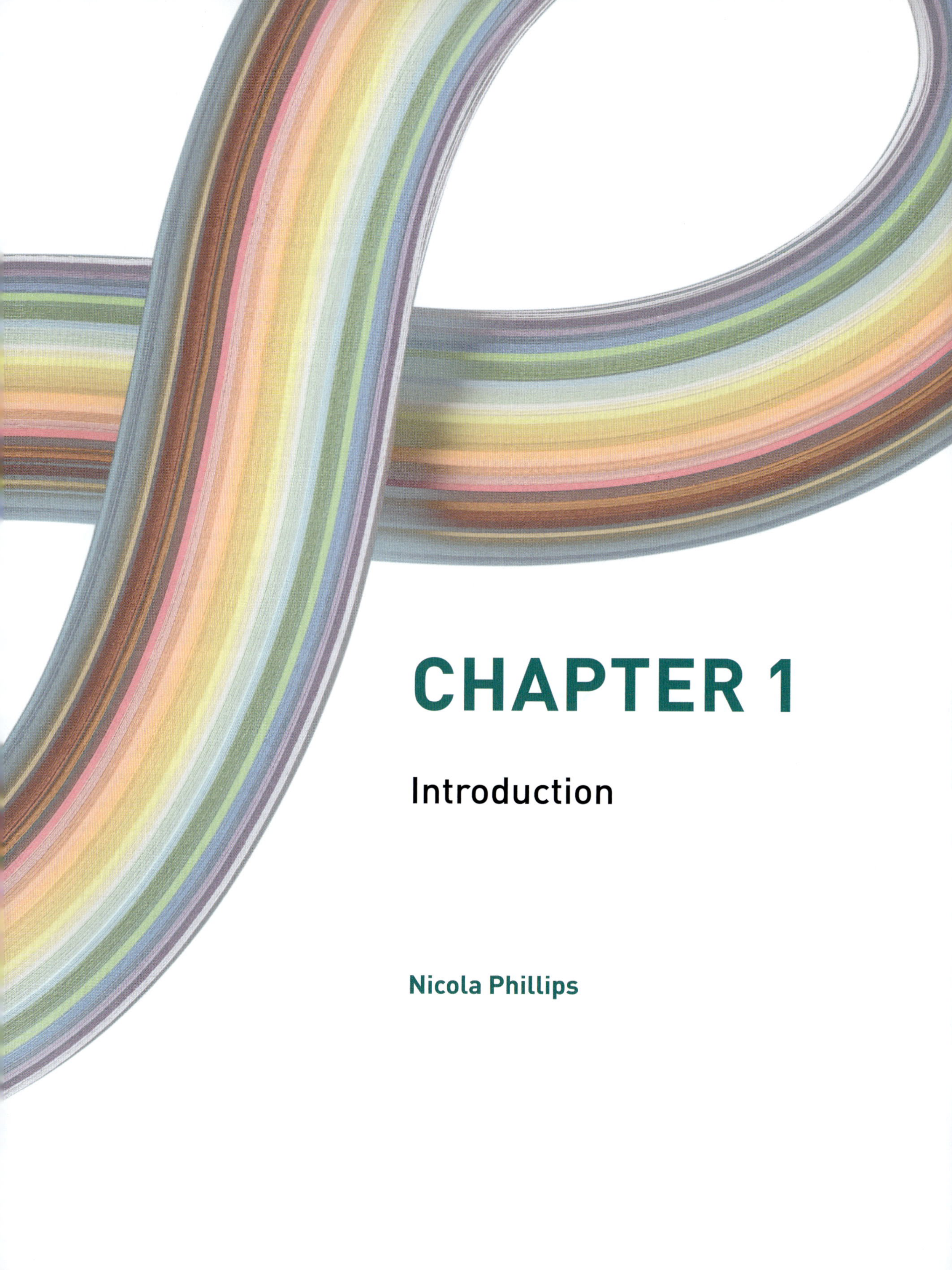

CHAPTER 1

Introduction

Nicola Phillips

Welcome to the fascinating world of Global Political Economy. Some of you may already be acquainted with our field (which from now on we will call GPE); others of you may be coming to GPE, and perhaps even the social sciences, for the very first time. Either way, you have made a great choice!

GPE is a marvellously rich, varied, and relevant subject for you to study. You will see its connections immediately to your own everyday life and the world we all live in together. It will stretch you intellectually in thinking about difficult questions, in understanding rich and often complex bodies of theory, and in being able to work with different approaches and methods to explore and analyse the subject matter that you will encounter in the field.

It is a wonderful place for people with open minds and curiosity, who want to be challenged and provoked into deeper thinking. It offers a set of debates which will stimulate you and often unsettle the assumptions you make about the world, and which will encourage you to understand how other people see the world. It doesn't contain easy answers, and you will need to push yourself to engage properly with it. But it is worth every bit of the effort.

We aim, with this textbook, to help you to dive into GPE and start to uncover for yourself its breadth, diversity, and interest. We will delve in the chapters of **Part I** into some of the foundations of GPE, with interesting discussions about the contours of the field, the big questions about how to go about studying GPE, and an introduction to the theories that you need to know. You can then stand on these foundations as you move into **Part II** of the book, which covers a wide array of some of the most important and interesting topics in contemporary GPE.

But before that, let's look briefly at the 'what, where, and who' of GPE, and then explore how this textbook is organized and how you can use it in your studies.

1.1 What is GPE?

GPE is a contemporary field of study which first took shape in the 1960s and 1970s, most often going under the label 'International Political Economy' (IPE). We will come back to the difference between IPE and GPE in just a second. Clearly, though, regardless of the adjective in front, it is a field which is rooted in the tradition of political economy. Those of you who have some familiarity with GPE might have come across the contention that political economy is about the interaction between politics and economics, or indeed that political economy is the study of the politics of economic relations. But, as Leonard Seabrooke and Kevin Young tell us (**see Section 2.2**), this definition doesn't capture the core of GPE, in the sense that you can't separate something called 'politics' and something called 'the economy'. Instead, GPE, at its core, is the study of the forms of power—economic, political, material, and social—which shape how the world operates.

So, what about the 'global' prefix? As noted, the field that has often come to be called GPE started out in its contemporary form as 'International Political Economy'. IPE, at least in the dominant form it took in the United States, was closely associated with the discipline of International Relations (IR), and many of the key scholars associated with the emerging field of IPE would identify themselves as scholars of IR. It follows, then, that many of the issues that most preoccupied them concerned relationships between national states—the 'inter-national'.

Over time, this dominant focus came to be challenged by those who argued that the field of IPE was, and needed to be, much more encompassing if it were truly to get to grips with the nature of power in the world. It needed to incorporate attention to a wide range of actors which were not states, and a wide array of processes which transcended the interplay between national states or governments. IPE evolved in this direction, becoming the broader and much richer field that we see today. But many people remained dissatisfied with 'international' as the adjective describing the field, and opted instead for the name GPE in order to capture this expanded scope of interest (**see Section 1.2**). We use GPE here as our preference, for these reasons.

Don't get too hung up on this point, though. Some people prefer IPE, some GPE, and some use them essentially interchangeably. Their preference often reflects the scholarly traditions in which they are working, but GPE and IPE are both often used and well recognized as names for this field of study, and you will encounter both names in your further reading.

These comments point to what, I expect, will strike you most about GPE, which is its breadth and scale. It is often remarked that it can feel hard to touch the sides of GPE, such is the richness and variety of its subject matter, the wide variety of people who cluster under its banner, and the diversity of theories, methods, and approaches. This is undoubtedly part of its charm and why you will find it so fascinating. But it would be a mistake to think that GPE is incoherent, or that it lacks a unifying core. The chapters in **Part I** of the book explore this point in more detail, and you will see GPE's central themes of power running through all of the chapters in **Part II**.

1.2 Where is GPE?

Despite their names, IPE and GPE have both—entirely fairly—been criticized for their lack of a 'global' viewpoint. This is meant in two senses. First, for a long time, most of the attention in IPE and GPE has been focused on the Anglo-American world, alongside parts of East Asia. This has meant that the topics of interest have been primarily about the processes and issues that most affect those parts of the world—and which emerge from and are shaped most by them—with the rest of the world being more of an afterthought.

Second, IPE and GPE have evolved as fields dominated by scholars from North America, the United Kingdom (UK), and Australia, with rather little room afforded for scholars in other parts of the world. This led to discomfort among many scholars with the specifically 'Western' character of IPE/GPE, and generated calls for much greater engagement with perspectives from people working in other parts of the world which would both enrich the field and challenge many of its core assumptions, premises, and interests.

It remains true that the majority of people who call themselves scholars of GPE are working in universities in North America, the UK, and Australia. But this is changing rapidly, and the calls for more engagement are being heeded. One of the aims of this textbook is to make a real contribution to this project of GPE as a genuinely 'global' field of study. You will see from the list of authors (**see About the Contributors**) that they have been drawn from many different parts of the world and diverse national identities, whether in relation to where they have lived, where they were educated, and/or where they now work as academics.

The reasons for this are perhaps obvious. Understandings of power are always going to be different when developed from the vantage point of the most powerful countries in the world, and often by the most privileged people within them, than if they emerge from the less powerful, or even powerless. In the chapters of this book, you'll be invited to reflect on the difference in thinking about global governance from the perspective of the global 'governors' compared with the globally 'governed', for instance, or about inequality from the perspective of rich countries as opposed to poorer and more marginalized ones, or about globalization through the lens of Asian development models rather than neoliberal models in North America or Europe.

While the value of such 'global' perspectives may seem intuitively quite clear to you already, it is worth reflecting on these issues carefully as you read this volume. Ask yourselves: what value is added in a traditionally Anglo-centric field by greater engagement between scholars from different parts of the world, with varied experiences and perspectives, and a greater array of intellectual traditions and normative frameworks to draw on? What would we miss if we did not have this diversity and geographical breadth? How would our understanding of the world be affected, and impaired? How is it enriched?

We still have some way to go and much work to do before our field is and feels genuinely 'global' in its profile and substance. It is so important for the next generation of students of GPE—which, I hope, will include some of you!—to continue positioning GPE within this project, and reflect the intellectual value of much greater diversity.

1.3 Who is GPE?

The discussion just now gives us a starting point as well in thinking about the 'who' question: whose voices are heard in GPE? Whose dominate? Whose are not accommodated? And with what consequences?

We have looked already at the 'who' question through the lens of the geographical reach of the GPE community. What about academic identities? As you will see from the profile of the authors in this book (**see About the Contributors**), GPE is—and needs to be—a genuinely interdisciplinary field, reflecting the best of the spirit of political economy. It offers a home for people with backgrounds as political scientists, international relations scholars, economists, sociologists, students of business and management, students of development, anthropologists, geographers, and many more. The point is that these people are brought together around the core themes in GPE which represent shared interests. And one of the hallmarks of GPE, at its best, is the way that different disciplinary perspectives interact with one another and offer different kinds of insight into the key issues and questions.

So GPE is not just one group of scholars who all share the same academic identity or academic background, but is by definition an interdisciplinary field.

Now, let's extend the 'who' question to the voices which traditionally have been less dominant in GPE. It was a long time ago now that feminist political economists started to argue that GPE was guilty of a complete neglect of gender, and this is a point which more recently has been made forcefully in relation to race. Thanks to the huge range of scholars and scholarship making the argument—again and again—about the importance of these perspectives over the years, we now have a field of study genuinely capable of accommodating ways of seeing the world that go beyond the dominant masculinized, White, Eurocentric perspectives. We can understand power in its many dimensions, including at the intersections of gendered and racialized forms of power, and our understanding of every issue and topic encompassed by GPE is enhanced: how otherwise could we possibly think properly, for instance, about inequality, or labour and work, or globalization, or trade and finance?

Again, this might seem intuitively obvious to you, but we encourage you to keep this question at the front of your mind as you read the chapters in this book, discuss and debate the issues with your peers and teachers, and start to think deeply about the issues.

The point about diverse perspectives connects more broadly to a need for diversity in the academy, and in our field. The value of diversity for our academic field cannot be disputed: the different light that is shed on the core questions, the new questions which are posed, the challenge to dominant ways of thinking that all come from diversity—all are critical to us as individuals and as a community in unsettling our own assumptions and causing us to seek deeper understanding of how others see the world in order to understand, decide, and continually question how we ourselves see it.

This textbook is designed with the aspiration to make a real contribution to all of these dimensions of diversity in GPE, and to capture the freshening of the field that greater diversity is starting to bring about.

But there is an important final point to make. GPE is a field that brings together people right across the spectrum of 'academic age', as it were—including students. We tend to assume that the people most worth listening to are those who have been working in the field for the longest and have reached the highest levels of academic achievement. And it is of course true that they often bring wisdom, perspective, and great learning to their teaching and research. But so much fresh thinking, challenge, and dynamism comes from people at all stages of their academic careers, and any good teacher will tell you how much they learn from their students.

So, you are also part of this field of GPE, and this textbook is designed to encourage you to take your place in it, to participate in the debates, and to think deeply about your own perspectives and the arguments you want to make.

1.4 How to use this book

Everything I have said above about the 'what, where, who?' question informs the way this book has been put together and what it offers you as a resource to support your studies. First, as mentioned in **Section 1.2** and **Section 1.3**, you will notice the diversity in the line-up of contributors: you will engage through your reading and the electronic resources with people working in different parts of the world, at different stages of their academic careers, of different genders and ethnicities, and from different disciplinary backgrounds.

Second, you will notice that in all of the chapters, the authors use many examples and case studies drawn from around the world, representing a wide range of issues, so that you are able to gain fuller insight into how the global political economy works and the impact of the key processes and dynamics across different parts of the world.

And third, you will notice that the chapters in **Part II** of the book cover a wide terrain of some of the most interesting topics in GPE at the present time, and offer you an early insight into how some of the theories and methods of analysis in GPE can help you to understand the questions that we—and you—are interested in as students and scholars of GPE. The 'concept' for this textbook is that the best and most interesting way for students new to the field to approach it is through the big questions, topics, and debates which animate GPE. It is by looking at big questions, and considering different ways of exploring them, that you will most easily understand and be able to assess the value of the different theories and methods that people use in the field.

This brings us to an important point about this book, which is that it is intended to be an *introduction*. No single volume can cover the full scope of GPE, and no single chapter can give you everything there is to know about a particular topic or question. There is a reason why people spend their entire academic lives studying particular issues! So, while we hope that you will rely on this textbook systematically as you approach your studies, it can't and won't be a 'one-stop shop' for everything you need or want to know.

It is intended instead to help open the door to you, to help you survey the landscape as you walk through it, and then assist you with resources for roaming across this landscape. Each chapter offers references and suggestions for further reading, and the electronic resources offer further guidance and suggestions for you to extend your learning.

Perhaps most importantly, our aim is to invite you to become an active participant in the discussions and debates which animate the field. This is precisely the idea of the *Roundtable features* which accompany each chapter in **Part II**. Their purpose is to give you an insight into how scholars in the field engage with one another, how they debate with one another over the big questions, and how different perspectives can be brought to bear on the issues that interest us.

It is often the case that the word 'debate' is taken to mean very different—often polarized—opinions and positions being brought into confrontation with one another. But that is not always what debate means in academic circles. You will see in the Roundtables some instances where people disagree with one another, others where there is basic agreement but people have different ways of approaching the question, others where people agree but for different reasons, and so on. 'I completely disagree with you and you are wrong!' doesn't always have to be the basis for debate. Equally valid are 'Yes, I agree with you, but there is a missing element to that argument' or 'I think what you are saying is valuable, but it still doesn't provide a full answer to the question for the following reasons' or 'I think about this issue in a very different way'. This is the approach to debate which is reflected in the Roundtables, reflecting *dialogue* between scholars on issues and questions, and the interplay of different opinions, different perspectives, and different vantage points.

Each Roundtable finishes with an *'Over to you'* section, inviting you to consider where you stand and what you think. You might start off by thinking about how persuasive you find the perspectives you have read in the Roundtable—which perspective leaves the greatest impression on you, and why. Who or what do you agree and disagree with, and why? Do you feel that what you *thought* you thought is no longer what you think?(!) What do you need to read more about, and talk to more people about, so that you understand better and are able to improve your knowledge and thinking? As you advance in your studies, you will hone your skills in thinking independently about your *own* position, and how you learn from having that position tested in debate and dialogue in the classroom and outside it.

So, with that, the door is open—welcome to the world of GPE!

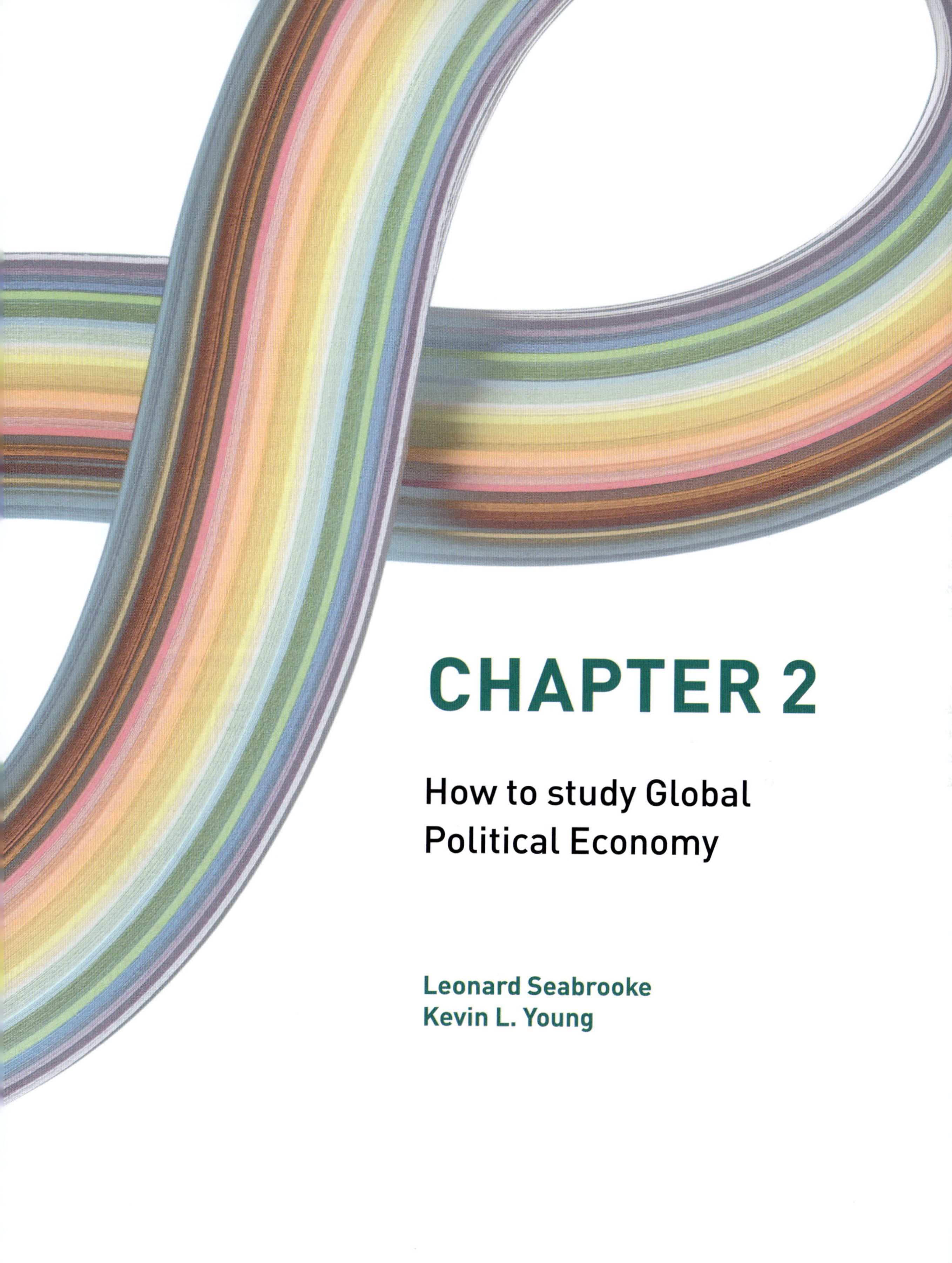

CHAPTER 2

How to study Global Political Economy

Leonard Seabrooke

Kevin L. Young

2.1 Introduction

The question of 'how to study Global Political Economy (GPE)' is a very broad one. It raises two kinds of possibilities for new students of GPE. The first approach is to study what other people have said about GPE already. What observations have they made? What are the dominant theories? Where are the controversies and debates? You gather up existing scholarship, including empirical studies, to get a vision of the field. You become literate in the main theories of GPE, as well as its defining questions and internal debates (see Blyth 2009; Payne and Phillips 2014; Pevehouse and Seabrooke 2022).

This first approach stands in contrast to a second kind of recommendation regarding the 'how to study GPE' question: how should we *go about* studying GPE? In other words, other than becoming 'literate' in GPE as it has been studied and written about to date, what kind of *orientation* should we have about the field? It is this second approach that we look at in this chapter. We walk through three arguments about how to study GPE.

First, we make the case for why the study of GPE is fundamentally exciting and wonderful. GPE is exciting because of its sheer scale and potential comprehensiveness in offering macrosocial explanations for the operation of the world. This fundamentally interdisciplinary orientation is very different from other areas of study, and it makes GPE a refreshing contrast to a lot of conventional thinking within the social sciences.

Second, we argue that the study of GPE is really hard. Yet it is hard for very specific and interesting reasons that you should be aware of as you approach your studies. In other words, far from being a reason for discouragement, understanding *why* GPE is hard can help you appreciate and value the field. We walk through the choices that must be made to produce a way of studying GPE. This includes thinking through ontological and epistemological assumptions, and it also distinguishes between the aims of theory and the choice of methods.

Our third argument is that, in order to navigate both the wonderfulness and the challenges of studying GPE, a particular conceptual device can be tremendously helpful. Specifically, we argue that it is useful to be able to identify the different 'modes' of intellectual activity that operate within GPE scholarship. In this regard, we differentiate the modes of *critique*, *advocacy*, and *discovery*. We argue that these 'modes' are useful both for being able to identify what existing scholarship is doing and, just as importantly, for identifying what you might want to be doing yourself, as a new student of GPE.

2.2 GPE is exciting and wonderful

[International Political Economy] is a vast, wide open range where anyone interested in the behavior of men and women in society [can] roam just as freely as the deer and the antelope. There [are] no fences or boundary-posts to confine the historians to history, the economists to economics. Political scientists [have] no exclusive rights to write about politics, nor sociologists to write about social relations.

Susan Strange 1984: ix

GPE is part of the broader tradition of political economy. Political economy involves the study of humans' material relationships with nature and with each other, and their enmeshment within social dynamics of power. Political economy is neither the study of politics nor the study of a separate sphere delineated as 'the economy', but is an orientation that recognizes that relationships of power are everywhere in the way the economy is organized. Global Political Economy (GPE) is a field of study which takes these considerations up with reference to global dynamics. While the distinction is admittedly a bit 'fuzzy', GPE might be differentiated from International Political Economy (IPE). IPE arguably tends to emphasize nation-states more as central actors of interest, in comparison to GPE, which operates more often at a more systems-level of analysis. The simplified version of this would be IPE that emphasizes the politics of inter-state economic relations. GPE subsumes that description but also seeks to go beyond it, for example by seeking to identify and understand dynamics that transcend inter-state relations, but which are nonetheless 'global' in orientation.

While the distinction might be somewhat challenging to make in some instances, scholarship that self-defines as GPE is arguably very expansive and at the same time yet more challenging. With a lot of IPE scholarship, the central locus of actors and agency are fixed: the central actors are states. The terrain upon which those actors inter-relate—the system, as it were—is also relatively fixed: the system is a system of states. Of course, a lot of scholarship calling itself IPE—or published in IPE journals—transcends this limitation. However, what is important to emphasize is that GPE explicitly transcends state-centrism as a matter of course (**see Box 2.1**)—as you can see across all of the chapters in this volume.

Why is GPE fundamentally exciting and wonderful? There are a few reasons. The first reason is that the scale of analysis is potentially so broad as to encompass the entire world. GPE 'leaves nothing out', and studies the world from the grandest possible scale. GPE is fundamentally about 'big structures, large processes, and huge comparisons' (Tilly 1984). Yet it is not simply social theory at a grand scale. GPE's core assumption is that politics and economics are intertwined and that this is expressed across the globe at multiple scales of analysis. The breadth of what can be included into GPE is enormous, which is exciting and wonderful, but also perhaps overwhelming unless there is a common conversation and a shared notion of standards of how inquiry should operate (Young 2021).

Box 2.1 Global, international, and transnational: what's the difference?

What does 'global' mean in GPE? Students of political economy who look at processes across borders often refer to the 'international political economy' and the 'global political economy', as well as 'transnational governance'. What do these spatial monikers signify?

'International' is between nations, and normally interpreted as cross-border behaviour that is primarily conducted between sovereign nation-states (Farrell and Newman 2016). An assumption here is that formal public authorities are in charge of decision-making and that the key drivers of change are powerful national governments and intergovernmental organizations (like the International Monetary Fund and the World Bank).

(Continued)

'Transnational' is across nations. This scholarship typically focuses on how key drivers of change are not only national governments and intergovernmental organizations, but also actors with a capacity to work with some autonomy from the 'international' (e.g., Henriksen and Seabrooke 2016). This includes multinational enterprises, non-governmental organizations, and multistakeholder organizations that combine public and private interests. This work often looks at how decision-making over matters like trading standards takes place at a transnational level, suggesting there are sources of authority that are not simply national and international.

Finally, 'global' refers to the globe, and to processes that have an impact across the world and are not isolated to particular governments or organizations. This suggests that sources of authority are multiple and the global system incorporates a mix of organizational types. Rather than formal politics between national governments, there is a broader focus on 'governance' between actors in the global system. As such, authority can be claimed by public organizations, like national governments and intergovernmental organizations, but also by multinational enterprises, elite groups and clubs, think tanks, and non-governmental organizations (e.g., Hopewell 2015).

Conceptually the range from 'international' to 'transnational' to 'global' can be thought of as a spectrum of theoretical delimitation, moving from parsimonious explanations of how governments interact to a more complex and systemic understanding of what creates change in the global political economy.

The second reason is that GPE accommodates a broad array of analytical goals. A shared concern is to analyse trends and behaviour in the global political economy. On top of this, for many GPE is also an emancipatory project where analysis can reveal how power asymmetries are replicated globally, including those related to gender, race, class, and other factors (Waylen 2006; Farrands and Worth 2005; Shields, Bruff, and Macartney 2011; Moolakkattu 2009; Murphy and Nelson 2001; R. Cox 1981). You will identify power asymmetries as a recurring theme in the chapters you will read in this volume.

A third reason why GPE is exciting and wonderful is that GPE is a scholarly field that has no fixed disciplinary boundaries, allowing scholars and students to apply insights from a range of disciplines, including political science, international relations (IR), economics, sociology, geography, and others. As such, those studying GPE have a wide range of options in developing their theoretical and methodological approaches to analyse the global political economy.

As Benjamin J. Cohen argues in **Section 3.1**, as a field of study GPE is 'vast and variegated, offering a colourful multitude of theoretical approaches and perspectives'. While GPE scholarship does often have a 'let thousand flowers bloom' approach, the community of scholars also certainly tends to focus on particular concepts and themes to avoid a situation of 'anything goes'. **Figure 2.1** presents the most frequent words used in GPE publications, with the size and centrality of the word illustrating its importance. To create this image, we took the most recent 500 journal articles and book chapters containing the topic Global Political Economy according to the Web of Science database. These came from a variety of

Figure 2.1 Wordcloud of key terms within recently published GPE scholarship

different publications—220 different journals and other types of publications, such as book chapters.

We can easily distinguish some key themes here in the meta-concepts 'power' and 'governance'—claims made by various actors to direct activity. We can also see terms such as globalization, networks, policy, and the state. This reflects a strong interest in how policy is composed at the global level, and for global issues. Policy direction is often articulated not by singular actors but through networks (see Stone 2019), often composed of different types of organizations and sometimes steered by elites working through 'clubs' (Tsingou 2015). Often these governance processes are associated with globalization: the extension of ideological, economic, military, and political power across the globe. This includes the spread of liberalism, capitalist finance and production, the extension of military range, and establishment of national governments as the common form of polity, which then created intergovernmental organizations (Mann 2012).

2.3 GPE is really hard

Learning about the operation of the global political economy is really hard. It is hard partly because political economy is a challenging area of social inquiry and carries with it a complex intellectual tradition. But there are also unique challenges to studying something which encompasses the entire world. You should be aware of these unique challenges when approaching the study of GPE. Emphasizing these challenges can help you appreciate how the study of GPE is different from the study of other things—and in particular how it is different from the kind of intellectual work and analysis in some other fields and disciplines.

It is worthwhile emphasizing that GPE is a field, and not a discipline. What's the difference? A discipline typically has an established set of theories, conceptual tools, and objects of analysis. Economics is an example of a discipline. So is sociology. Both are disciplines in the sense that there is canonical knowledge that is a prerequisite to engaging. The object of analysis is relatively clear: the economy (economics) or human social relations (sociology). Environmental studies is a field, and not a discipline, because it is oriented around a particular collection of topics. GPE has no clearly established set of methods or behavioural assumptions that are recognized as best practices across the world (Seabrooke and Young 2017).

Yet GPE is not simply hard because it doesn't have a clearly established set of theories, conceptual tools, or objects of analysis (we will help you think through some of these hurdles in **Section 2.3.1**, **Section 2.3.2**, and **Section 2.3.3**, as will Cohen in **Chapter 3**). GPE is hard for another set of reasons. We wish to emphasize that GPE is 'hard' because of a few different facets of this field of study that make it unique: scale, complexity, and the need to make theoretical and methodological choices in an interdisciplinary field. We explore these hurdles in turn.

2.3.1 Hurdle #1: Scale

The scale of GPE entails studying phenomena that either are global in nature or are related to global dynamics in some way. We do not necessarily study the 'global system' all at once in GPE, but that system is usually a referent to whatever scale of analysis is being conducted. For example, an analysis of pension reform in Kenya would make reference to global-level phenomena such as the financialization of the global economy. An analysis of local politics would make reference to the changing structure of global capitalism.

GPE is challenging to study because technically everything can potentially be situated within a 'global' framework, even if not equally so. This permits a very wide range of theorizing. For example, it is entirely possible to develop macrolevel theories that trace how the global political economy has been shaped by nomads and imperial forces (e.g., Van der Pijl 2007), just as it is possible to develop microlevel theories about how gender relationships in households reflect and impact the global political economy (e.g., Elias and Roberts 2016). Both of these arguments make sense. The challenge therefore is in identifying how a 'local' phenomenon is related to 'global' dynamics. This is not easy.

The scale of GPE means that one of the primary challenges of GPE is often relating particular 'local' phenomenon to global-level dynamics. This is not only challenging simply because of translations of scale, but rather because theories of GPE do not necessarily link to local phenomena directly. There is no one singular theory of GPE that allows you as a researcher to set local phenomena in context. Consider how this relates to other fields of inquiry. A biologist does not have this kind of problem. They can make sense of most things they study in light of evolution by natural selection. That is because they have an overarching grand framework: Darwinian evolution + Mendelian genetics. Physics has the same kind of grand framework, called the unified synthesis. For example, a particular phenomenon in physics—such as the charge of an electron—can be situated within a broader universe of entities and interactions that allow it to fit together in a meaningful way. The point is that situating a specific 'local' phenomenon in light of a larger system is not something that different disciplines and fields of inquiry do equally well. GPE has many arguments and trials for how this can take place, but this ground is far from settled around a grand overarching framework (although there are some interesting new contenders (see Oatley 2021)).

2.3.2 Hurdle #2: Complexity

The world is enormously complex. And the vaster our scale of analysis, the more complex it can get. Studying GPE entails leaning into complexity. GPE frequently deals with entities and dynamics that are themselves aggregations of other things—trade flows, investment banks, international organizations, and so on. Consider for example the kinds of issues this textbook covers, such as 'production and business' (**see Chapter 7**), 'poverty and inequality' (**see Chapter 10**), or 'global crime' (**see Chapter 11**), among the many others.

These and others are what might be called 'macrosocial' entities. They are collections of other things and are often systems of other systems. Yet they are not simple aggregations of things. These macrosocial entities we theorize about, such as 'global capitalism' or 'patriarchy' or 'the world system' at large, have their own unique properties that are arguably not fully reducible to their component parts. The systems we study within GPE also often *subsume other systems*. This makes it inherently difficult to engage in the kind of 'reductionism' that sometimes characterizes other fields of inquiry (see Winecoff 2017).

Most social systems are incredibly complex and as such are difficult to describe, explain, or predict. This does not mean that we cannot describe, explain, or predict anything at all, but it does mean that there is always going to be a diversity of phenomenon that we are unable to explain well, constantly bringing forth calls to include new variables, new concepts, new ways of thinking.

This complexity can make it difficult to study GPE because social scientists still do not understand a lot about the individual social systems they study, even when they study them one at a time. Understanding how different systems fit together thus requires the skill of *creative synthesis*. For example, in thinking about how migrant workers are exploited in parts of the global economy, we need to understand how international migration operates *and* how international business organizations utilize this labour *and* how local laws and customs regulate and produce situations for the international migrant that are used by the business. Thus, GPE at its best has an open orientation with regard to plural perspectives and different analytical strategies (see Wullweber 2019).

These two features of GPE—its scale and its complexity—mean that your scope of vision as a student must be extremely wide. Not only does it demand creative synthesis, but it also demands reading widely, so that synthesis can take place as robustly as possible. As noted in **Chapter 1**, much of this wide reading in GPE will cross some of the apparent boundaries between academic disciplines, reflecting the interdisciplinary character of the field.

Let's illustrate this point by thinking about the academic journals you will come across that produce a lot of GPE scholarship and consider the diverse areas that scholarship published within them draws on. We can start with one of the leading journals in the area of GPE scholarship, called *Review of International Political Economy* (*RIPE*), and then look at the journals where *RIPE* articles are cited most frequently in the references. Over the course of *RIPE*'s history, most citations to work published within *RIPE* have come from the journal *New Political Economy*, while the second is an economic geography journal called *Geoforum*, and the third is a development studies journal called *Third World Quarterly*. For each of these journals, we can then take *their* top citation-linked journals and represent the relationships among these journals in a network, as seen in **Figure 2.2**.

Figure 2.2 **Network of relationships between journals**

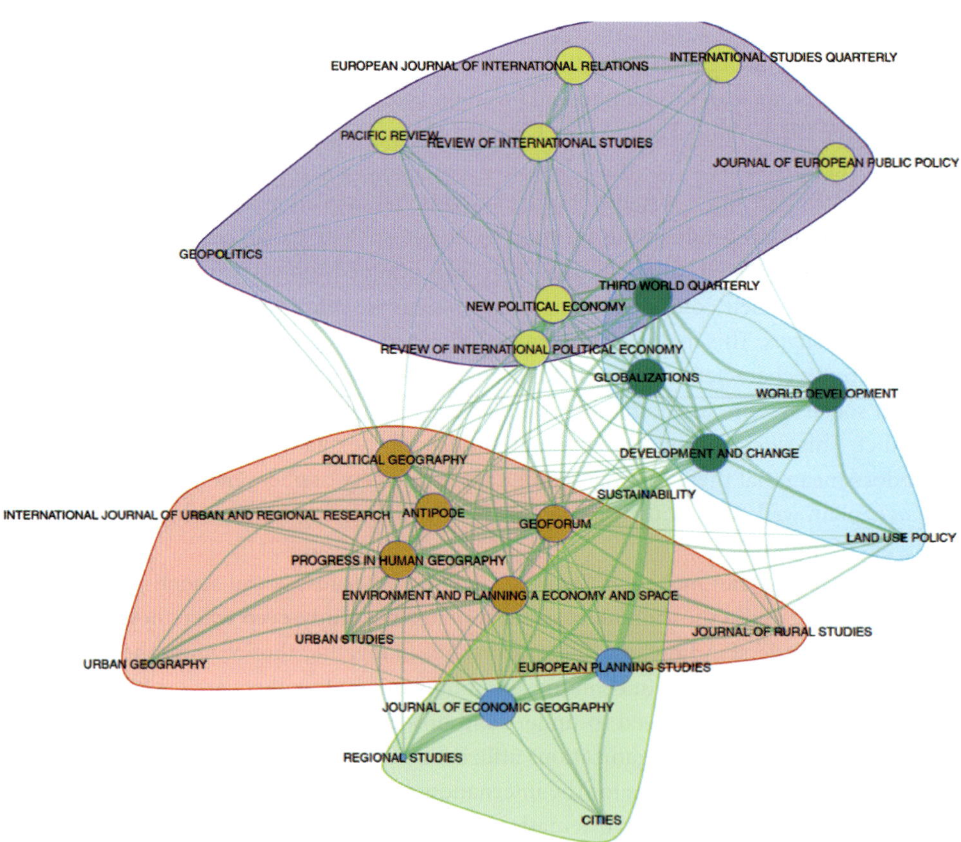

Doing so tells us something interesting about the field: that GPE is a scholarly field with no clear disciplinary home. The purple cluster at the top of the diagram is mainly associated with international relations and political science, but the large red cluster at the bottom is geography. To the right of the network, we can see development studies. While all of these journals publish work where there is a strong assumption that politics and economics are intertwined, and that global issues matter, there is no strict disciplinary home for GPE. This is both an immense opportunity and also a constraint.

Not only does GPE lack an overarching grand theory, within which most phenomena can be situated, but concepts are not always uniformly defined. They can also mean different things to different scholars. Take the example of 'gender'. For some scholars, especially those that study gender in a very focused way such as feminist IPE, gender refers to a complex set of social relationships and norms related to social position, status, and sexuality. In this vein, gender is seen as highly multidimensional. Yet for other scholars, gender is but a variable, operationalized as a (usually) binary indicator. Both sets of scholars take gender seriously in their analysis, but they are looking at the phenomena in different ways because of the way their analysis proceeds.

Not everything will be clearly defined in GPE. Few scholars provide a concise definition of what they mean by 'power', or 'the economy', or 'globalization' in their writing, for example. Yet not everything needs to be. Consider an example from a clearly defined area of study in which there has been enormous progress: the biological sciences. The concept of 'life'—and therefore what is alive and what is not—is probably the central concept within the biological sciences. Yet it is not an entirely settled definition. But this does *not* mean that there is no progress in the science of life. We know more than ever about how to treat disease, how biological systems operate, and how underlying processes operate. Thus, while GPE scholars can sometimes speak at cross purposes regarding what they mean by big concepts—capitalism, the economy, globalization, or gender—it does not mean that they cannot make progress.

2.3.3 Hurdle #3: Navigation

Studying complex phenomena not bound by a singular scholarly discipline requires the navigation of conceptual, theoretical, and methodological issues, as well as some self-care. When studying GPE we need to be aware of the assumptions we are making when it comes to how we see the world and what traits and characteristics we assume dominate it. We also need to ensure we have access to ways of knowing how to find information on the global political economy, as well as the skills to use this information in a way that is convincing.

Let us start with the basics that we need to consider, and which you'll hear some more about in **Chapter 3**: ontology, epistemology, theory, and methods. These four aspects can, and should, be distinguishable.

> **Key Concepts**
>
> **Ontology:** How we conceive of 'what is out there' in the world that we study: the concepts and categories we use when we model the world.
> **Epistemology:** An approach to how knowledge can be acquired.
> **Theory:** A way of thinking about what patterns and relationships are likely to exist in the global political economy.
> **Methods:** The ways of gathering information and the common forms of processing the information for analysis.

Ontology is all about how we conceive of 'what is out there' in the world that we study: the concepts and categories we use when we model the world. Does our model of the global political economy consist of a large collection of individuals, firms, and governments? Or are there other relevant categories like 'global capitalism', 'patriarchy', or 'social movements' in operation that we think are relevant to model how the global political economy is operating? Ontology relates to the set of assumptions we make about the world, and the nature of interactions among different aspects of the world we study. Ontological choices also include what kinds of actors are seen as the lens through which action happens. Is it states or groups or individuals? Ontological assumptions also sometimes operate at a high level of abstraction. Are the different components of the world we study 'really' out there (a 'realist' ontological frame) or are these components only 'constructed' in our heads, through the prism of language and our perspective (a 'constructivist' ontological frame)? As Cohen notes in **Chapter 3**, a key aspect of GPE's diversity is the different ontologies at play in the field.

Epistemology describes an approach to how knowledge can be acquired. Epistemological differences constitute differences in the way that we approach acquiring and synthesizing knowledge, with regard to methods, validity, and scope. It is in the area of epistemology that many scholars of GPE can fundamentally disagree, or just speak past one another. All scholarship makes claim to knowledge. However, it is the underlying basis to those claims to knowledge where key disagreements can persist, for they deal with the most appropriate way to study GPE and to synthesize knowledge about it (see Grieco 2019; Chaudoin and Milner 2017; H. Weber 2015; Waylen 2006; Agnew 2007; B. Cohen 2007).

Ontology and epistemology have consequences for how GPE scholarship gets done. Consider the example of race. Race was not widely considered in the ontologies of most GPE analyses for a long time outside of a few specialized areas, but a range of recent scholarship within GPE has been incorporating its importance (J. Singh 2021; Mosley 2021; Young et al. 2021; Shilliam 2018b; Hobson 2013). However, it is conceptualized and 'measured' in very different ways (Shilliam 2018a).

Theory is a way of thinking about what patterns and relationships are likely to exist in the global political economy. To work, theories require a series of assumptions that are grounded in ontological and epistemological choices. These assumptions provide shortcuts for the student to then propose what are likely patterns and relationships in the phenomena they are looking at. These shortcuts also require conceptual specification. For example, within GPE there is a lot of talk about 'hegemony'. For a realist scholar, this term refers to the leading state in the global political economy, which is able to dominate others and tries to maintain its power in the face of rivalry from other great powers (Lake 1993). For a liberal scholar, hegemony means the same, and the potential for conflict among great powers can be reduced through international cooperation (Keohane 1984). For a Marxist, however, the concept of hegemony often refers to the establishment of a common sense among the population, which secures their subordination to the benefit of transnational elites (Gill 1991; De Graaff and Van Apeldoorn 2021). The point here is that theories require conceptual clarity.

When you learn about GPE, it might be tempting to 'choose' a 'favourite' theory and become close to it such that you become an expert in that area and start to think more and more within the parameters it establishes. This can be very psychologically rewarding. But beware: becoming overly attached to a given theoretical perspective can mean inadvertently developing your own intellectual bias. This is perhaps most likely when a given theory becomes fused with your own individual identity, as in 'I am a *X*ist', or 'I identify with the *X* school of thought.' It used to be the case that most scholarship worked quite closely within a given theoretical tradition, but recently 'non-paradigmatic' approaches have been dominating the field of interdisciplinary fields like GPE. As such, theories still remain important vehicles through which scholars try to make sense of the world they study, but they are perhaps less wedded to theoretically driven 'paradigms' than they were in the past. There are many interesting recent debates on how to synthesize insights from a variety of theoretical traditions, as Cohen will also show you in **Chapter 3** (see Grieco 2019; Wight 2019) (**see Box 2.2**).

Box 2.2 Deduction, induction, or abduction?

An important choice for GPE students to make is the manner of reasoning in which they will acquire knowledge. We stress the importance of reasoning because the choices here ideally follow the analytical strategy, what is already known about the phenomena, and what tactics will pay off the most to obtain new knowledge. The classic positions for social science research are typically opposed as deduction and induction.

Deduction starts from the premise that knowledge about an empirical phenomenon can be validated or predicted by *theory-testing* against known relevant data. Theories can inform the creation of hypotheses to test against observations within the dataset. If the hypotheses align with observations in the data they can be confirmed, thus providing an *explanation*. If not, then they should be rejected or modified. Deductive approaches are often associated with quantitative analytical treatments, such as regression analysis. According to this deductive reasoning, theory-derived hypotheses can be specified to test the relationship, through regression analysis, between a dependent variable (the outcome) and one or multiple independent variables (explanations). If the relationship is strong, one can infer that there may be a causal relationship between the variables.

The reasoning behind *induction* works according to the opposite logic. It is not assumed that we have adequate knowledge on the phenomena of interest. As such, the scholar has to start with specific observations rather than hypotheses. As these observations are collected,

(Continued)

the scholar tries to observe patterns and regularities that give some stability to *understanding* the phenomena. On this basis, tentative hypotheses can be developed, primarily to assist *theory-building* in relation to understanding similar types of phenomena. This approach is typically associated with qualitative methods, where theoretical parsimony is less valued and thick empirical description is viewed as a way to improve knowledge.

While GPE scholars certainly use deductive and inductive reasoning, many also use what Charles Peirce referred to as *abduction* (Friedrichs and Kratochwil 2009). This is not stealing someone away. Rather, abduction refers to reasoning whereby an initial set of observations leads to assumptions and guesses about likely behaviour. This helps generate hypotheses that can be tested, but the process should not end once they are verified. Rather, the verification of these hypotheses should help with finding more observations, thus assisting in knowledge discovery. In GPE the use of typology and ideal types often follows this abductive logic, especially in building cases across which generalizations can be made.

Finally, the most important element here is honesty. If you are seeking knowledge about the world, then it doesn't matter that your prior assumptions are not confirmed. The best knowledge about the world is stuff that could be wrong but isn't. That's how we develop new insights in GPE

Theories are also used for different purposes. Some theories have the purpose of explaining phenomena based on predicted outcomes. Theory, in this fashion, leads to testable propositions that can be evaluated against empirical evidence. Scholars of GPE differ in regard to how precisely such testable propositions ought to be evaluated (e.g., see Young 2021; Chaudoin and Milner 2017; B. Cohen 2017). Theory can also be used to understand phenomena. Theory, in this mode, is the development of conceptual and analytical frameworks that help the student find information on the empirical case, with the aim of finding new knowledge to understand it. In general, theories operate on the basis of reason. Some would claim that theories should be based on particular assumptions about the rational agency of the actors being studied, but that is an assumption about behaviour linked to ontological and epistemological preferences. Reason trumps rationality in divining what theories are appropriate for discovering knowledge about the global political economy.

Finally, the means of getting to that knowledge comes through methods of collecting and analysing information. *Methods* refer to the ways of gathering information and the common forms of processing the information for analysis. For GPE students there are many methods to choose from. Some prefer fieldwork-based methods such as interviews and observation or sifting through archival materials. Others prefer desk-based methods such as statistical analyses based on available data or a range of computational methods. It is common to juxtapose qualitative methods with quantitative methods, but in reality, many GPE scholars use both. Importantly, theory and method are not one and the same. Theories and methods may have affinities, but should be distinguished.

Often, when students start learning about methodology and methods, they find themselves entering a contentious world of professional dividing lines and strong opinions on the 'best way' to do social science. One of the reasons why the area of methods and methodological assumptions is so contentious is because of the stakes involved in claim-making. Who is right? How do we know? Claims to knowledge are a big part of what scholarship is all about and so these are fundamental issues.

However, another reason why the area of methods is so contentious is for less grandiose reasons, only indirectly related to underlying concepts of epistemology. Many scholars—in GPE and beyond—are trained to think in terms of a certain set of methods and end up being relatively specialized users of them as a result. Because of such investments, they end up seeing the world through these methods. They also seek to protect those investments, by arguing that they can see things that others cannot, or that scholarship that uses these methods is superior. Such posturing is rarely very explicit, but becomes a cultural frame that informs how groups of academics see one another and see themselves.

At other times, GPE scholars disagree about the purpose of scholarship more broadly. Is it to find out stuff about how the world works, or is it about actually seeking to change the world? Some depictions of the field (see B. Cohen 2017 and **Chapter 3**) draw a dividing line between 'positivist' and more 'normative' work in GPE scholarship. The important thing to remember is that, as a student of GPE, you don't have to take sides in these issues. To be sure, many academic writers will try to draw you to their side. Some of your professors might try this too, such as in the ways that they depict the 'other side' in a given topical area. Rather than taking sides, it's always good to be aware of these issues, and to be able to read between the lines of what other people are saying, and how they are positioning their arguments.

Combining ontological and epistemological assumptions with theory and methods to study the global political economy is a challenge. It raises a few questions, such as:

- What is the right balance between parsimony and complexity?
- What actors, institutions, and organizations are important for the topic that interests you most in GPE?
- What is considered credible evidence?

How you answer these questions depends on what mode of intellectual engagement you adopt (**see Box 2.3**).

Box 2.3 Different paths to discovery: an example from international financial standards

Let us imagine seeing an empirical phenomenon from a range of methodological approaches, using a hypothetical example. You want to investigate the process through which a new international financial standard has been developed, and how this agreement made between experts and national representatives will be translated into regulations and laws. This can be tackled in a number of ways, depending on your ontological and epistemological assumptions, whether you prefer a deductive, inductive, or abductive approach, and whether you prefer field-based or desk-based research. For example, an inductive field-based approach might lean heavily on interviewing the known policymakers involved in the standard-setting, using *semi-structured interviews* to put the pieces together in how the standard was created, which interests were

(Continued)

disproportionately represented, and if the social organization among policymakers matters for outcomes (Macartney 2009; Tsingou 2015). A more deductive approach would establish *hypotheses* based on established interests and use interviews to confirm or dismiss the relevance of these hypotheses (Quaglia 2019).

An inductive desk-based approach may examine the *content* of the standard, looking for patterns in what issues are put forward as important to the standard-setting process, as well as who is most present in pressing for certain issues. Such work can be done through a *close reading content analysis* (Ban, Seabrooke, and Freitas 2016), as well as through *quantitative text analysis* (James, Pagliari, and Young 2021). A deductive desk-based approach may rely more on assumptions about the bargaining power of national representatives, based on *quantitative assessment* of the size of various financial sectors. Such an approach may posit that the policymakers have a delegated responsibility from national legislators and that the process of standard-setting can be seen as a *two-level game* where those negotiating must satisfy two constituencies at once (D. Singer 2004; Rixen 2013).

Those applying an abductive approach—which is what most GPE scholars actually do—can use any of the above, as well as combine methods in executing such investigations. For example, assumptions about who may be present in the standard-setting process can be assessed through the application of *social network analysis*, finding out who is not only involved in direct negotiations but also in the environment—and then developing propositions on how this network relates to the bargaining process and likely outcomes (Pagliari and Young 2014; Seabrooke and Tsingou 2021).

In short, there are many methodological avenues to explore in GPE.

2.4 Modes of intellectual activity in GPE

One way to approach the study of GPE is to learn a huge amount about the global economy, to learn lots of theories of power and governance, and to read lots of GPE scholarship. We can easily spend a long time traversing the different theories of how power operates in the global economy. There are many excellent suggestions throughout this book. But as for a general approach to how to study GPE, we think a useful starting point is to think about the kind of intellectual 'modes' that you might be encountering when you read a given piece of scholarship. This is doubly important as you engage in your own research: you need to think about what intellectual 'mode' you might want to operate in, at a given point in time (**see Figure 2.3**).

We conceptualize three *modes* of scholarship, depicted in **Figure 2.3**. They are interrelated and arguably all scholars operate in all of these modes. Yet they each represent fundamentally different ways of proceeding with academic work. If you are to understand the field of GPE, you need to be able to identify and properly situate scholarship operating in these different modes. You also need to be able to identify which corner of the triangle you want to focus on at a particular time, and which mode you want to develop, as a stronger assemblage of skills. Each of these modes has their own costs and benefits. Being able to 'decode' these modes is an important skill that we think will serve you well.

Figure 2.3 Intellectual modes triangle

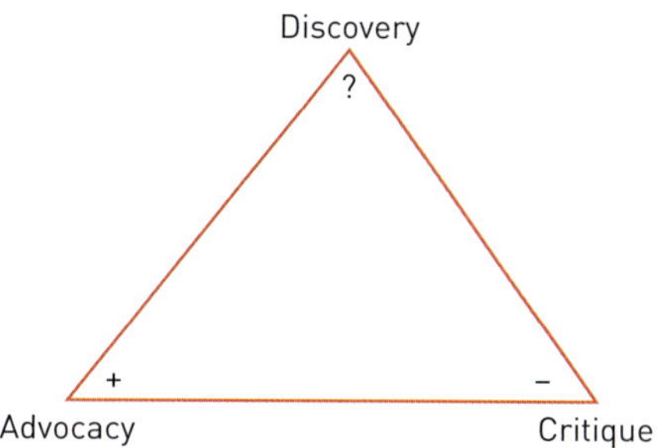

Advocacy is thesis driven. It entails the act of 'selling' an argument to others, by way of forceful argumentation and buttressing an argument. When students learn to 'develop a thesis', they are learning to operate in this mode. Indeed, most of the writing you will encounter—in blog posts, in essay writing, in most popular non-fiction writing—is a form of expository prose that entails advocating for a given position: 'Here is how the world works, and why you should believe me. Buy my argument.' This is actually where the social and political dynamics of knowledge are truly interesting because not everyone advocating a position can be correct simultaneously. Indeed, close attention to the real world of ideas and advocacy—about the operation of the GPE or anything else—often involves wading through highly motivated advocacy.

Advocacy, by its very definition, is *motivated*. Advocacy always has a particular goal. For example, an interest group is concerned to shape a conversation in a certain way to advance its own interests. A journalist with a particular well-known stance on a topic advocates for their particular stance. So too, academics engage in advocacy when they seek to advance a particular argument. Operating within the mode of advocacy within GPE, the writer *starts* with an argument, and the work entails formulating ways to best articulate that argument. Some of this advocacy is clandestine—for example, when an academic subtly advocates for the use of a particular method or in favour of a particular theory. But typically, the advance of a thesis in this way is easily discernible.

The mode of *critique* involves taking on existing claims. Most dramatically, it involves the intellectual act of 'tearing down'. Even 'deconstructing' someone else's argument—that is, picking apart its hidden assumptions, identifying faulty logic, or hidden bias—or criticizing an existing theory can be tremendously satisfying. When you think of your fellow students in an academic seminar offering reactions to a given piece of scholarship in that week's reading list, often what they are doing is operating in a critical mode. What academics do around each other in seminars, quite often, is to operate entirely within the mode of critique. Clever advocacy, it might be noted, prepares in advance for critique, for example by neutralizing potential objections to whatever is being advocated. Many teaching environments are set up to allow students to 'perform' different forms of critique. A lively seminar is full of people not just proposing ideas and asserting different conjectures, but also features a lot of knocking things down. The critical mode is also readily apparent when scholars engage with the world of policymaking, as many scholars are good at identifying problems within the existing architecture of power and policy.

These various 'modes' serve to differentiate ways that a lot of intellectual activity is approached. For example, advocacy entails advancing a claim, while critique entails interrogating a claim. They are often combined, and an effective arguer will move between these modes. For example, a good advocate for a claim might point out the ways in which 'the other side' advances a set of claims, but argue these are ultimately faulty in some way. Critique, too, is sometimes performed in a way that suggests that the thing we should 'buy' is not a particular claim, but a claim about a claim—for example, that X is wrong, or misleading.

A recent example of advocacy and critique in operation within GPE scholarship is Gurminder K. Bhambra's (2021) argument concerning the emergence of the modern global economy. Bhambra critiques existing depictions of capitalist development as self-contained and endogenous to Europe and North America, pointing to a 'failure to acknowledge, or regard as significant, the global connections forged through colonialism that are the condition of capitalist-modernity'. She advocates an improved interpretation of how the modern global economy came about, through dispossession and colonialism through private property, formal empire, and other mechanisms.

Being able to differentiate the different intellectual 'modes' of GPE scholars is important and valuable to you. That's because students can get mixed up if they do not know how to identify these modes in operation. When students read the big thinkers or 'central debates' within a given area of study or discipline, they encounter a collection of works operating both in the modes of advocacy and critique. A representative text from a 'realist' IR scholar, for example, is trying to advocate for a realist theoretical approach, and might be actively critiquing liberal institutionalism or idealism in the process.

The mode of *discovery* is very different from the other two modes. Advancing a particular position or argument is not its objective, although it could potentially be its consequence. Critical thinking is important in the mode of discovery, but discovery does not entail a formulated critique of anything necessarily. Discovery involves the uncovering of facts. If the mode of advocacy is equivalent to 'selling' and critique is about 'tearing down', discovery is about 'learning'. What most academics spend most of their time on when they are engaging in empirical scholarship in the actual research process is discovery.

Advocacy and critique modes are where facts are debated. Discovery is where facts are born. The tools you will learn in specialized methods seminars and workshops on research design are often tools of discovery. Academics spend a huge amount of time on discovery. Yet discovery is arguably underemphasized, and what we train students to do is to practise the modes of advocacy and critique. Yet when it comes to discovery, especially training in empirical research methods, students encounter a panoply of recommendations regarding research design, complex philosophy of science issues, and skills and methods training. Learning 'how' to discover empirical patterns about the world is what most methods are doing. Methods are trying to give you various 'tools for discovery'.

Each mode has a different set of emotional experiences. These are important to think about as you learn about GPE. Critique can be very empowering—especially when you are a student, and you 'knock down' existing research. Advocacy can be very self-affirming—when you feel you have a strong thesis to advance. However, advocacy can also expose you to a unique vulnerability: the imminent threat of critique. Sticking your neck out and advocating for a given position means that you can always be cut down, to so speak. Discovery, on the other hand, exposes you to a different kind of vulnerability, because you don't know what you will find. In a sense, the world decides for you. One way of thinking about this is to make sure you go out and hunt for information that might prove your favoured theory wrong, rather than just going out and collecting information that will support your favoured theory. Many students, locked and trained in the mode of advocacy only, fail to do this. But it is essential for operating well in the mode of discovery.

2.5 Conclusion

In this chapter we offered different recommendations for how to go about studying GPE. Other than gaining literacy in key theories and evidence, what kind of orientation should one have about the field of GPE? We argued, first, that GPE is fundamentally exciting and wonderful (**see Section 2.2**). This is true not only because of its sheer scale and potential comprehensiveness in explaining the operation of literally the whole world, but also because it is fundamentally an interdisciplinary area of study. In this sense, GPE both takes on, and outdoes, the rest of social science. Yet that is also why GPE is really hard (**see Section 2.3**). It is useful to think through basic concepts like ontology and epistemology and the assumptions that different forms of GPE scholarship make, and to distinguish these from theory and methods. Finally, we argued that in order to navigate the field of GPE, it is useful to identify and differentiate, different modes of inquiry (**see Section 2.4**). We argued that differentiating between advocacy, critique, and discovery can be useful both to identify what existing scholarship is doing and, just as importantly, to identify what you might want to be doing yourself, as a new student of GPE.

Key Points

- GPE is fundamentally exciting and wonderful, and is a highly interdisciplinary field of study. It encompasses social theory on a grand scale, but also contains the core assumption that power and the organization of the material world—politics and economics—are fundamentally intertwined.
- GPE is a scholarly field that has no fixed disciplinary boundaries, although some themes and concepts are more frequently used than others.
- GPE is hard, because of the scale and complexity involved, which can make choices about methods and theory challenging to navigate. This can be made more manageable if you can learn to recognize different assumptions about ontology, epistemology, theories, and methods that GPE scholars use.

- A useful skill when studying GPE is to be able to identify different 'modes' of intellectual activity that you encounter. The mode of 'advocacy' entails work that is trying to advance a specific claim or argument about some aspect of the global political economy. The mode of 'critique' is about knocking down or deconstructing an existing theory or assumption or empirical finding.
- A lot of scholarship moves between the modes of advocacy and critique, but a lot of what GPE scholars actually *do* involves another mode, the mode of 'discovery', in which they accumulate evidence and evaluate theories with that evidence.

Further Reading

Farrands, C., and **Worth, O.** (2005), 'Critical Theory in Global Political Economy: Critique? Knowledge? Emancipation?', *Capital & Class*, 29(1): 43–61. An interesting example of a critique of Global Political Economy scholarship on the basis of whether and how existing theory is sufficiently 'critical', which advances a set of principles for how global political economy in a critical tradition can improve.

Farrell, H., and **Newman, A.** (2016), 'The New Interdependence Approach: Theoretical Development and Empirical Demonstration', *Review of International Political Economy*, 23(5): 713–36. Offers an important intervention by presenting a new theory of change in GPE that emphasizes structural conditions between states that provide power games based on rule overlap, opportunity structures, and power asymmetries.

Montgomerie, J. (ed.) (2017), *Critical Methods in Political and Cultural Economy* (London: Routledge). Describes real-life accounts from academics doing empirical research, emphasizing a critical ethos. Includes short autobiographical vignettes from different scholars on the particular methods they use, as well as practical advice on researching and writing about political economy.

Oatley, T. (2021), 'Regaining Relevance: IPE and a Changing Global Political Economy', *Cambridge Review of International Affairs*, 34(2): 318–27. Outlines the limitations of current theories in explaining contemporary phenomena like anti-system politics and the reform after economic and financial crises. Proposes that GPE should focus more on uneven and combined development, as well as forms of complex interdependence, to get on track and maximize the power to not only explain but understand.

Paterson, M. (2021), 'Climate Change and International Political Economy: Between Collapse and Transformation', *Review of International Political Economy*, 28(2): 394–405. Argues that, in the context of global climate politics and their urgency, IPE scholarship can contribute some key theoretical and substantive knowledge, although the central challenge is for IPE scholars to deploy this knowledge.

Pevehouse, J. C., and **Seabrooke, L.** (eds) (2022), *The Oxford Handbook of International Political Economy* (Oxford: Oxford University Press). Provides overviews of contemporary scholarship in GPE/IPE, stressing cutting-edge contributions and controversies. Contains over forty chapters, based on themes like 'fields of IPE', 'methods', 'processes', 'forums', 'flows and stocks', 'actors', 'outcomes', and 'assets and resources'.

Singh, J. P. (2021), 'Race, Culture, and Economics: An Example from North–South Trade Relations', *Review of International Political Economy*, 28(2): 323–35. Argues that the way that North–South trade relations have operated reflects racialized cultural values at work, in the way that bilateral and multilateral trade negotiations have operated and the way that North–South trade gets framed more broadly.

Young, K. L. (2021), 'Progress, Pluralism and Science: Moving from Alienated to Engaged Pluralism', *Review of International Political Economy*, 28(2): 406–20. Argues that GPE/IPE often falls into a trap of 'alienated pluralism'. To have productive conversations we need to recognize a scientific ethos is fundamental to intellectual conversation and critique. Contends that we should move towards 'engaged pluralism' to allow more space for debate.

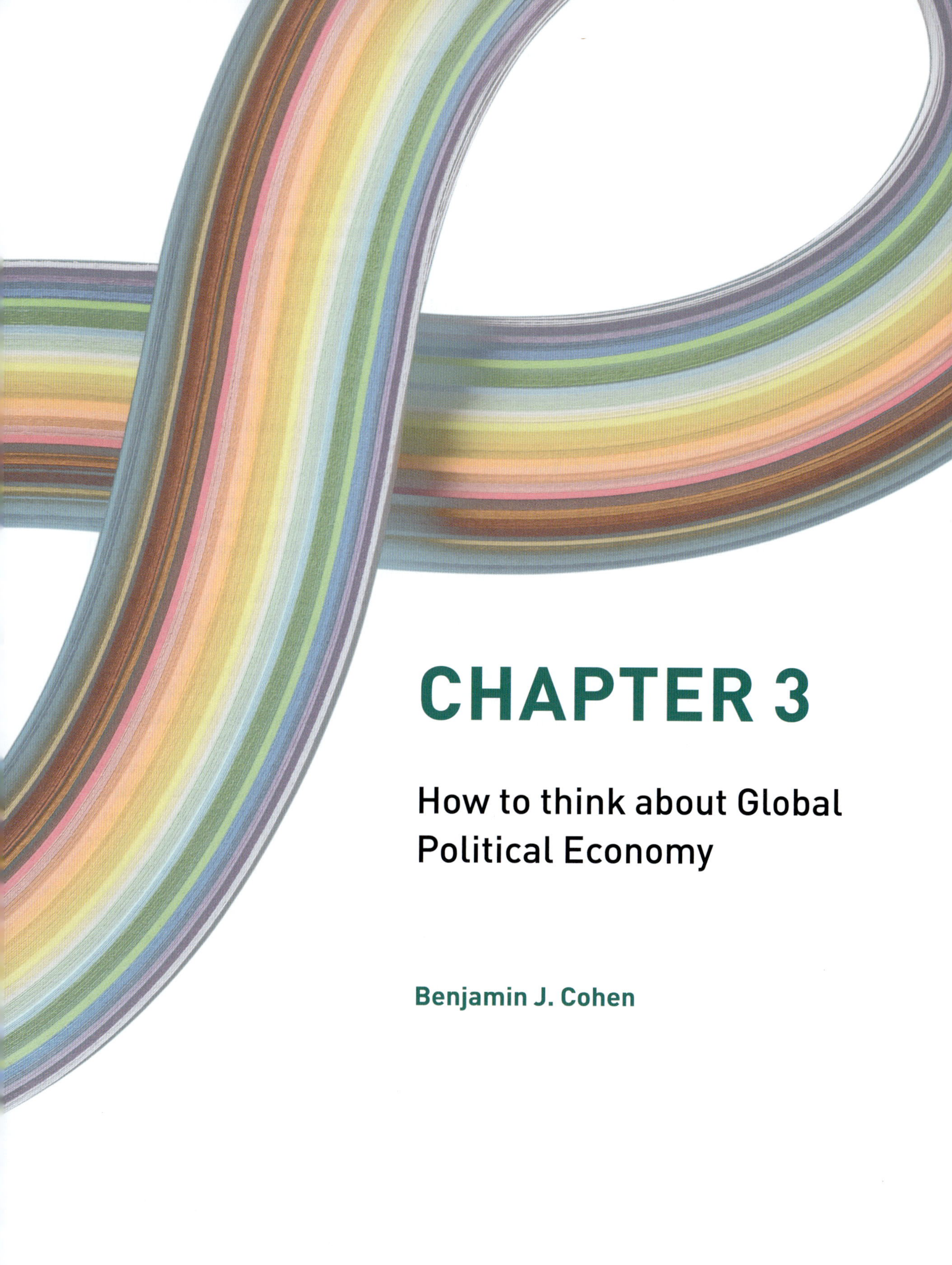

CHAPTER 3

How to think about Global Political Economy

Benjamin J. Cohen

3.1 Introduction

How should we think about Global Political Economy (GPE)? The question has no simple answer. As you read in **Chapter 1** and **Chapter 2**, and as you will see from the contents of this textbook, as a field of study GPE is vast and variegated, offering a colourful multitude of theoretical approaches and perspectives. Scholars agree on the basics. In principle, GPE is a multidisciplinary (or interdisciplinary) area of inquiry that has something to do with economics (economy), something to do with politics (political), and something to do with the world beyond the confines of the sovereign state (global). But that is about as far as agreement reaches. In practice, there seem to be almost as many conceptions of GPE—what we call paradigms—as there are specialists in the subject. Pluralism rules (B. Cohen 2022).

Diversity in an academic discipline is not necessarily bad. A budding of multiple paradigms, like the cultivation of diverse crops in well-tilled farmlands, can help to preserve a field's fertility. Much depends, however, on how well we understand the myriad of research traditions and what criteria we use to judge their respective contributions. GPE as a field of study can be thought of as a robust ecology where a hundred flowers bloom, each offering a distinctive intellectual perspective. The aim of this chapter is to harvest what we can from all this thriving diversity—in short, to learn how to think about GPE.

Two questions dominate. First, how do we *distinguish* among the many theoretical approaches that are available? What attributes are most salient in differentiating one perspective from another? In **Section 3.2** I suggest that in this respect five dimensions stand out: *ontology, agenda, purpose, boundaries,* and *epistemology.* Together, these five defining characteristics provide us with a useful lens for comparing and contrasting alternative conceptions of the field. Using this lens, the chapter will survey the principal paradigms that have flourished as the field has grown over time (**see Section 3.3, Section 3.4,** and **Section 3.5**).

The second question then logically follows: How do we *choose* among the available approaches for purposes of study? The answer, I submit, depends on our *goal.* What are we aiming for? Fundamentally, our thinking about GPE should be ruled by two paramount principles: *pragmatism* and *eclecticism* (**see Section 3.6**). Echoing some of the discussion you heard from Leonard Seabrooke and Kevin L. Young in **Chapter 2**, we must be prepared to be flexible in our choice of analytical perspective (pragmatism), and we must be prepared to draw on any combination of paradigms that seem right for the goal at hand (eclecticism). In a field of a hundred flowers, each problem deserves its own hand-selected bouquet.

3.2 Attributes

Flowers differ in all sorts of ways, of course, so in horticulture it is only natural to seek to identify a few distinguishing characteristics by which they can be compared—for example, colour, size, or shape. The same is true for the multitude of perspectives in GPE. We need to agree on a list of defining attributes that can be used for the purpose of comparative analysis. For our field, five dimensions stand out.

First is *ontology*, from the Greek for 'things that exist'. Ontology is about investigating reality: the nature, essential properties, and relations of being. What are the basic units of analysis in our research, and what are their key relationships? For many specialists, particularly in the United States, the proper focus is the state. Analysis is—or should be—strictly state-centric, which is why in America and often elsewhere our field of study is better known as *International* Political Economy (IPE) rather than *Global* Political Economy. The adjective 'international' signals that the focus is on nation-states and the relations between them, rather than on more global structures or processes. In many other research traditions, however, it is the overall system that is or should be of most interest—hence the preference for the label GPE rather than IPE. Both designations are legitimate, though representing distinctly different ontologies.

Second is *agenda*. What are the most salient issues to be addressed? Are we more interested in matters relating to material welfare—the production and distribution of goods and services for final use—as emphasized by the discipline of economics? Or is our interest more in issues of politics and governance—decision-making, cooperation, and the management of conflict—as stressed by political scientists? Do we emphasize more the role of power in determining economic outcomes, or rather the part that economics plays in shaping political behaviour? Should we focus on markets or hierarchies? Are our horizons primarily local or regional, or does our perspective extend to the intercontinental and global? And what are the links among these different geographic levels of analysis? In the real world, of course, everything is in a sense intertwined—'mutually endogenous', to adopt a phrase beloved of social scientists. Nonetheless, for analytical purposes it is necessary to establish priorities about what is to be considered more or less central.

Third is *purpose*. What is the goal of research? Is our aim 'positivist', intended primarily to enhance our objective understanding of how the world works? Or, rather, is it more 'normative', hoping to make the world a better place to live in? Do we study GPE to gain more insight into underlying causal relationships or to promote the cause of social justice? Is our motivation comprehension or compassion?

Fourth are *boundaries*. Where do we draw a line around our multidisciplinary field of study? How receptive are we to ideas or insights from other specialties beyond GPE's roots in economics and political science? How important are contributions from related disciplines like sociology, history, geography, or psychology? What role is played by culture or gender? And what about other more distant areas of scholarship such as anthropology, law, religion, or philosophy? Should the boundaries of our field be drawn tightly to provide a more parsimonious basis for theory-building? Or to quote Susan Strange, one of the pioneers of modern GPE, should inquiry be 'unfenced … open to all comers' (Strange 1984: ix)? The study of GPE, Strange argued, 'would do well to stay an open range, like the old Wild West, accessible … to literate people of all walks of life' (Strange 1991: 33).

Fifth, last but not least, is *epistemology*, from the Greek word for 'knowledge'. Epistemology has to do with the methods and grounds of knowing. What analytical techniques do we use to study the world? All theoretical inquiry, properly speaking, should begin with accurate observation of behaviour and a close reading of available empirical evidence. But must our understanding be grounded primarily in rigorous quantitative or qualitative research methodologies? Or can we rely as well, or instead, on less formal theoretical approaches that rely to a greater extent on logical inference, intuition, or even pure speculation? GPE is a social science, but should the emphasis be on the science or on the social?

3.3 Classifications

The aim of the list of defining attributes described in **Section 3.2** is to provide criteria for a comparative analysis of our field's principal theoretical approaches. But we know that differences can exist along all these dimensions, combining in a variety of complex ways. Hence it is not always easy to know where to draw the lines between competing perspectives. Any set of labels to categorize paradigms is bound in some degree to be arbitrary—and therefore controversial. 'Typologies are most useful,' the noted scholar John Ravenhill has remarked, 'when they have minimal within-type variance and maximum between-type variation' (Ravenhill 2008: 26). But classifications that achieve this ideal are hard to find. Alternative traditions may diverge along some dimensions even while converging on others; elements of several perspectives may overlap and intertwine, even in the minds of individual scholars. Like any healthy ecology, GPE's world is inherently messy.

Can all this diversity be 'mapped'? Many efforts have been made to capture the messiness of GPE in a single system of classification. But these usually result in taxonomies of such density that they make the head spin. A representative example is offered by two prominent scholars, Leonard Seabrooke and Kevin L. Young (2017), who used highly refined community-detection methodologies to distinguish numerous 'niches' in GPE's thriving ecology—as many as five to seven distinct clusters of intellectual style at any given time. We can admire the great scholarship underlying such an approach, yet respectfully question its usefulness. The purpose of any typology should be to simplify and clarify, not overwhelm.

Between these extremes lie many possible systems of classification, each stressing one or some combination of our five defining attributes. Most popular is an oft-noted dichotomy between what are described as either orthodox or heterodox theoretical perspectives (alternatively, 'mainstream' versus 'radical' perspectives) (**see Table 3.1**). The distinction between orthodoxy and heterodoxy is widely used by scholars in the field. Orthodox approaches tend to be state-centric in their ontology and agenda, positivist in their purpose, narrow in their conception of the field's boundaries, and demanding in their choice of methodology. Heterodox approaches, conversely, are less state-centric, more normative, more inclined towards the open range advocated by Strange, and more relaxed about methods. Following common practice, this chapter too will make use of the orthodox–heterodox divide to help learn how to think about GPE.

The advantage of using the orthodox–heterodox divide is that it maximizes between-type variance. It is easy to know where to draw a line between contending paradigms. The field

Table 3.1 **Key concepts**

Principal theoretical approaches to GPE	
Orthodox perspectives	**Heterodox perspectives**
These approaches share a preference for a state-centric ontology, positivism, closed disciplinary boundaries, and rigorous methodology.	These approaches, by contrast, are less state-centric; agendas are broader and more normative; boundaries are more open; and methodology is less formal.
Variants	**Variants**
Liberalism assumes that economics dominates politics and is more comfortable with a domestic level of analysis focusing on policy processes.	**System-level theories** centre on global structures and processes. Examples include classical Marxism, dependency, world-systems theory, and world orders.
Realism assumes that politics dominates economics and favours a systemic level of analysis focusing on state power and interests.	**Critical theory** challenges orthodoxy of every sort and is highly normative, with a focus on dominance and inequality.
Constructivism focuses on the role of ideas and social norms, emphasizing a logic of appropriateness rather than a logic of consequence.	**Extensions** seek to expand the boundaries of the field by adding an emphasis on some allegedly missing element such as history, non-elite actors, culture, gender, or complexity.

can be defined simply in terms of two sharply contrasting styles. One approach is conventionally termed mainstream, though that by no means implies better or preferred. The other challenges the mainstream to a greater or lesser extent. But dividing the field this way has an obvious disadvantage as well. The broad brush of a single dichotomy also obscures many crucial differences that can be found under each of the two headings. In each category there remains an enormous amount of within-type variance. To obtain a full appreciation of the range of perspectives to be found in GPE, therefore, the orthodox–heterodox divide must be treated as no more than a first approximation, helpful mainly as a starting point for more refined further discussion. Due attention must be paid as well to the many interesting variations that have been developed for each of the two broad themes. Each side of the dichotomy is home to a myriad of compelling interpretations.

3.4 **Orthodox perspectives**

Orthodox perspectives, as indicated in **Section 3.3**, share a preference for a state-centric ontology, positivism, closed disciplinary boundaries, and rigorous methodology. Because approaches of this kind got an early start well over a half century ago, they gradually came to acquire the mantle of scholarly orthodoxy. And because they are especially popular in the United States, where there are more specialists in GPE (or, as

Americans prefer, IPE) than anywhere else in the world, orthodoxy in the field has come to be most closely identified with the conventional standards of mainstream US social science. Though its adherents can be found worldwide, many in the field simply call it the American school (B. Cohen 2008).

The orthodox style, however, comes in many flavours, reflecting a multitude of intellectual traditions. Within the American school there are all sorts of debates over everything from the proper level of analysis to the salience of materialist versus cognitive motivations for behaviour. Orthodoxy may be based on common premises, but it is by no means unanimous over how to build on that foundation (B. Cohen 2009). For many years, a well-known American restaurant chain advertised itself as the home of twenty-eight flavours of ice cream. The American school of GPE has even more.

3.4.1 The American school

From the start, American-style GPE has seen itself essentially as a sub-specialty of the study of international relations (IR)—in effect, a branch of political science. Foremost this means that GPE in America is, above all, about sovereign states. As in the discipline of IR more generally, the state is seen as the fundamental locus of authority in world politics. No other actor enjoys the legitimacy that comes with internationally recognized sovereignty, nor can any other actor legally exercise the ultimate right of coercion. It is no surprise, therefore, that for the American style of GPE, ontology would be determinably state-centric. National governments are the core actors. State policymaking is the main concern. Other actors are not ignored but enter the picture only insofar as they exercise some form of influence or constraint on governmental behaviour.

Further, most scholarship in the American style tends closely to follow the methodological norms of conventional US social science. Priority is given to scientific method—what may be called a pure or hard science model. Analysis is based on the twin principles of positivism and empiricism, which hold that knowledge is best accumulated through an appeal to objective observation and the systematic evaluation of evidence using rigorous quantitative or qualitative techniques. Conjectures in some form are specified, based on deductive reasoning, and then tested for empirical accuracy—a process formally known as 'hypothetico-deductivism'. Grand comprehensive conceptualization on a global scale is generally eschewed. The style, instead, is essentially ahistorical. Most emphasis is placed on micro- or mid-level theory concentrating on key relationships isolated within a broader structure whose characteristics are unquestioned and assumed, implicitly, to be stable through time.

The purpose of analysis in the American school is to explain and understand how the world works, not to judge it. Normative concerns, for the most part, are downplayed. Serious scholarship is not to be sullied by personal values or policy advocacy. Theoretical inspiration is drawn largely from just two disciplines—modern GPE's twin ancestors, economics and political science. Ideas or insights from other scholarly specialties rarely draw much systematic attention. Analysis tends to concentrate on two major sets of issues. One is the question of state behaviour. How do we understand the policies of national governments in the global economy? The other is the question of system governance. How do states cope with the consequences of economic interdependence? These two issues constitute what, in formal language, may be called the American school's core 'problematique'.

In principle, three broad levels of analysis are distinguished, each a general theoretical orientation corresponding to one of the well-known 'images' of international relations initially sketched by IR theorist Kenneth Waltz. In his classic *Man, the State, and War*, Waltz (1959) sought to categorize the causes of war in as concise a fashion as possible. Any possible *casus belli*, he suggested, could usefully be ordered under one of three headings: (1) within individuals; (2) within individual states; or (3) within the structure of the inter-state system. The first of his three images stressed defects in human nature; the second, defects in the internal organization of states; and the third, defects in states' external organization (the anarchic inter-state system). Today these are referred to, respectively, as the first, second, and third images of international relations.

In practice, most attention in the American school is directed towards the systemic and domestic levels of analysis and the interaction between them. The style was codified by David Lake, a former president of the American Political Science Association, under the label Open Economy Politics (OEP). For the American school, Lake declared, the synthesis of second and third-image analysis is the 'dominant approach [that] now structures and guides research' (Lake 2006: 757).

Open Economy Politics, as Lake summarized it, is largely materialist in orientation and builds outward in linear fashion from the interests of individuals and other social units at the domestic level to policy preferences and strategic interactions at the international level. For analytical purposes, the paradigm is decomposed into a sequence of three distinct steps. First come individuals or groups—for example, enterprises, sectors, or factors of production—that can reasonably be assumed to share more or less the same interests, defined as preferences over alternative outcomes. Interests are derived from established economic theories that highlight the distributional implications of different national policies. Next, OEP turns to how interests are aggregated and mediated through domestic political institutions. Drawing on familiar models from political science, the approach theorizes how divergent interests may be translated through political processes into public policy. Finally, once policy preferences are determined, OEP assumes a stage of international bargaining as states seek to influence one another's behaviour, either explicitly or implicitly. At issue are the distributional consequences of alternative joint outcomes. Each state is naturally assumed to seek the best deal it can.

The strength of the OEP paradigm lies in its careful delineation of the microfoundations of government policy. A weakness is its choice to study policymaking from the inside out, largely in isolation from broader macro processes—a striking form of methodological reductionism. Causation, in effect, is assumed to run in just one direction, from domestic interests and institutions (steps one and two) to international outcomes (step three); the possibility of inverse outside-in influences tends to be downplayed or ignored. Thomas Oatley (2011), a noted US scholar, calls this the 'reductionist gamble'—a risky bet that results attained by reducing analysis to the driving force of domestic politics will not be moderated or distorted by developments at the international level. More recent scholarship acknowledges that in many cases the reductionist gamble may indeed miss important interactions between the domestic and international levels of analysis (Chaudoin, Milner, and Pang 2015).

Scholars working in the orthodox tradition have applied the OEP paradigm to virtually every issue facing governments in the world economy. Individual contributions, however, are typically more modest—what might be described as 'small-bore' in calibre—focusing on just bits of the picture rather than the whole. In technical language, analysis tends to be partial-equilibrium (holding many variables constant) rather than general-equilibrium in nature. Some discussions assume interests that are given in order to study how different domestic institutions aggregate or refract preferences under varying circumstances. Others set aside the complexities of domestic politics in order to isolate the direct impact of constituency preferences on policy. And yet others may simply assume a set of policy interests in order to evaluate the dynamics of international bargaining. In principle, nothing stands in the way of a more general-equilibrium approach that would bind the components together into a more complete whole. But as Lake (2009: 225) has ruefully acknowledged, 'in practice synthesis remains imperfect'. Theorizing, for the most part, remains determinedly micro- or mid-level.

3.4.2 Variations

Theorizing, however, is by no means monolithic. The American school does not want for within-type variance. Adherents largely agree on the need for a state-centric ontology, with an emphasis on positivism and empiricism; they concur as well on what constitutes the fundamental problematique for analysis. Yet there is also much disagreement on more specific questions, reflecting debates that have gone on among IR theorists for years. Orthodoxy, in practice, encompasses many variations—a multiplicity of traditions that can all claim a degree of intellectual legitimacy (B. Cohen 2009).

Perhaps the deepest split is the classic divide between liberalism and realism in mainstream IR theory (**see Table 3.1**). At issue between these two historical schools of thought is the nature of the underlying connection between economic and political activity—an age-old question that has long divided scholars of political economy. Does economics drive politics, or vice versa? Central to the many versions of liberalism (later, neoliberal institutionalism) is a belief that economics dominates politics—meaning, in particular, the forces of market competition and incentives for material advancement. Variants of realism (later neorealism), by contrast, have always retained faith in the capacity of political factors—especially the distribution of power among states—to shape economic structures. Correspondingly, realists have always favoured the systemic level of analysis, where power and politics are central. Liberals, on the other hand, are more comfortable with the domestic level of analysis, where economic factors mould the constellations of interest that are assumed to be at the heart of the policy process.

In time, the differences between liberalism and realism have come to seem less crucial than their similarities—in particular, their effective convergence around what John Ruggie, a US scholar, has called 'neo-utilitarian precepts and premises' (1999: 215). Both traditions share a preference for a purely rationalist, materialist, and individualistic approach to analysis (utilitarianism). Actors, whether states or non-state entities, are assumed to act in pursuit of clearly defined interests. Identities are well established and unchanging. Outcomes reflect a careful balancing of costs and benefits of alternative paths of behaviour. Today, by contrast, some of the most vigorous debates are between neo-utilitarianism of any kind and *cognitive* analysis (third-image analysis), which rests on a logic of appropriateness rather than a logic of material consequence. Collectively, cognitive approaches go under the label of constructivism, with roots in sociology and psychology (**see Table 3.1**).

Constructivism highlights the role of social relations in determining actor perceptions of identity and interests. In place of the autonomous individual, emphasis is placed on intersubjective understandings and the development of social norms. Prominent in scholarship along these lines is a growing literature incorporating core elements of feminist theory. Traditional neo-utilitarian perspectives, feminists contend, are innately androcentric, owing to the early dominance of the field by men (with the notable exception of Susan Strange). Dominant ideas in the field reflect masculine identities that were socially constructed from birth. Conventional analysis, therefore, is inherently biased, favouring male perspectives and interests. Research that neglects the role of gender is bound to yield a distorted understanding of how the global economy actually works.

3.5 Heterodox perspectives

Heterodox (or radical) perspectives differ from orthodoxy in terms of any or all of our five defining attributes. Ontology tends to be less state-centric; agendas, broader and more normative; disciplinary boundaries, more open; and methodology, less formal. Indeed, as the label of heterodoxy implies, approaches often define themselves explicitly in contradistinction to the conventions of the American style. But here too, as in orthodoxy, there are many variations on a set of common themes. Within-type variance, at times, is extreme.

3.5.1 Common themes

Five themes stand out, to a greater or lesser extent, to distinguish heterodox perspectives from orthodoxy, corresponding to our five defining attributes.

First is a rejection of the state-centrism of the American style. States still matter, but so too do many other units of analysis, ranging from the individual to the global. The state is just one actor of interest among many, and by no means the most central. Heterodox approaches question why the state must necessarily be prioritized for purposes of analysis. For the American school, with its roots in the discipline of political science, a focus on the sovereign nation seems natural. But for others, coming to the subject from other academic specialties such sociology, history, or international studies, other ontologies seem equally legitimate.

Second is a broadening of the research agenda to go well beyond orthodoxy's core problematique of inter-state politics and governance. For many heterodox scholars, it makes sense to concentrate instead on the evolution of the global system as a whole, understood in terms of vast and complex social structures, with particular emphasis on transcendent issues of power, inequality, development, and change. The core problematique, it is argued, should encompass the causes and consequences of systemic transformation in historical context—what has been labelled a 'historical-relativist paradigm' (R. Tooze 1985: 121). A wide-band historical-relativist paradigm contrasts sharply with the more fine-grained focus of the American school, where broader structures are rarely problematized.

Third is a departure from positivist analysis, with its emphasis on purely objective analysis. Most heterodox approaches tend to be more normative in ambition. Scholarship tends to be critical of established orthodoxies and more engaged with social issues, impatient with the status quo, and more eager to change attitudes or practices. The driving motivation is to make the world a better place. Where the mainstream American school aspires to the lofty impartiality of conventional US social science, heterodox approaches tend to be more openly value-driven in the tradition of classical moral philosophy.

Fourth is a greater receptivity to academic specialties other than economics and political science in the spirit of the open range advocated by Susan Strange. For heterodox scholars, GPE is about much more than simply the pursuit of material wealth or the processes of public governance. It is about society as a whole, with all its multiple disharmonies and complexities. So why limit ourselves to just what economics or political science can teach us? Analysis should seek illumination from wherever it can be found, regardless of traditional disciplinary boundaries.

Fifth, finally, is a more relaxed attitude towards analytical methods. Epistemology takes second place to purpose. Scholarship tends to be more qualitative than in the orthodox American style, attaching less importance to narrow hypothesis-testing or systematic evaluation of empirical evidence. Theorizing, instead, is typically more interpretive in tone and more institutional and historical in nature. The formalism of hypothetico-deductivism is valued less than a broad organic comprehension of the social context of GPE. Where the American school self-consciously restricts itself mainly to micro- or mid-level theorizing, heterodox approaches tend to aim for grander visions of structural transformation or social development.

For all that they share in common, however, heterodox approaches are no more monolithic than orthodoxy—perhaps even less so. Here too perspectives come in many flavours, reflecting sharp disagreements over all kinds of more specific questions. At the risk of over-simplification—and acknowledging again that any system of classification is bound to be, to some degree, arbitrary—it is possible to group most heterodox approaches roughly into three related sub-categories: system-level theories, critical theory, and a medley of more specialized contributions ('extensions') that seek to extend the boundaries of the field in one direction or another (**see Table 3.1**).

3.5.2 System-level theories

System-level theories are distinguished by their ontology, which centres on global structures and processes. The basic unit of interest is nothing less than the world as a whole. The preferred mode of analysis is a historical-relativist paradigm.

3.5.2.1 Marxism

Oldest among heterodox system-level perspectives is classical *Marxism*—the intellectual tradition tracing back to the writings of Karl Marx in the nineteenth century. As a body of theory, Marxism means, above all, a commitment to 'historical materialism', which Marx defined as the 'materialist conception of history'. The materialism in historical materialism means placing economic relations and the social organization of production (the 'modes' of production) at the very centre of analysis, with particular emphasis on the inherent 'contradictions' of capitalism and the 'commodification' of all aspects of life. For those working in the Marxist tradition today, such as William Robinson (2014) in the United States or Benjamin Selwyn (2015) in Britain, there is no difference between the global system and global capitalism. The global system *is* global capitalism. The focus of GPE, therefore, should properly be on class relations and the 'laws of motion' of contemporary capitalism.

3.5.2.2 Dependency theory

Over time the intellectual tradition bequeathed by Marx has proved to be a source of inspiration for a wide range of alternative system-level approaches, each combining elements of Marxist analysis with other ideas to offer its own heterodox vision of how the world works. One of the first of these was *dependency theory*, a school of thought that first emerged in Latin America in the 1950s seeking to explain the persistent poverty of peripheral regions around the globe. Long before, Marxist theorists had already promoted the image of a stratified world economy divided between a dominant core and a dependent periphery, extrapolating from V. I. Lenin's 1917 polemic, *Imperialism, the Highest Stage of Capitalism*. Global capitalism, according to Leninist ideology, naturally degenerates into a system of economic imperialism—rich nations exploiting the poor. Dependency theory added new insights about the constraints that bar improvements in the periphery. Dependency, it was argued, was self-perpetuating, offering no easy escape. Prevailing capitalist structures systematically deformed local economies and bound them to their fate—the 'development of underdevelopment', as Andre Gunder Frank (1966), a leading *dependentista*, later put it. Dependency theory remains popular today among scholars in the Global South, such as Brazil's Alexandre Rands Barros (2017) or Nigeria's Luke Amadi (2012).

3.5.2.3 World-systems theory

Another system-level perspective inspired in part by Marxism is *world-systems theory*, which grew out of the writings of the sociologist Immanuel Wallerstein (1974). Like Marxist GPE, world-systems theory concentrates on the evolution of the global capitalist system, but without the rigors of Leninist ideology. Generically, world-systems are conceived as comprehensive human interaction networks, encompassing everything from the individual and the household to national and global markets. The specific system that prevails today, the *modern world-system*, has origins that date back to the sixteenth century. The modern world-system is understood as a hierarchical and long-lasting structure composed of three distinct tiers: a dominant core along with dependent peripheral and semi-peripheral regions. Capitalism is assumed to contribute to the dynamics of the modern world-system, but only in part. Important as well is geopolitics, where corporations and governments compete vigorously for power and wealth. Competition among firms and states, in turn, is conditioned by an ongoing struggle among classes and by the resistance of peripheral and semi-peripheral peoples to domination and exploitation from the core. The world-systems perspective is especially popular with sociologists and other students of social change such as Christopher Chase-Dunn (1989) and Jason Moore (2015).

3.5.2.4 World orders

Elsewhere, another counterpoint at the system level was provided by the pioneering contributions of Robert Cox, a Canadian, who was also driven by a commitment to historical materialism to think in terms of a succession of complex social structures defined by their modes of production. He too had in mind a historical-relativist paradigm. But in place of the rigid stratifications characteristic of dependency theory or world-systems theory, Cox proposed a more fluid concept that he chose to call *'world orders'*—a succession of global systems that he saw as a function of three broad influences: material capabilities, ideas, and institutions. Historical change, he insisted, had to be thought of in terms of the reciprocal relationship of structures and actors within a much broader conceptualization of international relations, the 'state–society complex'. Outcomes would depend on the response of 'social forces', defined as the main collective actors engendered by the relations of production both within and across all spheres of activity. 'International production', he wrote, 'is mobilizing social forces, and it is through these forces that its major political consequences *vis-à-vis* the nature of states and future world orders may be anticipated' (R. Cox 1981: 147).

Cox's theories, encouraging interpretative historical analysis, have shaped generations of scholarship since they were first articulated in the early 1980s. Though largely ignored by the American school, his writings are still widely taught and debated in Britain and in Canada, his homeland. 'The work of Robert Cox', remarks one British observer, 'has inspired many students to rethink the way in which we study international political economy, and it is fair to say that [his] historical materialism is perhaps the most important alternative to realist and liberal perspectives in the field today' (Griffiths 1999: 118). To this day, numerous sources cite Cox as the starting point for their own theoretical contributions.

3.5.3 Critical theory

Heterodoxy's second sub-category is critical theory, ambitiously conceived as a form of inquiry aimed at attaining nothing less than general human emancipation. The agenda of critical theory is the broadest possible. The goal is to decrease domination and increase autonomy in all its forms. Though the approach overlaps with system-level theories, it also encompasses other levels of analysis down to social units as small as the family or the firm. At every level, the aim is to further human freedom.

Critical theory is distinguished by two related assumptions. First, empirical research cannot be separated from normative inquiry. Any notion that actors and processes in GPE can be treated in strictly objective terms is rejected. Rather, forms of agency must be understood as historically and socially dynamic and mutually constituted. And second, socioeconomic and political structures must be problematized. They are not neutral categories, given and immutable. Rather, they are potentially transitory and subject to evolutionary or revolutionary change.

Given the breadth of its ambition, critical theory is not easily summarized. Encompassed within the category are diverse variations on Marxist themes as well as all kinds of other heterodox schools of thought. Yet there remain ties that bind. One sympathetic source suggests that a more adequate label for critical theory would be 'ideologically oriented inquiry' (Griffiths 1999: 114). The common denominator, according to another commentary, is an 'oppositional frame of mind' (Brown 2001: 192). Critical theory challenges orthodoxies of every sort and is particularly averse to modern capitalism in all its guises. Proponents of critical theory can be found in every part of the world where GPE is studied (Cafruny, Talani, and Martin 2016).

3.5.4 Extensions

Finally, we come to a sub-category of more specialized contributions that seek to formally extend the boundaries of the field in one direction or another. The motive for these innovations is a sense that something important is missing from the path that scholarship has followed until now. The aim is to bring in insights from other disciplinary specialties in order to point research towards a fresh conception of GPE's ontology and purpose. The change is typically signalled by the addition of a novel descriptive label for the field.

For instance, a broader perspective on history has been pushed by numerous scholars across the globe. Prominent among them is the British scholar John Hobson, who argues for supplanting today's 'Eurocentric' GPE, rooted as it is in Western experience, with a much wider take acknowledging the role that other parts of the world have played in the past development of the field. His preferred label is either Inter-Civilizational Political Economy (Hobson 2013) or New Global Political Economy (Hobson 2021). The important contributions of early non-Western thinkers have also been emphasized by Eric Helleiner (2020), a leading Canadian scholar. Other history fans include a scattering of Continental European scholars motivated by a more comparative take on GPE—what they call Comparative Historical Political Economy (CHPE) (Boettke, Coyne, and Leeson

2013). The aim of CHPE is to develop a set of analytical tools that could be used to compare historical phases of global capitalism.

Another movement aims to extend analysis to incorporate a more sociological conception of the field. The movement has been given the name Everyday IPE (EIPE) (Hobson and Seabrooke 2009), and you will see the theme of the 'everyday' cropping up regularly in the discussions in this volume. The label signifies a shift from formal politics to a much greater emphasis on the dynamics of underlying social relations, both domestic and transnational. The proposed view is strictly 'bottom-up'. More traditional approaches, whether orthodox or heterodox, focus on elite 'power makers', whether they be hegemonic powers, international organizations, the capitalist class, or government policymakers. With EIPE, the spotlight turns to everyday folk, society's diverse masses of 'power takers'. Through their routine daily practices and patterns of behaviour, non-elite actors can confer or withhold legitimacy from elite dictates and thus exercise an independent influence on outcomes. An excellent example is provided by Kate Bedford (2019), a British scholar, in her prize-winning study of British bingo halls and their impact on systems of regulation.

Others call for a new cultural turn in GPE, comparable to the rise of constructivism as a challenge to neo-utilitarianism on the other side of the orthodox–heterodox divide (Best and Paterson 2010*b*). Cultural IPE seeks to highlight the importance of the cognitive level of analysis as a complement to more traditional rationalist and materialist approaches. A prime example is provided by a cohort of scholars aiming to make gender studies an integral part of the field—a Feminist IPE (Bakker 2007). At issue for feminist scholars are the gendered meanings that we attach to different kinds of economic activity. Traditional neo-utilitarian perspectives implicitly tend to value so-called masculine activities (e.g., competing, making money) more highly than activities commonly thought of as feminine (e.g., reproduction, family care). Hierarchies, therefore, tend to be gendered and to work to the disadvantage of women. The challenge is to highlight how understandings of masculinity and femininity shape behaviour and outcomes. The solution is to bring gender into the core of analysis as a key causal variable. In the words of one leading advocate, 'feminist work is not a digression from nor supplement to conventional accounts; rather, it is an *essential orientation* for advancing our theory *and* practice of political economy' (Peterson 2005: 518; emphasis in the original). As you heard in Chapter 1, gender offers a theoretical perspective and empirical theme that runs throughout the chapters in this book.

Lastly, we have an extension that has been prompted by concerns about climate change and its impact. The global environment, it is argued, can no longer be relegated to the margins of the field (**see Chapter 9**). The dangers of global warming and biodiversity decline are simply too great to be ignored. Damage is speeding up all around us. Greenhouse gas emissions continue to grow; temperatures are increasing, the oceans are acidifying; species extinction is spreading; permafrosts are melting; heatwaves are more frequent; the rainforests are disappearing, hurricanes are becoming more numerous and intense—all part of what earth scientists call the 'great acceleration'. A new Global Ecological Political Economy (GEPE), we are told, is needed to explore how all of this will shape the future of the world economy (Katz-Rosene and Paterson 2018). Nothing less than the survival of the human species may be at stake.

3.6 **Making choices**

In summary, it is evident that the ecology of GPE is indeed robust. The number of flowers that have bloomed over the years may not reach literally to a hundred, but the field's dense proliferation of perspectives is certainly impressive. Our five defining attributes—ontology, agenda, purpose, boundaries, and epistemology—help us to think about how to distinguish among the many approaches that compete for attention. But a critical question remains: How do we *choose* among all these contending paradigms for purposes of study? How can we make best practical use of all this diversity?

The answer, I suggest, depends first and foremost on our *goal*. What are we aiming for? Clearly, our choices among theoretical perspectives should seek to match up best with our analytical intentions. Is the historical evolution of global structures our concern? In that case, we would hardly want to limit ourselves to approaches that are designed more for exploring, say, the role of cognition (e.g., constructivism, cultural GPE) or the domestic politics of sovereign states (American school). Conversely, if applied policy interests us, we would hardly look first to heterodox system-level approaches (e.g., world-systems, world orders) for practical advice. An approach in the American style would certainly seem appropriate if our aim is limited to gaining objective understanding of some key aspect of the world economy as it operates today. But if our purpose is more normative, seeking to right wrongs or promote justice, we would undoubtedly be better off turning to any of a number of heterodox approaches, including critical theory in particular. Every perspective in GPE was developed with a particular problematique in mind, giving each a comparative advantage for certain specific applications. Our choices should be guided accordingly.

Above all, choice demands that we abandon dogmatic allegiance to any single research tradition, no matter how appealing. The rich diversity of GPE should be embraced, not rejected. As Rudra Sil and Peter Katzenstein (2010), two US-based scholars, have contended, our minds should remain open to all available perspectives, ruled by two paramount principles: pragmatism and eclecticism. *Pragmatism* means a willingness to be flexible in our choice of analytical approach. We must not be wedded to any single paradigm to the exclusion of all others. *Eclecticism* means a readiness to draw on any combination of paradigms that seem right for the research objective at hand. We must not overlook the value that might be added by any of the field's many traditions and styles. Differences of overall perspective do not exclude the possibility of creative synergies among specific elements of theory or methodology. The ambition, ultimately, is simply to get the best insight we can.

Katzenstein (2005) himself provides an instructive model in his monumental study *A World of Regions*. The book skilfully interweaves elements from a variety of traditions to explore the role of regions in an increasingly globalized world economy. Ours is a world of regions, he contends, each distinct in institutional form, type of identity, and internal structure. In the manner of constructivism and cultural GPE, he highlights the role of cognitive factors in determining how regions come to be defined. In the manner of hypothetico-deductivism, he uses systematic case-study methodology to test his arguments, carefully sifting all available evidence. And in the manner of a historical-relativist approach, he frames his discussion as a question of systemic transformation set in broad historical context. The book succeeds precisely because it is so pragmatic and eclectic.

That is the way to think about GPE.

Key Points

- Global Political Economy is a vast and variegated field of study, offering a multitude of theoretical approaches and perspectives. The most salient characteristic of the field is its diversity.
- Perspectives can be distinguished from one another along five key dimensions: ontology, agenda, purpose, boundaries, and epistemology. *Ontology* refers to the choice of unit of analysis. *Agenda* asks what issues are to be addressed. *Purpose* highlights the goal of analysis. *Boundaries* are about where to draw a line around the field of study. *Epistemology* is about the choice of methodology.
- At the most general level, the field is divided between two broad approaches, typically described as either orthodox or heterodox theoretical perspectives. *Orthodox* perspectives share a preference for a state-centric ontology, positivism, closed disciplinary boundaries, and rigorous methodology. *Heterodox* perspectives are less state-centric, agendas are broader and more normative, boundaries are more open, and methodology is less formal.
- Orthodox perspectives may be subdivided into three main variations: liberalism, realism, and constructivism.
- Heterodox perspectives include a variety of system-level theories, critical theory, and approaches that seek to extend the boundaries of the field in one direction or another.

Further Reading

Clift, B., and Rosamond, B. (2009), 'Lineages of a British International Political Economy', in M. Blyth (ed.), *Routledge Handbook of International Political Economy (IPE): IPE as a Global Conversation* (London: Routledge): 95–111. An insightful discussion of the richness and diversity of GPE scholarship in Britain, with an emphasis on the historical roots of the field going back to classical IPE. British GPE, Clift and Rosamond argue, evolved over time in intellectual conditions of loose disciplinarity, multidisciplinarity, and engagement with a variety of system-level theories.

Cohen, B. (2019), *Advanced Introduction to International Political Economy*, rev. 2nd edn. (Cheltenham, UK: Edward Elgar). A comprehensive *tour d'horizon* of GPE as it exists today across the globe, from mainstream and heterodox versions of the field in the United States to diverse variations in Britain, Continental Europe, Australia, Canada, Latin America, and China.

Phillips, N., and Weaver, C. (eds) (2011), *International Political Economy: Debating the Past, Present and Future* (London: Routledge). A compendium of brief commentaries on the alleged 'transatlantic divide' between the American and British schools of GPE. The collection includes the thoughts of prominent scholars from both sides of the Atlantic.

Seabrooke, L., and Young, K. L. (2017), 'The Networks and Niches of International Political Economy', *Review of International Political Economy* 24(2): 288–331. A highly refined empirical study of how social clustering operates within the broad field of GPE. Seabrooke and Young find that while in publishing GPE is highly pluralist and driven by a logic of 'niche proliferation', teaching is characterized more by a 'reduction to polarity' between orthodoxy and heterodoxy.

Vivares, E. (ed.) (2020), *The Routledge Handbook to Global Political Economy* (London: Routledge). A wide-ranging collection of essays representing multiple variations of heterodox GPE. The emphasis of the volume is on the diversity of radical contributions and insights to be found around the world. A majority of the authors are from Continental Europe and the Global South.

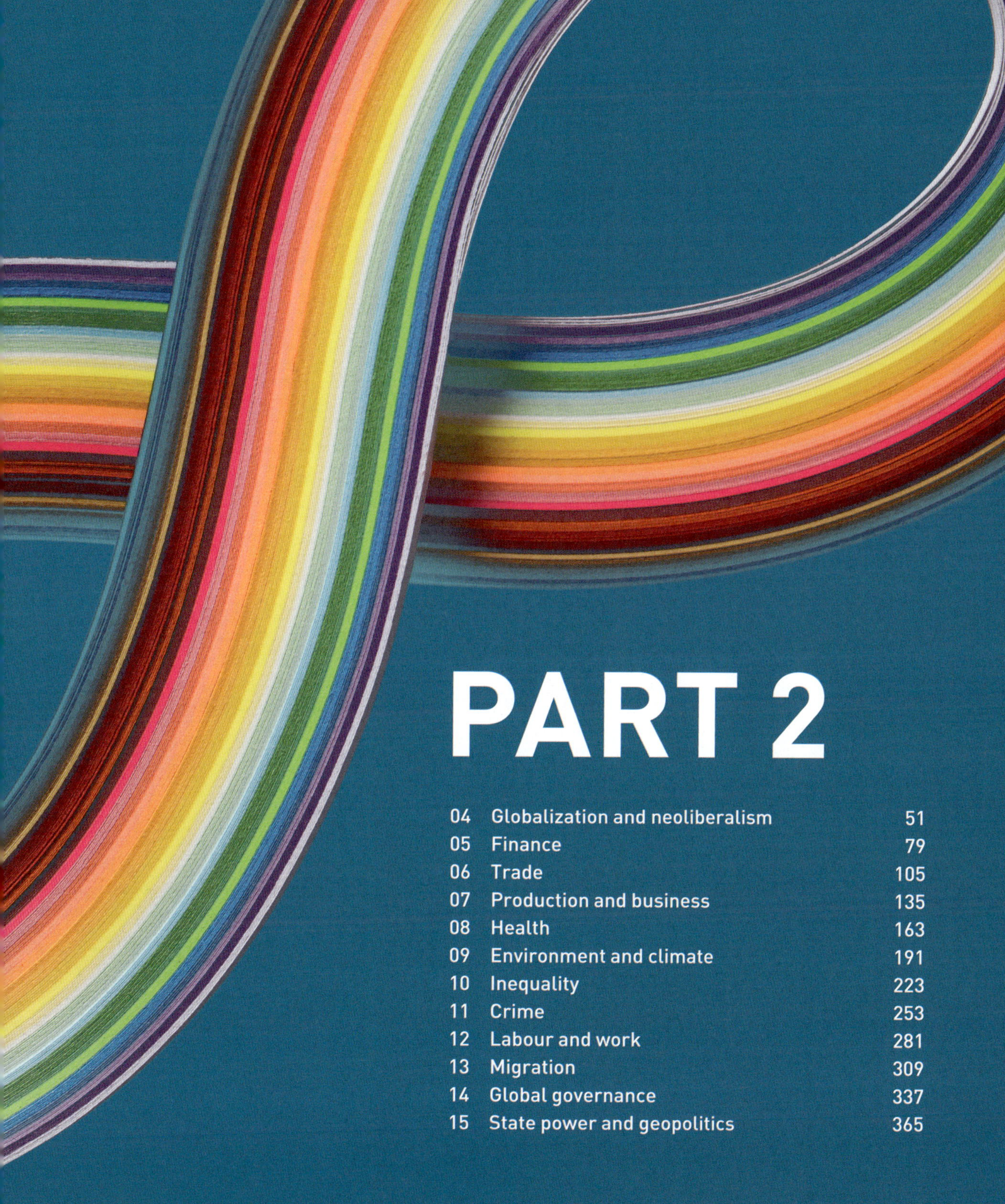

PART 2

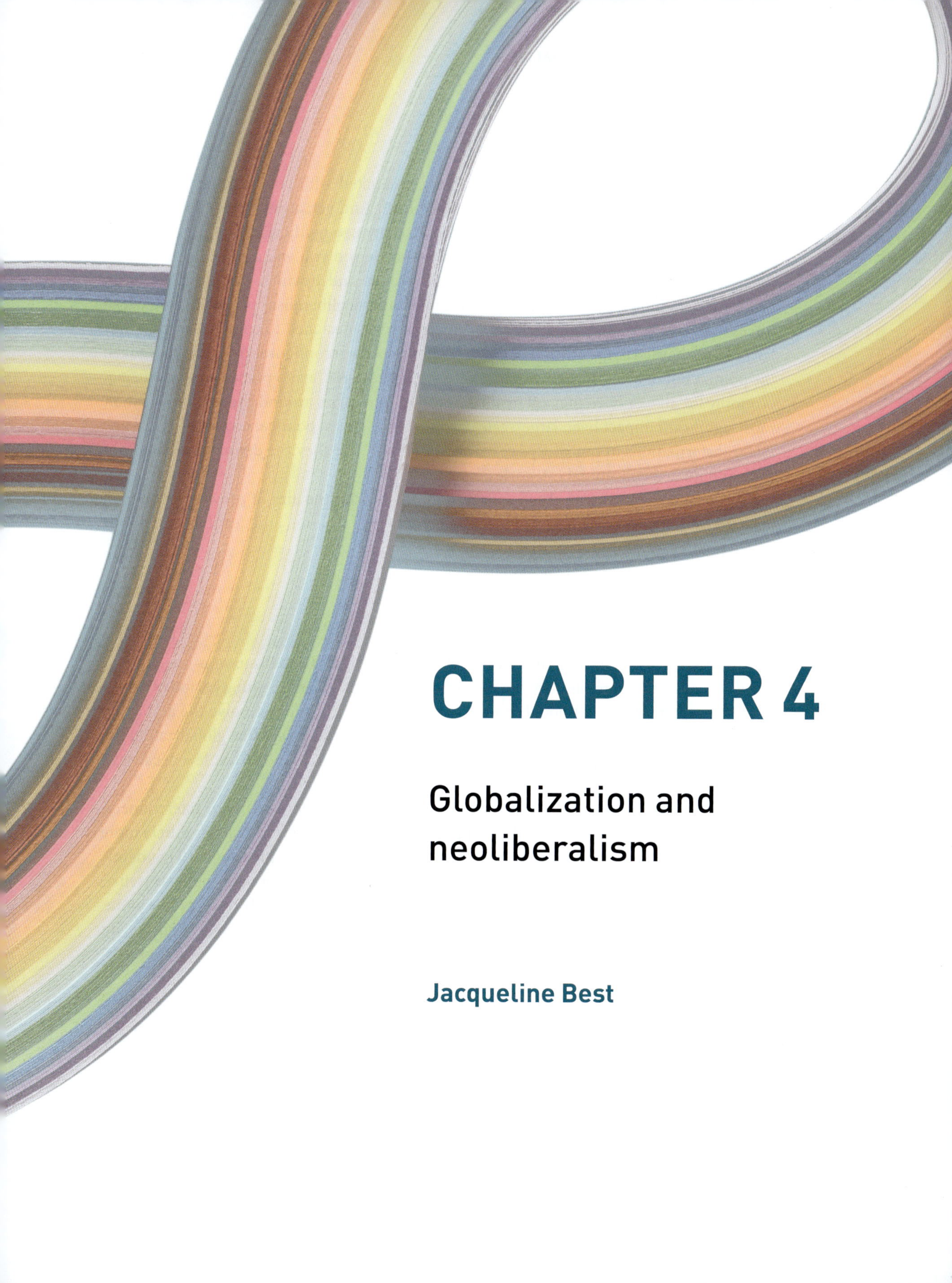

CHAPTER 4

Globalization and neoliberalism

Jacqueline Best

4.1 Introduction

There are probably no two words more closely associated with contemporary global political economy than globalization and neoliberalism. And yet, at the same time, there are few concepts that are as contested as these two. Ask any two political economists what they think these terms mean and what their significance is and you will almost invariably get different answers—a situation that Leonard Seabrooke and Kevin L. Young reflect on in **Section 2.3.2**. Should we understand globalization and neoliberalism primarily as material forces that have reshaped the world or as powerful ideas designed to convince us that they have? Have they led to the erosion of the state's power or its reconfiguration? Have they taken the politics out of economic governance by enabling technocrats to pursue a more efficient economy for all—or have they intensified power asymmetries around the world? Has their most significant impact been large-scale changes to the global political economy or less visible transformations in our everyday lives? And, finally, are they the defining forces of our time or outdated conceptual categories?

This chapter will take up these debates and others with the aim of providing you with an appreciation of the complex and contested role of globalization and neoliberalism in the global political economy.

4.2 What is globalization?

The former US Secretary of Labor Robert Reich once joked, 'Globalization is one of those words to have gone from obscurity to meaningless without any intervening period of coherence' (Kornbluth 2013). Although it may not be possible to entirely resolve the ambiguity of the term, we can at least map out some of the most important ways that globalization has been used since it first became widespread in the social sciences in the last few decades of the twentieth century.

One of the simplest ways of defining globalization is as an increase in our interconnectedness across the globe—so that what happens in one part of the world affects others more quickly and significantly than in the past. Just think of the way that the Covid-19 pandemic spread from one part of the world to another, as travellers brought it with them, as well as how scientific discoveries about the virus and possible responses quickly travelled the globe. While the 1918 influenza pandemic was also global in scope, it spread much more slowly. And although scientists developed a vaccine for polio as they did for Covid-19, it took decades rather than months to do so.

As this example reveals, another way of thinking about this growing interconnectedness is in terms of its spatial and temporal dimensions: the world is far smaller from a human perspective than it once was, as we can move ourselves, our money, and our ideas around more easily and quickly, shrinking the distances that once separated us (Harvey 1990).

Scholars have pointed to the impact of globalization on culture: music, fashion, ideas, and memes can spread rapidly around the world too, leading to greater cultural diversity in some areas (as we can enjoy a much wider range of kinds of food or styles of music than in the past), and more homogeneity in others (as the same brands and chains colonize every major city in the world).

Many scholars also focus on material objects, particularly various forms of technological innovation, as major forces driving globalization. They point to the ways in which objects both large and small, ranging from steam-powered trains and ships, airplanes, and standardized shipping containers to mobile phones and barcodes, have enabled the movement of people, money, goods, and ideas around the world far more easily than in the past (Thrift et al. 2014).

All of these different dimensions of globalization come into play when we focus on its role in the global political economy and look at how international finance, production, and trade have changed over the past decades.

Those who want to emphasize the dramatic impact of globalization on the world economy often point to international finance. Starting in the 1980s, as many governments decided to liberalize—or deregulate and open up—their financial systems, it became much easier to move money quickly around the world and to buy and sell securities from different countries, as **Chapter 5** explains. In 2019, foreign exchange markets (which allow investors to trade one currency into another) saw $6.6 trillion of funds changing hands in a single day, massively outpacing the trade in actual goods (BIS 2019).

Production processes have also been globalized over the past decades, as what were once largely nationally based supply chains have become spread out over many different countries, as **Chapter 7** and **Chapter 12** explain further. Corporations have found ways of cutting their costs by locating different stages in their products' design, production, and assembly in various countries.

Of course, in order for a company to be able to move its products from country to country multiple times before it sells them to consumers, it must be able to rely on inter-state agreements that allow the free movement of goods. Trade liberalization—or the removal of various tariffs, quotas, and other limits to trade—has also played an important role in increasing the globalization of production and consumption (**see Chapter 6**).

Although most scholars would agree that these economic changes are underway, they often disagree about how politically salient they are. To map these debates, some time ago David Held and his co-authors (1999) developed a typology which remains useful today, which includes 'hyperglobal', 'sceptical', and 'transformational' approaches to globalization.

As **Table 4.1** illustrates, *hyperglobalists* like Kenichi Ohmae (1995) argue that globalization is radically transforming the political and economic landscape, dramatically reducing the importance of state borders, eroding traditional North–South inequalities, and reducing the power of the state.

Sceptics like Paul Hirst and Grahame Thompson (1996) on the other hand dispute these claims, pointing out that global interdependence was in many ways higher in the nineteenth century than today and arguing that the state remains the key political economic actor. What we are witnessing today, they argue, is better described as 'internationalization' among sovereign nation-states who remain the key drivers of these economic processes.

Finally, those who take a *transformational* approach to the question see globalization as a profound social and political force but emphasize its role in transforming rather than eroding the power of the state (Cerny 1997; Sassen 1996).

Table 4.1 **Approaches to the politics of globalization**

	Hyperglobal	Sceptical	Transformational
Significance of globalization	Complete transformation	Significantly overstated	Real but complex
Power of states	Significantly eroded	Increased	Changed in quality
Main features	Global capitalism and governance	Less state interdependence than nineteenth century	Complex shifts in territory, sovereignty, and power
Synopsis	'The end of the nation-state'	States are key actors driving globalization	Globalization is transforming state power

Source: Adapted from Held et al. 1999: 10.

As you read this chapter, it is worth keeping these perspectives on globalization in mind and considering which (if any) of these positions is best supported by the evidence.

4.3 A contested history of globalization

When did globalization begin? There is little doubt that the global political economy has undergone some very significant changes over time and that these changes have accelerated since the 1970s. Yet not all scholars agree on whether we should focus on this most recent round of changes as the starting point for globalization or look further back in time to understand current dynamics. Others have gone further and have suggested that the concept of globalization itself has been compromised by the poverty of the historical assumptions that are embedded in the concept.

4.3.1 Globalization and empire

Ironically, one of the most powerful historical accounts of the ways that political and economic connections were forged around the world is one that actively resists the concept of globalization itself. In his article, 'What Is the Concept of Globalization Good For? An African Historian's Perspective', Frederick Cooper (2001) suggests that there are two problems with the term: 'first the "global," and second the "-ization"'. The problem with the term 'global', he argues, is that it suggests a universal set of connections linking people and countries around the world. The problem with the '-ization' is that it presumes that these changes are happening now for the first time.

In contrast, Cooper proposes that we take seriously the long, complex, and often 'lumpy' connections that were forged between the Global North and the Global South during the many centuries in which empires held sway. Two particularly important examples of this kind of transnational connection were the triangular trades through which European economies exploited the people and resources in the Global South (**see Case Study 4.1**).

Case Study 4.1: Early globalization and the triangular trades

Two intersecting systems of triangular trade played crucial roles in the early development of the global political economy: the Atlantic slave trade and Britain's imperial trade with India and China (Map 4.1).

The Atlantic slave trade lasted from the sixteenth through the nineteenth centuries, forcibly removing over 12 million African men, women, and children from their homelands to live and die under horrific conditions as slave labourers in the Americas (Blackburn 1997). The sugar, cotton, and tobacco that their labour harvested was then shipped to Europe where it was exchanged for guns, cloth, and other manufactured goods that were used to 'buy' the slaves in Africa. This trade was crucial for the early development of modern capitalism, generating the raw goods that Europe needed to fuel its rapid industrialization (Williams 1944). At the same time, economic ideas and techniques were also transmitted this way: as Raj Patel and Jason Moore (2017) have noted, many of the innovations in the division of labour that were pioneered in slave plantations were used much later in factories throughout Europe.

Beginning in the nineteenth century, a second triangular trade began to take shape, with imperial Britain at its heart. The first side of the triangle was Britain's import of tea from China, which had grown until it vastly outweighed China's desire to import goods from Britain (Liu 2020). This trade imbalance was solved through an indirect trade via India, which was then a British colony. The second side of the triangle involved India's import of British cotton, which was imposed through one-way tariffs that ensured that the Lancashire goods replaced locally produced textiles, ultimately leading to the de-industrialization of India (Davis 2017). The final side was China's import of Indian opium—a trade that Britain first encouraged and then imposed with its gunboats through the Opium Wars (1839–42 and 1856–60) when China sought to limit the addictive trade.

Map 4.1 Triangular trade

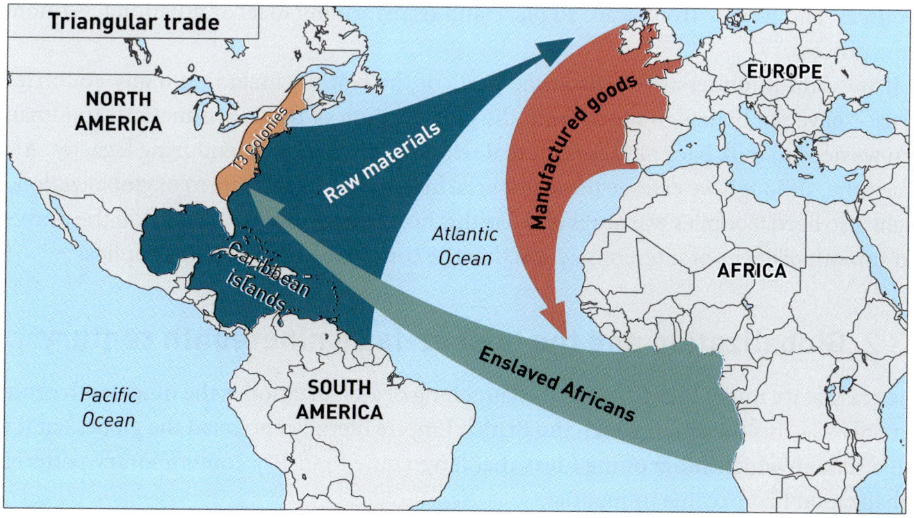

Source: *Encyclopædia Britannica, Inc.*/ Kenny Chmielewski.

(Continued)

Why are these much earlier patterns of global trade so important today?

Both triangular trades make it clear that it was not the natural functioning of the 'free market' that produced the modern global economy, but rather the ruthless application of force by colonial powers, whether in the form of gunboats or iron chains.

They also both reveal just how crucial colonialism has been to the Global North's dominant position within the global economic order. As Mike Davis notes, between 1850 and 1900, India and China's contribution to global GNP dropped from 65 per cent to 38 per cent (and then to 22 per cent by 1960) (2017: 204).

Finally, by recognizing the crucial role of these colonial practices in the early evolution of the global capitalist economy, we can begin to identify the lasting legacies of colonialism today (Bhambra 2021).

Questions

1 Should we see these triangular trades as early forms of globalization, or should we reject the concept of globalization altogether in favour of a concept that can appreciate the uneven character of global connections?
2 What are the legacies of these triangular trades today?

The most infamous—and heinous—of these triangular trades was the slave trade which, from the sixteenth through the nineteenth centuries, ensured a constant supply of forced labour in European colonies in North America and the West Indies, which in turn produced the raw goods that European countries needed to develop their economies. Imperial economic practices forged powerful new links between parts of the world, moving people, resources, and money from place to place and transforming local and national economies in the process.

If we want to understand why some parts of the world—including many countries in Africa—have not benefited much from the globalization of trade, production, and finance, then we need to look back at these colonial relationships and their enduring legacies. At the same time, although we can see these imperial linkages as an early form of globalization, we might also heed Cooper's warnings and use this historical evidence to question the universal and smooth patterns of interconnection that the concept of globalization implies.

4.3.2 Globalization and the laissez-faire nineteenth century

One era that we might identify with the launching of globalization is the nineteenth century. Not only was this the era in which the British Empire literally encircled the globe, but it was also a time in which some of the ideas that have come to justify contemporary patterns of globalization first became influential.

When the early imperialist powers sought to create new political and economic linkages around the world in the fifteenth through eighteenth centuries, they did so primarily as mercantilists (**see Chapter 6**). Mercantilism was a state-centric approach to economic relations that viewed exchanges in zero-sum terms. When Spain, Holland, or Great Britain first set out to build their empires or to trade with neighbouring countries, their ultimate goal was to enrich their nation—ideally by increasing their stock of gold. Although they were keen to expand trade, they privileged the kind of unequal trade that they could conduct with their own colonies—and put in place a wide range of tariffs and other forms of protection in order to ensure that they always came out ahead.

When Adam Smith published *The Wealth of Nations* in 1776, it was this mercantilist approach to international economic relations that he was challenging. In an early version of today's liberal arguments in favour of free trade, he insisted that free economic exchange between countries was positive sum, benefitting all involved (A. Smith 1776).

Although Smith did not live to see the tariffs that he argued against abolished, by the mid-nineteenth century, Britain had begun to remove many of its protectionist measures as it shifted away from mercantilism and embraced the liberal ideal of a laissez-faire economy. This was an economic philosophy that was highly sceptical not only of a government's place in the domestic economy but also of any attempts it might make to limit international trade or financial flows.

As Britain's political and economic power expanded in the nineteenth century, it sought to create a global economic system in which laissez-faire would be a core organizing principle. One of the institutional pillars of this economic order was the gold standard, an international monetary system in which countries agreed to exchange their currencies for a set amount of gold (such as the British official price in the late nineteenth century of £4.24 per ounce). This system made it easy for individuals or firms to move money among those countries on the gold standard, as their currencies were all exchangeable for gold.

The other institutional pillar of this global economic order was the British Empire, which ensured that even as Britain championed the virtues of a liberalized economy, the British economy benefited unequally from its global exchanges with its colonies and those countries, like China, that they had bound through unequal treaties (**see Case Study 4.1**). This was an era of 'free trade imperialism', in which liberal values combined with *realpolitik* strategies to forge a globally interconnected economy with clear winners and losers.

4.3.3 Globalization as a late twentieth-century phenomenon

As striking as the parallels may be between the nineteenth century and today, it would be a mistake to assume that we can simply draw a straight line between the early patterns of globalization that we see then and the present day. A great deal happened on the global stage between the late nineteenth century and the end of the twentieth century—including two World Wars, the Great Depression, and the slow move towards decolonization. These events had profound effects on the structure of the global political economy and led to a pull-back from global integration for a significant length of time.

Key Concept: The Great Depression

Precipitated by a stock market crash in 1929 and lasting a full decade, the Great Depression was the longest and most severe worldwide economic downturn. The intensity of this economic crisis was enough to force major rethinking in macroeconomic policy, ultimately contributing to the rejection of laissez-faire liberalism after the Second World War.

In his influential book on the crises of the first half of the twentieth century, *The Great Transformation*, Karl Polanyi (1944) argued that the First World War, the Great Depression, and the Second World War were linked to the global economic system of the time. He argued that the nineteenth century's laissez-faire capitalism had 'disembedded' economic relations from the national political and social systems upon which they were dependent, producing a highly volatile and unstable global order.

John Maynard Keynes, an economist and chief architect of the British proposals for the post-war economic order, had also argued some years earlier that the laissez-faire economic order that had dominated the international economy was a failure, insisting, 'It is not intelligent, it is not beautiful, it is not just, it is not virtuous—and it doesn't deliver the goods' (Keynes 1933).

When political and economic leaders from around the world, including Keynes, met in 1944 at Bretton Woods, New Hampshire, in the USA to decide on the structure of the post-war economic order, they sought to return to states the tools that they needed to manage their economies according to domestic political and economic priorities (**see Chapter 5**). Although political economists have often focused on the roles of the United Kingdom and the United States in these negotiations, Eric Helleiner (2014*a*) has revealed the central role played by countries in the Global South, including China, India, and a powerful contingent from Latin America, who sought to use this moment to create an international order that would be more supportive of their development.

Together, countries from around the world agreed to create a global economic system that would allow them to pursue their own state-led forms of development. Although governments sought to encourage global trade, they allowed one another to retain various controls on the free movement of money, or capital. This was an era of 'embedded liberalism' (Ruggie 1982), in which the liberal goal of creating an open global economic system was combined with an effort to embed those values and practices within a political system that gave significant autonomy to the nation-state.

By the 1970s, however, this post-war economic order was coming undone, as what had been a very stable and prosperous 'golden era' of growth gave way to a decade of high inflation, repeated recessions, and economic shocks. It was during this decade of huge political and economic instability that the seeds of the current globalized economic order were sown.

Key political economic actors—many of them espousing neoliberal ideas (**see Section 4.4**)—seized this moment of crisis to argue for the bankruptcy of the post-war economic system and to propose their own alternative, which harked back in many ways to the laissez-faire era. As neoconservative political leaders like UK Prime Minister Margaret Thatcher and US President Ronald Reagan came into office in the late 1970s and early 1980s, they moved quickly to deregulate their domestic economies and liberalize their international economic relations.

At the same time as the Anglo-American economic consensus shifted away from embedded liberalism and towards neoliberal globalization, international financial institutions including the World Bank and the International Monetary Fund (IMF) also began to impose conditions for their loans that required poorer countries to open their own economies up to international financial flows, trade, and production as well—a practice known as 'conditionality' (**see Section 15.2**).

4.4 What is neoliberalism?

From the 1980s onwards, neoliberalism and globalization become very difficult to separate out. Neoliberal ideas and policies have played three crucial roles in the evolution of globalization in recent decades: spreading globally and becoming embedded in institutional practices around the world; inspiring governments to embrace globalization; and emerging as a powerful set of ideas that suggests that globalization is not only universally beneficial but also inevitable.

Echoing Reich's quip about globalization (**see Section 4.2**), Stephanie Mudge (2008) has suggested that neoliberalism is an 'oft-invoked but ill-defined concept'. Mudge corrects this failure by providing a useful first cut at conceptualizing neoliberalism, suggesting that it has three intersecting 'faces': 1) an intellectual and professional face organized around a set of influential economic ideas that tout the free market as central to solving most political and economic problems; 2) a bureaucratic face that seeks to implement these ideas through a range of policies such as privatization, deregulation, and liberalization; and 3) a political face that gains political and electoral capital from a set of policy promises that emphasizes the centrality of market forces (Mudge 2008: 707). What all three faces have in common is a belief in the 'free market' as an absolute and unquestionable value in political and economic life.

Based on the historical account that I traced in **Section 4.3.2**, it is clear that these views have much in common with the laissez-faire politics of the nineteenth century. And yet, it is also important to note the differences as well as the similarities between 'liberalism' and 'neoliberalism'.

As Michel Foucault outlines in his lectures on the liberal and neoliberal logics of governing, liberals in the eighteenth century like Smith set out to establish a minimalist form of government in which the fear was always that *'on gouverne toujours trop'* [one always governs too much], and the answer was *'laissez-nous faire'* by letting the market do its job (Foucault 2004: 20). In contrast, he suggested, the twentieth century's neoliberals had lost their faith in the minimalist liberal vision of markets running themselves and saw the role of government in far more maximalist terms, as a means of actively producing a market-centred society (Foucault 2004: 120).

As Quinn Slobodian puts it, 'The core of twentieth-century neoliberal theorizing involves what they called the meta-economic or extra-economic conditions for safeguarding capitalism at the scale of the entire world' (2018: 2). The state has always played an important role in neoliberal politics, as Cemal Burak Tansel notes in **Roundtable 4.2**.

Watch the video on the online resources to take your understanding of this section further.

> ### Key Concept: Minimalist and maximalist forms of neoliberalism
>
> Neoliberalism takes both minimalist and maximalist forms today: on the one hand, we live in a world in which many governments have pared back labour legislation designed to protect workers in the name of greater labour market flexibility. On the other, many governments have reorganized the delivery of publicly funded education so that schools' performance is measured and compared, encouraging parents to 'shop around' for the best value. In the first example, the government is trying to 'get out of the way' of the market, while in the second, it is redesigning policies delivered by the state so that they function more like their idea of a free market.

4.5 A brief history of neoliberalism and its role in globalization

Although the term 'neoliberal' was coined in 1938, most scholars locate its intellectual origins in 1947, at the very first meeting of what was to become the Mont Pèlerin Society, a group of free-market economists that included Friedrich Hayek and Milton Friedman—the two figures most commonly identified with the neoliberal 'intellectual movement' as Slobodian notes in **Roundtable 4.4**.

While the early founders of neoliberal thought did not always agree with each other, they were united in their opposition to what they labelled 'collectivism'—which they saw as a broad trend underpinning much of the post-war economic order. The political and economic leaders who had built that order had put limits on global financial activity to give nation-states more autonomy (**see Section 4.3.3**). Many governments used that autonomy to involve the state more actively in the economy, through the creation of a welfare state in much of the Global North, and through the pursuit of state-led development in the Global South, as was advocated by the influential Argentinian economist, Raúl Prebisch (1959).

> ### Key Concept: The welfare state
>
> After the shocks of the Great Depression and the Second World War, many governments became more active in providing for the basic welfare of their populations, creating public pension plans, funding education and healthcare, and in other ways building the social infrastructure needed for a robust and more equitable economy.

While the early advocates of neoliberalism were ardently opposed to these policies and proposed their own market-based alternatives, they were unable to gain much political traction for their ideas until the late 1970s and early 1980s, when economic instability created an opportunity for neoconservative political leaders to try to put neoliberal ideas into practice.

Both the neoconservative British and American governments of the early 1980s were influenced by neoliberal ideas and drew inspiration and practical advice from neoliberal economists including Hayek and Friedman. Yet, it would be a mistake to assume that there was a straight line linking neoliberal theories with the economic policies that first took hold in the 1980s in the UK and the United States. Although some of the most important policies of the era were inspired by neoliberal ideas, including monetarism and public choice theory, many of the initial attempts to put them into practice failed. Friedman's monetarist theory, for example, predicted that it would be possible to dramatically reduce inflation by controlling the money supply, an idea that was put into practice in the United States, Canada, and the UK and that produced shockingly high interest rates, huge recessions, and continued high inflation, leading governments to give up on the experiment within a few short years (Best 2020).

It would also be a mistake to see early neoliberal policies as an exclusively Anglo-American phenomenon. Well before neoliberal policies were introduced in the UK and the United States, they were tried out in Chile, when a group of Chilean economists who had studied under Friedman at the University of Chicago (known as the 'Chicago Boys') set out to create a new free-market order after Augusto Pinochet took power in a brutal military coup in 1973. Between 1973 and 1980, they set about privatizing state-controlled companies, cutting education, health, and social services, and liberalizing the financial sector.

From the late 1970s onwards, neoliberalism and globalization became increasingly interconnected, as neoliberal policymakers began to push for financial deregulation, trade liberalization, the deregulation of labour markets, and the globalization of production. International financial institutions (IFIs) like the IMF and the World Bank, which had originally been created at the meeting in Bretton Woods in 1944 with mandates consistent with the principles of embedded liberalism (**see Section 4.3.3**), pivoted instead to become the enforcers of neoliberal globalization, making the adoption of neoliberal policies a condition of receiving development aid. In 1989, John Williamson, an American economist, famously coined the term 'the Washington consensus' to describe the major reforms that Western donors and IFIs were demanding.

Key Concept: The Washington consensus

The Washington consensus was a list of neoliberal reforms that IFIs demanded of borrowing countries in the Global South:

1. Fiscal discipline (reducing budget deficits)
2. Reordering public expenditure priorities (reducing and redirecting subsidies)
3. Tax reform
4. Liberalizing interest rates (and financial systems more generally)
5. A competitive exchange rate
6. Trade liberalization
7. Liberalization of inward foreign direct investment
8. Privatization
9. Deregulation
10. Property rights

Adapted from Williamson 2002.

By the 1990s, neoliberalism was no longer the preserve of right-wing governments. Across North America and Latin America, in the UK and throughout Europe, a growing number of centre-left parties embraced what became known as the 'Third Way' and sought to implement many of the tenets of neoliberalism—including the liberalization of finance, the deregulation of labour markets, and the push for greater globalization.

Yet, even as neoliberalism reached its peak globally in the late 1990s and early 2000s, there were already significant regional examples of difference and resistance.

The Asian financial crisis of 1997–98, discussed in **Section 5.3.1**, was a devastating blow to many East Asian and Southeast Asian economies, pushing many people back into a level of poverty that they thought they had left behind. This crisis, which had been driven by panicked foreign investors, not only revealed the dangers of following the neoliberal prescriptions of liberalizing financial markets, but also reinforced many Asian countries' conviction in the value of pursuing their own state-led approach to economic development.

In Latin America, the late 1990s and early 2000s were defined by a different form of resistance to neoliberalism—as newly elected left-wing governments in countries including Argentina, Brazil, Bolivia, and Chile set out a diverse range of policies that many have labelled 'post-neoliberalism' (Ruckert, Macdonald, and Proulx 2017).

When the 2008 Global Financial Crisis hit, beginning in the American housing market and spreading its devastation rapidly around the world with the help of an underregulated global financial system, many scholars (myself included) believed that it would serve as a major wake-up call. Although, as **Chapter 5** explains, some reforms were introduced in the wake of the crisis, on balance, it is hard not to see it as a failure that was largely ignored—at least in the Global North.

Among middle-income countries and in much of the Global South, the failure of the economies that had most strongly championed the virtues of neoliberal globalization has certainly tarnished its reputation. At the same time, we have begun to see the spread of a new kind of resistance to neoliberal globalization—one that is driven by the rise of populist nationalism in many countries around the world (Photo 4.1). Although these more populist

Photo 4.1 Anti-capitalist rally outside Bank of England and Royal Stock Exchange, City of London, October 2008

Source: Julio Etchart / Alamy Stock Photo.

political movements are led by political figures on the left and the right, they share a disillusionment with neoliberal globalization.

4.6 **Winners and losers**

Taking a political economic lens to the rise and spread of globalization and neoliberalism means paying attention to the political effects that they have had, and the winners and losers that they have created.

Those who champion the virtues of globalization tend to emphasize global, aggregate data that show significant rises in global economic flows through trade, investment, and finance. The volume of international trade, alone, for example, was forty-one times higher in 2019 than in 1950 (WTO 2021*a*).

Yet not all countries have been equally integrated into these growing global economic flows. When we focus on national and regional patterns instead, we find that integration into the global economy is quite uneven around the world. Many of the benefits of globalization have gone to countries in the Global North, as they leveraged the advantages that they gained during colonial times to ensure that regulations in trade, finance, and production worked in their favour.

Asian economies have also become more central to global trade and production networks in the past few decades (WTO 2013). Some emerging market countries—including those labelled as the 'BRICS' (Brazil, Russia, India, China, and South Africa)—have also become much more significant players in the global economy, as Andrew Hurrell discusses in **Chapter 15**. On the other hand, when poorer countries have been integrated into global production, investment, and trade networks it has often been on highly unequal terms and with perverse effects (Chang 2002; J. Ferguson 2005; **see Chapter 7**).

The picture gets even more complicated when we focus instead on levels of inequality—both within and among countries around the world. As Eduardo Ortiz-Juárez and Andy Sumner discuss in more detail in **Section 10.4**, since 1990, levels of inequality *within* countries have increased in countries with over two-thirds of the world's population, including most industrialized countries and many middle-income countries, such as China and India (UN 2020*b*). In the United States, the United Kingdom, Canada, and other English-speaking industrialized countries, the historical pattern of inequality has followed a clear 'U-shaped' curve, with the income share of the top 10 per cent declining from 1920 until the moment when neoliberal policies were adopted and then sharply increasing since then (Roser and Ortiz-Ospina 2016).

Branco Milanovic (2016) has developed some powerful statistical analyses of how levels of inequality have changed *among* different populations around the world. His famous 'elephant graph' looks at which individuals have gained the most income in relative terms between 1988 and 2008 (**see Figure 4.1**). The graph provides several insights into the effects of globalization on patterns of inequality around the world. First, the very poorest populations, concentrated in the Global South, have gained very little or nothing.

Figure 4.1 Branko Milanovic's 'elephant-shaped graph'

Source: https://catholicphilly.com/media-files/2016/08/branko-milanovice-global-inequality-elephant-curve-415x313.png

Second, some of the greatest increases have come from a growing 'global middle class' concentrated in emerging market economies, particularly in China. While these populations still earn much less than many low-income groups in the Global North, they have improved their global position considerably in the past two decades. Third, the Global North's middle class has done very poorly from globalization, achieving very few gains in real terms.

Finally, the very biggest winners in both relative and absolute terms are a growing group of global plutocrats, the richest 1 per cent (and particularly the very richest among them), who have gained enormously from neoliberal globalization.

Globalization and neoliberalism have also had important effects on different forms of inequality, as class, race, and gender *intersect* in complicated ways to increase the opportunities for some people while constraining those of others (**see Case Study 4.2**).

Social theorists have emphasized the ways in which neoliberalism operates at the micro-level, shaping everyday lives by inculcating particular forms of economic subjectivity, or ways of being in the world (Rose 1996). Drawing on Foucault's (2004) work, these scholars have pointed to how neoliberalism encourages us to see ourselves as entrepreneurs of our own lives who are responsible for every success and failure. Whereas after the Great Depression, unemployment was seen as a collective failure requiring state action, neoliberal governments have shifted responsibility to individuals who must invest in themselves and cope with the ups and downs of the economy.

Case Study 4.2: The everyday political economy of the Covid-19 pandemic

Although the Covid-19 pandemic was first and foremost a global health crisis, it has also revealed many of the political economic aspects of everyday life (see also Hiroko TAKEDA's analysis in **Roundtable 4.3**).

Although the rapid spread of Covid-19 and its variants indicates how globally we are connected today, once we focus in on the ways in which different people have experienced the pandemic, we find that it has not been universal at all. To be able to understand the differentiated impact of the pandemic, it is useful to draw on an intersectional analysis (Collins 1993), which looks at how intersecting forms of inequality, including those of gender, race, and class, can structure peoples' life chances.

In the early days of the pandemic, it quickly became evident how important essential workers were, risking their health every day to ensure that people had the necessities of life—working in manufacturing, at grocery stores, driving public transit, and providing childcare and basic healthcare (Photo 4.2). Yet these workers were not paid nearly as well on average as those who were able to work much more safely from home. In the United States, for example, almost half of low-wage workers are essential workers (Kinder and Stateler 2021).

Who got sick and who was more likely to die from Covid-19 also depended on race and class. In the UK, Black men were 3.3 times more likely to die from the virus than White men (White and Nafilyan 2020). In Canada, public health data showed that Black people, minoritized groups, and low-income earners were at considerably higher risk of testing positive for Covid-19 (CBC 2020).

Photo 4.2 **A thank you to key workers during the Covid-19 pandemic**

Source: Avpics / Alamy Stock Photo.

(*Continued*)

Although the reasons for this disparity are complex, they include the fact that racialized workers are less likely to be able to work from home and are more likely to take public transport and to live in close quarters where it is difficult to practise social distancing.

The economic impact of the pandemic was also gendered, with women disproportionately losing work or reducing their hours and taking on huge new caring responsibilities with school and childcare closures (Neely 2020). The economic recovery has taken a 'K-shape' in many countries, as Slobodian notes in **Roundtable 4.4**, with low-income workers (on the downward leg of the 'K') not recovering economically nearly as quickly as high-wage workers (on the upward leg of the 'K'). The Managing Director of the IMF, Kristalina Georgieva, has also warned that this 'K-shaped' recovery is increasingly taking a global form, with rich countries bouncing back far more quickly—with the help of rapid vaccination—while poorer countries lag far behind (Rappeport and Smialek 2021).

As TAKEDA makes clear in her analysis of the experience of Japan (**see Roundtable 4.3**), although the political economy of the Covid-19 crisis has taken different forms in different parts of the world, in many of these cases the crisis provides important insights into the everyday practices of neoliberal globalization.

Questions

1 Reflect on your own family and community's experience with Covid-19. In what ways might an intersectional analysis help you to make sense of it?
2 Does the Covid-19 crisis demonstrate the possibilities of globalization or point to its limits?

This logic of individualized responsibility makes it difficult to see systemic inequalities. As Isabella Bakker (2007) has chronicled, neoliberal cuts to social services like childcare and care for the sick and elderly have pushed those tasks back into the household where women take on a disproportionate share of caring labour.

The role of systemic racism in shaping the division of labour, the accumulation of wealth, and the distribution of property also becomes easier to ignore when the dominant way of viewing the economy is individualistic. As Lisa Tilley and Robbie Shilliam (2018) note, neoliberal subjectivity encourages us to see racism as an individual prejudice that deserves moral censure but does not require institutional change.

4.7 **Two essentially contested concepts**

I began this chapter by suggesting that globalization and neoliberalism are among the most contested concepts in the field of global political economy (**see Section 4.1**). Underpinning these various debates are three core puzzles: should we see globalization and neoliberalism as strategies for taking the politics out of economics or as deeply political strategies? Should we understand them as primarily global, macro-level processes or as having their greatest impact in reshaping everyday lives? And should we see them primarily as material phenomena or as powerful ideas?

We do not have to choose one answer over another in resolving these puzzles—but can instead use them to develop a better understanding of the complexity and power of these concepts.

4.7.1 **Beyond politics?**

In the final decades of the twentieth century, when support for neoliberalism and globalization was at its peak, many political leaders and policymakers believed in the possibility of a world in which voting for a government would be like choosing the most capable manager rather than deciding between starkly different political and economic visions. Governments signed global trade and investment deals designed to limit the ability of governments to control international economic flows (Gill 2002). They also adopted the neoliberal principle of central bank independence, protecting central bankers from democratic influence in the belief they might otherwise be pressured to allow too much inflation (McNamara 2002; J. Johnson 2016).

By adopting these forms of 'technocratic exceptionalism', governments argued that some aspects of the economy were just too important to leave to the democratic process (Best 2018). Yet, the term exceptionalism itself contradicts the claim that this was genuinely de-politicizing. Although political leaders might argue that some economic issues are too vital to subject to the uncertainty of democratic debate, the very act of exempting them from normal democratic processes is of course political. Much of the reasoning behind these policies was also political, aimed at both achieving particular political goals and values, and at gaining electoral support (Gamble 2021; Mudge 2018).

Some scholars like Ian Bruff and Cemal Burak Tansel (2019) go further and suggest that neoliberalism has always had an authoritarian flavour—one that has if anything become more pronounced in recent years with the rise of more authoritarian-leaning governments ranging from Donald Trump in the United States to Viktor Orbán in Hungary and Reçep Erdogan in Turkey.

4.7.2 **Global or everyday phenomena?**

So much of what is most visible about globalization and neoliberalism occurs at a global level, where we can track changes in economic flows and policies. At the same time, as I noted in **Section 4.6**, some of the most interesting scholarship on neoliberalism and globalization has focused on the ways in which they reshape everyday forms of economic subjectivity (TAKEDA 2008; M. Cooper 2017; Shilliam 2021).

Of course, it is not necessary to choose one or the other lens in studying globalization and neoliberalism. As **Case Study 4.2** demonstrates, it is only by linking macro-structural and everyday analyses of neoliberalism and globalization that we can better understand the complex intersections of race, class, and gender in the contemporary global political economy.

4.7.3 **Material or ideational?**

There is little doubt that both neoliberalism and globalization have had profound material effects, reshaping global political and economic patterns and changing how people live their lives. Yet neoliberalism and globalization are also clearly very powerful ideas, operating as a kind of political language.

Scholars of political economy have spent a great deal of energy debating the relative importance of ideas and material interests. In the case of the history of neoliberalism, for example, some have pointed to the election of Thatcher and Reagan as a moment of paradigm shift, in which neoliberalism eclipsed Keynesianism as the dominant theoretical framework for economic policy (Hall 1993). Others have argued instead that more mundane political, technical, and electoral concerns were really the main drivers of change (Krippner 2011; Prasad 2006).

But do we really have to choose between ideational and materialist approaches to these two concepts?

If part of the power of neoliberal ideas and practices is their ability to reshape how people experience their economic identity and relations with each other—to think of themselves as a specific kind of (self-interested, maximizing) economic citizen and to see themselves as part of a transactional rather than solidaristic political community—then we cannot easily distinguish between their power as ideas and as material effects.

And if political leaders spent much of the 1990s and early 2000s arguing (and believing) that globalization was an inescapable fact of life that must be adapted to, then acting on that claim had profound material effects—whether or not the claim was in fact true (Hay and Rosamond 2002). Ironically, the very ambiguity of neoliberalism and globalization as ideas is part of their continued practical success, allowing them to avoid responsibility for disappointments and to narrate 'quiet failures' as successes (Best 2020).

4.8 **Conclusion**

As this textbook demonstrates, the concepts of globalization and neoliberalism are key to understanding Global Political Economy. And yet they also remain profoundly contested. This chapter has provided some clues as to not only the power of globalization and neoliberalism today, but also the recent rise of new forms of opposition and protest. Neoliberal advocates' promise of a world beyond politics guided by technocratic experts who know everyone's best interest has also helped to generate a broader distrust of expertise, which has also fuelled populist critiques of elites.

At the same time, Milanovic's elephant-shaped graph (**see Figure 4.1**) makes it clear that even as the very rich have gained enormously from neoliberalism and globalization over the past decades, and a growing population in China and some other emerging market economies have made real progress, the middle classes in the Global North have seen very few gains at all.

Populist leaders on both the right and the left have tapped into the discontent produced by this economic stagnation in very different ways. Those on the right have often done so by galvanizing resentment against the new emerging global middle class in China and other countries that have gained from globalization (even if their absolute level of income remains vastly below that of the average American), while left-leaning political leaders have pointed to the inequity of the huge gains by the very wealthy.

Globalization and neoliberalism appear to be at a crossroads today. While they may have been among the most significant political economic forces over the past decades, will they continue to remain so in the decades to come? This is the central question that I and three other scholars will tackle in the **Chapter 4 Roundtable**.

Key Points

- Both globalization and neoliberalism are contested concepts. There are significant debates about the political salience of globalization, with hyperglobalists, sceptics, and transformationalists disagreeing on its implications for the power of the state.
- Scholars also disagree about when the era of globalization began: some suggest that it is a late twentieth-century phenomenon while others point to the nineteenth century as its origin point. Yet other scholars look back to the early days of colonialism and the slave trade for antecedents of modern patterns of global interconnection.
- Neoliberalism is a set of economic ideas and policies built upon a belief in the 'free market' as an unquestionable value in political and economic life. From the late 1970s onwards, neoliberalism and globalization became increasing interconnected.
- Neoliberal globalization has produced winners and losers, increasing living standards in many parts of the world while also intensifying inequality along the lines of class, race, and gender.
- At the heart of debates about neoliberalism and globalization are three core puzzles: whether they are primarily depoliticizing or repoliticizing strategies; whether they are best understood by looking at global-level processes or at changes in everyday life; and whether their power is primarily material or ideational.

Further Reading

Best, J. (2020), 'The Quiet Failures of Early Neoliberalism: From Rational Expectations to Keynesianism in Reverse', *Review of International Studies* 46: 594–612. Provides an overview of the early attempts by the Thatcher and Reagan administrations to put neoliberal theory into practice.

Brassett, J., Elias, J., Rethel, L., and Richardson, B. (2021), 'International Political Economy', in A. L. Atchison (ed.), *Political Science is for Everybody* (Toronto: University of Toronto Press). Provides an overview of the everyday approach to global political economy.

Cooper, M. (2017), *Family Values: Between Neoliberalism and the New Social Conservatism* (New York: Zone Books). Offers an analysis of the socially conservative gender norms at the heart of neoliberal economic theory and practice.

Davis, M. (2017), *Late Victorian Holocausts: El Niño Famines and the Making of the Third World* (London; New York: Verso). Chapter 9 provides an overview of the lasting global effects of the triangular trade linking Britain, China, and India in the nineteenth century.

Foucault, M. (2004), *The Birth of Biopolitics: Lectures at the Collège de France, 1978–1979* (New York: Palgrave Macmillan). Offers a powerful historical analysis of the emergence of liberal political economy and its transformation into neoliberalism.

Patel, R., and Moore, J. (2017), *A History of the World in Seven Cheap Things: Guide to Capitalism, Nature, and the Future of the Planet* (Oakland: University of California Press). Provides a critical analysis of the ways in which care, work, nature, and lives have historically been instrumentalized to forge globalized capitalism.

Tilley, L., and Shilliam, R. (2018), 'Raced Markets: An Introduction', *New Political Economy* 23: 534–43. Offers an incisive analysis of the ways in which contemporary neoliberal market economies are shaped by race.

Chapter 4 Roundtable discussion

Is neoliberalism now an exhausted model?

Roundtable 4.1
Opening contribution **Jacqueline Best**

Have the tumultuous events since the 2008 Global Financial Crisis reinforced the power of neoliberalism and globalization as concepts, demonstrated that they have reached the end of their useful life, or revealed their longstanding bankruptcy as analytic categories? Has the global political economy changed significantly since the financial crisis of 2008?

It is always hard to tell if we are living in a moment of epochal change, simply because when we are immersed in the moment, we cannot know what changes are truly significant and whether they will persist into the future. In 2008, for example, when the global financial system was brought to its knees, many scholars assumed that the crisis would inspire major changes as we had seen after the Second World War and the Great Depression. Over a decade later, it is very hard to see 2008 as any kind of turning point in the global economic order (Helleiner 2014*b*).

Yet, in the years since then, other changes have begun to occur which may well add up to a more significant shift in how the global economy works. Some of these changes, like the rise of new forms of anti-globalist nationalism and populism, can be thought of as aftershocks of the financial crisis as certain political leaders tapped into a growing frustration at the inadequacy of governments' responses to that crisis. Others, like the intensifying climate crisis and the growing recognition of systemic racism and sexism, have only recently taken up the space that they deserve in the political and economic conversation. As, year after year, we see average temperatures rise and climate-related disasters grow, it is hard not to see climate change too as a failure of the neoliberal passion for deregulation and growth at all costs.

And yet other events, most notably the Covid-19 pandemic, have simply blown up in our faces, forcing political leaders to confront difficult questions about who wins and who loses in the current Global Political Economy (McNamara and Newman 2020). The Covid-19 pandemic laid bare the everyday suffering that is produced by a global economic system that intensifies domestic inequality while laying responsibility for poverty on the shoulders of the individuals who bear it. What clearer indictment of the claim that globalization and neoliberalism will raise everyone's chances than the grim statistics that show that those living in predominantly racialized communities are often over twice as likely to die of the virus than those living in White communities (CDC 2021; CPHO 2021; White and Nafilyan 2020)?

The growing evidence of these failures has produced concrete changes that seek to reverse decades of neoliberal globalization. The response to the Covid-19 pandemic has included vaccine nationalism as well as a significant expansion of the welfare state in a range of countries as governments have stepped in to support the economy. The walls protecting central banks from democratic pressure—a core tenet of neoliberalism, as we discuss in **Section 4.7.1**—have also been eroding, as central bankers have been forced into increasingly politicized terrain in their efforts to keep the economy going in recent years.

Yet, there are also many indications that these changes are likely to be cosmetic. Finance is still resolutely global, and global supply chains, while facing very real challenges, have bounced back more quickly than many had predicted. Whether we look at the damage that is being caused by climate change or the likely costs of the pandemic, existing inequalities both between countries in the Global North and South and within them are only likely to be exacerbated in the coming years.

We have witnessed the failures of neoliberalism and globalization before. Yet, the result has not been to undo or erode these processes but to encourage their advocates to change the narratives they tell to avoid responsibility (Best 2020).

For all of these reasons, I would argue that a significant shift away from the broad patterns that we have labelled neoliberal globalization is unlikely just now.

That still leaves open the question of the usefulness of the concepts themselves. Since a great deal of the concepts' power comes from how they are used rhetorically to narrate a particular conception of the world, getting these concepts wrong has some very real practical effects.

Although the concept of globalization has provided useful analytic traction for mapping large macro-level processes over time, political economists have had a hard time using this concept without falling into Eurocentric tropes and missing the historical role of empire and the profound unevenness of global flows even today (F. Cooper 2001).

When political economists use the concept of neoliberalism, they also frequently give too much credence to its advocates—even when they set out to challenge its core tenets. They do so by too often treating neoliberalism as a coherent set of ideas and practices and ignoring its messy history of trial, error, and repeated failure. They also distort the character of neoliberalism by too easily accepting its claims to depoliticize policy, thus missing the role of power, its long historical relationship with social conservatism, and its core reliance on gendered and racialized forms of inequality (M. Cooper 2017; Shilliam 2021).

Neoliberalism and globalization may not be exhausted as concepts, but if we are to continue to use them to make sense of the times in which we live, we need to reconceptualize them so that they better capture the complexities of the world that they have helped to create.

Roundtable 4.2
Response **Cemal Burak Tansel**

It is undeniable that the Covid-19 pandemic and the unfolding climate breakdown—lamentably to a lesser extent—have compelled states and international organizations to reorient their economic management tools and priorities. In the words of the former UK Health Secretary Sajid Javid (2020), the pandemic has necessitated the deployment of 'the most significant fiscal firepower seen in modern times', with the United States alone spending about $5 trillion on stimulus and recovery packages as of mid-2021. Echoing this trend, the response from international financial institutions has coalesced around the need to scale-up public spending to mitigate the economic impact of the pandemic.

Looking at this picture, it is tempting for critical observers to proclaim that decades of neoliberal globalization and the associated privileging of the demands of capital over labour have come to an end (L. Cooper 2021). How else can we explain the 'return' of the state as the principal actor of economic management, or the apparent acquiescence of 'market forces' to popular public demands? Yet, as Jacqueline Best notes in **Roundtable 4.1**, we have been here before: Neoliberalism has repeatedly and publicly 'failed'—most recently, amid the tribulations of the global economic crisis of 2007–08—yet retained and even expanded its hegemony over domestic and international policymaking apparatuses.

There are important conceptual and empirical reasons to be cautious about equating greater public investment with a sudden retreat of neoliberalism. The so-called 'return of the state' is seen by some as a repudiation of a common-sense understanding of neoliberalism, where the term refers to the retreat or 'rollback' of the state. Yet, states have always been integral actors in the 'rollout' of neoliberalism. We possess a rich archive of evidence demonstrating that neoliberalism has never been about shrinking the state per se, but about reconfiguring it to safeguard capital and property (Tansel 2017). An increased role for the state in managing national economies is certainly compatible with neoliberal governance, and the current pivot towards public investment, in and of itself, does not invalidate neoliberalism's defining logics.

In other words, there is no guarantee that the current policy fixes will remain integral parts of a post-pandemic socioeconomic landscape, nor that they will usher in a more equal and sustainable reorganization of the global economy.

Where do we go from here then? In questioning the usefulness of neoliberalism as a concept, we might wish to focus on how neoliberalism has acted and continues to operate as a political language around which concrete public struggles are organized.

As Quinn Slobodian notes in **Roundtable 4.4**, the academic literature has spent a great deal of time thinking about and defining neoliberalism on the basis of shared ideas and policy templates, but the term has also been adopted by social movements as a way of articulating socioeconomic and political grievances. From the Zapatistas in Mexico to environmental social movements in the Middle East, from the Landless Workers' Movement in Brazil to anti-privatization campaigns in Europe, 'neoliberalism' has acted as a foil for communities and mobilizations to frame their political priorities, strategies, and antagonists. For those involved in those struggles, neoliberalism has not referred to a catch-all academic term, nor has it necessarily signalled the weakening or disappearance of the state apparatuses (Gago 2017; Koch 2018). On the contrary, the concrete struggles against neoliberalism waged by those movements have been defined by contestations with the state around clearly identifiable everyday issues, such as securing and maintaining access to land and public services, or claiming a 'right to the city'—to a lived environment shaped by social and ecological priorities.

Thinking about 'neoliberalism' in these explicitly political and practical terms gives us a productive way to reflect on what may or may not be possible in a post-pandemic world. For example, the fact that those who resist 'actually existing neoliberalisms' often have to do so by directly confronting state power should make us more wary of embracing a romanticized understanding of state supervision over the economy. We might also want to ask whether the current drive to bolster public investment is being led by social forces who are committed to a publicly and democratically owned and managed economy, or by those who regard redistributive state intervention as a necessary evil—a short-term crisis management strategy—to chart a route back to the neoliberal status quo as quickly as possible.

In short, we should focus on the responses and strategies of popular mobilizations to assess whether the pandemic represents the end of neoliberalism as we know it. This, as Hiroko TAKEDA puts it in **Roundtable 4.3**, necessitates a focus on 'lived experiences of neoliberal globalization embedded in particular contexts'. While we might not be able to offer a compelling forecast from our current vantage point, one thing is certain: We will either exhaust neoliberalism—by overcoming its clearly evidenced inability to coordinate global economic activity in sustainable and equitable ways—or we will exhaust ourselves and the planet.

Roundtable 4.3
Response **Hiroko TAKEDA**

The Covid-19 pandemic has certainly showed some signs of departure from the orthodoxies of neoliberal globalization. Restrictions placed on economic, social, and everyday activities to suppress the spread of the virus compelled states to engage in proactive management of the national economy and change the course of economic and social policymaking. Suddenly, austerity policies were replaced by large-scale financial assistance and stimulus packages, and neoliberal creeds seem to have lost relevance as governments acknowledged that the rebuilding of the national economy and people's everyday lives is the most pressing political task. This process of 'great transformation' reached a stage in which the world leaders at the G7 summit in June 2021 agreed to make a clear commitment to end the 'race for the bottom' through the introduction of the global minimum corporate tax rate.

Could these recent developments spurred by the Covid-19 pandemic signify that neoliberal globalization has finally become an exhausted model?

I approach this question by following the valuable lesson learned from Jacqueline Best's opening contribution to this debate (**see Roundtable 4.1**): we need to link macro-structural (big picture) and 'everyday' analyses of neoliberal globalization to better understand its complexity and power. Such an exercise cannot be conducted without considering lived experiences of neoliberal globalization embedded in particular contexts—and so, here, allow me to offer some experiences from Japan, a nation-state in which neoliberalism, as a doctrine underpinning political reforms, has been evolving with a time lag and a different focus compared with other industrially advanced countries.

Although neoliberalism as a school of political and economic thought was imported to Japan in the 1980s from the USA and UK, it was in the 2000s that the effects of neoliberal institutional reforms on the everyday lives of Japanese people became noticeable. Neoliberal political and economic reforms in Japan have exhibited distinctive normative characteristics that pressure individuals to mould their everyday lives and 'subjectivities' in a particular way (TAKEDA 2009).

One of the most frequently mentioned normative values mobilized in neoliberal political projects in Japan is the notion of 'self-responsibility'. This term generally refers to a state of responsible and capable individuals who are self-reliant without depending on state assistance and able to autonomously plan and manage their lives. The political emphasis placed on the term has grown since the 1990s, as the country started to face two sets of pressures imposed by the progress of globalization: on the one hand, the demand to expand Japan's international role, particularly by making a visible contribution to international military efforts; and, on the other, the impetus to shift to a model of small government, by off-loading the task of managing social risks onto individuals' shoulders (Hook and TAKEDA 2007: 94).

'Being self-responsible' epitomizes the Japanese government's handling of the Covid-19 pandemic. By July 2021, a 'state of emergency' had been declared four times in Tokyo; however, the terms of these 'emergency' measures were, unlike lockdowns implemented elsewhere, essentially voluntary. The light-touch approach can also be observed in the lukewarm promotion of remote work, the hesitant procurement of testing, and the slow, timid, and cumbersome provision of financial assistance to businesses and individuals. With lighter governmental measures, Japanese people have been encouraged to act prudently to avoid contracting the virus, but they did so in a circumstance of mutual surveillance in which the so-called 'self-restraint police'—namely, anonymous people who operate entirely of their own volition—attack and publicly humiliate those who they feel are acting irresponsibly.

One might say that what I have just described is an authoritarian surveillance society, not a globalized neoliberal rule. My counterargument is twofold. First, the light-touch approach did not cost as much as budgeted, as 30 trillion yen of the Covid-19 supplementary budget and contingency funds were rolled over from FY2020 to 2021. Then-Prime Minister Suga Yoshihide proudly reported this scale of underspending on the emergency budget at a parliamentary Party Leaders' debate in June 2021 as evidence of his government's prudence, suggesting that the Japanese government remained within the framework of austerity. Second, in the meantime the economic interests of global business have been prioritized, as demonstrated most notably in the holding of the delayed Tokyo Olympic Games in the summer of 2021 amid the state of emergency. In this way, neoliberal political values and goals (the ideal of a small government and the economic interests of global business) have taken precedence even during the course of implementing governmental measures to tackle the pandemic.

The non-death of neoliberal globalization in today's Japan can be attributed to the immature state of countermodels. As discussed, Japan is a latecomer to the realities of neoliberal globalization; hence, alternative models are also developing with a time lag. In addition, the one-dominant-party system, in which a change of government cannot be envisaged as a real possibility, does not help to stimulate the articulation and spread of alternative political programmes. Still, the most troubling issue is that, as discussed by Jacqueline Best in **Roundtable 4.1**, neoliberal values have been internalized within individuals—simply put, people still act on this idea. For example, journalist Nakamura Atsuhiko documented numerous cases of female university students who engaged in sex work, while being very much aware of the health hazards involved in the circumstances of the pandemic (Nakamura

2020). Sex work enables them to earn enough financial resources to cover tuition fees and living expenses between their busy university commitments, and a university degree is vital for young Japanese women to survive in a labour market internationally known for a high level of gender inequality. But in doing so, they expose themselves to manifold dangers and put themselves in at extraordinary risk of serious harm.

Looking from Japan, I have to conclude that neoliberal globalization as a political and economic model cannot be exhausted until it can be replaced by a countermodel of political economy based on care and mutual interdependency (The Care Collective 2020). Importantly, too, this requires the agency of the Japanese people to internalize and bring an alternative model into being.

Roundtable 4.4
Response Quinn Slobodian

Jacqueline Best is right to say that the Global Financial Crisis, the Covid-19 pandemic, and ongoing climate breakdown have forced us to look twice at the toolkit of concepts we use to make sense of the world (**see Roundtable 4.1**). Are terms like 'neoliberalism' still helpful given the intersection of diverse challenges, events, and threats? A helpful way to approach the problem is by returning to the categories again to ask exactly what we mean by them. That way, we can determine if they still have salience for our present.

In my experience, people tend to use the term 'neoliberalism' in one of four ways.

The first is to define neoliberalism as a *period in world history*. By this definition, sometime in the 1970s the world entered the 'neoliberal era', as Ronald Reagan and Margaret Thatcher came to power in the United States and United Kingdom respectively, and as the communist Soviet Bloc collapsed and left only one model of political economy remaining.

A second way neoliberalism is used is as a *policy package* that accompanied this epoch in global history, which would include the calls to liberalize, privatize, and deregulate, pushing free trade over protection, private ownership over public ownership, flexible over unionized labour markets, and personal responsibility over the welfare state.

A third definition sees neoliberalism as an *intellectual movement*, earning its name in a term coined and adopted first in 1938 by a group of intellectuals, journalists, and policymakers who have gathered in the Mont Pèlerin Society since 1947 to discuss the unfolding threats posed to the stability of the global capitalism they hold dear.

A fourth approach is to define neoliberalism as a *worldview*. By this definition, economics becomes the only meaningful measure of human life and every last thing on the planet is deemed available to be bought and sold.

The central problem of the scholarship on neoliberalism is the way that these four definitions are mixed, matched, combined, and collapsed into one another in ways that can lead to greater confusion than clarity. Addressing the question at hand gives an illustration of the potential pitfalls.

Take the first definition. We can rephrase the question by asking: is the neoliberal era over? But such a question itself implies a uniformity of Global Political Economy that never existed. The assumption that only one model of political economy existed after the fall of the Soviet Union discounts not only the mixed economies of European social democracy, 'Pink

'Tide' post-neoliberalism, and the smaller socialist states like Cuba that lived on, but also an enormous state that did too—the People's Republic of China. Though not socialist by any plausible measure, it is also not helpfully described as neoliberal either, using a very different language of legitimacy in its political rhetoric and disregarding the distinction between public and private ownership so central to neoliberalism (I. Weber 2018). The more one looks at the conduct of governments, the growth of state budgets, and the continued existence of social services in the face of opposition, the more one is tempted to agree with Kean Birch (2015) that, when it comes to actually existing state policy, 'we have never been neoliberal'.

If this is true, then what might it mean to ask if the neoliberal model is exhausted? We could follow the second definition and look at what *policies* are being proposed now and whether they differ from what preceded them. Here, the effect of the 2008 Global Financial Crisis is significant, not because of the re-regulation of the financial sector, which has been minimal, but because of a paradigm shift in the treatment of money. The US Federal Reserve Bank flooded world markets with liquidity to save global credit markets and, in the years that followed, the European Central Bank and the Bank of England followed suit. In the intervening decade, they discovered that they could do so without producing the inflation that had put the fear of state spending in the hearts of policymakers since the 1970s—although, of course, the re-emergence of inflation in 2022, associated with the disruption of the Covid-19 pandemic, once again began to challenge these orthodoxies.

As governments seek to 'build back better' (in the jargon of the early 2020s) after the Covid-19 pandemic, this has opened up the possibility of a departure from the austerity policies that were internalized by politicians for a generation. The multi-trillion-dollar spending plans announced by US President Joe Biden's administration suggest a renewed flexibility in policy circles about using the power of the state towards a broader range of ends.

Yet whether such ambitious policies ever translate into reality is another question again. The third definition of neoliberalism points not just to a small group of famous economists but to a 'think tank archipelago' of lobbyists and pressure groups, from the Heritage Foundation and American Legislative Exchange Council (ALEC) in the United States to the Institute of Economic Affairs in the UK, alongside hundreds more that have had considerable success in capturing policy agendas for their corporate backers (Jackson 2012). Legislative bodies and courts in the United States are filled with people dedicated to blocking the rollout of economic policy aimed at expanding a more equitable economic or environmental policy model.

This leaves the final definition, which differs little from Karl Marx and Friedrich Engels writing in 1848 that bourgeois society 'left remaining no other bond between man and man than naked self-interest and callous "cash payment"' (Marx and Engels 1848). Dubbed 'capitalism' later in the nineteenth century, this category remains adequate to describe a world where distribution is primarily determined by private rather than public actors through the institutions of private property and the price mechanism. Indeed, the further from the commanding heights of policy creation one travels, the less it seems that this way of organizing human affairs is faltering. The 'K-shaped recovery' from the pandemic compounded the K-shaped one that followed the Global Financial Crisis, when families with assets saw their wealth boom but those without saw their wages stagnate along with their life chances.

Even if the neoliberal model is exhausted and, in defiance of all premature obituaries, happens to perish this time, then the capitalist model would live on in a different guise.

Over to you ...

1 You have heard clear arguments here from our contributors that we are still some way from the 'exhaustion' of neoliberal globalization. How do you account for its resilience in the face of repeated crises?

2 All four of the authors here invoke the Covid-19 pandemic in their discussions of the continuing resilience of neoliberalism as a way of organizing the world, and you have read about the resurgence of state spending and state direction of economies to manage its effects. The authors generally do not think that this amounts to a major shift away from neoliberalism—what do you think? And is the more significant role for nation-states in the pandemic a good thing, or something we should reverse as soon as possible?

3 We have heard much in **Chapter 4** and the **Chapter 4 Roundtable** about the inequalities associated with neoliberalism (**see Chapter 10** for more on this topic). Do you think that these inequalities signal the long-term unsustainability of neoliberal globalization, or are they 'bugs' in the system, so to speak, that simply need to be addressed through better policy fixes?

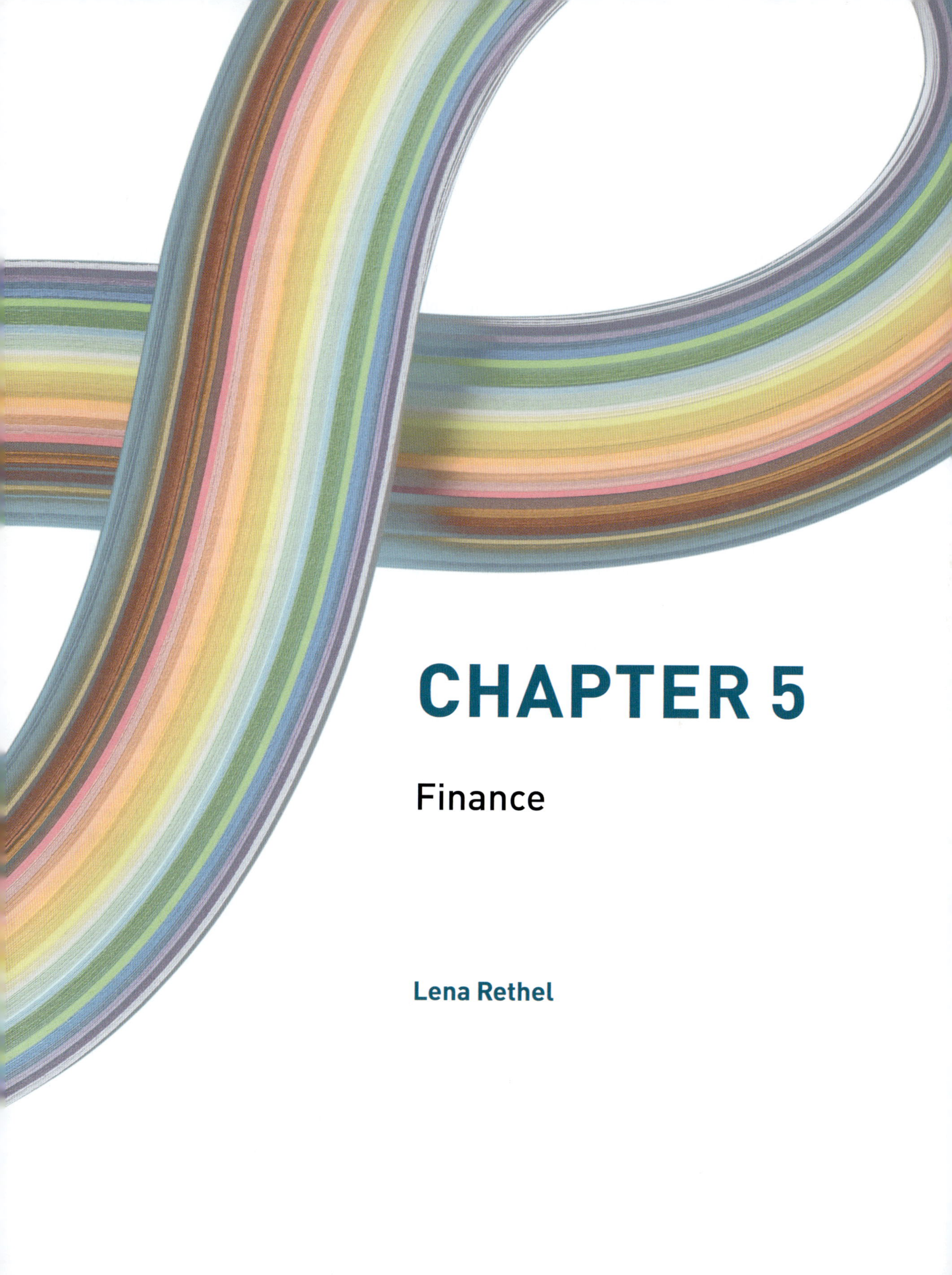

CHAPTER 5

Finance

Lena Rethel

5.1 Introduction

The Global Political Economy (GPE) of finance examines the politics of both money and debt. Enhancing our understanding of the crisis-prone nature of global finance is one of the core contributions of GPE scholarship. Since the formalization of the research field in the 1970s, financial crises and their management have remained very much at the heart of contemporary GPE analysis. At the same time, there have been significant changes in how we study the global politics of money and debt, including the field's approach to the foundational question: *what and who matters?*

In **Section 5.2**, we will explore key pillars of the GPE of finance. First we will look at money, currencies, and the international monetary system (**see Section 5.2.1**), before examining in more detail dynamics of credit and debt (**see Section 5.2.2**). While money is ubiquitous, its usages are characterized by great variety and so are the practices—economic, political, and cultural—to which money gives rise. In the third part of this section, we will look at both public and private mechanisms that have been established to govern global finance (**see Section 5.2.3**).

In **Section 5.3**, we will explore the claim that global finance is inherently crisis-prone. In the period since the 1970s, financial crises, linked to both money (currency) and debt, have been a recurring phenomenon. However, there have also been important shifts. For example, at least until the Covid-19 pandemic, sovereign debt crises—involving the debt owed by governments—were on the decline, whereas for a growing number of people, personal debt—accrued, for example, via student loans or credit cards—had become unsustainable. Much of the economics literature on financial crises is concerned with the typical anatomy of a crisis—its causes, cures, and prevention. In this literature, it is a widely held assumption that economies follow an equilibrium path, periodically disrupted by financial crises. Efforts to contain and resolve a crisis, then, are seen as primarily shaping an economy's return to its equilibrium path, mitigating broader adverse effects such as spillovers into other sectors. By contrast, GPE scholarship has been more sceptical of the efficiency of global financial markets. You will be introduced to the work of key thinkers drawing attention to the inherently unstable nature of finance, which we will then put in the context of current developments to illustrate both continuity and change when it comes to the GPE of finance and its crises.

In **Section 5.4**, we will consider examples of doing and studying global finance differently. One example of doing finance differently is Islamic finance (**see Section 5.4.1**). It constitutes a principled approach to finance, drawing on the teachings of Islam. What sets it apart from many other, often quite localized, alternative approaches to finance is the establishment of a global architecture for governing Islamic finance. This has played a significant role in the mainstreaming of Islamic finance, but has also had an impact on the degree to which it presents a substantive alternative to the current, crisis-prone global financial order. We will then move on to a new set of approaches to the GPE of finance that use the 'everyday' as an analytical entry point (**see Section 5.4.2**). (Jacqueline Best discusses this concept in **Chapter 4**.) Everyday approaches to finance broaden the range of actors and practices under consideration when examining the global politics of finance.

5.2 **Key pillars of the GPE of finance**

5.2.1 **Money, currencies, and the international monetary system**

The history of money—as a medium of exchange, as a unit of account, and as a store of value—is long and varied. By contrast, the idea of national currencies is of much more recent provenance and linked to states establishing economic control over their territories. Decolonization from the 1940s onwards played an important role in the increase of the number of national currencies. For many countries having their own money has been a key marker of their sovereignty. As Supriya Singh succinctly summarizes, '[c]urrency has become one of the important symbols of national identity' (2013: 1). In modern times, the relationship between states and money has become intricately linked.

Sovereign states usually claim a monopoly over the issuance of currency, defining what is to be accepted as legal tender. Most currencies nowadays operate as *fiat money*, which means they are not backed by a commodity such as gold or silver. As a consequence, states expend much effort on maintaining monetary stability (as opposed to inflation) and the value of their currencies in global exchange markets. If a currency's value depreciates rapidly, this can result in a currency crisis, as happened for example in East Asia in the late 1990s.

Following the liberalization of exchange rates from the 1970s onwards, many countries, especially in the Global South, had adopted the practice of pegging their currency to the US dollar, as a way to integrate with the global financial system and make themselves attractive to investors. However, this then also made these currencies especially vulnerable to speculative attacks, with investors effectively betting on a country's inability to maintain this peg. Once a central bank would run out of foreign currency reserves, it would be forced to abandon the peg and the currency would plunge as a result. This would then be compounded by liabilities—such as government and corporate debt—being denominated in foreign currency, which could quickly turn a liquidity crisis—the lack of US dollar reserves—into a full-blown economic crisis.

For the past century, the US dollar has occupied a hegemonic position in the international monetary system in that many countries hold US dollar reserves and many international transactions, including the trade in oil, are conducted in US dollars. This has reflected both US military might and economic strength. In turn, being the issuer of such a global reserve currency has further shored up US power. Not surprisingly, GPE scholars have paid significant attention to the power relations that underpin the international monetary system—and how currency competition and currency statecraft affect countries at the top of international currency hierarchies (B. Cohen 2019). In the 1980s, much of this literature focused on the relationship between the US dollar and the Japanese yen, followed by US dollar–Euro relations in the 1990s and early 2000s. More recently, interest has turned to how the ongoing liberalization of the Chinese currency, the renminbi, will affect the monetary system and inter-state relations, both in the Asian region (Grimes 2009) and at the global level (B. Cohen 2019).

Other work, however, has focused more on the countries and regions at the lower ends of international currency hierarchies. This work explores the dependencies created by an international monetary system organized around a small number of core currencies and traces its colonial origins (Kvangraven 2021). From this perspective, monetary sovereignty is very much a spectrum, creating differentiated dependencies on the size of—and vulnerabilities to—swings in international flows of aid and investment (Bonizzi, Kaltenbrunner, and Michell 2019). It further analyses how the unevenness of monetary sovereignty and distribution of power can be reinforced by international financial regulatory frameworks and the unilateral policy decisions of central banks in core currency countries (Bortz and Kaltenbrunner 2018). However, there has also been resistance to state-controlled money, especially at times of crises (**see Case Study 5.1**).

Case Study 5.1: Alternative currencies

Despite governments' attempts to monopolize the issuance of money, around the world there have been numerous experiments with *local currencies* and alternative forms of money (Photo 5.1). Some of these initiatives take place in response to government failure to control the money supply and guarantee the stability of the national currency, often in the wake of financial and economic crisis. One example is the case of Argentina (North 2005). In response to recurring economic crises in the 1990s and early 2000s, barter networks emerged in Argentina. When the economy collapsed in 2001, the Argentine government limited access to cash, making an increasing number of people dependent on these networks. Markets issued their own money—*creditos*—to facilitate trading.

However, there are other reasons for creating local currencies. Often, local currency initiatives are driven by a commitment to the local economy—the Bristol Pound, the Chiemgauer and the (now defunct) Ithaca HOURS are all also about keeping money in the local area as a deliberate counterpoint to the increasingly globalized world of finance. These schemes share a focus on money as a means of payment. A similar use could be ascribed, for example, to corporate schemes that can be used for purchases, such as loyalty points and airmiles.

These local initiatives stand in contrast to efforts to create global currencies at a remove from state control. A prominent example in this regard are *cryptocurrencies* such as Bitcoin. Bitcoin is a form of digital money that operates without a central bank and is instead produced in a decentralized manner. Computer users around the globe help to 'mine' it and validate transactions. Supporters of digital currencies say that they are difficult to counterfeit and leave little room for government interference. However, critics point to the use of digital currencies in illegal transactions as well as their high energy consumption—one energy consumption index put the global energy consumption of Bitcoin in early 2021 above the amount of energy consumed by all of Sweden (Cambridge Bitcoin Electricity Consumption Index, n.d.). Different from local currencies, cryptocurrencies have been put to further uses than just as a means of payment. Effectively, they have increasingly been the target of financial speculation causing volatility—not just of cryptocurrencies themselves but also spilling over into other segments of global financial markets. Nevertheless, both local currencies and cryptocurrencies have in common that they largely seek to function outside the state—in some cases specifically with the aim of challenging state control over the monetary system. In response to the growth of cryptocurrencies, states have begun to consider issuing their own electronic money, so-called central bank digital currencies.

Photo 5.1 Bitcoin is a form of digital currency

Source: © iStock/dulezidar.

Questions

1 Do local currencies provide a viable alternative to national money?
2 How do cryptocurrencies challenge state control over money?

5.2.2 Finance, debt, and the international organization of credit

The international organization of credit has undergone significant changes since the 1970s. Despite a resurgence in government-directed lending since the Global Financial Crisis, especially loans linked to China's Belt and Road Initiative (its major regional infrastructural development programme), governments, multilateral organizations, and commercial banks are by far no longer the only players in town when it comes to global financial markets. Instead, there are a growing number of pension funds and other institutional investors that have become increasingly active on a global scale. Similarly, non-financial corporations access global financial markets not only as borrowers but also as investors to manage their cash flows and seek speculative returns—Tesla's investment in Bitcoin being a case in point.

Even so-called retail investors have come to increasingly invest and speculate in global financial markets.

Moreover, there have been significant changes in the modalities of financial instruments, from bank loans to bond finance to a whole slew of financial products that have at best a very tenuous connection to other aspects of the global economy such as trade and production. When private international capital flows resumed in the decades after the Second World War, it was primarily in the form of loans extended by syndicates of commercial banks to country borrowers. However, following the fallout from the international debt crisis of the 1980s, this shifted to bonds. Essentially, bonds are debt certificates that specify the relationship between creditor and debtor, including the sum that is lent and the debtor's obligation towards the creditor. What distinguishes bond debt from bank loans is that bonds are easily transferable. Through bonds, a loan is broken up into smaller denominations and usually claims are marketable, meaning that they can be sold and bought in a secondary market. Bonds also allow people to bundle together a range of assets, say mortgages or student loans or credit card receivables, and sell them on to investors. This technique is known as 'securitization', and contributed to excessive risk-taking in the run up to the Global Financial Crisis of 2008–09 (Rethel and Sinclair 2012). One form of finance that in the past received little attention from GPE scholars is equity finance; this has been changing in recent years with the growth of state-led cross-border investment, including of sovereign wealth funds (Babic, Garcia-Bernardo, and Heemskerk 2020).

Moreover, states are not the only borrowers; in the wake of the Global Financial Crisis, GPE scholars have begun to pay more attention to the borrowing behaviour of corporations and, importantly, households. Some of this is facilitated by financial innovations such as securitization that connect, for example, domestic consumer finance with global financial markets. However, it is important to remember that there exist significant hierarchies of difference about who can access credit, in what manner (for example, currency denomination of loans and tenure), and at what cost. Nevertheless, there have been efforts to challenge this, for example with regard to the currency denomination of debt (**see Case Study 5.2**).

Financial instruments are not mere tools, but crucial components of the organization, efficiency, and governance of international credit relations. The re-emergence of the international bond market from the late 1980s onwards and the development of domestic bond markets since the turn of the twenty-first century have fundamentally changed the borrowing practices—and opportunities—of developing countries. However, at the same time many countries in the Global South, especially in the group of least developed countries, have very little access to international financial markets. They remain dependent on bi- and multilateral sources of credit such as concessional loans provided under the umbrella of official development assistance or lending by multilateral development banks. With the Covid-19 pandemic, their need to access funds to pay for medical equipment and vaccines, as well as to fund basic social safety nets and economic recovery programmes, has only increased at a time when well-off countries such as the UK are cutting their aid budgets.

Case Study 5.2: The development of domestic bond markets in Asia

In the aftermath of the Asian Financial Crisis of 1997–98, regional policymakers identified two overall root causes of the crisis: volatile, short-term portfolio investment flows (that is cross-border investment in equity and debt securities); and a dependence on bank finance in Asian financial systems. Their solution was to strengthen the role of domestic bond markets—that is, markets in which funds are raised via the issuance of debt securities which can then be traded in so-called secondary markets. Bonds were seen as having the advantage over bank loans in that they can be purchased in smaller denominations and thus would be easier to trade, a feature referred to as liquidity.

The development of local bond markets, in which bonds are issued in local currency and subject to domestic jurisdiction, was thus seen as a means to address vulnerabilities exposed by the crisis, specifically to deal with the double mismatch of short-term, US dollar-denominated borrowing for long-term, domestic currency investments (Katada 2009). The development of domestic bond markets was seen as an important means of financial development and generating the long-term investment deemed necessary to address the infrastructure needs of the region.

One major initiative undertaken at the regional level has been the establishment of the Asian Bond Markets Initiative (ABMI), endorsed by ASEAN+3 Finance Ministers in 2003. Under this framework, a number of working groups have been set up to address core areas of bond market development. ABMI has played a crucial role in facilitating regular exchange among Asian financial policymakers; it has become a central mechanism for the diffusion of best practices and technical expertise with regard to bond markets. In September 2010, the ASEAN+3 Bond Market Forum was established. It brings together policymakers and market practitioners, seeking to incorporate market expertise in developmental efforts. The Asian Development Bank (ADB) acts as a facilitator of ABMI by providing technical and research assistance as well as hosting AsianBondsOnline, an electronic information platform. Furthermore, as an issuer in Asian domestic bond markets, ADB also takes on a role as market player and seeks to build developmental capacity (Dent 2008).

The second major development has been the Asian Bond Funds (ABF) initiative launched in 2003 by the Executives' Meeting of East Asia Pacific Central Banks (EMEAP), a regional grouping that also includes Australia and New Zealand. Its first fund, ABF-1, was initially endowed with $1 billion. ABF-1 was managed by the Bank for International Settlements and invested in the US dollar-denominated sovereign and quasi-sovereign bonds of eight EMEAP countries; it was closed in 2016. In 2004, ABF-2 was launched. It invests in Asian local currency bonds. It consists of two elements, the Pan Asia Bond Index Fund and eight single market funds. ABF-2 is a public initiative, endowed by the EMEAP central banks with a seed capital of $2 billion, but most of the country funds are managed by private-sector providers.

Questions

1 What are domestic bond markets?
2 What do people mean when they refer to liquid financial instruments?

5.2.3 Global financial governance: From architecture to infrastructures

Given the recurrent dynamics of financial crises, it is no surprise that the international community has expended considerable effort on establishing frameworks and mechanisms to govern global finance. However, increasingly since the 1970s, private actors and associations have also come to play more important roles in global financial governance, in particular in the area of standard setting. At the same time, public authorities such as central banks and treasuries have become significantly involved in the provision of market infrastructures.

The two most prominent international organizations tasked with governing global finance are the International Monetary Fund (IMF) and the World Bank, both located in Washington, DC. They were created in 1944 as part of the Bretton Woods Agreement and formed the basis of the Bretton Woods system (**see Section 4.3.3**). While the IMF was set up to support international monetary cooperation, the World Bank was established to provide loans to fund post-war reconstruction and the development of production capacity in less developed countries. The Bank for International Settlements (BIS), already established in 1929, also has the mandate of supporting international financial cooperation, although its focus is on supporting central banks in this endeavour.

> ### Key Concept: Bretton Woods system
>
> This term refers to the international financial order agreed at the end of the Second World War. The core pillars of the system were:
>
> - Currency convertibility in support of international trade;
> - Fixed, but adjustable exchange rates, pegged to the US dollar, which in turn was backed by gold;
> - Capital controls.

Both the World Bank and the IMF played important roles as emergency lenders during the financial crises of the 1980s and 1990s, and again during the Covid-19 pandemic. However, they have also come under significant critique for their actions—the harsh criteria they have been imposing on developing countries seeking assistance, the (in)adequacy of their policy solutions during the Asian crisis, and the concentration of voting power in the hands of a small number of countries, in particular the United States, to name but a few examples. Nevertheless, despite repeated calls for reform, they have remained the mainstays of the global financial architecture.

The BIS's part in global financial governance gained more attention from the late 1980s onwards in its role as host to the Basel Committee on Banking Supervision (BCBS), a body tasked with developing minimum capital requirements for internationally active banks. Moreover, it also hosted the secretariat of the Financial Stability Forum, established in the wake of the Asian crisis in 1999, with the aim to promote international financial stability, and its successor, the Financial Stability Board. As you can see from this very brief overview, the existing global financial architecture largely reflects the global distribution of power at the end of the Second World War. However, this status quo has been increasingly challenged by the rise of new emerging powers, specifically the group of countries known as the BRICs—Brazil, Russia, India, and China. Collectively, and in their capacity as members of the Group of 20 (G20), they have sought to change the global financial architecture both from within and without (Roberts, Armijo, and Katada 2018). This includes advocating for reform of quota systems and expanding membership of existing international organizations and frameworks, as well as the—individual and collective—creation of new institutions such as the Asian Infrastructure Investment Bank. Their efforts are part of a wider transformation of the institutions of global financial governance in the aftermath of the Global Financial Crisis of 2008–09 (Grabel 2018).

In the wake of the 2008–09 crisis, scholarly attention has increasingly moved beyond the inter-state foundations of the global financial architecture to pay closer attention to financial infrastructures provided by both state and market bodies. This reflects the growing importance of private financial market actors not just about the financing they provide but also with regard to the governance functions they have come to assume. On the one hand, this extends to the growing number of intermediaries involved in the running and governance of global financial markets. Work in this direction interrogates, for example, how rating agencies, and increasingly also index providers, pass judgement and channel funds into specific markets and sectors (Sinclair 2005; Petry, Fichtner, and Heemskerk 2021). Furthermore, it extends to groups of professionals and their networks: take the example of accounting professionals and the development of a new accounting framework via the International Accounting Standards Board (IASB) (Perry and Nölke 2006). On the other hand, it also revisits the work of key state agencies in governing finance, most importantly of central banks and the ways in which they inject liquidity into domestic and global markets (Gabor 2016).

More generally, sharp distinctions between a public sphere of governance and a private sphere of markets do not fit easily with current global financial dynamics. With a greater range of actors being part of the GPE of finance, it is little surprise that there exist significant differences in how finance is done in different parts of the world and in different segments of global financial markets. One important aspect is the changing role of the state—not just as a public authority governing markets, but as a market player itself (Datz 2008). It is open to debate how this in turn will affect dynamics of international financial cooperation and contestation and the institutional frameworks that underpin it.

5.3 Are financial crises inevitable?

Crises have been a recurrent phenomenon in the GPE of finance. At the same time, both their frequency and intensity have increased as financial markets have become ever more globalized. In this section we will first examine major financial crises of recent decades (**see Section 5.3.1**), before discussing major explanations for crises advanced by GPE scholarship (**see Section 5.3.2**).

5.3.1 Financial crises and the globalization of financial markets

The GPE of finance covers both monetary and debt relations. One important way to distinguish between the two is the time horizon—monetary transactions have a short time horizon, usually less than a year, whereas credit and debt are intended to be of longer duration and contribute to a country's capital formation. This distinction is also reflected in how political economists categorize financial flows between countries, via the balance of payments.

Key Concept: The balance of payments

On the one hand, there are short-term flows such as payments received in exchange for goods and services or interest payments on an investment. Political economists refer to this as the *current account*. By contrast, there are a country's assets and liabilities, such as investments in factories or sovereign debt. Political economists refer to this as the *capital account*. Together, current account and capital account, as well as the international reserves that a country may have accumulated, constitute its balance of payments.

For much of the post-war period, international capital mobility—the ability to move capital from one country to another—was significantly restricted (Sinclair and Thomas 2001). Following the international economic turmoil of the interwar period, policymakers in the 1940s had been very aware of the harm caused by volatile international capital flows. In 1944, they had agreed on a system to regulate international financial flows, the Bretton Woods system (**see Section 5.2.3**).

Nevertheless, over time, restrictions on international capital mobility were successively dismantled, resulting in its collapse in 1973. Following a rise in primarily US bank lending to Latin America, a spiral of international debt crises was set off in 1982 when Mexico declared that it would suspend payments on its debts (Madrid 1992). The crisis rapidly spread to other countries. All in all, more than twenty countries defaulted on their debts in the 1980s, some repeatedly so. The ensuing reversal in economic development led commentators to refer to the 1980s as Latin America's 'lost decade'. A period of protracted debt renegotiations took place. Ultimately, the resolution of the 1980s international debt crisis did not put a stop to the unshackling of global financial markets. Instead, its major remedies—the conversion of existing bank debt into bonds and the introduction of common minimum capital requirements for internationally active banks—contributed to the further globalization of finance in two significant ways. It initiated a wider shift towards bond finance within international portfolio investment flows. And it further institutionalized the practice of global banking, seeking to create a level playing field in particular for internationally active US and UK banks, rather than a return to national financial systems insulated from each other via capital controls.

If the 1980s were marked by financial crises arising from international indebtedness and overlending, then the 1990s witnessed a series of very prominent currency crises. This started in 1992 when Britain had to withdraw from the European Exchange Rate Mechanism, a scheme that had been introduced by European countries as a semi-flexible exchange rate system and that Britain had joined in 1990. It continued with the Mexican peso crisis of 1994–95 and peaked with the Asian Financial Crisis of 1997–98. Financial liberalization made currencies more vulnerable to speculation. International speculators can bet against a currency by entering agreements to sell it at a lower value in the future; this can then create downward pressures, with central banks ultimately no longer able to support the value of their currency.

The Asian crisis in particular highlighted the pernicious dynamics of crisis contagion as it rapidly spread from the Thai baht to the Philippine peso, the Indonesian rupiah, and the Malaysian ringgit, followed by the Korean won and even the Russian rouble coming under attack. As the value of East Asian currencies fell, borrowers who had raised loans in foreign currency were caught out as suddenly these loans had become much more expensive. Notably, China was spared much of the fallout from the Asian Financial Crisis, given its lower integration with global financial markets, having kept its capital account closed and exchange rate carefully managed.

Financial globalization accelerated in the 1990s through a combination of regulatory reforms, the rapid growth of non-bank financial institutions such as pension funds and venture capital, and technological change. The search for yield drove a series of overinvestment crises, channelling more and more money into specific assets, such as the shares of new technology companies or residential housing. This resulted in speculative bubbles that were often barely warranted by the quality of underlying investments. Ultimately, these bubbles were not sustainable—resulting in the Dot.com crisis of 2000 and the subprime mortgage crisis of 2007. The latter then morphed into the Global Financial Crisis of 2008–09, followed by the Eurozone crisis. Policy responses to these crises combined a continued commitment to monetary expansion (increasing the money available) and, especially in response to the global financial and Eurozone crises, fiscal retrenchment—more popularly known as austerity. Not surprisingly, this in turn accentuated wealth inequalities at both within-country and global levels, further widening the gaps between the winners and losers from financial globalization.

 Watch the video on the online resources to take your understanding of this section further.

Key Concepts: Crisis terminology

Debt crisis: A crisis that is set off when a borrower (for example, a government, corporation, or household) does not repay interest and/or principal according to the schedule agreed with the lender (for example, another government, international organization, or private commercial bank).

(Continued)

> **Currency crisis:** A crisis that is caused when currency values decline rapidly and significantly as happened in a number of Asian countries during the late 1990s. In turn, this can make foreign currency debt more expensive and lead to defaults. It may also prevent a government (or other national actor) from acquiring important goods in global markets, such as fuel or personal protective equipment, as we saw during the Covid-19 pandemic.
>
> **Overinvestment crisis:** A crisis that emerges when money gets channelled into assets or sectors that become increasingly overvalued. A bubble builds up with significant consequences when it bursts, including business failures and bankruptcies. Moreover, it means that financial resources have not been allocated efficiently across the economy which can have further social and economic consequences, such as preventing people from accessing affordable accommodation in the case of a housing bubble.

5.3.2 The inherent instability of global financial markets

We can see from the overview in **Section 5.3.1** that financial crises have been an inevitable feature of financial globalization. Studying the causes and consequences of crises has been a core theme in the GPE of finance, which widely recognizes the inherent instability of global financial markets. Nevertheless, scholars differ in the explanatory power they grant to both structural and conjunctural factors regarding both the causes of crises, as well as what they deem to be suitable policy and regulatory responses. Let's look at different approaches to studying crises and theorizing the inherent instability of global financial markets.

One school of thought focuses on power relations among states and their impact on international financial stability. Charles P. Kindleberger (1973) points to the relative stability of the international financial system in the period prior to the First World War, which he attributes to British hegemonic leadership. In later work, Kindleberger also examines the typical anatomy of financial crises over centuries—*manias, panics, and crashes*: speculative booms, followed by a reversal of sentiment and the collapse of the market (Kindleberger and Aliber [1978] 2005). Kindleberger emphasizes the importance of country leadership in ensuring financial stability, calling for government to step in as a (domestic and international) lender-of-last-resort as market mechanisms fail.

Another school of thought focuses on the changing *relationship between states and markets*. Susan Strange (1986), a prominent scholar of the GPE of finance, traces the shifting balance between states and markets back to the liberalization of foreign exchange and interest rates, and the accumulation of petrodollars—that is, US dollars acquired through oil sales. In her eponymous book, Strange describes the global financial system as one of 'casino capitalism', marked by volatility engendered by the practices of private market actors. Moreover, she points to significant information gaps and 'the ignorance among the controllers and regulators of what the bankers and speculators are up to', a view that was to be vindicated once more during the 2008–09 financial crisis and its aftermath (Strange 1986: 192; see also Mattli 2018).

A third school of thought focuses on *institutional dynamics* of finance in the contemporary system of global capitalism. Hyman Minsky [1986] 2008 draws attention to the inherent instability of modern financial systems operating according to the principle of profit maximization. According to his view, the search for yield can mean that 'financial innovation and aggressive seeking of borrowers outpaces the demands for funds for investment financing' (Minsky [1986] 2008: chapter 10). This is compounded by further rises in the return on speculative capital. In such a context, monetary expansion—governments stepping in as lenders-of-last-resort—does not stabilize the system but rather sets off yet another speculative cycle. Financial instability is thus an endemic feature of financial systems and should be addressed by limiting the activities that banks can engage in.

It is important to note that much of the GPE scholarship on financial crises is situated at the intersections of these approaches. And of course, there has been significant conceptual development, further enriching GPE analyses of financial globalization and its crises. This includes, for example, the impact of technology and digitalization, the volatility generated by global financial cycles, and the challenges posed by regulatory capture, veto players, and group think among policymakers when it comes to meaningfully re-regulating global finance. Indeed, one could argue that this diversity in thought and approach, underscored by the recognition of the limits of one-size-fits-all explanations and policy solutions, is another important contribution that GPE scholarship makes to the study of Global Financial Crises.

While financial crises have been frequent and with significant impact since the collapse of the Bretton Woods system, power relations between countries, the shifting balance between states and markets, and the systemic features of global capital remain core staples of GPE approaches to finance. Especially from the vantage point of the Covid-19 pandemic, it is important to note that not all financial crises are rooted in the financial system. They can also arise from changes in the so-called 'real economy': take, for instance, Strange's reference to the oil price shocks of the 1970s (1986: 17–20). And indeed, the Covid-19 pandemic is an example of shocks in the real economy triggering multiple and very protracted financial crises—illustrated, for instance, by a new wave of sovereign debt crises, the impact of the collapse of remittance flows (money that is sent back by migrant workers) on household budgets, and the surge of non-performing loans (loans where borrowers have stopped paying the interest that would be due, let alone repaying the loan) in the corporate sector (Photo 5.2).

5.4 Are there other ways of doing and studying global finance?

There have been significant changes afoot in the GPE of finance since the 1970s, resulting in a greater pluralism of actors, ideas, and practices. Much work on the GPE of finance focuses on major actors such as banks, investors, and international organizations. However, when it comes to crises, the characteristics of different aspects of finance are important, both in terms of causes of and vulnerabilities to crisis dynamics. This in turn also impacts who and what is thought to matter in the GPE of finance. Let us look in more detail at how this has impacted both how global finance is done and how it is studied. We will focus on two examples in particular: the emergence and global governance of Islamic finance (**see Section 5.4.1**) and everyday approaches to the study of the politics of global finance (**see Section 5.4.2**).

Photo 5.2 **In 2022 fuel prices in the UK reached a record high, adding to the national inflation figures and creating more stress on household budgets**

Source: © iStock/dulezidar.

5.4.1 **An alternative global financial order? The example of Islamic finance**

The pluralization of finance, aspects of which we traced in **Section 5.3**, is not just restricted to different institutional formations and market dynamics, but extends to the very values that underpin global finance. One approach that very explicitly positions itself as part of an alternative value system is Islamic finance (Pollard and Samers 2007). Islamic finance constitutes a principled approach to finance in that it draws on the teachings of Islam, both in terms of its prohibitions and its requirements. The development of modern Islamic finance gained momentum in the 1970s as a result of the rising wealth of the Gulf countries. In 1974, the Islamic Development Bank was established, swiftly followed by the emergence of private commercial banks operating according to Islamic principles, foremost the prohibition of *riba*—that is, the taking and paying of interest (Warde 2010).

Further Islamic financial principles include the prohibition of *maisir* (gambling) and *gharar* (contractual ambiguity). In so doing, Islamic finance takes issue with the asymmetric transfer of risk, where one party gains at the cost of another, often through speculative activities. Instead, Islamic finance emphasizes risk-sharing and the need for economic reward to be associated with tangible contributions to the economy. This is promoted by the requirement of linking financial transactions to real assets and/or economic effort. Islamic finance has also a significant social dimension, including stipulations regarding lenience with borrowers in distress and charitable giving. For example, many Islamic banking apps allow users to donate automatically to charity. Both these prohibitions and requirements ostensibly set Islamic finance apart from the current global financial order, and its speculative nature. Since the 1970s, Islamic finance has become a mainstay of the global financial system. Islamic financial assets were estimated to stand at $2.88 trillion in 2019, a share of roughly 1.8 per cent of global financial assets (DinarStandard 2020: 62).

Although Islamic finance potentially offers resources and strategies to mitigate and resist the speculative bubbles to which global finance has been prone, it has not been immune to crises. Islamic finance largely avoided the sort of speculation in financial instruments that was an important factor in the Global Financial Crisis of 2008–09. Nevertheless, the requirement that Islamic financial transactions be linked to the real economy has resulted in a significant exposure to real estate and thus property bubbles, as we saw for example in Dubai in 2009. There is also much debate in Islamic finance circles about whether financial products comply with Islamic principles in both form and substance. Product innovation in Islamic finance has tended to start with existing financial products, from which elements not compatible with Islamic values are stripped. Many of these products are in the categories of personal and consumer finance; yet in a country such as Malaysia, seen by many as leading the development of Islamic finance, its expansion has coincided with a significant rise in levels of household debt (Ariff 2017; DinarStandard 2020: 15).

Islam is by no means the only religion that espouses significant strictures when it comes to finance, especially in its more speculative guises (Sen 1991). Similarly, Islamic finance is certainly not the only values-based approach to finance. Nevertheless, one of the key aspects setting Islamic finance apart from other alternative financial economies is the rather elaborate global Islamic financial architecture that has been developed. As a result, Islamic finance has achieved a significant degree of institutionalization that many other alternative approaches to finance arguably lack. At the same time, this institutionalization has led to a blurring of the distinction between global finance and its Islamic counterpart (Rethel 2011; Sandal 2019).

Similar to the governance of global finance, shared standards play an important role in the governance of Islamic finance. One of the main standard setters in Islamic finance is the Islamic Financial Services Board (IFSB). Established in 2002, the IFSB was originally tasked with developing capital adequacy rules for Islamic financial services, akin to those developed by the Basel Committee on Banking Supervision (BCBS). And indeed, IFSB cooperated closely with the BCBS in the first years of its inception. However, over the years IFSB broadened its mandate, developing standards not just for Islamic banks, but also capital markets and *takaful* (insurance). As a consequence of its efforts, the IFSB is well integrated in global regulatory networks, counting the BIS, the IMF, and the World Bank among its associate members. Another standard setter is the Accounting and Auditing Organization for Islamic Financial Institutions (AAOIFI). It is tasked with the development of accounting rules for Islamic financial institutions, a function similar to that fulfilled by the International Accounting Standards Board in the global financial architecture (**see Section 5.2.3**). Like in the case of the IFSB, over the years its remit has broadened. While in most countries Islamic financial institutions abide by AAOIFI standards on a voluntary basis, in some jurisdictions they have been made mandatory by regulators.

One of the challenges for many Islamic financial institutions is managing their liquidity. In the international monetary system, liquidity is provided by US Treasury securities, short-term US dollar-denominated bonds, which financial institutions can easily buy and sell. But of course, these are interest-bearing instruments and therefore not compliant with Islamic financial principles. Yet, even here, an Islamic alternative has been developed with the International Islamic Liquidity Management Corporation. This is a body set up by the central banks and monetary authorities of a group of Muslim-majority countries, tasked with the issuance of short-term interest-free Islamic debt securities denominated in US dollars. In so doing, it helps Islamic financial institutions to manage their cross-border liquidity.

In sum, while Islamic financial institutions operate according to somewhat different principles, there exists significant overlap with the institutions and practices of global finance. Examining the development of Islamic finance and its governance thus also casts light on the significant challenges faced by attempts to develop alternatives to the existing global financial order.

5.4.2 An alternative approach to the study of global finance? The everyday turn

In an important intervention, John Hobson and Leonard Seabrooke (2006) have argued that much of the IPE literature has been focused on top-down understandings of the global political economy, guided by questions such as 'who governs?' and 'how is international order regulated?' They call this approach 'regulatory IPE'. Hobson and Seabrooke contrast regulatory IPE with the emerging approach of 'everyday IPE' that instead focuses on 'who acts?' and how their actions either promote or serve as acts of acquiescence, contestation, and resistance to economic transformation. The GPE of finance is a case in point.

Despite the high politics of finance—financial crises, sovereign debt, and currency contests—remaining a mainstay of GPE, since the Global Financial Crisis of 2008–09 a new research field has emerged that can be called 'everyday' approaches to global finance. It draws on an interdisciplinary body of scholarship ranging from social anthropology to cultural studies to economic geography. It examines how everyday practices—how we borrow, how we save, how we invest, and so on—shape and, in turn, are shaped by the dynamics and structures of the global political economy. Moreover, much of this literature is inherently intersectional in nature in that it recognizes hierarchies of difference—including of class, gender, and race—and their impact on how we experience finance in our daily life (Brassett et al. 2021).

Such a view—of finance as not just an abstract category, but something that is both constituted through our daily practices and has significant implications for our daily lives—broadens the range of both actors and topics of interest to the GPE of finance. So, for example, we could explore the causes and consequences of student debt, its often racialized dimensions (as in the USA, with Black students more likely to have to take on loans to fund their studies), and how it is wrapped up in precisely those sorts of securitization transactions that went wrong so badly in the run up to the Global Financial Crisis of 2008–09 (Montgomerie 2019). Or we could examine the impact of a growing number of people having to save for their own retirement, with new forms of pension accounts giving rise to emerging cultures of mass investment (Langley 2008). Or we could look at bingo, and how it intersects with the speculative practices of the global gambling industry (Bedford 2019). And so on.

In particular, feminist political economy has for a long time taken the everyday as one of its core foci. With regard to finance specifically, feminist political economists have explored such issues as the rationalities that link debt and social reproduction (Rankin 2001), or the practices that turn transnational families into financial customers and entrepreneurs (Kunz, Maisenbacher, and Paudel 2021) and their connections to international flows of aid and remittances, as well as resistance to them. Everyday approaches to the GPE of finance may also draw attention to its cultural production through books and films, and even board games such as *Monopoly* that normalize speculative practices (de Goede 2005). This can include heavily gendered tropes like that of the reckless banker or of the prudent housewife that underpin global finance (Brassett and Rethel 2015). However, it also includes the cultural productions of financial actors themselves, such as HSBC marketing itself as the world's 'local bank' in its advertising campaigns (Best and Paterson 2010*a*).

It is important to emphasize that while the everyday presents a distinct entry point in the GPE of finance, it by no means rejects the idea that there are other levels of analysis. Analyses tend to cross from the everyday to the global and back. In so doing, they open the GPE of finance up to new sets of questions and pathways of inquiry. For example, how can we compare campaigns for sovereign debt relief and those for abolishing student debt (Tooker 2017)? What lessons can we draw from domestic social sources of legitimacy for the legitimacy of the global financial order and vice versa (Seabrooke 2007)? Or to what extent do diversity initiatives in the global financial industry both embrace and foreclose diversity in economic thought and practice (Griffin 2019)? These are just some of the questions that adopting an everyday approach to the politics of global finance allows us to ask.

5.5 **Conclusion**

This chapter has offered you an overview of how global finance has developed since the 1970s. Examining the international monetary system, credit and debt relations, and their governance at the global level (**see Section 5.2**), it focused on the question of why financial crises seem inevitable (**see Section 5.3**). The three main pillars of the global financial system are the international monetary system and the international credit system as well as the international architecture that has emerged to govern them. Given the frequent recurrence of financial crises, there have been considerable efforts geared towards designing frameworks to govern global finance and rein in its worst excesses—but their impact has been limited.

We looked at Islamic finance as a non-Western approach to finance (**see Section 5.4.1**), but saw how it has nevertheless become very much entangled with the mainstream global financial system. We also explored how everyday approaches change how we think about who and what matters in global finance (**see Section 5.4.2**).

Key Points

- Recurring financial crises are a key feature of the Global Political Economy. These crises can be triggered in different segments of the global financial system, including currency and debt markets, and can result from shocks outside the financial economy such as the Covid-19 pandemic.
- As a result of financial liberalization since the 1970s, financial markets around the world have become increasingly interconnected, which allows for the easier transmission of crises from one financial system to another.
- The recurrence of financial crises has led to calls for its re-regulation, including reforms of the global financial architecture. However, despite these efforts, global finance remains largely unfettered.
- The emergence of new actors in the GPE of finance also draws attention to different ideas that may shape the international organization of credit. One such example is that of Islamic finance, which adopts a principle-based approach to finance that explicitly rejects speculative practices.
- Everyday approaches to the GPE of finance allow us to consider a greater range of actors, objects, and practices constitutive of global finance, ranging from households, to films about money, to student debt.

Further Resources

Cohen, B. J. (2019), *Currency Statecraft: Monetary Rivalry and Geopolitical Ambition* (Chicago: University of Chicago Press). A rich discussion of money and state power, charting both the history and future of the international currency system.

Grabel, I. (2018), *When Things Don't Fall Apart: Global Financial Governance and Developmental Finance in an Age of Productive Incoherence* (Cambridge, MA and London: MIT). A detailed examination of the changing global financial governance landscape in the wake of the 2008–09 financial crisis.

Inside Job (2010), film, 108 minutes, directed by C. Ferguson. An excellent account of the intricacies of financial securitization and wider dynamics of regulatory capture.

Langley, P. (2009), *The Everyday Life of Global Finance: Saving and Borrowing in Anglo-America* (Oxford: Oxford University Press). Another take on the everyday politics of finance, with a focus on the rise of mass investment.

Roberts, C., Armijo, L. E., and Katada, S. N. (2018), *The BRICS and Collective Financial Statecraft* (New York: Oxford University Press). A detailed analysis of the ways in which the BRICs challenge the existing global financial order.

Singh, S. (2013), *Globalization and Money: A Global South Perspective* (Lanham and Plymouth: Rowman & Littlefield). A Global South perspective on money, including mobile money and remittances.

The Big Short (2015), film, directed by A. McKay. Elucidates links between the worlds of global finance and local mortgage markets.

Warde, I. (2010), *Islamic Finance in the Global Economy*, 2nd rev. edn (Edinburgh: Edinburgh University Press). An excellent overview of the development of Islamic finance.

Chapter 5 Roundtable discussion

Has anything changed in the global financial system since the crash of 2008?

Roundtable 5.1
Opening contribution **Lena Rethel**

The financial crisis of the late 2000s had significant economic, political, and social implications, but not just in the two countries that were at its core—the UK and the USA. The collapse of export markets, including of China and the wider Asian region, and the decline in remittance flows, harshly felt in particular in South Asia and Latin America, quickly turned a crisis caused by excessive risk-taking in the UK and US financial sectors into a global economic crisis.

I do not want to rehash the causes of the 2008–09 crisis. Films such as *Inside Job* and *The Big Short* do excellent jobs at chronicling the maelstrom of speculative financial excess, hypermasculinized financial culture, and regulatory and epistemic capture—compounded by greed—that brought the global financial system close to collapse.

Instead, I want to look at the question of impact, and to suggest that, fundamentally, little has changed since 2008 in how global finance works, and who gains and loses as a consequence.

The crisis of the late 2000s resulted in greater scepticism towards claims that markets function efficiently. Regulators in the Global South felt vindicated in their more cautious approaches to global finance. After two decades of untrammelled support for international capital mobility and a global focus on financial development, the 2008–09 crisis highlighted the dangers of financial overdevelopment. At the same time, the crisis did little to change the structural power features of the global financial system: dollar dependency; the dominance of the USA and Europe in global regulatory networks and institutions; and the fragilities—the boom and bust cycles—of speculative financial markets, of which the global crisis had been such a spectacular example.

In the wake of the crisis, a loose coalition of actors called for fundamental reforms to the global financial system. Emerging market economies, led by the BRICs, called for a more inclusive global financial architecture, reflecting both the shifting dynamics of the global economy and the need to distribute the gains and costs of financial globalization more evenly. Financial regulators agreed on the necessity to prevent excessive and damaging risk-taking. And at a societal level, there were demands for redistribution aimed at reducing inequality—the 'we are the 99%' chants of the Occupy Wall street movement.

And there was some reform. The G20, a grouping of nineteen large economies and the EU, founded in 1999 as a forum for policymakers to meet, was upgraded in 2008 into a venue for heads of governments to coordinate their crisis responses. Importantly, it included the four BRIC countries (Grabel 2018; Roberts, Armijo, and Katada 2018). Similarly, the Financial Stability Board was created in 2009 by the G20, elevating financial stability to the top of the international reform agenda (Moschella 2013). And there was talk about breaking up the banks that had become 'too big to fail'. But the cracks in the system would soon become visible again.

If the motto of 2008–09 was that 'we are all in this together', this solidarity turned out to be a rather temporary phenomenon. When global financial volatility returned with a vengeance in 2013, following the US unilateral announcement that it would taper the liquidity support it had provided to financial markets, emerging countries such as India and Indonesia were told to 'bring their house in order' (Basri 2017). Banks turned out not only to be too big to fail, but also too big to break up. And at the domestic level, rather than reducing inequality, governments implemented austerity policies that left many people struggling.

As a result, since the crisis of the late 2000s, there has been recovery for some, but not for everyone. This was different from previous crises which also acted as economic levellers—reducing asset prices and thus the wealth of asset-holders, as in the Asian crisis (Ragayah 2008) or by giving momentum to progressive distributive policymaking, as in the Great Depression (Piketty 2014).

And now again, we are worrying that the world is at the brink of yet another Global Financial Crisis, triggered by the Covid-19 pandemic. The changes post-2008 have not fared well in the test of time. The G20 has been largely irrelevant in the fight of the pandemic and concomitant economic fallout. The lack of a coordinated crisis response has been compounded by the rather tepid attempt to stall a looming sovereign debt crisis by introducing a short-term moratorium on the debt service of the world's poorest countries. This does not tackle structural issues, let alone address financing requirements caused by the pandemic—to afford vaccines or basic safety nets. The global financial architecture remains far from inclusive.

At the onset of the pandemic, policymakers were quick to inject liquidity into global financial markets to stave off their collapse (A. Tooze 2020). Yet since then, financial markets hit new record highs—but there was little effort, let alone political will, to make them share the burden of the crisis, for example by imposing a windfall tax. (The situation was slightly different at the domestic level, where countries ranging from Malaysia to the UK introduced loan moratoria, whose costs were also, and in some instances predominantly so, borne by the banks.)

Moreover, a decade of austerity left many countries in the West ill-prepared for dealing with the pandemic (Jones and Hameiri 2022). High burdens of personal debt and precarious employment, direct consequences of the fallout from the late 2000s crisis, made it even more challenging, if not impossible, for poorer households to weather the shock of the pandemic. This is indicated, for example, by the significant increase of households depending on food banks for their basic needs in the UK and USA.

So, the impact of the crash of 2008 has been severe and far-reaching, and is far from over. But at the same time, there has been little change—apart from even further entrenching existing injustices and inequalities.

Roundtable 5.2
Response Giselle Datz

Lena Rethel convincingly argues that little has changed when it comes to the financial sector's prevalence and role in perpetuating inequalities since 2008, particularly in the USA (**see Roundtable 5.1**). She was also correct in pointing out that we seemed to be on the brink of a financial crisis, this time prompted by the Covid-19 pandemic. Indeed, in the first quarter of 2020, investors largely pulled back from risky assets, running to cash in response to uncertainty about the economic effects of the pandemic.

Yet a financial crisis did not materialize in 2020 or 2021, largely thanks to a trend in monetary policymaking established *because of* the 2008 financial crisis: systematic injections of liquidity in the financial system by emboldened monetary authorities. Therefore, as Rethel suggests, acknowledging broad continuities in the prevalence of the dollar in the global economy, the lack of truly diverse representation in global economic governance and the continuous financialization of the everyday life may lead to the conclusion that not much has changed since 2008. However, policy patterns inaugurated then have stayed with us, shaping the past decade and likely the near future.

Rethel mentions that bold interventions on the part of advanced economies' central banks managed to avert the collapse of the global financial system in 2008 (A. Tooze 2018; Eichengreen 2016). The goal of liquidity provision was not only technical, but, importantly, to restore confidence in financial institutions, dispelling the notion that the financial panic could render many of these insolvent.

Since then, given lingering political difficulties in expanding government spending prior to the pandemic and a slow recovery from the 2008 crisis, central banks have taken on an extraordinary role in trying to propel recovery, particularly in the USA and Europe. This meant keeping interest rates low, and in some cases negative, in an unprecedented move to encourage lending that could fuel economic growth. Unprecedented too was the expansion of these central banks' balance sheets—the result of their purchases of financial assets such as government bonds and even mortgage-backed securities (known as quantitative easing) on a large scale to prevent further financial turmoil and spur economic activity.

The 'unconventional' monetary policy levers created to deal with the 2008 crisis were pulled again (at times even more forcefully) in 2020 in order to prevent financial instability as a result of the Covid-19 pandemic. In the USA, the Fed revived initiatives originated in 2008, such as the Primary Dealer Credit Facility (allowing primary dealers to facilitate the availability of credit to businesses and households), the Money Market Mutual Fund Liquidity Facility (meant to cushion money market funds in early 2020 as investors questioned the value of the securities held by these funds), and repurchase agreement operations (repo) to also add liquidity to money markets (Martin and McLaughlin 2021; Milstein and Wessel 2021). Fed chairman Jerome Powell acknowledged in April 2020 that the Fed was 'deploying [its] lending powers to an unprecedented extent' (quoted in Milstein and Wessel 2021).

A 'tapering' of asset purchases came in November 2021 when unemployment numbers recovered and inflation rose to 6.8 per cent—the fastest annual pace since 1982 (C. Smith 2021). In fact, rising inflation is now a worldwide phenomenon thanks to 'pandemic-related supply–demand mismatches and higher commodity prices compared to their low base' in 2020. Particularly in some developing countries, fiscal policy is bound to shift from the expansion propelled by the pandemic to new austerity goals (IMF 2021*b*).

It is clear that one of the legacies of the 2008 crisis is a world economy now used to large scale, consistent central bank interventions that go beyond customary monetary policy instruments and objectives (Goodhart et al. 2014: 4). The resultant high levels of liquidity led to handsome gains for investors who benefited from higher asset prices and experienced 'their most profitable period since the 2007–09 financial crisis' (Scuffham 2021). In fact, US equity markets alone returned around 80 per cent in 2020, recording annual performances in excess of 15 per cent (Merrill Lynch 2021). Wall Street's top five investment banks (JPMorgan Chase & Co., Goldman Sachs, Bank of America, Morgan Stanley, and Citigroup) accumulated an additional $51 billion in trading revenues in 2020 and the first three quarters of 2021, compared with the year prior to onset of the pandemic (Scuffham 2021).

The resilience and—more to the point—remarkable profitability of key financial institutions remain inextricably tied to monetary authorities' interventions since 2008. At the end of 2021, the IMF sounded an unsurprising alarm: this 'prolonged period of extremely easy financial conditions, while needed to sustain the economic recovery, may result in overly stretched asset valuations and could fuel financial vulnerabilities' (IMF 2021a: ix).

Rethel is right to be sceptical about whether any fundamental change in the financial system has been propelled by the 2008 crisis. Nonetheless, policy patterns set in 2008 have been reinstituted in the midst of the Covid-19 pandemic. This is not only a sign of a 'new normal' in monetary policy levers, but a clear reminder that active states and markets are far from antagonists. Bold and systematic government interventions in financial markets since 2008 clearly have not spelled a redesign of financial market operations. Yet they have unequivocally contributed to buoyant financial returns even amid a confounding global pandemic.

Roundtable 5.3
Response **Hongying Wang**

The central question for the **Chapter 5 Roundtable discussion** is whether anything has changed since the crash of 2008. Lena Rethel's opening contribution answers this question largely in the negative (**see Roundtable 5.1**). In particular, she contends that the Global Financial Crisis (GFC) 'did little to change the structural power features of the global financial system: dollar dependency; the dominance of the US and Europe in global regulatory networks and institutions; and the fragilities—the boom and bust cycles—of speculative financial markets'. Her argument echoes the perspectives of many other scholars, one of whom labels the GFC as 'the status quo crisis' (Helleiner 2014*b*).

A challenge in debating this question is the lack of a common understanding of where the threshold for identifying 'change' lies. As Manuela Moschella points out, there are not clear indicators or precise measures that we can use (**see Roundtable 5.4**). While I broadly agree with Rethel's view that the GFC did not lead to a transformation *of* the global financial system, I suggest that it did bring about important changes *within* the system. I would argue that the GFC was a turning point in developing countries' view of neoliberal economic policies and Western dominance of the global economy. In China, for instance, the GFC prompted a reassessment of the international economic order and China's role therein. This reassessment, in turn, has reshaped Chinese politics and the Chinese economy, as well as Chinese foreign policy. The Covid-19 pandemic has reinforced the post-GFC Chinese mentality, which has important implications.

The fact that the GFC originated in the United States and had its greatest impact on Western industrialized countries made this crisis very different than many previous financial crises, especially the Asian Financial Crisis (AFC) a decade earlier. The AFC upended the economic miracles in East and Southeast Asia and revealed serious problems of their state-led development model. Many critics blamed state meddling with the market and 'crony capitalism' (close connections between the state and businesses) for the crisis. In contrast, the GFC laid bare the flaws of neoliberalism. A consensus quickly emerged that overzealous financial liberalization was a key culprit of the crisis and the resulting social and economic dislocations.

Following the AFC, the Chinese government continued the economic liberalization measures encouraged by Western countries and international financial organizations such as the World Bank and the IMF. But the GFC had the opposite effect. It gave Chinese policymakers and analysts a new outlook on the international order. The crises—financial and economic—that engulfed the United States and Europe confirmed their view that the West was in irreversible decline. China's financial stability and sustained economic growth through it all boosted their confidence in its heavily statist development model (Wan 2010; Naughton 2015).

Indeed, in the post-GFC era the Chinese government strengthened its support of the state sector and intensified its use of industrial policy, issuing its 'Industrial Revitalization Plans' in 2009 and a plan for 'Strategic Emerging Industries' soon thereafter. With policies favouring state-owned enterprises, the operating environment for private enterprises deteriorated. A trend of 'the advancing state and the retreating private sector (*guojin mintui*)' in the following years undermined the most dynamic elements in the Chinese economy (Naughton 2015; Lardy 2019).

In this process, the Chinese Communist Party (CCP) increased its control of the country's economic and financial systems. The Party also used the GFC as an opportunity to enhance its legitimacy and squash any advocates of Westernization. At the 18th Party Congress in 2012, CCP leader Hu Jintao set forth the confidence (*zixin*) doctrines, calling the population to be confident in the Chinese pathway, Chinese theory, and Chinese institutions. Later, his successor, Xi Jinping, added a fourth doctrine—confidence in Chinese culture.

On the international front, China's strong economic performance during and after the GFC propelled it to the centre of global economic governance. Some observers went so far as to suggest that China had become a major partner with the United States, forming a de facto G2 within the G20 (Garrett 2010). Basking in the glow of greater international respect, the Chinese government began to take a more assertive approach in its foreign policy. It demanded a greater voice in international organizations, notably at the IMF and the World

Bank. In 2013, Xi unveiled an ambitious Belt and Road Initiative, encompassing trade, investment, and infrastructure projects in Europe, Africa, Asia, and Latin America. In 2014, China led the creation of the Asian Infrastructure Investment Bank. In 2015, Xi called for the creation of 'a centre for international knowledge on development to research and communicate with other countries on development theories and practices suitable to their respective national conditions'. Two years later, Beijing established the Center for International Knowledge on Development.

The outbreak of the Covid-19 pandemic in early 2020 threw the world into chaos. Although China was the first to suffer the onslaught of the coronavirus, with draconian policy measures and mass mobilization, the CCP quickly brought the situation under control. The Chinese economy and society initially returned to a level of normalcy much earlier than other regions in the world, and the government and the public in China alike have celebrated the institutional superiority of the Chinese system (Buckley 2020). China's triumphalism borne out of the GFC has become further consolidated. A more assertive China has not yet changed the structural power features of the international economic (including financial) system, but it has already changed the power balance within the system.

To summarize, on the question of whether the world has changed since the 2008 crash, Rethel has provided a rich argument that the glass, as it were, is almost empty. However, I suggest that the glass is fuller than it seems.

Roundtable 5.4
Response Manuela Moschella

If there is something that has not been in short supply for scholars of Global Political Economy, it is a 'crisis'. The evolution of the discipline, and especially the study of money and finance, has been deeply shaped by the history of financial crises and their economic consequences. Few events are as imprinted in the collective memory of the discipline as the historical record of the Great Depression in the 1930s. Financial crises are so central to the study of GPE because their causes and effects are inherently linked with distributional issues and institutional design problems that stand at the core of the discipline. Besides, a crisis usually serves as a kind of 'critical juncture', that is a 'window of opportunity' that leads to political and institutional change.

Has the expected change materialized in the wake of the 2008 Global Financial Crisis and of the more recent Covid-19 crisis? Lena Rethel's conclusions are rather gloomy: the recent crisis period was largely a wasted opportunity. In her words, 'fundamentally, little has changed since 2008 in how global finance works, and who gains and loses as a consequence' (**see Roundtable 5.1**).

Although I largely share Rethel's disappointment, her writing inspired me to think further about this common sense of frustration. I would like to expand on Rethel's insight into what the 2008 crisis has changed by reflecting on two major issues, which I organize around the following questions: What kind of change would have been a 'fundamental' transformation in how global finance works? And is the Covid-19 crisis different than the 2008 Global Financial Crisis?

First, Rethel rightly notes that the impact of the 2008 crisis has not basically altered the balance between states and markets, with markets able to benefit from the crisis and its aftermath much better than governments and societies at large. While I see Rethel's point, I also wonder what exactly an indicator of fundamental change in the balance of power between states and markets would be. Indeed, I think that much of the literature, including my own contributions, has mainly focused on the indicators of continuity with the past, usually measured in terms of the scope of post-crisis financial regulatory changes (Moschella and Tsingou 2013; Pagliari and Wilf 2021). However, much less attention has been devoted to clearly articulating what policy actions are required to bring about a more profound transformation to the status quo.

To be fair, the adoption of a global financial transaction tax (FTT) is one of the policies that is usually invoked as an example of such a transformation process. However, it is not entirely convincing to maintain that the introduction of a single but important measure like the FTT can really reverse the balance between states and markets. Besides, finance adapts and evolves over time.

The limited attention devoted to exploring the measures that would amount to a fundamental post-crisis transformation also lead me to wonder whether we are not somehow under-appreciating the extent of the political change brought about by the crisis. Much of the debate on the post-crisis changes expects a dynamic of change that can be described as 'punctuated'—namely a big, concentrated moment of change. Yet, in the global political economy, change can also take a long time to unfold and become visible (Moschella 2015). Even Bretton Woods—the archetypical example of a marked regime shift in GPE—was not exactly a moment but a drawn-out period of transformation (Helleiner 2010).

The second point I would like to dwell on regards the differences between the two recent crises. Rethel argues that the Covid-19 crisis is not significantly different from the 2008 crisis in terms of its political consequences: 'there has been little change', she argues, 'apart from even further entrenching existing injustices and inequalities'. While I agree that one of the most serious consequences of the Covid-19 pandemic is growing inequalities both within countries (especially based on gender and race) and among countries (with the poorest countries the most constrained in confronting the health crisis), I also think that some important differences between the 2008 crisis and the Covid-19 crisis are worth stressing.

Two differences stand out. The first is about the use of the fiscal lever to shield households and businesses from the negative impact of the crisis. Of course, as Rethel suggests, the fiscal space was available for some countries only—that is, high-income countries and some emerging market countries. While this imbalance is undeniable and needs to be addressed, it should not obscure the transformations that have taken place since 2020. If in the aftermath of the 2008 crisis, austerity became the standard policy response, the rejection of fiscal austerity became the new mantra in the 2020 crisis (Ban 2015; Clift 2018).

Second, and connected, the crisis has reinvigorated the debate on the role of the state in supporting domestic economies not only in traditional areas such as industrial policies but also in new areas such as climate change and green finance. The fact that public authorities such as central banks are at the front-end of attempts at greening finance tells us a lot about potential changes in the balance of power between public and private authority and between states and markets in the Global Political Economy.

Of course, the big question is whether these important and embryonic signs of change will stick. But that's for another Roundtable conversation.

Over to you ...

1 You have seen some differing points of view in the **Chapter 5 Roundtable**: Lena Rethel argues that little has changed since the 2008 Global Financial Crisis (**see Roundtable 5.1**), but the other three contributors suggest that there may have been more change than first appears (**see Roundtable 5.2**, **Roundtable 5.3**, and **Roundtable 5.4**). Where do you stand? Can you see clear signs that the responses during the Covid-19 pandemic were shaped by changes which took place in the aftermath of the 2008 Global Financial Crisis? Or do you think they are very different crises and cannot be easily compared?

2 You have seen that some of the contributors here, like many people, are worried that we would see another financial crisis after the Covid-19 pandemic began. However, one did not immediately emerge. Why not? Thinking about the present day, what have been the economic effects of the pandemic, and how are governments and banks trying to manage them? How do you evaluate the arguments our contributors have presented here in that light?

3 What sort of change do you think we would need to see in order for the repeated cycles of financial crisis to be interrupted in the global economy? Or are they simply inevitable?

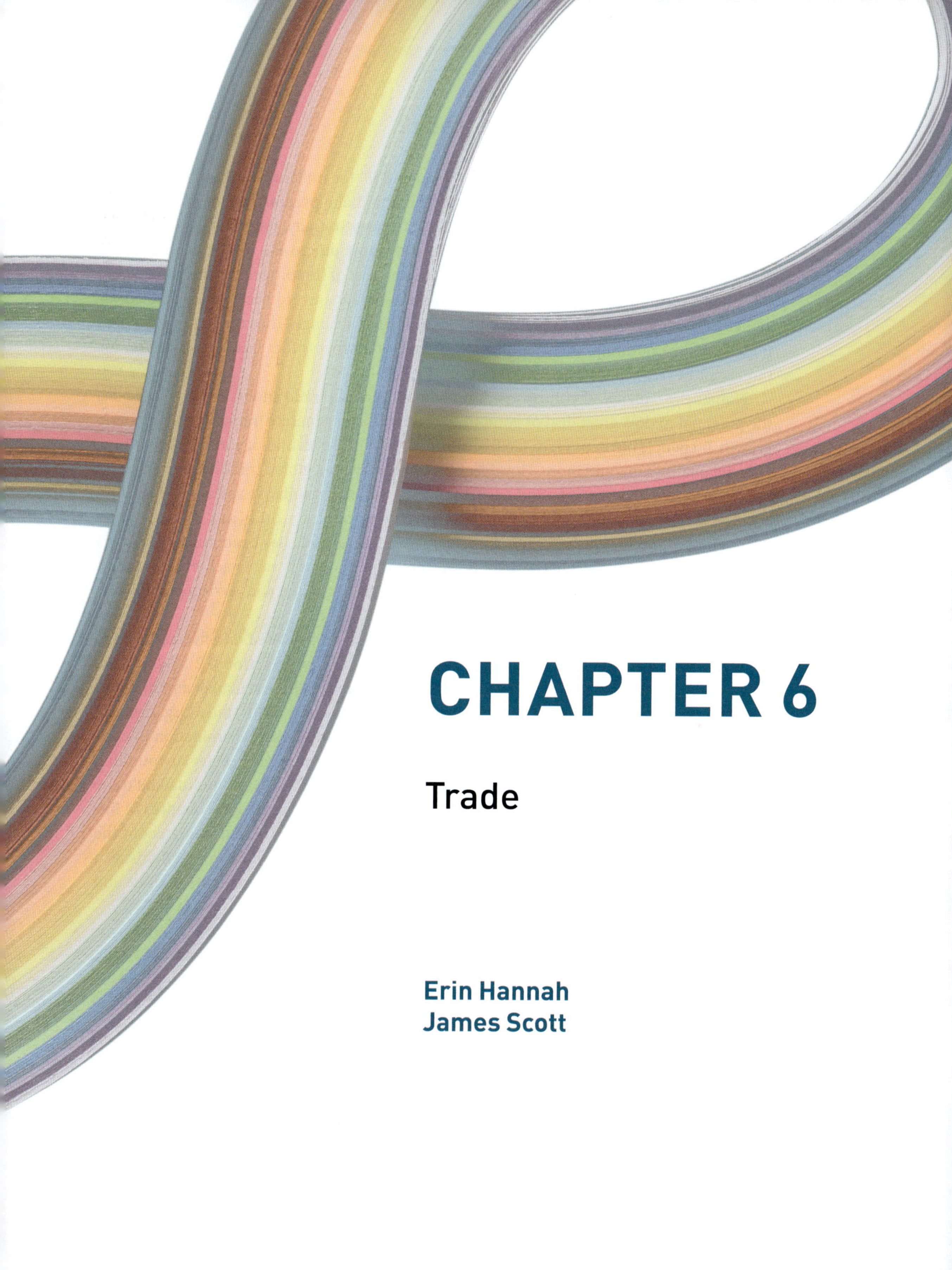

CHAPTER 6

Trade

Erin Hannah
James Scott

6.1 Introduction: What is trade?

Trade has shaped the world around us, for good and ill, for millennia. It has thrived wherever sufficient political stability allowed merchants to make perilous journeys across land and sea to exchange goods for (often very large) profit. Initially, long-distance trade was restricted to luxury commodities such as silk and spices due to the difficulty and cost of shipping in bulk, but as technology advanced and the cost of shipping fell to the point where it is often almost insignificant for even low-value goods, the world has been connected together in ever more complex chains of production and exchange. The contemporary global trade system is nothing more than the latest stage of a process that has been going on for thousands of years (Bernstein 2009).

Nonetheless, plenty of controversies remain concerning trade and its effects. Trade has the potential to do a great deal of good in the world. It can generate tremendous economic growth, lift people out of poverty, facilitate the uptake of green technology, empower women, close inequality gaps, and more. However, throughout history, global trade has been characterized by unequal power relations, structural inequalities, exploitative social relations, and ecological crises that are unfolding highly unevenly across the world (Kim 2011; J. Singh 2016; Findlay and O'Rourke 2009). This is largely because trade has been pursued in ways that align with the interests of the most powerful, rather than as a way to achieve important social goals such as development, human rights, gender equality, and environmental sustainability (Hannah, Roberts, and Trommer 2022*c*).

This chapter introduces you to the global trade system. It is divided into five parts. First, we will look at the debate over free trade and protectionism (**see Section 6.2**). Second, we will explore the evolution of the multilateral trade system, with particular emphasis on the General Agreement on Tariffs and Trade (GATT) and the World Trade Organization (WTO), highlighting the centrality of trade liberalization and non-discrimination in contemporary trade relations (**see Section 6.3**). We will then consider the debates surrounding the relationship between trade and development, particularly around how multilateral trade rules reflect unequal power relations (**see Section 6.4**), and the social consequences of liberalized trade (**see Section 6.5**). We will also take the opportunity here to think about the recent backlash against neoliberal trade and the ostensible turn towards protectionism in some parts of the world. Finally, we will put a spotlight on the gendered nature of trade and how it affects gender equality (**see Section 6.6**).

Key Concepts

Protectionism: The use of policies to restrict imports. The most important method is the use of tariffs, taxes applied to goods and services at the border. States have also often used quantitative restrictions, where goods can be imported only up to a specific quota. Non-tariff barriers are domestic rules and regulations such as product standards that restrict trade flows. Free trade agreements increasingly focus on tackling these barriers to trade.

Trade liberalization: The removal or reduction of barriers to the flow of goods and services across borders.

Tariffs: Taxes on goods and services as they cross borders. Historically these were sometimes charged on exports, but today that is extremely rare and tariffs are charged only on imports. There are two key types: ad valorem tariffs, which are charged as a percentage of the value of the good as it crosses into a country; and non-ad valorem tariffs, which are charged based on anything other than value, such as weight, quantity, etc.

Free Trade Agreements (FTAs): Reciprocal trade agreements between two or more countries aimed at facilitating the flow of goods and services across borders and coordinating national rules and regulations that impinge upon cross-border trade. FTAs often include legal frameworks for resolving disputes among contracting states or between a contracting state and foreign investors.

6.2 **Free trade and protectionism**

6.2.1 **The case for free trade**

In what is termed the mercantilist way of thinking (**see Section 4.3.2**), which dominated Europe until around the eighteenth century, trade was seen in simple terms. Exports were considered beneficial because they meant that money (specifically gold and silver) was flowing into the economy, while imports were seen as harmful because they led to an outflow of currency.

Adam Smith's *The Wealth of Nations*, published in 1776, revolutionized this thinking. Smith demonstrated that a country can make itself better off if it concentrates on producing the goods that it can make most efficiently—those in which it has an advantage—and imports goods that it cannot produce efficiently. Imports are not to be deterred or feared, because they enable a country to specialize in making the goods it is best at producing, which creates economic gains. David Ricardo subsequently built on Smith's insights in his 1817 *On the Principles of Political Economy*. He explored a hypothetical example consisting of two countries and two commodities (cloth and wine), where one country was more efficient at producing *both* commodities. Ricardo demonstrated that even in this scenario, specializing in producing the goods in which they are comparatively most efficient—those in which they have a 'comparative advantage'—will still leave both countries better off. Moving towards free trade in this analysis is a win-win, positive-sum situation for each country as a whole, however adversely affected groups such as those who lose their jobs will need to be compensated if no individual is to be harmed.

China is a good contemporary example of a country that has utilized liberalization to drive economic development (Lin and Wang 2012). Following the death of Chairman Mao, China embarked on a process of opening itself to foreign trade and investment, greatly reducing its tariffs from an average of around 40 per cent in 1992 to just 5 per cent in 2020 (**see Figure 6.1**). Through this process it has generated millions of jobs and achieved the fastest poverty reduction in human history. This could not have happened without engagement with global trade—although there is another side to this story, which we will explore shortly.

At its root, Smith and Ricardo's argument is one about consumption. Free trade allows a country to maximize the amount that it can consume at a given level of income because it allows consumers (individuals and businesses) to buy products at the lowest globally available price. If T-shirts made in the UK cost £10, but imported T-shirts from, say, Bangladesh cost £5, then in a context of free trade UK consumers can purchase their T-shirts at half the cost. The savings they make can then be spent on other goods and services, enabling them to consume more at a given level of income. This increased consumer spending drives more investment, which in turn creates new jobs and thereby drives economic growth and higher wages.

There are many other arguments in favour of free trade (Wolf 2005: **Chapter 10** provides a good overview). From a Global Political Economy (GPE) perspective, one of the key arguments is that free trade encourages more peaceful international relations. This is for two key reasons. First, pursuing free trade ensures that states cannot discriminate between trade partners because all countries are receiving the same tariff-free treatment. Conversely, favouring some over others typically breeds resentment and tensions which can spill over into conflict. Second, greater trade flows increase interdependence between states, making conflict more costly.

For these and other reasons the pursuit of free trade often sits at the heart of liberal approaches to GPE (**see Section 3.4.2**).

Figure 6.1 China's applied tariff, simple mean, percentage

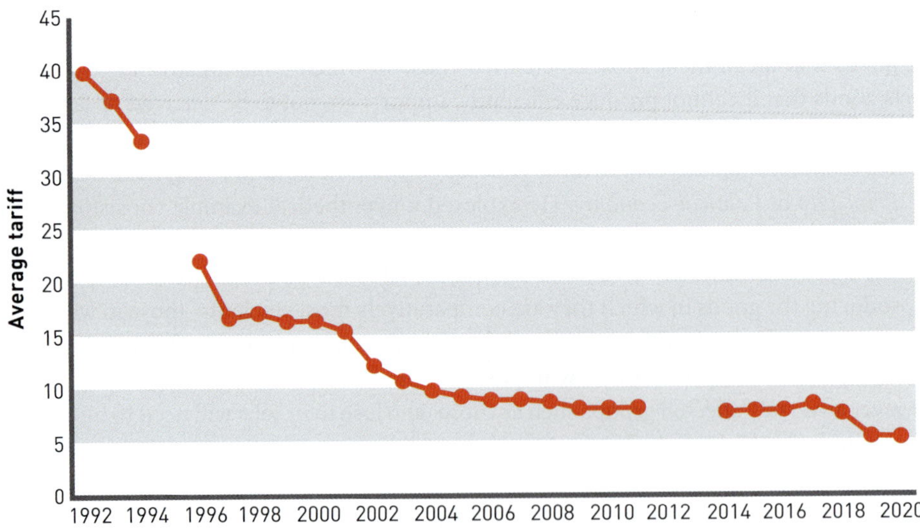

Source: World Bank, www.worldbank.org. Data unavailable for 1995 and 2012–13.

6.2.2 **The case for protectionism**

Nonetheless, liberal trade theory is not without its critics. Here we need to consider arguments in favour of protectionism relating to economic development. Adam Smith's arguments had a profound effect on economic thinking and his core concepts were accepted by many critics. However, other theorists emerged in countries that were seeking to catch up with the UK following the industrial revolution, and they came to a different conclusion on trade policy (Shafaeddin 2000).

The two theorists who gained the greatest attention are Alexander Hamilton from the United States and Friedrich List from Germany, but we should add Sun Yat-sen, who wrote independently along very similar lines in the early twentieth century concerning China's catch-up with the West (Sun 1922; Helleiner 2021). These scholars argued that industrialization was crucial if their respective countries were to be able to compete, both economically and militarily. Subsequent history has provided support for this intuition. As Adam Szirmai has found, 'there are no important examples of success in economic development in developing countries since 1950, which have not been driven by industrialisation' (Szirmai 2012).

List, Hamilton, and Sun asked themselves what trade policy was most effective in driving industrialization. They argued that simply relying on free trade would not lead to industrialization, since their respective countries could not compete with Britain's highly efficient industrial sector. Free trade would therefore inevitably lead to manufacturing continuing to be concentrated in Britain (or the Global North in general) while the rest of the world largely exported raw materials. Instead, they argued that the state should (among other things) use protective tariffs on industrial goods to raise the cost of imported manufactures and enable domestic producers to compete. This idea has become known as infant industry protection. It advocates temporary, targeted protection to help drive economic transformation, driven by an interventionist state.

In **Section 6.2.1** we noted how China has used liberalization to drive economic development, but it is, perhaps paradoxically, also a good example of a country that has also used a highly interventionist state to achieve its success. The government has provided widespread support for targeted industries to try to achieve competitiveness in new sectors, set out most clearly in the Made in China 2025 programme (Agarwala and Chaudhary 2021). Far from relying exclusively on its current areas of comparative advantage, as liberal theorists would suggest, China has actively sought to shape where its future comparative advantages will lie.

The China example highlights the complexity of trade policy. This complexity is also to be found in the works of the theorists on both sides of the debate on trade, but all too often their arguments are caricatured, used to suit purposes and arguments that do not do justice to the nuances of their thinking (Harlen 1999; Shafaeddin 2000; Ho 2010). For example, Adam Smith noted several exceptions to the case for free trade, while List and Hamilton both advocated free trade to be the optimal policy for countries once they had achieved industrialization (see Helleiner 2002). Care must be taken not to create silos of opposing, simplified versions of these bodies of thought. Nonetheless, two differing approaches to trade policy can be identified through these works and both became elements of the global trade system, as we will see in **Section 6.3**.

6.3 How did the contemporary multilateral trade system evolve?

The contemporary global trade system has its roots in the post-Second World War period. The United States emerged from the Second World War as the global economic hegemon as demonstrated by the establishment of the US dollar as the global reserve currency and its growing preponderance in international trade and foreign investment. By 1944, the United States was in a unique position to exercise economic leadership and, together with its Second World War allies, sought to create a new, global economic architecture that would help avoid the devastating recurrence of war and economic depression.

Trade protectionism was widely thought to have contributed to both the Great Depression of the 1930s and the Second World War. The introduction of tariffs on more than 20,000 imported goods by the USA in 1930 sparked a period of retaliation and counter-retaliation, which led to a massive contraction in the value of global trade, heightened joblessness in industrialized countries, and the concomitant rise of both communism and fascism in the interwar years (Siles-Brügge 2014).

In the aftermath of the Second World War, the United States and its allies embraced the principle of multilateralism and resolved never again to resort to 'beggar-thy-neighbour' trade policies—that is, policies which benefit one country or a group of countries while (or by) adversely affecting another—which had so fundamentally destabilized the global economy. They also recognized that with more open global markets can come increased risks for citizens—including increased competition from foreign firms, associated local business closures, declining wages, and job losses—and that it is the government's duty to cushion citizens from such shocks and risks.

> ### Key Concept: Multilateralism
>
> Institutionalized or rule-governed cooperation between three or more states that is underscored by non-discrimination, reciprocity, and indivisibility—the idea that all participants are equal and cannot be divided—in pursuit of a common goal such as economic growth or development.

As outlined in **Section 4.3.3**, the post-Second World War economic architecture was finalized in 1944 at Bretton Woods, New Hampshire and sought to strike a balance between an open global economy and movement towards free trade on the one hand, and the active public management of national economies on the other. Coined 'embedded liberalism' by John Ruggie (1982), the Bretton Woods system prioritized free trade and multilateralism but also recognized that governments should play an active and interventionist role in national economies through redistributive and welfare policies in order to ensure economic growth, equity, and full employment.

This embedded liberal compromise between unfettered economic liberalism and Keynesian-style domestic interventionism was underpinned by a fixed exchange rate regime—a new kind of gold standard—that was designed to bring stability and predictability to global trade (**see Chapter 5**). Governments committed to pegging their currencies to the US dollar which was convertible into gold at a rate of $35 per ounce. No longer could they competitively and unilaterally devalue their currencies in order to increase their trade competitiveness or improve trade imbalances. Instead, they were subject to the oversight of the newly created International Monetary Fund (Helleiner 2020). This system persisted until the US abandonment of the gold standard in 1971, after which global currencies would largely float in relation to each other and global capital would travel freely across borders.

6.3.1 The General Agreement on Tariffs and Trade (GATT)

It might seem obvious that a global economic system designed to prioritize free trade and multilateralism would be supported by a formal, multilateral trade organization. Indeed, an agreement to form an International Trade Organization (ITO) was signed in 1948; however, citing concerns over the loss of sovereignty, the United States Congress refused to ratify the agreement. In its place, twenty-three countries agreed to rely on the General Agreement on Tariffs and Trade (GATT), a treaty established during a round of tariff negotiations in 1947 (see Kim 2011). Meant to serve as a temporary agreement until political will shifted in the USA and the ITO could be ratified, the GATT was a negotiating forum in which trade liberalization was pursued in a series of 'rounds' of multilateral negotiations. GATT rules effectively covered industrial and manufactured goods only and negotiations primarily concerned the reduction of tariffs and non-tariff barriers. Major gains were made in liberalizing trade, particularly in the Uruguay Round (1986–94) where the average tariff cut was 39 per cent on $3.7 trillion of trade (Trommer 2020). As we will see in **Section 6.3.2**, the Uruguay Round vastly expanded the scope of multilateral trade rules beyond just covering manufactured goods.

The GATT was predicated on the principle of non-discrimination, which has two dimensions: national treatment (Article I) and Most Favoured Nation (MFN) (Article II). National treatment means that imported and locally produced goods should be treated the same in the market; preferential treatment that would enhance domestic producers' competitiveness such as tax breaks were no longer allowed. General exceptions to this rule were only permitted in limited circumstances to serve very specific public policy goals such as the protection of public morals, the protection of human, animal, or plant life, or the conservation of exhaustible natural resources (GATT 1947: Article XX).

MFN simply means that countries cannot normally discriminate between their trading partners; any advantage such as lower tariffs granted to one trading partner must be extended to all trading partners. Exceptions included preferential trade arrangements for former colonies such as the countries of Africa, the Caribbean, and the Pacific (ACP) and for customs unions and regional trade agreements such as the European Economic Community (EEC), the predecessor of the European Union (EU).

The principle of reciprocity basically says that when one country lowers its barriers to trade against the exports of another country, they will be granted equal trade concessions in return such that liberalization is 'mutually advantageous'. Exceptions to this principle include Special and Differential Treatment (SDT) for developing countries, which lessens some of the rules and disciplines of the GATT and permits development assistance and preferential market access for developing country exports. Notably, under the GATT, countries could selectively apply the rules by using exemptions and escape clauses, and dispute resolutions were ad hoc and non-binding. This changed radically with the creation of the WTO in 1995.

6.3.2 The World Trade Organization (WTO)

The creation of the WTO marks one of the most significant advances towards legally rigorous economic integration in the global political economy. With 164 current members, all of which are states, the WTO aims to reduce discrimination and promote progressive trade liberalization among its members. It also seeks to promote fair, undistorted competition and encourage economic reform and sustainable development. The WTO monitors and reports on national laws and regulations in order to promote transparency and predictability in international trade. It provides a forum for dialogue and for settling trade disputes among members. Importantly, the principles established under the GATT system—non-discrimination and reciprocity—remain the cornerstones of the WTO system and the GATT remains as one of the WTO Agreements (now GATT 1994).

The creation of the WTO significantly expanded the scope of international trade rules beyond trade in manufactured goods to include intellectual property, services, and investment. Agriculture—the key strategic interest of most developing countries—was also brought into the fold of multilateral trade agreements for the first time. Moreover, WTO rules expanded well beyond removing barriers to trade at the borders to touch on national social and regulatory policies including: labour, environment, human health, food safety, and development policies.

One of the most significant developments in 1995 was the creation of the dispute settlement system under the WTO. The WTO enjoys a legal personality that the GATT did not; the dispute settlement system makes WTO rules legally binding and members have legal recourse to ensure their trade partners comply with the rules. Since members cannot apply the range of obligations contained in the WTO Agreements selectively, nor can they appeal to pre-existing national legislation to avoid adherence to the WTO Agreements, WTO members must bring their national laws into compliance with international trade rules or face costly and compulsory adjudication. Adding this legal character to the international trade regime was aimed at promoting security and predictability in global trade.

The creation of the WTO marked a so-called 'Grand Bargain' between developed and developing countries; in exchange for the inclusion of new issues such as intellectual property rights and services and the new organization with its strengthened dispute settlement system, developing countries were granted inclusion of agriculture and textiles—two areas of key economic interest. They were also promised greater SDT which includes exemptions from the principle of reciprocity and preferential market access for developing country exports to industrialized countries. Given these institutional changes, members of the WTO are far more deeply bound to international trade rules than signatories to the GATT ever were: the rules are more intrusive, they are more formalized, and there is increased enforceability through the enhanced dispute settlement system. Partly as a consequence, the successful conclusion of trade negotiations has been made increasingly difficult.

 Watch the video on the online resources to take your understanding of this section further.

6.4 Does the WTO support development?

The relationship between trade and development is, like almost every interesting question in GPE, complex and at times contradictory. More or less by definition, countries at a low level of economic development have low per capita income and consequently relatively small market sizes (with the partial exception of the likes of India and China which were able to compensate for low income with large populations, and the USA in the nineteenth century). This means that internal markets are unable to provide the economies of scale required to propel a transformation of the economy. *All* countries that have successfully moved from low-income status to high per capita income, with the exception of a handful of tiny tax havens, have relied on trade to provide demand for goods as they transform their economies.

The economies that have made the transition to industrialization and high per capita income since the 1960s, including Japan, South Korea, Taiwan, and China, have relied on export markets to drive rapid economic transformation. Exporting manufactured goods has driven transformational growth by moving economic activity out of low-productivity sectors such as agriculture into the high-productivity industrial sector, providing higher-paid jobs in the process. Nevertheless, these jobs are often very low quality by Western standards, involving long hours of repetitive and dispiriting work in 'sweat shops', and often have been akin to modern slavery (**see Chapter 7** and **Chapter 12**).

Even where countries have managed to use trade to drive economic development, these should not be taken as unequivocal instances of free trade. In all of these cases, the state played an important role in channelling economic activity, including through the targeted use of trade protection. That is, they followed something more closely associated with the thought of Friedrich List and Alexander Hamilton than that of Adam Smith (Wade 1990) (**see Section 6.2.2**). Trade expansion formed a component of a broader set of state policies designed to foster economic transformation. At times, this included trade liberalization, while in other instances it involved protectionism.

Moreover, these states are the exception. Far more developing countries have failed to make the transition to sustained economic growth, and the trade system has been structured in ways that have made that fate more likely. Even when states have managed to begin the process of industrialization, all too often they have found themselves locked into low-paid, low-value production, often in textiles and clothing, and been unable to diversify into more profitable sectors (Bernhardt and Pollak 2016; Lockwood 2021).

Other countries have remained primarily producers of agricultural goods, but the agricultural sector was largely excluded from the push towards trade liberalization undertaken by the GATT and WTO (Hoda and Gulati 2008). Agricultural subsidies paid in rich countries depress global prices of agricultural goods, and as a consequence farmers in poor countries receive less for their produce. Furthermore, opportunities for exporting to rich countries are severely curtailed by the combination of high tariffs, subsidies, and restrictive quality requirements on things like pesticide residues on food (called sanitary and phytosanitary standards). **Figure 6.2** illustrates this by comparing the average tariff rates on agricultural goods with those on non-agricultural goods. Global trade rules allow these policies because they treat agriculture very differently to manufactures, and developing countries are consequently unable to take advantage of their key area of comparative advantage (**see Case Study 6.1**).

This situation is largely a consequence of the way in which the GATT/WTO were designed and the central place given to power politics in the liberalization process. The process determining which products will be liberalized is one of competitive bargaining between members. When there are such large inequalities between countries around the world, this inevitably means that the commercial interests of the powerful are favoured at the expense of the rest. The result is a system that structures trade opportunities in ways that work against the developing world and the global poor (Wilkinson 2014).

It is clear that trade can certainly aid development in some situations and indeed has been an essential component of the development process for many successful countries. However, the current configuration of the global trade system is not one designed to repeat these successes. In many regards it could be argued to do the opposite, contributing to the exacerbation of inequalities between countries. Even if such problems are fixed, however, we need to pay attention to the impact of trade on inequalities *within* countries, to which we now turn.

Figure 6.2 **Simple average applicated tariffs, percentages, select countries, 2020**

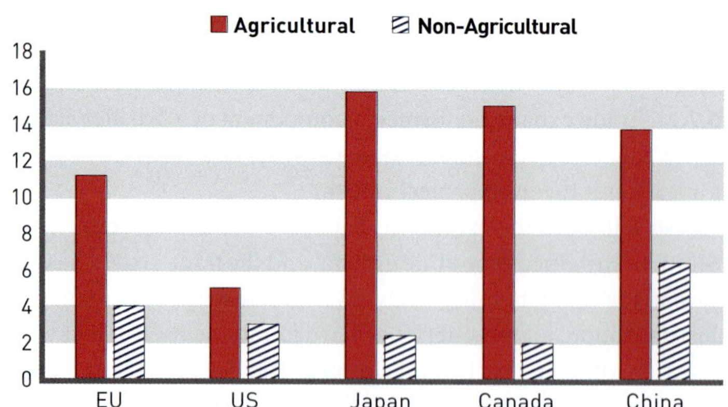

Source: WTO Tariff Profiles, available at www.wto.org.

Case Study 6.1: Cotton

During the WTO's ultimately failed round of trade negotiations, the Doha Development Agenda or 'Doha Round', trade in cotton came to be one of the most controversial issues and a litmus test of whether the negotiations could deliver on their promises for developing countries. The issue was driven by a group of four African countries—Benin, Burkina Faso, Chad, and Mali—which became known as the Cotton Four. Their climate makes them among the most efficient producers of cotton globally and some are heavily reliant on cotton exports (Photo 6.1). In Benin, for instance, cotton comprised fully half their exports when the Doha Round was launched in 2001 (OEC n.d.).

The United States is one of the largest exporters of cotton. However, the Cotton Four, backed by non-governmental organizations such as Oxfam, argued that the USA achieves this only because it pays billions of dollars a year in subsidies to its farmers, enabling them to undercut farmers in Africa who receive minimal support from their cash-strapped governments (Oxfam 2002). Though justifications for these subsidies typically appeal to the idea of 'Mom and Pop' small-scale farms and defending the traditional way of life, in reality 80 per cent of subsidies are paid to just 10 per cent of producers—huge agri-business corporations—while two-thirds of US farmers receive no support (Cross 2006: 159). Estimates made by the International Cotton Advisory Committee during the Doha Round suggested that these subsidies depressed world cotton prices by around 26 per cent (2002: 8).

The overall picture was one in which the roughly 10 million farmers in West and Central Africa, often living in poverty, who relied on cotton for their livelihoods were having their earnings significantly diminished by the massive subsidies being paid to a handful of giant corporations in

Photo 6.1 Freshly harvested cotton in Burkina Faso

Source: © iStock/ALEXANDER BEE

(*Continued*)

the USA. They were unable to make use of their comparative advantage because of the distortions to the market brought about by US subsidies.

Cotton is just a single example of a far broader critique of the trade system as it operates in agriculture. All major rich countries (and, increasingly, emerging countries such as China) have a raft of subsidy programmes to support agricultural producers to overcome the fact that their farmers cannot compete on global markets. **Figure 6.3** shows the estimated producer support for a selection of countries, measured as the percentage of total farm income that comes from government support, to illustrate the extent to which governments interfere in agricultural markets. These same countries tirelessly advocate free trade to poor countries, but then practise the exact opposite when it suits them.

Redressing these inequalities was at the heart of the Doha Round, the WTO's first (and, as of the early 2020s, only) round of multilateral trade negotiations, which was launched in 2001 and effectively abandoned in 2015. Also known as the Doha Development Agenda (DDA), it put poverty alleviation and the needs of poor countries at the centre of the agenda. Agricultural liberalization and the reduction of protectionist policies such as domestic subsidies in industrialized countries were seen as key to delivering on these priorities.

As noted in **Section 6.3**, agriculture was outside the purview of the GATT system, and while the Uruguay Round included an Agreement on Agriculture, bringing the sector under WTO law, little liberalization was achieved. Rather, the Agreement was written by the USA and EU in such a way as to minimize the market openings required of them. Even the WTO Secretary General Mike Moore, who is obliged to remain neutral on all WTO matters, said that developing countries were 'fobbed off' by the Agreement on Agriculture (WTO 2000).

The DDA was meant to redress this failure. However, it quickly became clear that the rich world had little intention of overhauling their agricultural support regime. The best they were

Figure 6.3 **Producer support estimates, selection of countries, 2010–20**

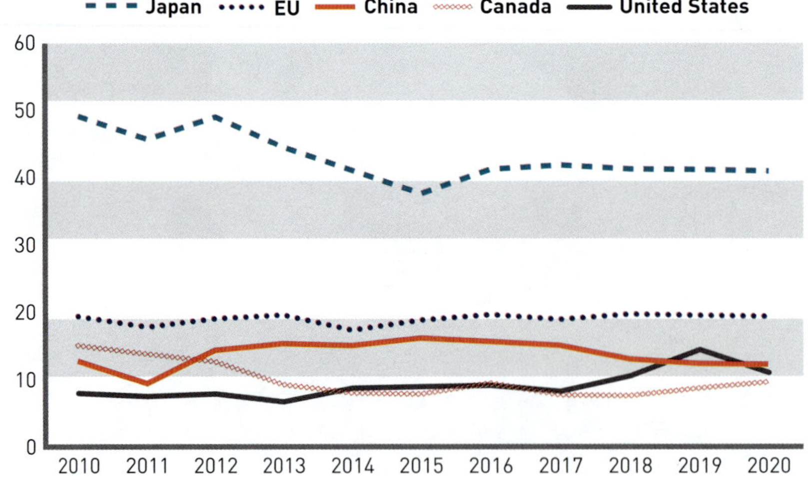

Source: OECD, www.oecd.org.

willing to offer was to lock in the permitted level of agricultural subsidies to roughly what they were currently paying. In return, however, the USA and EU demanded steep new market openings by the likes of China, India, and Brazil (Scott and Wilkinson 2011).

The inability to reach a compromise led the Doha Round negotiations to be put on hold in July 2008 and finally, after a further seven years of stasis, terminated in 2015. Unable to secure a WTO deal to their liking, the USA and EU further shifted towards regional trade agreements as alternative forums for pursuing their trade agenda. However, such agreements never include sections tackling agricultural subsidies, leaving those developing countries that rely on agricultural goods for their export revenue little hope of securing greater opportunities to utilize their comparative advantage (Scott 2017).

The Cotton Four managed to get the issue of cotton subsidies onto the agenda as a particularly egregious case, leveraging the supposed development focus of the DDA (Eagleton-Pierce 2012), but when the Doha Round was abandoned so was hope for any significant action. Since then, cotton subsidies have continued to grow, most notably in China, which is now the world's largest subsidizer, paying out more than twice the amount of the USA, which is in second place (International Cotton Advisory Committee 2020).

Questions

1 Why do countries provide so much protection for their agricultural sectors?
2 How can this protection be reconciled with the principles of free trade?

6.5 What are the social consequences of global trade?

Trade liberalization has long been recognized as having unequal impacts on different social groups. Some will lose out, notably through jobs being lost to cheaper imports, but others gain, through expanding job opportunities in export industries and through the reduction in prices. Economists point out that since there is a net gain, losers can be compensated such that everyone is left better off. In practice, however, this may prove to be impossible for a variety of reasons: politically, if such tax and redistribution policies do not have widespread support; economically, if the benefits are inaccessible to governments through, for example, being shunted into tax havens; and administratively, if it is impossible to identify who has lost out, or if there is a small tax base and weak state capacity as is typically the case in developing countries. Little attention is paid to these problems and indeed to the whole idea of directly compensating losers from liberalization.

Concern over the impacts of trade growth on inequalities became a major focus of academic and political attention in the 1980s and 1990s following the emergence of highly competitive, low-wage exporters across East Asia, and the outsourcing of industrial production from the Western countries to these new centres of manufacturing. More recently, this strand of the literature has re-emerged, this time examining the impact of China's export-led growth and its growing penetration of Western markets and the growth of global value chain-based production. A key contribution is Autor, Dorn, and

Hanson (2013), who found that increased trade between China and the USA had caused higher unemployment and reduced wages in areas that have import-competing manufacturing industries. Further work found that such areas took at least a decade to adjust (Autor, Dorn, and Hanson 2016).

Such experiences fuel anti-trade sentiments within Western countries, particularly with regard to trade between them and low-wage industrializing countries, and formed a key element in the election of Donald Trump in the USA in 2016. De-industrialization in much of the Western world has destroyed long-established livelihoods and created areas of economic decline, even as other sectors and localities, such as financial centres and Silicon Valley, have thrived, resulting in inequalities and political resentment against the 'establishment' that presided over this outcome. Trade becomes an obvious target of anger, driving populist pressure for protectionism. The resulting prospect of trade war between the USA and China has increased international tension and threatened a full-scale dismantling of the global trade system (Hopewell 2020).

However, the backlash against trade liberalization is not altogether justified. Nor is it necessarily the most appropriate response to the suffering of communities facing increased unemployment. Trade is often the primary target of blame for de-industrialization, but is in truth responsible for only a relatively small proportion. The main driving force is technological change and increased productivity in factories, allowing more to be made with a smaller workforce. Even Autor, Dorn, and Hanson's (2013) study found that increased China–USA trade was responsible for only around a quarter of the lost industrial jobs in the USA.

Furthermore, part of the problem is the lack of assistance given to workers who are displaced. Re-training schemes exist but are usually chronically underfunded and unfit for purpose. Broader support packages—meaning a much more comprehensive social safety net—would cushion workers against job losses and help them to seek out new opportunities, avoiding the often catastrophic impact on people, particularly those with lower levels of education, that currently accompanies economic adjustment to trade and technology changes (Posen 2021; see **Chapter 12**).

Equally, a more active policy stance is necessary to avoid some of the other inequalities created by trade liberalization. One key area of attention is gender inequalities.

6.6 Is global trade gendered?

Recall that non-discrimination is the cornerstone of the contemporary global trade system. Until recently, conventional wisdom among trade policymakers was that trade is gender neutral, in the sense that it targets neither women nor men (Roberts, Hannah, and Trommer 2019). Open markets and free trade were seen as engines of economic growth and thus desirable ends in themselves, as opposed to other social goals such as gender equality, human rights, environmental protections, and so on (Hannah, Roberts, and Trommer 2022c). In other words, trade was considered a technical matter and goals like gender equality and human rights were seen as totally separate from trade policy, and certainly not the business of trade institutions such as the WTO.

This began to change in 2017 when policymakers started to talk about the importance of gender mainstreaming in trade policy. This shift in thinking gained traction with the signing, in December 2017, of the WTO Joint Declaration on Trade and Women's Economic Empowerment (WTO Declaration) by 118 members and observers. Since then, more than 100 gender and trade initiatives have been developed globally (Hannah, Roberts, and Trommer 2018).

> ### Key Concept: Gender mainstreaming
>
> A strategy of achieving gender equality which involves ensuring that gender perspectives and the goal of gender equality are pulled all the way through institutional practices in state and global governance, in ways that transform conventional ways of developing and implementing policy.

6.6.1 What does it mean to say global trade is gendered?

Global trade is and always has been gendered (Hannah, Roberts, and Trommer 2018, 2021, 2022*c*; Roberts, Hannah, and Trommer 2019). Trade policy affects almost every area of public policy and it impacts people in their multiple roles as business owners as well as workers, consumers, users of public services, paid and unpaid carers, citizens, and more. These different roles are shaped by gender norms and power relations in society (Roberts, Hannah, and Trommer 2019). For example, gender norms in a country can impact women's access to education, employment, and earnings relative to men. They are also shaped by other, intersecting identities, such as class, caste, race, ethnicity, nationality, citizenship status, sexuality, age, and ability (Hannah, Roberts, and Trommer 2022*c*). The impacts of trade policy are gendered as a result of the different position of women and men in these roles and policymakers are increasingly attuned to the differential impacts of trade in four key areas—paid work, consumption, public services, and care work (Roberts, Hannah, and Trommer 2019).

It is important to emphasize that trade does not cause gender inequalities. Trade can improve the lives of women and other vulnerable groups by redressing existing gender inequalities, or it can make them more precarious by exacerbating already existing gender inequalities (Roberts, Hannah, and Trommer 2019).

6.6.1.1 Paid work

Trade liberalization often results in an increase in jobs, particularly in those countries that specialize in production for export, and this may give women increased income and purchasing power. However, women are responsible for the majority of unpaid care work for children and the elderly the world over. This means that they are over-represented in precarious and temporary forms of work. Countries that specialize in goods for export may also have wide gender wage gaps as the payment of low wages or poor working conditions in feminized sectors of the economy are the ways that countries are able to compete in a global economy—their comparative advantage, so to speak (Roberts, Hannah, and Trommer 2019).

The 'feminization' of labour that occurred in Mexico following the signing of the North American Free Trade Agreement (NAFTA) in 1994 is one example of the complex ways in which trade liberalization can impact the conditions of paid work for women and other vulnerable communities. The impacts are often complex and context specific. An often-rehearsed argument is that greater employment opportunities for women, even if initially poorly paid and precarious, will in time reduce gender pay inequalities when wages begin to rise in response to declining unemployment. However, the evidence for this is rather weak. To take one example, Lilia Domínguez-Villalobos and Flor Brown-Grossman (2010) find that after twenty years of Mexican export production (primarily by women), '[t]here is consistent evidence of the negative impact of export orientation on men's and women's wages and the gender wage ratio, signifying that women lose in both absolute and relative terms'.

That said, there may be important positive effects on women's position in society that come through their greater incorporation into paid employment. For instance, in Turkey, even though women are integrated into textile and clothing production on the basis of long hours, low pay, and low security, it nonetheless opens some limited opportunities for positive change, such as enabling greater personal choice of whom they marry (Dedeoglu 2010: 22–23).

6.6.1.2 Consumption

Generally speaking, trade liberalization is thought to benefit consumers by lowering prices of goods and services, but the picture in practice is not always so clear. For example, sometimes trade liberalization leads to increases in the cost of food imports, which disproportionately affect the poorest households and women, who tend to have less access to and control over income while also being the primary persons responsible for food purchase and preparation (Roberts, Trommer, and Hannah 2019). Moreover, when there are dramatic price fluctuations in international markets for food staples like rice, as occurred in 2007–08 and 2022, those costs of provisioning households tend to be borne most heavily by women.

6.6.1.3 Public services

Women, along with Indigenous and other racialized groups, are overrepresented among those who use public services. This is often due to their disproportionate responsibility for care work. Women also tend to make up the majority of workers in public service sectors like health, education, and social work. If public services are privatized and opened to global competition through trade liberalization, these groups will be most heavily impacted. Sometimes trade liberalization leads to improved access to public services, including those that are essential for women's reproductive health. At other times the capacity of governments to invest in public services are undermined through its marketization or privatization and this makes it more difficult for women and other vulnerable groups to access public services (Roberts, Hannah, and Trommer 2019).

6.6.1.4 **Care work**

When new trading arrangements succeed in drawing women into formal work, there is a need for additional resources—either from the state or from families—to make up for the potential reduction of care work that was previously performed by women. Unless governments dedicate additional resources to support the provisioning of public services in the health and care sectors, there may be a decline in levels of care overall, with poor households experiencing the greatest losses (Roberts, Hannah, and Trommer 2019).

6.6.2 **How can trade policy be levered for gender equality?**

As noted in **Section 6.6.1**, trade policy has the potential to make women's lives better or worse by either mitigating or exacerbating existing gender inequalities. Governments and international organizations have begun to use trade policy to improve gender equality globally. Existing gender and trade governance mechanisms include aspirational statements such as the 2017 WTO Declaration, women's entrepreneurship programmes such as the International Trade Center's 'She Trades' initiative, and the inclusion of gender chapters in FTAs such as the Chile–Uruguay FTA, all of which are geared to removing obstacles and bolstering the role of women in global trade.

Assessing and monitoring the gendered impacts of trade policy is another way that policymakers have begun to mainstream gender into global trade governance (**see Case Study 6.2**). Providing effective gender-based impact assessment and continuous monitoring is key to ensuring that trade policies can be used to improve gender equality, produce no harm, and that the sort of negative impacts discussed in **Section 6.6.1** can be remedied (Roberts, Hannah, and Trommer 2019). The United Nations Conference on Trade and Development's (UNCTAD) gender and trade toolbox, for example, offers a comprehensive framework for gender-based impact assessment (UNCTAD 2017).

The development of these types of gender and trade governance mechanisms in recent years indicates that there has been a fundamental shift in thinking within trade policymaking communities about the ways in which trade policy can be used to improve gender equality, and the need to identify and mitigate the potentially adverse effects of trade policies on vulnerable communities. If they are to work to improve the lives of women and other vulnerable communities they should be attuned to 1) existing gender norms and structural inequality; 2) the impacts of trade on different groups of people in their multiple roles; 3) the dynamics of social reproduction, including the environment and care work that constitute the global economy; and 4) the need for more inclusive and democratic trade governance, which includes opportunities for the participation and representation of a diversity of women (Hannah, Roberts, and Trommer 2022*b*).

Case Study 6.2: Canada's Gender-Based Analysis Plus (GBA+)

Canada is a country that is leading the global agenda on gender and trade. Assessing and monitoring the gendered impacts of trade policy is one way that Canadian policymakers have attempted to mainstream gender into global trade governance. This is key to ensuring that trade policies can be used to improve gender equality and that they produce no harm. They are also useful for identifying how trade policy can be combined with appropriate social policy so that it works to reduce gender inequality (Roberts, Hannah, and Trommer 2019; see Hannah, Roberts, and Trommer 2022a).

In partial fulfilment of its ratification of the United Nations (UN) Beijing Platform for Action, Canada committed to using Gender Based Analysis Plus (GBA+) to advance gender equality. This promise was made actionable in 2018 when Canada committed to applying GBA+ to all federal budget items, including FTAs. GBA+ is an analytical process to examine potential impacts of FTAs on gender and a range of other intersectional identity characteristics including race, religion, mental and physical ability, Indigenous heritage, and socioeconomic status (Hannah, Roberts, and Trommer 2018). GBA+ has no prescribed methodology. It is described, rather, as a 'way of thinking' that draws on a range of methods and approaches including computer generated equilibrium modelling, descriptive statistics, interviews, and community forums. It is conducted alongside, and is informed by, environmental impact assessments and economic impact assessments.

Photo 6.2 Some of the identity factors considered in GBA+

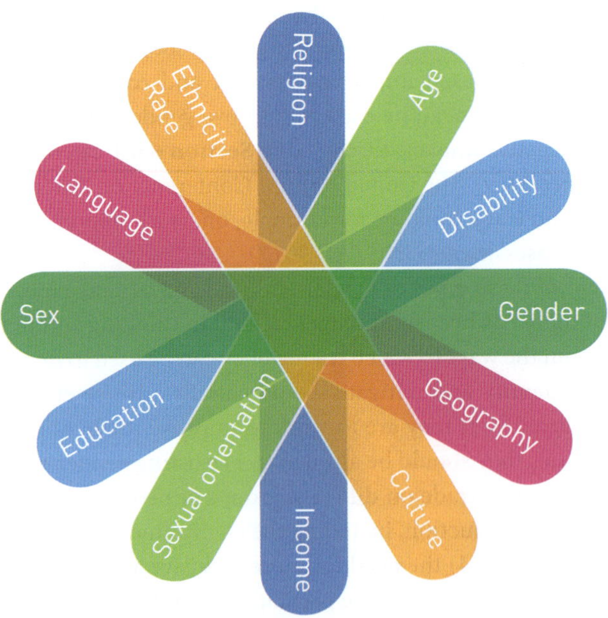

Source: Government of Canada.

In 2019, Canada became the first country to conduct a comprehensive, chapter-by-chapter GBA+ of its ongoing trade negotiations with Mercosur.

Canada's GBA+ is, by definition, intersectional. It aspires to 'go beyond biological (sex) and sociocultural (gender) differences to consider overlapping identity factors', paying particular attention to the impacts of the FTA on women, Indigenous, and LGBTQ2 (lesbian, gay, bisexual, transgender, queer, two-spirit) communities. The focus is on integrating 'traditionally under-represented groups'—women; micro, small, and medium enterprises (MSMEs); and Indigenous peoples—into the global economy rather than on mitigating the adverse impacts of trade agreements on vulnerable communities (Photo 6.2).

The predominant emphasis of Canada's GBA+ on removing obstacles and barriers to market entry notwithstanding, Canada is the first country to consider the impacts of FTAs on unpaid work and various dimensions of family caregiving responsibilities. The distinct vulnerabilities of migrant women, those working in the informal economy, and/or with irregular status are also put into view in Canada's GBA+ of FTAs and they are attuned to social goals such as environmental protections, labour rights, and gender equality. Nevertheless, Canada has not yet considered the impacts of FTAs on the provision of public services which, as we outline in **Section 6.6.1.3**, is of crucial importance to the well-being of women and other vulnerable communities.

Finally, Canada has set the bar high for conducting regular and iterative consultations with a broad cross-section of Canadian stakeholders, including non-governmental organizations, women's groups, and gender experts. It should do more to integrate the voices of those people who are potentially adversely affected by FTAs in partnering countries (particularly developing countries) and commit to monitoring the impacts of FTAs after they are implemented.

Questions

1 Why did it take policymakers so long to recognize that the impacts of trade are gendered, despite the fact that gender equality was a policy norm in other areas of global governance for decades?
2 Are social goals—such as development, human rights, gender equality, and sustainable development—matters for trade institutions such as the WTO?

6.7 Conclusion

Too often, trade is treated in reductionist and simplistic terms, and reduced to a debate about 'free trade' versus 'protectionism'. The discussion in this chapter suggests that this is unhelpful. Trade policy affects different countries differently and different groups within countries differently. Context is everything. Trade has facilitated development in many countries, helping to provide the opportunity for transformative economic growth and moving from low to high productivity sectors. Yet it can also disrupt communities and destroy livelihoods.

Trade can create opportunities for women, empowering them by creating new employment options, increasing their bargaining position within the family, and enhancing their position in society. But even where this is the case, opposing forces simultaneously pull in the other direction. Trade liberalization can increase the burden on women, exacerbating the 'double burden' women face—of having to contribute financially through paid employment while also taking on an unequal share of unpaid caring responsibilities—and negatively impacting the public services on which women disproportionately rely.

Key Points

- Policy and academic debates have, for too long, been centred on an unhelpful dichotomy between free trade and protectionism.
- The contemporary multilateral trade system is predicated upon the principles of progressive trade liberalization, non-discrimination, reciprocity, and legalization.
- Despite attempts to place development at its heart, existing WTO rules continue to reflect unequal power relations among its members and exacerbate global structural inequalities.
- While de-industrialization, technological change, and increased productivity are partly to blame for the contemporary backlash against free trade in countries such as the United States, weak social supports for those who are most adversely impacted by trade are a big part of the problem.
- Trade policymakers are increasingly attuned to the gendered impacts of trade, but gender mainstreaming will only work to improve gender equality if it is attuned to 1) existing gender norms and structural inequality; 2) the impacts of trade on different groups of people in their multiple roles; 3) the dynamics of social reproduction; and 4) the need for more inclusive and democratic trade governance.

Further Reading

Bernstein, W. (2009), *A Splendid Exchange: How Trade Shaped the World* (New York: Grove Press). An accessible book which covers the history of trade over the last 1,000 years and which includes many fascinating details.

Hannah, E., Roberts, A., and Trommer, S. (2022), 'Gender in Global Trade: Transforming or Reproducing Trade Orthodoxy?' *Review of International Political Economy*, 29(4): 1368–93. Builds upon critical trade and feminist IPE literatures to assess whether the new gender and trade agenda marks a transformative shift in global trade governance or reproduces the trade orthodoxy, thereby perpetuating existing inequalities.

Hopewell, K. (2016), *Breaking the WTO: How Emerging Powers Disrupted the Neoliberal Project* (Stanford, CA: Stanford University Press). Explores the ways in which the rise of Brazil, India, and China disrupted the US-led project of neoliberal globalization.

Rodrik, D. (2018), *Straight Talk on Trade: Ideas for a Sane Global Economy* (Princeton, NJ: Princeton University Press). Examines the anti-globalist, populist backlash to neoliberal globalization and argues that solutions can only be found in a middle path between economic nationalism and global trade.

Trommer, S. (2020), 'The Evolution of the Global Trade Regime', in J. Ravenhill (ed.), *Global Political Economy*, 6th edn (Oxford: Oxford University Press): 111–37. Provides a detailed overview of the evolution of the global trade regime.

Wilkinson, R. (2014), *What's Wrong with the WTO and How to Fix It* (Cambridge: Polity). Argues that the WTO has failed to deliver on its promise to produce welfare gains for all and, instead, has exacerbated inequalities between wealthy and developing countries because it is a system predicated upon bargaining among equals. The only way to fix the problem is to radically overhaul the WTO.

Chapter 6 Roundtable discussion

Does the renewed prospect of global trade conflict re-validate the argument for free trade?

Roundtable 6.1
Opening contribution **Erin Hannah and James Scott**

For too long, policy and academic debates have been centred on a false dichotomy between free trade and protectionism. Many see free trade as either the route to economic growth and welfare for all or, worse still, an end in itself. Others decry free trade as perpetuating an inherently unjust system of economic and social relations. Anti-globalizers and populists alike call for the 'return of the state' and the abandonment of the rules-based multilateral trade system.

As the smouldering prospect of a possible trade war between the United States and China makes clear, there is nothing inherently progressive about protectionist policies. Nevertheless, it is incontestable that contemporary trade policy has exacerbated structural inequalities, undermined ecological systems, and left behind the world's most vulnerable people.

Trade has the potential to do a lot of good in the world—it can lift people out of poverty, empower women, and facilitate the adoption of green technology. But to fulfil these promises, trade policy should prioritize social goals such as sustainable development and gender equality over economic goals. It should put into view the needs of vulnerable communities, and it should consider the impacts of trade on people in their multiple roles as workers, producers, consumers of goods and services, providers of unpaid care work, and more.

We would not argue for a return to 'embedded liberalism' as conceived by the architects of the post-Second World War global economic order. This was of its time and relied on entrenching, rather than addressing, global inequalities. As John Ruggie (1982) openly noted, the embedded liberal compromise entailed the marginalization of developing countries in the international trade system, as it was their exports that were taken to be undermining social stability in rich countries. All too often, the 'embedded' side of the embedded liberal compromise meant restricting exports of such things as agricultural goods and low-technology manufacturing—precisely the areas of comparative advantage within the developing world. Furthermore, the system was constructed to afford powerful states policy space to manage their economic and social affairs—while denying the same space to poorer developing states.

This led to outcomes that were deeply unequal from a global perspective. Even if international trade rules had allowed all countries to use domestic intervention and protectionist policies in equal measure to protect people from the adjustment shocks associated with more global, open markets, 'bringing the state back in' would continue to render invisible essential forms of inequality in the global political economy if the state, the market, and society are treated as distinct spheres (as they are in all liberal thinking).

This implies that we need to approach trade not as an end in itself, but as a means to an end. And likewise, protection is not an end in itself, but a means to an end. Rarefied debates pitching the one against the other start from the wrong analytical position and lead to weak policy. Rather, we should be determining what social, economic, or political aims need to be addressed and asking what trade policy, accompanied by appropriate social policy, will help to achieve these aims. This demands an approach that is far more context-specific than simple free trade vs protectionism dichotomies, and the policies that ensue will be a mix of trade liberalization alongside regulation, protectionism, and other forms of state intervention.

Some brief examples help to illustrate our point. If our central policy aim is to empower women and address gender-based inequalities, context is crucial. The first step is to ask where and how women are incorporated into the economy, as this will be a key determinant of how trade policy affects women's livelihoods. A country in which women are largely working in agriculture, such as Rwanda, is very different to one in which women are found in industrial textile and clothing production, such as Lesotho. The effects of liberalization of agricultural trade, for instance, will be very different in these two contexts. Since liberalization will push down food prices, this may squeeze the incomes of women whose livelihood comes from supplying food to local markets, but would benefit women engaged in manufacturing as it makes their wages go further in provisioning households. In either case, if women are to benefit fully from the international trade system, the government will need to put in place domestic policies to enable this to happen, such as training programmes, access to capital, support for the elderly and childcare, quality public services, and so on.

Second, much has been made of the shift since the 1990s to global value chain (GVC)-based production (see **Chapter 7** and **Chapter 12**), with some (including the WTO, Organization for Economic Co-operation and Development (OECD), and the World Bank) claiming that this renders obsolete previous industrialization policies based on state intervention. The path to industrialization is said to lie firmly with free trade and opening the economy to foreign capital and factories serving export markets. Protectionism simply impedes this. But this kind of approach is, again, too dichotomized. Engagement with GVCs may well require a degree of liberalization. But making GVC-based production work toward poverty alleviation or other social goals, such as gender equality, demands state intervention and policies aimed at pushing economic activity into higher value-added activities. At times, this may include targeted, temporary tariff protection or positive discrimination for women and other vulnerable communities. Once again, context is everything.

For too long trade policy has been approached in overly simplistic ways. Sophisticated statistical analysis and modelling have been deployed to supposedly demonstrate that free trade generates higher growth, with insufficient attention to complexity and the actual policies pursued by the most successful countries. This matters, because constructing the debate in dichotomized terms generates bad policies, driven by politics and ideology.

If we are to dampen the social tensions that have generated current trade conflicts, we need to move beyond simplistic free trade vs protectionism divides.

Roundtable 6.2
Response **Evgeny Postnikov**

Free trade promises to deliver huge macroeconomic benefits, generate economic development, and reduce poverty. It also creates winners and losers and can cause social and economic dislocation, contributing to inequality within and across countries. These effects, exacerbated by domestic austerity policies and technological change, have resulted in a recent backlash against trade liberalization. Voters, particularly in the developed world, are increasingly sceptical about the arguments made by free trade proponents. Their grievances are exploited by populist leaders—think of Donald Trump in the United States, for instance—vowing to reverse trade liberalization, bring back lost jobs, and regain domestic autonomy. The multilateral trade system and the liberal international order as a whole are in crisis, with the WTO stalling and the prospect of future trade deals remaining uncertain.

A real danger exists that countries driven by economic nationalism will resort to the beggar-thy-neighbour policies of the interwar era, further enabled by the rising geo-economic competition between China and the West. History tells that such political responses are dangerous. To avoid conflict, we need to restore the perception of free trade as a public good, so new thinking is required on how to design trade policies at this critical juncture.

Hannah and Scott propose to conceive new trade policies that would go beyond a simplistic free trade/protectionism dichotomy and imbue trade with wider social purposes (**see Roundtable 6.1**). This is a welcome proposal: indeed, for decades free trade has been the vestige of neo-classical economic thinking which fails to look beyond economic utility and acknowledge the importance of workers' dignity and identity, trying to neatly separate it from larger social and environmental concerns. It should not surprise us then that the legitimacy of the global order built on such shallow foundations has been shaken. The erosion of domestic compensation for free trade losers (low-skilled workers) through social expenditure that occurred in the earlier decades has caused much of the recent protectionist surge (Bisbee et al. 2020).

Admittedly, restoring it would not be sufficient today, as Hannah and Scott say. The current politicization of trade is as much about compensation for lost jobs as it is about conflicts over societal values. New trade deals reach deep into the domestic regulatory space, threatening to damage hard-won social and environmental policies aimed at protecting public interest through the democratic process. Policymakers are then faced with a particularly wicked problem: domestic compensation is essential but is not enough (and often difficult to achieve politically in debt-ridden economies), while defining the boundaries of free trade and protection is certain to re-ignite old ideological battles about the extent of state authority.

Which steps could then be taken to move beyond a simplistic free trade/protectionism dichotomy? Compensation of free trade losers remains important, and there is a wealth of empirical evidence in Global Political Economy (GPE) scholarship confirming that. Job losses need to be offset through increased social expenditure and innovative labour market policies. The state remains important and its hollowing out has contributed to the current systemic crisis. But increasingly, free trade winners (high-skilled workers) are also critical of its consequences, concerned with a lack of domestic and global fairness as trade agreements are believed to side-line human rights, the environment, and consumer protections and prioritize corporate interests (Ehrlich 2018). Therefore, avoiding the erosion of national regulatory autonomy through trade deals when core societal norms are involved is also a politically pragmatic strategy for governments wishing to de-politicize trade and restore public trust in trade and investment agreements.

But Hannah and Scott are also correct to assert that a truly global perspective is needed, and compensation at the expense of poorer nations must be avoided. Thus, some form of regulatory convergence between the Global North and South around shared norms and values is required. Traditional compensation through social expenditure can be supplemented with broader, non-monetary mechanisms before a need for welfare payments arises. For example, trade agreements can be designed to preclude a race to the bottom in the Global North and induce a race to the top in the Global South, helping to level the playing field (Bastiaens and Postnikov 2020). This would involve strengthening the social dimension of the myriad preferential trade agreements (PTAs) through which current trade liberalization occurs and may eventually necessitate a social clause in the WTO, as was envisioned in the 1990s.

Fortunately, there is some convergence of expectations taking place across the North and the South around appropriate PTA templates, including their regulatory depth (Gamso and Postnikov 2021). This indicates that PTAs can be designed to win the hearts and minds (and pockets) of constituents across the world, rehabilitating their image as both free and fair.

Ultimately, the legitimacy of future trade deals hinges on greater public participation. More representation of all societal segments in trade policymaking is needed. The permissive consensus around trade liberalization is dead, especially its regulatory dimension, and today's trade agenda mobilizes multiple civic actors. So public deliberation through domestic and global stakeholder dialogues should help form a new consensus on the larger purposes of free trade that Hannah and Scott suggest, and help remedy the democratic deficit of the global trade system.

Finding appropriate ways for the meaningful inclusion of local communities affected by trade into trade policymaking across the developed and developing world is a crucial task for GPE scholars and policymakers interested in preserving the rules-based order. State *and* society need to be brought in to restore the good name of free trade and change the perception of its procedural and substantive fairness.

Roundtable 6.3
Response **Lay Hwee Yeo and Xianbai Ji**

In an enlightening and thought-provoking piece, Erin Hannah and James Scott argue against a seemingly reductionist, simplistic dichotomy of free trade versus protectionism in trade policy deliberation (**see Roundtable 6.1**). To them trade policy is more of a means to an end than an end in itself. Charting out a third path, they advocate a context-specific trade policy to advance certain social goals such as gender equality and the protection of vulnerable communities.

While we agree with the general sentiment that there is scope for trade policy contributing to a more efficient attainment of human progress and societal well-being, we would like to bring the spotlight back to the inherent tension between free trade and protectionism. This is because trade policy by definition, predominantly if not entirely, concerns trade.

Let us explain that statement. Trade policy per se aims to regulate two kinds of cross-border economic flows—exports and imports—through two policy instruments, tariffs and subsidies.

That means that governments engage in four activities when wielding trade policy: taxing exports; taxing imports; subsidizing imports; and subsidizing exports. How the inflows and outflows of goods, services, and investment relate to other socioeconomic objectives of the government, while important, falls largely outside the purview of *trade* policy per se.

The distinction between free trade and protectionism remains relevant, especially when protectionism has been on the increase since the Global Financial Crisis (GFC) of 2008–09. The WTO Trade Monitoring Database shows that from October 2008 to October 2019 a stockpile of 3,824 trade-restricting and trade-remedial measures like tariffs, quotas, new border regulations, and export controls were put in place by the WTO member states. Data from Global Trade Alert paint an even bleaker picture of the situation, putting the total number of trade-harming policy interventions implemented globally at close to 18,000 since November 2008 (Global Trade Alert, n.d.).

Due in part to this sharp upward swing in protectionism, the expansion of international trade as the driving force of global economic integration is losing steam. For much of the post-Second World War period, global merchandise trade was growing twice as fast as the world's total gross domestic product (GDP). However, since 2012, the ratio has been equalized to approximately 1:1. At the same time, cross-border flows of intangible goods, services, data, technologies, and labour mobility have all decelerated—from globalization to 'slowbalization', as some have put it (Economist 2019). Moreover, in the shadow of protectionism, trade conflicts have become a frequent feature of the contemporary global trade landscape, plaguing international commercial relations while running the risk of worsening slowbalization into de-globalization. The average number of active trade disputes at different stages of the WTO settlement process nearly tripled from 15 to 42 in just a decade from 2009 to 2018 (WTO 2022).

The sources of trade tensions and conflicts have also proliferated from conventional border barriers to cover a diverse set of behind-the-border policy issues involving, among others, safeguarding measures, renewable energy policy, 'buy national' directives, technical standards, forced localization and technology transfer demands, special licensing requirements, intellectual property rights infringement, state aid, and export subsidies.

Exacerbating the rise in protectionism are the geopolitical tensions between the two largest economies—the USA and China. In turn, the crude tariff policies pursued by the Trump administration in the USA from 2016–21—against both allies (such as the European Union and Canada) and strategic competitors (such as China)—threatened to derail the liberal global trading order.

The supply chain disruptions and trade conflicts brought about by the efforts of the USA to decouple its economy from China in the midst of a global pandemic were the alarm bells necessary for other economies in the world to re-evaluate the importance of free and open trade. The Covid-19-induced market volatility and the damage to the economic growth trajectory actually go against the grain to illustrate the need and importance for trade to continue to flow. This was an additional push factor that led to the conclusion of the Regional Comprehensive Economic Partnership (RCEP) agreement, and the increasing interest expressed by countries such as the United Kingdom, South Korea, and most recently China to join the Comprehensive and Progressive Agreement for Trans-Pacific Partnership (CPTPP).

Multilateral trade negotiations may take a backseat, but plurilateral and regional free trade agreements may become even more important in the face of uncertainties and volatility in global supply chains.

In the midst of trade conflicts and the Covid-19 pandemic, there is a sliver of hope that after decades of integration, the world has become so interconnected and trade has developed such a complex web of supply chains that it would be difficult to completely decouple economies from one another. While global supply chains will be reformed with pressures to become more localized and regionalized, the more important question that faces many economies is whether the supply chains are resilient and reliable—and that requires diversification and interdependence, not autarky or self-sufficiency.

Hence, what is likely to replace the global liberal trading order is a network of mini-lateral, regional, sub-regional, and bilateral free trade agreements. Such free trade agreements may not be the comprehensive, high-quality agreements that have been pushed for by groupings such as the EU, but more focused and pragmatic ones with an emphasis on reciprocity, locking in mutual liberalization commitments, and provisions for rules-based trade and investment disputes resolution.

The liberal trading order informed by the neoliberal Washington consensus of the 1990s is not likely to be resuscitated any time soon, but free trade and regionalization will survive. Moreover, as C. Fred Bergsten's (1996) famous 'bicycle theory' goes, trade policy is likely to slide back to protectionism if countries cannot sustain the momentum towards freer trade. The debate on free trade versus protectionism thus should continue actively in academic circles and inform the policymaking world.

Roundtable 6.4
Response **John Ravenhill**

In his first formal news conference in March 2021, newly-elected US President Joe Biden repeated Otto von Bismarck's aphorism that 'politics is the art of the possible' (Karni and Rogers 2021). All governments, especially those that face regular elections, are constrained by domestic constituencies, which dictate the limits of possibilities. This truism applies as much to trade policies as to those in other sectors. In international affairs, matters are complicated by the need to balance the benefits of cooperation, not always immediately obvious to constituencies at home, with the need for autonomy to pursue domestic priorities.

As Erin Hannah and James Scott note, John Ruggie coined the term 'embedded liberalism' to refer to the compromise in international economic relations between respecting international norms and retaining autonomy to pursue domestic social and economic policies, a reconciliation of the efficiencies of markets with the values of social community (**see Roundtable 6.1**).

The extension of international trade disciplines with the advent of the WTO (to cover agriculture, services, and intellectual property), and through multiple preferential trade agreements (which often focused on 'behind-the-border' barriers such as regulatory standards), increasingly threatened this delicate balance. International obligations became more intrusive; those governments that wanted to shield their populations from the disruptive effects of international markets found it more and more difficult to do so.

By the turn of the twenty-first century, anti-globalization was rife among those on the political left in many industrialized economies. In the second decade of the new millennium, this discontent was no longer confined to the left, frequently finding expression in right-wing populism (Rodrik 2019).

It seems an appropriate time, once again, to re-examine the cases for protection and for free trade. As Hannah and Scott argue, the theoretical arguments are more nuanced than often portrayed. The international trade regime (first the GATT and then the WTO) had acknowledged the *political* importance of the embedded liberal compromise through a number of significant provisions that enabled countries to opt out of their obligations if they put at risk important domestic policy objectives. Some of these measures coincided with exceptions to the argument for free trade that have been acknowledged in *economic* theory for at least two centuries. Adam Smith (1789: Book IV Ch. II) asserted that protection was justified 'when some particular sort of industry is necessary for the defence of the country'. The 'national security' argument often overlapped with another justification for protection allowed by classical economists, that is, the temporary protection of infant industries until they had acquired the 'skill and experience' to compete with established industries elsewhere (Mill 1909: 92).

The onset of the Covid-19 pandemic in March 2020 exacerbated trends towards increased protectionism (see, for instance, the reports produced by Global Trade Alert). These had been driven in countries as disparate as India and the United States by concerns about trade imbalances, that some countries (notably China) persistently failed to play by the rules of the global trade and financial systems, and that 'de-industrialization' caused by globalization increasingly threatened national security.

Is this a bad thing? Let's look at how this resort to protectionism was justified and the challenges that it posed.

The WTO's rules enable countries to circumvent their obligations through a number of 'exceptions' that are potentially sweeping in their scope. The most important of these are the various elements of the 'General Exceptions' listed in Article XX, which include the protection of public morals, the protection of human, plant, or animal life or health, the conservation of natural resources, and the acquisition or distribution of products in short supply, and Article XXI, which refers to 'Security Exceptions'.

The legitimization of a country 'taking any action it considers necessary for the protection of its essential security interests' (Article XXI(b)) appears to be so open-ended that it could be used to justify almost any action. Indeed, some countries, notably the United States, have consistently argued that this article is 'self-judging', that is, a member's decision that its national security is at risk should not be subject to WTO review. In two important cases, however, the WTO Appellate Body rejected these interpretations, asserting that any use of Article XXI must be consistent with countries' overall obligations under the WTO. And efforts by the Trump administration to justify bans on imports of steel from allies such as Canada and several other NATO members on national security grounds were ridiculed (and by increasing costs to downstream users of steel actually hurt the US economy).

More persuasive during the Covid-19 pandemic have been justifications for protectionism that mixed the infant industry and national security arguments in asserting the need to build national industrial capacity in critical sectors—particularly health—in the context of disruptions to global supply chains. In some instances, this was a reaction to a hollowing out of manufacturing capabilities that had occurred under globalization. Those industrialized economies (such as Australia and Canada) that now lacked the domestic capacity to develop and mass-produce vaccines were left behind in the unseemly scramble to secure supplies of vaccines and personal protective equipment (PPE). A typical response was the decision by the Canadian government in 2021 to provide $2.2 billion Canadian dollars to *re*-establish domestic manufacturing capabilities. Two of the other 'General Exceptions' also came to the fore during the pandemic. The 'public health' and 'distribution of products in short supply' clauses were used to justify restrictions on companies exporting vaccines.

Whatever the morality of such actions, it appears that they are legitimate as far as the WTO is concerned (Pauwelyn 2020). And they directly addressed the assertion we started with—that politics is the art of the possible. Who, after all, would vote for governments that were perceived to be putting the health of their domestic population at risk by exporting scarce vaccines?

Over to you ...

1 You have heard about how anti-globalist political trends since the mid-2010s have been associated with calls for a return to protectionism in trade policy. You will have also noted, as Evgeny Postnikov put it in **Roundtable 6.2**, how even the proponents of free trade—and the people who 'win' the most from it—are increasingly critical of its consequences. What do you think the most important of these consequences are? Do you think they are the direct outcomes of free trade? Or are they more indirectly related issues, which, recalling Lay Hwee Yeo and Xianbai Ji's arguments in **Roundtable 6.3**, cannot fully be addressed by trade policy?

2 You have heard much about the looming trade conflict between the United States and China, with consequences for the whole world. What are the causes of this tension between the world's two largest economies? And if the world erupted into full-blown trade conflict, resulting in resurgent protectionism and disrupted supply chains, what do you think would be the consequences for people around the world? Who would gain and who would lose?

3 Erin Hannah and James Scott (see **Roundtable 6.1**), echoed by others, set out an argument for a trade system that is more responsive to its own social, environmental, and economic impacts. Think about how you can continue their line of thought—what would such a system look like, and how economically and politically viable are the options you can imagine?

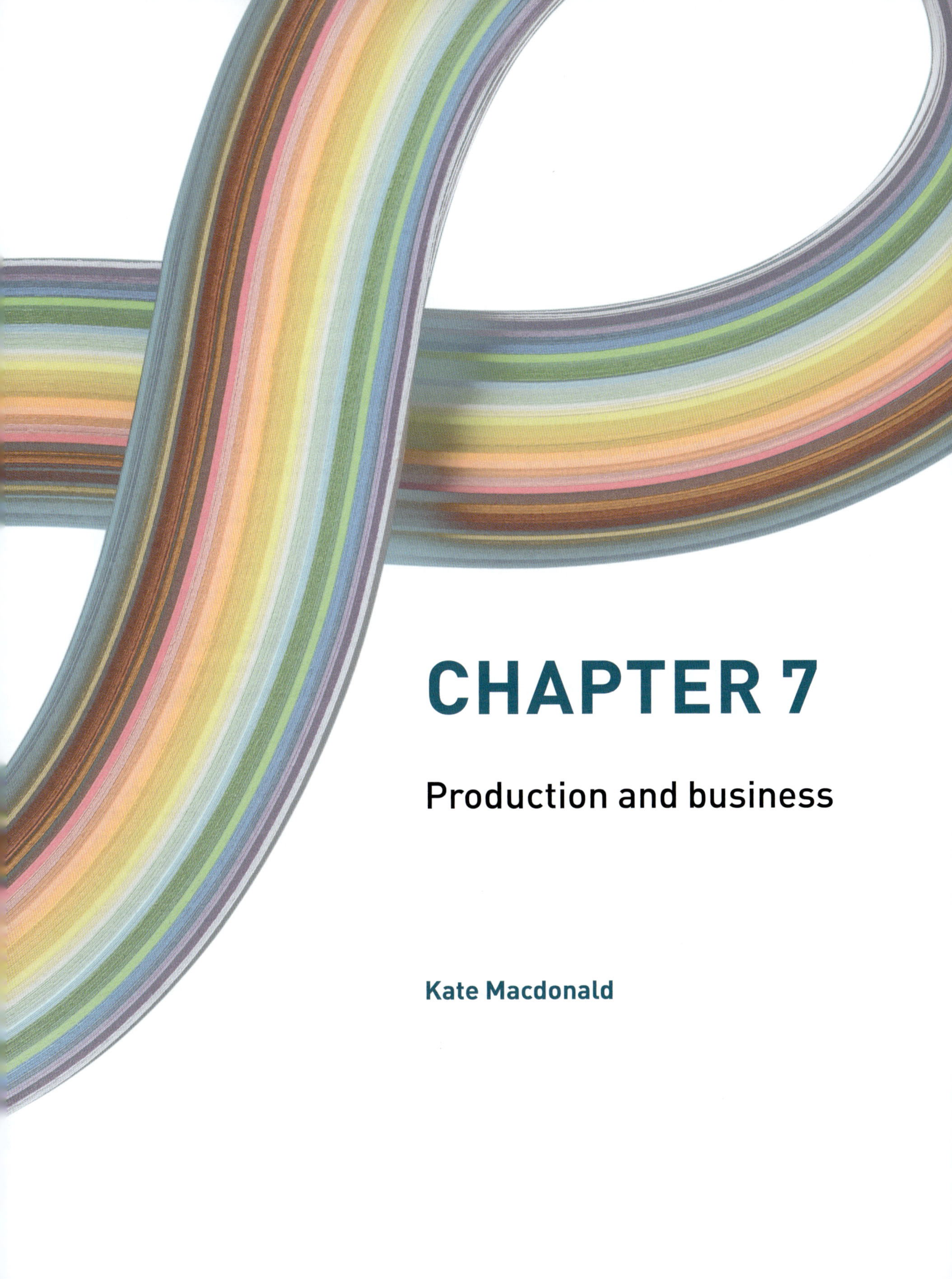

CHAPTER 7

Production and business

Kate Macdonald

7.1 Introduction

There are few areas of the global political economy that have such a tangible connection to our everyday lives as global production. Many of us wake up in the morning and check the latest news on our smartphone, constructed from components provided by suppliers in thirty-six countries across six continents. Then we stumble to the kitchen for a coffee, perhaps from Brazil or Vietnam, get dressed—parts of our outfit being likely to have come from major apparel manufacturing locations in China, the European Union, or Bangladesh—and sprint outside to leap into a car or bus manufactured in turn from tens of thousands of components sourced from many different parts of the world. Complex systems of production are fundamental to creating the goods that we consume—transforming economic inputs such as raw materials and labour hours into other highly valued goods or services that shape our daily lives.

Production is also a dimension of economic life in which most individuals participate in some form through their paid or unpaid work. As a result, the organization and governance of global production has powerful effects on the incomes, working conditions, and development opportunities of populations around the world. While global production systems have provided some workers with new income-earning opportunities and pathways out of poverty, such systems have been widely condemned for the exploitation of hired labour and contributions to global inequality (**see Chapter 10** and **Chapter 12**). The processes through which raw materials are sourced and transformed also have significant implications for the environment, through pollution, extraction of non-renewable resources, disruption of landscapes and ecosystems, and contributions to climate change (**see Chapter 9**). It is perhaps not surprising then that the ways in which we organize and regulate production of the goods and services that we all enjoy consuming have become one of the most contentious subjects of debate within the field of GPE.

In this chapter we will confront a number of difficult questions linked to these debates: Who does the work of global production, and how has its organization changed over time (**see Section 7.2**)? Who exercises power within evolving systems of global production, and what winners and losers do such arrangements produce (**see Section 7.3**)? How is global production governed, and with what consequences for labour rights and the environment (**see Section 7.4**)? In exploring these questions, analytical lenses drawn from a range of political economy perspectives (**see Chapter 2** and **Chapter 3**) help us to make sense of the complex economic and political forces through which the organization and governance of contemporary global production is shaped and contested.

7.2 Who does the work of global production and how has this changed over time?

7.2.1 The globalization of production

The changing organization of global business systems through which production is coordinated has been one of the most striking features of a globalizing political economy over recent decades. While globalized trade and investment flows during the last quarter of the twentieth century were not in themselves new, the cross-border production systems that emerged during this period were in many respects unprecedented. During the 1960s and 1970s, a rising tendency among major companies to shift production facilities offshore began to attract significant attention, prompting analysts to develop new concepts—such as 'global value chains' (GVCs)—for thinking about how production, distribution, and exchange were coordinated across borders.

Key Concept: Global value chains (GVCs)

The concept of a 'chain' of global production gained influence during the 1980s and 1990s as a broad heuristic for analysing 'the full range of activities that firms, farmers and workers carry out to bring a product or service from its conception to its end use, recycling or reuse' (Ponte, Gereffi, and Raj-Reichert 2019: 1; Hopkins and Wallerstein 1986; Gereffi 1994). Focusing on one product at a time, GVC analysts map the consecutive stages of the production process—encompassing activities as diverse as design, financing, production, processing, distribution, repair, and disposal—and examine how these activities are distributed across different geographical locations and between firms. Analysts can thereby gain new insights into the changing organization of production and the distributional consequences of such changes.

The concept of a GVC developed in close critical dialogue with the related concept of *global production networks*—a lens that emphasized the importance of history, geography, social relations, and political and institutional systems in shaping production processes and their governance (Dicken and Thrift 1992; Hess and Yeung 2006; Bair 2008).

Rather than relying primarily on in-house production facilities, powerful firms increasingly outsourced simple yet labour-intensive production activities like cutting, sewing, and packaging jeans to countries where such activities could be carried out at lower cost, while retaining more profitable activities such as product design in their home countries (Neilson, Pritchard, and Yeung 2014). Outsourced production processes were then managed through chains of purchasing or sub-contracting relationships spread across multiple firms and countries.

Such outsourcing strategies became common in rapidly globalizing sectors such as clothing and footwear, electronics, automobile assembly, agri-food systems, and some service sectors. Iconic companies such as Nike, Walmart, or Apple now tend not to own and operate the factories in which products sold under their brand or label are produced. Rather, they specialize in design, marketing, distribution, and after-sales service, then arrange the manufacture of their products through chains of suppliers who work to their specifications (Neilson, Pritchard, and Yeung 2014; Gereffi 2014).

Production processes are now not only fragmented and distributed organizationally between firms, but also much more spread out geographically. Production in manufacturing sectors has evolved in recent decades away from the industrialized core economies of the rich world—generating what some have referred to as a 'new international division of labour' (Fröbel, Heinrichs, and Kreye 1980). During the 1970s and 1980s, globalizing manufacturing systems began to shift to parts of the developing world—a trend that accelerated dramatically during the post-Cold War decades of the 1990s and 2000s. By 2015, 47 per cent of global manufacturing exports were estimated to originate from the Global South (Horner and Nadvi 2018: 208).

Two seemingly competing tendencies can be observed. On the one hand, production has become dispersed across many geographical locations. At the same time, production has become clustered in specific regions. Although we often speak of 'globalized' production, in fact production activity remains concentrated in major regional hubs which are then intensively interlinked through trade and investment flows (Coe et al. 2004; Mikler 2018).

China now occupies a unique position at the centre of East Asian clusters of trade and investment, and its corporations have rapidly climbed lists of the world's largest corporations (Mikler 2018: 56). China has accumulated a critical mass of infrastructure and factory capacity that has made it a highly attractive location for manufacturing production (Thun 2008). Particularly in labour-intensive manufacturing sectors such as clothing, rapidly rising wages in China have contributed to recent manufacturing shifts towards countries such as Cambodia, Vietnam, and Bangladesh. Nonetheless, China remains a central global manufacturing hub, accounting for 31 per cent of global clothing exports in 2018 (Altenburg et al. 2020: 5). China also operates to some extent as a regional production base, with large proportions of inputs for China's processing activities coming from Hong Kong, Japan, South Korea, and Taiwan. Important regional concentrations of global production can also be found in Mexico, South America, and Eastern and Central Europe (Cattaneo, Gereffi, and Staritz 2010: 8).

Over time, such shifts have produced what has been referred to as a 'global value chain world', in which fragmented chains of production are spread across many countries, coordinated by 'lead firms' such as large retailers, brands, or manufacturers (Mayer and Phillips 2017; Mayer and Gereffi 2019). While a consumer may purchase a new car from a dealership linked to a major car 'manufacturer' such as Ford or Toyota, in fact these companies now specialize largely in the design, assembly, and marketing of cars, while most of the materials, systems, and components that go into making the car have been produced by other companies around the world. As different firms and countries specialize not just in producing different products, but in producing different *parts* of different products, patterns of world trade have significantly changed (**see Chapter 6**). Over 50 per cent of world trade is now in intermediate products (parts and components that are neither raw materials nor finished products), in contrast to previous periods in which trade was largely in finished goods (Mayer and Gereffi 2019: 571; Gibbon and Ponte 2005).

Globalized production systems continue to evolve in response to ongoing processes of global turbulence and change. In the last decades, global production systems have confronted numerous political and economic disruptions, including the 2008–09 Global Financial Crisis, intensifying trade tensions between major economies such as China and the United States, and the Covid-19 pandemic. Together, these have placed sustained pressure on the multilateral free trade system and exposed the vulnerabilities of global supply chains to disruption. The globalization of value chains peaked around 2008; growth in globalized production then levelled out following the 2008–09 financial crisis (World Bank 2020*b*). Since that time, some governments have signalled interest in relocating crucial manufacturing activities back to home countries or to a smaller number of relatively low-risk sourcing locations (Barbieri et al. 2020; Gereffi 2020; Golgeci, Yildiz, and Andersson 2020).

While future trends remain uncertain, globalized production systems have proved resilient in the face of such pressures. Indeed, in some respects GVCs have supported responses to the Covid-19 pandemic by enabling production to shift rapidly between production locations in the face of shifting waves of localized lockdowns and facilitating rapid innovation and knowledge-sharing in response to crisis (Williamson 2021).

7.2.2 Drivers of reorganized global production

Changes in the organization of global production over recent decades have been profound. But what actors or forces have produced such changes? Globalized production has emerged in response to interacting economic and political drivers, in part as a result of the strategic decisions of transnational companies (**see Section 7.2.2.1**), but also as a result of shifting policies promoted by governments around the world (**see Section 7.2.2.2**).

7.2.2.1 Firm strategies and incentives

Changing firm strategies have contributed importantly to new patterns of globalized production. One simple reason that many firms globalized their production activities was a desire to lower production costs in the face of competition from foreign manufacturers facing cheaper labour costs or enjoying efficiency savings linked to economies of scale. US and European firms found themselves struggling in the face of competition from emerging East Asian economies, prompting the transfer of production to locations that facilitated access to large pools of cheap—and in some cases also highly trained and weakly unionized—labour (Gereffi 2020; Ponte, Gereffi, and Raj-Reichert 2019).

Such changes were further propelled by popular management theories that advocated extensive outsourcing of activities outside of a firm's core competencies. Walmart, for example, transformed from a company that originally trumpeted its support of US producers to one that sourced up to 70 per cent of its product from Chinese factories where goods could be produced more cheaply (Schell 2011). The attraction of shifting production towards major emerging markets was enhanced in some cases by the potential to position production facilities close to large emerging consumer markets such as China, India, or Brazil, where increasing wealth among the middle and upper classes created new opportunities to expand sales of consumer products (Sturgeon and Kawakami 2011; Cattaneo, Gereffi, and Staritz 2010; Gereffi 2014).

Expansion of foreign production was further facilitated and incentivized by advances in communication and transport technologies (Ponte, Gereffi, and Raj-Reichert 2019). The development of containerized freight was one seemingly mundane but highly influential technological innovation that dramatically lowered the costs of international shipping.

By packing goods in shipping containers of standardized size, it became possible to stack them, unload them, and shift them between different kinds of ships, trains, or trucks without opening them, while registering their movement via computerized tracking systems. By avoiding the need to manually sort and re-package shipments, this innovation facilitated both faster and cheaper international trade.

A further innovation that helped to stimulate and facilitate globalized production was modularization, which enabled separate teams of engineers to ensure compatibility of different parts of a complex product (such as a car or computer system), thereby dramatically increasing the feasibility of product components being produced by different companies in different places (Thun 2008).

Key Concept: Modularization

The term *modularization* refers to an approach to design and production in which a given product is disaggregated into components that can be separately manufactured and then assembled in different ways.

Just as the standardized design of Lego enables blocks from different Lego sets to be mixed together and used to create new Lego masterpieces, a product based on a modular design, such as a personal computer, is made up of components such as a processor, hard drive, and monitor that can be developed and produced by different companies and then later assembled into different versions of a finished computer.

7.2.2.2 Government policies

While such economic and technological shifts provided powerful motivations for firms to globalize production, such changes were further spurred by government policies (Mayer and Phillips 2017; Mayer and Gereffi 2019; Horner 2017). Globalized production depends on a range of policy conditions supplied by states individually and collectively. States actively promoted globalized production through enabling policy conditions developed and sustained over many decades, propelled in part by broader ideological shifts towards (neo)liberal modes of economic organization.

At the international level, intergovernmental agendas of trade and investment liberalization, particularly following the end of the Cold War, played a central role in creating a favourable environment for globalized production. A proliferation of new international agreements helped to facilitate freer international trade and investment flows and to provide legal protections for transnational businesses wanting to establish production facilities outside their home country bases (**see Chapter 6**). The boundaries of such agreements shaped evolving geographies of global production. For example, the North American Free Trade Agreement (NAFTA)—a free trade agreement between the United States, Canada, and Mexico which came into force in January 1994—encouraged significant expansion in apparel sector production networks linking US lead firms with Mexican suppliers, while later multilateral liberalization of apparel trade subsequently led production to shift to other exporting countries (Bair and Gereffi 2001).

Globalized production was embraced by the governments of many emerging economies, which viewed connection into GVCs as a potential means of spurring industrial development. Many national governments sought to facilitate the expansion of global production through policies of market deregulation and liberalization, alongside tax concessions and other incentives designed to attract foreign investors. Governments sought actively to enhance national competitiveness through a range of policy interventions. Numerous governments established export processing zones (EPZs), which incentivized export-oriented production facilities via a range of favourable regulatory and tax policies, direct subsidies, and liberalized wages policy and labour laws. Other governments invested in infrastructure, transport, or communication facilities, or supported local producers through provision of credit facilities or research and training capabilities (Neilson, Pritchard, and Yeung 2014).

Key Concept: Export processing zones

Export processing zones (EPZs) are special economic zones in which national governments seek to encourage foreign (and sometimes also domestic) investors to build large-scale production facilities in which goods to be sold into export markets can be manufactured. Incentives are provided through policies such as tax concessions and duty-free import of materials used in the production of exported goods, alongside direct government investment in required infrastructure.

The establishment of EPZs became increasingly widespread from the 1970s, as many governments in emerging economies sought to create jobs, boost exports, and encourage the inflow of capital and technology from foreign firms. EPZs played an important role in facilitating the rapid industrial development of a number of East Asian economies, including Taiwan, South Korea, Singapore, and the coastal zones of mainland China. The proliferation of EPZs accelerated across the world from the 1990s, with new concentrations emerging not only in East Asia but also in North and Central America, particularly around the USA–Mexico border.

7.3 Who are the winners and losers of global production processes?

'Who wins and who loses?' is one of the classic questions motivating the work of political economists. Changing patterns of global production have contributed to dramatic shifts in distributions of power, resources, and opportunities at many levels: between governments and firms; countries and populations in different countries and regions; firms focused on different stages of the production process; individuals and households with different occupational, socioeconomic, or citizenship status; men and women; and people with different racial and cultural identities.

While debates about the consequences of globalized production for distributions of wealth, power, and opportunities are often highly polarized, a careful consideration of evidence suggests a more nuanced picture in which globalized production contributes to a range of complex and often contradictory distributional impacts—for economic inequalities and development opportunities (**see Section 7.3.1**), and for labour, human rights, and the environment (**see Section 7.3.2**).

7.3.1 Implications for economic development and inequalities

Champions of globalized production have often highlighted the potential for emerging economies to engage with global production systems as a means of expanding economic growth, job creation, and poverty reduction (Mayer and Gereffi 2019; Humphrey and Schmitz 2002). Bangladesh offers a striking illustration of such opportunities. Its apparel and footwear exports grew by an average of almost 18 per cent per year between 1988 and 2018, by which time the sector accounted for 89 per cent of the country's exports and 14 per cent of GDP—employing 3.6 million workers. In Mexico and Vietnam, research showed that provinces or municipalities more connected to global value chains experienced faster reductions in poverty than other locations (World Bank 2020*b*).

Others have highlighted the potential for emerging economy suppliers to move away from reliance on relatively unprofitable production activities towards higher value-added activities (a progression often referred to as 'economic upgrading'). For example, apparel and electronics firms in some East Asian economies were able to progress from relatively low value-added work assembling imported inputs in EPZs towards an increased role for local suppliers in manufacturing inputs and designing products—thus capturing greater profits and development opportunities within the local economy (Gereffi and Lee 2016; Van Biesebroeck and Sturgeon 2010).

Yet while some firms and countries in regions such as East Asia have benefited from participation in global production systems, others have remained steadfastly excluded—unable to attract foreign investment or connect with global trading networks. Many companies have chosen to concentrate their offshore sourcing in relatively large, low-cost production sites close to major East Asian manufacturing centres. Smaller countries that are geographically further away from these hubs, such as less-developed countries in sub-Saharan Africa, find it increasingly difficult to compete with large and established suppliers (**see Chapter 10**).

In industrialized countries too, the hollowing out of manufacturing following extended processes of outsourcing has produced significant economic hardship in areas such as the USA's 'rustbelt', in which persistent de-industrialization has been associated with large-scale unemployment and poverty (World Bank 2020*b*).

In the absence of economic upgrading possibilities, some analysts have highlighted risks that global production systems will generate 'immiserizing growth', in which an increase in economic activity delivers lower standards of living (Shaffer, Kanbur, and Sandbrook 2019; Selwyn, Musiolek, and Ijarja 2020; Kaplinsky 2004). Economists have long been aware of the possibility that growth in productive output may be associated with falling incomes, where expanding supply causes prices to fall so much that overall income declines despite increased output (Bhagwati 1958). Early analyses of immiserizing growth focused on exporters of tropical agricultural commodities. Later, researchers started to document cases in which the expansion of manufacturing capacity in developing countries led supply to outstrip demand, significantly lowering the prices of manufactured products such as clothing, furniture, or car components, and associated incomes for producers (Kaplinsky, Morris, and Readman 2002).

Such uneven patterns of opportunity have fuelled inequality not only 'horizontally' between countries and regions, but also 'vertically' between firms, farmers, and workers occupying different positions within GVCs. This is discussed further in **Chapter 10**. To analyse such inequalities, value chain analysts first identify the different functional stages of the production process for a given product, and then analyse how income-generating opportunities are distributed across these stages. Let's take the example of coffee. To produce coffee, coffee farmers first grow the coffee beans, which are then processed and dried into green coffee beans (Photo 7.1). They are then transported, exported, and finally roasted and packaged for either retail sale, formulation into processed food and beverage products, or sale through wholesale markets to cafes, restaurants, and other institutional buyers. While precise distributions of costs, revenues, and profits vary between firms and countries and over time, coffee roasters and retailers tend to capture large proportions of the profit generated across the supply chain, while farmers growing the coffee struggle to make a living from the very low prices they receive (Gresser and Tickell 2002).

Photo 7.1 It is often the coffee farmers who struggle in the supply chain

Source: © iStock/wundervisuals.

This example is illustrative of a broader tendency for higher profits to flow to more powerful firms engaged in stages of production such as product design, marketing, retail, or after-sales service, in which there are high barriers to entry (meaning that few firms can participate in these activities) and correspondingly lower levels of competition between firms. Conversely, those supply chain activities with lower barriers to entry must contend with high levels of competition from rival producers, which drive down bargaining power, prices, and associated incomes (Macdonald 2012; Kaplinsky 2000; Gereffi and Lee 2012). As a result, large brands such as Walmart (Photo 7.2) tend to exercise significant power over those directly producing the goods they sell, enabling them to capture the lion's share of profits while lowering prices, wages, and working conditions for suppliers and workers (**see Case Study 7.1**).

Such unequalizing dynamics are often reproduced at the level of individual workers and producers (Kaplinsky 2013; Phillips 2011, 2017; Selwyn 2015). For example, major disparities frequently exist between workers on permanent or casual contracts, as casual workers experience more precarious employment, lack of access to social protection coverage, and limited opportunities to organize or participate in trade unions (Rossi 2013). The situation is even worse for workers who are not hired through legal employment contracts, such as undocumented migrant workers, or those engaged to produce goods through informal sub-contracting arrangements. Such workers are often paid below legal minimum wages, are more vulnerable to arbitrary dismissal, and lack access to trade union membership or other legal mechanisms designed to protect their labour rights.

Photo 7.2 **Walmart has consistently ranked first or second in Fortune 500's list of the world's largest corporations**

Source: © iStock/Niloo138.

Case Study 7.1: The power of large retailers

Inequalities of income associated with participation in global production chains are often underpinned by power disparities between large firms and their suppliers and workers. Walmart occupies a somewhat emblematic status as the embodiment of a broader trend towards the concentration of power in a small number of huge retail companies. Walmart has repeatedly been ranked as the world's largest retailer, commanding around 16 per cent of the global retail market (Retail Information Systems 2020), and has consistently ranked first or second in Fortune 500's list of the world's largest corporations (Elder and Dauvergne 2015).

The company's annual revenues are often compared to the gross domestic product (GDP) of whole countries. Mikler (2018) showed that in 2013, Walmart's annual sales of almost $500 billion were roughly equivalent to the GDP of Taiwan, and greater than the GDP of other major national economies such as Austria, Iran, Pakistan, or Finland.

How does this enormous scale of business activity translate into power over the organization and governance of global production?

The large market share of a company like Walmart, and the relative ease with which it can switch between different suppliers around the world, enables it to dictate the terms of how, when, and by whom goods are produced. Major retailers like Walmart use sophisticated point-of-sale data regarding precisely what consumers are buying at a given time and place, and then relay this information electronically through their supply chains to initiate replenishment orders almost instantaneously. Lichtenstein puts it well: 'when Walmart sells a tube of toothpaste in Memphis, that information flashes straight through to Bentonville, then on to the P&G headquarters office in Cincinnati, the Ohio home-product manufacturer, which then immediately sends the electronic impulse directly to an offshore toothpaste factory, which adjusts its production schedule accordingly' (2011: 17–18).

Walmart's enormous purchasing power further enables the company to negotiate low prices with the farmers and factories from which the company sources its products. Yu and Ngai (2011) showed how Walmart's ascendence to become the largest toy retailer in the US market led to intensified price competition among toy retailers and downwards pressure on prices paid to suppliers and workers. One official from the Guangdong Toy Association was reported complaining that 'U.S. buyers demand prices that are not reasonable, considering the growing labour costs. Walmart in particular puts a lot of pressure on prices, and it orders so much from China, it has a large influence' (Yu and Ngai 2011: 59).

Such downwards price pressure then contributes to pervasive violations of international labour rights in toy factories supplying major retailers, in the form of hazardous or unhealthy working conditions, forced overtime, illegally low wages, or abusive labour discipline.

Larger retailers also have significant influence over the social and environmental rules that govern global production. Not only does Walmart directly control the ethical, social, and environmental standards laid out in its own contracts with suppliers, its ability to act as a 'gatekeeper' to its huge networks of suppliers also gives the company significant bargaining power when negotiating over the definition of broader sector-wide social and environmental standards (van der Ven 2018). Such power could be used to water down the stringency of social and environmental commitments (Fuchs, Kalfagianni, and Arentsen 2009), though at times Walmart has used its substantial market power to push for strengthened social and environmental protections, either

(Continued)

in response to NGO pressure or to help secure consistent ongoing supply of the goods needed for sale in their stores (Elder and Dauvergne 2015).

Questions

1 Commentators have claimed that companies like Walmart have become more powerful than many governments. Do you agree?
2 Is the power of large corporations like Walmart inevitable or even desirable within a 'free market' system of production?

Inequalities between workers often have significant gendered and racialized dimensions—the precise contours of such inequalities varying depending on hierarchies of social difference in particular contexts. Systematic patterns of inequality are often linked to sociocultural inequalities and patterns of discrimination associated with gender, ethnicity, social class, caste, cultural identity or language, or migration status (Phillips 2011). Marginalized groups are more likely to experience informal, casual, or precarious employment, lower pay, excessive overtime, denial of entitlements, and high levels of health risks (Dunaway 2014; Werner and Bair 2019; Phillips 2011).

For example, in India, Nepal, and Pakistan, where social caste plays an important role in shaping socioeconomic hierarchies, it has been estimated that over 80 per cent of those in bonded labour or child labour producing products such as garments, carpets, agricultural products, or stones and minerals are either Dalits (members of the lowest caste) or from Indigenous groups (Wright 2019).

Such inequalities have also been documented in global production networks in service sectors such as tourism. In Kenya's highly internationalized tourism sector, Indigenous African, Maasai, and female workers were found to occupy the lowest-paying positions, while jobs with greater income and status were dominated by whites, expatriates, and Kenyan-Asians (Christian 2016).

7.3.2 Impacts of global production on labour, human rights, and the environment

The organization and governance of global production also has significant implications for the human rights and labour conditions of workers, and for the environment.

GVC researchers have documented a range of harmful or exploitative labour practices in manufacturing and agricultural facilities connected to global value chains, including low pay, precarious work, excessive or forced overtime, harassment, unsafe working conditions, and restrictions on worker organizing (Barrientos, Kabeer, and Hossain 2004; Kidder and Raworth 2004). Such conditions raise concerns not only regarding violations of nationally and internationally recognized labour rights, but also 'exploitation', understood as unfair extraction of economic surplus created through workers' labour. **Chapter 12** focuses at greater length on these implications for labour in global production.

While it is often suggested that workers' low wages are a function of their employment in low-productivity industries, researchers have shown that in fact many supplier firms and associated workers have similar levels of productivity to their equivalents in the Global North yet are not remunerated for the value they produce. For example, one study showed US firms in the Mexican *maquila* sector to be 85 per cent as productive as their US-based counterparts while paying their workers only 6 per cent of the wages that US workers received for comparable tasks (Henwood 1995: 33; Selwyn 2019).

Such conditions of exploitation are sometimes intensified by the loss of control that workers experience—in the most extreme form through various forms of forced labour, but also through other constraints on workers' control over their lives, bodies, and working conditions (Phillips 2017; Harriss-White 2006). In some cases, such conditions have resulted in serious mental health consequences for workers, as evidenced by repeated incidents of worker suicide in Chinese factories producing electronics products for major companies such as Apple, Samsung, and Nokia (Chan and Pun 2010).

Such labour conditions are generated in part as a function of the purchasing strategies adopted by powerful brands or retailers. In the garment sector, many large fast fashion brands seek not only to lower costs but also to reduce the turnaround time of their orders, so that they can keep new fashion trends moving quickly through their retail stores and respond quickly to changing demand for products (**see Case Study 12.1**). As a result, they demand that their suppliers not only manufacture clothing at low cost, but also respond quickly to demands for last minute orders. Such practices have been linked to low wages and precarious employment, and to excessive and forced overtime for workers (Anner 2020; Gereffi and Frederick 2010).

These practices are in turn facilitated by huge pools of cheap labour produced by large-scale poverty in many countries, leaving many people with little choice but to sell their labour as a means of survival. The labour pool available to global production systems increased enormously during the 1990s following the entry of China, India, and former Soviet bloc nations into global markets (Phillips 2017; Kaplinsky 2013; Freeman 2007). The expanded supply of cheap labour helped to keep wages low. Low wages in turn created pressure on workers to work additional hours or find other sources of income to sustain themselves, furthering opportunities for labour exploitation (Selwyn 2019; Werner and Bair 2019).

As feminist economists have long argued, the capacity of firms to keep wages and prices low is further enhanced by the subsidization of formal sector production by unpaid work done by women within the household—an issue introduced in **Chapter 6**. The formal economy could not function without a huge amount of what is known as 'reproductive labour', not only involving biological reproduction and child rearing but also unpaid caring or domestic work that provides ongoing support to waged workers (Pearson 2007; Dunaway 2014). Yet such work is rarely recognized as a factor of production.

Globalized production also generates a range of environmental impacts (**see Chapter 9**), which vary between economic sectors. For example, agri-business and forestry production chains have been associated with widespread deforestation, land degradation, biodiversity loss, and climate change. Almost 80 per cent of deforestation worldwide has been attributed to land clearing for agriculture—some to support the livelihoods of subsistence farmers, but much to support the expansion of large-scale commercial agriculture (Kissinger, Herold, and De Sy 2012; FAO 2020). In the Brazilian Amazon, the clearing of forests to create land for ranching cattle and growing soybeans used for animal feed is a major contributor to dramatic rates of ongoing rainforest loss. Mining and other natural resource or land-based sectors are also frequently linked to air and water pollution, disruptive impacts on river and forest systems, and over-exploitation of fisheries, soil, water, and other resources (Bolwig et al. 2010). Across a range of sectors, intensive energy use linked to production and transportation of goods is a major contributor to climate change and other environmental harms (Kagawa et al. 2015).

Despite such negative social and environmental impacts, some analysts of GVCs have expressed optimism regarding the potential for economic upgrading to translate into benefits for the working and living conditions of individuals and communities, a process sometimes referred to as 'social upgrading' (Barrientos, Gereffi, and Rossi 2011; Barrientos et al. 2016; Rossi 2019). More recently, some analysts have also scrutinized the potential for environmental upgrading, such as through developing eco-friendly products or improving the environmental impacts of global production (Ponte 2020; De Marchi et al. 2019).

Key Concept: Social upgrading

The process of improving the rights and entitlements of workers involved in global production processes is often referred to as 'social upgrading'.

The extent to which participation in globalized production systems generates opportunities for improving social and economic welfare depends not only on opportunities for expanded economic growth and profitability, but also on the extent to which economic opportunities translate into improved social standards for workers. Such improvements can take the form of improved wages, health, and safety practices, working hours, or employment security, alongside 'enabling' rights to collective bargaining, non-discrimination, voice, and empowerment.

There are several potential pathways through which social or environmental upgrading might occur: for example, where economic upgrading is associated with transitions of workers from casual to more secure employment, or where knowledge transfer and training activities jointly produce economic, social, and environmental upgrading. More often, however, economic upgrading has not been accompanied by social and environmental upgrading and may sometimes even be associated with social or environmental downgrading, such as through a rise in casualization or other forms of precarious work, or increased environmental harms created through rapid industrial growth.

7.4 Governing the social and environmental impacts of global production

Given the significant distributional implications of globalized production, it is not surprising that the governance of globalized production systems has become highly politicized. Intense debate has focused on the appropriate relationship between state and non-state actors, as traditional state-led regulatory processes increasingly operate alongside voluntary or mixed (public and private) governance mechanisms designed to protect workers, communities, and the environment.

Despite persistent concerns about the weakness of national systems of social and environmental regulation, national governments continue to play an important role in governing global production. At the intergovernmental level, legal instruments such as the International Labour Organization (ILO)'s core labour conventions—which address forced labour, child labour, the rights of workers to organize and engage in collective bargaining, and rights to equality and non-discrimination—also play a significant role in defining internationally recognized social and environmental standards (Posthuma and Rossi 2017).

Nonetheless, many national and international regulatory instruments remain poorly implemented as a result of weak capacity among labour and environmental regulators, large power imbalances between employers and vulnerable workers, and strong incentives for business to cut corners on wages, labour standards, or environmental management systems as a means of increasing profits or simply staying in business (Ruggie 2014). In some cases, regulatory enforcement is further weakened as a result of fears by government policymakers that businesses might shift their operations to other countries if faced with significant regulatory costs (Duanmu 2014).

Against this backdrop, there has often been increased reliance on largely voluntary mechanisms of regulatory governance in which intergovernmental or non-governmental organizations play a central role in setting social and environmental standards and establishing systems to monitor and promote compliance (Buthe 2010; Cashore 2002; Mayer and Phillips 2017). Efforts to develop voluntary intergovernmental codes specifically designed to govern global production activity can be traced back to the 1970s, when both the Organization for Economic Co-operation and Development (OECD)'s Guidelines for Multinational Enterprises (MNEs) and the ILO's Tripartite Declaration of Principles concerning Multinational Enterprises and Social Policy were adopted (Alston 2004; Macdonald 2012).

International standards to govern global production have continued to evolve since that time. International human rights standards have been reformed in recent years to support demands for strengthened transnational business regulation, most notably through negotiation of the non-binding United Nations Guiding Principles for Business and Human Rights, which were adopted by the United Nations Human Rights Council in 2011 as a means of defining both state and business responsibilities for human rights abuses linked to business operations (Ruggie 2014).

Significant reliance is now also placed on market-based regulatory systems in which companies contribute to the development of voluntary systems of social and environment regulation. Contracts regulating the terms of business relationships between buyers and suppliers now commonly incorporate obligations relating to social and environmental practices (Wright and Rwabizambuga 2006). Many large companies have created new policies and supply chain management systems through which commitments to social and environmental responsibility can be operationalized. Prominent examples include Starbucks' Café Practices Program and the Cocoa Life Program developed by Mondelēz (Macdonald 2007; Krauss and Barrientos 2021).

Many businesses also participate in multistakeholder standard-setting, auditing, and capacity-building schemes in which firms work together with governments and civil society organizations to strengthen elements of their social and environmental performance. Such initiatives include well-known consumer labels such as Fairtrade and Rainforest Alliance, alongside multistakeholder forums promoting sustainable production standards such as the Forest Stewardship Council or Fair Labor Association, and a range of single-commodity sustainability roundtables such as the Roundtable on Sustainable Palm Oil (Cashore 2002; Auld, Renckens, and Cashore 2015; Bartley 2011; Vogel 2010).

The willingness of companies to participate in such market-driven governance systems has been fuelled in part by pressure from civil society campaigners—encompassing grassroots worker or farmer movements, trade unions, national and transnational activist networks, and campaigners targeting consumers or investors. Private regulatory systems have been particularly widespread in consumer-facing sectors such as electronics (**see Case Study 7.2**), food-based commodities, garments, and sportswear, which more commonly attract activist attention. Corporate participation in such initiatives has sometimes been further motivated by concerns about access to critical raw materials and commodities, and an associated desire to strengthen direct sourcing relationships with suppliers (Gereffi 2014). Together with more traditional governmental and intergovernmental regulation, such schemes now play a prominent role in regulating the social and environmental impacts of global production activity across a range of economic sectors (Hale and Held 2011; Braithwaite and Drahos 2000; Partzsch 2020).

Have these governance systems worked? They have indeed contributed to achieving some improvements in labour and environmental standards within GVCs, particularly on issues such as child labour and occupational health and safety. Yet, as you see also from the discussions in **Chapter 9** and **Chapter 12**, they have been widely criticized as inadequate. By their nature, they are not legally or coercively enforceable. Many private governance schemes have limited coverage across sectors and geographical locations, with a tendency to concentrate in highly politicized, consumer-facing sectors, and to focus largely on issues consumers or investors in the Global North are concerned about, such as child labour, while neglecting issues that may be of more concern to ordinary workers or farmers. These schemes often contain weak provisions for independent monitoring and enforcement, and many have been criticized for being unaccountable to the workers and communities who are the supposed beneficiaries of the schemes (Koenig-Archibugi and Macdonald 2013).

A number of scholars have also drawn attention to the failure of many private regulatory systems to address gendered forms of disadvantage experienced by workers in global production systems, as a result of their focus only on workers who are directly employed in a particular supply chain, and the frequent lack of attention to issues of particular concern to women, such as reproductive rights, freedom from abuse, and gendered health and safety issues (Pearson 2007; Barrientos, Dolan, and Tallontire 2003).

Growing recognition of the limitations of private governance as a means of protecting social and labour standards has led many to call for the reassertion of state authority and regulation (Esbenshade 2012; Anner 2017; Bartley 2010). An increasing number of governments, particularly in Europe, are now passing legislation that requires

Case Study 7.2: Making an iPhone

Making an iPhone has become a truly global undertaking (Photo 7.3). The iPhone's value chain relies on factories and sub-contractors spread across dozens of countries around the world, with the greatest concentration located in East Asia (Petrova 2018). Product development and design takes place at Apple's headquarters in California, and some parts are manufactured in the United States. A range of other specialized components are manufactured in Japan, Taiwan, South Korea, Germany, and Switzerland, before the iPhone is assembled in factories in China. These manufacturers are in turn provisioned by complex networks of raw materials suppliers, who extract and transport an array of precious metals, rare earth elements, and other crucial production inputs from around the globe.

Apple's control over design, branding, and technology enables it to exercise tight control over its complex global supply chain, though significant power is also exercised by major suppliers such as Foxconn, which operate the vast Chinese factories in which iPhones are assembled.

Many observers have pointed to the example of Apple's iPhone to illustrate broader distributional trends in global value chains. Despite intense politicization of China's role as a global manufacturing base for products such as smartphones, the majority of value in the iPhone supply chain is in fact not captured there. Using data from 2009, it was estimated that while the

Photo 7.3 **Apple's headquarters in California**

Source: © iStock/P_Wei.

(*Continued*)

iPhone 4 was sold for $495 retail in the United States, it was assembled in China and exported at a unit value of $175. But the share of final value added in China was only $6.50, reflecting the fact that most of the components and capital goods involved in production were imported into China from other East Asian or European countries; the phones were then assembled in China from these pre-produced components. Meanwhile, more than half of the total value created in the iPhone production process was captured by Apple as profit (Phillips 2017; Kaplinsky 2019: 160; Gereffi 2014).

Apple's supply chains have also been controversial with respect to labour conditions associated with the assembly of Apple products. Foxconn factories in China have received significant attention surrounding highly publicized claims of forced or child labour and other labour rights violations in their factories (**see Section 12.2.2**). Intense human rights controversies have also surrounded the sourcing of raw materials used to create solder and other electronics components, including coltan, tin, and other so-called conflict minerals. Extraction of such minerals has been associated with child labour, forced labour, and the fuelling of violent conflict funded by minerals sales (Phillips 2017; Clarke and Boersma 2017; Hofmann, Schleper, and Blome 2018; Diprose et al. 2020).

Environmental harms associated with Apple supply chains have also been extensive, encompassing environmental destruction associated with mineral and rare earth extraction, intensive energy use and carbon emissions throughout the supply chain, and problems of waste management and water contamination linked to the disposal of electronic products (Suckling and Lee 2015).

In response to such concerns, Apple has developed a range of in-house responsible sourcing initiatives, such as programmes promoting water and energy conservation; due diligence and reporting systems designed to comply with international rules targeting conflict minerals, human trafficking, and slavery; and a Supplier Code of Conduct that is broadly aligned with international standards such as ILO core labour conventions, the OECD's due diligence guidance, and the UN Guiding Principles on Business and Human Rights. The company has sometimes also engaged with multistakeholder initiatives, such as inviting the Fair Labor Association to carry out audits of labour standards in its suppliers' factories or participating in industry forums such as the Electronic Industry Citizenship Coalition.

Watch the video on the online resources to take your understanding of this case study further.

Questions

1 Who do you think are the biggest winners and losers from Apple's globalized production strategies?
2 Taking the example of Apple iPhones, what are the strengths and drawbacks of voluntary and hybrid (public–private) governance arrangements in addressing social and environmental risks?

companies operating in other countries to publicly report on the measures they are taking to guard against adverse impacts of their activities on human rights and the environment (Palpacuer and Smith 2021). There have also been attempts to use private law instruments relating to unfair business practices or misleading advertising as means of holding corporations to account for their social or environmental impacts in other countries

(McBarnet, Voiculescu, and Campbell 2007). Nonetheless, such private law mechanisms were designed for very different purposes and have rarely given rise to successful legal rulings in such cases, though favourable out-of-court settlements have sometimes been achieved (Macdonald 2012).

Watch this video to explore the social and environmental consequences of global supply chains:

https://www.ted.com/talks/lena_partzsch_alternatives_to_multilateralism

7.5 **Conclusion**

We have seen in this chapter that global production systems have evolved dramatically in recent decades, giving rise to highly globalized but also very uneven geographies of production. While economic and technological drivers have played an important role in motivating these shifts, relationships of political power and interest have played a decisive role in reshaping global production.

Globalized production has been associated with significant distributional consequences for both people and the environment. As competing countries, firms, and individuals wrestle for advantage, new governance systems are developing in ways that redistribute power and authority between a range of public and private, domestic, and international actors. Within the resulting political struggles to control these processes, neither businesses nor governments have full control over the organization, governance, and distributional consequences of globalized production.

Key Points

- Production continues to be highly globalized, despite recent economic crises and rising trends towards economic protectionism.
- Patterns of global production have been shaped by a mix of technological change, firm strategies, and intentional political choices by governments around the world.
- The distributional effects of globalized production are mixed: global production systems have offered new opportunities for economic growth and development for some people and places, while others have remained excluded or exploited.
- In many GVCs, a small number of very large companies exercise substantial power over networks of suppliers, enabling them to control product design, quality, and pricing, as well as many social and environmental conditions of production.
- New forms of state and non-state global governance have been developed as a means of mitigating some of the worst effects of globalized production on labour, human rights, and the environment. Nevertheless, the adequacy of such governance arrangements has been widely questioned.

Further Reading

Bair, J. (2005), 'Global Capitalism and Commodity Chains: Looking Back, Going Forward', *Competition & Change*, 9(2): 153–80. Offers a detailed survey of major theoretical frameworks that political economists use to analyse the dynamics and consequences of globalized commodity production.

Barrientos, S. (2019), *Gender and Work in Global Value Chains: Capturing the Gains?* (Cambridge: Cambridge University Press). Reviews the implications of changing gender patterns of work in contemporary global production systems and explores potential ways that global sourcing systems might support more gender-equitable outcomes.

Chan, S., Boran, I., and van Asselt, H., et al. (2019), 'Promises and Risks of Nonstate Action in Climate and Sustainability Governance', *Wiley Interdisciplinary Reviews: Climate Change*, 10(3): e572. Drawing on the perspectives of a diverse group of scholars and practitioners from developing and developed countries, this paper reviews and scrutinizes a range of common arguments in support of non-state engagement in sustainable business governance.

Gereffi, G., Humphrey, J., and Sturgeon, T. (2005), 'The Governance of Global Value Chains', *Review of International Political Economy*, 12(1): 78–104. Elaborates an influential theoretical framework that both categorizes and explains varied patterns of global value chain governance.

LeBaron, G., and Lister, J. (2021), 'The Hidden Costs of Global Supply Chain Solutions', *Review of International Political Economy*, 29(3): 669–95. Presents a critical review of debates about both the effectiveness and the potentially unintended consequences of private systems of global supply chain governance, focused on social and environmental problems.

Mayer, F. W., and Phillips, N. (2017), 'Outsourcing Governance: States and the Politics of a "Global Value Chain World"', *New Political Economy*, 22(2): 134–52. Develops a framework to support an understanding of how state power interacts with the power of business in shaping and governing globalized production.

Chapter 7 Roundtable discussion

Do we need stronger global governance arrangements to hold big business to account?

Roundtable 7.1
Opening contribution **Kate Macdonald**

Stories of big business poisoning rivers, appropriating land from Indigenous communities and small farmers, or exploiting vulnerable workers remain disturbingly commonplace. Yet in place of strong regulatory responses, the picture is too often one of persistent corporate impunity and the inability of affected people to seek redress. Are current global governance arrangements to blame for such problems, and if so, can stronger global governance arrangements help to hold big business to account?

Stronger global governance arrangements are certainly needed to hold big business more effectively to account. But I want to argue that the concentration of academic and political attention on formulating institutional blueprints for global governance reforms often diverts attention from underlying problems—the deep power imbalances and significant accountability gaps that underpin persistent global governance failures.

In part, power imbalances can be seen in the influence business exerts over the very governance systems that should in theory be supporting efforts to hold big business to account—the classic idea of the fox guarding the hen house. Politicians and government officials can sometimes retain the autonomy needed to exercise regulatory leadership in the face of resistance from powerful business interests. Yet governments depend on business interests—to support their political candidature or post-political careers, finance their political campaigns, empower their political allies, support high-profile policy initiatives, and fuel the underlying processes of capitalist economic growth on which the legitimacy of national governments (and, in some cases, the personal enrichment of individual government officials) so often depend.

For example, some of you might have followed vigorous debates in many countries about the power of large pharmaceutical companies to shape public health policies relating to issues such as drug pricing, availability, and safety regulation, or the influence of lobbyists paid by large fossil fuel companies in holding back progress on tackling climate change. The balance between regulatory autonomy and regulatory 'capture' varies between contexts and over time. But in the overwhelming majority of cases, powerful business interests have the power to restrict the political space within which governance reforms can be implemented (Levy and Prakash 2003; Fuchs and Lederer 2007).

Big business is also able to constrain the content and scope of non-governmental regulatory initiatives in ways that are aligned with the interests of business, reflecting the reliance of such schemes on both the operating revenue derived from business membership or licensing fees, and business support for the acceptance, dissemination, and implementation of private regulatory norms (Dauvergne and Lister 2010; van der Ven 2018).

This often leads to a situation in which governance actors assigned responsibilities for holding business to account are symbolically applauded while being in practice disempowered.

Governments around the world enthusiastically endorse international norms that require protections for labour rights and the environment, but the regulators who are assigned responsibility for ensuring that businesses comply with such standards are then denied the resources and enforcement powers that would enable them to do their job effectively.

Increasingly, both governmental and non-governmental regulatory initiatives rely on voluntary corporate participation, putting the onus on civil society organizations and others to scrutinize, shame, and pressure companies into regulatory compliance. And sometimes this works. But just as often, communities remain largely unsupported in their efforts to hold big business to account, civil society groups promoting corporate accountability agendas struggle to gain funding from business-friendly foundations and governments, and human rights and environmental defenders can even find themselves subject to violent intimidation, lawsuits, or government repression (Matejova, Parker, and Dauvergne 2018; Haines and Macdonald 2020).

So, we have a circular problem: strengthened corporate accountability requires the presence of both state and civil society actors who are motivated and empowered to hold business to account. Yet the civil society actors which take on such a role are systematically disempowered, and government regulators are routinely neutralized or captured to a greater or lesser extent by precisely the powerful business interests they are called upon to regulate.

Perhaps somewhat paradoxically, solutions to institutional failings therefore cannot be achieved exclusively or even primarily through the pursuit of institutional reforms.

Instead, the goal of holding big business to account involves not only generating and promoting creative institutional reform proposals, but also directly challenging the power imbalances between companies, governments, and other social interest groups. We need not only strengthened global governance arrangements, but also strengthened strategies of mobilization and coalition-building that 'facilitate the exercise of countervailing power' by civil society organizations and other pro-regulatory and pro-accountability social forces (Rodríguez-Garavito 2017: 26; Fung 2003; Levy and Newell 2002).

We might therefore imagine virtuous webs of strengthened accountability, in which governance institutions provide strengthened symbolic and material support for pro-accountability social coalitions; market pressure is brought to bear by consumers, institutional investors, and international financial institutions in support of such coalitions; and these cumulative pressures in turn help to create political conditions within which institutional reforms that would strengthen global governance arrangements become more politically possible and sustainable.

For example, many of you may be familiar with efforts to pressure major shareholders and financial institutions to withdraw investment from companies involved in extracting fossil fuels, in which student activists in many countries have played a significant role. In such cases, there have been important mutually reinforcing interactions between principles articulated in intergovernmental agreements such as the Paris Agreement, policies of individual governments designed to encourage reduced fossil fuel dependence, and social and market activism demanding stronger corporate, governmental, and intergovernmental action, in which individual citizens participate.

While we should indeed continue to advocate for strengthened global governance arrangements, we need to be careful not to take our eye off an equally important objective: to empower pro-accountability social forces to weave together the political conditions that are needed to hold big business more effectively to account.

Roundtable 7.2
Response **Tim Bartley**

Do we need stronger global governance arrangements to hold big business to account? Yes, but rectifying power imbalances is ultimately more important than tweaking global governance, argues Kate Macdonald (**see Roundtable 7.1**). We are currently stuck in a vicious circle, in which corporate power defangs the kinds of regulatory capacities and civil society organizing that would be necessary to hold companies to a higher standard. What is needed, Macdonald argues, is not merely reform of global governance arrangements, but a strengthening of social movements through which marginalized groups can gain more power in domestic and transnational arenas. Only then will reforms to global governance make a big difference, by helping to translate small successes into durable accomplishments and forging 'virtuous webs of strengthened accountability'.

I concur completely. While some scholars see existing corporate responsibility initiatives as promoting real progress in difficult circumstances (Short and Toffel 2021), I see the evidence as pointing more toward failures than successes. I therefore agree with Macdonald that is it time to consider new approaches.

But Macdonald's diagnosis overlooks another vicious circle that plagues global governance of corporate accountability: As reformers look at the places where controversies arise—such as the factories of Bangladesh, the forests and palm oil plantations of Indonesia, or the mines of the Democratic Republic of the Congo—they too often imagine the local context as an 'empty space', essentially devoid of governance and waiting to be filled by global norms and standards. Describing these locations as regulatory voids, governance gaps, and 'areas of limited statehood', scholars and reformers end up looking to the private sector as the saviour (Abbott and Snidal 2009; Börzel and Risse 2010; Braithwaite 2006). Diagnosing national and local governments as uniformly incapacitated, corrupt, or illegitimate, they hope that global companies can bring some order to this setting by pushing standards through their supply chains.

This further empowers big companies, which are asked to become quasi-regulators of their suppliers but dictate many of the terms of this activity, as Macdonald notes. Even when promoting standards developed by multistakeholder initiatives, large corporations can decide whether and how to reward compliance or penalize noncompliance, whether to adhere to their stated targets (for example, 100 per cent certified by a particular year) or revise them quietly, and whether to reform or retain pricing and production strategies that make it difficult for suppliers to improve (Amengual, Distelhorst, and Tobin 2020; Anner 2020; Bartley 2022; Grabs and Ponte 2019).

The places where controversies occur are not empty spaces—they are crowded with competing agendas and actors, including social movements, policy reformers, and labour unions. Domestic and local governments are not uniformly devoid of capacity or interest to address problems of labour exploitation, environmental degradation, and human rights abuses. They vary dramatically in this regard, but scholars are finding pockets of effective, reform-minded governance in some surprising places—such as in the enforcement of labour and environmental law in parts of Latin America (Coslovsky 2011; Perez-Aleman

2013; Schrank and Piore 2018). Of course, governments are also relevant when they oppose these goals, restrict rights, and repress social movements (Bartley 2018; Malets 2015; van Rooij, Stern, and Fürst 2016). Recent crackdowns on civil society and rising authoritarianism must be acknowledged as we think about the possibilities for linking global governance, corporate accountability, and challenges to existing power imbalances.

What would you do in these circumstances? Would you attempt to bypass these national and local forms of governance in order to bring factories and farms up to global best practices? Or would you see it as impossible to stimulate real reform without acknowledging the local contexts in which factories and farms are enmeshed—some of which are more aligned with your goals than others?

My position is that we must acknowledge these crowded and varied spaces, and that once we do so, we can think more clearly about how global governance could provide leverage for social movements and strengthen webs of accountability. Existing forms of private governance have rarely provided useful leverage. Activists have waged cross-border 'brand boomerang campaigns' only to see apparent gains vanish when a factory moves, a brand withdraws, or a government intervenes to co-opt or repress the effort. This has become a common story in the supply chains of Nike, Adidas, and other major brands (Bartley and Egels-Zanden 2016).

Local NGOs' attempts to utilize the stakeholder consultation and complaint mechanisms of multistakeholder initiatives have likewise produced more frustration than meaningful remediation and recognition. This can be seen in research on the Roundtable on Sustainable Palm Oil, among other initiatives (Macdonald and Balaton-Chrimes 2016).

With this in mind, we can go beyond Macdonald's plea to prioritize power imbalances to think about *how* global governance might become more consistent with this goal.

First, global governance institutions must acknowledge that domestic law on the books is relevant, often stronger than imagined, and highly salient to domestic social movements, even when it is poorly enforced. Regimes that penalize *illegality* in global supply chains have some potential to do this, though their likelihood of proving progressive rather than repressive is by no means guaranteed.

Second, global governance must not simply encourage corporations to promote standards, manage risks, or exercise 'due diligence'. It must push corporations to prioritize locations where progress is being made, negotiate with local actors, and face penalties when violations persist.

Third, institutions governing global trade, such as the World Trade Organization, should expand rather than restrict the space for governments to address labour, environmental, and human rights concerns in novel ways.

Ultimately, perhaps the 'protect, respect, and remedy' triumvirate of the UN Guiding Principles on Business and Human Rights needs to be supplemented with a more basic prescription to 'recognize and tolerate'. That is, global governance must *recognize* that domestic orders matter, with some settings more conductive to meaningful corporate accountability than others. And it must push companies to *tolerate* and negotiate with social movements rather than fleeing them for the sake of risk management.

Roundtable 7.3
Response **Surya Deva**

Chapter 7 highlights adverse impacts of ever-changing global production models on human rights, labour rights, and the environment. The current regulatory frameworks are clearly inadequate to hold (big) businesses accountable for human rights abuses, including those linked to their global supply chains. These frameworks are perhaps not meant to be effective because they do not even attempt to address root causes of corporate impunity.

Businesses are good at turning models of innovation into models of irresponsibility. And regulation of such models of irresponsibility by private, public, and hybrid approaches is often either playing a 'catch up' game to newer models of production, or is content with operating within inherently imbalanced and unfair power structures. We should see failure of various regulatory approaches to humanize global supply chains in this wider context, as they do not address the power imbalances that are the root cause of exploitation in global supply chains—the issue that, like Macdonald (**see Roundtable 7.1**), I believe is at the heart of the problem.

These power imbalances arise due to multiple intersectional factors such as poverty; discrimination based on gender, religion, language, caste, and migration status; absence of independent trade unions; and lack of awareness about one's rights as well as remedial mechanisms (Overeem, Theuws, and Heyl 2021). Irresponsible purchasing practices of brands also contribute to this power imbalance, and were exposed further by the Covid-19 pandemic (LeBaron et al. 2018; Sherman III 2021).

Despite well-documented exploitation of the principles of separate corporate personality and limited liability by parent companies to deny, delay, or altogether avoid responsibility for human rights abuses by their subsidiaries, there is not much appetite to modify these principles in both soft and hard regulatory regimes (Mares 2017). While no efficient solution has yet been found to regulate corporate groups, companies started using supply chains to outsource their risks and responsibilities to suppliers spread across the globe. The creation of gig platforms is taking the distancing of responsibility to the next level. In the future, the automation of manufacturing may result in no work for many people, despite them having the right to work on paper (**see Chapter 12 Roundtable**).

Moreover, although various non-state regulatory approaches offer some potential to regulate supply chains abuses in certain situations, they again try to operate within contours of exploitative business models rather than disrupting them. The general failure of reporting regimes, certification schemes, and social auditing in addressing an issue as serious as modern slavery is a case in point, as innovative business models of modern slavery continue to mushroom at will (Crane et al. 2021).

Several regulatory shifts are, therefore, needed to hold business actors to account and create supply chains that are free from exploitation.

First, the dominant narrative of supply chains creating jobs and facilitating the development of economies in the Global South should be challenged. Unless supply chains create 'decent' jobs, assist in reducing economic inequality, and contribute to sustainability generally, they should face regulatory 'red lines'. For this reason, regulating the gig economy may be a superficial and symbolic exercise, as this business model is rooted in exploiting vulnerabilities and converting workers into independent contractors in the guise of flexibility and empowerment.

Second, greater attention should be given to companies utilizing complex supply chains to be able to demonstrate certain 'outcomes'. The human rights due diligence (HRDD) 'process' introduced by the UN Guiding Principles on Business and Human Rights is a useful tool for companies to identify, prevent, mitigate, and show how they account for adverse human rights impacts through their operations. Yet, it merely places a responsibility of means and does not guarantee outcomes—that is, the non-violation of human rights. Similar to product liability regimes, it may be desirable to hold companies strictly accountable for human rights abuses in their supply chains (Deva 2021).

Third, while non-state actors have a vital role in regulating corporate behaviour, states should not adopt a 'hands off' approach in monitoring supply chains' transparency. As part of their duty to protect against human rights abuses by businesses, states must exercise effective oversight and enforcement over corporate disclosure and reporting of information concerning their supply chains (Chambers and Yilmaz Vastardis 2021). This may require building a strong political will for states to act on these lines.

Fourth, 'in order to contest the unequal distribution of power and resources along supply chains, the workers and local communities most directly affected by supply chain capitalism should be at the forefront' of private regulatory initiatives (Brinks et al. 2021: 268). In many cases, trade unions—if independent and gender-responsive—could go a long way in addressing these power imbalances between brands and their business partners on the one hand, and workers on the other hand.

Fifth, a significant number of workers in vulnerable situations—such as migrant workers, workers who are part of the informal economy or unorganized sector, and undocumented workers—face additional risks of exploitation. Regulatory regimes should be responsive to this sad reality and try to mitigate some of these vulnerability-causing factors.

In short, the current regulatory approaches neither pay adequate attention to various asymmetries at play in global supply chains, nor question the inherently exploitative nature of certain business models operating in a neoliberal market economy. Unless these structural issues are resolved, regulatory initiatives are likely to continue struggling to protect the human rights of workers and communities from the effects of global supply chains.

Roundtable 7.4
Response **Lena Partzsch**

We've seen in **Chapter 7** and from my colleagues' contributions to the **Chapter 7 Roundtable** how supply chains have become fragmented and complex. As global markets become more integrated, governments have become increasingly hesitant to enforce arrangements to regulate business. At the same time, multilateralism has proven unsuccessful in coordinating states' responses to global challenges, such as labour rights, human rights, or environmental degradation.

Yet I want to take an optimistic view and argue that there *are* emerging—alternative— forms of private, public, and hybrid social and environmental regulation which do allow us the possibility of holding big business to account.

The most well-known alternative is private regulation based on voluntary certification. Non-state initiatives guarantee producers' compliance with specific standards, and consumers are willing to pay a higher price for goods and services in return. You find certificates on a wide range of goods and services, from organic food and textiles to sustainable banking. Fairtrade coffee is the most well-known example. Besides workers' rights, safer working conditions, and fairer pay, fair trade initiatives guarantee that there was no child labour used in the process of production, and consumers respond positively to this reassurance.

The advantages of this form of governance are that certification is voluntary for business and that it is transnational in scope. Its disadvantages include free-rider problems, where certain companies 'piggy-back' on certification schemes and benefit from them, but make no meaningful change of their own (Partzsch 2020). And we know that most private standards are defined by and for corporations from the Global North, often disadvantaging smallholders in the Global South (McDermott, Irland, and Pacheco 2015). There are very few exceptional cases, such as fair trade programmes, which are designed to empower smallholders and which demonstrate real 'normative' power (Barratt Brown 2007). However, fair trade is restricted to small segments of the market and therefore cannot be an encompassing solution.

A second alternative to govern the social and environmental impact of global production is through national laws relating to supply chains. These laws require pertinent information from importers to be disclosed. A good example is the United States and the European Union (EU) demanding due diligence from importers of so-called conflict minerals, designed to withdraw money from armed forces in the Democratic Republic of the Congo and other conflict regions (Partzsch and Vlaskamp 2016). Similar laws already exist for illegally logged timber (Bartley 2018).

Unlike private regulation, supply chain laws apply equally to all importers and therefore have no free-rider problem (Sarfaty 2015). But they are based merely on transparency and disclosure—requiring business to declare relevant information. They do not influence standards themselves or promote particular schemes such as those relating to organic farming programmes. Moreover, monitoring and control in many countries is very difficult, particularly, for instance, where much activity in supply chains takes place outside formalized markets. Supply chain laws may well demonstrate a 'regulatory renaissance' (Alford and Phillips 2018), but in their current form they can only be considered first steps to hold big business to account.

Finally, hybrid governance means that states encourage private regulation, such as voluntary certification. The EU Renewable Energy Directive, which determines sustainability standards for biofuels contributing to the EU's renewable energy targets, is one example of this. Companies prove compliance with these standards, including zero deforestation, through certification. Private certification in effect becomes mandatory for imports.

Moreover, if non-governmental organizations (NGOs) are often involved in multi-stakeholder certification schemes, they can give a voice to otherwise marginalized groups (Partzsch 2020). However, this amounts only to 'accountability-by-proxies' (Koenig-Archibugi and Macdonald 2013), and externally enforced standards prevent exporting countries from setting their own priorities.

So, I want to suggest that alternative forms of governance already allow for holding big business to account. They demonstrate a new normative power: consumers use their purchasing power to enforce norms such as peace and sustainability. However, the key challenge is that they count on private actors for implementation. Only a few programmes improve social and environmental impacts on the ground and these programmes have so far been limited to niche markets. More normative power would be necessary to enforce social justice and environmental sustainability in the global economy. And we need to more prudently combine private with public regulation in new hybrid arrangements.

Alternative forms of regulation in this sense address but do not solve global challenges. However, there is no need, or excuse, for any individual consumer, corporation, or Western country to purchase goods and services produced under unacceptable conditions. Alternatives are available.

Over to you ...

1 The contributors to this debate all agree on the need for corporate accountability and appropriate governance arrangements to achieve it, but they offer quite different views on both what those arrangements would be, and how viable the alternatives are. Are you optimistic or pessimistic about the possibilities of increasing the accountability of big business for social, labour, and environmental standards? Why?

2 All of the contributors signal the importance of social movements and civil society actors in achieving corporate accountability. But NGOs and other actors don't make policy and don't run corporations. So, what kinds of action can they take? And how effective can they be? Can you think of instances where pressure from consumers and civil society has brought about genuine change? What do you think are the main barriers we face in doing so?

3 Kate Macdonald kicked off the Roundtable by pointing to the issue of power imbalances (see Roundtable 7.1). Do you agree with her and other contributors that this is a core problem that needs to be addressed if we are to achieve higher levels of accountability? Which power imbalances are the most influential? And how do we go about addressing them? What do you make of the different suggestions offered in this debate?

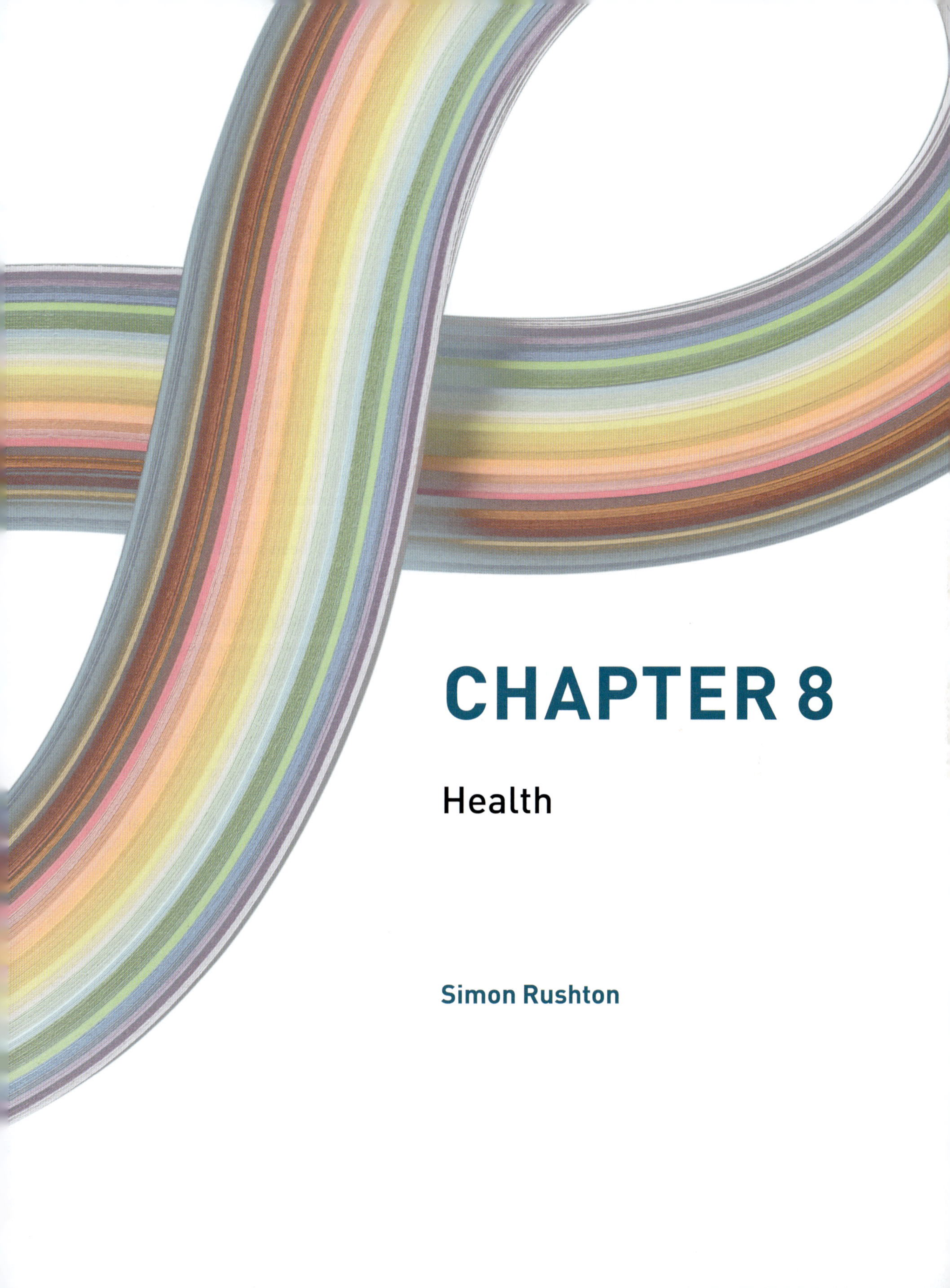

CHAPTER 8

Health

Simon Rushton

8.1 Introduction

The Covid-19 pandemic—by far the most high-profile global issue at the time this chapter was written in 2021–22—has focused the attention of the entire world on issues of health and disease. Although it is not yet clear precisely when, how, or where this novel coronavirus jumped the species barrier from animals into humans, the health impacts of what became known as the SARS-CoV-2 virus first began to be noticed in Wuhan, China in late 2019. Within weeks there were cases of this new disease in every country of the world: a clear illustration of some of the downsides of life in a globalized world. Just as goods and people move rapidly across national borders, so do diseases.

The pandemic, and the response to it, have also brought to the fore and shed new light on many of the issues that are core to Global Political Economy (GPE) and addressed in other chapters of this textbook. These include questions of poverty and inequalities in gender, race, and class (**see Chapter 10**); trade (**see Chapter 6**); global governance (**see Chapter 14**); business (**see Chapter 7**); labour (**see Chapter 12**); and many more. The economic impacts of Covid-19 on individual nations, and on the global economy as a whole, have been huge, as have the political tensions created both within and between countries. In short, the pandemic has not only been a medical or public health crisis: it has also been a political and economic crisis, and gives you as students of GPE much to think about.

We won't focus only on the Covid-19 pandemic in this chapter, although we will return to that subject in the **Chapter 8 Roundtable**. Instead, we will look at a wider range of contemporary health challenges and ask some questions that seem simple, but in fact turn out to be fiendishly complex, namely:

- How is the health of people around the world affected by the Global Political Economy?
- In what ways does the ability of people to access healthcare when they need it depend on global political and economic structures and processes?
- How can we improve global health and reduce health inequalities, both within and between countries?

8.2 What does it mean to be healthy?

The most commonly used definition of health is the one set out in the Constitution of the World Health Organization (WHO), agreed by member states at the time of the WHO's creation in 1946:

> Health is a state of complete physical, mental and social well-being and not merely the absence of disease or infirmity. (WHO 1946)

In many ways, this was a progressive and wide-ranging definition for its time. It explicitly addressed not only physical health but also mental health—a subject that at the time was far less discussed in most countries than it is today, and which even now remains a taboo topic in many societies. It argued against a 'negative' view of health as simply the absence of illness. But even more than this, the definition includes within the scope of health 'social well-being', which we might take to include things like the ability of the elderly to live independent lives, or of people with a disability to participate fully in the workplace.

Over time, this definition has been subjected to critique on a variety of grounds. Huber et al. (2011) usefully set out three of the most common critiques. First, it has been argued that applying the standard of 'complete physical, mental and social well-being' means that almost all of us are unhealthy almost all of the time—something that some have feared promotes a creeping 'medicalization' of society in which more and more of the problems we face become redefined as 'health issues', for which we then seek medical solutions such as pharmaceuticals rather than trying to address the underlying causes.

Second, following from this, if most of us are deemed to be 'ill' most of the time, the burden placed on health systems could easily become unsustainable when we would be better off (some claim) promoting 'the human capacity to cope autonomously with life's ever changing physical, emotional, and social challenges' (Huber et al. 2011: 236).

And third, it has been argued that the definition is so broad that it has been difficult to operationalize or measure in practice, making it a less than useful tool for making good policy. For the time being, however, the WHO Constitution is as close as we have to an internationally agreed definition of health.

The things that threaten people's health vary widely over time as a function of geography, scientific and social developments, and people's different social backgrounds and economic circumstances. Historically, infectious diseases (for example, those caused by viruses or bacteria) were the biggest causes of mortality and morbidity. But as medical knowledge and technologies have advanced, and as other changes in our lifestyles have taken place, this has begun gradually to shift towards non-communicable diseases (**see Box 8.1**).

Box 8.1: What are the world's biggest health problems?

There are a variety of ways of answering this question. One of the easiest measures to consider relates to causes of death. The WHO's list of the 'Top 10 Causes of Death' shows that, globally, the following are the world's biggest killers (WHO 2020):

1. Ischaemic heart disease
2. Stroke
3. Chronic obstructive pulmonary disease
4. Lower respiratory infections
5. Neonatal conditions
6. Trachea, bronchus, lung cancers
7. Alzheimer's disease and other dementias
8. Diarrhoeal diseases
9. Diabetes mellitus
10. Kidney diseases.

(Continued)

However, this global 'Top 10' looks very different across countries. Among low-income countries, for example, neonatal conditions are the leading cause of death; HIV/AIDS, malaria, and tuberculosis are all in the Top 10; and road injuries are seventh. But even in poorer countries, non-communicable diseases are on the rise, leading to what is often called a 'double burden' of disease (Marshall 2004).

The problem with focusing on causes of mortality is that it doesn't tell us much about people's quality of life when they are alive. In response, a range of new measures have been developed including 'Healthy Life Expectancy' (HALE, the number of years that a person can expect to live in 'full health'), 'Disability-Adjusted Life Years' (DALY, the number of lost years of healthy life), and 'Quality-Adjusted Life Years' (QALY, the number of years of healthy life gained). Unsurprisingly, these measures also vary hugely between different countries. One of the leading global attempts to incorporate these wider measures of health is the Global Burden of Disease study (IHME 2019).

Improving health around the world is a challenge that needs to be tackled on a variety of scales. Some threats to health are extremely localized, but many are closely connected to much larger global-level social and economic trends. This will become clear in **Section 8.3**, where we will look at the social, economic, and commercial determinants of health.

8.3 The (global) social, economic, and commercial determinants of health

The idea that 'prevention is better than cure' is a very old one indeed, but it still has profound implications for how we think about health, and what we do in our attempts to improve it. The idea of 'medicalization', which was introduced in **Section 8.2**, emerged from a wider trend over the course of the nineteenth and twentieth centuries in which new knowledge and technologies were created, and proved to be powerful ways of addressing disease and illness at both the individual and population levels (Conrad 2007). New medicines revolutionized our ability to cure diseases—one obvious example being the creation of the first antibiotics in the 1920s, which enabled people to recover from infections which would previously have been fatal. As we will see in **Section 8.4**, the benefits of these advances have been unevenly distributed, but they have been remarkable nonetheless.

This medical approach to addressing health problems—in which an individual patient receives treatment for their condition, often through the use of pharmaceuticals—sits alongside public health efforts that have primarily sought to address the causes of ill health at the population level. The aim of such interventions is to address the conditions that threaten health—in other words, *prevention*. Early examples of this included the creation of urban sanitation systems in the nineteenth century and the clearance of slums that created the conditions for rapid spread of disease (and, crucially, in doing so reduced the productivity of urban industrial workers).

Over time, the role of medical technologies, most notably vaccinations, have supplemented public health's preventative efforts, and have led to significant reductions in the prevalence of vaccine-preventable diseases worldwide, including the global eradication of smallpox—a disease that had caused 500 million deaths in the century before it was declared to have been eradicated in 1980 (Bazin 1999). Technology keeps moving forwards, with more recent developments in understanding the human genome allowing for the identification of genetic predispositions to particular conditions, new screening methods, and advanced forms of 'personalized medicine' that are tailor-made for an individual patient. As medical science develops, we are getting better at predicting, preventing, and treating disease.

Alongside the advances in medical technology, in recent years there has also been a renewed interest in tackling the 'external' factors that impact people's health, which we can term the social, economic, and commercial determinants of health.

The work of the WHO's Commission on the Social Determinants of Health (CSDH), which was established in 2005, played a major role in kickstarting global-level policy discussions around these issues. Led by the eminent epidemiologist Michael Marmot, the CSDH published its final report in 2008 (WHO 2008). This was a wide-ranging report that was far from being a dry, technical document of the kind that might be expected from a body like the WHO. Instead, it engaged head-on with big issues of Global Political Economy and focused its recommendations on forwarding an agenda of social justice and health equity. Because of this, it was highly controversial: some of the WHO's member states felt that the organization had overstepped its health remit and strayed into 'political' areas that were beyond its mandate. But even for those who welcomed it, the report raised real questions as to how the wide range of challenges the Commission pointed to could be prioritized and tackled (Lee 2010).

The three 'Principles of Action' set out in the CSDH's report give a flavour of their approach:

1. Improve the conditions of daily life—the circumstances in which people are born, grow, live, work, and age.
2. Tackle the inequitable distribution of power, money, and resources—the structural drivers of those conditions of daily life—globally, nationally, and locally.
3. Measure the problem, evaluate action, expand the knowledge base, develop a workforce that is trained in the social determinants of health, and raise public awareness about the social determinants of health. (WHO 2008)

How these principles relate to the workings of the Global Political Economy should be immediately clear. Globalization (**see Chapter 4**) has resulted in huge economic and social changes across the world that have fundamentally altered the conditions of daily life for billions of people, with consequences for health. Here I will give just two examples, but there are countless more.

First, the development of global value chains (GVCs) has led to a huge growth in manufacturing industries in many countries, fundamentally altering employment markets and driving rapid (and often unplanned) urbanization (**see Chapter 7**). This has created new health problems in many cities, often resulting from the inadequacy of basic infrastructure such as water and sanitation, large numbers of people living in sub-standard and closely packed housing, air pollution, and traffic-related injuries. Urbanization has also been associated with people changing their behaviours in terms of diet, physical activity, and consumption of harmful substances such as tobacco and alcohol (Galea and Vlahov 2005).

Second, environmental destruction associated with the exploitation of earth's natural resources is creating significant new risks to health. Rising global temperatures pose direct threats—for example, from heat and drought—but also indirect ones as mosquitoes and other 'vectors' of disease spread to new regions, expanding the geographical range of diseases such as malaria and dengue fever. Other forms of environmental destruction such as deforestation and mining have their own impacts, causing health-threatening environmental pollution and increased levels of contact between humans and wild animals, which raises the risk of 'zoonoses' (new diseases that cross the species barrier from animals to humans) (Morand and Lajaunie 2021).

In all societies, poverty and inequality are closely correlated to health outcomes. Poorer and more marginalized groups, such as ethnic or religious minorities or people with disabilities, are more likely to live and work in environments that are damaging for their health and are more likely to suffer from long-term health conditions (including 'multimorbidities'—where people have multiple physical or mental health conditions). They are also less likely to be able to access high-quality treatment and care.

This is just as true in the world's richest countries as it is in the world's poorest. The work of scholars such as Danny Dorling and Michael Marmot has shown the ways in which high levels of inequality in countries like the UK and the USA have created huge differentials in health outcomes (Dorling 2013; Marmot 2015). Research in Sheffield, the northern English city in which I live and work, has found that life expectancy in the least deprived parts of the city (86 years for women; 83.1 years for men) is significantly higher than in the most deprived parts of the city, less than 5 km away (78.7 years for women; 74.4 years for men). Infant mortality rates in the city are highly unequal across ethnic groups: 5.5 per 1,000 live births for White British mothers, compared with 10.9 for Black and Black British mothers and 13.4 for Asian and Asian British mothers (NHS Sheffield Clinical Commissioning Group 2012). Although there has often been a tendency to blame the disadvantaged for their own poor health—criticizing food 'choices' or rates of tobacco, alcohol, and drug use, for example—the structural roots of these inequalities have long been clear (Marmot 2015).

It has also long been clear that tackling these health inequalities across the world will require actions not only by the health sector, but by a whole range of different actors at sub-national, national, and global levels. The concept of 'Health in All Policies' (HiAP) is one attempt to use policy to address the wider structural determinants of health. Originally developed by the government of Finland, HiAP is intended to ensure that the impacts of health are considered in the making of policy across all sectors, even those that at first glance do not appear to be health related (Godziewski 2020).

> **Key Concept: Health in All Policies (HiAP)**
>
> 'Health in All Policies' is an approach to addressing the wider social, economic, and commercial determinants of health. It is defined by the WHO as 'an approach to public policies across sectors that systematically takes into account the health implications of decisions, seeks synergies, and avoids harmful health impacts in order to improve population health and health equity' (WHO 2013). At the heart of the concept of HiAP is the idea that policymakers should take health considerations into account when making policy in all fields.

Such initiatives have faced significant opposition in many countries. On the one hand, there have been libertarian arguments against increased government intervention in the name of health. Is it right, for example, for the government to adopt policies limiting the availability of unhealthy foods, or to ban the advertising of tobacco or alcohol products? On the other hand (and often the two hands have worked together), there has been determined lobbying by businesses that have an interest in avoiding or softening regulation.

This brings us to a newer concept in the literature: the 'commercial determinants of health' (Kickbusch, Allen, and Franz 2016). The focus here is on how some kinds of firms are responsible for activities that, while profitable, are detrimental to health, even while the private sector in some areas makes significant contributions to health improvement. That includes firms whose products are directly damaging to people's health, such as producers of tobacco products, fast food, or high-sugar drinks. But it can also include firms in myriad other sectors, from mining to clothing, whose activities have negative health consequences either for their own workers, or more widely. Although some firms have sought to reduce the health impacts of their activities (for example, through better environmental protection, or reformulation of food and beverage products), there have also been many instances in which they have sought to protect their profits, including through lobbying against regulation and/or expansion into new (and less regulated) markets.

> **Key Concept: Commercial determinants of health**
>
> There is often a tension between firms' desire to pursue profit and public health. Although there are various definitions of 'commercial determinants of health' in the literature (de Lacy-Vawdon and Livingston 2020), the acknowledgement of the health harms that can result from private companies pursuing their profit-maximizing interests is a common thread through all of them. Where the definitions often differ is over whether those harms need to be intentional: Kickbusch, Allen, and Franz (2016) limit their definition to 'strategies and approaches used by the private sector to promote products and choices that are detrimental to health'; another widely-used definition from West and Marteau (2013) is somewhat broader, referring to 'factors that influence health which stem from the profit motive'.

Case Study 8.1 shows an example of lobbying, in which the tobacco industry sought to push back against attempts by the WHO to agree on a global framework on tobacco control.

Case Study 8.1: The tobacco industry's opposition to the WHO Framework Convention on Tobacco Control

The Framework Convention on Tobacco Control (FCTC) was the first international treaty to be concluded under the auspices of the WHO. The multiple damaging health impacts of tobacco smoking had already been well-evidenced for several decades, and policy efforts to reduce tobacco use, including through taxation, had already been implemented in some countries. But the negotiation of the FCTC was nevertheless a long and highly politicized one, beginning with an initial World Health Assembly resolution in 1996 through to the Convention eventually being opened for signature in 2003. The political challenges have continued at the national level in a series of disputes about the implementation of the FCTC's provisions.

Photo 8.1 A poster from the FCTC highlighting the negative impact tobacco use has on the environment

Source: © WHO.

As the WHO says in the foreword to the treaty:

The WHO FCTC was developed in response to the globalization of the tobacco epidemic. The spread of the tobacco epidemic is facilitated through a variety of complex factors with cross-border effects, including trade liberalization and direct foreign investment. Other factors such as global marketing, transnational tobacco advertising, promotion and sponsorship, and the international movement of contraband and counterfeit cigarettes have also contributed to the explosive increase in tobacco use. (WHO 2003)

The heart of the FCTC is a pledge by WHO member states to implement policies to reduce tobacco consumption. A wide range of such measures are set out in the treaty, including the use of taxation and price controls, the introduction of safety warnings on packaging, measures to reduce exposure to second-hand smoke (such as indoor smoking bans in public places), education efforts (Photo 8.1), and banning tobacco advertising and sponsorship.

Given that the FCTC was explicitly aiming to reduce consumer demand in a large and profitable global market, it came as no surprise that the tobacco industry (and a number of WHO member states with a significant stake in tobacco production) was strongly opposed to the FCTC and made extensive efforts first to prevent its adoption, and later to water down its implementation.

During the negotiation process, industry bodies such as the International Tobacco Growers' Association sought to lobby governments to oppose the treaty, to discredit research showing the health consequences of tobacco use, and to argue that the agreement would have a particularly detrimental effect on workers in developing countries.

Even long after the FCTC was concluded, efforts to undermine it continued. A leak of internal documents from Philip Morris International, the world's largest tobacco company, which was made available by the Reuters news agency in 2017, showed what many anti-tobacco advocates had long claimed: sophisticated and ongoing attempts by the company to persuade governments around the world not to fully implement the provisions of the FCTC (Reuters 2017). In many cases, these efforts appear to have been successful, with the WHO regularly bemoaning the lack of progress on implementation of some of the treaty's key provisions.

According to the WHO's figures, 8 million people die each year as a result of tobacco smoking and 80 per cent of the 1.3 billion tobacco users in the world now live in low and middle-income countries—a sign of the industry's strategy of expanding into new markets as smoking rates in the Global North declined in the late twentieth and early twenty-first centuries.

Watch the video on the online resources to take your understanding of this case study further.

Questions

1 Are corporate lobbies too powerful in global health? If so, how could their influence be reduced?
2 How should governments strike the balance between individual liberties and the need to reduce the consequences of health-harming products?

This was far from an isolated example. The very nature of lobbying is that it often takes place 'behind the scenes' and can, as a result, be difficult to research. Nevertheless, there are countless examples of the different strategies businesses have pursued to fend off the perceived threat of tougher regulation. These include financial or other support for legislators to encourage them to oppose new laws, or the use of legal action to argue that particular forms of regulation are in breach of domestic or international law (as the tobacco company Philip Morris did in a six-year legal case against the government of Australia's introduction of plain packaging laws (Mitchell and Studdert 2012)).

Many of those same companies have used the new opportunities provided by the globalization of markets to expand into new territories. The Global Fund to Fight AIDS, TB and Malaria partnered with Coca-Cola on 'Project Last Mile', using Coca-Cola's vast distribution network to get essential medicines to places that weren't being reached by existing medicine supply chains—but were being reached by Coca-Cola. Many in public health questioned the ethics of a health organization partnering with the producer of a high-sugar beverage that is harmful to health (Lauber, Rutter, and Gilmore 2021). A similar partnership between the Global Fund and Heineken in Africa attracted even more criticism (Marten and Hawkins 2018). The tobacco industry has also deliberately sought to expand into new markets in the developing world as public health measures in the Global North have started to lead to declining rates of smoking (Saloojee and Dagli 2000).

All in all, the health of every individual in the world is closely bound up with the operation of the global economy—both directly through the things we consume, and indirectly through structuring the environments in which we live and work. While we have made quite remarkable advances, life in the global village has not always proved to be good for our health.

8.4 Access to healthcare

Even those who take the highest possible degree of care over their own health are highly likely at some stage of their lives to need healthcare of one form or another. Yet there are huge global disparities in people's ability to access healthcare—and continuing debates over the best means of providing it to populations (for example, over the appropriate mix of public and private provision). Once again, we find that adopting a GPE lens allows us to more fully understand the possibilities and challenges people face in getting the care they need.

Across the world, healthcare is provided by a varied mix of public and private actors and there is no agreement on the best model of paying for health services. Some countries, like the UK and some other European countries, have health systems that are largely publicly funded from general taxation or national insurance schemes, and that are available to all, free or at low cost at the point of delivery. Elsewhere, as in the USA, healthcare is largely a private industry funded through medical insurance, with a much more limited publicly funded 'safety net' for the uninsured and elderly.

It is certainly the case that healthcare is now a global market. Both multinational and domestic companies operate to provide services in most countries in the world, and have in many ways increased the availability of high-quality—often technologically advanced—healthcare. Through approaches based on New Public Management, even many publicly provided services have attempted to learn from the private sector in an effort to drive greater efficiency and operate in a more 'business-like' manner. In the Global North, private providers are often able to offer more advanced forms of treatment, or in some cases quicker access to services, than over-stretched publicly funded systems. In many poorer countries in the Global South, private providers often offer standards of healthcare comparable to those that are available in wealthier countries, often far beyond what government health providers can manage—to those who can afford it.

The direct private provision of services is only one of the ways in which global and national markets impact healthcare. Let's look at two further issues: the global market for healthcare workers (**see Section 8.4.1**) and the role of corporations in developing new drugs and medical technologies (**see Section 8.4.2**).

8.4.1 **The global market for healthcare workers**

The WHO estimates that the world will have a shortage of 18 million health workers by 2030, with most of the shortage being in low- and middle-income countries (WHO n.d.*b*). This shortfall is increasing over time as life expectancy increases and the elderly, who on average have higher care needs, make up a larger proportion of the population. The differences between richer and poorer countries are stark. To take the example of nurses and midwives, data available from the WHO's Global Health Observatory shows that there are six territories in the world that have over 150 nurses/midwives per 10,000 population (Sweden, Monaco, Norway, Switzerland, Iceland, and the United States). Meanwhile, there are four countries in the world with less than two nurses/midwives per 10,000 people (Cameroon, Somalia, Guinea, and Chad) (WHO n.d.*a*).

A similar picture emerges in the data on the number of medical doctors per 10,000 people, with one significant exception: Cuba—a country that has invested significantly in medical training both for its own doctors and those from elsewhere in Latin America—is at the top of the list, with 84 doctors per 10,000 population. Twenty-two countries (all on the African continent) have fewer than one.

How can we explain these disparities? A country's overall wealth, and its consequent ability to invest in training and employing health workers, is clearly a huge factor. The Cuban example, however, shows that government priorities play a big part, and that even relatively poor countries can, with sufficient investment, significantly improve their health workforce (Kirk 2015). Global training capacity for health workers is notably insufficient and unevenly distributed. It is probably also relevant that 70 per cent of the health workforce globally are women (would we see the same levels of underinvestment in training if it were 70 per cent male?). But also important is health worker migration, as poorer countries are subject to a 'brain drain' of skilled and trained health professionals moving to take up positions in health systems in the Global North.

The ethics of this global market in highly trained (and often highly mobile) health workers are complex. On the individual level, the factors that would encourage a health worker to seek employment overseas are immediately obvious, and most of us would probably make the same choice: better wages and employment conditions, better resourced healthcare facilities, and better opportunities outside of work (such as access to high-quality education for a health worker's dependants) have all been found to correlate with health worker destination choices (Botezat and Ramos 2020). The benefits for the health systems in which they work are also clearly enormous. Yet, the effects that outward migration has on the health systems (and, by extension, the health of populations) that those workers leave behind are profound and raise real issues of global justice (Gostin 2008).

8.4.2 The global market for pharmaceuticals and medical technologies

Another global market—in pharmaceuticals and other medical products—has a similarly profound impact on the ability of people around the world to get effective treatment for their health conditions. Advances in medical technologies over the last 100 years have been spectacular, with new drugs, diagnostic techniques, surgical procedures, and much more playing a large part in reducing the burden of illness and extending lives around the world. Both private companies and publicly funded research institutions have played important roles in the research and development that has underpinned this revolution in healthcare.

Yet, the benefits of those discoveries have not always been equitably shared among those in need of them. Here we will focus on pharmaceuticals, but it is just one example of a much wider range of medical products, including diagnostic tests and advanced medical equipment.

The global pharmaceutical industry is dominated by a handful of so-called 'originator firms' that develop and market new drugs. The process of creating new drugs and getting them through stringent regulatory processes is extremely costly: a 2020 study found that the average cost of bringing a new drug to market is $1.3 billion, although previous studies had put the average much higher, at closer to $3 billion (Wouters, McKee, and Luyten 2020). This means that only extremely large corporations (the vast majority of which are based in Europe, North America, and Japan) generally can bring new drugs to market.

Intellectual property (IP) rules, set out in the WTO's 1994 Agreement on Trade-Related Aspects of Intellectual Property Rights (the TRIPS Agreement), mean that in return for their investment, those firms retain a monopoly on selling the new drug—and, as a result, the ability to set the price for which it will be sold (**see Box 8.2**). Only once a new drug's patent has expired (usually after twenty years) can so-called 'generic' versions be produced by other firms, with the resultant rebalancing of supply and demand often leading to a dramatic lowering of the cost.

This system has obvious implications for the affordability of medicines, but the problem of unequal access in fact starts much earlier in the drug development pipeline. Long before a drug is brought to market and IP rules come into play, decisions are made about the allocation of research and development (R&D) resources. To invest large sums of money in the development of new drugs, firms need to be convinced that there is an economic case for doing so: usually, that there will be a substantial demand for the drug if they succeed in creating it (remember, of course, that a large proportion of drug research efforts—as

Box 8.2: The TRIPS Agreement and the Doha Declaration

The TRIPS Agreement (reached in 1994), which has legal status between all members of the World Trade Organization (currently 164 states and territories), was an attempt to harmonize intellectual property (IP) rules across the globe. It applies not only to medicines and health products, but across a huge range of areas such as copyright on computer software and patents in all fields of technology. The Agreement includes the possibility of enforcement through the WTO dispute settlement mechanism in cases in which a government fails to abide by the terms of the TRIPS Agreement.

Opposition to TRIPS was especially heated in the case of medicines, where the new global rules were seen to be severely limiting the ability of the poor to access life-saving drugs (Ragavan and Vanni 2021). In response, in 2001, the Doha Declaration introduced some new flexibilities into the TRIPS regime, allowing governments in some circumstances to override IP protections for the purposes of protecting public health.

These flexibilities again became a huge global political issue during the Covid-19 pandemic, in which controversy over the global supply of vaccines erupted. With vaccination rates in poorer countries lagging far behind those in richer ones, South Africa and others argued strongly for an emergency waiver of IP rules to allow manufacturers in the Global South to produce vaccines. This was blocked by a coalition of countries with big domestic originator industries (the UK, EU, USA, and Switzerland)—although a more limited compromise agreement was eventually reached in June 2022, eighteen months after the first vaccines came onto the market (Oxfam 2022). The trade politics surrounding vaccines are a notable illustration of the dynamics noted in **Chapter 6**, where you will find discussion of the enduring power inequalities that underpin world trade, and how trade is consistently controlled in the interests of the most powerful rather than mobilized for social good.

many as nine out of ten—fail, and no new product results). Where there are no effective markets—for example, in the case of 'neglected tropical diseases' that largely affect people in poorer regions of the world—there has often been very little incentive to generate any R&D investment at all.

Even where new products to treat a disease do make it to market, there continue to be huge global disparities in access to them. The inability of people living with HIV and AIDS in poor countries to access life-changing medicines became a cause célèbre in the early 2000s (Photo 8.2) (**see Case Study 8.2**). But it was by no means an isolated example. The WHO estimates that nearly 2 billion people have no access to essential medicines—some of which are widely available elsewhere in the world in inexpensive generic versions (WHO 2017: 14). It will be no surprise to learn that the lack of access to medicines disproportionately falls on women, the poor, people with disabilities, and other marginalized groups.

Again, a variety of efforts have been made to try to correct this market failure. Global public–private partnerships such as the Global Fund to Fight AIDS, Tuberculosis and Malaria and Gavi, the Vaccine Alliance have been created in an attempt to ensure that medicines and vaccines are available even in the poorest countries. Largely funded by the wealthy

Case Study 8.2: Access to anti-retroviral medications for people living with HIV and AIDS

First identified in the United States in the early 1980s, by the late 1990s the Human Immunodeficiency Virus (HIV) which causes Acquired Immunodeficiency Syndrome (AIDS) was present in every country in the world, and had reached epidemic proportions across large parts of sub-Saharan Africa. Although data in many countries was still relatively poor, by the year 2000 it was estimated that there were over 34 million people living with HIV/AIDS worldwide, causing close to 3 million deaths per year. 24.5 million of those people lived in sub-Saharan Africa (UNAIDS 2000: 6).

The first AIDS drug to gain regulatory approval was AZT in 1987—a drug that did show some efficacy, although with significant side effects. A breakthrough came in the mid-1990s with the development of new combinations of 'anti-retroviral' (ARV) drugs that came to be known as 'highly active anti-retroviral therapy' (HAART). Although not a cure, these drugs proved to be effective in extending the lives of people living with HIV and reducing the prevalence of opportunistic infections. The major issue was cost: these drug cocktails cost $10,000–$15,000 per patient per year—a sum far in excess of what was affordable for health systems in the Global South in particular, and impossible for most people to cover through out-of-pocket expenditure.

A major impediment to reducing the cost of anti-retrovirals was the TRIPS agreement which had come into force in 1995 and, for the first time, set global standards for patent protection that required WTO member states to introduce twenty-year patent protections on medicines

Photo 8.2 People get tested for HIV at a hospital in Jakarta; testing is the gateway to treatment and support

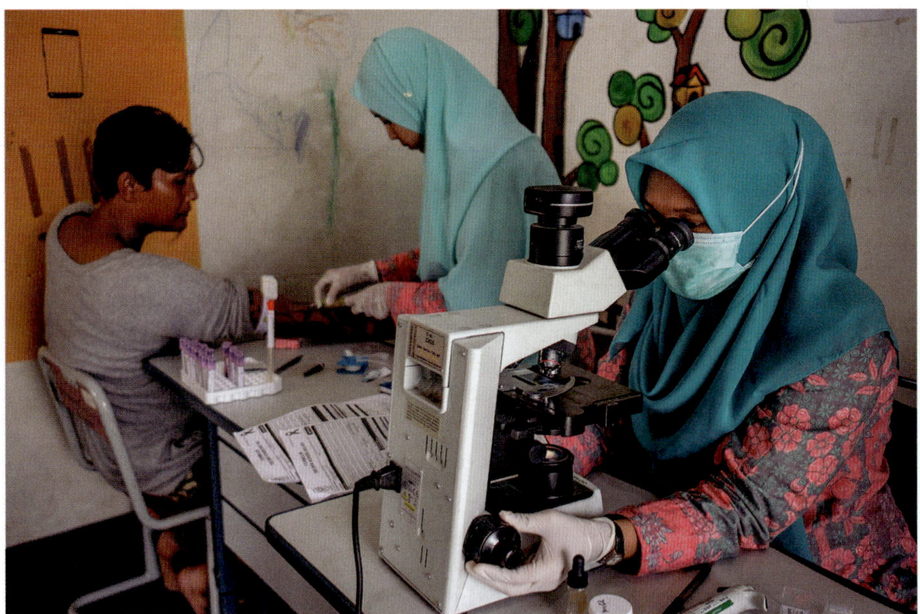

Source: The Global Fund / Jiro Ose.

(see Box 8.2). This meant that AIDS drugs could only be produced by the firms that had developed them—indeed, it was widely argued that, without strong patent protections, the investment needed would never have been made. Yet, while those firms did agree to price reductions through programmes brokered by the WHO and others, there was no opportunity for generic producers to enter the market with lower-cost versions. Gradually, this began to change.

The Indian company Cipla was the first generics manufacturer to enter the market. After publicly offering to produce a triple-drug cocktail for Médecins sans Frontières for $1 per patient per day (hugely below the cost of these drugs from the originator firms), the pharmaceutical industry's efforts to block this on the basis that it violated their patents led to a public relations catastrophe, and ultimately an agreement that they would waive their intellectual property rights on these particular drugs (Roemer-Mahler 2013).

Even though the entry of generics rapidly reduced the cost of ARVs, the scale of the pandemic meant that universal access to ARVs for those who needed them remained far in the future. Even at the lower cost, governments were not managing to provide them for all. New international efforts emerged to finance global access. One of the most significant was the Global Fund to Fight AIDS, Tuberculosis and Malaria, which received financial donations from donor countries (largely G7 members) and used these to fund countries to implement programmes in prevention, treatment, and care. Another large initiative was the United States' President's Emergency Plan for AIDS Relief (PEPFAR), the largest bilateral health programme of all time which, as of the end of 2021, claims to have invested over $100 billion and saved over 20 million lives (HIV.gov 2021).

In many ways, these initiatives have been transformative. By 2020, 27.4 million people were taking anti-retroviral therapies, compared to 7.8 million in 2010 (UNAIDS 2021). Yet, there is still a long way to go to achieve the global commitment to universal access to these medicines for all those who need them.

Questions

1 Should everyone in the world have the right to access the medicines they need? How could such a right be realized?
2 How could pharmaceutical innovation be incentivized in a way that does not make products unaffordable for the poor?

G7 countries and philanthropic donors such as the Bill & Melinda Gates Foundation, the Global Fund and Gavi have made huge strides in improving access. But they have done so largely through a charity-based model which does not disrupt the dominant private, for-profit nature of drug development.

8.5 **How can we improve global health?**

How can we improve the health of people around the world and reduce the huge health inequalities that exist both within and between countries? You will now understand that this is a difficult task given that health is so closely bound up with a much wider set of social, economic, and environmental issues, and that a wide variety of political and corporate interests can stymie action. How, theoretically, can we best understand these challenges? How might the variety of orthodox and more critical approaches introduced in **Chapter 3** lead us to think differently about problems and solutions in global health? What new light can a focus on 'everyday GPE' shed on the political and economic determinants of health and illness?

In this section, we will examine the dominant global approaches to improving health over the last three decades and some of their shortcomings. But first, it is worth thinking about why governments should care about health beyond their borders, given that we might think their primary responsibility is to their own citizens.

There are three key reasons—each of which might lead to different types of efforts to improve the health of people around the world. The first are what might be called the 'overspill' consequences of health crises around the world—most vividly seen in the case of infectious diseases that cross international borders to become wider threats to the world. Governments in the Global North in particular have increasingly come to see such disease events as national security threats. 'Lessons learned' reports following successive disease outbreaks have pointed to investing in health globally as a priority action for preventing or mitigating the transnational threat of new pandemics (see, e.g., Moon et al. 2015).

A second reason is the promotion of international development. High-profile economists such as Jeffrey Sachs have been arguing since the late 1990s that there is a positive relationship between health improvements and wider economic development, and the report of the WHO's Commission on Macroeconomics and Health (which Sachs chaired) became highly influential in policy circles (Commission on Macroeconomics and Health 2001). As populations get healthier, the logic goes, they become more productive, wealthier, and in turn health improves again. The Sachs commission argued that investing in health can kickstart a virtuous circle of poverty reduction and health improvement—and that those countries with an interest in expanding global markets therefore should see investing in health worldwide as a matter of enlightened self-interest. In no small part as a result of such ideas, health has been prominent on the international development agenda in the twenty-first century (seen in both the Millennium Development Goals (MDGs) (2000–15) and the Sustainable Development Goals (SDGs) (2015–30)) and development assistance for health has increased substantially (**see Case Study 14.2**).

A third reason—this time less bound up with conceptions of self-interest—is the humanitarian imperative to address disease and suffering. Most often evident in the case of high-profile events such as epidemics, famine, or natural disasters, both publics and governments have in many cases chosen to respond with humanitarian aid in order to alleviate the health effects of such crises.

All three of these motivations have been visible in the liberal approaches to global health that have predominated in the post-Cold War era. The result has been a huge expansion in the range of global health institutions as new institutions have been created and existing institutions have broadened their remits to include health. New global public–private partnerships have been created to address specific global health problems, as with the Global Fund to Fight AIDS, Tuberculosis and Malaria, and Gavi, the Vaccine Alliance. At the same time, philanthropic donors have once again come to the fore—the most prominent by far being the Bill & Melinda Gates Foundation, which has become a hugely influential actor in global health. Meanwhile, existing institutions such as the World Bank have adopted a new focus on strengthening health systems and responding to diseases such as AIDS, and the UN Security Council has shown an increasing interest in the international security consequences of disease outbreaks.

All this activity and investment has certainly created improvements in health in a number of areas. But have they fundamentally addressed the underlying issues of political economy that cause health inequalities in the first place? Current efforts have been criticized on three principal grounds.

First, in terms of priorities, it has widely been noted that global health efforts have tended to be 'vertical' in orientation, focused on addressing particular high-profile diseases, rather than 'horizontal', which would entail strengthening health systems around the world to allow them to better cope with a whole range of health issues. The result has been that efforts to address many of the everyday health threats faced by the global poor have continued to be under-resourced, with investment focusing on high-profile campaigns such as those against HIV/AIDS that have attracted attention and interest from the world's wealthiest states (Ollila 2005).

Second, it has been argued that global health interventions have too often carried with them uncomfortable echoes of the colonial era. This is unsurprising given that concern in wealthy countries with international health largely arose out of the desire of the colonial powers to manage health risks in the colonies—especially diseases such as malaria which threatened the health of the colonizers and undermined their ability to extract the economic riches of their colonial 'possessions'. Many would argue that, while explicitly racist tropes about an unhygienic and disease-ridden global poor are far less often expressed openly, many of those assumptions persist not far beneath the surface. The result is that countries of the Global South become 'targets' for 'Western intervention'—or at best 'partners' in Western-driven efforts—rather than sovereign actors in their own right (Packard 2016).

Third, while we have seen a rapid expansion of global health institutions and funding, especially since 2000, we have not seen a simultaneous halting of the processes that undermine health. The international expansion of markets for health-damaging products such as high-fat and high-sugar foods and beverages, tobacco, and alcohol have continued. Intellectual property rules have continued to inhibit access to essential medicines (including Covid-19 vaccines) (**see Section 8.4.2**). Health systems in the Global North have continued to rely on importing trained health workers from the Global South (**see Section 8.4.1**). Environmental destruction has continued apace, raising all manner of new health threats.

So, what are the alternatives? Some have identified opportunities for raising more resources for global health efforts. Suggestions have included 'Tobin taxes' on financial transactions, which could raise money to fund health, education, and water-related investments (Stewart 2011), a levy on airline tickets (which was indeed introduced by France) to fund disease programmes (UNITAID 2013), or heavier taxation of those global corporations that damage health (Summan et al. 2020). But while these might make a difference, critics have argued that they would not fundamentally challenge the social, economic, and commercial determinants of health. Some global health justice campaigners have made the case that it is global capitalism itself that is bad for health, and that any real change for the better can only come about if there are much wider changes to the structure of the global political economy (People's Health Movement 2018). So far, however, health has consistently lagged behind economic concerns as a policy priority. Really addressing the huge health inequalities around the world would require this to change.

8.6 Conclusion

This chapter's core message is a simple one: health and illness is determined not only by biology, but by a wide range of political and economic factors. Healthcare systems and services are only one part of what determines our health—and often a much smaller part than we might assume. The list of other factors is almost endless and includes all of the basics of everyday life: the food and drink we consume, the environment in which we live, the work we do, the ways in which we travel, and whether we are subjected to discrimination and disadvantage.

The result of this is that, while investment in good quality and accessible health systems is a vitally important task, improving health and addressing health inequalities requires a broad range of social, political, and economic interventions. This necessitates actions from governments, the private sector, and international actors. Unfortunately, those actions often come into conflict with other political and economic interests and priorities. Although, when surveyed, people consistently rank their physical and psychological health as one of the most important aspects of their quality of life (see, for example, Eurofound 2016), when it comes to policymaking health often finds itself far down the pecking order.

Key Points

- Despite spectacular advances, there are huge inequalities in health in the world today, both within and between countries.
- Improving health requires both prevention and cure: public health efforts to protect and promote the health of populations, and healthcare services that are accessible to all in times of need.
- The social, economic, and commercial determinants of health can best be understood by adopting a GPE lens.
- A GPE framework can also reveal the challenges the world faces in its attempt to achieve universal access to quality healthcare.
- Improving health requires action on all scales: from the local up to the global.

Further Reading

Chigudu, S. (2020), *The Political Life of an Epidemic: Cholera, Crisis and Citizenship in Zimbabwe* (Cambridge: Cambridge University Press). Looking in detail at a major cholera outbreak in Zimbabwe in 2008, Chigudu manages to show both the experiences of those who lived through the epidemic, and the ways in which it was intimately connected with the wider political and economic crisis the country was facing.

Farmer, P. (2001), *Infections and Inequalities: The Modern Plagues*, rev. edn (Berkeley: University of California Press). A classic text in global health, Farmer draws on his extensive experience of delivering healthcare in some of the world's poorest countries, setting these experiences within the wider context of the global political and economic forces that create health inequalities.

Marmot, M. (2015), *The Health Gap: The Challenge of an Unequal World* (London: Bloomsbury). A highly readable and engaging book that shows the ways in which social disadvantage impacts health, both within and between countries.

Prah Ruger, J. (2018), *Global Health Justice and Governance* (Oxford: Oxford University Press). A book that engages both with theoretical ideas on global health justice and with the global governance institutions that might be our best chance of creating a more just world.

Schrecker, T., and Bambra, C. (2015), *How Politics Makes Us Sick: Neoliberal Epidemics* (Basingstoke: Palgrave Macmillan). A trenchant critique of neoliberal capitalism, from two of the leading scholars on the political economy of health.

Chapter 8 Roundtable discussion

Has the Covid-19 global pandemic been a 'great leveller' across countries and societies?

Roundtable 8.1
Opening contribution **Simon Rushton**

Since the 1990s, there has been increasing global concern about the threats posed to health, economies, and societies by so-called 'emerging infectious diseases'—those diseases that are either new in humans or expanding in their range to infect people in previously unaffected parts of the globe. The idea that, in a globalized world, the rapid and widespread transmission of pathogens will be extremely hard to prevent has informed the development of policy efforts around 'global health security' to mitigate their impacts.

Two elements of this global health security discourse have been striking: first, the view that global pandemics are inevitable, and the best we can collectively do is to mitigate their impacts; and second, the idea that this inevitability binds the world together as a 'community of common fate', with rich and poor countries alike at risk and needing to work together for the good of humankind as a whole.

The Covid-19 pandemic—by far the most high-profile health emergency in living memory—has vindicated some of these ideas. This new coronavirus rapidly spread around the world from its apparent origins in Wuhan, China. Within a matter of weeks, there were epidemics ongoing in almost every country of the world. Border controls and domestic measures such as lockdowns were relatively effective in slowing the spread in some countries, but in a global economy it was impossible to keep the virus out.

It was also true that the pandemic affected both richer and poorer countries. In stark contrast to previous health emergencies such as the Ebola outbreaks in West Africa and the Democratic Republic of the Congo in the years preceding Covid-19, this was not an emergency confined to the Global South. Indeed, to the surprise of most people, some of the world's richest countries were most seriously affected and seemed least able to cope.

This globally shared experience, combined with the fact that both rich and poor people within countries were becoming infected, led to the idea that the Covid-19 pandemic was a 'great leveller'. In the UK, for instance, the hospitalization of Prime Minister Boris Johnson with Covid-19 was taken as a sign that everyone was vulnerable, no matter their position in society. 'We are all in this together' became a regularly uttered phrase. A few months later, as vaccines began to be rolled out, a new phrase that sounded equally solidaristic began to be heard: 'No one is safe until we are all safe.'

Neither of these phrases stood up to scrutiny, nor did they reflect the policy decisions that were being made at the time they were uttered. Far from being a great leveller, the pandemic has made national and global inequalities worse than ever. I want to make three main points to substantiate this argument:

First, despite the 'in it together' rhetoric, risk has been highly unequally distributed. On a biological level it is true that anyone can be infected by viruses. But the social and economic determinants of health play a huge part in determining health outcomes. Prime ministers and paupers alike could contract the disease, but their chances of doing so were not equal—and the likelihood of them suffering serious illness or death were similarly uneven. It very quickly became apparent that the elderly and those with pre-existing medical conditions were especially prone to severe disease, and also that some sections of society were more likely than others to become infected in the first place.

This leads to my second point: as the virus spread more widely, some familiar patterns of vulnerability emerged. Let's take the example of employment. That health workers would be more at risk of contracting the virus was obvious, but around the world other 'key workers' and those in insecure jobs also found themselves more vulnerable. The fact that such workers continued to work as normal while many office-based professionals switched to working from home was one obvious factor. But it was not the only one. Those in low-paid or insecure roles, whether they be warehouse workers in the Global North or daily-waged labourers in the Global South, often found that they were unable to adequately protect themselves due to shortages of personal protective equipment or unsafe working conditions, and were often unable to afford to take time off work to self-isolate if they had symptoms. It was no surprise that around the world this meant that risk tended to closely track pre-existing social and economic inequalities. The poor, those from lower castes, and ethnic and religious minoritized groups all found themselves disproportionately likely to become infected and—just as in normal times—found it more difficult to access high-quality treatment if they were infected.

And finally, if these inequalities challenged the 'all in it together' claims, the global distribution of Covid-19 vaccines made a mockery of the idea that 'No one is safe until we are all safe.' Long before Covid-19 vaccines gained regulatory approval, wealthy countries around the world had bought up supplies through contracts that guaranteed they would get doses first—often many times more doses than were needed to cover their entire populations. Many of those same countries fought against any relaxation of intellectual property rules that would allow for vaccines to be produced by other companies, potentially increasing the overall global supply (**see Box 8.2**). Global efforts to ensure vaccine supplies were available around the world through the World Health Organization (WHO)'s COVAX system remained underfunded and unable to purchase the vaccine supplies they needed to achieve their aims. Again, the result was a reinforcing of pre-pandemic inequalities.

Only after everyone in the richest countries had been vaccinated could the focus switch to the majority of the world. 'No one else can be safe until we are safe' would have been a more accurate phrase.

Pandemics reveal the societies that we are, and cruelly expose the stories we tell ourselves about the societies we think we should be.

Roundtable 8.2
Response **Susan K. Sell**

Despite all the talk of how 'we are all in this together', the Covid-19 global pandemic is one of the sharpest and most devastating reminders of the deadly inequalities that pervade the global political economy (GPE). Yes, the virus knows no borders. It does not care about class, race, sexual identity, or belief systems. But structural inequality means that we are not all equally vulnerable to this deadly virus.

Simon Rushton offers important insights, especially about the inadequacies of the 'global health security' narrative (**see Roundtable 8.1**). But while I agree with his points, I nevertheless think he underplays the structural power of contemporary capitalism and systemic racism in accounting for the uneven devastation that Covid-19 has brought across communities. This pandemic reflects the concentrated power of capital and vestiges of colonialism that span the globe, but also infiltrate cities in the Global North.

Structural inequality has many dimensions—and can be seen on every level. Internationally, states do not have equal access to life-saving treatments, equipment, and disease-preventing vaccines. Nationally, citizens do not have equal access to protections from the virus. Locally, residents are not equally vulnerable to the virus and its devastating effects.

Internationally, rich countries hoarded vaccines, and some obtained many more doses than they needed to vaccinate their entire populations. Meanwhile, most of the Global South was left to wait for scarce supplies. Vaccine nationalism demonstrated the very real limits of the professed global solidarity around the pandemic. Enthusiasm for booster shots after full vaccination in rich countries raised new ethical concerns when millions around the globe were needlessly dying for want of even a first dose.

International rules protecting intellectual property in the World Trade Organization meant that newly minted 'vaccine billionaires' could restrict access to vaccine technology and know-how, ensuring scarce supplies and huge profits (**see Box 8.2**). Patent protection increases prices and reduces access to medicines, diagnostics, vaccines, medical devices, and personal protective equipment. By restricting the number of potential suppliers to whom vaccine producers were willing to issue licences, producers were responsible for numerous unnecessary deaths. Qualified would-be producers reached out to these firms, but they refused to license them to produce vaccines.

The ability to exclude others from using a firm's intellectual property ensures higher profits for the firm than would be the case in a fully competitive market in which multiple firms had access to that intellectual property. Developing countries fought for a pandemic waiver of intellectual property restrictions at the World Trade Organization, and as debates dragged on many continued to die for lack of vaccines. Furthermore, vaccine producers benefited from massive public funding to develop and produce the vaccines, yet most also enjoyed tremendous private profits, in effect making taxpayers pay twice for vaccines.

States are unequal in their abilities to acquire, produce, and pay for vaccines, treatments, and essential equipment. National health systems are not equal in their capacities to administer and distribute the necessary healthcare and protective measures to keep their citizens safe and well. National hospital capacities are vastly unequal, with even relatively well-resourced and provisioned hospitals overwhelmed by the demand for skilled personnel, intensive care unit (ICU) beds, and ventilators. The New York City hospital system barely coped with the surge in admissions of winter and spring 2020.

Within countries, and even within cities, the virus exploited persistent racial and economic inequalities. In the USA, one of the richest countries in the world, hospital workers in Chicago's inner city were forced to re-use single-use N95 masks for forty-five days (Jaffe and Chen 2020: 138). Some had to wear plastic garbage bags because personal protective equipment and clothing were in short supply. Covid-19 disproportionately killed people in lower socioeconomic areas, often Black, Brown, migrant, and precariously employed, within cities, such as tower blocks in Melbourne and Western Sydney in Australia. In these communities, multiple family members often became infected. The disease spread quickly and easily in crowded apartments.

Covid-19 amplified systemic racism and low socioeconomic status. The US Centers for Disease Control and Prevention (CDC) found that hospital rates for Black people, Native Americans, and Latinos were four times higher than for whites (Fault Lines 2020). These communities have suffered from living in food deserts, where fresh produce is scarce and junk food abundant, in more polluted areas, and at greater distance from health facilities. This has meant that many suffer from underlying health conditions such as diabetes, hypertension, and heart disease. Such conditions have made them disproportionately vulnerable to the virus.

While the language of 'essential workers' implies some exalted or special status, in fact it means those least able to protect themselves from the virus. In many cases, 'essential workers' are risk workers who have no choice but to show up for work and often are not provided with protective equipment on the job. For example, first responders, aged care workers, childcare workers, bus drivers, delivery drivers, agricultural workers, cleaners, supermarket stockers, and Amazon warehouse employees did not have the luxury of taking time off or working from home.

The meat processing industry reflects the structural dynamics of contemporary capitalism. It is highly consolidated, dominated by a handful of global corporations including Cargill, JBS, Smithfield, and Tyson. Since the 1980s this industry has pursued the financialized model of consolidation, 'aimed at increasing profits through efficiency and low wages' (Van der Zee, Levitt, and McSweeney 2020). Some of the most devastating workplace Covid-19 outbreaks occurred in large meat packing plants around the globe. Many of these workers are recent migrants, People of Colour, and undocumented. Crowded working conditions, cramped housing, lack of paid sick leave, and low wages all exacerbated the spread of Covid-19 in these environments. Indeed, Tyson was offering workers $500 bonuses to keep working during plant outbreaks (Van der Zee, Levitt, and McSweeney 2020).

The rhetoric of solidarity rings hollow in the face of this pandemic. Rather than acting as a 'great leveller', it has served as a potent reminder of structural inequality, systemic racism, and the devastating health impacts of contemporary global capitalism.

Roundtable 8.3
Response **Adam J. Ferhani**

In my response, I want to explore the linkages between global health security and national borders, and suggest, in agreement with Simon Rushton in **Roundtable 8.1**, that Covid-19 has been far from a 'great leveller'.

One of the most common expressions in the burgeoning global health literature, to the point of becoming a cliché, is that 'diseases know no borders'. The idea is simple and makes sense: history is replete with instances of pathogens spreading around the world. Think about the Black Death or the 1918 influenza pandemic, frequently known by the misnomer 'Spanish flu'. And many historical methods of attempting to mitigate contagion—the spread of zoonotic, foodborne, and/or emerging infectious diseases—proved so effective that they are still used today. Following the onset of the Black Death in 1348, the Venetian authorities appointed three 'guardians of public health' whose responsibility was to 'detect and exclude ships which had infected people on board' (Delich and Carter 1994: 285). Not only were primitive forms of prevention and surveillance apparent, 1377 saw Venetian authorities introduce exclusionary border controls and quarantine measures for the first time (Delich and Carter 1994: 285; Tognotti 2013).

But owing to ever-increasing global mobility and 'interconnectedness', infectious diseases are now able to spread further and quicker than at any other time in history, and it is all but 'impossible for any state to isolate itself from the global circulation of viruses and other disease-causing microbes' (Ferhani and Rushton 2020: 458).

Given this global interconnectedness—and despite the World Health Organization vehemently advising *against* border controls—states' self-protection through measures at borders should come as no real surprise. However, this reliance on border controls to control the spread of infectious disease outbreaks is deeply problematic. I say this for four key reasons.

First, border controls have generally been regarded as ineffective at keeping (especially respiratory) diseases out of countries and doing little beyond delaying the inevitable.

Second, the International Health Regulations (IHR) are the 'primary international instrument and governance mechanism that guides collective behaviour in the event of a disease outbreak' and were revised in 2005 following the SARS outbreak in 2003 (Davies and Wenham 2020: 1235). Part of the rationale behind the 2005 revision was to discourage non-reporting. Governments tended to keep outbreaks secret due to fear of the economic consequences of travel and trade restrictions that might be imposed on them. The new IHR sought to prevent this by creating a new 'deal': 'openness about outbreaks in exchange for other countries promising not to implement unnecessarily punitive travel and trade restrictions' (Ferhani and Rushton 2020: 465).

Third, it has often been suggested that border closures actually hinder responses to outbreaks as it makes it harder for essential supplies and personnel to enter the country.

Finally, and the crux of this contribution: border restrictions raise significant issues of human rights and civil liberties, including the potential for discriminatory practices at borders and restrictions on free movement that were not justifiable in public health terms (Ferhani and Rushton 2020: 465).

In many respects, the Covid-19 pandemic has followed the historical trajectory of infectious disease control of attempting to prevent the entry of pathogens at national borders. This has been made especially conspicuous with 'traditional' methods such as border controls and quarantine. Yet with Covid-19, something else was also going on—away from national borders—which was no less concerned with 'bordering' and no less exclusionary or discriminatory.

An unusual form of 'bordering' can be seen in the Wuhan evacuations. In early 2020, Wuhan was the epicentre of the outbreak, and—as is common following various kinds of disaster (natural or otherwise)—states arranged flights to evacuate citizens. However, the evacuation flights from Wuhan saw disputes over who could evacuate their citizens (the evacuations required permission from the Chinese government, as Chinese airspace was closed). More importantly for our discussion, these disputes concerned *who was eligible to be evacuated by a particular national government*. Almost invariably, 'governments strictly imposed citizenship requirements to ensure that they only "rescued" their own nationals from Wuhan, and not the nationals of other countries' (Ferhani and Rushton 2020: 465).

Similarly, export bans were introduced to prevent certain commodities from 'getting out' of countries (which, consequently, secured their domestic availability). This unusual form of 'bordering' was especially visible with medical technologies that were vital for providing treatment and care for those with severe symptoms—equipment such as ventilators and personal protective equipment—as well as with altogether more banal products such as face masks, soap, and disinfectant (Ferhani and Rushton 2020: 465).

During the early days of the pandemic, travel restrictions became commonplace. Numerous states imposed bans on arrivals from *all* countries (for example the European Union closed all of its external borders), while a number of states imposed bans on travellers from specific countries. For example, the United States banned arrivals from most European countries and China. While by mid-2022 borders were increasingly open (though some countries still required a period of isolation), the 'openness' of international borders remained largely predicated on Covid-19 vaccination status—automatically excluding those who have chosen to not receive vaccines, and discriminating against those who are unable to receive vaccines.

Covid-19 has seemingly resulted in a reinforcement of traditional 'bordering' practices, as well as the introduction of new, novel, and deeply worrying practices. We have still to see whether these will stick and persist.

Covid-19 has far been far from a 'great leveller'.

Roundtable 8.4
Response **Seye Abimbola**

Nothing prepares you for a pandemic. At the onset of the Covid-19 pandemic, there was a sense in high-income countries that a certain level of solidarity would be essential for a successful response. Even then, solidarity or success meant was vague. But if one thing has been true across human history, it is that all lives have never been deemed equal.

The notions that the Covid-19 pandemic was a 'great leveller', that 'we are all in this together' or that 'no one is safe until we are all safe', were also vague, perhaps inevitably. Were they vague because 'we' referred to a limited group, which was best left unnamed by its members who were declaring solidarity? On the contrary, were they vague because they point to something intangible, a moral advance in human relations? If the latter is true, then I suggest that Simon Rushton's claim that calls to solidarity 'do not stand up to scrutiny' can be only partly true (**see Roundtable 8.1**).

Even if these statements of solidarity may not be fully true—a point I'll come back to—they are not fully false either. But the fact that such declarations of solidarity were made especially by privileged people, groups, and countries deserves attention. Less privileged people, groups, and countries were instead asking—sometimes pleading—for solidarity. In what seems like an enduring historical pattern, some were declaring or faking solidarity, while others were demanding or wishing for it.

The history of equity in health has been one about relations between the privileged and the disadvantaged, one in which the circle of 'we' has progressively embraced those who were previously excluded, through acts compelled by the threat of force, or devised to serve the needs of the privileged. This has been true from dynastic states, to nation-states, and the current globalized non-state.

Why would a dynastic state ruled by monarchs want to make its subjects believe that 'we are all in this together' or that 'no one is safe until we are all safe'? The dynastic state has ample incentives to ensure that a larger proportion of an otherwise disadvantaged population are brought into the circle of solidarity. But far from being a 'great leveller', such solidarity is content to leave the large mass of people behind, bringing within its orbit only people who can serve the interests of the monarchy or an expansionist dynastic state.

In nation states, people who would have been subjects in a dynastic state are now citizens. Powered by a narrative about rights, there is a social contract between the state and its citizens. Sovereignty is invested in citizens, and so more people join the circle of solidarity. But the wealthy, bourgeois class is still more equal than others, as the saying goes. Women, ethnic minorities, immigrants, enslaved people, disabled people, Indigenous people in colonized territories, and others on the margins of society remain excluded. Threats of uprising by the growing working class compel the expansion of solidarity to more citizens. Even then, such expansions serve to preserve the order that placed the new wealthy class on top.

A globalized world imposes its own need to expand the circle of solidarity. Epidemics easily become global; they become pandemics. Even then, solidarity is local before it is global. Solidarity begins at home, and hardly kicks in until the disease, like the working class, threatens the privileged. Enter Covid-19, and HIV/AIDS before it. When does an outbreak elsewhere trigger a solidarity response at home? Is there still a 'we' when only the disadvantaged are affected? Does a pandemic teach moral lessons? Long before there was a vaccine for Covid-19, the urgent need for global solidarity was clear to those who remember the fight to ensure that people with HIV in low- and middle-income countries have access to anti-retroviral drugs—the fight to waive intellectual property rights and to create new financing mechanisms (**see Case Study 8.2**).

These were inadequate solutions for HIV/AIDS, but the early anticipation and similar action for Covid-19 suggests a moral shift. That pre-emptive considerations for global solidarity kicked in much earlier in the Covid-19 timeline compared to HIV/AIDS perhaps says something about how far humanity has come. So far, expanding the circle of solidarity has required proximity and a sense of direct threat to privileged people, groups, and countries. But in a globalized world, the privileged can be diffuse and distant. The global power of distant headquartered corporations or the legislature of foreign governments is far less visible, as are the forces they wield—capitalism and coloniality among them. The threats to health and equity provoked by their action and position can be so indirect, they often seem insignificant. But they are significant.

To expand the circle of solidarity, we'd have to name and confront those diffuse people and forces. What's more, it requires a moral shift that recognizes that just as enslavement damages the slaveholder, privilege damages the privileged when it is wrought from the suffering of others. The privileged and the disadvantaged are inevitably yoked.

So, this is a glass-half-full kind of response. Simon Rushton is right to argue that the Covid-19 pandemic reinforced old inequities—the argument speaks to a physical reality. But that is not the entire story. There was also the reality of a shift in the moral landscape, say, from the HIV/AIDS response to the Covid-19 response. What we need to tackle pandemics, health inequities, and climate change is the same—a solidarity that recognizes that within and across states, our destinies are inextricably linked, just as human health is linked to the health of the planet. We must learn to see one another and the consequences of our actions and inactions clearly, no matter the distance, whether physical, social, or temporal.

If humanity has a future, what 'we' means, that circle of solidarity, must include all of us. We may ask why it takes so long for the circle of solidarity to include all of humanity. But we may also draw attention to how far we've come. We mustn't do one without the other.

Over to you . . .

1 You have heard a range of arguments in the **Chapter 8 Roundtable** about how Covid-19 can't be thought to have been a 'great leveller'. Which kinds of existing inequalities do you think were reinforced or worsened by the pandemic? How did this happen? Did the pandemic create new inequalities as well? And what do you think the pandemic tells us in particular about gendered and racialized forms of inequality across the world?

2 Seye Abimbola finds some positive progress in the handling of the Covid-19 pandemic when compared with the handling of the HIV/AIDS crisis in the 1980s and 1990s, demonstrating to his mind the signs of a shift in the moral landscape (**see Roundtable 8.4**). What kinds of evidence can you see of this shift? Do you share his optimism that, albeit slowly and in fits and starts, we can see the signs of a new moral landscape that reflects (or arises from) our globalized world?

3 Rather than 'no one is safe until we are all safe', says Simon Rushton, a more accurate phrase to describe the international politics of the development and distribution of vaccines would be 'no one else can be safe until we are safe' (see Roundtable 8.1). Do you agree? What do you think the story around Covid-19 vaccines tells us about power in the global political economy? What do you think it tells us about the prospects for international cooperation the next time we have a global health emergency or pandemic?

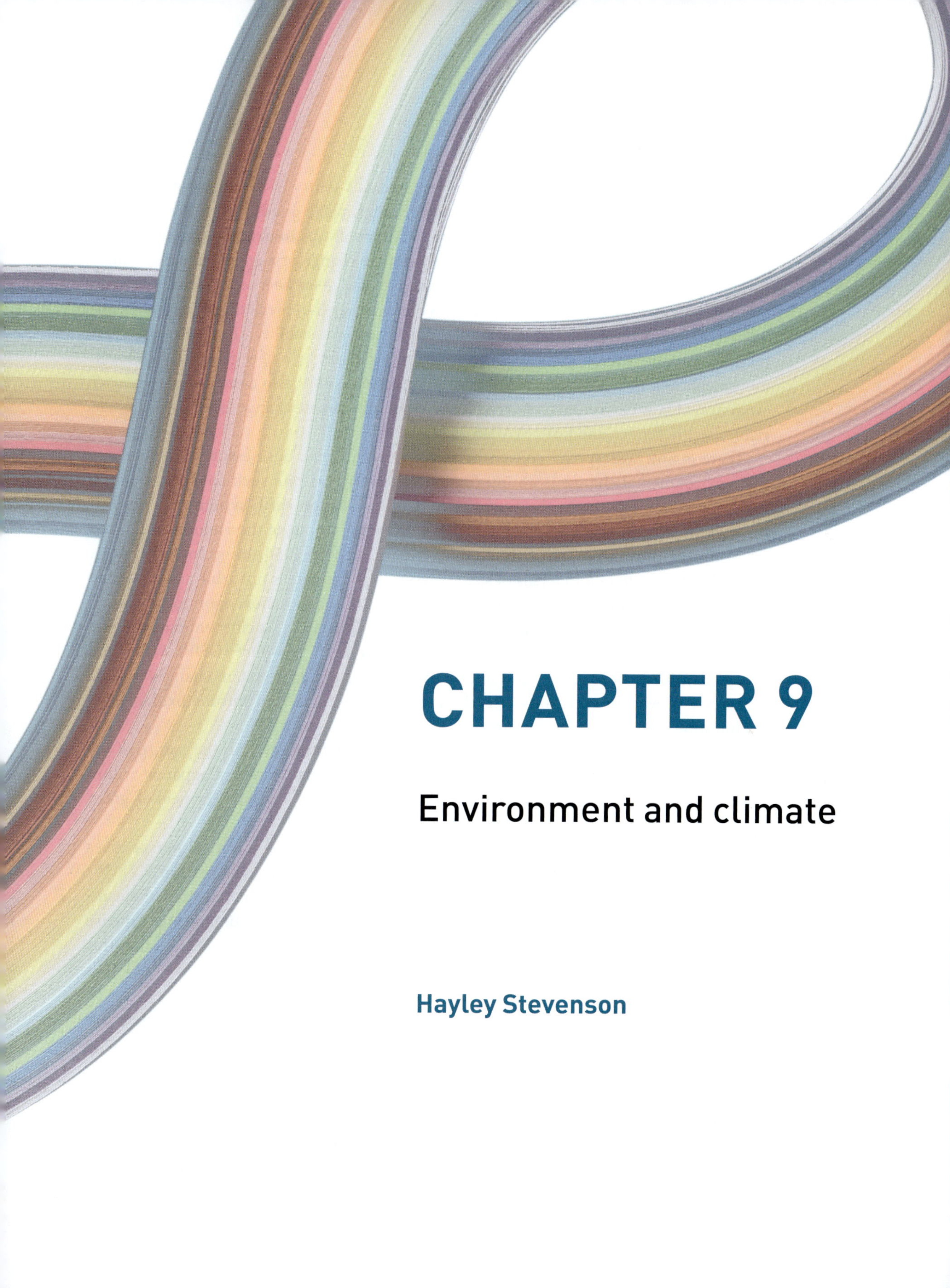

CHAPTER 9

Environment and climate

Hayley Stevenson

9.1 Introduction

Traditionally, the environment has been understood as a source of natural resources available to societies to build infrastructure, produce consumable goods, and fuel economies. Until recently, when environmentalists voiced concern, it was to demand preservation of pristine areas and species. For example, when climate change first appeared on the international political agenda in the 1980s, the image of the polar bear was typically used to motivate action. In the twenty-first century, we have a deeper appreciation of how environmental change undermines human well-being and economic stability. The environment has therefore become a mainstream political concern. Activism by a new generation of social movements and non-governmental organizations (NGOs) has also contributed to greater awareness of how environmental change, and especially climate change, is linked to human rights, health, gender, and justice (Allan 2021).

There is now widespread consensus across governments, business, and civil society that environmental change is an international concern. Despite such consensus, action and cooperation fall short. The extent of human impacts on earth systems has reached the point that scientists warn of an epochal shift taking us out of the Holocene and into the Anthropocene. This 'era of the human' began in about 1950. In geological time, it makes little sense to talk in terms of specific years, but this date is not arbitrary. As we see in **Figure 9.1** and **Figure 9.2**, a 'Great Acceleration' of many socioeconomic and earth-systemic trends began in this period (Steffen et al. 2015: 82). Socioeconomic changes include significant increases in population, gross domestic product (GDP), water and energy use, paper production, and international tourism. Earth-system changes include significant growth in emissions of carbon dioxide, methane, and nitrous oxide, ocean acidification, and marine life capture.

Despite consensus about the importance of sustainability, views on the nature of the problem and appropriate solutions diverge considerably. This is not just apparent within efforts to coordinate international action, but also in scholarly analysis. The field of 'green political economy' is very broad.

In this chapter, you will first be introduced to mainstream and critical perspectives on the relationship between globalization and the environment (**see Section 9.2**). We will see how race and gender are implicated in the distribution of environmental harms, and how clean and safe environments in the Global North often come at the expense of communities in the Global South. A case study of green technology reveals that this asymmetry also characterizes efforts to transition to more sustainable societies (**see Case Study 9.1**).

We then turn to the topic of global governance to see how environmental multilateralism has developed over the past five decades (**see Section 9.3.1**), and the tensions that remain between global rules on trade and the environment (**see Section 9.3.2**). A second case study on clashes between the United States and India in the World Trade Organization (WTO) reveals how tensions between local development priorities and liberal economic norms affect the shift to sustainable energy systems (**see Case Study 9.2**).

Figure 9.1 Socioeconomic trends from 1750 to 2010

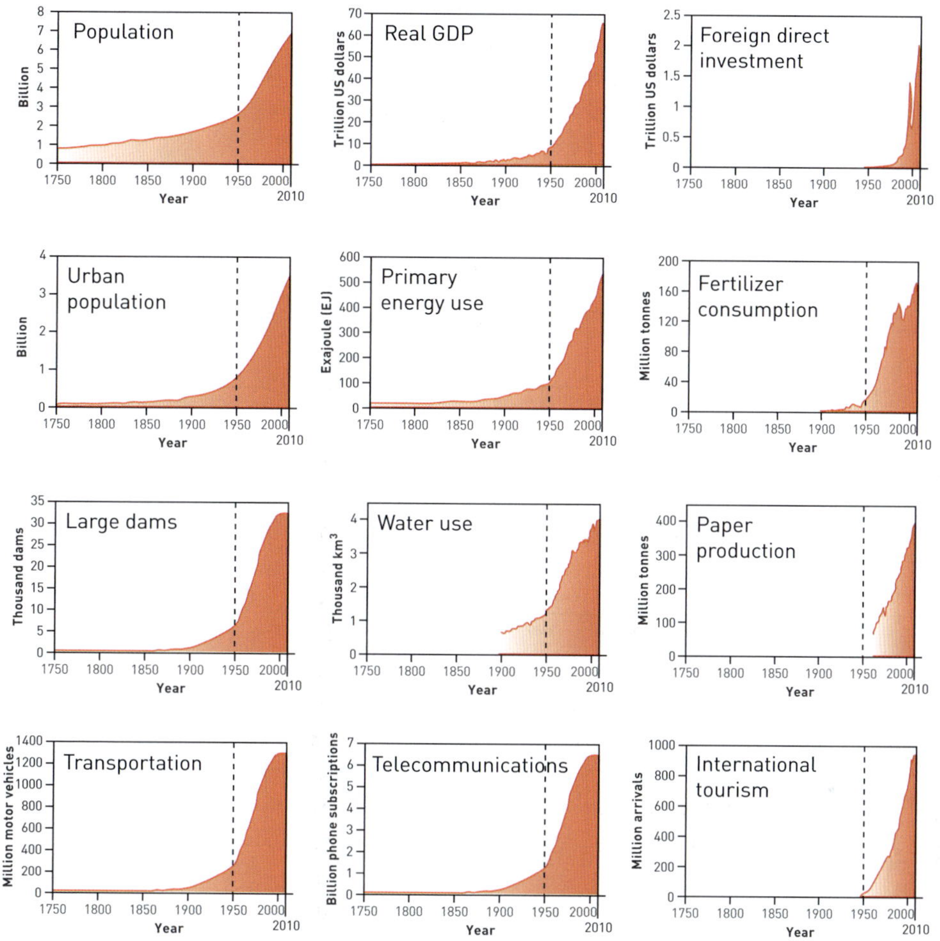

Source: Steffen et al. 2015: 84.

9.2 Perspectives on globalization and the environment

Global environmental problems are political problems. Neither the condition of unsustainability nor discrete environmental problems can be defined in purely objective ways and resolved with purely technical solutions. The solutions proposed depend on how the problem is understood. Some theories offer an optimistic view of the potential to reconcile economic systems with the necessary conditions for environmental sustainability. Others make power a more central concept in their analysis and, in doing so, reveal the winners and losers in both historical and contemporary systems for using and managing the environment.

Figure 9.2 Earth system trends from 1750 to 2010

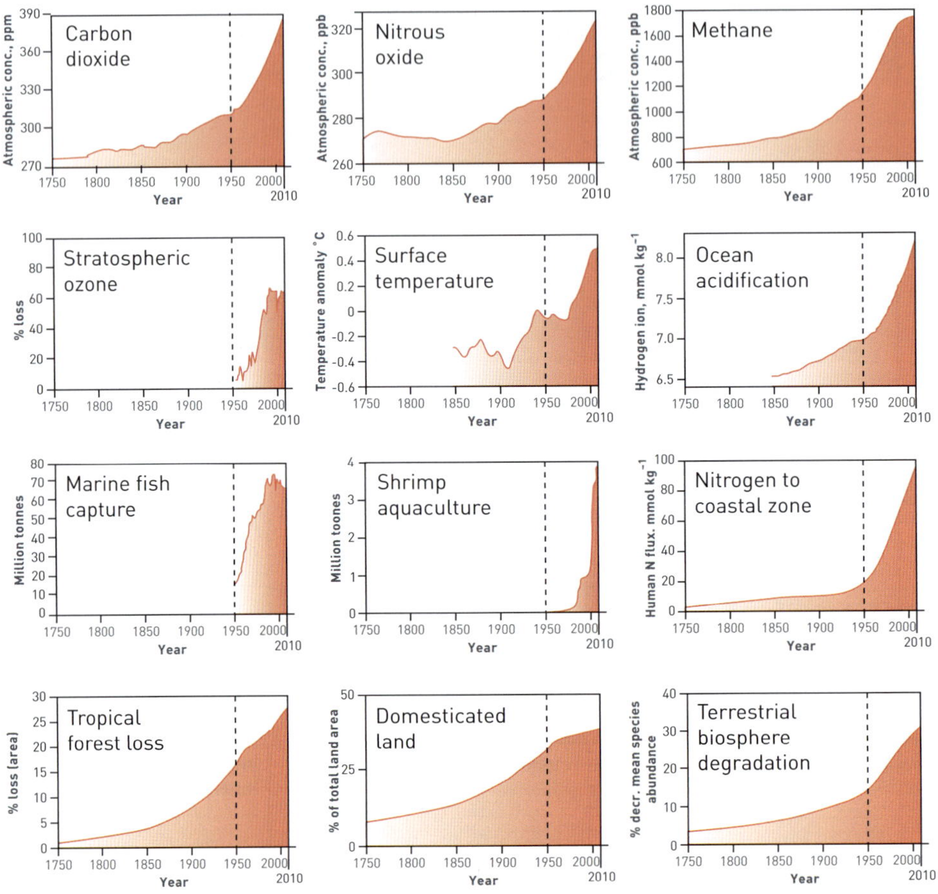

Source: Steffen et al. 2015: 87

9.2.1 Liberal environmentalism

Contemporary global environmental governance is built on the assumptions that continued economic growth is necessary for environmental protection and that the liberal economic order offers the strongest foundation for promoting sustainable economic growth (S. Bernstein 2001). This perspective is informed by several economic theories. Some expand the concept of capital, while others aim to show that capital accumulation is compatible with environmental sustainability.

Traditional economics is based on two forms of accumulated assets: financial and manufactured capital. Environmental economists argue that this narrow understanding overlooks the importance of social capital (families, communities, businesses) and natural capital (renewable and non-renewable resources, seas and forests, and natural systems that regulate the climate) (Porritt 2007: 139). Based on these forms of capital, Hawken, Lovins, and Lovins (1999) describe 'a future in which business and environmental interests increasingly overlap, and in which businesses can better satisfy their customers' needs, increase profits, and help solve environmental problems all at the same time'.

Proponents of sustainable capitalism and the 'green economy' argue that GDP can continue to grow by reinvesting in natural capital, focusing on providing services instead of products, radically increasing resource productivity, and re-using waste as a resource. Such changes are promoted primarily through economic instruments such as taxes, markets, and subsidies. These ideas are also prominent in the idea of 'net zero' (or carbon neutrality), which assumes that excess greenhouse gas emissions can be partly offset by measures that remove emissions from the atmosphere. Such measures may be natural (tree planting) or technological (carbon capture and storage). Despite the considerable uncertainty that surrounds the effectiveness of such measures, this idea now underpins many national climate change goals.

Key Concept: Green economy

These are policies that promote economic growth while minimizing resource use and pollution. Examples include investing in public transport infrastructure, incentivizing compact urban planning, transitioning workers into 'green' sectors, and reforming tax systems to favour 'environmentally friendly' activities.

Optimism is found in observed trends of 'dematerialization', which refers to a reduction in the amount of energy and resources required to produce a good or service. This means that economic growth is 'decoupled' from resource use and pollution. On a global scale, today's global economy is less 'energy-intensive' than in previous times—meaning that we use less energy to produce each unit of GDP. By 2015, many countries were improving the 'energy intensity' of their economies by at least 2 per cent per year (IEA 2016: 13). Unfortunately, in 2020, the International Energy Agency warned that global improvements in efficiency were declining, putting a dent in optimism (IEA 2020).

Environmental economists point to decoupling trends in pollutants as well as resources. The so-called Environmental Kuznets Curve (EKC) shows that environmental quality deteriorates as a country's economy grows but starts to improve when it reaches a certain level of development. This inverted U curve is shown in **Figure 9.3**.

Figure 9.3 shows sulphur dioxide (SO_2), which is emitted from vehicles and many industrial processes, and contributes to respiratory problems in urban populations. American economists introduced the EKC in the 1990s with the aim of quelling fears about the environmental effects of a free trade agreement between the USA and Mexico (Grossman and Krueger 1991, 1994). Expanding economic activity and international markets would not be environmentally detrimental because as countries modernize and grow, they adopt cleaner technologies. They pointed to pollution data in many countries which showed

Figure 9.3 The Environmental Kuznets Curve (EKC)

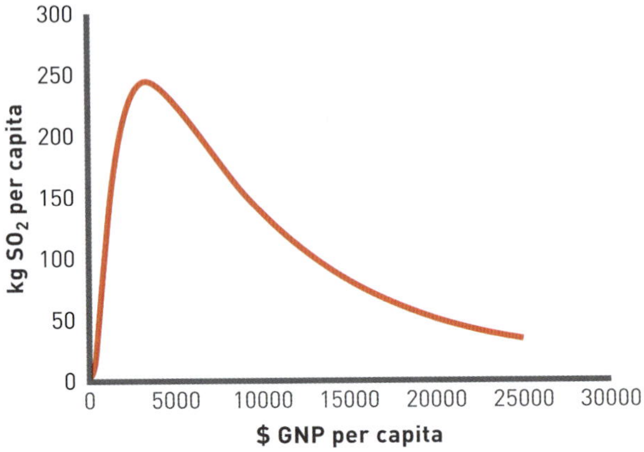

Source: Stern et al. 2006: 1152 (Stern Review: The economics of climate change, https://www.osti.gov/etdeweb/biblio/20838308).

that SO_2 emissions grew at lower levels of development but began to fall at higher levels of development.

Critics dispute these findings (see, e.g., Kaika and Zervas 2013). They show that many pollutants, including greenhouse gas (GHG) emissions, continue rising and are not decoupled from income at any practical level. It appears that an EKC exists for problems that are visible in the short-term and are relatively affordable to address, such as urban air pollution, urban sanitation, and water pollution. But pollution that is not immediately visible, has little or no short-term impact, and is costly to reduce tends to continue rising as incomes rise.

9.2.2 Eco-Marxism

Some scholars question whether the global capitalist system can ever be sustainable (Foster, Clark, and York 2010; Barry 2012). From this perspective, searching for capitalism-compatible solutions to problems like climate change, deforestation, biodiversity loss, and toxic waste will fail because they ignore the role of capitalism in producing and exacerbating these problems. Not only will they fail, but they also generate additional problems, usually for people in distant places and times.

In nineteenth-century Western societies, nature was valued almost exclusively as natural resources. Marx was no exception; his theory is certainly anthropocentric, meaning that it gives primacy to human beings and human interests. Nevertheless, contemporary scholars draw important insights from Marxist theory to explain environmental degradation and its connection to globalization (Foster, Clark, and York 2010; J. Moore 2003).

Marxists see capitalism as a contradictory system. The traditional tension between production and consumption is well known. Less well known is the system's ecological contradiction (Stevenson 2017: 60–68). Materially there is a tension between the planet's natural limits and the limitless material expansion required in a capitalist system. The earth is a 'closed system' that cannot support infinite growth, but capitalism cannot survive without continual growth. When natural resources are used for productive purposes (like fossil fuels for energy) they generate waste or pollution. Biophysical systems may eventually convert this waste into a more useful resource, but these natural processes are out of sync with capitalist productive processes. As a result, capitalism undermines its own 'productive conditions'.

In his critique of industrialized agriculture, Marx observed that capitalism interrupted the natural dynamic processes that connected humans with the earth. Traditional agriculture kept production and consumption in close proximity: crops and natural wastage were returned to the land as fertilizer, thus sustaining its nutrient base and productive capacity. Driven by capitalism's accumulative imperative, industrial agriculture concentrated land ownership, depopulated rural areas, increased the density of urban living, and ultimately created an urban–rural divide that resulted in soil nutrients accumulating as urban waste (Foster, Clark, and York 2010: 77). This is one example of how capitalism undermines its own productive conditions.

In the short- and medium-term, this tension is hidden in two ways. First, technological solutions delay or transfer problems into the future. For example, industrial-scale farms use large amounts of artificial nitrogen fertilizer to compensate for the loss of organic soil nutrients. But nitrogen compounds are released into the atmosphere and into waterways (Foster, Clark, and York 2010: 81–82). Second, the 'core' continues producing wealth by drawing on the resources of the 'periphery', a practice called 'ecological imperialism'. Marxist scholars argue that the pursuit of profit at the 'core' has destroyed social and ecological systems at the 'periphery' for several centuries.

Key Concept: Ecological imperialism

Marxist scholars understand environmental degradation in the context of relations between the 'core' and 'periphery'. Colonial and post-colonial countries have become locked into unequal relations whereby they incur most of the costs of environmental degradation and resource depletion in order to supply raw materials to industrialized countries.

Environmental degradation is not just a consequence of commodity production. It has also been a driver of further expansion and globalization of the capitalist economy. As Jason Moore explains, 'Degradation and relative exhaustion in one region after another were followed by recurrent waves of global expansion aimed at securing fresh supplies of land and labor, and thence to renewed and extended cycles of unsustainable development on a world-scale' (J. Moore 2003: 309). Historically we can see this in commodities such as silver, sugar, and guano (seabird dung, a phosphate- and nitrogen-rich resource which has become emblematic of ecological imperialism). In the nineteenth century, large volumes of guano were transferred from South America to Europe and North America to enrich depleted soils.

Over thousands of years, guano had accumulated to depths of 45 metres on islands off the coast of Peru. But it was exported far more rapidly than it could replenish, and the resource was quickly depleted.

Ecological imperialism is not a purely historical phenomenon. There is a rich literature on contemporary 'ecologically unequal exchange', a practice which allows the Global North to ignore capitalism's ecological contradictions. While mainstream economic theory measures trade flows in monetary terms, ecological economists observe asymmetrical flows of resources by considering biophysical metrics such as raw materials, energy, and ecologically productive space (Hornborg and Martínez-Alier 2016). Such analysis shows that low- and middle-income developing countries tend to export natural resources and commodities to wealthy developed countries. The latter enjoy the benefits of these resources, while the former experience the environmental costs of extraction (the externalities). These costs are not reflected in the prices paid by importing countries.

By tracing resource inputs and contamination at different points along global supply chains, ecological economists present more nuanced pictures of where the ecological contradictions of capitalism may be hidden. As Thomas Wiedmann and Manfred Lenzen explain:

> When production takes place beyond countries' borders, associated impacts are displaced away from the point of consumption. One example is bauxite, which is mined in Australia and processed into raw aluminium in China, which is in turn exported to a German car manufacturer that uses aluminium for the chassis of cars destined for the United States (US) market. Energy used, pollution caused and employment generated by mining in Australia and manufacturing in China and Germany then becomes 'embedded' in the purchase of a car by a US consumer. (2018: 314)

In **Case Study 9.1**, we will see how ecological and economic asymmetries are also present in efforts to transition to more sustainable societies.

Case Study 9.1: Green technology: Lithium mining in the Andes

Sustainable development theories and policies paint diverse visions of the future but share an understanding that green technologies will replace polluting and resource-depleting technologies. The viability of certain technologies is debated but, with the exception of nuclear power, the political-economic and socioecological aspects of green technologies remain almost invisible. Eric Bonds and Liam Downey (2012) point out that green technology supply chains look very similar to traditional, exploitative supply chains: they fit the pattern of unequal ecological exchange that has enriched the Global North at the expense of the Global South for centuries. This is because green technologies rely on metals and minerals that are mined mostly in the Global South, and often in places where governments use or ignore violence to quell resistance, and where multinational corporations pay scant attention to workers' safety.

Paying attention to North–South dynamics should not prevent us from noting the divisions within countries. Illustrative is the case of lithium mining in Chile, where some 30 per cent of global production originates (Photo 9.1). Successive administrations have permitted

Photo 9.1 A lithium mine supervisor inspects lithium-rich brine in the Atacama Desert, Chile

Source: Photo by John Moore/Getty Images.

multinational corporations to mine lithium without conducting full environmental impact assessments. They have rejected proposals to nationalize and industrialize the sector to ensure that greater benefits of this increasingly lucrative resource accrue to the nation and not international firms (Chile 2012; Leiva 2019). In contrast to these broadly neoliberal and nationalist discourses, communities most directly affected by lithium mining have called for a halt on further extraction.

In the Global North, lithium is seen as key to sustainable futures. Due to its capacity to store energy, it is an essential element in the production of rechargeable batteries and electric vehicles. The World Bank estimates lithium production will need to increase by nearly 500 per cent by 2050 to limit global warming to 2° C (Hund et al. 2020: 12). But while it permits more environmentally friendly practices in the Global North, the ecological impacts at sites of extraction are considerable and potentially irreversible. Despite being one of the most arid places on the planet, agricultural production has been possible in the Atacama Desert due to its important groundwater resources. But this has also become the largest site for lithium mining in Chile. Competition from private mining companies in recent years has led to excessive extraction of groundwater, depleting this resource and limiting access for agricultural irrigation (Boddenberg and Mortensen 2020). Every year, mining companies extract 63 billion litres of groundwater (Boddenberg and Mortensen 2020). This mining activity also encroaches on the rights of Indigenous communities, whose collective ownership and use of water is recognized by law (Romero Toledo, Videla, and Gutiérrez 2017). These communities maintain cultural connections with their territory that go beyond its productive use and material value (Gundermann and Göbel 2018).

(*Continued*)

Some affected people are calling for changes to policies that prioritize economic benefits over the protection of ecosystems and local communities (OCMAL 2020). Their demands have found support in the scientific community. In 2018, a group of eminent scientists published the 'Acta de Tarapacá' (Tarapacá Manifesto), which warns that the current rate of water extraction endangers ecosystems, traditional practices, and the viability of future economic activity. The Manifesto calls for a fundamental revaluation of water, recognizing it not as a commodity but as an inalienable human right ('Acta de Tarapacá' 2018). The idea that sustainability requires a shift in consciousness is echoed in the words of Jorge Álvarez Sandón, whose community is affected by lithium mining: 'They came to tell us that the solution was electric cars . . . but . . . that won't save us . . . If all of us consciously respected the earth, we would not have to say that electric cars are going to save the planet' (Boddenberg and Mortensen 2020; translated by the author).

The idea of 'supply chain justice' takes these local voices seriously. It is an idea that connects the choices of consumers with impacts at sites of production to avoid treating those places as 'sacrifice zones' (Hernández 2015). Focusing on justice would force citizens in the Global North to challenge the assumption that lithium production needs to increase by 500 per cent. This would require reducing energy demand, for example by favouring investments in electrified public transit over the promotion of private electric car ownership (Aronoff et al. 2019).

 Watch the video on the online resources to take your understanding of this case study further.

Questions

1 Thinking about the different perspectives presented in **Section 9.2**, how could green technology production be improved?
2 Is greater awareness of the social and environmental impacts of production likely to change consumption patterns?

The concept of ecologically unequal trade captures not just asymmetrical biophysical indicators, but also asymmetrical valuation. The most polluting and resource-intensive points on the supply chain (at the periphery) tend to receive less monetary reward than the cleaner points (at the core). Take the example of motor vehicles consumed in the USA. The USA (where some parts of vehicle production take place) is directly responsible for about half the CO_2 emitted during production. The USA also gains about half the monetary value of total production. China, by contrast, is directly responsible for about 13 per cent of the CO_2 emitted in producing vehicles for US consumers, but only receives about 2 per cent of the monetary value (Prell and Feng 2015: 542). In other words, 'China pollutes substantially more than it gains in value added, and China is . . . sharing the largest proportion of the U.S. overseas emissions for U.S. consumption' (Prell and Feng 2015: 542).

However, the place of China in core–periphery relations has undergone considerable changes in recent years. Recalling Wiedmann and Lenzen's terminology, China exports large amounts of embedded emissions to North America, Europe, and East Asia, but less developed countries in Southeast Asia, South Asia, and Africa now export large amounts of embedded emissions to China.

> ### Key Concept: Embedded emissions
>
> These are the sum of greenhouse gases emitted in the production of a good. When countries calculate their emission reductions, they only count what is produced within their territory, not what is emitted in producing the goods consumed in their territory.

Asymmetrical trade patterns should lead us to question claims made by developed countries that their economic growth has been 'decoupled' from pollution and resource use. This phenomenon has high relevance for climate change because large amounts of GHG emissions are embedded in trade. This means they appear on the emissions inventories of exporting countries and give the misleading impression that importing countries are making greater progress on reducing emissions than is actually the case. For example, the UK claims to show 'evidence of absolute decoupling' because between 1985 and 2016 GDP grew by 70.7 per cent per capita, while carbon dioxide emissions fell by 34.2 per cent (ONS 2019). In recent years the EU has begun to acknowledge that its 'ecological footprint' extends beyond European territory and draws on carbon, water, land, and materials of other regions (Tukker et al. 2016: 171). This means that the goods imported into the EU contain greater quantities of these elements than the goods that the EU exports to other countries.

9.2.3 Environmental justice

A rich body of scholarship that builds on the insights and concepts of eco-Marxism—although it doesn't always explicitly identify with that tradition—is environmental justice. Environmental justice movements emerged in the United States in the 1980s as people became aware that environmental risk was distributed along racial and class-based lines (Bullard 2000). Poor people and racial minorities, including Indigenous communities, have long been disproportionately exposed to environmental risks and degradation relative to the rest of the US population.

This is not limited to the USA. Studies of pollution in London and Delhi, for example, show that low-income residents are more exposed to fine particulate air pollution than average and high-income residents, leaving them at greater risk of respiratory and cardiovascular disease, and shortened lives (Garg 2011; S. Moore 2012). This occurs because firms often choose the 'path of least resistance' when making investment decisions, a path which they have often found in 'economically poor and politically powerless' communities. In the USA, Robert Bullard highlights the primacy of racism over classism because racial segregation results in affluent, middle-income, and poor African Americans living close together and confronting the same environmental threats (Bullard 2000: xv–xvi).

Activists and social movements have played a leading role in advancing understanding of environmental injustice. However, scholars have caught up and begun to explain how race and class shape global environmental politics. Peter Newell explains that race and class are 'relevant to understanding causation (the distribution of benefit from environmental destruction), process (which social groups make these key decisions and through what decision-making structures) and distribution (of hazard and harm)' (Newell 2005: 70).

> ### Key Concept: Environmental injustice
>
> People living in poverty, and racial minorities, are disproportionately exposed to environmental risks and degradation relative to the rest of the population.

Globalization has globalized environmental injustice. Firms often seek the 'path of least resistance' in developing countries because economically deprived communities are perceived as having higher tolerance thresholds for dirty industry that provides jobs and investment. This is not just a question of the Global North and Global South. Regions and countries tend to have their own asymmetries of political and economic power. Indigenous communities in both the Global North and Global South are particularly vulnerable to injustice. Within Europe, asymmetries are evident in Eastern Europe where many agro-food corporations shifted polluting plants following expansion of the EU. While distant consumers and shareholders enjoy the benefits and profits of production, local communities suffer the health and environmental consequences of, for example, industrial pig farming (Juska 2010: 250).

Scholars and activists of environmental injustice often raise concerns that governments and the international community allow some areas to be used as 'sacrifice zones' for national development or to satisfy the demands of distant consumers at least cost. This is visible in the US–Mexican border region where US companies own the majority of *maquiladoras* (foreign-owned factories producing goods for export to the country of ownership). Sara Grineski and Patricia Juárez-Carrillo show that the level of industrial hazard (measured in terms of factory density) is twenty-four times higher in the Mexican city of Ciudad Juarez than in El Paso, just a few kilometres away, on the US side of the border. This means that residents of Ciudad Juarez are disproportionately exposed to a variety of health and environmental hazards. Grineski and Juárez-Carrillo explain:

> This represents a global environmental injustice, as it reflects how unequal political-economic relations between the United States and Mexico have produced divergent trajectories of industrialization. Specifically, deindustrialization in El Paso combined with a maquiladora boom in Ciudad Juarez has resulted in a highly disparate cross-border industrial risk profile. (2012: 181)

Uneven political-economic relations also determine how waste is handled and distributed. National and international inequalities in power and wealth provide 'systematic opportunities and motivations to shift ecological ills onto others rather than to prevent their generation in the first place' (Plumwood 2002: 81). Countries in the Global North have typically 'solved' the problem of excessive and hazardous waste by exporting it to the Global South. Such problem displacement is a classic case of environmental justice (Stevenson 2017: chapter 10). Modern production requires large amounts of chemicals and metals which generate multiple health and environmental hazards. While there are multilateral agreements governing the use and disposal of hazardous substances (such as the Basel Convention), weaknesses and loopholes in these agreements have allowed the North to 'dump' its waste on the 'South' and shift the burden to distant people and places.

Part of the problem is that material for 'recycling' is not counted as waste, allowing considerable volumes of discarded goods to pass under the radar. Another part of the problem is the failure to control illegal waste trade. Much of the illegal trade goes undetected because hazardous substances are either mislabelled or mixed with non-hazardous substances. There are push and pull factors involved. The main factor pushing actors to pursue illicit trade channels is the cost differential: it is more expensive to dispose of hazardous materials in the Global North than in the Global South. Pulling the shipments 'southward' are weak regulations, corruption, and structural disadvantage. Countries in a weaker financial position are more likely to accept the higher levels of risk that hazardous shipments carry, especially given that those individuals who sign off on deliveries are not those who will be exposed to its harmful effects (Stevenson 2017: chapter 10).

The framing of this issue as 'waste dumping' and environmental injustice is not universally accepted. Some commentators suggest that the waste trade is mostly a legal and legitimate form of international trade that supports development and livelihoods in the Global South. But this argument overlooks how economic and political power asymmetries condition what weaker actors are willing to accept as legitimate forms of trade.

As its position has strengthened, China has proven less willing to 'be the dumping ground for the world's recycled waste' (Katz 2019). In 2018, China unexpectedly announced that it would no longer accept imports of plastics and other discarded materials, and over the following year plastic imports fell by 99 per cent (Katz 2019). This move had a drastic impact on the global recycling industry, with exporting countries rapidly searching for alternative trading partners, including with Indonesia, Malaysia, Thailand, and Vietnam (Parker 2018). Local communities in these countries soon began complaining of the toxic fumes produced by burning plastic waste (Schauenberg 2019). The rise of China is affecting where waste ends up, but the dynamics of international environmental injustice remain unchanged insofar as wealthier, high-consuming countries continue displacing their waste onto poorer developing countries.

Scholars are increasingly paying attention to environmental injustices in South–South relations. Chinese and Taiwanese investments attract particular attention (see, for example, Siciliano et al. 2019), and these investments are often interpreted as a form of neocolonialism (Bayo 2011). Mei-Fang Fan, Chih-Ming Chiu, and Leslie Mabon have studied the case of Taiwanese conglomerate Formosa Plastics Group, which constructed a steel mill in Vietnam after Taiwanese authorities raised environmental impact concerns about constructing the plant within their own territory. Anti-Formosa protests broke out in Vietnam when about 100 tonnes of dead fish washed up along the coast in 2016, a disaster which locals linked to the steel mill operations. After initial cover-ups of the firm's responsibility, Formosa 'admitted it had caused the environmental disaster and pledged US\$ 500 million to clean up the environment and compensate the affected people' (Fan, Chiu, and Mabon 2022).

9.2.4 Ecofeminist political economy

Ecofeminism is a broad church. Ecofeminist *political economists* distance themselves from approaches which assume a natural affinity between women and the environment, and instead focus on 'women's position in society, particularly in relation to male-dominated economic systems . . . (and see) a material link between the externalisation and exploitation of women and the externalisation and exploitation of nature' (Mellor 2006: 140). From an ecofeminist perspective, resolving the tensions between globalization and environmental degradation is not just a matter of transitioning to greener technologies but requires acknowledging how current economic systems externalize and exploit the natural world in the same way they externalize and exploit women's lives and work (Mellor 2006, 2017).

Current economic systems value what is marketable. The tasks historically associated with women ('women's work') make marketable activity possible, but traditionally exist outside the market: caring for children and the elderly, domestic work, subsistence work, and community activities (Mellor 2006: 139). These tasks are 'embodied', which means they are directly connected to the human body and its basic needs. They are also 'embedded' in local places, centred around the home. The modern global economy is both disembodied and disembedded. It undervalues its own natural support structures. It is built on the idea of 'economic man', who

> is fit, mobile, able-bodied, unencumbered by domestic or other responsibilities. He is fed and rested. The goods he consumes appear to him as finished products or services and disappear from his view on disposal or dismissal. He has no responsibility for the life-cycle of those goods or services. (Mellor 2006: 143)

Economic processes are disembedded from ecosystems and out of tune with 'biological time', which is based on the knowledge that the body—and the rest of the natural world—has natural limits: it requires rest and care, it becomes sick and takes time to recover, it ages. Failure to recognize and respect biological time leads to depleted resources, species loss, and disrupted ecosystems. It leads to problem displacement (like exporting hazardous waste) and unequal ecological exchange to transcend local limits.

From an ecofeminist perspective, a sustainable economy would be based on the *provisioning* of human needs in ways that respect biological time. As Mellor argues, 'Central to this would be the idea of sufficiency and not the dynamics of the market or the profit-motive' (Mellor 2006: 145–46). There is no single vision of what a provisioning economy would look like. Challenging the neoliberal slogan of 'There Is No Alternative' (TINA), ecofeminist political economists tell us that 'There Are Many Alternatives' (TAMA). What these alternatives would share is a focus not on greening the economy, but on 'sustaining livelihoods to ensure nutrition, ecological balance, clean water, secure housing, gender equality, meaningful and diverse approaches to labour' (Harcourt and Nelson 2015: 10–12).

9.3 Global environmental governance

The complex relationship that we have just seen between globalization and the environment creates unique challenges for the international community. The global scale of many environmental problems means that impacts are global and everyone is ultimately affected. But like most problems in international politics, environmental change generates winners and losers. Many powerful actors in the international system have vested interests in maintaining the unsustainable status quo. The result is tensions between international economic and environmental institutions.

9.3.1 Environmental multilateralism and sustainable development

There is no overarching international environment organization in the sense that we have a World Health Organization (WHO) or WTO. Global environmental governance is highly fragmented across over 1,000 multilateral environmental agreements (MEAs) and across different international institutions. Some argue that this signals a lack of commitment to environmental protection, while others argue that integrating environmental concerns into existing international institutions is more important that centralizing governance in a single organization (Biermann and Bauer 2005).

What the international community does have is the United Nations Environment Programme (UNEP), but its status as a subsidiary organ of the UN General Assembly gives it limited resources and authority. The decision to establish UNEP as a 'light' institution was made in 1972 when states were still getting to grips with the implications of environmental change and did not want to commit too many resources (Ivanova 2010). In 2012, UNEP was upgraded, resulting in an expanded membership (from fifty-eight states to universal membership), an increased budget, and an annual assembly. Nevertheless, its authority still largely remains in the realm of knowledge and research, with no power to make demands, resolve disputes, or enforce international agreements.

Still, environmental concerns have been slowly integrated into international agendas and institutions since 1972. North–South tensions were apparent from the earliest conversations during plans for the 1972 United Nations Conference on the Human Environment. Some developing countries threatened to boycott the conference, fearing that an international environmental agenda would curtail their economic development aspirations. This led to a merging of development and environmental agendas, which eventually produced the concept of sustainable development (Stevenson 2017: chapter 6). Based on three pillars (environmental, social, and economic), this concept is defined as 'development that meets the needs of the present without compromising the ability of future generations to meet their own needs' (WCED 1987).

Although many indicators of environmental quality continue to decline, there has been progress towards institutionalizing norms of sustainability in international institutions. Robert Falkner argues that international society has been 'greened': '(o)ver the last century, the ideas and values of global environmentalism have slowly but steadily moved from the margins towards the centre of the international agenda' (2012: 504–05). We can witness this in state-based diplomacy. North–South tensions have not disappeared in international environmental negotiations. Countries in the Global South typically acknowledge the importance of addressing global environmental problems, but they stress their limited capacity and tend to peg their ambition to promises of financial and technological support from the Global North.

Contrarian voices are not entirely absent. Former Brazilian president Jair Bolsonaro, for example, elected in 2019 with an explicitly anti-environmental perspective of development, openly criticized international agreements and boasted about opening up protected territories for production.

Perhaps most visibly, these kinds of positions found a powerful platform with the election of Donald Trump to the presidency of the United States in 2016. Yet environmental multilateralism proved more robust during the Trump administration than many feared. The return to a Democratic administration in 2021 certainly mitigated the damage. Another important factor was the cooperation of many state-level governments within the United States, which make many of the decisions that impact international pollution. When Trump announced the withdrawal of the USA from the Paris Agreement on climate change, leaders across the country assured the international community that 'We Are Still In' and committed to work towards fulfilling the country's GHG emission targets. Other key players, including China and the EU, also remained committed to the Paris Agreement despite the recalcitrance of the USA. Their continued goodwill was aided by a move towards 'bottom-up' global climate change governance, whereby states decide their own level of ambition and only commit to what is politically feasible in their own domestic context. Such flexibility has become an important characteristic of global environmental governance.

We can also see the greening of international society when we look at international economic institutions. This is not to say that norms of environmental protection are given equal standing, nor necessarily harmonized with the core work of these institutions, but there is now an expectation that attention be paid to environmental impact and climate change. The Organization for Economic Co-operation and Development (OECD) has embraced the concept of green growth; the World Bank has adopted social and environmental safeguards and placed restrictions on funding for fossil fuel-based projects; and the International Monetary Fund (IMF) has become an advocate of the reduction and removal of fossil fuel subsidies. The Paris Agreement, which aims to limit global warming to 2° C above pre-industrial levels, is now frequently cited in the declarations, strategies, and agendas of economic institutions, including informal groupings like the G20. So, the challenge now is not getting the issue of environmental protection on the agenda, but rather reconciling it with existing priorities and resolving contradictions (Stevenson 2021).

One of the most important expressions of 'environmental mainstreaming' has been the replacement of the Millennium Development Goals (MDGs) with the Sustainable Development Goals (SDGs) in 2015. The MDGs comprised eight goals with the aim of reducing global poverty and improving quality of life. Environmental sustainability constituted one goal. The SDGs, by contrast, integrated sustainability into seventeen objectives and 169 goals (**see Case Study 14.2**). There are signs that these goals have been somewhat incorporated into the work of many international institutions, with the aim of implementing and achieving them by 2030.

> **Key Concept: Sustainable Development Goals (SDGs)**
>
> These are seventeen objectives containing 169 goals adopted by the UN to reduce poverty, improve well-being, tackle climate change, and preserve the environment.

Nevertheless, the fragmentation of environmental governance continues to be a problem. Frank Biermann, Philipp Pattberg, and Harro van Asselt (2009) explain that fragmented governance in itself is not a problem. It can be synergistic, cooperative, or conflictive. But the fragmentation of environmental governance across many institutions tends to result in gaps, duplication, and contradictions in policy and action. There is conflictive fragmentation with the norms and rules of some institutions clashing with those of other institutions. This is evident, for example, in the case of trade and global environmental governance.

9.3.2 Trade and global environmental governance

The relationship between international regimes for trade and environment is characterized by frictions. Existing multilateral and bilateral trade agreements foster the expansion of energy-intensive industries and industrial-scale agriculture. As we saw in **Section 9.2.1**, the mainstream paradigm of liberal environmentalism requires that environmental measures be compatible with the liberal economic system. International trade is, of course, the bedrock of this system.

The 2030 Sustainable Development Agenda identifies trade as key to fulfilling the SDGs. It urges countries to 'Promote a universal, rules-based, open, non-discriminatory and equitable multilateral trading system under the World Trade Organization' (UN 2015). Many environmentalists believe that production and consumption have to be localized for environmental, economic, and social sustainability. International trade is not absent from this vision, but it would have considerable restrictions and regulations to ensure that sustainability is prioritized over profit (see, e.g., Friends of the Earth Europe 2018). These different perspectives on trade and sustainability explain why the same trade agreement can be described by some as 'environmentally conscious' and by others as an 'ecological disaster' (Morin, Dür, and Lechner 2018: 122–23).

In theory, there is considerable scope to 'green' international trade by introducing stronger environmental standards into global value chains and by expanding markets for environmental goods and services. Environmental goods and services are those that prevent or minimize pollution and resource depletion, and repair damage to natural environments, as well as activities that monitor and control environmental change, or enhance the capacity to do so (Eurostat 2020). We can point to some multilateral environmental agreements that contribute to the greening of trade, such as the Convention on International Trade in Endangered Species of Wild Fauna and Flora (CITES), the Montreal Protocol on Substances that Deplete the Stratospheric Ozone Layer, the Convention on Biological Diversity (CBD), and the Basel Convention on the Control of Transboundary Movement of Hazardous Wastes and their Disposal (IISD and UNEP 2014). These agreements restrict and regulate trade in certain goods.

Generally, however, efforts to green trade have stumbled on various obstacles. The basis of international law on climate change, the UN Framework Convention on Climate Change, states that 'Measures taken to combat climate change, including unilateral ones, should not constitute a means of arbitrary or unjustifiable discrimination or a disguised restriction on international trade' (UN 1992: Article 3.5). This reluctance to sacrifice free trade for environmental benefit is common when these two bodies of law are in tension.

The core principle of the international trade regime, as institutionalized in the WTO, and its predecessor, the General Agreement on Tariffs and Trade (GATT), is non-discrimination (**see Section 6.3.1**). This requires that states treat foreign goods and services in the same way as equivalent, or 'like', products in the local market, and that if an advantage is extended to one country it must be extended to all WTO members. States have appealed to this principle to criticize and repeal proposals to impose tariffs on goods that do not meet local environmental standards.

Trade law under the WTO does actually provide exceptions that, in principle, allow states to prioritize environmental protection. According to Article XX, 'WTO members may adopt policy measures that are inconsistent with GATT disciplines, but necessary to protect human, animal or plant life or health (paragraph (b)), or relating to the conservation of exhaustible natural resources (paragraph (g))' (WTO n.d.*b*). But the application of this article is rarely protected in disputes between members of the WTO.

In 1991, for example, Mexico registered a complaint against the USA in a case that became known as the Tuna–Dolphin case. In response to local concerns about the number of dolphins carelessly killed during tuna fishing, the USA decided to ban tuna fish imports from countries whose 'incidental kill ratio' of dolphins was greater than their own. Mexico claimed that this decision violated the principle of non-discrimination and constituted an unjustified restriction on trade. The panel ruled in favour of Mexico, finding that the ban was not justified by Article XX (Ekins and Voituriez 2012: 281). The Tuna–Dolphin case sparked strong environmental campaigns in the United States.

A few years later, another classic case—the Shrimp–Turtle case—raised hopes that the balance of priorities was shifting in favour of environmental protection rather than free trade. India, Malaysia, Pakistan, and Thailand brought a similar complaint against the USA, claiming that a measure to protect sea turtles was being unfairly used to ban shrimp imports from their countries (WTO n.d.*a*). This time, the WTO legal panel found the measures justified on environmental grounds (thereby endorsing the application of Article XX), but ruled against the USA because the ban had been applied to some countries but waived for other countries (thereby violating the principle of non-discrimination) (WTO n.d.*a*). This was perceived as a win for environmentalists. However, in hindsight we can see that its impact was limited because since this time the vast majority of disputes over Article XX have ruled in favour of the complainant, thereby favouring free trade over environmental protection (Moran 2017).

As negotiations have stalled in the WTO (**see Chapter 6**), states have increasingly sought trade liberalization through bilateral and regional agreements. In this arena, we see greater progress in institutionalizing environmental norms; indeed, the vast majority include environmental provisions (Jinnah and Morin 2020). In one study of environmental provisions in trade agreements, Jean-Frédéric Morin, Andreas Dür, and Lisa Lechner found that Article XX-style provisions appear in nearly half of the 630 agreements included in their database. They feature most prominently in North–South agreements (with an average of thirty-two provisions compared to twelve provisions in North–North agreements), and the USA is the most active country in promoting such provisions (Morin, Dür, and Lechner 2018: 127–28). The motives for such activity include placating domestic pressure, protecting the competitiveness of local industry, and exporting domestic environmental norms (Jinnah and Lindsay 2016).

US leadership on trade and environmental provisions is not only evident in the substance of its own trade agreements, but also in its influence on how other countries approach environmental provisions when negotiating preferential trade agreements (PTAs) (Jinnah and Morin 2020: 130). Given the USA's performance in international negotiations on climate change, many observers would baulk at the suggestion of its environmental leadership. Developing countries might look at the data on North–South versus North–North agreements and feel justified in their longstanding fears that environmental norms would be used to their disadvantage. The trade wars launched during the Trump administration had multiple 'environmental casualties', with the price of electric vehicles and solar panels (Photo 9.2) rising significantly (Rauber 2018). The Biden administration is less hostile to environmental regulations but the extent to which this will affect trade relations remains unknown (Ellerbeck 2021). What is clear is that transitions to more sustainable energy

Photo 9.2 **A solar energy plant in Texas, USA**

Source: © iStock/Roschetzky.

systems will be very difficult if the international community fails to resolve tensions between environmental, economic, and development objectives. **Case Study 9.2** provides greater insight into this challenge in the context of trade disputes between the USA and India in the WTO.

Case Study 9.2: Environment–trade tensions: the USA–India solar panels disputes

Environmentalist visions of sustainable economies often stress local production. Shipping is a major source of greenhouse gas emissions and localization can often help to reduce the environmental impact of consumption. Promoting local investment and the creation of 'green jobs' can also make environmental regulations more palatable and appease resistant sectors of society. Fostering the local production of environmental goods and services is also an option for countries in the Global South that need to develop their economies while complying with international environmental agreements.

But such localization clashes with international trade law that has the aim of expanding rather than restricting trade in goods and services. Efforts to establish coherent norms that would facilitate trade in environmental goods and services have stalled in the WTO. Without clear rules, states tend to apply tariffs and non-tariff measures to environmental goods and services in an ad hoc manner. This is particularly concerning for developing countries whose efforts to promote local green industry can be undermined by cheaper imports. Disputes over tariffs on environmental goods and services are also concerning for advocates of a Green Economy and Green New Deal in North America, who stress local job creation and economic development (USA Congress 2019; Ontario 2009).

The challenge of reconciling competing interests of trade, development, and environmental protection is evident in a case of tit-for-tat between the USA and India. In 2010, the Indian government launched the Jawaharlal Nehru National Solar Mission 'to establish India as a global leader in solar energy' (IEA 2018). The USA took issue with the initiative's requirement that solar power developers purchase and use nationally produced solar panels. The USA, under Barack Obama's leadership, complained that this violated WTO rules and discriminated against imported solar cells and modules. While this was true, what was surprising about the complaint was that the USA already had in place its own 'domestic content requirements', including through loans tied to obligations to purchase US-produced solar panels (Kumarankandath 2015). Such 'doublespeak' by the USA provoked retaliation by India (Issac and Menon 2017: 43). After the WTO ruled in favour of the USA in 2015, India filed its own case against the USA. In 2017, the WTO ruled that measures designed to promote the solar power industry in seven USA states were also inconsistent with international trade rules.

For some observers, this is good news all round: domestic content requirements make equipment and installations more expensive, and the taxpayer ultimately foots the bill for such subsidies (Worstall 2016). Others, however, will be concerned that such rulings against local support ultimately harm sustainable transitions in all countries.

Questions

1 Should WTO rules permit 'domestic content requirements' in environmental goods and services sectors?

2 How could global environmental governance be improved to avoid contradictions between trade rules and environmental norms?

9.4 Conclusion

Awareness of the extent of human impact on the earth and its implications for human well-being has never been greater. You have seen in this chapter how scholarship on green political economy and global environmental governance helps us to understand the considerable challenges faced by the international community in addressing environmental change. Some scholars have more optimistic views on the potential for sustainable capitalism. Others are concerned that environmental improvements for some are won at the expense of environmental damage for others. Countries in the Global South have long feared that the global environmental agenda would consolidate inequalities and rob them of opportunities for poverty reduction and economic growth.

Efforts to integrate environmental concerns into the international development agenda (most recently in the Sustainable Development Goals) have somewhat mitigated these concerns. However, tensions between environmental and development priorities remain, and this is further complicated when incompatibilities with trade rules arise. The fragmented nature of global environmental governance has made it difficult to reconcile competing interests. Transitioning towards sustainable societies in the Global North and Global South is one of the most important challenges we face this century.

Key Points

- Environmental degradation and resource depletion undermine human well-being, but environmental harm is unequally distributed across the Global North and South. The distribution of environmental harm is often structured by class, race, and gender.
- Some theories are optimistic about the potential to reconcile economic growth and environmental degradation, while others highlight how progress in some countries comes at the expense of environmental quality in other countries.
- Four key perspectives on globalization and the environment are liberal environmentalism, eco-Marxism, environmental justice, and ecofeminism.
- There is no World Environment Organization and global environmental governance is highly fragmented. Over several decades, the international community has sought to integrate environmental concerns into economic and development agendas, but tensions between rules and priorities remain.
- The relationship between international regimes for trade and environment is characterized by frictions. In theory, there is considerable scope to 'green' international trade, but often efforts to green trade have stumbled on various obstacles.

Further Reading

Clark, D. B. (2018), 'Why Is China Treating North Carolina Like the Developing World?' *Rolling Stone*, 19 March, www.rollingstone.com/politics/politics-news/why-is-china-treating-north-carolina-like-the-developing-world-122892/. A thought-provoking essay about the changing position of China in patterns of environmental injustice.

Gupta, J. (2014), *The History of Global Climate Governance* (Cambridge: Cambridge University Press). Provides important historical context for understanding how international climate change negotiations have evolved over several decades.

Harcourt, W., and Nelson, I. L. (eds) (2015), *Practicing Feminist Political Ecologies* (London: Zed Books). An excellent collection of contributions from academics and activists that reveals the diversity of feminist perspectives on environmental problems and strategies.

Newell, P. (2021), 'Race and the Politics of Energy Transitions', *Energy Research & Social Science* 71, 101839. Calls on scholars and students of sustainability transitions to recognize the racialized foundations of modern energy systems.

Nixon, R. (2011), *Slow Violence and the Environmentalism of the Poor* (Cambridge, MA: Harvard University Press). An extraordinary book that engages the voices of writer-activists to expose how environmental impacts often unfold slowly and invisibly, and disproportionately burden poor and disempowered people.

Stevenson, H. (2021), 'Reforming Global Climate Governance in an Age of Bullshit', *Globalizations* 18(1): 86–102. Highlights the extent of insincerity and indifference to truth in contemporary global climate change governance.

Zografos, C., and Robbins, P. (2020), 'Green Sacrifice Zones, or Why a Green New Deal Cannot Ignore the Cost Shifts of Just Transitions', *One Earth* 3(5): 543–46. A short text that highlights the importance of making justice a foundational element of strategies for transitioning to sustainable economies.

Chapter 9 Roundtable discussion

Is responsible consumption the solution to the environmental crisis?

Roundtable 9.1
Opening contribution **Hayley Stevenson**

From time to time, a familiar debate plays out in the Twittersphere. It has become the chicken-and-egg conundrum of environmental politics. Which comes first: individual responsibility or collective action?

Michael Maniates was one of the first to raise concerns about the 'individualization of responsibility', doubting that 'knotty issues of consumption, consumerism, power, and responsibility can be resolved neatly and cleanly through enlightened, uncoordinated consumer choice' (2002: 45). But what could possibly be wrong with comparing tissue brands, or the carbon footprints of tofu and T-bone steaks?

It might be a simple question of time. Every action has opportunity costs. An hour spent pondering an individual purchase is an hour not spent on democratic action to demand better environmental regulation. But it is also a question of how different actions engage our 'environmental imagination' (Dowie 1996: 7).

Some actions encourage us to adopt a consumer rationality (thinking in terms of what benefits us privately and individually) and other actions encourage us to adopt a citizen rationality (thinking in terms of what benefits society collectively). Thinking as consumers, we may resist the option of spending 20 per cent more on sustainably produced paper. Thinking as citizens, we may support regulation to ban paper production from virgin rainforests, even if this raises prices by 20 per cent. Our individual purchases cannot signal this preference for regulation—only collective and democratic action can do that.

Those who defend the importance of individual responsibility point out that individual and collective action are not mutually exclusive. We can consider individual habits without 'depoliticizing' environmental problems. In other words, we can think and act as consumers *and* citizens. Indeed, evidence suggests that individuals who engage in environmentally responsible consumption see this action as part of 'a larger repertoire of strategies and actions oriented toward social change' (Willis and Schor 2012: 161).

But even if we accept the argument that individual action and collective action are mutually supportive, there are some constraints that we ought to recognize. Optimism in responsible consumption is based on the idea of 'consumer sovereignty': power lies in the hands of consumers because, if demand for environmentally damaging goods drops, the production of such goods will drop. However, although many of us may have good intentions to be responsible consumers, many forces affect our decisions and actions.

Our capacity to engage in responsible consumption is limited by *incomplete* information, *manipulated* information, and *unnecessary* information.

Incomplete information: When economists talk of 'bounded rationality' they are acknowledging that decisions are always made on the basis of incomplete information. Many of the goods purchased by the typical Western consumer have complex production chains. Understanding the environmental implications of each potential purchase is hardly straightforward. Reducing consumption is the simplest option, but how do we make decisions about the food, clothing, and gadgets that we do wish to purchase?

We may consider the carbon emitted in transporting tomatoes from Málaga to Manchester, and on the basis of these 'food miles' decide to purchase locally grown tomatoes. But then we would have to consider whether local tomatoes have a higher 'carbon footprint' because they are grown out-of-season in heated facilities.

The task of understanding the impact of each item we consume can become paralysing. Does my soap contain triclosan? How dangerous is the perchloroethylene used to dry clean my coat? Should I be worried about the praseodymium in my smartphone? Were my cornflakes grown with cadmium-based fertilizers? Few people have the information, time, or interest to make such determinations.

Manipulated information: 'Ecolabels' have proliferated in recent years to help consumers make more informed decisions. If we look out for a recognized logo (like a green tick), we can make our purchases with a clear conscience. There are many sincere initiatives, but we must be alert to 'greenwashing', or misleading virtuous statements.

One study of sustainability-related claims found that the majority of large companies are guilty of some form of misrepresentation, ranging from vague language like 'eco-friendly', selective information, and lack of evidence, to outright lies (Pearse 2012; Stevenson 2017: chapter 9).

Unnecessary information: We should not exaggerate our capacity to exercise free will as consumers. Over several decades, the advertising industry has fine-tuned the art of influence. Spectacular sums of money are spent convincing us to engage in excessive consumption that undermines environmental sustainability. In 2020, over \$716 billion was spent globally on advertising (Statista 2021*a*).

Planned obsolescence goes hand-in-hand with advertising in undermining our capacity to be responsible consumers. There is more bang for your advertising buck if the product that fulfils a desire becomes prematurely obsolete, thereby requiring a replacement. If you ask your grandmother how many times her family replaced the home phone when she was growing up, the answer is likely to be never. One phone served its purpose over many years. These days, over 1.5 billion smartphones are sold each year across the world (Statista 2021*b*). A smartphone's average lifespan is just 2–3 years. New phones are continuously produced, while the old ones mostly end up in landfill rather than being recycled, contributing to pollution and depletion of valuable and non-renewable metals.

Confronting the impact of *incomplete*, *manipulated*, and *unnecessary* information on our capacity to consume responsibly ultimately requires us to think as citizens and not as consumers. We cannot resist these forces individually. Creating the conditions that enable responsible consumption will require multiple new policies and regulations. No single collective action will be sufficient, but together they can build momentum.

One example is the growing movement to ban public advertising in cities (Rushton 2020). In 2007, the Brazilian city of São Paulo became the world's first to ban advertisements with its 'Clean City Law'. Some questioned whether banning 'visual pollution' was a misplaced priority given the lack of restrictions on polluting vehicles and industrial waste (Da Silva 2020). Nevertheless, the case inspired actions in other cities. Grenoble became Europe's first ad-free city in 2014 when its Green Party mayor decided to ban public advertising panels and plant trees in their place.

Such movements show that, ultimately, individual action and collective action go hand-in-hand in creating responsible consumption.

Roundtable 9.2
Response Jane Lister

The planet is in crisis. Global environmental problems are pressing and catastrophic. Policy solutions have, so far, failed. Climate change and biodiversity loss are worsening. Interventions have not been strong or fast enough. Consumption is a major contributor to the environmental problem. Exponentially increasing resource extraction is destroying habitats. Globally expanding manufacturing and distribution systems are polluting ecosystems. And run-away consumerism is generating mountains of waste. Scientists warn that we are in the age of the earth's sixth mass extinction and that it is happening faster than projected.

What can be done? Hayley Stevenson argues that individuals acting as both responsible 'consumers' and 'citizens' is important and can be mutually reinforcing, but limited by incomplete, imperfect, and manipulated information which the state must intervene to correct (**see Roundtable 9.1**). In alignment but going beyond Stevenson's argument, I want to contend that while responsible consumption is necessary, it is an insufficient solution to the environmental crisis.

We cannot simply commoditize nature and 'responsibly' shop our way out of the environmental crisis. Solutions will need to go deeper, and go beyond markets. Ultimately, the solution to the environmental crisis will challenge rather than reinforce consumerism, directly protect ecosystems, and transform the systems and values underlying the capitalist paradigm.

Governments have acknowledged the importance of responsible consumption. However, with some exceptions, like regulated health and safety consumer protections, the state has largely handed off environmentally responsible consumption solutions to industry. Corporate social responsibility (CSR) has been the main vehicle for this, covered in more detail in **Section 7.4** and **Section 12.3**. CSR broadly refers to corporations voluntarily adopting environmental and social sustainability measures.

Since the 1990s, CSR has boomed. Under different labels, it has been enabled and encouraged by states and civil society under the neoliberal narrative that markets are more efficient, faster, and more innovative than resource-constrained governments. There are now hundreds of market-led voluntary codes and eco-certification standards. Big-brand retail companies like Walmart and Unilever in particular have embraced CSR and loudly promote their ambition to be 'corporate sustainability leaders'. Companies are incorporating recycled content, redesigning lighter and smaller packaging, and adopting renewable energy. Shoppers are encouraged to look for and purchase the eco-labelled products.

Yet, despite the surge in CSR, global environmental problems are worsening. Why?

Sceptics argue that CSR is a complete fairy tale and 'greenwash'. This is not just in terms of eco-label misrepresentation and failure of commitments, but also the role CSR plays in guarding the business status quo and distracting from stronger regulation.

On the other hand, proponents stress that in the absence of a world government to design, implement, and enforce transnational environmental policy, CSR is a potentially powerful global governance lever. Multinational corporations have the resources and research and development (R&D) capacity to drive changes to producers and consumers through their global supply chains.

Companies' voluntary efforts *are* lessening the environmental intensity of some products and industrial processes, but they are also driving consumerism which places greater rather than less stress on the planet. 'Responsible consumption', as defined by business, is in the interests of business. It is about using environmental sustainability to sell more and to make more profit—what Peter Dauvergne and I refer to as *eco-business* (Dauvergne and Lister 2013). The consequences of CSR are some incremental per unit improvements and efficiency gains, but at the greater cost of worsening global environmental impacts due to the expansive growth of sales and production.

Responsible consumption as a policy solution would be more effective if the aim were to lessen non-essential consumption and if it included redistribution to address the unevenness of consumerism. Wealthy communities around the globe over-consume, while impoverished communities lack basic essential provisioning. Stronger policy would place the regulatory responsibility back in the hands of democratically elected governments that have broader societal goals.

The problem is that states and non-governmental organizations endorse and enable the CSR approach (of encouraging responsible consumption through more consumption), now under the banner of 'green growth'—a presumed win-win policy solution that assumes environmental impact can be decoupled from economic growth through green innovations. So far, though, decoupling is more an ideal ambition than an empirical reality. In fact, the rate of expansive consumptive growth typically far exceeds the incremental environmental improvements. In some cases, the improvements are even spurring a worsening 'rebound effect' of even more household consumption.

The truly effective solution to the environmental crisis will have to be much more transformative (Raworth 2017; Hickel 2020; Jackson 2021). It will need to go beyond consumption to challenge the economic growth imperative of the capitalist paradigm. And it will need to reimagine the economic signposts of success (such as gross domestic product or sales) that we unquestionably accept as measures of societal well-being, progress, and development. In practice, it will constitute a shift in policy emphasis from producing and consuming more and more sustainable goods to embracing de-growth priorities such as avoided extraction, dematerialization and reduced throughput, decarbonization, and a redistribution of resource use to essential provisioning instead of affluent consumerism.

CSR efforts that encourage more responsible consumption will play a role in this respect. But it is unrealistic to expect that corporations including the big brand 'sustainability leaders' would lead this type of disruptive policy that changes the fundamental rules of the game which keep them in business. And to a large degree, states are similarly challenged given the immediate, uncertain impact on jobs and prosperity of any intervention that aims to reduce consumption.

So, how a de-growth policy objective might be practically achieved, to safeguard environmental values and not just business interests, is an essential public policy question and a critical future global governance challenge.

Roundtable 9.3
Response Peter Ferguson

Many of the key barriers to responsible consumption have been noted in Hayley Stevenson's opening comment (**see Roundtable 9.1**). These stem from the limits to informed consumer behaviour imposed by incomplete, manipulated, and unnecessary information. All of these mean that the idea of the rational environmentally conscious consumer—or *green Homo economicus*, upon which all arguments for green consumerism ultimately rest—is largely illusionary. Rather, it is only when we behave not as consumers, but as green citizens, that we can be expected to act rationally in the best interests of both human and non-human nature (Plumwood 2002).

However, even in a world populated by rational green citizens, would consumption patterns and their environmental impact be shaped by our ecologically enlightened political agency, or by broader political and economic structures? If it is the former, perhaps responsible consumption might reduce aggregate environmental degradation. If it is the latter, individual consumer choices, however ecologically enlightened, are unlikely to significantly reduce humanity's impact on the biosphere.

We can think about drivers of this impact by using the equation:

$$I = P \times A \times T$$

where **I** represents environmental *impact*; **P** represents the size of the *population*; **A** represents gross domestic product (GDP) per capita or *affluence*; and **T** represents the level of *technology* deployed in the production process, expressed in terms of the throughput of natural resources and the waste generated per unit of GDP (Eriksson and Andersson 2010). Put simply, in order to lessen environmental impact, one or more of P, A, or T must be reduced.

Let's consider each of these. Take **P** first. Deliberately reducing global population is obviously not an option. Even actively slowing the rate of population growth is practically, let alone morally, fraught. This is especially so because even though the rate of population growth has been declining naturally since the late 1960s (Dorling 2020), the United Nations (2019) predicts that the global population will still increase from 7.9 billion in 2021 to 9.7 billion by 2050. Nevertheless, empowering women to control their own fertility offers numerous social and ecological benefits (Stephenson, Newman, and Mayhew 2010; *The Lancet* 2009).

Then what about **T**? In fact, the rate of technological innovation across many sectors, including fossil fuel-intensive areas such as transport and stationary energy, has declined steadily since the middle of the last century (Bardi 2011; Dorling 2020), which illustrates the limits to purely technological solutions to ecological problems. Unfortunately, similar declines in rates of ecological degradation have not materialized, as average global temperatures and other drivers of environmental destruction such as biodiversity loss continue to increase with alarming rapidity.

This just leaves **A**—affluence—as the only variable that realistically can be manipulated. For this reason, substituting renewable energy for fossil fuel-based energy sources and halting the destruction of biodiversity, while reducing overall levels of resource consumption, are the inescapable prerequisites for reducing humanity's ecological footprint. However, leaving this up to the enlightened choices of individual consumers will not take us very far down this path, for two main reasons.

First, in affluent societies, *consumerism* has replaced *consumption* as the major driver of production and, by extension, ecological degradation. Before the Great Acceleration of economic activity, resource extraction, population growth, and environmental degradation following the Second World War (Steffen et al. 2015), products were largely standardized and developed to become more efficient and/or affordable. The consumption of these products had little to do with the personal identity of consumers, which instead derived primarily from traditional notions of culture and/or class. However, since the Great Acceleration, 'the reversal of the relationship between production and consumption has seen consumption and marketing become the dynamic force of the system' (Hamilton 2010: 572).

For many people today, individual identity is shaped chiefly by the goods they consume, which are characterized by differentiation rather than standardization. This whole wasteful system is fuelled by the easy availability of consumer credit and rapacious marketing, as Hayley Stevenson notes, which seeks to create insatiable *wants* rather than serving fundamental *needs*. Meanwhile, the penetration of market values into almost all aspects of social and cultural life has created the misconception that the only way to reduce ecological degradation is through individual, environmentally conscious consumption decisions (Hamilton 2010).

But while the motives for these choices might be commendable, green consumerism actually constitutes the 'privatization' of responsibility for ecological degradation and the obfuscation of the deep-seated social, economic, and political structures that drive global environmental change. In doing so, it shifts the blame for these dynamics 'from state elites and powerful producer groups to more amorphous culprits like "human nature" or "all of us"' (Maniates 2001: 43).

This points to a second set of barriers to shifting the scale and composition of consumption, which are a consequence of the commitment of most of the world's governments to the pursuit of economic growth. For modern nation-states, growth fuels the imperative of generating sufficient revenue from taxation to finance government functions, from welfare provision to national security, and providing the profitable business conditions demanded by the corporate sector. And by expanding the overall economic pie rather than cutting it into smaller slices, governments can avoid addressing politically intractable issues of how wealth is distributed across societies (Ferguson 2018).

Overcoming all these barriers to more responsible consumption requires us to envisage a world in which we are not defined by consumer choices and nation-states can function without the socioeconomic lubricant of economic growth. In other words, we need to imagine a future that is not structured by consumer capitalism. But this will be no small achievement, because contemporary pro-growth, pro-consumerism economic discourse has attained an almost 'full spectrum' domination of public policy debates (Barry 2012) and become one of the central 'myths' of Western culture (Cato 2012).

Therefore, to rephrase Fredric Jameson's (1994) well-worn aphorism, imagining the end of the world is perhaps easier than imagining the end of consumer capitalism.

Roundtable 9.4
Response **Ana Carolina Evangelista Mauad**

When faced with a problem, most people will try to answer the following questions: 1) who is responsible for this (or who is to blame)? and 2) how can we fix it? It is no different with the urgent environmental crisis that we are facing.

For most of the 1990s, the global debate regarding environmental degradation was focused on the first question. It was important to understand the trajectory that led humanity to put the earth system in danger. Nation-states, together with other key actors such as non-governmental organizations (NGOs), civil society, the private sector, subnational governments, and youth coalitions, debated in multilateral conferences which actors had historically contributed most to environmental degradation. It was concluded that the most industrialized countries had historically contributed most and therefore should be responsible for taking bold actions and bearing the costs of changing path. This idea was evident in the concept of 'common but differentiated responsibilities' in the climate regime (K. O'Neill 2017; Stevenson 2017).

Fast forward to 2022, in a context of rapid environmental degradation in multiple areas—oceans, air, forests, biodiversity—combined with a pandemic. The question of who is to blame is no longer the centre of the debate because it is recognized that we need to solve this crisis to safeguard our existence on this planet. The transition in the climate regime from the logic established by the Kyoto Protocol to the 'nationally determined contributions' (NDCs) logic present in the Paris Accord reflects this change (Falkner 2016). How we fix this environmental mess we all have created is now central and urgent.

Hayley Stevenson offers a provocative argument in response, inviting us to question the role of our individual actions and their potential impact when compared with collective action (**see Roundtable 9.1**). Because environmental problems are complex and interconnected, it is of course very difficult to trace the impact of individual actions at a global scale. However, that is not an excuse to not reflect on our lifestyle choices, once we are informed about the situation and have the means to make changes.

Finding solutions to the environmental crisis in individual or collective action leads us to question the problem of scale, and furthermore the question of responsibility comes back into the debate.

One of the main environmental crises we face today is climate change and, by its nature, it is a crisis in which scale matters. To avoid catastrophic climate change, we need to reduce greenhouse gas emissions to prevent exceeding 1.5–2.0° C warming by the end of the twenty-first century. So, although changing our diet to be less intense in carbon has an important point in terms of moral and social behaviour, it is so small in scale that it cannot make any discernible mark on the direction we're heading in. Therefore, in this case, individual action has a very limited impact in solving the global climate problem, although it may be important as a moral choice depending on one's lifestyle (Wapner and Willoughby 2005; Markowitz and Shariff 2012).

So, does our power to promote change reside only in our social roles as consumers and voters (in democracies)? Of course not. We are social animals, and we learn and change by interacting with others; feeding those interactions with information can be powerful. Information and education are key elements to understand environmental problems and their possible solutions. But what do we do with the knowledge that we have? After knowing the facts, our choices become moral ones, generating endless environmental anxiety, and leading us almost to the point of paralysis, as Hayley Stevenson wryly observes.

Maybe it is not even optimism that drives our sustainable choices as consumers, but the fear of doing something wrong—an internal moral pressure, and indeed sometimes an external one related to our social groups, especially for globalized, urbanized young people.

So, if we want to say that responsible consumption is the key, we have to ask whether we're actually solving the global environmental crisis or just feeding environmental anxiety, especially in young people? Individual and collective actions need, first of all, good quality information to allow us to determine the severity of the problem and its possible solutions, generating the will to change among citizens. Afterwards, the will to change needs to find material conditions for the change to happen. So, individual actions such as biking to work, recycling, and trying meatless Mondays are an important sign that there is awareness of the problem and willingness to change it.

However, without the means to sustain a truly transformative action represented by public policies, these individual actions will get lost, generating frustration and more environmental anxiety. For example, the same São Paulo that banned advertising—as we read in Stevenson's **Roundtable 9.1** contribution—also approved a very ambitious climate law in 2009. But this vision of a more sustainable city was never implemented. More than ten years later, the city of São Paulo still hasn't complied with its 2009 climate regulations and outdoor advertising is once again all over the city (Mauad and Betsill 2019).

In this light, I want to put forward a different response to the question we are debating in the **Chapter 9 Roundtable** and suggest that the most transformative action may instead be connected with political choices, which in democratic regimes take the form of the right to vote into office a candidate and/or party that is committed to addressing the environmental crisis.

To secure environmental change, especially in the less developed regions of the world, it is crucial to foster democracy, education, and rule of law. Bringing the state, the private sector, and civil society back into the debate regarding responsibility, scale, and the urgency to solve our environmental crisis is vital if individual actions are to make any real difference.

So, go and try a less carbon-intensive diet, use more sustainable transportation options, and reduce your waste, but don't forget to get information and promote debates among your community. And most importantly, go and vote.

Over to you . . .

1 All of the contributors to the **Chapter 9 Roundtable** have offered distinctive reflections on the role of consumer responsibility in addressing the environmental injustices produced or exacerbated by globalization. Are you optimistic or pessimistic about the influence of consumers in this space? How achievable do you think a move away from our current system of 'consumer capitalism' is? And can we, as Jane Lister puts it in Roundtable 9.2, 'shop our way out of the environmental crisis' if we make the right choices?

2 You have heard some strong arguments in the **Chapter 9 Roundtable** that sustainable capitalism is a contradiction in terms, and that we have few prospects of moving towards sustainability without fundamental systemic change—in Jane Lister's terms, towards 'de-growth' (see Roundtable 9.2), and in Peter Ferguson's terms, towards the end of consumer capitalism (see Roundtable 9.3). Do you think environmentally sustainable capitalism is an oxymoron, where the two things could never be reconciled, or do you have more confidence that we could achieve sustainability through international cooperation, public policy, political choice, corporate responsibility, and/or consumer choices?

3 Ana Mauad forcefully argues for the importance of political choices made through democratic processes (see Roundtable 9.4). What do you think about the political alternatives on offer in countries or places that you are familiar with? Do we have viable forms of 'green' politics that electorates can choose to vote for? Are the green credentials of parties and politicians real or just window-dressing? And looking back to Hayley Stevenson's discussion in **Section 9.3.1**, how do you account for the electoral popularity of the environmentally destructive politics represented by figures like Donald Trump and Jair Bolsonaro?

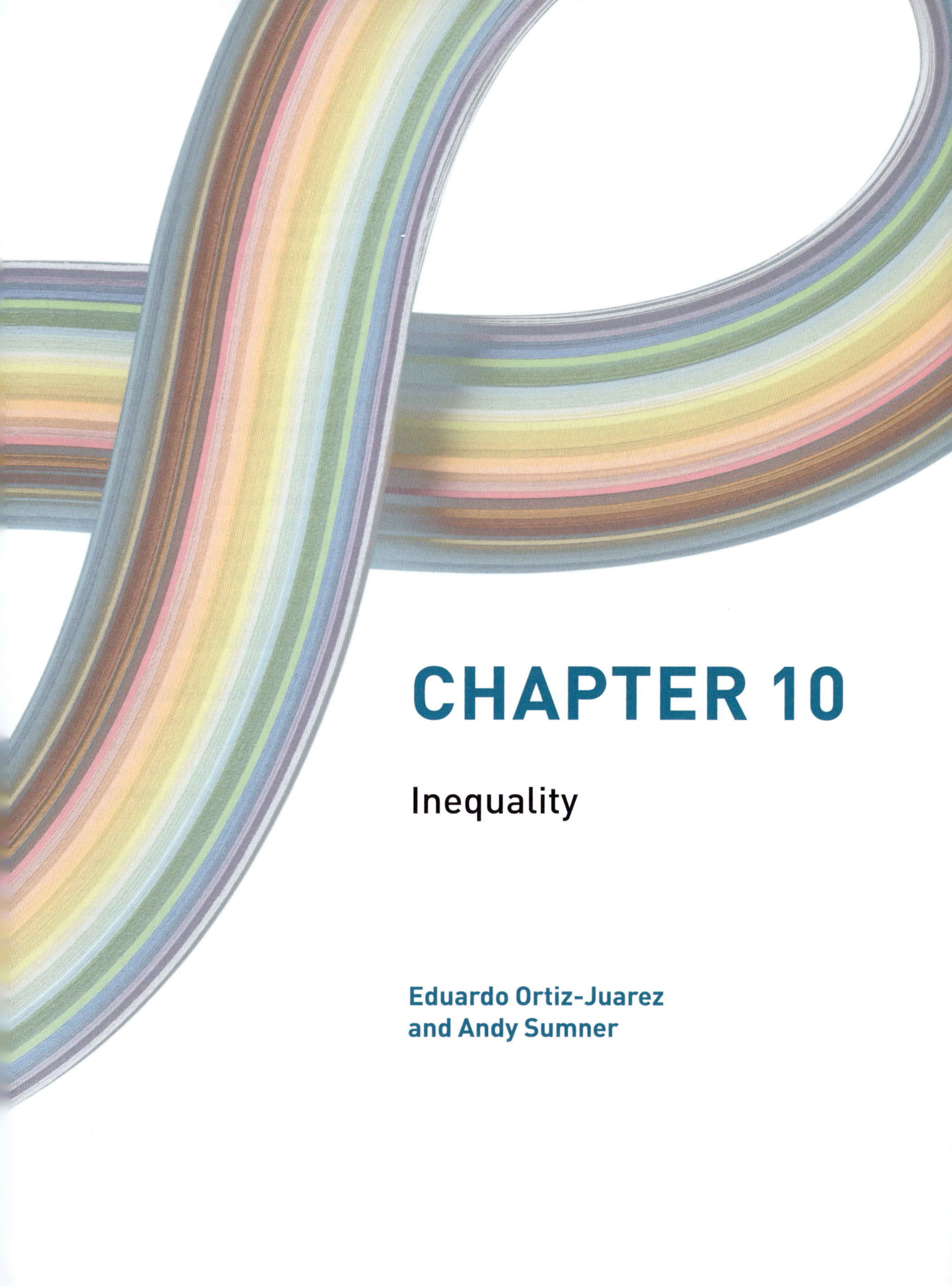
CHAPTER 10
Inequality
Eduardo Ortiz-Juarez
and Andy Sumner

10.1 Introduction

Income inequality has attracted intense interest from the global media, non-governmental organizations (NGOs) like Oxfam International, the United Nations, and political activists around the world, as the coverage of the meeting of the super-rich at the annual World Economic Forum in Davos, Switzerland testifies every year. But what exactly do we mean by income inequality? Income inequality between whom? Is income inequality rising or falling? How is poverty linked to income inequality? Has the Covid-19 pandemic made poverty and inequality worse or simply brought existing structural inequalities between and within countries to the fore?

This chapter is about income inequality—its concepts, measurement, trends, and drivers. Different forms of inequality also matter, as you will see in this chapter and in the **Chapter 10 Roundtable**, and it is often the intersection of various dimensions of inequality which shapes outcomes for people in societies. Note that much of our discussion relates to what has happened since the Cold War. This is largely because available, consistent, better-quality data on the issues at hand is usually available from the late 1980s, though there is some data available from the early 1980s. The end of the Cold War also represents a key juncture in terms of developments in the global political economy and the neoliberal resurgence becoming more evident in economic policy (**see Chapter 4**). Specifically, global production and trade have been radically reshaped by the emergence of global value chains (GVCs, **see Chapter 7** and **Chapter 12**), which play an important role in shaping contemporary income inequality at the national and global levels and reinforcing global inequalities between the rich countries and the Global South.

All of this points to a set of big and important questions for considering income inequality in the global political economy. In **Section 10.2**, we will start with the question of why inequality matters. Then we will discuss international, world, and global inequality in **Section 10.3**; national inequality in **Section 10.4**; and poverty in **Section 10.5**. Finally, in **Section 10.6**, we will sum up the overall story of inequality in the global political economy.

10.2 Why does income inequality matter?

There are intrinsic as well as instrumental reasons for why anyone should care about income inequality. Intrinsically, inequality is concerning since it impedes meritocracy or fairness in life opportunities. The first article of the Universal Declaration of Human Rights (UDHR) asserts: 'All human beings are born free and equal in dignity and rights.' The UDHR's preamble furthermore outlines that 'recognition of the inherent dignity and of the equal and inalienable rights of all members of the human family is the foundation of freedom, justice and peace in the world' (UN 1948).

Two influential thinkers on inequality are John Rawls and John Roemer. In *A Theory of Justice*, Rawls (1971) argued in favour of evening out any 'undeserved' attributes, such as wealth that is inherited and thus not one's own accomplishment. Equalizing the unfair distribution of these factors at birth makes inequality tolerable, according to Rawls, suggesting higher taxes on the rich and inheritance as well as equal access to education. Roemer (1998) in turn established the principles of equal opportunity and non-discrimination in *Equality of Opportunity*. Both principles imply that individuals must be provided—for example, through public intervention—with equal opportunities to achieve positive outcomes, such as high incomes. When opportunities are equalized, income—or rewards in general—should be determined by effort.

Next to the intrinsic rationale, we should also care about high or rising income inequality since both are associated with negative societal outcomes. Inequality of opportunity occurs when factors that cannot be influenced—such as race or gender—shape things like individuals' access to university education. High and rising inequality has been associated with weaker economic growth (Alesina and Rodrik 1994; Deininger and Squire 1998; Ravallion 1998) as well as with ills such as social marginalization or reduced physical and mental health, as Kate Pickett and Richard Wilkinson's (2010) influential *The Spirit Level* outlines in depth. We should care about inequality of opportunity since it implies that people face different life chances through no fault of their own.

Nancy Birdsall (2006) introduces at least three instrumental arguments as to why high or rising income inequality is problematic in developing countries. First, it impedes economic growth by creating unequal opportunities and thus blocking potential. Second, in settings where the government is weak, inequality makes it more challenging to build and sustain government accountability, which in turn increases the likelihood of economic and social policies that hamper growth and poverty reduction. And third, in institutionally fragile settings, inequality weakens the civic and social life that constitutes the backbone of healthy societies by encouraging and enabling effective collective decision-making.

Income differences between countries also have consequences at a global level. For instance, they may contribute to 'brain drain' by encouraging migration from poorer countries to richer ones (**see Chapter 13**), or may lead to the marginalization of developing countries in global decision-making bodies, such as the International Monetary Fund (IMF), where the number of votes is conditional on a country's financial contribution (**see Chapter 14**). You can debate over whether you agree with these arguments.

So, there are compelling intrinsic and instrumental reasons why high or rising income inequality matters. But Anthony B. Atkinson (2005) challenges the widely held belief that high or rising income inequality is inevitable (a belief which originates in interpretations of the oft-cited work of Simon Kuznets (1955)). Some have even argued that inequality is good for societies because it rewards those who work hardest, or that it might eventually benefit the poor since that income and wealth will 'trickle down' to them (see, e.g., Aghion and Bolton 1997).

So, who is correct? Is high or rising income inequality inevitable? To answer this question, we must look at the 'types' of income inequality.

10.3 International, world, or global income inequality

There are three ways to think about income inequality at a global level. These are 'international inequality', 'world inequality', and 'global inequality'.

International inequality is based on comparing the differences in income among the *average* citizen of each country around the world. This is typically done by contrasting gross domestic product (GDP) per capita, a measure that provides a proxy of the living standard enjoyed by the average citizen, at least in economic terms.

World inequality takes population size into account. For instance, China has 1.4 billion inhabitants while Brazil has only 210 million. If we do not take these differences into account, we are using international inequality. If, on the other hand, we weight for population size (so that China is seven times more important than Brazil), this is known as world inequality.

Instead of relying on national averages of countries, *global inequality* assesses income disparities among all individuals across the whole world as if the whole world is considered a single country (Milanovic 2005). This is usually assessed based on household surveys that collect individual incomes rather than on GDP per capita from national accounts. For this survey-based approach to work (relatively) well, individual incomes across countries should be made comparable. This involves a standardization through complex adjustments, although some degree of discrepancy between surveys has to be accepted. Surveys across countries differ in a number of ways. Some collect information on incomes whereas others focus on expenditures. Surveys also differ in their collection frequency, in the sources of income (for example, labour incomes or transfers), in the expenditure items they collect (for example, food and non-food items), or in the magnitude of the *unavoidable* measurement error.

For all three approaches, incomes in each country, typically collected in the national currency, must be converted into a unit that is *common* across countries. Ideally, this unit should allow the cross-country comparison of currencies while being sensitive to the standard of living within each country. This is only possible by collecting detailed information on prices and consumption patterns for the same basket of goods and services in all countries, from which a particular type of exchange rates, known as purchasing power parity (PPP) rates, can be derived. These rates allow the conversion of national currencies into the required common unit, and are indicative of what a country's currency can buy in another country.

The intuition is simple: in 2018 the PPP exchange rate for Brazil was R$2.2 (according to the World Bank's (2022) World Development Indicators), indicating the quantity of *reals* required to buy the *same* amount of goods and services in the country that could be bought with US$1 in the United States (see World Bank 2013). Of course, the use of PPP exchange rates is not free of problems. Perhaps the most evident is the assumption that the list of goods and services included in the common basket is representative of individuals' preferences and behaviours in all countries.

> ## Key Concepts: Ways of thinking about inequality
>
> **International inequality:** This approach is concerned with the differences in average GDP per capita between countries regardless of the size of their population. This is equivalent to saying that each country is represented by its *average* citizen.
>
> **World inequality:** This concept is similar to international inequality but acknowledges that each country has a different share of the total population in the world, thus the differences in per capita GDP matter and should be weighted by population.
>
> **Global inequality:** This is a relatively new idea and measures income differences from household-level data among *all* individuals in the world as if the world was one single country.
>
> **Purchasing power parity (PPP) rates:** These 'exchange' rates allow for the conversion of national currencies into an 'international dollar' and are indicative of what a country's currency can buy in another country (typically the amount of a national currency required to buy the same amount of goods and services that 1 dollar can buy in the US). PPP rates are therefore used to convert GDP per capita, or income amounts, to enable international comparisons of inequality under the concepts of international inequality, world inequality, or global inequality.

10.3.1 Is inequality at a global level rising or falling?

The received wisdom is that inequality has fallen at a global level in the era of neoliberalism since the Cold War. This is a fragile narrative, as it depends on how income inequality is measured at a global level. So, what is measured? Income inequality is usually measured by the 'Gini coefficient' (also called 'Gini index' or simply, 'the Gini'). Since this is not a very intuitive measure, it needs some explanation.

The value of the Gini coefficient can range from 1 (maximum inequality) to 0 (everyone has the same income). The Gini is related to and can be derived from a curve known as the 'Lorenz curve', which depicts the distribution of income across a given population. In South Africa, a society with high inequality, the Gini value was around 0.669 (sometimes also expressed as 66.9) in 2017. In Sweden, a more equal society, the Gini was about 0.287 (sometimes referred to as 28.7) in 2018 (UNU-WIDER 2022). The Gini coefficient may take the individual as the unit of analysis and is based on data from household surveys, which provide information on the total amount of income within a household.

> ## Key Concept: The Gini coefficient
>
> The Gini measure of income inequality is related to the Lorenz curve. This curve indicates the share of total income in a society held by each part of the population ranked from the poorest to the richest. You can see in **Figure 10.1** that the poorest 50 per cent of the population accrue
>
> *(Continued)*

less than 20 per cent of the total income. When there is no inequality, the Gini coefficient is zero and the Lorenz curve will lie on the 45-degree line (also known as the 'equidistribution line'). The more distant the Lorenz curve is from the 45-degree line, the higher the level of inequality. In **Figure 10.1** the Gini coefficient is the ratio of the area A (the area between the 45-degree line and the Lorenz curve) and the total area of the triangle below the 45-degree line (the sum of the areas A and B).

Figure 10.1 **The Lorenz curve**

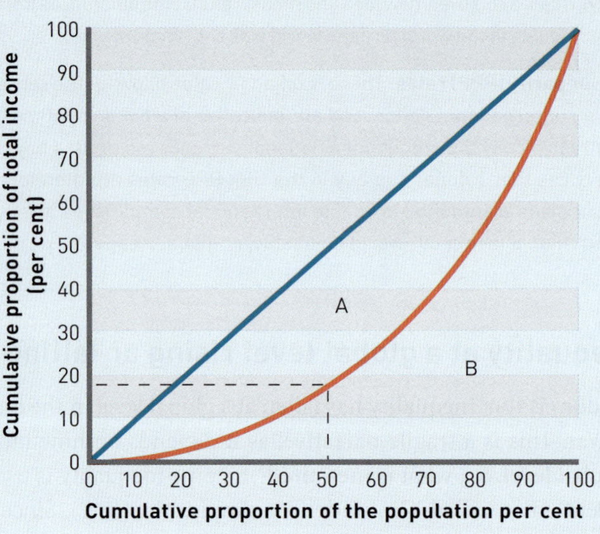

Other measures of income inequality are available. In fact, there are many. For instance, we can also look at the share of total national income accrued by the super-rich, often defined as the top 1 per cent (**see Case Study 10.1**). For the moment, let's focus on the Gini. If we take the Gini, what has happened to international inequality, world inequality, and global inequality over time?

Since 1980, international inequality and world inequality (both measuring inequality between countries) have unambiguously declined (**see Figure 10.3**). However, the magnitude of the decline depends on whether the size of the countries' population is taken into account. In the case of *international inequality*, in which each country weights the same, the Gini coefficient has fallen from 0.621 in 1980 to about 0.518 in 2019. Over the same period, *world inequality*, which applies population-weights, exhibits a decline from a Gini of about 0.636 to about 0.441.

However, at closer inspection, the change is largely due to the startling rise in per capita GDP in a handful of populous developing countries, such as China and India. What would

Case Study 10.1: Are changes in income inequality driven by the super-rich?

Our interest in the share of national income captured by the top 1 per cent—the richest in a given society—has been stimulated by better quality data. Usually, household surveys are used to make inequality estimates. These surveys tend to *not* capture the incomes of the richest households because households at the top 1 per cent of the income distribution are less likely to appear in survey data than those in the middle which comprise the majority of the population. This implies that standard measures of income inequality based on survey data are not capturing the *actual* level of income inequality in a society.

In the *World Inequality Report 2018* (Alvaredo et al. 2018) and *2022* (Chancel et al. 2021), the evidence shows that the income share going to the top 1 per cent, although varying substantially across countries, has increased since about 1990 in some contexts, in particular in the United States. At the global level, this share was above 15 per cent in 1980 but reached almost 20 per cent by 2021. The use of tax or financial records to capture those at the top of the distribution, however, is limited to a relatively small number of countries, mostly advanced economies, while data across the developing world is available only for fewer than thirty countries, mainly because most governments are reluctant to publish such tax data.

Using different methodologies for this reason, the World Inequality Database has produced information on the share of income going to the top 1 per cent for about 120 countries.

Figure 10.2 Share of national income accrued by the richest 1 per cent of the population

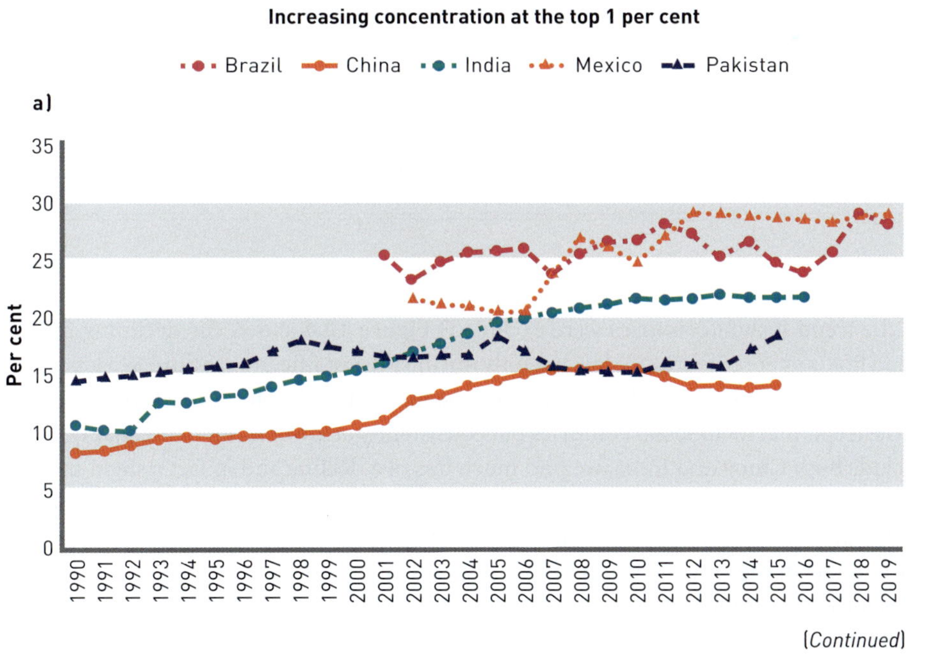

(Continued)

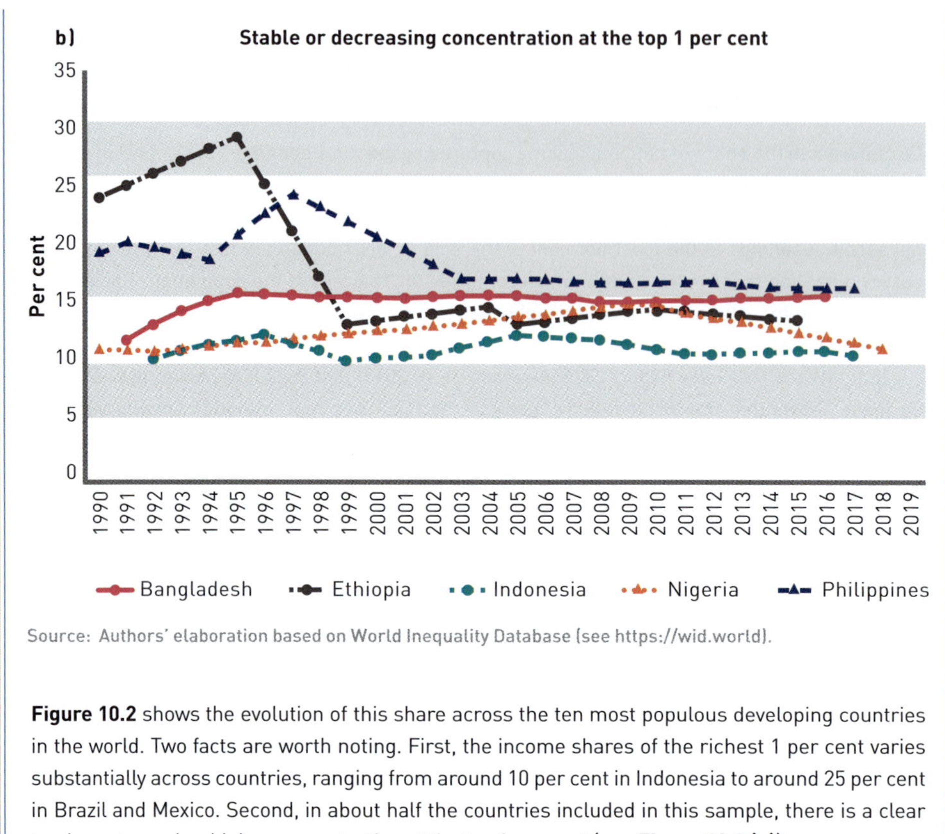

Source: Authors' elaboration based on World Inequality Database (see https://wid.world).

Figure 10.2 shows the evolution of this share across the ten most populous developing countries in the world. Two facts are worth noting. First, the income shares of the richest 1 per cent varies substantially across countries, ranging from around 10 per cent in Indonesia to around 25 per cent in Brazil and Mexico. Second, in about half the countries included in this sample, there is a clear tendency towards a higher concentration at the top 1 per cent (**see Figure 10.2 (a)**).

Questions

1 Are top income shares a preferable measure of income inequality than the Gini coefficient?
2 Should the richest 1 per cent in society pay more or less tax?

be the trend if such countries were excluded? **Figure 10.4** shows the declining inequality trend holds after removing China, but only during the last fifteen years and to a lesser extent. If, instead, India is removed, the declining inequality trend holds as well, running parallel to the trend that includes all countries but consistently at lower levels of inequality. But if we exclude both China and India, we find much less of a decline and in fact a slight increase in world inequality since the 2010s.

What is the trend in inequality according to *global inequality*, that is, between all individuals in the world? We find that the Gini coefficient has declined over the two decades for which comparable survey data is available, from around 0.645 in 1995 to around 0.580 in 2015. Again, the fall is less if we exclude individuals living in China and India (**see Figure 10.5**).

Figure 10.3 **Trends in international inequality and world inequality, 1980–2019. Gini coefficients**

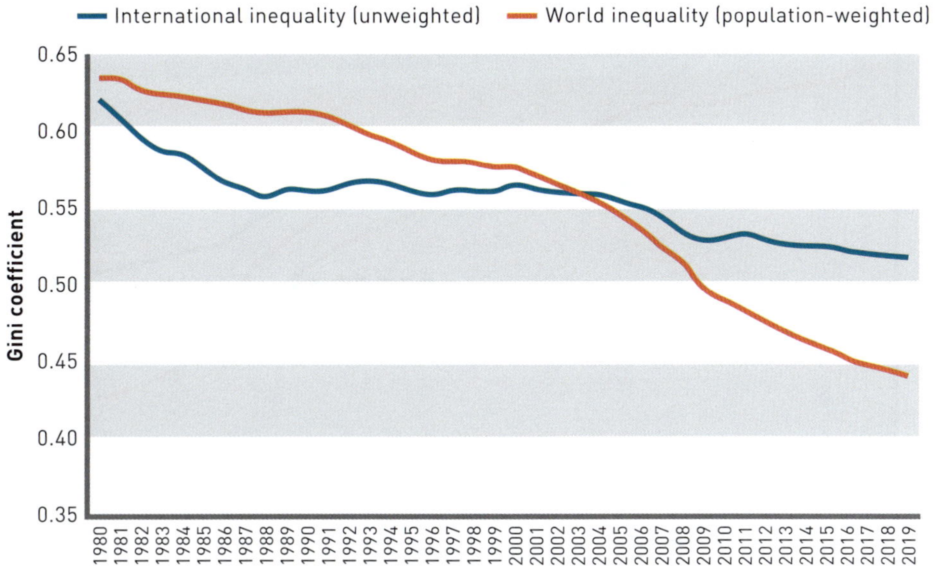

Source: Authors' estimates based on per capita GDP (PPP at 2011 prices) from IMF, World Economic Outlook Database (version October 2019).

10.3.2 **Why is global inequality rising or falling?**

So, we can say trends in inequality at a global level are not as simple as the 'global inequality is falling' narrative suggests. Instead, the salient issue is the persistence of world, international, and global inequality. What factors can explain this persistence despite much economic growth across the Global South? Two factors relating to globalization and the workings of the global economy are particularly important in illuminating why income inequality between countries persists once China and India are excluded from the analysis (Sumner 2021).

First, as discussed in **Chapter 7** and **Chapter 12**, transnational corporations (TNCs), predominantly from rich countries, coordinate global production through GVCs. To pursue economic development, developing countries seek to participate in GVCs but are subordinate to TNCs because power lies with the companies' orchestrating production. The good news is that developing countries may initially accrue some benefits, such as job creation, from exporting via GVCs. However, these benefits may be difficult to sustain because only a limited number of firms from developing countries are internationally competitive and thus capable of participating in global production.

Furthermore, job creation is limited and often favours higher-skilled workers. There may be fewer benefits for low-skilled workers who make up much of the population in developing countries. As a result, economic development may stagnate and be stunted in the

Figure 10.4 **Trends in world inequality with and without India and China, 1980–2019. Gini coefficients**

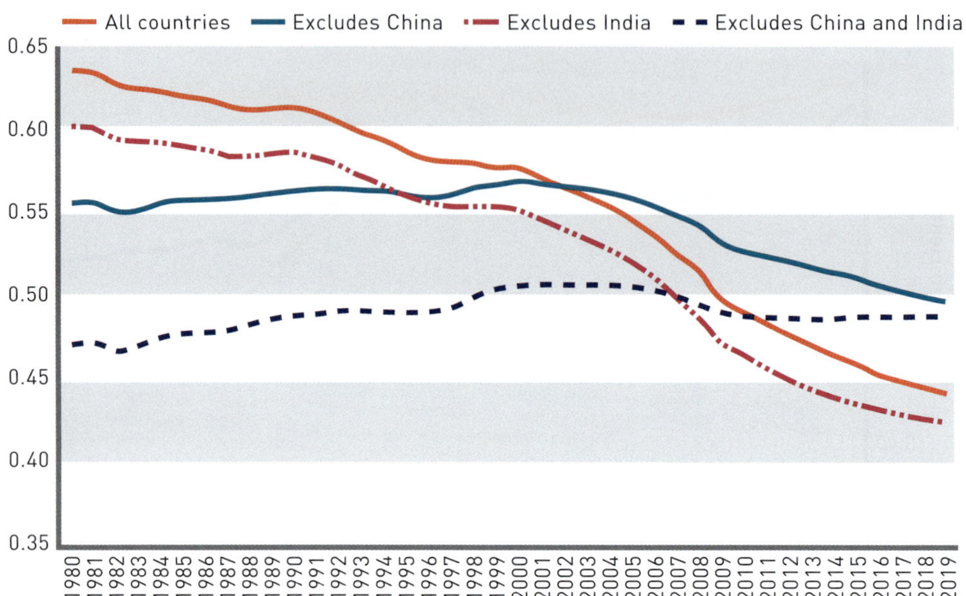

Source: Authors' estimates based on per capita GDP (PPP at 2011 prices) from IMF, World Economic Outlook Database (version October 2019).

long term, perpetuating the gap between developing and advanced countries and thus also perpetuating world, international, and global inequality, despite a handful of countries developing substantially.

The second factor is the extreme competition between developing countries over export markets and access to GVCs. In short, many developing countries compete over similar entry points to global production and trade. Their domestic manufacturers attempt to distinguish themselves through, for example, higher quality and reliability or lower costs. Therefore, manufacturing tasks have been dispersed across more and more developing countries over time (Felipe, Kumar, and Abdon 2014; Felipe, Mehta, and Rhee 2018), making it difficult for each individual country to secure sufficient economic activity to attain and sustain substantial economic development. Furthermore, certain developing countries may attract large shares of the manufacturing, such as China has since the early 2000s, making it much harder for other developing countries to compete in specific tasks and markets, thus diminishing opportunities for economic development.

An important issue is that developing countries are seeking economic development 'late', meaning many years after other states industrialized. This entails several challenges for developing countries to achieve sustained economic development, which the concept of 'late development' aims to understand. Specifically, the pursuit of economic development for developing countries takes place in a global economy dominated by richer states

Figure 10.5 Trends in global inequality with and without India and China, 1995–2015

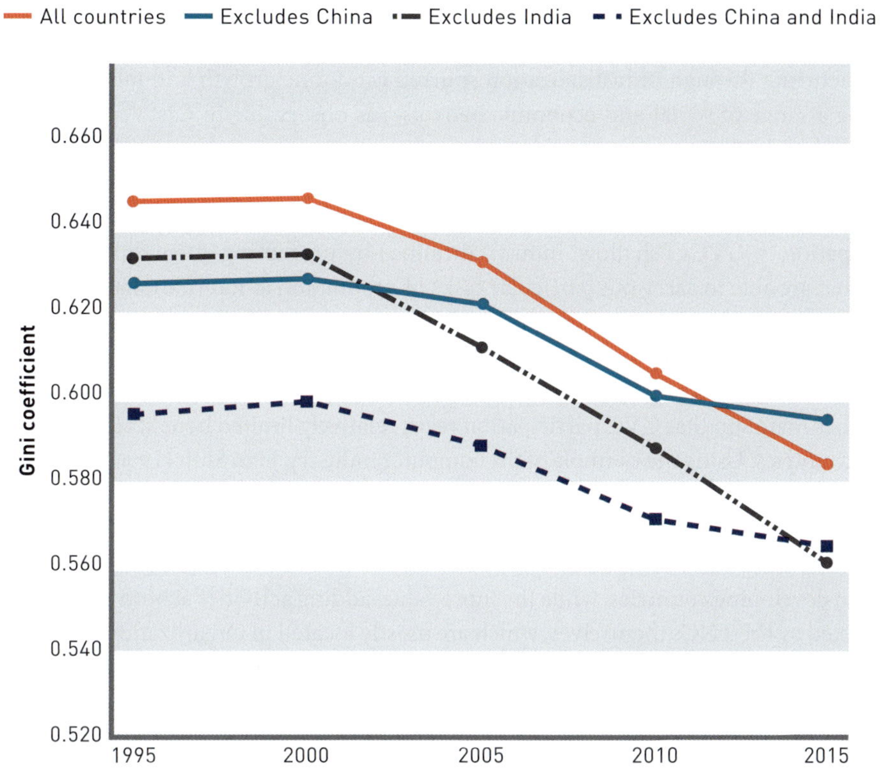

Source: Authors' estimates based on the World Bank's PovcalNet dataset on the basis of household surveys on income or consumption (PPP at 2011 prices) (World Bank 2021*d*).

and large TNCs, which are also predominantly headquartered in richer states. TNCs own most modern technology, meaning developing countries must pay for the use of such technology due to patents and royalties. In fact, the *net* cost for use of intellectual property paid by developing countries in 2018 amounted to approximately $250 billion per year and has grown since 1990 from about $35 billion per year (constant 2011 prices) (Sumner 2021).

Key Concept: 'Late development'

Alexander Gerschenkron (1962) is typically credited with coining the term 'late industrialization'. He argued that only the UK was an example of 'early' industrialization, meaning relatively uninfluenced by the global economy. All other countries were 'late' industrializers. The concept is predicated on the sense that late industrializers face structural constraints due to the timing of their development.

International development agencies have promoted (albeit with caveats) an economic development model according to which developing countries should expand their manufacturing output by participating in GVCs (UNCTAD 2013; UNIDO 2018; World Bank 2020*b*). The rationale behind this recommendation is that, in the past, the expansion of manufacturing through industrialization spurred economic growth and job creation, thus yielding a range of social and economic benefits—as observable in East Asia between the 1970s and mid-1990s.

However, with the emergence of GVCs post-1990, industrialization has changed. Instead of building entire domestic industries ('deep' industrialization), developing countries pursue participation in GVCs ('shallow' industrialization) by promoting a few domestic supplier firms that are able to carry out particular tasks of production at internationally competitive conditions in terms of costs, standards, and logistics. Optimists argue GVCs facilitate industrialization, as developing countries no longer have to master the entire production of a product to start exporting (Baldwin 2016).

Critics maintain that GVC participation reaps relatively limited benefits for many developing countries. Using the example of the computer industry, Stan Shih (1996) demonstrates that the tasks performed at the beginning (design) and end (marketing) of the production process add more value to the product than the actual assembly in between. The less value-adding assembly tasks in the middle of the value chain, however, are frequently executed in developing countries, while the more value-adding activities at both ends tend to be conducted by the TNCs themselves, which are mostly located in Organization for Economic Co-operation and Development (OECD), meaning rich countries (Mudambi 2008).

It can therefore be hard for some developing countries to achieve economic development through participating in the global economy, and the opportunities and costs of participation are distributed unevenly. By impeding development in this way, the dynamics of the current global economy contribute to the persistence of world, international, and global inequality.

 Watch the video on the online resources to take your understanding of this case study further.

10.4 National income inequality

National income inequality is more straightforward to define: it refers to differences in income between individuals within a country. It can be measured—like international, world, and global inequality—by the Gini coefficient.

However, income differences between individuals often intersect and overlap with differences between groups, creating complex patterns of exclusion and disadvantage. A common metric of gender disparities in income is the 'gender pay gap', which summarizes the difference between, say, average hourly wages of women as a proportion of average hourly wages of men. Data from the International Labour Organization (ILO) shows that in general women earn less than men. The average gap among the OECD countries, for instance, is about 13 per cent. This suggests that women, on average, earn 13 per cent less than men.

The gender pay gap can reach as much as 30 per cent in South Korea, about 20 per cent in the UK, Russia, and Chile, and about 7–8 per cent in countries such as Poland, Mexico, and Bolivia (ILO 2018*a*).

While income differences by gender can be the result of differences in some characteristics such as education or experience, they can also be the result of discrimination. In countries where gaps are relatively low, such as lower-middle-income Bolivia, the value of the gap may simply reflect women's selection of jobs (Olivetti and Petrongolo 2008). That means only women with specific high-wage characteristics are entering the workforce whereas those with low-wage traits are not entering the labour market; thus, the latter are not captured in the wage distribution.

While the data suggest that gender pay gaps have reduced slightly over recent decades, the Covid-19 pandemic could erase some of this progress. Studies suggest various channels for this (ILO 2021*b*; Montoya-Aguirre, Ortiz-Juarez, and Santiago 2021). First, the closure of non-essential sectors (such as hospitality and retail, which globally concentrate 40 per cent of female employment) to contain the spread of the virus disproportionately affected women's jobs and earnings losses. Second, the closures of nurseries and schools substantially increased the demand for care, making women shift from paid work to the unpaid economy, thus driving women out of the labour force.

Estimates by the ILO suggest that the loss of women's jobs in 2020 reached 64 million globally (ILO 2021*b*). Inactivity may be especially acute in places with strong social norms that impose on women the responsibility to stay at home to undertake domestic and unpaid care work. This might limit their voice in household decisions, including the control over resources. At the macro level, some of these norms may translate into the exclusion of women from decision-making and managerial positions, either in the private sector or in the public and legislative spheres.

These patterns of exclusion resulting from overlapping inequalities, especially in places where income inequality is high, are concerned not only with between-group differences due to gender but also with racial or ethnic disparities. In fact, all over the world, Indigenous and non-White people are overrepresented in poverty statistics. Some data from the World Bank's Equity Lab for Latin America is quite revealing. While poverty affected only 27 per cent of all non-Afro-descendant and non-Indigenous people in Colombia in 2019, it reached 60 per cent among Indigenous people, that is, 2.2 times the poverty rate. Similar ratios of about 2 times the poverty rate are to be found among Indigenous people in Peru and Mexico, whereas in Ecuador, this ratio reaches 2.5 times, in Brazil 3 times, and in Panama 6 times (World Bank, Equity Lab for Latin America 2021).

10.4.1 Is national income inequality rising or falling?

The dominant narrative on national income inequality suggests that it is rising within countries around the world. However, taking the most recent data, there is a more complex picture in which more equal countries have become less equal (the Asia story), while less equal countries have become more equal (the Latin America story). National inequality has fallen in general in Latin America from a very high level and risen in South and East Asia from a previously low level. In sub-Saharan Africa trends are mixed (**see Figure 10.6**). However, we should also note that these figures are based on the available household survey data, which often does not capture the incomes of the rich (**see Case Study 10.1**) and thus almost certainly underestimates the real level of inequality.

So, what happened in Latin American countries? Latin American countries experienced a significant decline in income inequality after national inequality peaked during the second half of the 1990s. The Gini coefficient for household per capita income fell in all eighteen countries for which there are comparable data, and it did so at an average annual rate of −0.85 per cent regionally, ranging from −1.57 per cent in Bolivia to −0.26 per cent in Costa Rica (**see Figure 10.6**). In contrast, over the same period income inequality among the rich countries (the OECD countries) increased by an average rate of 0.26 per cent annually (this excludes the following Latin American countries that are OECD members: Chile, Colombia, and Mexico). In contrast, the *annual* increase was 0.5 to 0.7 per cent in India and Pakistan, above 1 per cent in Ethiopia and Nigeria, and a startling 2.7 per cent in Indonesia, where national inequality has risen dramatically in the 2000s.

That said, income inequality in Latin America is still among the highest in the world. The *World Inequality Report 2022* shows that the richest 10 per cent of the Latin American population accrues about 55 per cent of total national income, whereas the bottom 50 per cent

Figure 10.6 **Changes in national inequality, 2000–15**

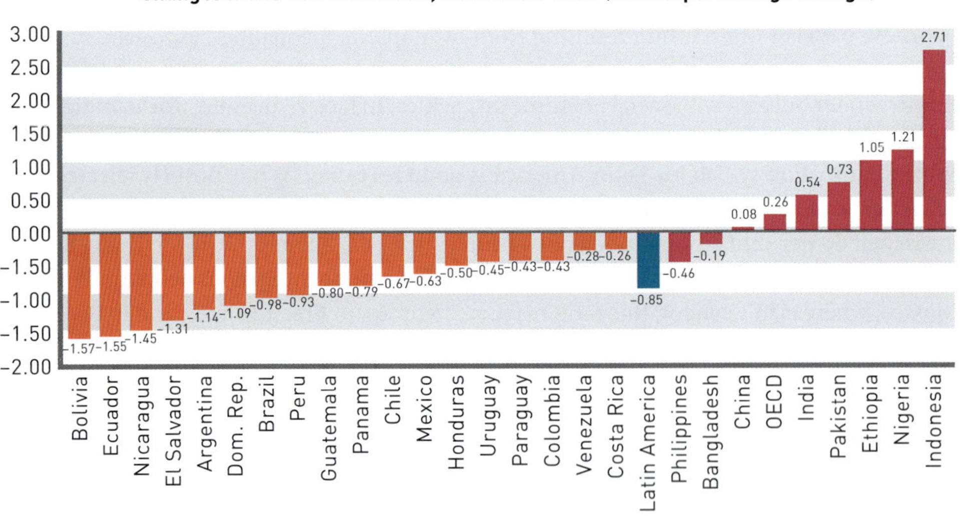

Source: Adapted from Lustig, López-Calva, and Ortiz-Juarez (2016) for Latin American countries with authors' update based on the Socio-Economic Database for Latin America and the Caribbean, SEDLAC (CEDLAS and The World Bank 2021), authors' estimates based on the OECD Income Distribution Database for the aggregate of the OECD (OECD 2021*b*), and PovcalNet for the rest of developing countries (World Bank 2021*d*).

captures only 10 per cent. These figures are very similar to those observed in sub-Saharan Africa, and just slightly 'better' than those recorded in the Middle East and North Africa, where the richest 10 per cent and the poorest 50 per cent capture, respectively, 58 per cent and 9 per cent of national income (Chancel et al. 2021).

10.4.2 Why is national income inequality rising or falling?

What factors can explain the different trends of rising national inequality in Asia and falling national inequality in Latin America? Asia's entry into the global economy has exerted downward pressure on wage labourers' share of the overall national income. This is because developing countries' intense price-based competition for manufacturing tasks in the global economy has increased the bargaining position of capital owners compared to that of workers, given that TNCs can easily threaten to switch their suppliers (and sometimes actually do). A lower income share of wage labourers in turn means higher returns to capital, which tends to increase income inequality because capital is mostly owned by richer segments of society. Consequently, if governments do not counteract it, inequality within countries is likely to rise with participation in the global economy.

Furthermore, participation in the global economy often entails modern technology, which reduces the demand for low-skilled workers who are the majority of the developing-country population, thus perpetuating or worsening within-country inequality (**see Chapter 12**).

Why does Latin America display such different trends from those identified in Asia? Many countries in Latin America enjoyed additional income during the 2000s due to the commodity boom. Alongside leftist parties in power, this has led to more generous and progressive government transfers (Azevedo et al. 2013; Cornia 2014; Lustig, López-Calva, and Ortiz-Juarez 2013, 2016). Additionally, many governments have increased minimum wages, which resulted in higher hourly wages among workers at the bottom of the income distribution. This has been further supported by a large expansion of education, which has reduced the income divergences between lower- and higher-skilled workers.

10.5 Where does global poverty fit?

Income inequality is an indicator used to assess *differences* in people's living standards. In contrast, income-based poverty evaluates whether the individuals with low living standards lack the monetary resources necessary to meet their needs. This assessment is typically based on a 'poverty line', whose value is determined by the price of a number of goods (referred to as a 'basket of goods') presumed to be indispensable for life—usually food items allowing each individual to consume 2,100 calories per day (as recommended by the World Health Organization (WHO)) plus crucial non-food items. Individuals with per capita incomes below the poverty line are considered poor. The percentage of poor in a given society yields the society's total poverty level, called the 'poverty headcount'.

People living in poverty lack items considered indispensable for survival and live with less than the minimum standard of living. Concretely, this means they are unable to meet basic needs such as nutrition, basic education, and access to healthcare, sanitation, and drinking water. The specific definition and measurement of poverty matter in practice because they usually determine who has access to welfare services.

Influential voices in debates on poverty include Amartya Sen (1992, 1999), Martha Nussbaum (2000), and the United Nations Development Programme (UNDP) (which has issued the annual *Human Development Report* since 1990), who argue that poverty measures should examine individuals' 'capabilities'—that is, what people can do with the resources and opportunities that are available to them. These ideas were discussed during the major UN Social Development Summit in 1995, which shaped the poverty-related objectives included in the Millennium Development Goals for 2015 and the subsequent Sustainable Development Goals (SDGs) for 2030 (**see Case Study 14.2**). During a participatory process including people from sixty countries, it became evident that this conceptualization of poverty also resonates with individuals experiencing poverty themselves (Narayan et al. 1999: 4–5).

In addition to monetary measures of poverty, UNDP and the Oxford Poverty and Human Development Initiative (OPHI) developed a global Multidimensional Poverty Index (MPI). This index aggregates ten non-monetary indicators across three dimensions: health (undernourishment and child mortality), education (years of schooling completed and school attendance), and living standard (type of cooking fuel; access to sanitation, drinking water, and electricity; adequate housing materials; and household assets) (Alkire and Foster 2011; Robles Aguilar and Sumner 2019).

10.5.1 Is poverty rising or falling?

There is a well-cited storyline that global poverty has fallen since the Cold War in the neoliberal economic policy era. However, this narrative is fragile too because it depends on where the poverty line is drawn and the dominant role of China in global figures for poverty reduction.

Globally, and to compare across countries, the World Bank uses three poverty lines ($1.90, $3.20, and $5.50 a day per person in 2011 PPP). The lowest line, $1.90 a day, is the global threshold for what is called *extreme* poverty and is derived from the average of the national poverty lines of a set of the poorest countries globally, which represent the 'low-income countries' (Ferreira et al. 2016). The $3.20 and $5.50 a day lines correspond to, respectively, the average of the national poverty lines of 'lower-middle-income countries' and 'upper-middle-income countries' (Jolliffe and Prydz 2016).

It is frequently argued that $1.90 a day (or even $3.20 or $5.50) is insufficient to afford essential goods or to be healthy and educated. In fact, the number of people with moderate or severe food insecurity globally was above 2 billion in 2020, according to the Food and Agriculture Organization (FAO 2021). Moreover, being temporarily out of monetary poverty does not imply being free of the risk of falling back in the future. On the contrary, longitudinal studies have been used to estimate a 'security from future poverty' threshold, which was found to be much higher than the World Bank's poverty lines, at about $13 a day in 2011 PPP (World Bank 2018).

What has happened since the 1980s? According to the lowest poverty line, global poverty unambiguously declined (**see Figure 10.7**). Yet, many previously poor people have simply moved just above the poverty line and thus the record of poverty reduction is rather fragile. Only a much higher threshold, namely $13 a day per person, is associated with a very low likelihood—10 per cent or less—of falling back into poverty. However,

Figure 10.7 Population (per cent) of the world (a.) and the world excluding China (b.) by daily income or consumption per capita group, 1981–2018

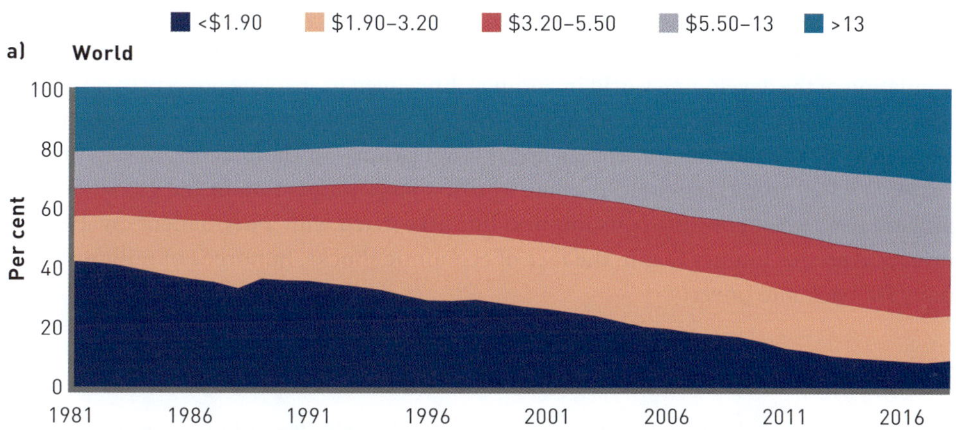

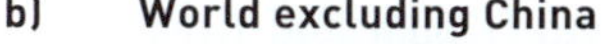

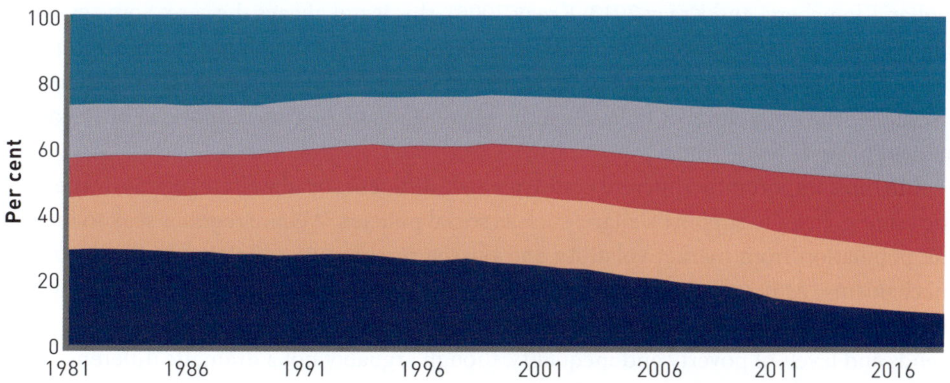

Source: Authors' estimates based on World Bank's PovcalNet dataset (World Bank 2021d).

more than 70 per cent of the world's population currently live below that threshold. In fact, when $13 a day is used as the poverty line, global poverty has not changed that much since the 1980s: it fell from about 80 per cent of the world's population in the early 1980s to about 70 per cent in 2018. If we consider the world excluding China, less has changed since the early 1980s.

Think about it in this way: in the late 1980s, the distribution of the world's countries and the world's people resembled what Danny Quah (1996) called the 'twin peaks' of a polarized world. The distribution showed a hump at the poorer end (encompassing the countries and people living in the homogenous 'Third World'), a hump at the upper end (developed countries and their population), and weak prospects for convergence of the poorer group with the richer one. But since the 1990s, that twin peaks world with a poorer and a richer hump has transitioned into one hump in the middle, in that most of those moving out of poverty have moved into a stage between poverty and security which we will call 'precarity', with incomes between $3.20 and $13 a day.

This in-between group has grown dramatically: in 2018, almost a quarter of the entire population of the developing world including China lived in absolute poverty (below $3.20 a day) while about 30 per cent lived in security (above $13 a day), leaving the remainder—nearly half of the developing world's entire population—in the precarious new middle (between $3.20 and $13 a day). In other words, a large proportion of the global population still lives well below the consumption line associated with a permanent escape from poverty. And this implies that in the face of economic shocks, hundreds of millions could easily fall back into poverty.

10.5.2 Why is poverty rising or falling?

Why does poverty rise or fall? Changes in income poverty depend on economic growth and changes in income inequality. While, on average, the poverty headcount falls and the incomes of the poorest rise in line with average income growth (Dollar and Kraay 2002; Dollar, Kleineberg, and Kraay 2013; Kraay 2006), this is not always the case. Some evidence suggests that reducing poverty depends on *changes* in income inequality and the *initial* level of inequality (Ferreira and Ravallion 2011; Ravallion 1997). The rationale is straightforward: the higher the initial level of inequality, the higher the rate of growth that will be needed to achieve poverty reduction.

But most importantly, different countries have different social welfare regimes—meaning the set of policies to support welfare, such as social policies. Welfare regimes seek to insulate the population from market volatility and pursue security via collective, public insurance mechanisms. Although the global economy is the major driver of poverty and inequality overall, there *is* scope for national policies such as social policy to make some difference to trends and levels of poverty and inequality, though arguably not a dramatic difference. That said, the Covid-19 pandemic has created a greater level of complexity for national social policy given debt repayments and has brought to light a range of inequality-related impacts (**see Case Study 10.2**).

Case Study 10.2: What will be the Covid-19 pandemic's lasting impact on inequality?

The Covid-19 pandemic has brought inequality-related issues to the fore (Photo 10.1). These include the weak, fragmented, and easily overwhelmed public health systems in developing countries versus developed countries (**see Chapter 8**), and the precarity of informal labour (**see Chapter 12**), notably the question of who can work from home. Other inequality-related issues include the fact that most of the world's population lives only barely above the (contentious) global poverty lines defined by the World Bank, meaning that economic disruption or ill health can easily push millions of people back below those poverty lines or into deeper poverty, and the importance and persistence of harmful gender inequality in terms of division of labour.

The pandemic has highlighted the global inequality of modern technology development, manifested in vaccine patents ownership being located largely outside the Global South, with the exception of China (and Russia, which is not typically classified as within the Global South), and the consequential unequal distribution of vaccines globally (**see Box 8.2** and the **Chapter 8 Roundtable**). The pandemic has also facilitated opportunities for autocratic-leaning governments to squeeze democratic participation with restrictions and lockdowns of varying degrees.

Photo 10.1 **Despite the efforts of COVAX in countries such as Colombia, we are a long way from an equitable distribution of Covid-19 vaccines; this is just one example of the inequalities the pandemic has highlighted**

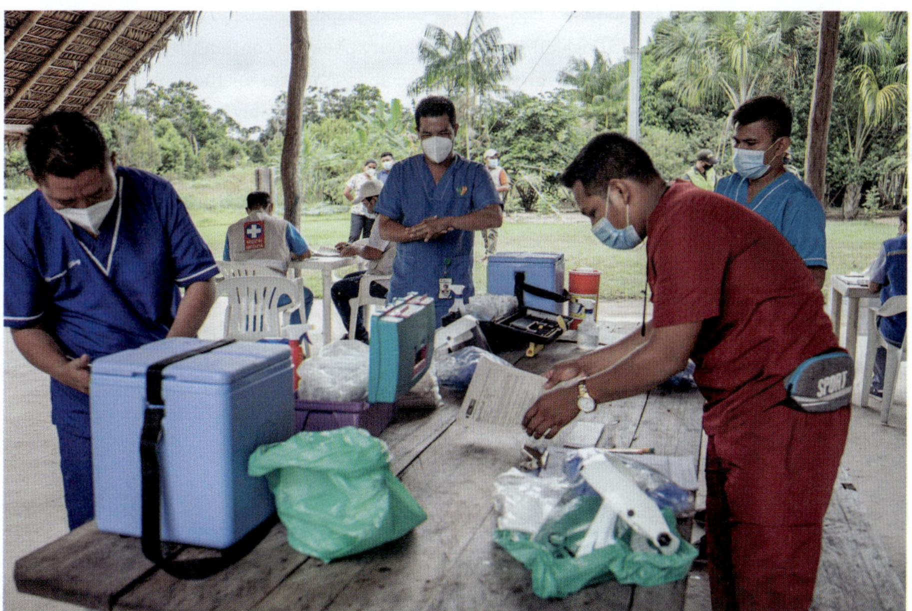

Source: WHO / Blink Media - Nadège Mazars.

(Continued)

The pandemic has accelerated the expansion of external debt servicing levels due to the cost of managing the pandemic and vaccination programmes, and the cost of economic disruption. Higher levels of debt servicing and the need to finance and logistically deliver vaccines will divert spending from other areas, given that the annual service on external debt for developing countries will be more than $3 trillion between 2022–25. Of this, half is public debt (World Bank 2021c), although the risk of outright default has been managed by a huge expansion of Special Drawing Rights (SDR) 'overdrafts' at the IMF. Even this may not be enough for some countries.

Moreover, the increase of investments in digitalization in OECD countries, which were put in place so rapidly during the pandemic, may lay the groundwork for tradeable services and a potentially large movement of employment from OECD countries to some developing countries. Again, this suggests new hierarchies in the Global South will emerge, especially as this sits alongside a contorting global economy for manufacturing as a result of unsynchronized waves of infection in different countries. This leads to late components delivery or missing components disrupting value chains, not least micro-chips. This in turn impacts prices of key commodities (and volatility) in many countries, already on an upward trend given increased demand and supply restrictions, and made worse by the war in Ukraine. The potential for acute development, conflict, and political tension is high.

Finally, the pandemic has given rise to a set of 'new' within-country fractures, in the sense that such considerations did not exist prior to the pandemic. Think of the split between those who can work from home and those who cannot. There is a likely a close fit to the informal/formal sector demarcation, but working from home in a sense is different as it is an extra layer of hierarchy and privilege. Some formal sector workers can work from home (office workers, clerical staff) while others in the same private or public company cannot work from home (such as employees of state or private railways or buses). Further, a distinction between agricultural and non-agricultural work is important, given that in some countries half or more of the working population are self-employed in small farms around the home.

Lockdowns of various kinds have often been a primary policy to contain the virus, but usually entail an income loss (in the absence of sufficient social assistance) for those who cannot work from home. Existing estimates of the proportion of jobs that can feasibly be done from home vary dramatically between countries. Jonathan I. Dingel and Brent Neiman (2020) estimate that the share of non-agricultural jobs that could be performed at home is less than 25 per cent in many developing countries. This again suggests accentuated inequalities within developing countries.

Questions

1 What have been the biggest impacts of the pandemic on developing countries?
2 Who are the winners and losers from the pandemic?

10.6 Conclusion

What is the overall story that has emerged in this chapter about inequality in the global political economy? It is this: since the Cold War, income inequality between countries has fallen overall, although the decline in global inequality is largely due to the development of China and India. In contrast, national inequality has risen in some countries while falling in others. Put simply, rising inequality in countries with relatively low initial inequality in Asia, such as China, was counterbalanced at a global level by falling national inequality in countries with higher initial inequality in Latin America during the 2000s. However, it is not clear whether this latter trend is likely to continue.

As students of GPE, we have seen that inequality between countries and its persistence in the global political economy can be explained by the following factors: first, the dynamics of a world where production is spread more and more thinly across countries and controlled by TNCs headquartered in rich countries, thus making it harder to capture sufficient activity to achieve economic development; second, developing countries' positions in global production, specifically their execution of mostly lower value-adding assembly activities in GVCs; and third, the intense price-related competition between numerous developing countries, which makes it harder for each country to sustain economic development.

The persistence of national inequality can also be explained by factors such as the provision of modern, labour-saving technology—especially regarding low-skilled labour—which leads to stagnating real wages over time, the relatively low redistributive impact of tax systems, and the relatively low levels of wealth taxation. Governments can enact and expand social policy and provision to mediate some of the extremities of poverty and inequality, although the position of developing countries in the global economy places limits on this.

An important issue, finally, is that developing countries are seeking economic development 'late', meaning many years after the advanced nations industrialized. This entails several challenges for developing countries (or the 'periphery') to achieve sustained economic development, which the concept of 'late development' aims to understand.

The Covid-19 pandemic may make many matters worse. It is likely to impact national inequality because the pandemic likely affects poorer parts of the population more than richer parts—informal sector workers are more impacted by lockdowns, increasing the number of people at risk of falling back into poverty. The pandemic will also impact global inequality as supply chains are disrupted and manufacturers in developing countries find it harder or more costly to source imported inputs due to economic disruption elsewhere. The likelihood is that economic growth will be start-stop, possibly with waves of infection in the absence of universal vaccine coverage in developing countries. And over 100 developing countries have signed new IMF agreements involving unambiguous austerity or declines in social spending, greater debt servicing to finance the costs of pandemic management and ongoing vaccination programmes. For all these reasons, inequality is not just here to stay, but may even become more marked as a defining feature of the global political economy.

Key Points

- Income inequality matters for intrinsic and instrumental reasons, and intersects with inequalities between social groups based on gender, race, and other factors.
- There are three ways to think about income inequality at a global level: 'international inequality', 'world inequality', and 'global inequality'. We can say that international inequality and world inequality have unambiguously declined since 1980. However, the magnitude of the decline depends on whether the size of countries' populations is taken into account. Furthermore, when we exclude both China and India, we find much less of a decline and in fact a slight rise in the 2010s.

- National inequality refers to differences in income between individuals within a country. Overall, we can say national inequality has followed different trends in different regions: in Latin America it has declined, albeit from very high initial levels. The trend of national inequality in sub-Saharan Africa has been rather mixed and thus depends on the specific country. Lastly, national inequality has unambiguously risen in South and East Asia.
- According to the lowest poverty line of $1.90, the decline in global poverty is unambiguous. Yet, many previously poor people have simply moved just above the poverty line and thus are not secure from the risk of future poverty. Hence, the record of poverty reduction is fragile.
- Explanations for patterns of inequality in the contemporary period can be traced to many of the dynamics associated with globalization, particularly the reorganization of the global economy around GVCs and the implications for countries pursuing 'late development'.

Further Reading

Global inequality

Alvaredo, F., Chancel, L., Piketty, T., Saez, E., and Zucman, G. (2018), *World Inequality Report 2018* (Paris: World Inequality Lab). Discusses trends in global inequality between and within countries with a focus on the richest.

Phillips, N. (2017), 'Power and Inequality in the Global Political Economy', *International Affairs*, 93(2): 429–44. Offers a critical perspective on global income inequality.

National inequality

UNDP (2013), *Humanity Divided: Confronting Inequality in Developing Countries* (New York: United Nations Development Programme). Discusses what inequality is, why it matters, and which kinds of policies can address it.

UNDP (2017), *Income Inequality Trends in Sub-Saharan Africa: Divergence, Determinants and Consequences* (New York: United Nations Development Programme). Discusses trends, drivers, and costs of income inequality across sub-Saharan Africa.

UNESCAP (2018), *Inequality in Asia and the Pacific in the Era of the 2030 Agenda for Sustainable Development* (Bangkok: United Nations Economic and Social Commission for Asia and the Pacific). Discusses trends, drivers, and costs of income inequality across Asia and the Pacific.

Poverty

Alkire, S., Foster, J. E., Seth, S., Santos, M. E., Roche, J. M., and Ballón, P. (2015), *Multidimensional Poverty Measurement and Analysis: Chapter 1—Introduction*, OPHI Working Paper No. 82 (Oxford: Oxford University Press). Introduces the empirical analysis of poverty from a multidimensional perspective.

Ravallion, M. (2016), *The Economics of Poverty: History, Measurement, and Policy* (New York: Oxford University Press). Addresses the question of why poverty matters, reviewing the history of thought as well as current and future challenges.

Chapter 10 Roundtable discussion

Is global poverty really falling?

Roundtable 10.1
Opening contribution **Eduardo Ortiz-Juarez and Andy Sumner**

Why does a technical issue—how poverty is measured—matter so much? It matters because there is a dominant and widely held belief that global poverty has fallen dramatically since the early 1980s, and it is not without foundation: the data show that global poverty has fallen since the 1980s when measured at both the 'extreme' poverty line of $1.90 per day and 'moderate' poverty line of $3.20 per day. But has global poverty *really* fallen?

One can argue that the fact that many previously poor people have moved just above the $1.90 or $3.20 poverty line, or even above the $5.50 one, only tells us people have crossed a consumption line (and life is not that much different between $1.89 and $1.91 per day). Further, people may easily fall back into poverty in the future due to economic shocks or ill health. Only a much higher threshold is associated with a low likelihood of falling back into poverty in the future.

As we saw in **Section 10.5.1**, longitudinal studies estimate this 'security from poverty' line to be at approximately $13 per day in 2011 PPP (World Bank 2018). However, more than 70 per cent of the world's population currently live under that threshold. In other words, they may live above the global poverty lines of $1.90 and $3.30 but not sufficiently far above them to be certain that they will not fall back into poverty in the future.

In fact, if we take a 'security from poverty' line of $13 a day, the decline in global poverty is much more modest. In reality, not too far from half of the developing world's entire population lives in a precarious new middle (between $3.20 and $13 a day).

The implication of this is that, in the face of economic shocks, hundreds of millions could easily fall back into poverty—indeed, this is what likely happened as a result of the loss of jobs and incomes imposed by the Covid-19 pandemic (Sumner, Ortiz-Juarez, and Hoy 2020).

Further, making assessments solely based on developing countries rather than the world picture casts further doubt on the idea that global poverty is now low or may be eradicated by 2030 as the UN Sustainable Development Goals aim to do. As **Table 10.1** shows us, even at the $1.90 line, on average, one in five people in the countries of the developing world live in poverty. At the $3.20 line—on average—about one in three of the people in the countries of the developing world live in poverty. The corresponding poverty counts at $5.50 and $13 per day are higher, respectively half of the population and 80 per cent of the population.

So, we think the widely held view that global poverty has seen a dramatic reduction is questionable. It is important to quickly add that we are *not* saying that the income growth among the poorest people in the world has not been positive in general, but rather that it has been slow and of a modest order, and many people remain below the income line associated with a permanent escape from absolute poverty.

To return to our starting point—why does this all matter?—we need to look at the consequences of poverty measurement. This all matters because there is a narrative that global

Table 10.1 **Average poverty rates by countries' income groupings (per cent of population below the poverty line), 2018**

Income group/poverty line	$1.90	$3.20	$5.50	$13
Unweighted averages				
Low-income countries (LICs)	43.5	68.7	87.0	98.0
Middle-income countries (MICs)	8.4	20.5	40.6	76.0
Lower-middle-income	13.5	31.8	57.5	89.1
Upper-middle-income	3.4	9.5	24.0	63.2
All LICs and MICs	17.0	32.3	51.9	81.4
High-income countries (HICs)	0.4	0.8	1.9	10.1
Population-weighted averages				
Low-income countries (LICs)	44.5	71.0	89.4	98.6
Middle-income countries (MICs)	7.7	24.3	46.8	78.5
Lower-middle-income	13.1	40.9	71.5	94.4
Upper-middle-income	1.6	5.1	18.3	60.2
All LICs and MICs	11.6	29.3	51.4	80.6
High-income countries (HICs)	0.7	0.9	1.7	6.8

Source: Authors' estimates based on World Bank (2021*d*).

poverty has fallen and could even be eradicated by 2030, and thus the current global economic development model—of economic liberalization and the participation of developing countries in the global economy—has lifted millions of people out of poverty. But in fact, absolute poverty is an endemic feature of contemporary global political economy and of much of the world's population, if we take a poverty line associated with a permanent escape from poverty.

Further, estimates of the end of poverty at this or other higher lines suggest it will be hundreds of years before the end of poverty, and that a completely new global economic model is required based on enormous redistribution globally and nationally (see projections in Edward and Sumner 2019).

So, the setting and use of low poverty lines may lead to a simple movement of people from one side of the line to the other, which is communicated as a trend of falling global poverty. But what has really changed beyond a few cents more? Are people really living above a minimum standard of living that is meaningful? Highlighting these questions often ignites tempers and fierce debate. But we should not shy away from asking uncomfortable questions.

Roundtable 10.2
Response **Arief Yusuf**

Is global poverty declining? Well, it depends on how we accurately define 'absolute' poverty—the absolute number of people living in conditions of poverty. Absolute poverty has been indeed declining if we define the incidence of poverty in terms of the proportion of the global population who live with less than \$1.90 per day in 2011 PPP. The threshold of \$1.90 was decided by the World Bank based on the median of national poverty lines of low-income countries. So, it is pretty arbitrary.

The arbitrary selection of such an important threshold typically needs some sort of sensitivity analysis. That is why Eduardo Ortiz-Juarez and Andy Sumner's suggestion to be more flexible in defining the line is important. They suggest that if we take a 'security from poverty' line of \$13 a day, the decline in global poverty is much more modest than the poverty incidence based on the \$1.90 line (**see Roundtable 10.1**).

I agree with Ortiz-Juarez and Sumner that there are big dangers in rushing to claim that we have been successful in reducing global poverty when using only one definition of poverty. One of the dangers is that we may, despite a low incidence of absolute poverty, overlook the population who live near the borderline, namely the large economically vulnerable population, those who live above the poverty line but below the vulnerable and security-from-poverty lines. These people have a high risk of falling back into poverty whenever there are shocks, one such shock being of course the Covid-19 pandemic.

Let's look at this from the vantage point of Southeast Asia. Indonesia is one of the best examples of such a situation. Indonesia, which was upgraded to upper-middle-income status in 2020, has a 10 per cent national poverty incidence and a 7 per cent incidence of extreme poverty. However, if we use the \$5.50 line (the median poverty line of upper-middle-income countries, sometimes referred to as the 'security line'), the incidence of poverty is in fact an arresting 52 per cent (World Bank 2022). For Indonesia, we are talking about 140 million people.

When the Covid-19 pandemic crisis hit, suddenly this vulnerable population was in dire need, and not only those who are officially defined as poor. Most of these people are outside the social protection system, and the Indonesian government quickly needed to devise additional social assistance to cover this vulnerable population, given that its existing social protection programme is normally designed for the lowest three deciles. With the pandemic, new programmes suddenly needed to be created to cover people in need even to the sixth decile. Needless to say, this created enormous pressure on the existing social protection system.

Placing too much focus on the sub-standard poverty line is also inconsistent with the sub-national heterogeneity of one country's poverty profile, and the important point here is that it may lead to less progressive poverty reduction policies at the sub-national level. For instance, Jakarta has comparable income per capita to a country like Portugal, but some provinces in Indonesia are similar to the least developed regions in sub-Saharan Africa. Other (geographically) large countries such as India or China are characterized by the same heterogeneity.

Focusing on an absolute low level of the poverty line may reduce the opportunity of those regions to focus on better poverty reduction policies. In a democratic country such as Indonesia, political leaders of more advanced regions should be elected or re-elected on the basis of achieving higher standards of poverty reduction. In short, we should make sure that we use a higher bar to judge their development performance.

Ortiz-Juarez and Sumner correctly point out the need to look at higher poverty lines. Focusing solely on extreme poverty may have delayed high-growth economies from upgrading their national poverty line (like Indonesia, for example), with a consequence of delaying the development of better social protection systems. Instead of attempting to revise the poverty line, which has lagged behind in comparison to other benchmarked countries, Indonesia has had its eyes only on the extreme line ('Jokowi Eyes' 2021). Indonesia's national poverty line remains comparable to the extreme poverty line of the lowest income economies (Yusuf 2021). Contrast this situation with what has happened in Malaysia, where the government recently changed the national poverty line quite radically (Kaos and Zainal 2020).

Of course, it is a good thing to celebrate the numbers showing the decline of extreme poverty. However, poverty has many dimensions, and many are not represented in the monetary/income poverty indicators. Some initiatives have suggested, for example, the Multidimensional Poverty Index as a much better alternative. This index looks beyond income poverty and considers health, educational dimensions, and other standard of living indicators to determine the incidence and intensity of poverty (Alkire and Foster 2011; **see Section 10.5**). Recently OPHI (2022) found that multidimensional poverty and monetary trends ($1.90 a day) do not necessarily match. This indeed highlights the need to measure multidimensional poverty separately, and suggests that there are different drivers for progress in poverty reduction.

We also have the Sustainable Development Goals (SDGs)—the post-2015 development agenda—and agendas like this are necessary (**see Case Study 14.2**). It is commonplace in national development policies that despite stated strong commitments to particular objectives, progress is not achieved due to a lack of measurable and quantifiable targets. The SDGs help national governments with these quantifiable targets. With the SDGs we can broaden our dashboard of development indicators beyond poverty. The SDGs include seventeen goals and also outline 231 unique indicators (UN Department of Economic and Social Affairs, Statistics Division 2021). Extreme absolute poverty is only one of them, and that is entirely a good thing.

Roundtable 10.3
Response Juanita Elias

Eduardo Ortiz-Juarez and Andy Sumner make a powerful intervention into debates on poverty measurement (**see Roundtable 10.1**). First, in emphasizing the extremely useful concept of 'security from poverty' they challenge accepted wisdom around what constitutes the point at which absolute poverty kicks in. Second, they establish how widely held ideas about what poverty is, and how best to measure it, reinforce perceptions that everyone is benefitting from neoliberal development policies. In this short response to these ideas, I draw upon research undertaken in Jakarta, Indonesia, into the everyday experiences of poor women evicted from their homes. I reflect on what it means to identify the poor as lacking 'security from poverty' and emphasize the need to more systematically integrate a concern with the feminized nature of poverty into this concept.

Consider the following extract which concerns a woman, Siti, who in 2016 was evicted from her home in the *kampung* (informal urban settlement) of Bukit Duri in Jakarta:

> Siti had lived in Bukit Duri her whole life. She lived in her grandmother's house which had been bought in the 1950s. Her mother had been born in the house and four generations had lived there. Kampung life prior to the evictions revolved around numerous routine activities

and gatherings—including some in which women played a prominent role such as arisan [savings cooperatives] . . . They received three warning letters about the eviction with the notices stating that eviction was necessitated for the 'public interest'. She was offered rental accommodation in the Rawa Bebek public housing site . . . over 14 kilometres away from her old house, a one-hour journey by the TransJakarta bus . . . . She ran a small snack shop from her home in Bukit Duri selling sticky rice—this would not be permitted in public housing and she would have had to rent a plot in order to sell her products and would find it difficult to combine work away from her home work with her childcare responsibilities. (Elias et al. 2018: 11)

This is the story of a woman who had made a life for herself in the *kampung*. Being able to combine running a business with looking after her children, she experienced some income growth and was able to save money. Security from poverty in this case is nonetheless about far more than just income. Siti's security stemmed from what she perceived to be a stable housing situation because her home was built on land her family understood that they owned and had long paid taxes on. Her security was also tied to an ability to access the 'social infrastructure' of the city—the forms of informal 'economic collaboration' that make life manageable for the urban poor (Simone 2004: 407). This included being able to access childcare support from trusted neighbours and a community-level savings collective.

Plans to modernize the city, by bulldozing the *kampung* and rehousing residents in high-rise accommodation on the city's fringes, an act of violent dispossession, changed all this. She no longer had security from poverty and faced significant new financial costs. Income matters, but this cannot be separated out from the wider networks of support and sources of security that contributed to *kampung* residents' ability to plan for and pursue a life for themselves and their families in the city—that is, to use a phrase introduced in **Section 10.5**, their 'capabilities'.

Ortiz-Juarez and Sumner rightly point out that poverty measurement has wider political effects. It can also be suggested that poverty measurement *in and of itself* has political effects in the sense that when poverty is *only* defined in monetary terms, we lose sight of the multidimensional nature of poverty, as well as the multiple sources of security from poverty, such as the ways urban women in Jakarta access the informal social infrastructures of the city. Taking a top-down measure of poverty based on income alone that is not disaggregated by sex may well serve to ignore women's needs, interests, and day-to-day activities (Bessell 2020).

Taking issues of the feminized nature of poverty seriously also means that we need to consider how inequalities are reproduced *within* the household itself. To understand women's experiences of poverty, it is necessary to think about the bargaining relationships, deep-rooted inequalities, and patriarchal gender norms that are at work within households. Specifically, unpaid domestic labour is vitally important labour that cannot be captured in measures of monetary income, but is undertaken overwhelmingly by female household members. Many women's experience of poverty is as much about time poverty (for example, increasing women's monetary income through work outside of the home does not necessarily lead to reductions in their household labour), a lack of access to land, the experience of gender-based violence, and other forms of oppressive household relations that render women powerless, as it is about income.

The question remains, then, whether or not alternative measures of poverty can better recognize the *gendered* nature of inequality and whether such measures might have political consequences in terms of tangible improvements for poor women around the world. Certainly, many feminist political economists have made the case for better recognition and measurement of women's unpaid domestic labour both in terms of its value (Waring 1988) and the costs associated with its non-recognition (Rai, Hoskyns, and Thomas 2014). Measures of gender (in)equality have also been built into existing frameworks for measuring poverty (Bessell 2020) and have informed the Sustainable Development Goals (SDGs).

But to what extent will the political effects of these efforts to *gender* how we measure poverty serve to undermine actually existing feminized forms of global poverty? Efforts to reduce gendered poverty are certainly far from straightforward. This is not least because when we look at poverty from a gender perspective, we are challenged to rethink what poverty is: to see how poverty is related to more than just monetary income and to recognize how poverty is experienced via unequal gendered social relations.

Roundtable 10.4
Response Craig N. Murphy

Since the 1970s, the World Bank and other development agencies of the United Nations system have considered the elimination of poverty a central goal. Since the turn of the twenty-first century, those agencies with the least interest in questioning global capitalism have touted evidence that poverty has dropped throughout the period of globalization that began around 1980. Eduardo Ortiz-Juarez and Andy Sumner correctly question that evidence (**see Roundtable 10.1**).

I'd like to take their argument further by recalling lessons of the first attempts to treat poverty as a measurable problem, more than a century ago, and by considering efforts to measure precarity that are sophisticated, consistent with the original definitions of the problem, and more useful in pinpointing relevant policy interventions than the supposedly universal income poverty lines.

The late nineteenth-century pioneers of the study of poverty understood that destitution was not required to create a proletariat. What we now call 'precarity' was enough to maintain the flow of exploitable workers into the job market. Thus, for the pioneers, ending destitution was far from a radical goal. After all, paternalistic capitalists, including the Quaker chocolate manufacturers, the Rowntrees, the Cadburys, and the Frys, had proven that profit could be made by firms that provided good working conditions, decent housing, and educational opportunities—in fact, almost everything short of the security of a lifetime income. It was in this context that Seebohm Rowntree began his ground-breaking research.

It had two parts. The first involved the direct observation of the concrete conditions of the life of workers in the city of York, in part by employing his famous checklist basket of goods essential for a decent life. The second involved a simple income measure: the amount of money necessary to purchase those goods.

The first part was primary; the income measure was just an easy-to-obtain indicator that Rowntree knew underestimated real conditions because it overlooked all the reasons why a household's available cash might not be used to purchase the basic basket of goods (for example, because the income-earners were also supporting other households). Rowntree and his followers also understood that what was necessary for a decent life would differ from place to place, which was another reason for preferring multiple concrete measures rather than a universally applied single indicator.

Some of today's longitudinal studies of poverty maintain this focus on concrete measures and they focus on the line of precarity. Consider the county-level reports of Stephanie Hoopes's United Way studies of the Asset Limited, Income Constrained Employed (ALICE) in the United States (Hoopes et al. 2020). These examine local needs and costs relative to a complex household budget that includes childcare, necessary transportation, and savings to cover the most common emergencies.

In New York State, for example, while the US federal poverty line would identity only 14 per cent of the population as poor, an additional 31 per cent are below the ALICE line of precarity (Hoopes et al. 2020). The ALICE studies let us see that even in the 'developed' world, many more people are no more than a pay-cheque away from life-altering poverty than even the 'generous' $13 a day poverty line would suggest.

Attention to multiple concrete measures of precarity makes it much easier to identify the policy changes likely to make a real difference. The Robin Hood strategy of just taxing the rich and giving the money to be poor would work, but we have no global government capable of taxing the world's wealth where most of it is, in the Global North, to give it to the poor of the Global South. Everyone should read Thomas Piketty's 'A Global Tax on Capital' (2014: chapter 15), but we also need to pay attention to the ways in which real-world policy can and has transformed specific contributors to precarity.

In doing so, we will be reminded of some incontrovertibly real positive changes in material life and its security over the last century: life expectancy has doubled. Since the 1960s, the annual rate of death by famine has fallen to historical lows and the related probability of dying in war is tiny now compared to the first half of the twentieth century.

There is dispute about why these changes have happened (S. Johnson 2021; Shaw 2011; Goldstein 2011), but students of Global Political Economy (GPE) should consider the roles of decolonization and the work of the UN system. Post-colonial governments certainly had a great deal more interest in health and famine relief and prevention than their predecessors ever had. Meanwhile, the World Health Organization, World Food Programme, and the UN proper have had these problems as their jobs.

Perhaps the World Bank and other UN development organizations have had less success with the harder-to-measure problem of poverty because so many believe that the poor will always be with us. The great achievement of the World Bank under Robert McNamara, and of Kofi Annan's Millennium Development Goals, was to question that verity and turn poverty into a problem that needed to be solved.

The historian Deborah Cadbury (2010) might add that this was a particularly difficult task after 1980, when the ideological tenor of the times and public policies of the most powerful governments made it impossible for socially responsible companies to survive. Seeking every advantage, even if it led to the impoverishment of others, just looked like good business practice. And firms run like the old Quaker chocolate manufacturers found it hard to survive.

Over to you . . .

1 All of the contributors to the **Chapter 10 Roundtable** agree that simple measures of poverty are inadequate to measure it properly, and they offer distinctive perspectives on why that is the case. What do you see as the shortcomings of conventional poverty measurements? What do they miss about the dimensions, profile, and causes of poverty? What do you think might make better measurements?

2 In explaining some of the roots of persistent poverty in the world, Craig N. Murphy makes a strong argument that dominant political and economic thought, along with the policies of powerful governments, 'made it impossible for socially responsible companies to survive' from the 1980s onwards (**see Roundtable 10.4**). Thinking about what you have learned in **Chapter 10** and other chapters in this textbook, do you think that globalization and neo-liberalism provide a compelling explanation for the persistence of poverty? Or do you see globalization and neoliberalism instead as offering the solutions to poverty? Why?

3 Juanita Elias (**see Roundtable 10.3**) and Arief Yusuf (**see Roundtable 10.2**) both illustrate their arguments with reference to different Southeast Asian countries, and Elias in particular comments on the gendered dimensions of poverty. How do you think the dynamics of poverty vary across different social groups? How are they shaped by gender and race? And how and why do they differ across distinct parts of the world?

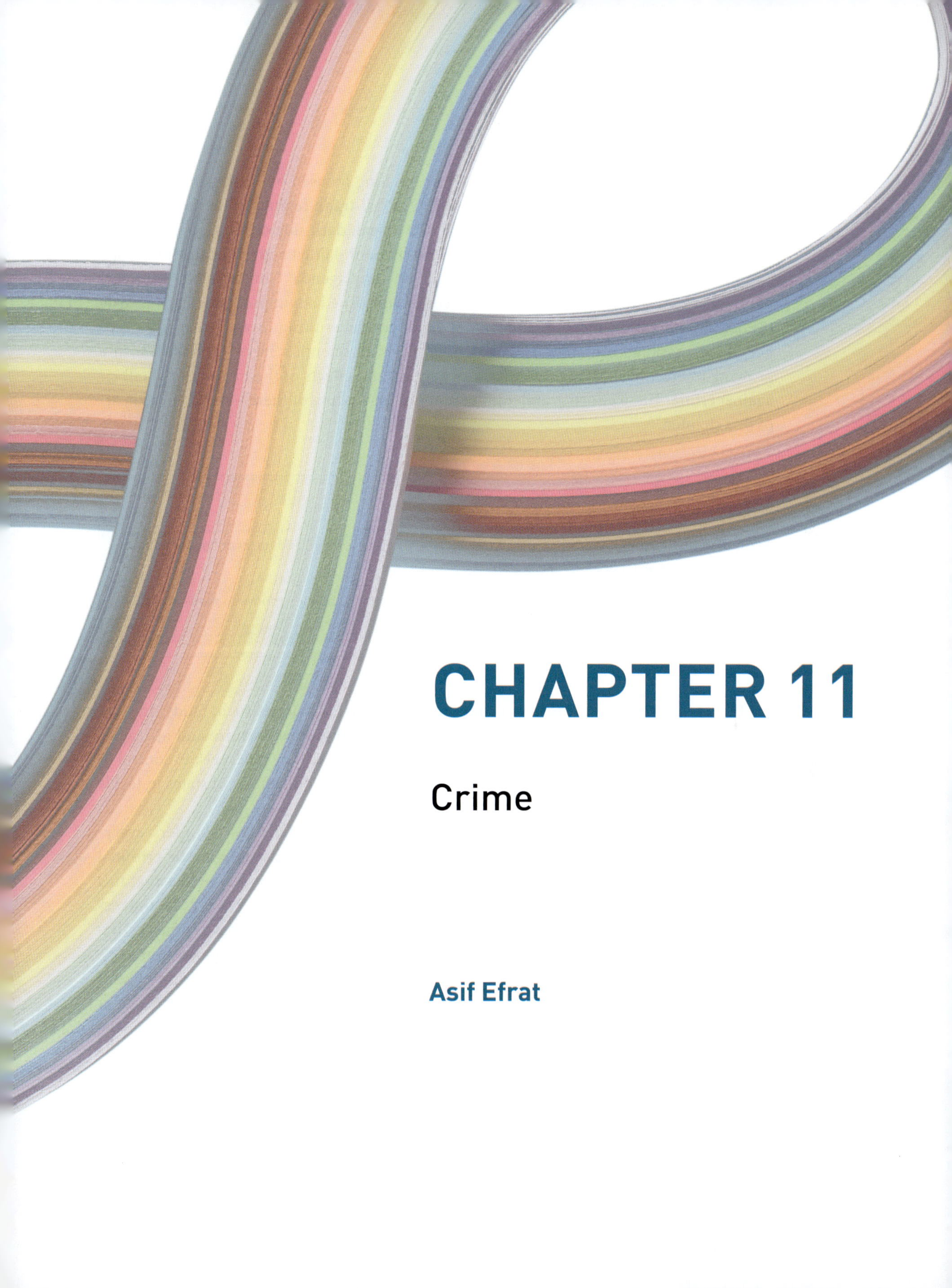

CHAPTER 11

Crime

Asif Efrat

11.1 Introduction

The study of Global Political Economy (GPE) has long focused on the legitimate, visible dimensions of economic integration: from the global trade regime to the international monetary and financial system. By contrast, the illegal, dark side of the global economy had been neglected by scholars. This changed as crime and illicit activities came to occupy a more central place on the international policymaking agenda. Governments and international organizations have become increasingly concerned about problems such as drug trafficking, human trafficking, and money laundering, resulting in an increasing number of international initiatives to curb crime. Political scientists have responded with a growing interest in studying the causes, dynamics, and effects of the international efforts against crime. These efforts—and our current understanding of them—stand at the heart of this chapter.

> ### Key Concepts
>
> **Human trafficking:** exploiting a person—typically, through force, fraud, or coercion—to obtain labour or sexual services.
>
> **Money laundering:** the concealment of the origins of illegally obtained money to make it appear legitimate.

This means that our focus here is *not* on the criminal activity as such. Studying what motivates individuals to engage in crime or how criminal groups organize and operate is the domain of criminologists. Rather, our goal is to understand how states seek to control or suppress crime. Even more specifically, we focus here on the joint efforts of states to tackle crime through bilateral or multilateral action.

Of course, every country also tackles crime independently within its own borders: everyday, national police, prosecution, and the courts deal with a variety of domestic criminal offences ranging from burglary to rape and homicide. Yet the criminal activities that fuel global concern are *transnational* in nature; they involve more than one country and thus require an internationally coordinated response. Typically, these transnational criminal activities involve illicit *flows*; that is, the movement between countries of people, goods, or money. What makes these flows illicit is that they are prohibited by the laws of the country that is the source of the flows and/or the laws of the country receiving them. Smuggling drugs or firearms across borders; laundering illegally obtained funds through international financial transactions; the sale of women to engage in prostitution—these are some examples of the transnational flows that constitute the illicit global economy. Let us briefly examine each of these flows (**see Section 11.2**), the challenge of measuring them (**see Section 11.3**), and their relationship with globalization (**see Section 11.4**), before turning to the efforts against them (**see Section 11.5** and **Section 11.6**).

11.2 Illicit flows

11.2.1 Illicit drugs

According to estimates, in 2018 roughly 270 million people worldwide used illicit drugs at least once. This figure represents 5.4 per cent of the global population aged 15–64 or nearly one in every nineteen people (UNODC 2020*a*). Drug use, especially in a pattern that is harmful or involves drug dependence, increases the risk of adverse health consequences, such as contraction of infectious diseases or premature death. Drug use can also harm one's educational attainment, increase the difficulty in finding and maintaining employment, and imperil one's financial stability. Beyond the damage they cause to individual users, drugs negatively affect the broader environment that includes the user's family, neighbourhood, and community at large. Drug abuse can lead to the neglect of the user's children or to a family breakup; users are more likely to engage in crime—under the influence of drugs or to fund the purchase of drugs; and the healthcare costs of drug use are ultimately borne by the community.

The contemporary drug market includes the traditional plant-based substances—cannabis, cocaine, and heroin—alongside synthetic drugs and non-medical use of pharmaceutical drugs and prescription medicines. Cannabis is by far the most commonly used drug, although greater threat to the user's health comes from opioids. Opium—from which heroin is made—is primarily produced in Afghanistan, and to a lesser extent in Myanmar and Mexico. Colombia accounts for most of the worldwide production of the coca leaf, from which cocaine is made, with smaller-scale production taking place in Peru and Bolivia. Cannabis is produced in nearly all countries worldwide. The production of methamphetamine—a synthetic drug—also takes places globally. From 2014 to 2018 some 28,000 clandestine methamphetamine laboratories were dismantled in twenty-eight countries (UNODC 2020*b*: 41). Trafficking routes connect drug-producing countries with the countries where the drugs are consumed. For example, heroin from Afghanistan flows to neighbouring Iran and Pakistan, as well as to Europe, the Middle East, and Africa; cocaine from Colombia flows to Central America and Mexico and onwards to the United States.

11.2.2 Human trafficking

Human trafficking serves as an umbrella term for situations in which one person compels another to provide a service. Such an exploitative provision of service is often obtained through force, fraud, or coercion, and it may take advantage of the victim's vulnerability as a result of poverty, unemployment, being an immigrant, and so on. Two primary forms of human trafficking can be distinguished by the type of compelled service: labour trafficking and sex trafficking. Labour trafficking involves exploitative and coercive employment, typically under harsh working conditions and meagre pay, in sectors such as agriculture, construction, and domestic work in cleaning or care to the elderly. The victims in such situations often find themselves under the full control of the employer, unable to leave. Sex trafficking involves the forcing, coercing, or deceiving of a person into prostitution or the use of pressure and coercion to maintain them in prostitution.

While much of human trafficking takes place within national boundaries, it sometimes involves the movement of victims from their own country for the purpose of exploitation in a foreign country. Examples include the trafficking of women from the former Soviet Union into prostitution in Europe, and trafficking of men and women from Mexico, Central America, and South America into the United States for sexual or labour exploitation. Growing awareness of human trafficking has led to an increasing number of victims being identified. In 2013, roughly 45,000 trafficking victims were identified worldwide; in 2019, that number reached nearly 119,000 (US Department of State 2020: 43). Most of those victims suffered sexual exploitation, but according to estimates, trafficking for labour exploitation is more prevalent. Note, however, that the number of identified victims represents only the tip of the iceberg: the actual number, while unknown, is likely far higher. Also note the gendered dimension of human trafficking. According to the UN (2020*a*), the majority of detected victims are female: adult women and increasingly girls, trafficked primarily for sexual exploitation. Women's economic inequality and poverty makes them vulnerable to traffickers. Racial inequality and discrimination against minority groups also increase individuals' vulnerability to trafficking (US Department of State 2021: 38–39).

11.2.3 The illicit arms trade

The illicit arms trade consists mostly of a category of weapons labelled 'small arms and light weapons': weapons intended for the use of a single person (such as handguns and rifles) or a small crew (such as heavy machine guns). We will refer to both categories as 'small arms'. Small arms are produced and exported by some forty countries worldwide; the leading exporters are Austria, Belgium, Brazil, Germany, Italy, Russia, South Korea, Switzerland, and the United States.

Most of the small-arms trade is legal: weapons are exported legally and reach authorized recipients. This trade becomes illicit when legally produced weapons end up on the black market and reach the hands of criminals, rebels, or terrorists. Weapons may reach these unauthorized recipients in different ways, including the obtaining of an export licence for the weapons through false information; purchasing guns in gun shops and selling them to criminals (which is how guns often flow from the United States to Mexico); or theft of arms from national arms stockpiles. While the illicit arms trade is mostly conducted by private actors, governments may contribute to this trade by arming groups of insurgents, rebels, or terrorists they sympathize with, sometimes in violation of UN arms embargoes. Overall, the illicit arms trade fuels civil wars and crime, undermines stability and economic development, and results in numerous deaths. Used for homicide or during armed conflict, guns kill approximately 200,000 people every year worldwide (Geneva Declaration on Armed Violence and Development 2015: 74).

11.2.4 Money laundering

Criminals typically commit crime for the purpose of generating profit. But if criminals generate large sums of money and then spend them, this could raise suspicion. In order to enjoy their ill-gotten gains and guarantee useable funds for further illegal activities, criminals must disguise the 'dirty' nature of the money and conceal its criminal origins. In other words, they need to launder the money to make it appear legal. In the laundering process, the dirty money enters the legitimate financial system and its illegal origin is then erased through a series of transactions. Examples include electronic transfer of funds between countries and into and out of offshore bank accounts; moving funds between banks or financial institutions; converting cash into financial instruments such as money orders, stocks, and bonds; and investing in real estate or legitimate business interests. As the money passes through additional layers of transactions or financial instruments, its illegal origins become more distant and obscure. Once the funds are no longer traceable to their source and have acquired legitimacy, the criminals may use them.

What are the negative effects of money laundering? Most directly, it encourages and facilitates crime. The ability to launder funds and protect them from possible confiscation makes crime more profitable and provides further incentive for criminal activity. The laundering of criminal proceeds also makes it harder for law enforcement to detect and suppress crime. In addition, money laundering can produce a host of adverse consequences for the economy, such as the corruption of financial institutions.

11.2.5 Counterfeits

Counterfeit goods are fakes: unauthorized copies of the real product, from shoes to perfumes to medicines. The selling of counterfeits typically violates the intellectual property rights—copyright, trademark, or patent—of the brand's owner. As first sight, counterfeiting seems harmless: What's wrong with purchasing a fake Louis Vuitton bag (Photo 11.1) or using a pirated copy of Windows? But counterfeiting causes significant

Photo 11.1 **What's wrong with buying a fake Gucci bag? Counterfeiting causes significant harm**

Source: © Antonio Batinic/Shutterstock.

harm. The direct victims of counterfeiting are the producers of the legitimate goods, who suffer lower sales, downward pressure on prices, and damage to the value and reputation of the brand. Counterfeiting may also inhibit future innovation: if creators of artistic works or technological inventions cannot reap the fruits of their labour, they will have weaker incentives to innovate, and society will lose the many benefits that come with creative works and products. And the counterfeit products themselves may be inferior in quality or even carry health and safety risks to consumers, especially from substandard food, medicine, cosmetics, and electronics.

> ### Key Concept: Counterfeiting
>
> This is the production and sale of unauthorized copies of consumer goods, typically at a lower quality than the authentic product.

11.2.6 Other types of illicit flows

These include:

- **Conflict diamonds** (or 'blood diamonds'): diamonds that originate in areas controlled by rebel groups and are used to fund their military campaigns. Diamonds illegally mined in African countries such as Angola and Sierra Leone were integrated into the world diamond trade, and the proceeds were used for financing civil wars.
- **Wildlife trafficking:** illegal hunting of protected species of animals and the selling of the live animals or their parts—to be used as food, medicine, ornaments, and so forth. Examples include the poaching of elephants for ivory and tigers for their skin and bones. This illegal trade threatens many types of species possibly to the point of extinction. It also negatively affects surrounding communities, for example by depriving them of tourism income or by leading to the killing of rangers in anti-poaching operations.
- **Organ trafficking:** trading in human organs—most commonly, kidneys—for the purpose of transplantation, contrary to national and international rules that prohibit commercial transactions in organs. The organs are typically purchased from vulnerable individuals through pressure or fraud and are transplanted into wealthier patients. The paid organ donors often suffer deterioration of their health, and the economic improvement they hoped for may fail to materialize.
- **Trade in looted antiquities:** the clandestine excavation and removal of antiquities from archaeological sites, typically in developing countries, and the flow of these antiquities to rich countries, where they are sold to private collectors and museums. The looting of sites and monuments often damages them considerably, and it deprives communities of parts of their heritage.

11.3 The problem of measuring illicit flows

How significant are illicit flows in magnitude and monetary value? Measuring illicit flows is important for establishing a policy response: the larger and more lucrative is a criminal activity, the more important it is to curb that activity. But herein lies a major problem. Illicit activities are, by definition, clandestine and invisible, and the individuals involved in them actively seek to hide them. This greatly complicates any effort to measure—or even roughly assess—illicit flows.

Yet the thirst for data—our need to get a sense of just how big a problem is and to have clear indicators of policy progress—results in the production and consumption of numerical estimates of illicit flows, even when these estimates are speculative, exaggerated, or lack a sound empirical basis. Such questionable estimates often come from respectable organizations, such as the UN, Interpol, and the US Department of State, and are accepted as true with little sceptical scrutiny. This produces a distorted understanding of illicit flows that gets perpetuated as unreliable numbers are repeatedly cited in the media and policy debates (Andreas 2010: 23–24). One also must remember that estimates of illicit flows may serve the interests of the actors producing and spreading them. For example, law enforcement agencies wishing to draw public attention to a crime problem—and obtain the resources to combat it—may provide inflated assessments of the magnitude of the crime. Furthermore, the difficulties in obtaining credible data on illicit flows and the methodological challenges inherent in assessing flows lead to widely different estimates by different agencies.

Consider human trafficking. In 2004, the US government estimated that between 600,000 and 800,000 people—primarily women and children—are trafficked across international borders every year. In 2006, the Government Accountability Office cast doubt on the reliability of this estimate (Government Accountability Office 2006). However, the wide reporting of that number by the media and the prestige of the agency that published it—the US State Department—turned this figure into an established 'fact' that is commonly cited in discussions of human trafficking. Other organizations—including the International Labour Organization, UN Office on Drugs and Crime (UNODC), and the International Organization for Migration published different estimates of the scale of human trafficking based on different methodologies (Feingold 2010: 54).

11.4 Crime and globalization

Even if we cannot estimate the magnitude of illicit flows with any certainty, there is general agreement that they have grown in the era of globalization. Indeed, globalization has unintentionally boosted illicit flows. In a globalized world, transportation between countries has improved considerably: there are more routes for moving people and goods at lower costs. In particular, the use of standardized containers that can be carried by ships, trains, or trucks has made trade easier and more efficient. These transportation developments facilitate legal, legitimate trade, but they also provide more opportunities for smuggling. Sealed containers, for example, might be used for smuggling drugs, guns, and even people. Improvements in communication and technology—such as cellular phones and the Internet—have similarly made it easier to move goods illegally and distribute them to consumers. So has the growing openness of borders (Kacowicz et al. 2021).

Globalization is also characterized by liberalization: relaxing government control of the national economy and opening it up to global market forces. Aiming to enhance economic activity and national welfare, liberalization policies may unintentionally facilitate illicit flows. The lowering of trade barriers, for example, increases the volume of trade between countries: a desirable outcome in itself, but one that also creates more places to hide smuggled goods and lowers law enforcement's capacity to detect and seize them. The reduction of customs checks and regulatory burdens, meant to support legitimate business, is a boon for criminals who face a lower risk of being caught. And the easing of controls on the cross-border movement of money, alongside the growing volume of international financial transactions, has made it easier to launder the proceeds of crime (Raustiala 1999; OECD 2018*a*). In another manifestation of unintended effects, liberal policies that reduce government support for the economy could make people poorer and desperate enough to turn to the illicit economy. For example, the shrinking safety net in Russia in the 1990s led many women, who were often the sole breadwinners, to work as prostitutes abroad, where they fell victim to sex trafficking.

11.5 How governments counter transnational crime

Efforts to curb illicit transnational flows begin at the national level. Governments put in place national legal frameworks to prevent illicit flows and to punish those involved. At the centre of these frameworks stand criminal prohibitions, such as bans on the illegal import and sale of guns or counterfeit products or a ban on the unauthorized export of antiquities. Other criminal offences may be more generally related to illicit flows, such as prohibitions on corruption or membership in a criminal organization. But while we often equate fighting crime with criminal legislation, it is important to remember that the efforts against illicit flows rely, to a considerable extent, on an array of bureaucratic and regulatory measures which are *civilian* in nature. For example, governments can implement systems of import or export licences to ensure that goods are imported and exported legally. The licence subjects transactions to government scrutiny and approval and lowers the likelihood of unauthorized transfers of goods. To counter money laundering, governments can require banks to implement various measures, such as verifying the identity of customers or ongoing monitoring to detect unusual, potentially suspicious transactions. On a broader level, governments can stem illicit flows by addressing the root causes that fuel them. For example, the demand for guns often comes from personal security concerns, poverty, and lack of educational and professional opportunities. Measures to enhance security or provide education and employment can somewhat mitigate the demand for guns and reduce gun violence.

Yet national efforts to fight illicit flows are only partially effective at best. Criminals can adapt to anti-crime measures and find ways around them, but the bigger problem is that the criminal prohibitions and regulatory measures are often not fully implemented or enforced.

The challenge is particularly acute in weak states with underfunded and understaffed law enforcement and administrative agencies. In such states, the government might lack effective control over parts of the territory, control of borders might be poor, and official corruption may further hinder effective enforcement. But even in developed countries with a well-functioning government, law enforcement agencies are often overstretched and may lack the human, financial, or technical resources for suppressing illicit flows. US authorities, despite their efforts, have not stemmed the flow of drugs into the United States nor have they eliminated the trafficking of persons into the country. Private institutions tasked with identifying criminal activity, such as banks in the case of money laundering, may similarly lack the necessary resources and capabilities for such a complex and challenging task, or they might be concerned about disruption to their business practices. Similar problems of cost and complexity plague efforts to address the root causes of illicit flows, for example by enhancing education or reducing poverty and unemployment. Such efforts may curb criminal activity only in the long run, if at all.

National efforts to curb illicit flows might fail for yet another key reason. Curbing illicit flows requires action both by the countries that are the source of the flows and by the countries to which the flows are destined. The United States makes enormous efforts to stem the illicit import and circulation of drugs, but if drug-producing countries keep sending drugs to the United States, the United States will find it extremely difficult to keep them out. African countries will similarly struggle to prevent the illicit import of guns if arms-exporting countries continue to sell guns indiscriminately. International cooperative arrangements are therefore necessary for coordinating the efforts to control illicit flows in source, transit, and destination countries.

11.5.1 Multilateral agreements against illicit flows

As in other areas of international cooperation, international efforts against crime rest on a set of international agreements negotiated and adopted by governments. The earliest agreements to prohibit a cross-border practice and commit states to its eradication concerned slavery and the slave trade. In the eighteenth century, Britons played a dominant role in the transatlantic slave trade, transporting enslaved Black Africans into the Americas. Yet in 1807, the British parliament banned the slave trade and later abolished the institution of slavery in Britain's colonies. Throughout the nineteenth century, the British government waged an anti-slavery campaign that included efforts of the Royal Navy to suppress the slave trade, as well as a set of bilateral agreements in which African rulers and European governments agreed to prohibit that trade (Andreas and Nadelmann 2006: 27–33).

International efforts to prohibit and curb certain cross-border flows intensified in the twentieth century. The year 1904 saw the signing of the first international agreement against sex trafficking, known then as the 'white slave traffic', and the first treaty on drug control—the International Opium Convention—was signed in 1912. In following years, throughout the twentieth century and into the twenty-first century, governments negotiated and signed additional agreements against drugs and human trafficking, as well as agreements aimed at other flows. This resulted in a patchwork of agreements that require states to put in place criminal prohibitions and a variety of civilian or bureaucratic measures to prevent and suppress illicit flows. Consider the following examples:

- The Agreement on Trade-Related Aspects of Intellectual Property Rights (TRIPS)—the primary international agreement against counterfeiting, in place since 1995—requires states to enforce intellectual property rights through criminal sanctions, civilian court proceedings in which the counterfeiter may be ordered to stop or pay damages, and border measures to intercept counterfeits and prevent their release into circulation.
- The 2000 UN human trafficking protocol—Protocol to Prevent, Suppress, and Punish Trafficking in Persons, Especially Women and Children—requires states to criminalize human trafficking, to take action to prevent that crime (for example, through mass media campaigns), and to provide assistance and protection to victims.
- Seeking to suppress the production of and trade in conflict diamonds, the Kimberley Process Certification Scheme, established in 2003, is based on a system of certificates that accompany international shipments of diamonds, guaranteeing that the diamonds are not tainted by conflict.

Note the delicate task of the Kimberley Process Certification Scheme: to separate the illicit, conflict-associated diamonds from legitimate diamonds; to allow the legitimate trade while preventing and suppressing the illicit trade. Other domains pose a similar challenge of separating the legal and the illicit: control of narcotic drugs seeks to allow the export, import, and distribution of narcotics for medical and scientific purposes while prohibiting and preventing any other use of these substances. The efforts against the illicit trade in small arms aim to prevent criminals, rebels, and terrorists from obtaining guns while allowing legitimate buyers to acquire them. But distinguishing between legal, legitimate transactions and those that are illegal may prove difficult. It requires significant efforts to ascertain the identity of buyers and sellers and to identify the purpose of transactions. And the challenge becomes greater when some of the private actors tasked with countering illicit flows have little incentive to do so, as **Section 11.5.2** explains.

11.5.2 **The actors**

International campaigns against criminal flows are typically initiated and led by governments concerned about the negative effects of such flows. Worried about widespread drug abuse in the United States, the US government has been at the helm of the international efforts to control drugs since the early twentieth century; it has also spearheaded the international campaign against money laundering to prevent criminals from enjoying their drug profits. The US government also initiated and promoted the TRIPS agreement on behalf of American industries whose products fell victim to counterfeiting. Developing countries, on their part, played a key role in pushing for international action against illicit flows of concern to the developing world, such as the illicit trades in small arms, antiquities, and conflict diamonds.

But illicit flows are ultimately commercial activities in which goods or services are provided and consumed. This means that the key actors in illicit flows are *non-state actors*: actors that are not a part of the state apparatus. Transnational crime obviously involves a host of malign non-state actors: mafias; drugs cartels and drug dealers; clandestine arms smugglers; sex traffickers and brothel owners; brokers who arrange the sale and purchase of kidneys; and looters of antiquities are but a few examples of criminal actors who make a profit—often, a hefty one—by engaging in prohibited cross-border transactions (Naím 2005). Groups of rebels, insurgents, and terrorists may also participate in illicit markets to obtain funds for their violent campaigns. All these malign non-state actors sometimes receive assistance from corrupt governments and law enforcement officials who ignore illicit flows or facilitate them in exchange for a bribe or under threat.

Illicit flows, however, also involve actors that we typically consider as legal and legitimate. Examples include arms manufacturers that sell guns indiscriminately, including to questionable buyers who might misuse the weapons; banks that launder the proceeds of crime; pharmacies that distribute prescription drugs likely to be abused; museums that acquire and display looted antiquities; or diamond companies that trade in conflict diamonds. Such legitimate actors feed, fuel, and assist illicit trade—knowingly at times, but often out of wilful neglect to ensure the integrity of their business. They ignore the dubious origin of goods and the questionable nature of transactions, and their unscrupulous conduct allows illicit flows to flourish.

Lastly, at the end of an illicit flow often stand individuals who do not fit the description of criminals: otherwise law-abiding citizens who consume drugs or buy prostitution services from victims of sex trafficking; farmers and contractors whose exploitation of workers amounts to labour trafficking; patients suffering severe kidney disease, willing to illegally pay for a kidney to save their lives; and people buying fake designer bags or using pirated software. The illicit economy, in other words, is not only the domain of criminals or shady dealers and smugglers. Rather, it encompasses a wide array of actors widely considered as legitimate and even socially respectable.

Accordingly, the efforts against illicit flows aim to suppress the activity of malign actors and also to regulate the conduct of legitimate actors to make sure they behave responsibly. If the arms industry implements measures to prevent guns from reaching criminals and terrorists, and if financial institutions take actions to ensure the legitimacy of transactions, this should reduce the illicit arms trade and money laundering, respectively. Yet, the legitimate actors involved in illicit flows are often reluctant to accept constraints on their business that would make it less profitable: complying with bureaucratic requirements can be costly and burdensome; ensuring that transactions are clean ultimately means having fewer of them. And these actors often receive the support of their governments. Seeking to protect business interests and to enhance employment and income, governments might be unwilling to accept international commitments against illicit flows or to enforce them. More broadly, governments might hesitate to view otherwise legitimate, respectable actors as criminals and punish them. This means that efforts against crime require pressure on governments to compel them to curb illicit flows. This pressure may come from the United States (**see Section 11.5.3**) or from civil society (**see Section 11.5.4**).

11.5.3 **The role of the United States**

One might hope that challenges such as human trafficking and drug trafficking would inspire the countries of the world to fashion a concerted response, but this has hardly been the case. Governments have often resisted efforts against crime for a variety of reasons. **Section 11.5.2** highlighted one such reason—concerns for the interests of legitimate businesses—and the **Chapter 11 Roundtable discussion** will identify additional reasons.

The upshot is that cooperation against crime requires cajoling and pressuring to bring governments to curb illicit flows. Throughout the twentieth and into the twenty-first century, this task fell to the United States.

First and foremost, the United States has led international campaigns against illicit flows that directly threaten American society: drugs; money laundering that fuels the drug trade and other crimes; and counterfeiting, which harms the commercial interests of American corporations. But the United States has also joined or led other campaigns where Americans were not the primary victims of crime. In those cases, moral or humanitarian sentiments motivated the United States to tackle crime problems abroad. In 2000, the United States launched a global campaign against human trafficking, aiming to curb the sexual exploitation of women and children abroad; since the 1970s, the United States has played a key role in the efforts against the illicit trade in antiquities—not to protect archaeological sites in the United States but to stem the looting of archaeology in foreign countries.

US policies against global crime consist of a mix of multilateral and unilateral measures. By spearheading multilateral agreements against crime and by working through international bodies, the United States can lend greater legitimacy to its efforts and make them look like a reflection of a world consensus rather than a US dictate. Unilateral measures, in contrast, allow the United States to set standards and enforce them with no need for other countries' consent, which is exactly what makes these measures controversial. Both the multilateral and unilateral efforts involve significant US pressure and coercion. An example of coercive multilateralism is the US domination of the UN's policymaking body on drugs—the Commission on Narcotic Drugs (CND)—in the 1950s and 1960s. By linking drug control to economic and political support, the United States brought other member states of this body to accept stringent drug regulation. Developing countries, especially from Latin America, faced threats of aid withdrawal if they did not align their votes on drug resolutions with the United States (Bewley-Taylor 2001: 65–73). The use of *unilateral* coercive pressure has been manifested most clearly in the drug certification process, which the United States introduced in the 1980s and employs to this day. As part of this process, the US president submits an annual report identifying drug-producing and drug-transit countries that failed to take anti-drug measures prescribed by international agreements and US law. Those countries might be penalized through the suspension of US economic assistance.

Following the drug 'blacklist', the United States established several other annual blacklists. Each of these lists identifies countries that, in the US view, failed to curb illicit flows; those countries then face a threat of penalties. Since 2001, the Department of State has published the annual *Trafficking in Persons Report* which ranks countries of the world in three tiers: countries whose governments fully comply with the minimum standards for combating human trafficking, as laid out in US law; countries whose governments do not fully comply with the standards but make significant efforts to comply; and countries whose governments do not make significant efforts to comply. Countries in the latter category could face withholding of US economic aid and US opposition to them receiving assistance from international financial institutions; they also suffer a blow to their international reputation (**see Case Study 11.1**). In a similar unilateral fashion, the United States annually designates countries that fail to take action against money laundering and counterfeiting.

Case Study 11.1: Coercion in the efforts against global crime: Israel and sex trafficking

The case of sex trafficking in Israel demonstrates how coercion through the tarnishing of a state's reputation can motivate efforts to tackle crime (Efrat 2012: 185–209).

The number of women trafficked into prostitution in Israel reached 3,000 in the late 1990s and early 2000s, with the number of brothels ranging between 300 and 400. The women typically came from post-Soviet countries, including Russia, Ukraine, and Moldova. Motivated by poverty and unemployment, these women arrived in Israel in search of work. Some had been promised jobs in cleaning or childcare. Most women knew they would be prostitutes, but were unaware of the inhumane and exploitative employment conditions: serving up to 30 clients per day, with nearly all the money ending up in the traffickers' pockets; and enduring threats and violence if they wished to leave.

Israeli law enforcement did little to tackle sex trafficking. As prostitutes, trafficked women found themselves on the margins of society and were not seen as deserving help. Several domestic actors in Israel—a parliamentary committee and civil-society groups committed to the rights of women and migrant workers—raised awareness of the women's plight and called for action. Yet the primary trigger for change came from the US State Department, which released its first *Trafficking in Persons Report* (TIP Report) in July 2001. The report gave Israel the lowest ranking—Tier 3—arguing that 'The [Israeli] government recognizes that trafficking in persons is a problem, but devotes limited resources to combating it.' Furthermore, Tier 3 countries faced a threat of suspension of US economic aid.

Israeli officials reacted to the American report with concern and alarm, but not necessarily because of the economic threat of aid suspension. It was assumed that the close and special relationship between the United States and Israel would prevent the United States from carrying out the economic threat. Rather, it was the threat to Israel's international reputation that worried the government, bureaucracy, and law enforcement agencies. Contrary to Israel's claim to be a rule-of-law country that protects women's rights, the report criticized Israel's failure to enforce the law against traffickers and its indifference to the abuse of trafficked women. Such criticism threatened to complicate Israel's delicate situation in the international arena and to damage the special bond between the United States and Israel, which builds on US appreciation for Israeli democracy.

These reputational concerns triggered a dramatic policy shift. The previous indifference toward sex trafficking was replaced by serious efforts to eliminate this problem. The police boosted efforts to raid brothels and arrest and investigate traffickers, and efforts were made to provide medical services and legal aid to victims. The culmination of Israel's efforts came with the enactment of a comprehensive anti-trafficking law in 2006. In 2012, the TIP report ranked Israel in the top tier: Tier 1.

Questions

1 To motivate governments to act against human trafficking, the TIP report combines two types of coercion: threats of aid suspension and tarnishing of the state's reputation. Which types of countries are more likely to be sensitive to each type of coercion?

2 Some have criticized the United States for appointing itself to be 'the world's policeman' on human trafficking. Is such criticism justified?

Coercion has also been key to US bilateral efforts against drugs, demonstrated most clearly in the US invasion of Panama and overthrow of accused drug trafficker Manuel Noriega in 1989. But the bilateral channel also includes assistance to countries in their anti-crime efforts, for example by providing funding and training to forces fighting the drug industry in Latin American countries and helping these countries strengthen their law enforcement institutions. In another expression of bilateralism, the Federal Bureau of Investigation (FBI) and the Drug Enforcement Administration (DEA)—agencies whose mission is to fight crime in the United States—have offices in dozens of countries worldwide. Through their contact and cooperation with local law enforcement in the foreign countries, these offices help their agencies to investigate international criminal and terrorist acts against US citizens and interests (FBI) and to stem the illicit flow of drugs into the United States (DEA).

It should also be noted that in some cases the United States *resisted* the efforts against illicit flows. Most notably, the United States has declined to join the 2013 Arms Trade Treaty which seeks to curb the illicit arms trade—out of unfounded concerns about the treaty's impact on the right to bear arms.

11.5.4 **The role of civil society**

Civil society groups—both domestic and transnational—play a key role in the efforts against illicit flows. These groups—sometimes labelled 'moral entrepreneurs'—are committed to worldwide suppression of flows that they deem harmful and repugnant, and they lobby governments to suppress these flows. Their motivation for doing so typically comes from values and normative principles, including religion, human rights, peace, development, and environmental protection. For example, in the late 1990s evangelical Christians teamed up with women's groups to demand US action against sex trafficking, which they considered immoral and abhorrent (Efrat 2012: 179–85). At roughly the same time, American and European non-governmental organizations (NGOs) began demanding that governments and the diamond industry halt the trade in conflict diamonds—for the sake of peace, development, and human rights.

To encourage governments to take action, moral entrepreneurs seek to educate policymakers and raise their awareness about the detrimental consequences of illicit flows. The provision and dissemination of information serves as the entrepreneurs' key strategy for gaining influence and shaping policy. Their provision of information involves various techniques, such as meeting with policymakers, sending letters, giving oral and written testimonies, and publishing reports. While the entrepreneurs' advocacy often highlights moral and normative reasons for suppressing harmful flows, it may also identify self-interested motivations—for example, warning policymakers that failure to take action would tarnish the country's international reputation.

In addition to influencing policymaking directly, moral entrepreneurs exert influence indirectly by fostering public opinion favourable to their efforts. Through such means as publications and lectures, the entrepreneurs can raise public awareness and galvanize popular concern, increasing the pressure on policymakers to take action. To encourage action against conflict diamonds, the campaigning NGOs distributed posters, leaflets, videos, and published reports. They called upon the public to ask governments and diamond companies for effective controls (Grant and Taylor 2004).

11.6 International mechanisms against crime

Combating global crime requires governments to establish norms aimed at prohibiting and suppressing cross-border flows, but it also requires mechanisms of cooperation to help put these norms into effect by facilitating the investigation and prosecution of crime and apprehension of criminals. This section discusses two of these mechanisms: extradition (**see Section 11.6.1**) and Interpol (**see Section 11.6.2**). **Case Study 11.2** discusses challenges in establishing mechanisms to combat cybercrime.

> ### Key Concept: Extradition
>
> This is a legal process through which persons accused or convicted of crime are surrendered from one country to another for prosecution or punishment.

11.6.1 Extradition

Extradition prevents criminals from escaping justice by fleeing to a foreign country. It is a formal legal process through which persons accused or convicted of crime are surrendered from one country to another for prosecution or punishment. Through extradition, drug traffickers from Colombia, Mexico, and other countries have ended up in a US courtroom. Perhaps the most infamous of these is Joaquin 'El Chapo' Guzman, the leader of the Sinaloa Cartel and among the leading drug lords globally. After a series of prison escapes and manhunts, Mexico extradited El Chapo to the United States in January 2017, and a New York court convicted him in February 2019.

Extradition typically takes place on the basis of formal treaties. Most often, these are bilateral treaties, that is, agreements between pairs of states. The United States, for example, has extradition treaties with more than 100 countries. But sometimes extradition involves regional treaties, such as the European Convention on Extradition. Both bilateral and regional treaties lay out a series of standards and procedures for carrying out extradition, and they seek to reconcile the tensions and mitigate the sensitivities inherent in this process. After all, prosecuting and punishing offenders is a prerogative of the sovereign. By transferring suspected offenders to stand trial abroad, a country limits its own legal sovereignty, and these limitations must be drawn carefully, so as not to compromise states' interests and their legal standards. For example, an extradition is typically possible only if the relevant conduct is criminalized in both countries involved in an extradition; this allows a country

Case Study 11.2: The challenges of cooperation against crime: The case of cybercrime

The spread of computer technology in recent years has given rise to cybercrime (Photo 11.2). 'Cybercrime' does not actually refer to a single type of offence. Rather, it is an umbrella term for various crimes that involve computers. Cybercrime can target persons (for example, online harassment or identity theft); it can target property, such as a computer or server (for example, destruction of information stored on a computer or transmission of a computer virus); and it may also target the government (for example, hacking into or sabotaging government networks).

Fighting cybercrime presents a unique set of challenges. For example, due to privacy concerns, law enforcement may be denied data relevant for criminal investigation; criminals may use encryption to prevent incriminating data from falling into the hands of the police; and new technologies, such as cryptocurrencies and cloud services, may also facilitate criminals' goal of escaping the law. Another challenge comes from the short time available to carry out cybercrime investigations: whereas illicit drugs take days or weeks to reach their destination, emails can be deleted in seconds, and large files can be downloaded in minutes.

Another challenge to tackling cross-border cybercrime comes from the differences in national legal policies. Many countries have been slow to enact laws criminalizing computer offences, and the national cybercrime laws that do exist may differ in the types of computer-related activities that they criminalize. This could hinder international cooperation in criminal investigations, since it may require criminalization of the investigated act in all countries involved. A global

Photo 11.2 Cybercrime can target persons, property, and the government

Source: © iStock/matejmo.

treaty would have harmonized cybercrime legislation, creating similar legal rules across countries and facilitating cooperation. Yet such a treaty has not yet been established, since countries vary in their thinking on the control of cyberspace: some prefer an open and free Internet, while others (like China and Russia) would like greater state control of the Internet.

Currently, the most significant multilateral agreement on cybercrime is the Convention on Cybercrime, established by the Council of Europe in 2001. The Convention requires countries to:

- *Define criminal offences and sanctions under their domestic laws for four categories of computer-related crimes:* fraud and forgery, child pornography, copyright infringements, and offences against the integrity of computer systems, such as hacking and illegal data interception.
- *Establish domestic procedures for detecting, investigating, and prosecuting computer-related crimes.*
- *Establish a rapid and effective system for international cooperation,* for example by assisting foreign authorities to obtain electronic evidence of a criminal offence (Archick 2004).

Countries that have joined the convention come primarily from Europe, but the convention does have several members from other regions, including the United States, Australia, and Argentina.

Watch the video on the online resources to take your understanding of this case study further.

Questions

1 Some argue that an international agreement on cybercrime without the participation of Russia and China would be ineffective, since much cybercrime originates in these two countries. Do you agree?
2 What other unique challenges may arise in the control of cybercrime that do not exist in the control of 'real-world' crime?

to avoid extraditing a person for conduct which, in its view, should not be considered criminal. Extradition treaties can also include provisions to guarantee the human rights of the individual being extradited. For example, they may allow extradition to be refused if the surrendered person could be punished with the death penalty.

11.6.2 **Interpol**

In every country, the primary task of detecting and investigating crime and catching offenders falls to the police. When the criminal activity crosses borders, suppressing crime requires police agencies in multiple countries to coordinate their activities and assist each other. Promoting such coordination and assistance is the purpose of the International Criminal Police Organization known as Interpol. A common mistake is to view Interpol as an international police force. This, however, is not the case. In a world of sovereign states, the authority to tackle crime and apprehend criminals rests with national police forces; Interpol does not send agents to carry out law enforcement within the territory of a country. Rather, the organization fulfils its coordination and support mission through its General Secretariat, housed in Interpol's headquarters in Lyon, France, and through national points of contact—named National Central Bureaus—in each country. These bureaus are run by national police officials and usually sit in the government ministry responsible for policing.

What does Interpol do? To carry out successful cross-border investigations, police require up-to-date global data on criminals. Interpol meets this need through nineteen databases, managed by the General Secretariat and searchable by the police in each country. These databases contain various types of information on crimes and criminals, including names and fingerprints of individuals; stolen items such as passports and vehicles; and weapons. These databases provide a tool for police forces to share sensitive information with their counterparts around the world. Furthermore, through Interpol, police can also obtain the assistance of foreign counterparts in bringing offenders to justice. Upon the request of a National Central Bureau, Interpol issues a Red Notice for fugitives wanted either for prosecution or to serve a sentence. A Red Notice requests law enforcement worldwide to locate and provisionally arrest a person pending their surrender to the requesting country.

11.7 Conclusion

Transnational crime poses a growing problem in the era of globalization, and its adverse economic, social, and political effects are felt by societies worldwide. This chapter has surveyed a range of cooperative tools through which the international community seeks to prevent and curb crime; it has also introduced key actors in this area: from the non-state actors involved in illicit flows to the US government and moral entrepreneurs who are seeking to suppress such flows.

A key takeaway point is that the illicit economy presents significant challenges of international cooperation: governments may be unable to suppress transnational criminal activities, or they may be unwilling to do so. Combating transnational crime requires us to give governments both the means and the motivation to take action.

Key Points

- Illicit flows are difficult to measure, but they seem to have increased in the era of globalization.
- While states typically seek to curb crime through national means, curbing illicit transnational flows also requires international cooperation among states.
- There is no single, integrated international framework for suppressing crime. Rather, global crime governance relies on a patchwork of agreements, each addressing a specific crime: from drug trafficking to the looting of antiquities.
- Illicit flows involve malign actors, such as criminals and terrorists, but also otherwise legitimate actors, such as banks and museums.

- Governments often have little incentive to suppress illicit flows. The efforts against illicit flows may therefore require coercion (exercised by the United States) or the advocacy of moral entrepreneurs.

Further Reading

Andreas, P. (2019), *Killer High: A History of War in Six Drugs* (New York: Oxford University Press). Examines how six drugs—alcohol, tobacco, caffeine, opium, amphetamines, and cocaine—shaped conflict and war.

Felbab-Brown, V. (2017), *The Extinction Market: Wildlife Trafficking and How to Counter It* (New York: Oxford University Press). Examines the causes, means, and consequences of poaching and wildlife trafficking, seeking to find ways to suppress this practice.

Jakobi, A. (2013), *Common Goods and Evils? The Formation of Global Crime Governance* (New York: Oxford University Press). Explains the evolution of global crime governance as a process of rationalization in world society, based on sociological institutionalism.

Jakobi, A. (2020), *Crime, Security and Global Politics: An Introduction to Global Crime Governance* (London: Macmillan Education). Introduces global crime governance, including drugs, human trafficking, the crime–violence nexus, environmental crime, financial crime, and cybercrime.

Sharman, J. (2011), *The Money Laundry: Regulating Criminal Finance in the Global Economy* (Ithaca, NY: Cornell University Press). Examines how anti-money laundering policies have spread to so many countries and whether these policies work.

Chapter 11 Roundtable discussion

Does international crime control work?

Roundtable 11.1
Opening contribution **Asif Efrat**

In **Chapter 11**, we reviewed a set of international agreements and mechanisms aimed at suppressing transnational crime. The key question is: Do these crime-fighting instruments fulfil their goal effectively? Do they actually curb illicit flows or at least motivate governments and other relevant actors to try and tackle these flows? The evidence is mixed.

More than a hundred years have passed since the signing of the first drug control treaty, and the drug trade continues to flourish. In 2019, a UN Task Team concluded that:

> Drug markets are evolving at unprecedented speed. The range of substances and combinations available to users has never been wider, and the amounts produced have never been greater. Cultivation and manufacturing of heroin and cocaine have reached record highs, synthetic drugs continue to expand … Drug-related deaths are on the rise. (UN System Coordination Task Team 2019: 5)

The effectiveness of international efforts against money laundering has also been called into question. A key tenet of the anti-money laundering regime is the regulation of shell companies: companies that exist on paper only, with no significant assets or operations. Such companies often facilitate a range of serious crimes, from corruption to drug trafficking. To prevent that, corporate service providers (CSPs)—the firms that establish and maintain shell companies—are required to demand notarized identification documents from their clients. Through an experiment, a team of international relations scholars examined whether CSPs actually comply with this requirement. The experimental design included sending 7,456 emails—under alias identities—to 3,771 firms in 181 countries. All emails asked for confidential incorporation of the shell company, but the researchers randomly assigned treatments to learn if targets' behaviour changed in response to different conditions, such as being informed about international legal requirements. The results were rather bleak: nearly half of the replies, many of them from US CSPs, did not request appropriate identification. Even when the email to CSPs mentioned that international rules require disclosure of identifying information, this did not motivate greater compliance with the requirement (Findley, Nielson, and Sharman 2014). This leads us to question not just the anti-money laundering regime but any efforts against crime that require private actors to implement rules contrary to their self-interest.

Yet experience in other areas offers some signs of hope. In **Case Study 11.1**, we saw how Israel, under US pressure, cracked down on sex trafficking. Judith Kelley (2017) shows that Israel was far from alone. Since 2001, the US process of monitoring and ranking governments on their actions against human trafficking has motivated many countries to tackle this problem. Concerned for their reputation and about maintaining US economic support, governments responded to US criticism by rushing to criminalize human trafficking and boosting their efforts against it.

The fight against the illicit trade in antiquities has also made some progress. US museums previously fuelled this trade by indiscriminately purchasing antiquities with little effort to verify their legitimate origin. A 1970 convention established by UNESCO—the UN's agency for cultural matters—imposed controls on the movement of antiquities and sought to induce more ethical behaviour in the art market. Archaeologists and the media reinforced the UNESCO Convention by documenting the looting of antiquities and exposing the role of museums (Efrat 2012: chapter 4). Today, museums make greater efforts to ensure the legality of their acquisitions and in some cases have returned illegally obtained antiquities to the countries of origin (Povoledo 2008).

This record presents two questions: First, to what extent are the international efforts against crime effective? Is the glass half empty (as the cases of drugs and money laundering would suggest) or is it half full (as the cases of human trafficking and antiquities would indicate)? Second, why is it that transnational crime often persists, despite governments' efforts? Why is it so difficult to tackle transnational crime?

We can consider different answers to this second question. One answer would focus on the capacity and sophistication of criminals as opposed to the constraints of governments. Criminals, empowered by enormous profits and technological innovations, can evade law enforcement. The flexible, non-hierarchical, and adaptive nature of criminal networks also allows them to avoid detection and suppression. Governments, by contrast, are bureaucratic and hierarchical entities, slow to respond and adapt to criminal challenges. They operate within the limits of public budget and of the law—constraints not applicable to criminals. Due to their limited resources, governments cannot implement the full extent of measures necessary for tackling crime and they are also susceptible to corruption by criminals seeking to buy political influence. These challenges intensify in weak states, where an underdeveloped bureaucracy and political instability hinder government action.

A second explanation for the persistence of crime would emphasize societal resistance to criminal prohibitions. Activities that the law proscribes may be seen as legitimate and acceptable by large segments of the population; at times they reflect deeply rooted social practices (Andreas and Nadelmann 2006). Poverty and limited social and economic opportunities may also turn crime into an 'attractive' option, with governments struggling to offer alternatives.

A third explanation would highlight governments' disincentives to curb illicit flows that harm other countries yet benefit domestic actors. Drug-producing countries may be reluctant to stop drug cultivation and exports that harm foreign countries but provide local employment and income. Arms-exporting countries might similarly be unwilling to restrict arms exports that fuel conflicts abroad but increase the profits of arms manufacturers at home.

My view is that the third explanation holds more power than commonly recognized. While we intuitively tend to identify 'crime' with 'criminals', we should recognize that many legitimate actors take part in illicit activities and that these actors, and their governments, may have little incentive to curb harmful flows. Yet the international community has managed to motivate various actors—from banks to museums—to behave more responsibly, and governments have increased their efforts to fight crime. While the eradication of transnational crime is not within reach, we have clearly made some progress.

Roundtable 11.2
Response **Anja P. Jakobi**

International crime control is a fascinating topic, and an area in which cooperation intensifies despite many political faultlines in international affairs. As Asif Efrat shows in **Chapter 11** and **Roundtable 11.1**, international agreements led to many important areas being included in international crime control—often including a better understanding of these crimes in politics and society. Comparable to other forms of international cooperation, international crime control works well in many respects, yet it carries significant limitations and some unintended consequences. Crime can be considered to be the 'dark side' of social activity. It evolves with social, technological, and normative developments, and it is likely to persist— even if diplomats were to draft ideal agreements and police forces were to enact ideal forms of international cooperation.

Inherent limits exist with regard to what the international crime control can contribute to make the world a better place. Moreover, crime control is not only an instrument for tackling societal evils—it is an instrument of control that can be used for different purposes—including purposes that seem to counter the original intentions of international cooperation.

To start with, crime control is the result of a political process, and priorities may not necessarily correspond with the damage caused by crime. Many efforts in crime control focus on the governance of illicit markets, but these markets do not necessarily represent the most dangerous crimes: preventing the trafficking of antiquities from war zones might be effective, but this kind of crime control does little to prevent war crimes, genocide, or other crimes against humanity in zones of conflict. Moreover, the illicit trade in arms, a major driver of sustained armed conflict, is a widely ineffective part of global crime control, although it has been the subject of a UN protocol and the arms trade treaty. Many aspects of international crime control focus on crimes that are somewhat easier to control due to the actors involved (antiquities traders versus war criminals), or because cooperation against these crimes is easier to establish (human trafficking versus weapon trafficking). Whether or not crime control works thus not only depends on specific crimes, but also on whether one talks about all severe crimes or just the control of those crimes that are the subject of intense international cooperation.

The political nature of global crime control is particularly visible in areas where states elect not to cooperate against specific crimes, although the instruments are available and es- tablished: as mentioned by Asif Efrat, crime control is linked to economic interests of states and states might be reluctant to cooperate against economic profits derived from crime. The global anti-money laundering regime has expanded since the turn of the twenty-first century and has been stretched to cover a growing number of financial crimes, relying on a growing number of private actors as part of policing efforts, and including almost all coun- tries worldwide (Nance 2018). Yet, the regime's toolbox has yet to be applied in full to tax evasion—a crime that many financial centres profit from. Any assessment of whether crime control works or not depends on whether we include crimes that are internationally relevant but remain outside the scope of global crime control.

When Asif Efrat refers to the relation of crime and the state, it is also important to realize that this relation is not necessarily antagonistic: many states are, unfortunately, involved in what others—even parts of their own population—consider to be a crime. These crimes, labelled 'state crimes' by some criminologists, range from war crimes to corrupt public officials and states building an economy on taxes evaded elsewhere. State leaders can easily ignore specific crimes when they profit from them, or if it is questionable whether specific actions can be classified as crime at all. After all, the definition of crime is not a technical exercise, but rather includes normative statements. Is it an environmental crime to exploit the Amazon forest in a way that benefits economic growth but does irreparable damage to the livelihood of Indigenous people and the tropical rainforest? Answers to that question will vary, and international cooperation against environmental crimes is therefore likely to suffer in its effectiveness.

In many areas of international crime control, ideas and instruments reflect some states' interests more than others. Global drug control is mainly focused on the production of drugs, and, particularly regarding drugs like cocaine and heroin, this means that producing countries in the Global South are more affected by an effective anti-drug regime than wealthier countries where the demand for these drugs is located. Countering drugs worldwide has also meant that traditional, Indigenous consumption of cocaine by local communities in the Andes was prohibited through international drug control, reflecting the normative demand of the United States and other Western countries to prohibit countries worldwide, but impacting local culture (Andreas and Nadelmann 2006). International crime control includes normative frictions that can result in economic and political disadvantages, and that can provoke national contestation with regard to international treaty obligations.

Finally, crime control is not only an instrument for tackling societal evils—it is an instrument of control that can be used for different purposes. Even if states widely accept crime control and include instruments in their national legal code (which is still a basic challenge for global crime governance), authoritarian states, in particular, can use them for purposes that were not originally intended—using the fact that crime is based on political definitions. For instance, countries like Turkey and Russia targeted political opposition as supporters or financers of terrorism and used Interpol to find political opponents abroad—misusing this international police cooperation that is keen to keep itself outside political involvement (European Parliament 2019). In these cases, international crime control is turned into an instrument of political control.

While these aspects do not deny many positive results of global crime governance, they are a reminder that whether you think that international crime control works or not ultimately depends on what you think the ideal form of international crime control would look like.

Roundtable 11.3
Response Lorraine Elliott

The illegal trade in wildlife is one of the more complex forms of transnational criminal flows that make up what is termed transnational environmental crime (Elliott and Schaedla 2016). Illegal wildlife trade (IWT) involves live specimens of species protected from international trade, and dead animals and parts thereof, such as skin, hair, bone, horn and tusks, organs, and eggs. It also includes products that have been produced using these components, such as tiger-bone wine, powdered rhino horn or dried seahorse. Much of the publicity around IWT has focused on charismatic and apex species, particularly elephants, rhinos, big cats, and great apes, as Asif Efrat outlines in **Section 11.2.6**. The trade includes lesser known but highly endangered animals, birds, and reptiles that are traded in significant numbers. Such a list includes (but is far from limited to) tokay geckoes, totoaba, pangolins, saker falcons, slow lorises, and glass eels. The trade is motivated by collector demand for high-status goods, by a global trade in unusual pets, by private and public zoological collections, by demands from medical research laboratories, and by often-misleading pharmaceutical expectations.

Guesstimates put the *annual* value of IWT at anything upwards of USD\$7 billion. Both developed and developing countries are implicated in the supply and demand sides of this illegal trade. Some IWT is small-scale and opportunistic. It is also increasingly systematic and well-financed, involving organized groups, sophisticated smuggling chains, and complex trade routes.

From a political economy perspective, these illicit chains of custody constitute production networks that can involve illegal or criminal activity at the point of extraction and harvest (poaching), warehousing, transportation, transformation (such as carving of ivory or tanning of skins), marketing, distribution, and retail, including into legal markets. The trade is also enabled by cross-over crimes such as corruption, fraud, tax evasion, and money laundering, involving corrupt officials and so-called delinquent professionals of the kind identified by Efrat—accountants, lawyers, and financiers, for example. While some of those involved in extraction, harvesting, or poaching might be in conditions of 'poverty and limited social and economic opportunities', as Efrat suggests (**see Roundtable 11.1**), the illegal wildlife trade is primarily driven by greed rather than need. Little or no financial benefit accrues to those who are at the most vulnerable end of the supply chain.

Concerns about the dire environmental, biodiversity, security, and social consequences of IWT have resulted in international declarations and resolutions calling for governments to declare IWT a serious crime in accordance with the provisions of the UN Convention Against Transnational Organized Crime. Yet many governments have been slow to do so, and there is no consistency in the way that IWT is included in criminal codes and wildlife protection legislation across countries. Indeed, there is no dedicated international legal framework on the criminality of illegal wildlife trade.

The Convention on International Trade in Endangered Species of Wild Fauna and Flora (CITES) is designed to ensure that species are protected from endangerment by international trade and to ensure that the legal wildlife trade is conducted in a sustainable way. It is not a crime convention. It also contains loopholes that permit trade in listed species if they are bred in captivity, if they were 'captured' prior to the convention entering into force for that species, if they are personal or household effects, or if they are for scientific collections. It is not hard to see how these loopholes invite the extensive use of fraudulent CITES documentation and false declarations of compliance.

As with other forms of illicit trade, successful crime control of IWT relies on inter-agency cooperation within and between countries. Within countries, the relevant agencies and actors who need to work together include police forces, conservation rangers, customs agencies, and government departments with responsibility for environmental protection. These agencies will often have differing regulatory, legislative, and material capacities to investigate, conduct searches, seize goods, and make arrests which makes cooperation both important and challenging (White and Pink 2017).

Between countries, international IWT crime control demands good intelligence and operational coordination, as well as due diligence support from the corporate world, including airlines and shipping agencies and financial institutions. Some intelligence efforts work better than others. Seizure reporting to CITES is uneven and generally inadequate for crime control purposes. Interpol's confidential Ecomessage reporting system and database is voluntary and it relies on data that comes from scattered multiple sources within countries. The European Union Trade in Wildlife Information Exchange (EU-TWIX), managed by the wildlife NGO TRAFFIC, provides a more operationally useful access-restricted repository of EU-wide wildlife seizures and a mailing list that enables approved enforcement agencies to share real-time intelligence and advice. Since 2010, CITES, Interpol, the World Customs Organization, the UN Office on Drugs and Crime, and the World Bank have worked together under the banner of the International Consortium on Combating Wildlife Crime (ICCWC) to provide targeted law enforcement support along the entire criminal justice chain. NGOs have also been more than moral entrepreneurs in this space, with some working independently and in formal arrangement with governments and international organizations on intelligence gathering and operational support.

Have these crime control efforts worked? We don't know how much illegal wildlife trade goes undetected, nor how quickly disrupted smuggling networks adjust and re-establish their activities, shifting their operations to 'less-regulated spaces' or to other species (UNODC 2020c: 12). There is reasonable evidence that training and capacity building for enforcement personnel can support better seizure rates with appropriate levels of government support, although, as Efrat notes, that support is often limited and constrained. Time-bound operations, such as those coordinated by ICCWC and Interpol, have led to significant seizures and arrests although the translation of arrests into successful prosecutions is uneven. Nevertheless, IWT crime control efforts can and should do more to address the whole supply-and-demand chain, leverage forensic capacities, and follow the money to disrupt illegal income streams.

Roundtable 11.4
Response **H. Richard Friman**

Asif Efrat's Roundtable response uses questions concerning extent and causality to frame the inquiry into the effectiveness of international efforts against transnational crime (**see Roundtable 11.1**). Although offering important insights, there are two shortfalls in his arguments. First, the discussion of the extent of effectiveness in meeting the goals of international crime control agreements risks treating criminalization as a constant standard against which enforcement has fallen short. Second, the discussion of causality—the reasons why enforcement is uneven—captures critical aspects of state capacity and political will, but risks narrowly framing the latter in terms of a reactive state constrained by domestic pressures. My response addresses both of these shortfalls.

Efrat begins by briefly reviewing the uneven track record of enforcement successes in four issue areas. Here, despite longstanding international treaties and conventions, illicit flows and practices persist. Clearly a gap exists between criminalization and enforcement, but the essay risks treating criminalization as a constant standard. Pointing to the time that has passed since the initial efforts at criminalization, particularly in centuries-old issue areas of concern such as drugs and human trafficking, is misleading. Criminalization has not been constant. International agreements, and their domestic implementing legislation, have expanded the scope of criminalization over time. With each new treaty and modification of international agreement more drugs have been added to the list of restricted substances, more financial practices and precursor offences to the list of money laundering, more methods of exploitation to understandings of human trafficking, and more dimensions to antiquities trafficking. Enforcement has clearly lagged behind these expanding parameters of criminalization.

Thus, when assessing whether the glass is 'half empty' or 'half full' when it comes to progress in the effectiveness of efforts to suppress transnational crime, one must not lose sight of the fact that the size of the glasses and their number have expanded over time.

That said, the gap between criminalization and enforcement is not simply a function of the escalation of criminalization. As Efrat correctly notes, insights into the persistence of transnational crime require exploring factors that impede enforcement efforts. The second part of his contribution essentially frames this discussion of causality in terms of state capacity and political will. Capacity limitations are a central theme in arguments concerning the challenges states face in dealing with transnational crime. This is perhaps best illustrated by the influential work of Moisés Naím (2005) which posits that bureaucratically and sovereignty-bound governments of even the most powerful states lack the relative capacity to respond to technologically empowered and highly flexible transnational criminal networks.

Along with state capacity constraints, Efrat points to societal resistance and economic disincentives. Both of these explanations address governments' political will to engage in enforcement in the face of domestic pressures. Insights into societal resistance hinge on a broader understanding of what societal groups see as legitimate practices and the extent to which such practices are criminalized by the state. The greater the tension between the two, the greater the societal resistance to enforcement of criminalization (Van Schendel and Abraham 2005). The extent to which governments act contrary to this resistance becomes an issue of political will in the face of the political power that such societal resistance can muster. This helps to explain why enforcement is often directed at politically weaker groups such as ethnic and racial minorities even though the criminal activity (for example, drug consumption) may be widespread.

Efrat's final explanation of causality—and the one he places most emphasis on—points to the domestic pressure on governments, often from legitimate economic actors such as drugs or arms producers and economic sectors more broadly, that benefit from illicit activities. Although presented in his contribution as economic disincentives to enforcement, the challenge is ultimately political. State contestation with powerful domestic economic actors again raises issues of political will.

These three explanations of causality capture important constraints on the effectiveness of governments in enforcing criminalization. Yet I would argue that we need a broader understanding of political will, one that looks beyond the state as reactive to bottom-up political pressures and instead explores governmental actors' own preferences for selective patterns of enforcement. For example, although the US government has been at the forefront of international efforts to establish an array of global prohibition regimes it has often violated the very agreements it created. National security concerns help to explain the roles of US intelligence agencies in facilitating the Southeast Asian and Afghan opium trades at the same time as US drug enforcement agencies were seeking to control it (McCoy 2003). National security considerations shaped US presidential decisions to certify countries including Panama and Mexico during the 1980s, and Afghanistan after 2001, as fully cooperating with US and international drug control efforts even though this was far from being the case (Friman 2015).

Also, such practices of selective international enforcement are not limited to drug control. As argued in a scathing report by the Government Accountability Office (2006), broader foreign policy considerations in the US Department of State resulted in intra-agency deals that inflated the tier rankings of countries in the annual *Trafficking in Persons Report* despite their questionable records in complying with the US minimum standards against human trafficking.

The history of global prohibitions notes the interaction between the efforts of moral entrepreneurs stressing societal harm and broader interests of the governments of powerful states, both economic and strategic, in bringing prohibition regimes to fruition (Andreas and Nadelmann 2006). Assessing the effectiveness of efforts against the problem of transnational crime requires an exploration of the goals of criminalization and enforcement, their origins and evolution, and their relative importance to the state and non-state actors charged with realizing them. Insights here lie in supplementing problem-solving with critical theory approaches to better capture the broader political, economic, and social structures within which policy problems emerge (R. Cox 1981). These dimensions are often missing when seeking to understand and solve the problem of transnational crime, but are indispensable.

Over to you ...

1 A common theme across the contributions to the **Chapter 11 Roundtable** has been the intensely political nature of crime control efforts, including the suggestion that it's not simply that states or governments are limited in their *capacity* to restrict transnational crime, but rather that it's often not in their interests to do so. Does this surprise you? Do you think effective transnational crime control comes down to an issue of political will, or do you think that, even with political will, the very nature of transnational crime puts it beyond comprehensive control?

2 NGOs, consumers, and other actors are described in this discussion as 'moral entrepreneurs'. On the basis of what you have read here, and what you know about the various types of transnational crime, what role do you think moral entrepreneurs do or should play in this space? What are the possible limits to their influence?

3 The responses draw attention to the debate about where the locus of crime control can and should rest. Does it depend on multilateral coordination by international organizations? Should we be looking to a powerful state or states, as in the idea of the US being the world's police officer, as the only viable option? Can we leave this in the hands of national governments? Where do you think most effort should be focused in order to make more progress on transnational crime control, and who should carry primary responsibility?

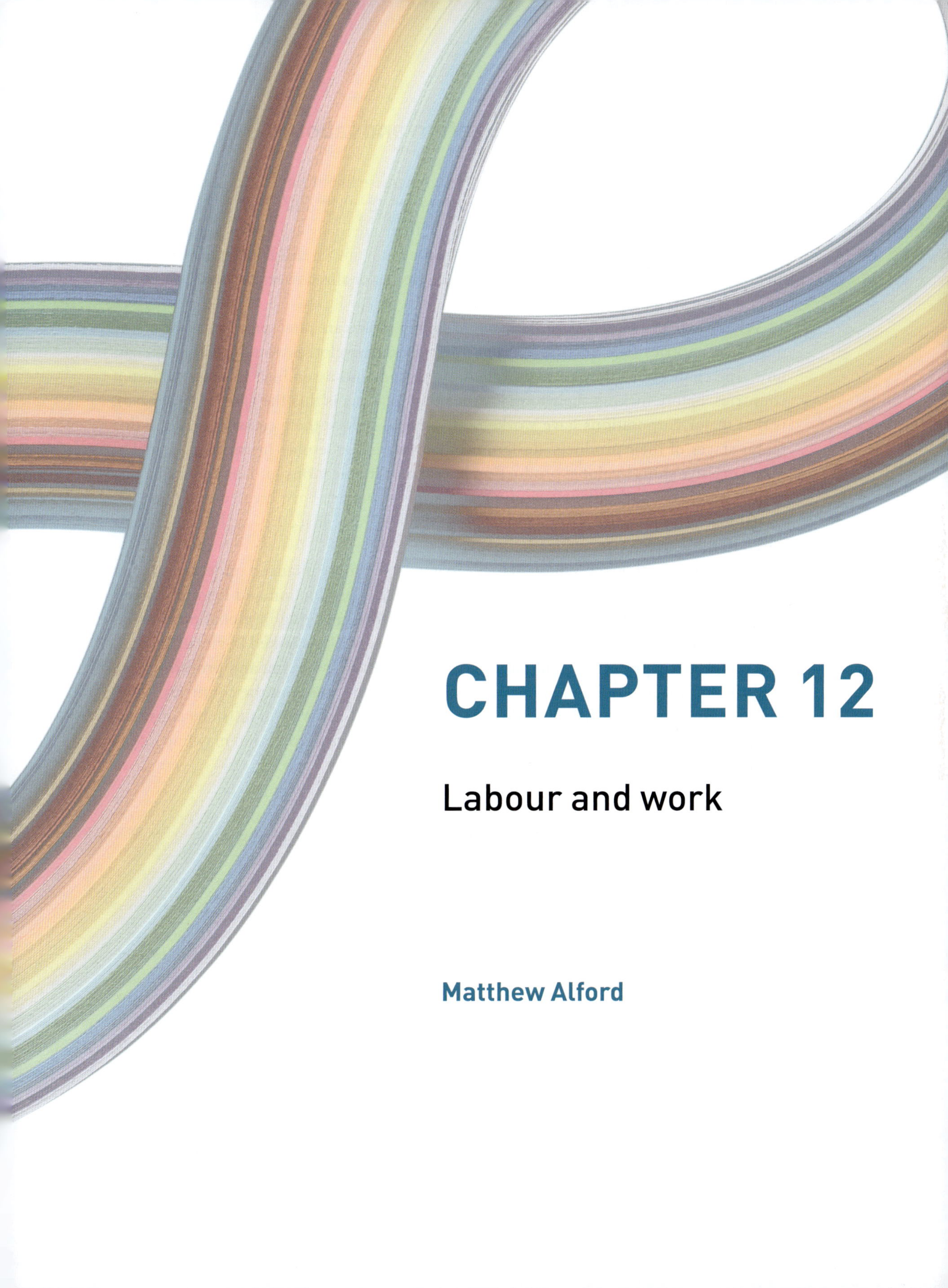

CHAPTER 12

Labour and work

Matthew Alford

12.1 Introduction: Globalization and labour

Globalization—in its simplest form—refers to an increase in our interconnectedness across the globe. Actions and events in one part of the world affect others much more quickly than they did before. As described in **Chapter 4**, there are many aspects to globalization—cultural, material, financial, and political, to name but a few. In this chapter, we will focus on how the production of goods and services has been globalized over the past decades and what this means for labour.

What used to be largely nationally based supply chains are now spread out over many different countries (**see Section 7.2.1**). Think about the clothes you are wearing right now. The chances are they were designed, produced, and assembled in many different countries, before making their long journey to you. Why is this the case? A big reason is that major corporations have worked out ways to reduce their costs by locating different stages of their products' design, production, and assembly in various countries. These massive shifts in global production have major implications for labour. On the one hand, complex supply chains spanning numerous countries have created many jobs in the Global South. On the other hand, most of these jobs are insecure and low-paid compared to those in the Global North.

This chapter will take up these debates to give you a more nuanced understanding of the complex and contested relationship between global production and labour. We will discuss whether (and which) workers win or lose from engaging in global production (**see Section 12.2**). Whose responsibility it is to ensure workers linked to global production are properly protected? Should it be the corporations sourcing and profiting from the products made? Or should it be national governments based in the countries where the goods or services are being produced (**see Section 12.3**)? We will finish by considering the very current issue of how technological advances and automation may impact the future of work (**see Section 12.4**).

12.2 Labour in global production: key concepts and debates

12.2.1 Changing dynamics of global production

In the past, corporations tended to make their own products, or at least source them through nationally based supply chains. Since the 1990s, they have delegated the production and assembly of goods to suppliers in distant countries—often based in the Global South. A significant and straightforward explanation for this is that corporations want to increase profits to appease their shareholders. The simple fact is that labour and production costs tend to be much cheaper in developing and emerging countries based in the Global South. But although corporations tend not to make the products and services they sell, they *do* remain heavily involved in the production process. In fact, corporations such as Nike, Apple, HP, and Walmart are able to use their powerful position as global buyers of goods and services to 'shape what is done and by whom . . . at what price, using what standards, to which specifications, and at what point in time they are delivered' (Ponte, Gereffi, and Raj-Reichert 2019: 1 (quote); Gereffi 1994; Gibbon, Bair, and Ponte 2008). After all, they want to make sure they retain their brand value, reputation, and attract us as their customers in what is a fiercely competitive global environment.

This means that the global supply chains linking suppliers and workers to powerful corporations are highly coordinated and interconnected. If a supplier based in the Global South wants to supply a major corporation, they must meet many standards and specifications laid down by the buyer. This can include the quality of the product and how it is produced—whether an item of clothing, electronic device, fruit, or vegetable. Following pressure from global civil society organizations such as Human Rights Watch and Oxfam, corporations also demand that suppliers meet a raft of social and ethical standards, ensuring decent and safe working conditions.

At the same time, this particular form of global industrial organization contains significant power asymmetries. Global corporations that demand these specifications from suppliers are positioned to capture most of the profits (Anner 2019; Milberg 2008; Phillips 2017). Consider the fact that a corporation such as Nike Inc. has almost 500 factories and over 1 million workers that span nearly forty countries. Yet very few (if any) are directly owned or employed by Nike itself—a point we will return to later on. Now consider a scenario where one of those factories fails to meet Nike's specifications and/or wants to increase production costs. It will likely be Nike that has the upper hand in the negotiation process. This is because powerful corporations are able to use technologically advanced sourcing strategies, economies of scale, and branding, which give them significant bargaining power over their geographically dispersed supplier base (Anner 2019; Nathan and Kalpana 2007; Milberg and Winkler 2013). They can pressure suppliers to reduce production costs, while demanding that they meet strict production and social standards—sometimes referred to as a 'Catch 22' (Barrientos and Kritzinger 2004).

All of this enables corporations to increase profits by offloading risk onto suppliers, who in turn transmit these pressures to smaller producers and workers (Anner, Bair, and Blasi 2013; Kaplinsky 2005). As we will explore more thoroughly in the following discussion, these power asymmetries that underpin global production—which are discussed at greater length in **Chapter 7**—have significant implications for labour (**see Section 12.2.2**), including how labour is governed and by whom (**see Section 12.3**).

12.2.2 **Labour exploitation and adverse incorporation**

The most frequent and effective way suppliers can offset the sourcing pressures inherent in global production described in **Section 12.2.1** is by managing labour costs. This is the case across many different types of supply chains, and especially those sectors that are price-sensitive and labour-intensive (such as agriculture, garments, footwear, and electronics) (Phillips 2016). Put simply, global buyers' demands for high-quality products at low cost have pushed suppliers to restructure their workforce to reduce costs. They do so by employing increasing numbers of casual workers on insecure, fixed-term contracts, alongside a shrinking core of permanent workers. This is to reduce both wage and non-wage costs (for example, social insurance or housing costs) associated with regular employment (Barrientos and Kritzinger 2004; Kaplinsky 2005).

The result has been a massive rise of 'precarious' work across the world. 'Precarious' work is used here as a broad term denoting a shift towards more insecure, non-standard forms of employment (Raworth and Kidder 2009). It is mainly undertaken by informal, migrant, third-party-contracted, and female workers (Alford, Barrientos, and Visser 2017; Barrientos 2019), with the most extreme forms involving the purposeful use of forced labour (Phillips 2013).

This has important implications for how we think about labour conditions in the contemporary global economy. Up until the 1970s, poverty and exploitation were thought to stem from certain groups being 'socially excluded' from the labour market (de Haan 1998; Hickey and du Toit 2007). Workers were presumed to be better off if they were directly employed by a large transnational corporation, and worse off if they were excluded from that same corporation's sourcing networks (R. Cox 1976). However, the changing dynamics of global production in the subsequent five decades meant that many more workers have become incorporated into corporations' sourcing networks (ILO 2015), despite very few being directly employed by the corporation itself (Phillips 2016: 598)—as we saw in the case of Nike (**see Section 12.2.1**). In reality, huge proportions of lower-tier suppliers and workers located in the informal economy are incorporated into global production, despite these same actors being possibly subcontracted by registered, upper-tier suppliers of global corporations.

This means that in the contemporary global economy, conditions of poverty and marginalization can be attributed not only to social exclusion from employment linked to global production, but also to the adverse incorporation of increasing numbers of precarious workers (Hickey and du Toit 2007; Phillips 2011, 2013). For example, while recent estimates indicate that global extreme poverty fell from 10.1 per cent in 2015 to 9.2 per cent in 2017, equivalent to 689 million people living on less than $1.90 a day (World Bank 2020*b*), it is also the case that those who are employed are equally likely to live in poverty relative to those outside the labour market (ILO 2019). Notice the small difference between working poverty rates and general poverty rates in **Figure 12.1**, indicating that the employed are not significantly more or less likely to live in poor households relative to those excluded from the labour market (ILO 2019). This reinforces the argument that poverty is significantly shaped by processes of adverse incorporation.

Key Concepts

Social exclusion: The process through which social groups or individuals are wholly or partially left out of the society in which they live.

Adverse incorporation: The notion that poverty can result from the (adverse) conditions in which people work in the global economy.

Precarious work: A broad, generic term denoting a shift towards more insecure, non-standard forms of employment, mainly undertaken by informal, migrant, third-party-contracted, and female workers, with the most extreme forms involving forced labour.

Figure 12.1 **Poverty rates and working poverty rates for the world and by income group (2015)**

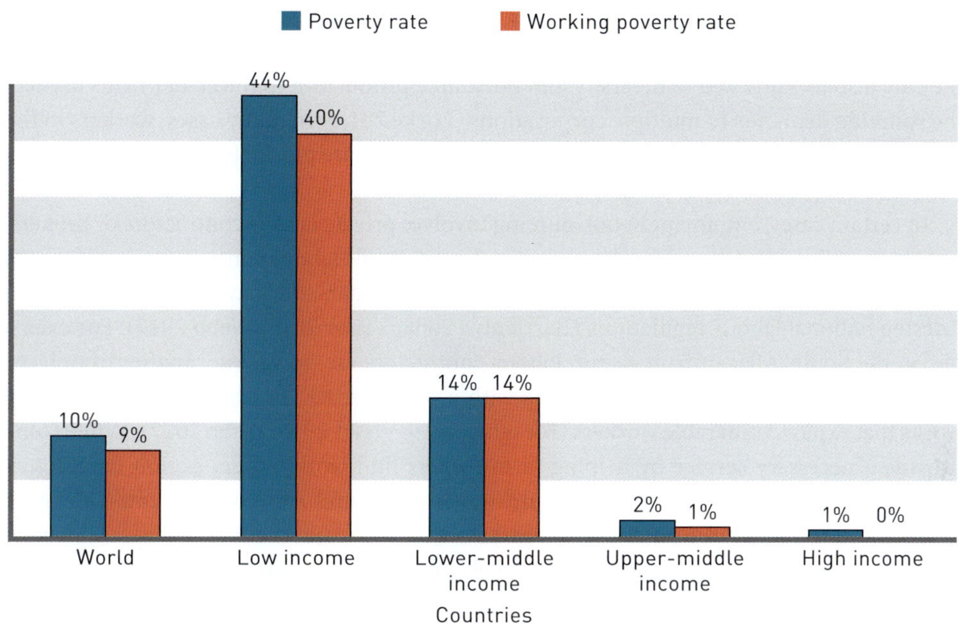

Source: ILO 2019.

Note: The poverty rate reflects the share of the total population living in poverty, at $1.90 per day. The income groupings refer to the World Bank classification of countries by income group (ILO 2019).

Having looked at these aggregate trends, we will now dig deeper into the specific dynamics that underpin the adverse incorporation of precarious workers into global production. The first of these relates to how global corporations *outsource* the production of goods and services to lower-tier firms, often based in the Global South (Mosley 2017). Rather than make the product themselves, corporations like Apple, HP, Gap Inc., and many others will transfer this work to outside suppliers. However, the situation becomes more complex when we consider that outsourcing often involves a number of subcontractor relationships that go beyond corporations' upper-tier suppliers.

To give a well-known example, Foxconn is a Taiwanese company and one of the oldest and largest 'first-tier' suppliers of Apple products—iPads, iPhones, and iPods. Apple has a longstanding relationship with Foxconn, and yet the electronics supply chain is vast, complex, and extends well beyond this 'first-tier' relationship. Many of the components and raw materials that make up the Apple product will be produced by lower-tier firms much further down the supply chain than Foxconn (**see Case Study 7.2**). This means that global corporations such as Apple actually have relatively limited knowledge of how and where goods are produced (Bartley and Child 2014).

To return to another famous example of outsourcing, Nike Inc's apparel, equipment, and footwear goods are produced in 486 factories located across thirty-nine countries, which themselves employ over 1 million workers in total (Nike n.d.). While some of these sub-contracted firms are large, upper-tier firms that are multinationals in their own right, such as the Vietnam Ching Luh Shoes Company, a subsidiary of Taiwan-based Ching Luh Group, they are also incentivized to diversify and outsource production to lower-tier firms to meet the sourcing demands of multiple corporations (Locke 2013). In many cases, workers in the lower tiers of global production will have no idea that they are producing goods and services for a branded global corporation.

In certain cases, employment outsourcing involves private labour contractors or brokers, used by supplier firms to manage labour recruitment. While labour contractors can of course be 'honest' and registered, they can also be informal, illegal, and may enable employers to sidestep national labour regulations (Barrientos 2008; Visser 2016; Webb 2017). For example, in the South African fruit sector, labour contractors are prevalent, ranging from large employment agencies, to ex-farmworkers with a pickup truck, to organized criminal networks that exploit vulnerable workers (Meagher 2019; Visser 2016; Webb 2017). While some provide a necessary service by helping farmworkers find work, others exploit contractual loopholes to undercut national minimum wages and avoid statutory benefits (Meagher 2019). More extreme cases can involve contractors paying workers advance wages which are then owed as debts, further exacerbating levels of vulnerability and exploitation (LeBaron 2014; Phillips 2017).

A second dynamic that poses challenges for labour relations connected to global production is the issue of *labour migration* (Phillips and Sakamoto 2012)—broadly defined as the movement of persons from their home state to another state for the purpose of employment (IOM 2019*a*). As discussed at greater length in **Chapter 13**, it is now commonly recognized that migration is a global phenomenon, with the International Labour Organization (ILO) estimating that 169 million people were migrant workers in 2019—an increase of 13 per cent since 2013 when the number was 150 million (ILO 2021*a*). **Figure 12.2** provides a useful breakdown of the distribution of migrant workers in 2019 by region.

Labour migration therefore involves the movement of people both from the Global South to the Global North, as well as across countries within the Global South (ILO 2021*a*). For instance, the 2010s saw vast swathes of internal migration to industrial zones within China; a fall in migrant workers in high-income countries; and an increase in migrant workers travelling to emerging economies across Eastern Europe, Southeast Asia, and sub-Saharan Africa (ILO 2021*a*).

Global migration has also been strongly linked to precarious work and adverse incorporation, partly due to the transient and vulnerable status of migrant workers, and particularly those without documentation (Phillips and Sakamoto 2012; Alford, Kothari, and Pottinger 2019). Migrant workers tend to lack recourse to rights and representation afforded by regulatory frameworks, which restricts their access to welfare and labour protections and their ability to bargain for improved wages and conditions (Phillips 2017). Unsurprisingly, there are countless examples of migrant exploitation across the Global South. They include the

Figure 12.2 **Distribution of migrant workers in 2019, by region**

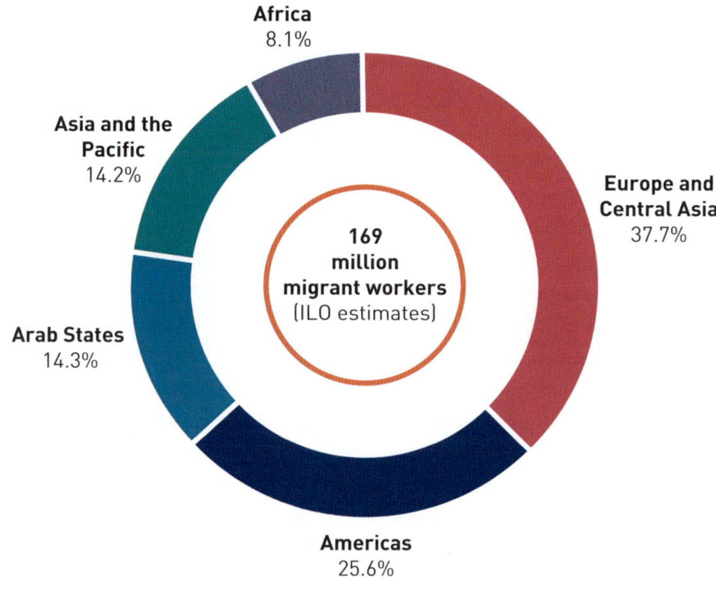

Source: Migration Data Portal 2022 citing ILO 2021a statistics.
Available online https://www.migrationdataportal.org/themes/labour-migration

'dormitory system' in China, where internal migrants' movements are heavily restricted to factories and factory accommodation, and workers experience forced overtime and labour-intensive 'sweatshop' conditions (Ngai and Smith 2007); agricultural migrant workers in Brazil and India being subject to conditions of debt-bondage (Phillips 2011; Phillips and Sakamoto 2012); and the exploitation of South Asian migrant workers during Qatar's preparations for the 2022 football World Cup (Donini 2019).

These conditions of precarity and adverse incorporation are often considered to be confined to developing countries in the Global South. However, the transnational nature of global production means that parallel examples of labour exploitation due to pressure on wages, contracts, and conditions, and examples of forced labour, occur everywhere in the world. We could take as just one illustration an incident that took place in Greece in 2013, where supervisors opened fire on groups of mostly undocumented migrant strawberry pickers from Bangladesh who were demanding their wages (Stringer and Michailova 2018). Twenty-eight workers were injured, seven of them seriously, with one left in critical condition (Chrysoloras and Penna 2013). Despite entering the employment relationship freely, these workers had not been paid for six months, and were subsequently detained by their employers and threatened with deportation (Stringer and Michailova 2018).

In considering why these problems are so widespread, a central issue concerns how work is governed in today's global economy and by whom (**see Case Study 12.1**).

Case Study 12.1: Squeezing workers' rights in global supply chains: the Bangladesh garment sector

Bangladesh is the second largest apparel exporter in the world, behind China (Photo 12.1). In 2015, the garments sector made up 76 per cent of its exports in goods and services, which accounted for 13.64 per cent of its gross domestic product (GDP). More than 4,000 suppliers and 4 million direct workers make a living from the sector (Anner 2020; Anner and Bair 2016). Supplier factories and workers are heavily integrated into global supply chains. Production workers often encounter precarious working conditions, including wages insufficient to meet living standards, excessive and sometimes forced overtime, unsafe factory conditions, and limited trade union representation (Locke 2013; Nathan, Tewari, and Sarkar 2016; Mezzadri 2017; Bair, Anner, and Blasi 2020; Kumar 2020).

A major study of the Bangladesh garment sector found that the pressure global corporations put on their suppliers to produce consistent volumes of high-quality, low-cost products contributed to driving down worker wages and eroding working conditions in supplier factories (Anner 2020). For instance, buyers demanding shorter lead times resulted in supplier firms then requiring their workers to undertake excessive overtime. Large fluctuations in buyers' order volumes were also found to exacerbate overtime demands during peak periods, as overall volume uncertainty meant factories hired fewer workers. Order volume uncertainty also drove some suppliers to cut their fixed costs by operating in cheap and often substandard factory buildings, as well as outsourcing orders to other factories. Factory owners also reported that lead firms repeatedly and increasingly ordered a wider variety of product styles and commonly changed

Photo 12.1 **Garment workers and supervisors in a clothing manufacturing plant in Bangladesh**

Source: Marcel Crozet / ILO.

orders even after production had begun. This reduced production efficiency and contributed to substantial worker overtime.

A follow-up study found that such power asymmetries in Bangladeshi garments global supply chains were both elucidated and exacerbated by Covid-19 (Anner 2022). At the outset of the pandemic, Anner found that major apparel brands and retailers cancelled billions of dollars' worth of orders, with critical implications for suppliers and workers (**see Table 12.1**).

Table 12.1 Brand and retailer initial order cancellations with Bangladeshi suppliers

Buyer (major brands)	Headquarters	Amount cancelled, March 2020 (US$)
Arcadia Group	United Kingdom	25 228 461
Bestseller	Denmark	69 659 250
C&A	Germany/Belgium	170 240 990
Carter's (Oshkosh)	United States	24 161 333
Edinburgh Woollen Mill (Peacocks)	United Kingdom	28 679 145
Gap (Old Navy)	United States	19 239 003
H&M	Sweden	172 807 508
Inditex (Zara)	Spain	72 941 131
JCPenney	United Kingdom	24 618 447
Kiabi	France	57 933 226
Kohl's	United States	38 761 950
Kontoor (Lee, Wrangler)	United States	27 926 686
LPP	Poland	43 079 137
Marks & Spencer	United Kingdom	50 240 214
Mothercare	United Kingdom	61 601 272
New Yorker	Germany	15 305 114
Next	United Kingdom	22 754 000
Primark	Ireland	311 883 607
PVH (Tommy Hilfiger, Calvin Klein)	United States	38 625 650
J Sainsbury	United Kingdom	22 231 690
Target	United States	25 489 848
Tesco	United Kingdom	56 405 999
Varner (Dressmann)	Norway	28 830 842
VF (Jansport, Timberland)	United States	67 075 555
Walmart	United States	68 690 721
Large, multibuyer entries*		361 392 729
Subtotal		1 905 803 508
Other (smaller buyers)		1 241 353 959
Grand total		**3 147 157 467**

Source: Anner 2022: 67.

*'"Multibuyer entries" are entries for which a supplier listed several buyers as a part of one entry; these were mostly for large buyers (for example, "Primark, H&M and C&A: US$5 million"). Grouping them together in one category prevented such cancellation amounts being registered with a single buyer' (Anner 2022: 67).

(*Continued*)

Figure 12.3 Impacts of cancelled orders on workers (percentages)

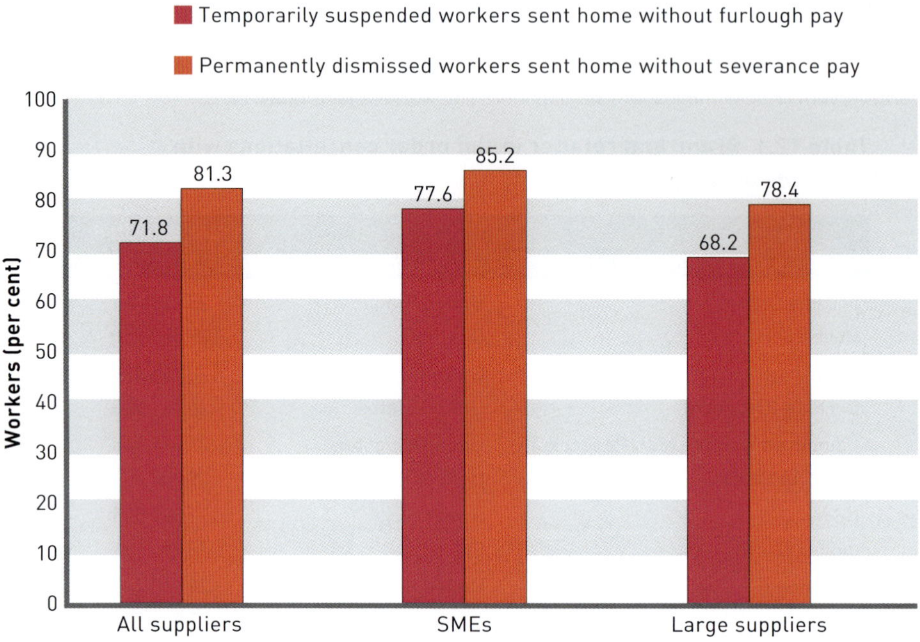

Source: Anner 2022: 70, based on survey of Bangladeshi suppliers, March–April 2020.

The study found that 71.8 per cent of suppliers that suddenly lost contracts with buyers and received no payment stated they were unable to furlough workers with some income and 81.3 per cent said they could not provide severance pay when cancelled orders resulted in permanent worker retrenchment. As reflected in **Figure 12.3**, the impacts were even more severe for workers employed by small- and medium-sized enterprises (SMEs).

All of this suggests that if branded corporations are to be serious about addressing labour contraventions in their supply chains, they must closely examine whether and how their purchasing practices might be undermining their efforts to ensure that suppliers comply with codes of conduct.

Watch the video on the online resources to take your understanding of this case study further.

Questions

1 What are the key drivers of adverse incorporation in the context of garments' supply chains in Bangladesh?

2 In what ways do retailers' purchasing practices need to change?

12.3 Governance of labour in global production

As discussed in **Section 12.1** and **Section 12.2** (and **Chapter 7**), major shifts in the global economy have featured, and facilitated, the exploitation and adverse incorporation of precarious and vulnerable groups of workers.

Neoliberal policies imposed by major international financial institutions (IFIs) in the 1980s and 1990s put pressure on nation-states to liberalize their economies and deregulate their labour markets (**see Chapter 4**). Unsurprisingly, this severely hampered states' ability to regulate labour conditions linked to global production. This has led some to suggest that today's global economy is characterized by governance 'gaps' (Gereffi and Mayer 2006; MacDonald 2014). Nation-states are severely restricted in their ability to govern due to the adoption of neoliberal policies and the fact that corporations' sourcing networks span many different countries (Mayer and Gereffi 2010). Some have described the dismantling or absence of national labour laws and regulations as a 'race to the bottom' in terms of social standards and protections (Esbenshade 2012; P. Robinson 2009; Utting 2008). This has prompted a strong backlash from global civil society organizations, such as Labour Behind the Label, Solidaridad Network, and Human Rights Watch, demanding corporations clean up their supply chains and governments put in place effective regulation to protect labour standards.

Global corporations have responded by developing their own company codes of conduct and corporate social responsibility (CSR) strategies, which cover—to varying degrees—labour conditions. For example, major corporations such as Apple, Walmart, HP, Nike, Tesco, and Gap Inc. all have some form of supplier code of conduct. These codes often refer to internationally accepted labour standards—including the ILO's core conventions. If a supplier wants to win a contract to supply one of these big corporations, they have to agree to the standards outlined in the code of conduct, which is often enforced through regular audits. This involves a third-party agency visiting the farm or factory to ensure compliance with the code of conduct and that no labour violations are found.

Given that these 'private' strategies are implemented by 'private' corporations (as opposed to national governments and public agencies), they are sometimes collectively referred to as *private governance* (Neilson and Pritchard 2010: 1849). We can distinguish this from *public governance*, which refers instead to labour laws and regulations drafted and enforced by nation-states.

Given their monumental rise since the 1990s, private governance initiatives have unsurprisingly come under intense scrutiny. It is now widely acknowledged that modes of private governance have been largely unsuccessful in improving labour standards. Private audits have been found to be more effective in protecting measurable conditions that are more easily seen (such as health and safety, working hours, or contractual arrangements) as opposed to those less visible, such as a worker's right to join a trade union (Barrientos and Smith 2007; Oxfam 2013). Put simply, it is very difficult for an auditor to tell which workers are being pressured—directly or indirectly—to refrain from joining a trade union. Auditing has also been found to be less effective in monitoring working conditions and contraventions in subcontracted, lower-tier firms, located further away from the global buyer (Nadvi and Raj-Reichert 2015). The sourcing demands of global corporations also often appear contradictory, insofar as they squeeze costs while demanding compliance with labour codes without providing any financial support (Barrientos 2013).

For example, Indian factory workers supplying major brands—Marks & Spencer, Tesco, Sainsbury's, and the fashion brand Ralph Lauren—have alleged routine exploitation by their employer (Vaidyanathan 2020). Allegations range from forced overtime, including working overnight to complete orders; a lack of toilet breaks; verbal abuse; poor working conditions; and extremely low wages, exacerbated by a virtual absence of union representation. In response to the allegations, all brands in question expressed their deep concern and pointed to the fact that they all demand adherence to labour codes of conduct, monitored through regular, third-party audits. However, one owner of a clothing supplier instead blamed poor working conditions on the brands, for wanting to maximize profits and pushing suppliers to exploit their workforce in order to survive. This is a very clear example of a contradiction in branded corporations' sourcing demands. On the one hand, brands demand suppliers adhere to their codes of conduct. At the same time, brands demand consistent supplies of high-quality, low-cost goods with short lead times. The result is downward pressure on working conditions.

These insights regarding the rising significance and pitfalls of private governance are extremely valuable. However, some argue that this major focus on private governance has drawn attention away from the ongoing importance of nation-states and the *public governance* of labour—that is, the formal rules and regulations set by governments to protect workers incorporated into global value chains (GVCs) (Mayer and Phillips 2017; Alford and Phillips 2018; De Marchi and Alford 2021). National labour legislation, for example, can directly affect working conditions in supplier firms linked to global production by regulating different aspects of labour conditions and standards (Alford 2016, 2020).

Rather than replacing the state, many observers have actually found that public and private governance work in combination. Researchers have tried to capture the complex ways in which private standards intersect with public regulations at production sites (Bair 2017). When this occurs, one potential outcome is 'displacement', where one form of governance can displace or crowd out other forms (Amengual 2010; Gereffi and Lee 2016). Private codes of conduct may in fact replace public laws and regulations and threaten local labour institutions and union movements (Amengual 2010). For example, in their criticism of private governance initiatives in the plantation districts of South India, Jeff Neilson and Bill Pritchard found that fair and ethical trade schemes tended to supplant national laws and regulations and protect only a small minority of workers, who were not actually the most disadvantaged (2010: 1847).

A different possibility is that public and private forms of governance can 'complement' one another, whereby private governance positively reinforces compliance with public regulations (Amengual 2010; Bartley 2011; Coslovsky and Locke 2013). In a study of the Dominican Republic's export processing zones, private auditing was found to complement public governance by helping to release limited government resources for labour monitoring and redirecting them to firms that would otherwise be less likely to draw regulatory attention (Amengual 2010). In similar cases of private governance in apparel factories located in Mexico and Guatemala, close scrutiny by third-party auditors was able to bring government actors, branded lead firms, labour unions, and factory managers to negotiate for improved compliance with labour standards (Rodriguez-Garavito 2005).

Taken together, these insights show that even with the rise of private forms of governance, the state remains integral to the governance of labour in global production. Despite the understandable interest in private codes of conduct and CSR which burgeoned in the 1990s, the evidence shows they are 'always and everywhere underpinned' by interactions with state regulatory frameworks (Phillips 2017: 443). However, although state capacity may be critical for better regulation, it alone is not sufficient to achieve improvements in labour rights, given that the root cause of violations is the sourcing practices of global corporations (Anner, Bair, and Blasi 2013). This point will be elaborated further in **Case Study 12.2**, which looks at the case of the South African fruit export sector.

Some final caveats are necessary. So far, we have explored the different combinations of public and private governance designed to improve labour standards. But not all firms are constantly looking to undermine public regulations, and some do work proactively to take ethical responsibility for their supply chains. For example, Unilever has pledged to go beyond the national minimum wages found in its supplier countries and ensure a living wage for all supply chain workers worldwide by 2030 (Unilever 2020). It is also important to note significant changes in the geography of global production (Horner and Nadvi 2018), which have major implications for the governance of labour. Dominant lead firms are not only those based in the UK, Europe, or North America (Cattaneo, Gereffi, and Staritz 2010), but are increasingly found in China, India, and Africa, in line with the massive growth of middle-class consumers in these regions (Guarin and Knorringa 2014). Recent work has challenged assumptions of a 'race to the bottom' on standards demanded by lead firms in Southern markets (Barrientos et al. 2016; Langford 2019). Equally, certain states are more politically motivated than others to challenge big business through regulation, taxation, or other mechanisms. For example, in early 2022 the European Union (EU) published its long-awaited directive imposing a duty on major companies operating in the EU to carry out human rights and environmental due diligence in their global supply chains. And without a doubt, intense political contestation constantly plays out between states and firms as they vie to capture the value of global production and each blame the other for contraventions in labour standards (Phillips 2017).

With those caveats in mind, let's now explore the issues of e-commerce and automation, which could have major implications for the future of work.

Case Study 12.2: Governing labour in GVCs: the case of South African fruit

The South African fruit sector has undergone a period of rapid change following the end of apartheid in 1994. On the one hand, the government decided to deregulate the sector, which resulted in South African fruit producers exporting to the UK and Europe. This happened at a time when supermarket retailers such as Tesco, Asda, and Sainsbury's were becoming increasingly dominant (Alford and Phillips 2018). Many of the retailers sourcing fruit from South Africa had, on paper, codes of conduct covering labour conditions. At the same time, the South African government sought to overturn exploitative employment practices associated with apartheid. This included strengthening labour laws and regulations in order to enhance workers' rights and modernize agricultural labour relations (Du Toit 2004; Ewert and Du Toit 2005).

From 2010–2015, research into fruit farms in the Western Cape serving UK and European supermarkets shed light on the governance of labour (Alford 2016; Alford and Phillips 2018). It found that some dimensions of labour regulation were delegated to private agencies. A lack of capacity on the part of the Department of Labour meant that the enforcement of labour standards was filled by private auditing companies. Yet the *content* of labour regulation, particularly in relation to wages, was determined much more strongly and actively by the South African government.

Despite apparently complementary combinations of public–private governance, large numbers of casual workers on short-term, insecure contracts still faced poor working conditions. In interviews, farmers explained that they were unable to meet supermarkets' demands for high-quality, low-cost produce without reducing labour costs. This meant that fruit producers used increasing numbers of low-paid casual workers alongside a shrinking 'permanent' workforce (an average of 68 per cent casual relative to 32 per cent permanent workers was found on the farms under study). Not only that, farmers explained that they were unable to pay casual workers more than the minimum wage, which prior to the 2012–13 labour crisis was extremely low at 69 rand per day, considered well below the cost of living (Bureau for Food and Agricultural Policy 2012).

This contributed to unprecedented labour protest in the Western Cape fruit sector that ran from 2012 to 2013, mainly led by casual workers who downed tools and demanded increased wages and better working conditions. The strikes were characterized by violence—farms were torched, roads blocked, arrests made, workers injured, and tragically some lost their lives. The eventual regulatory response by government to the crisis was to increase wages from 69 rand to 105 rand per day, which came into effect in early 2013. However, a government-sanctioned report during the crisis acknowledged this level to be still below living costs. At the same time, farmers argued that the sourcing pressures put on them by UK and European supermarkets made it impossible to pay any higher wages without shutting down their farms or shedding more jobs (Alford 2020).

This case shows how difficult it is to simply increase wages and improve working conditions on supplier farms serving powerful global corporations without compromising suppliers' competitiveness in what is a fiercely competitive global sourcing landscape. Even with supermarkets demanding that labour codes of conduct be met and the South African government putting in place a strong raft of labour legislation, wages remained below living costs and working conditions became increasingly insecure.

12.4 The changing nature of work: e-commerce and automation

12.4.1 E-commerce platforms on the rise

The way that we live our lives and buy things is changing dramatically. Be it laptops, phones, clothes, groceries, or almost any other consumable item one can think of, we are increasingly buying them online. During the Covid-19 pandemic, people in most corners of the globe were asked, told, or simply decided to stay indoors and purchased what they wanted or needed online.

Quite unsurprisingly, this has hugely accelerated the growth of e-commerce platforms—which are essentially websites—and the underlying software that enable buying and selling of goods and services over the Internet. The most famous of these is Amazon, which has strengthened its foothold in Northern markets such as the USA, UK, and Europe and is expanding worldwide. To give a broader picture of the rise of e-commerce, globally it stood at 14 per cent of worldwide retail sales in 2019 (Statista 2020) and by 2040, around 95 per cent of all UK purchases are expected to be via e-commerce (Nasdaq 2020).

All of this has led to a move away from shopping in 'brick and mortar' (physical) stores. Generation Z and millennial shoppers who represent future growth tend to have vast personal debts, less disposable income, and an increasing tendency to shop online in search of the most competitive prices (Barrientos 2019). This is changing the way we buy our products, giving us immediate access to pricing information and offers across platforms and greatly increasing competition between retailers (eMarketer 2017).

Exacerbated by the huge cost advantages that e-commerce companies accrue by avoiding tax on a global scale (Sweeney 2017), traditional physical retailers such as Marks & Spencer, Tesco, and Walmart are coming under even more pressure to reduce their sourcing costs so as to deliver high-quality products at low prices, with a likely adverse effect on the workers who make those items (Barrientos 2019).

The same can be said about the competitive pressure e-commerce platforms are putting on well-known brands, many of which are sold on the platforms themselves. On the one hand, e-commerce platforms could potentially disrupt more direct relationships between branded corporations, consumers, and suppliers. The platform (rather than the brand) hosts the products being sold, along with extensive data on consumer activity and demand.

Consider the fact that Amazon hosts a huge array of products, including those made by well-known brands. Let's take running shoes as a specific example. Brands such as Nike,

Reebok, Adidas, and many others all sell their shoes on Amazon. But so does Amazon, which now has its own line of running shoes. And because Amazon has such a vast array of data on us, as consumers, in terms of the style of shoe we want and prices we're willing to pay, it can price its products very competitively relative to branded firms. That is not to say that online shoppers won't keep on buying brands; in fact, recent consumer reports indicate they will (Feedvisor 2019). But it might well mean that brands such as Nike, Adidas, and Reebok respond to this pressure by lowering prices to remain competitive and maintain profits. The fear is that this may result in downward pressure on suppliers to make goods at ever-lower costs, while retaining product and brand quality. As we saw in **Section 12.2** and **Section 12.3**, the likely loser in this scenario will be the insecure, low-cost workers required to meet such demand.

At the same time, platforms can coordinate a much wider range of lower-tier suppliers based in low-cost production locations across the Global South. For example, Amazon provides a selling outlet for a huge number of third-party sellers who use Amazon's marketplace platform. Not all, but some of these are suppliers that may previously have been unable to meet stringent social standards required by branded corporations (as discussed in **Section 12.3**) and are more likely to use precarious workers to cut costs. In 2019, the *Wall Street Journal* reported that Amazon Marketplace sold clothes from Bangladeshi factories that other retailers had blacklisted. Two-thirds of the factories blacklisted were being used by third-party sellers. Of particular concern was the fact that Amazon does not require third-party sellers to disclose the factories where products come from. All of this indicates that working conditions in supply chains linked to e-commerce platforms may be less subject to ethical scrutiny.

The rise of e-commerce is also leading to the expansion of precarious work in the Global North, where employment is traditionally seen as better regulated and more secure. This includes the insecure employment status of gig economy workers at the 'sourcing' end of e-commerce platforms, such as delivery couriers and warehouse workers subject to low pay and intensive working conditions (Bergvall-Kåreborn and Howcroft 2014), and at the 'production' end, with recent reports of below-minimum wage payments and exploitation of garment workers by clothing suppliers in the UK, serving well-known e-commerce platforms based in the same location (Bland and Kelly 2020).

However, the rise of e-commerce platforms is not left unchecked by national governments. While e-commerce platforms such as Amazon are increasingly powerful and operate all around the world, state policymakers are beginning to challenge their market dominance through increased taxation and other mechanisms. For example, in a landmark case the European Commission charged Amazon for using data on third-party sellers to boost sales of its own-label goods, with South Africa and India taking similar regulatory steps (Goga and Paelo 2019).

12.4.2 Automation, robotics, and artificial intelligence

You are likely to have come across headlines such as 'Will robots take our jobs?' You may have noticed that such news stories, while clearly designed to draw readers in, are often posed as questions not statements. That is because *whether* robots will replace human workers is a highly contested issue, with opposing viewpoints that we will discuss here and in the **Chapter 12 Roundtable**.

First, it is worth taking a step back and noting that for many centuries machines have replaced jobs. The spinning jenny made weavers obsolete, buttons replaced elevator operators, and the Internet put many travel agencies out of business (Semuels 2020). However, the loss of jobs to machines has rapidly accelerated since the turn of the twenty-first century. Approximately 1.7 million manufacturing jobs are thought to have been lost to robots since 2000, including 400,000 in Europe, 260,000 in the USA, and 550,000 in China (Oxford Economics 2019).

Needless to say, the impact of robotics, automation, and artificial intelligence (AI) is felt differently depending on the sector and type of job in question. While drastic predictions indicate that all jobs, from factory workers to lawyers and white-collar workers, are vulnerable to automation, there is consensus that more repetitive, labour intensive, and factory-based jobs are most at risk (ILO 2016). Think of the images you may have seen of automated factories, where long rows of highly sophisticated-looking robots are seen making anything from cars to laptops to clothes. This means that countries and regions where there are more people with limited access to skills and education are much more vulnerable to losing jobs to robots. Indeed, by the end of the 2030s it is predicted that while almost half of existing jobs in the United States (Frey and Osborne 2017) and 15 million jobs in the UK will be vulnerable to automation (Spencer 2017), as many as three-quarters of jobs in China and two-thirds in India may be at risk (Frey and Osborne 2015).

All of this could potentially lead to a mass shrinkage in work opportunities, as firms opt to use more cost-effective machines over humans (Brynjolfsson and McAfee 2014; Ford 2015). The prospect of a decline in work has generated obvious concerns around the potential for rising unemployment and deepening inequality. An article in *Time* told the story of a man, Larry Collins, who worked for twenty-three years in a booth on the Carquinez Bridge in San Francisco, collecting tolls. Over time, the fare changed from a few dollars to $6, but the work stayed the same. Collins would greet commuters, answer questions, give directions, and make conversation. But one day in March 2020, as the Covid-19 pandemic escalated, Collins' supervisor called to say he and around 185 other toll collectors in Northern California weren't needed any more. Drivers would now pay bridge tolls automatically using windshield-mounted tags or receive bills sent to the address linked to their licence plate (Semuels 2020). If workers such as Collins are not able to rely on work for income, they may face economic hardship, resulting in higher inequality as the benefits of automation are channelled to a select few, including the owners of technological infrastructure (Ford 2015).

A contrasting and more radical argument is that automation is immensely positive, with the potential to liberate humanity from the shackles of work (Mason 2015; Srnicek and Williams 2015). Proponents of this view argue that work is increasingly regarded as bad for one's health for a myriad of reasons—overwhelming to-do lists, long hours sitting at desks, and vital human tasks such as looking after children or elderly relatives neglected. Some writers in this camp argue for a 'post-work' future which includes something akin to a universal basic income (UBI) paid by the state to all working-age people so they can survive the onset of a 'full-automation' society (Spencer 2017).

Both of these perspectives have been criticized because, as in the past, technological innovations are much more likely to *augment* productive work than to replace it (Spencer 2018). For example, there are innumerable jobs linked to new technologies, 'from the mining of raw materials that go into their production, through the sales functions in their consumption, to the task of disposing of them when they are no longer required' (Spencer 2018: 7, citing Huws 2014). While automation may not necessarily require physical labour, it does need a skilled workforce. However, it is very important to note that societal norms play a key role in shaping who gets access to the necessary skills and training to benefit from technological advancements in the workplace, with women and other groups of more vulnerable workers often losing out (Barrientos 2019; Wacjman 2010).

This latter point draws attention to the fact that far from being apolitical, the rise of digital technologies is a highly political and contested process. At supplier sites linked to global production, employers increasingly use digital technologies to drive up productivity. Employers use electronic devices such as Fitbit, Nike+, FuelBand, and Jawbone UP to measure and monitor worker behaviour as part of 'wellness' programmes (Spencer 2017). Some view this as a positive development. Employers will be equipped with a dashboard of employee performance trajectories, including their fatigue and sleep levels. They will be able to select the fittest and most work-ready individuals for important business negotiations, meetings, or presentations.

Others believe this increased surveillance, which extends to off-duty hours, is unethical and intrusive, comes at the expense of worker well-being, and leads to a more stressed, anxious, and exploited workforce. A brief look through the history books tells us how this might happen. One of the first employee health-tracking programmes was trialled in 1913 by Ford Motor Company, which was struggling with high worker turnover after introducing a moving assembly line (D. Cox 2020). Ford tried to retain more staff by doubling their wages, which came with strict conditions—that workers adopt a healthier lifestyle. Ford set up a sociology department to check that workers were complying with its rules. Investigators made impromptu home visits and even spoke to workers' neighbours to gather information. Workers that Ford deemed insufficiently healthy had their wages reduced. By the early 1920s Ford abandoned the scheme. Competition from other carmakers rendered higher salaries unaffordable, and staff increasingly complained that Ford was encroaching into their private lives (D. Cox 2020).

A century later, this case study provides a relevant indicator as to how worker-tracking can backfire. The term 'digital Taylorism' has been used to describe the use of digital technologies to consistently monitor workers' performance in Amazon warehouses, resulting in a dehumanized workplace ('Digital Taylorism' 2015). These examples point to the uneven implications of digital technologies and work, involving both the generation of highly skilled jobs for those fortunate to access them, alongside the potential growth of insecure, intensive, and low-paid work (Dyer-Witheford 2015). The extent to which different workers benefit, or are increasingly exploited, will greatly depend on the interplay of private and public governance, alongside enhanced representation of workers' interests within the political system (Berliner et al. 2015)—points which we will return to in the **Chapter 12 Roundtable** discussion.

12.5 Conclusion

We began this chapter by discussing significant changes in how goods are produced in the global economy, and how corporations increasingly outsource the production of goods to suppliers in different countries (**see Section 12.1 and Section 12.2.1**). This helped us to consider whether (and which) workers win or lose from engaging in global production. Through various examples, we observed that processes of poverty and exploitation are shaped not only by workers' *exclusion* from global production, but also by their *adverse incorporation* into them (**see Section 12.2.2**). We dug deeper into the more specific dynamics underpinning the adverse incorporation of precarious workers into global production and looked at the interrelated processes of *outsourcing* and *migration*, which have been associated with the exploitation of workers linked to global production.

We built on this discussion in **Section 12.3**, by considering whose responsibility it is to ensure workers linked to global production are adequately protected. Here, we observed that while branded corporations play an increasingly prominent role in the governance of labour, it is equally true that private governance initiatives have been widely regarded as ineffective. We questioned claims that the rise of private governance has caused the nation-state to 're-treat' or 'roll back', and instead focused on the intertwining of public and private governance with varying implications for labour.

We turned in **Section 12.4** to discuss nascent and yet highly significant shifts towards e-commerce and automation, which promise to have major implications for the future of work. How we purchase products is moving online, with pricing competition a key factor and evidence to suggest that supply chains linked to e-commerce platforms may be less subject to ethical scrutiny (**see Section 12.4.1**). While nation-states are already trying to push back against increasingly powerful e-commerce platforms, this will become an important arena of struggle between private and public actors. Our discussion closed by considering the substantial implications that automation, robotics, and AI have for future patterns of work (**see Section 12.4.2**). While some have assumed that the rise of digital technology will replace work—either for better or worse, depending on your viewpoint—this chapter presented the more likely scenario of technology *augmenting* work. The extent to which workers will win or lose from these developments will depend on the interplay of private and public governance, and the extent to which workers' interests are adequately represented within the political system.

Key Points

- The mode of global production has changed dramatically since the 1970s. In the past, corporations tended to make their own products, or at least source them through nationally based supply chains. Since the 1990s, they have outsourced the production of goods to suppliers around the world.

- At the core of this contemporary form of global production is the ability of lead firms to profit through advanced sourcing strategies, economies of scale, and branding. This gives corporations significant bargaining power over their fragmented and geographically dispersed supplier base.

- In the contemporary global economy, conditions of poverty and marginalization can be attributed not only to exclusion from employment, but also to the adverse incorporation of precarious workers into global production.
- Despite the rise of private forms of governance, the state remains integral to the governance of labour in global production.
- The extent to which workers will win or lose from technological shifts in terms of e-commerce and automation is a political question, requiring close scrutiny from academics and policy-makers alike.

Further Reading

Anner, M. (2020), 'Squeezing Workers' Rights in Global Supply Chains: Purchasing Practices in the Bangladesh Garment Export Sector in Comparative Perspective', *Review of International Political Economy*, 27(2): 320–47. An excellent account of how corporations' sourcing strategies shape working conditions in global production.

Barrientos, S. (2019), *Gender and Work in Global Value Chains: Capturing the Gains?* (Cambridge: Cambridge University Press). A rich analysis of issues surrounding gender and work in global production, drawing on a range of case studies.

Bartley, T. (2018), *Rules Without Rights: Land, Labor, and Private Authority in the Global Economy* (Oxford: Oxford University Press). An engaging analysis of the tensions and contestation between private and public governance of labour in global production.

Mayer, F., and **Phillips, N.** (2017), 'Outsourcing Governance: States and the Politics of a "Global Value Chain World"', *New Political Economy*, 22(2): 134–52. An engaging analysis of the role of politics and states in governing work in contemporary global production.

Spencer, D. A. (2018), 'Fear and Hope in an Age of Mass Automation: Debating the Future of Work', *New Technology, Work and Employment*, 33(1): 1–12. A nuanced account of the implications of automation for work.

Chapter 12 Roundtable discussion

Is increased automation the solution to global labour exploitation?

Roundtable 12.1
Opening contribution **Matthew Alford**

The relationship between machines and humans has permeated popular and academic debates for centuries (**see Section 12.4.2**). Recent technological advances in robotics, automation, and artificial intelligence have propelled these issues to the fore (ILO 2018*b*). Let's now debate what automation means for labour worldwide.

Very different and often opposing responses to automation have been put forward. Some influential empirical research (Frey and Osborne 2017) has fuelled a growing belief that it will lead—for better or worse—to the abolishment of work (Ford 2015). For some, this scenario paints a bleak and unwelcome picture of jobs being lost, higher unemployment, and worsening inequality, reflected in popular press headlines such as: 'Will a robot take your job?' (BBC 2015), 'Will robots steal all our jobs?' (Samuelson 2017), and 'Robots will take our jobs' (Elliott 2018). Policy solutions to redress this erosion of work range from upskilling workers to enhancing social protection in the form of a basic income (Brynjolfsson and McAfee 2014).

For others, the prospect of automation should be actively encouraged as a means to achieve a 'post-work', post-capitalist utopia (Mason 2015). This more radical perspective emphasizes the potential benefits of mass automation in terms of increased leisure time and freedom from the toil of work.

An alternative perspective predicts that rather than reducing or displacing work, technological advances in automation will 'augment' (Spencer 2017) or even 'complement' it (Dahlin 2019). Many people highlight the huge number of jobs stemming from new technology. These range from the many millions of roles involved in the 'manufacture, sale and disposal of technologies such as iPhones which can be connected to vast value chains . . . across different countries and sectors' (Spencer 2018: 7) to assembly-line employees working alongside robots in industrial engineering, car and aeroplane manufacturing plants (Dahlin 2019). Significantly, these latter examples illustrate the 'complementary' generation of work alongside automation in manufacturing settings, thought to be most vulnerable to displacement by robots. This has led some to suggest policy interventions such as investing in education, worker upskilling, and infrastructure to create 'new and better' quality jobs in the future, combined with a 'basic income' tax to assist the most vulnerable, lower-paid members of society (Brynjolfsson and McAfee 2014).

While agreeing that automation can indeed augment rather than displace work, a more critical strand of literature highlights that digital technologies 'are themselves products of unequal power . . . created, harnessed and reproduced under conditions where power resides with capital, not labour' (Spencer 2017: 145). This viewpoint critiques the so-called 'complementary' automation/work thesis for being essentially apolitical, as it fails to account for how technologies can and will be used to exacerbate worker exploitation. Consider the various examples of the use of wearable technology to measure, monitor, and control workers, leading to increased surveillance, work-rates, and anxiety (Delfanti 2019; 'Digital Taylorism' 2015).

I concur with this more critical take on automation, with the previous examples showing that it can in fact lead to 'more and worse jobs', as opposed to 'new and better'. Returning to the original **Chapter 12 Roundtable** question—'Is increased automation the solution to global labour exploitation?'—for me, the answer would have to be a resounding 'no'. That is because the types of digital technologies (including automation) that are produced, how they are used, and who benefits from them, will continue to depend on (and be shaped by) the dynamics of global production and governance discussed in **Chapter 7** and **Chapter 12**. In other words, existing structures of global production wherein big business is able to 'control how, where and by whom value is *created*, and how, where and by whom it is *captured*' will remain firmly in place (Phillips 2017: 432).

These points are crystallized in attempts to unionize at Amazon warehouses. Amazon claims its corporate social responsibility commitments and use of robots in warehouses have made jobs easier and safer. Yet, workers highlight constant tracking and surveillance, insufficient break times, and one-sided termination policies. This prompted 'the first attempt to unionize a large US Amazon facility in the tech giant's 25-year history', at a warehouse in Bessemer, Alabama (Del Rey 2021). This attempt received support from senior members of the US government, who signed a public letter demanding the company overhaul its 'profit-at-all-costs culture', such as by reducing workers' quotas and speed requirements. After the Alabama unionization vote failed twice, an Amazon warehouse in Staten Island, New York with 8,300 employees ultimately became the first to successfully form a union (Weise and Scheiber 2022).

This example clearly shows that increased automation is not necessarily the solution to global labour exploitation. The example also highlights that the governance of labour will continue to be highly political and contested. The evolution of working conditions in line with technological innovations will evoke a response by firms and states as they vie for control over the terms of production and the future of work. Some states may be more politically willing to challenge powerful firms, through regulation or other mechanisms. Firms will likely continue to lambast states for weak regulations, perpetuating a 'politics of blame' that does little to address the continued exploitation of workers operating in ever more automated environments (Phillips 2017: 444).

These are the kinds of issues which political economists have grappled with over the centuries, and close scrutiny will continue to be needed in the coming years.

Roundtable 12.2
Response **Mark Anner**

Matthew Alford is clear and eloquent in his answer to the question: Is increased automation the solution to global labour exploitation (**see Roundtable 12.1**)? The answer, he writes, is a resounding 'no'. This is because automation takes place in a context of global production that is marked by power imbalances. I concur both with his conclusion and with the reasoning behind it. This is particularly the case of the global garment sector, where brands and retailers—with and without advanced technologies—squeeze suppliers, and suppliers squeeze workers.

Mass-produced ready-made garments began to grow in the late 1800s following Isaac Singer's development of the sewing machine, which could sew nearly one thousand stitches a minute (Carlson 1952). By 1920, the sewing machine became widely diffused around the world (Godley 2006). In addition to use in homes, sewing machines allowed for the development of mass manufacturing of garments, a sector that has long been seen as the first step in the path to development.

Today, the global garment export sector is made up of approximately 35 million workers, most of whom are women from vulnerable sectors of society (young, migrants, religious and ethnic minorities, etc.). Many of these workers labour under extremely harsh conditions, including below-poverty level wages, long hours of work, extreme work intensity, verbal abuse, and gender-based violence (Anner 2020). Thus, the question of whether automation will create or reduce jobs, and augment or decrease worker exploitation, is of crucial importance for garment workers.

More than 170 years since the development and global dispersion of the Singer sewing machine, most garments are still made by female workers using this relatively simple machine. The reason why the sewing of garments has not become more automated is due to the difficulty of machine handling of cloth and constantly changing fashions (Nayak and Padhye 2017). It is also a result of extremely low wages. The sector has been so successful in keeping wages low that in most cases it is not cost-efficient to automate.

This does not mean that automation has not impacted garment production around the sector's large edges. The spinning of yarn and weaving and knitting of textiles has become highly automated and capital intensive, displacing millions of workers in the process. Cotton harvesting on some farms is done by tractors the size of barns. Yet, elsewhere on cotton fields large-scale use of child labour (for example, in India and Mali) and forced labour (for example, Uyghurs in China) persist. The two processes are linked: automation by some puts intense cost pressures on those who are unable to automate, which contributes to child and forced labour.

Logistics and distribution are other core components of the sector that are affected by automation and work intensity. An average port crane operated by a single worker can load 65 tonne containers on massive ships. The largest of these ships, such as the one that got stuck in the Suez Canal in early 2021, are the length of four football fields. Despite their size, they have relatively small crews. This does not mean that these workers are treated well. During the Covid-19 pandemic, as countries enthusiastically received needed goods in their ports, they were remarkably inhospitable to the workers who delivered those goods. In country after country, workers were denied the right to disembark, condemning 300,000 seafarers to months at sea past the expiration date of their contracts (Almendral 2020). When products (if not seafarers) leave ships, they then pass through distribution centres, last-mile delivery, and retail sales, sectors that largely remain labour intensive. Unsurprisingly, in these sectors we also find high levels of worker exploitation, as noted in the discussion in **Section 12.4.2** and **Roundtable 12.1** of the conditions of labour for Amazon distribution centre workers.

Driving these trends are the financial firms, retailers, and brands that sit at the top of global supply chains. Here, automation, digitalization, and data analytics have allowed for the tremendous consolidation of power among those at the very top (for example, BlackRock, Nike, Walmart, H&M, and Amazon), which gives them ever-growing power over the suppliers and workers at the bottom. With fast fashion and other forecasting pressures, the industry has become obsessed with speed to market. Data analytics, 3D prototyping, and other forms of digitization and automation improve forecasting, reduce unsold inventory and thus the need for mark downs, and increase profits. They also place increased pressure on workers to work longer and faster. In India, hourly production targets have been pushed up from 60, to 80, and to even 100 operations per hour (Anner 2019). Hence, automation at the top contributes to greater work intensity and exploitation at the bottom.

Observing Amazon workers with buzzing bracelets that keep them on pace to work faster, the question might not be whether robots will replace workers, but rather if technology is forcing humans to be more robot-like in how they work. No doubt, technology can be conducive to greater worker productivity, but it most certainly does not guarantee greater worker income or more humane conditions of work. Without strong labour unions, collective bargaining, and supportive state structures, the gains from technology (particularly in labour surplus economies) will accrue to the top at the expense of hyper-worker exploitation at the bottom. What this suggests is that the question of whether automatization, digitization, and robotization will bring humankind greater freedom and well-being, or intensify forms of subordination and exploitation, will be the result of a political process.

Roundtable 12.3
Response **Samanthi Gunawardana**

I agree with Matthew Alford that increased automation is not a straightforward solution to global labour exploitation (**see Roundtable 12.1**). Gender, race, and class are central to the social construction of labouring bodies and the different types of labour tasks deemed appropriate for different workers. Reducing labour exploitation would therefore involve unravelling and transforming the gender, class, and racial power relations underpinning manufacturing processes.

Alford's discussion shows that systems of inequality are constitutive elements of employment systems found across many different export sectors. I want to focus here on the apparel sector, where factories' predominant employment of women from low-income countries has been integral to the development of complex global supply chains. These employment opportunities have been generated in tasks and roles termed 'low-skilled'. Employment has been both liberating (potential to earn an independent income, decision-making power over its use) and exploitative.

Well-documented labour exploitation issues within these factories include underpayment, wage theft, excessive overtime, job segregation, sexual violence, poor health and safety systems, and the suppression of worker voice by the state and employers (Anner 2019). Many of the workers in apparel are domestic or international migrant workers. They reside in temporary housing spaces such as hostels and boarding houses, which may also be informal workplaces (Mezzadri 2016). Living conditions are part of the picture of labour exploitation, as the substandard conditions under which *social reproduction* occurs (that is, unpaid labour associated with maintaining human life) result in gendered harm. Overcrowded hygiene facilities, lax security, being subject to violence and harassment in their neighbourhoods, and the lack of childcare all contribute to the experience of exploitation. In recent times the Covid-19 pandemic increased care work and threats of gender-based violence for women workers (Castañeda-Navarrete, Hauge, and López-Gómez 2021). Global governance measures and national-level legislation to address these forms of exploitation have yielded uneven results (McCarthy, Soundararajan, and Taylor 2021).

And the experience of labour exploitation is not only gendered, but also racialized, as certain groups of women and men are considered more predisposed to the discipline required of repetitive assembly line work and are comparatively more vulnerable to exploitation (Bonacich, Alimahomed, and Wilson 2008).

Can more automation dissolve these kinds of labour exploitation? Automation in the apparel sector is already found in design, fabric cutting and inspection, sewing and knitting functions in traditional labour-intensive assembly lines, and 3D printing (Nayak and Padhye 2017). Human input is needed to design and program the machinery and systems, and to deploy, control, and guide this technology in the production process. A large body of work examines how the underlying infrastructure of automation (for example, the design of algorithms) can replicate, reinforce, or deepen existing power relations based on gender or race (Wellner and Rothman 2020).

The argument that automation will lead to the substitution of human workers highlights its potential for deepening rather than alleviating inequality. Automation can imply freedom from the need for human labour, but it still requires human interaction. Research over four decades has shown that recruiters rely on localized gender norms and stereotypes in order to maintain control over the production process and lower labour costs. For example, my research in Sri Lankan export processing factories over two decades reveals the rigidity of gendered assumptions, where recruitment managers saw young women as more acquiescent and uninterested in unions, unlikely to challenge management authority, and less likely to demand higher wages. Men were perceived as less controllable, even though women participated in collective action, and factories continued to hire some men into sewing roles (Gunawardana 2016).

These attitudes are found in other South Asian countries; it is not surprising that apparel factories in Bangladesh are reported to have started replacing workers with robots for the explicit reason of countering rising wages (Seric and Winkler 2020). Stephanie Barrientos notes that apparel is particularly susceptible to job displacement owing to automation (Barrientos 2019: 258). However, sewing roles are not less likely to be automated than electronics roles. Recent evidence shows that technological upgrading in labour-intensive industries such as apparel is a significant driver of 'de-feminization' in the sector—referring to the declining number of women employed (Tejani and Kucera 2021).

Who gets to participate in automated processes? Women have traditionally been relegated to more 'unskilled' assembly tasks, while men were often put in charge of 'complex' machines and functions such as cutting. Automation may see women being channelled into jobs that do not require expertise in smart technologies, as technology may still be considered a stereotypically masculine domain. As such, women may not be targeted for digital, technical, and vocational training, and the advantages that higher skill levels would bring.

However, even *if* women are substituted by automated machines, or by men selected to operate smart technology, automation does not diminish the forms of labour exploitation outlined at the start of this response. I'm reminded of the saying *'a solution in search of a problem'*. Automation and smart technology are often pitched as the solution to many wicked problems including gender, class, and racial inequality. But these solutions alone don't go far enough to address the underlying systems of inequality that drive labour exploitation. Only if we challenge and intentionally seek to transform gendered and racialized power relations in global production can automation diminish labour exploitation.

Roundtable 12.4
Response Shane Godfrey

Automation is not new. It has been around since the beginnings of industrialization, particularly after electrical power began to be applied to mechanical equipment in the late 1800s. As such, there is empirical evidence spanning over 150 years to draw on to debate this question. In broad terms we can say that there have been winners and losers, and overall the standard of living of people has risen significantly—but unevenly. So, I would agree with Matthew Alford that increased automation is not the solution to global labour exploitation (**see Roundtable 12.1**), but I would still argue that automation will benefit some workers.

Like automation, labour exploitation has also been around for a long time, but it is probably only since the 1970s that capitalism, and therefore labour exploitation, has been increasingly framed by a global lens. This lens has emphasized unevenness, in the degree of inequality (over time and between political systems), and in the geography of development and inequality. The global lens has also emphasized the immense diversity in the forms of work and employment around the world.

What does history tell us? Marx argued that automation saw a nuanced interaction between workers and powered machinery and the production systems within which they were organized: automation saw expertise and skills being extracted from workers and jobs, and then partly embodied in machines and broken down into simpler, less skilled jobs. This radically changed the role of workers in the labour process, but it did not end work or even reduce the number of workers. In fact, there was a huge increase in the workforce because the automated processes saw enormous increases in productivity and economies of scale that enabled the mass production of relatively cheap goods in large factories.

Further, the increases in productivity allowed for rising wages and improved conditions of employment, which went along with the growth of trade unions, the spread of collective bargaining, and legislated labour standards. These improvements, in turn, created the demand for more goods and services. A virtuous circle was therefore created—termed Fordism—which saw a rising standard of living and the creation of many relatively 'good' jobs.

But Fordism did not eliminate labour exploitation and, most importantly, did not spread uniformly across the globe. How wealth and jobs were spread across countries and between men and women, citizens and immigrants, and different ethnic groups laid the foundations of the inequality with which we currently live. Although we did not see what Marx's theory predicted, there is much evidence that automation in fact contributed to global labour exploitation.

But the question for this Roundtable asks us to look into the future and predict how the next phase of automation will impact workers across the globe. Let's therefore look at three examples of the complexity and unevenness that we have mentioned:

Uneven development: Advanced economies of the Global North achieved high standards of living as a result of their early industrialization, primarily on the back of their expanding manufacturing sectors and continuing technological advances. They are now de-industrializing and transforming into high-tech service economies. Arguably, increased automation will accelerate the transformation of such economies, which will drive further growth and create more wealth (although not for all).

On the other hand, many poorly developed economies of the Global South are still predominantly agricultural, with very limited industrialization, and with extremely high levels of poverty. Even if automation has a positive impact on such economies, it will certainly not be as great as the impact it will have on the high-tech service economies of the Global North, which means widening global inequality.

Low-tech sectors: As Mark Anner points out in **Roundtable 12.2**, the centre of the mass manufacture of garments is the industrial sewing machine. These machines have become much faster over time and have additional functions, and some are partly computerized—but all still require an operator to manipulate the fabric. Most garment manufacturing has relocated to less developed countries in South and East Asia, Central America, and sub-Saharan Africa, where it has created jobs for millions of workers, mainly women, and has the potential to catalyse industrialization. These are not pleasant jobs: they are low-paid, hours of work are long, the pace of work is intense, and garment production is highly regimented.

If sewing machines can be automated so that they do not require a human operator, it is likely that much garment manufacture will move back to the Global North. This will mean garment workers in developing countries will lose their jobs and millions will be plunged into poverty. And these countries will be without a low-tech starting point for industrialization. On the other hand, further automation in the sorts of high-tech sectors that are located in the Global North would likely create more highly skilled and paid jobs.

Informal employees: Fordism in the Global North saw labour regulation reach its pinnacle: well protected jobs, wide collective bargaining coverage, and comprehensive welfare benefits. It took research in Ghana and Kenya in the early 1970s to develop the concept of informal employment (Hart 1973; ILO 1972), that is, unregulated work, often of a very low-paid survivalist nature with predominantly 'own-account' workers. The challenge of addressing informality is huge: in the global South one finds many countries with over half of the total labour force in informal employment (Stuart, Samman, and Hunt 2018).

What will increased automation mean for such workers? Will it even reach them? Even an optimist would not envisage more than a small proportion of them benefitting from automation. The majority will likely be passed by and will remain stuck in a precarious hand-to-mouth existence.

So, rather than a resounding 'no' in response to this question, I suggest that the answer is more complicated. We do know that global labour is not in an advantageous position to deal with 'increased automation', which should make us worry about its consequences. But we shouldn't ignore the politics and agency in all this. We should consider how resistance by workers might change this picture, and what kinds of political choices will shape this uncertain future.

Over to you . . .

1 Matthew Alford (see Roundtable 12.1), Mark Anner (see Roundtable 12.2), and Samanthi Gunawardana (see Roundtable 12.3) all argue that automation cannot offer the solution to labour exploitation, and Shane Godfrey (see Roundtable 12.4) paints a mixed picture. Are you more optimistic about the potential impact of automation than they are? And if not from increased automation, where do you think the solutions for labour exploitation can come from in today's world?

2 Do you agree with all our contributors that automation may be more likely to reinforce existing inequalities—particularly gendered and racialized inequalities—than to lessen them? Why or why not?

3 All the contributions underline, in different ways, the fact that the impact of automation will be shaped by political decisions. Who should be making those decisions? Should we be seeking to control automation through greater regulation?

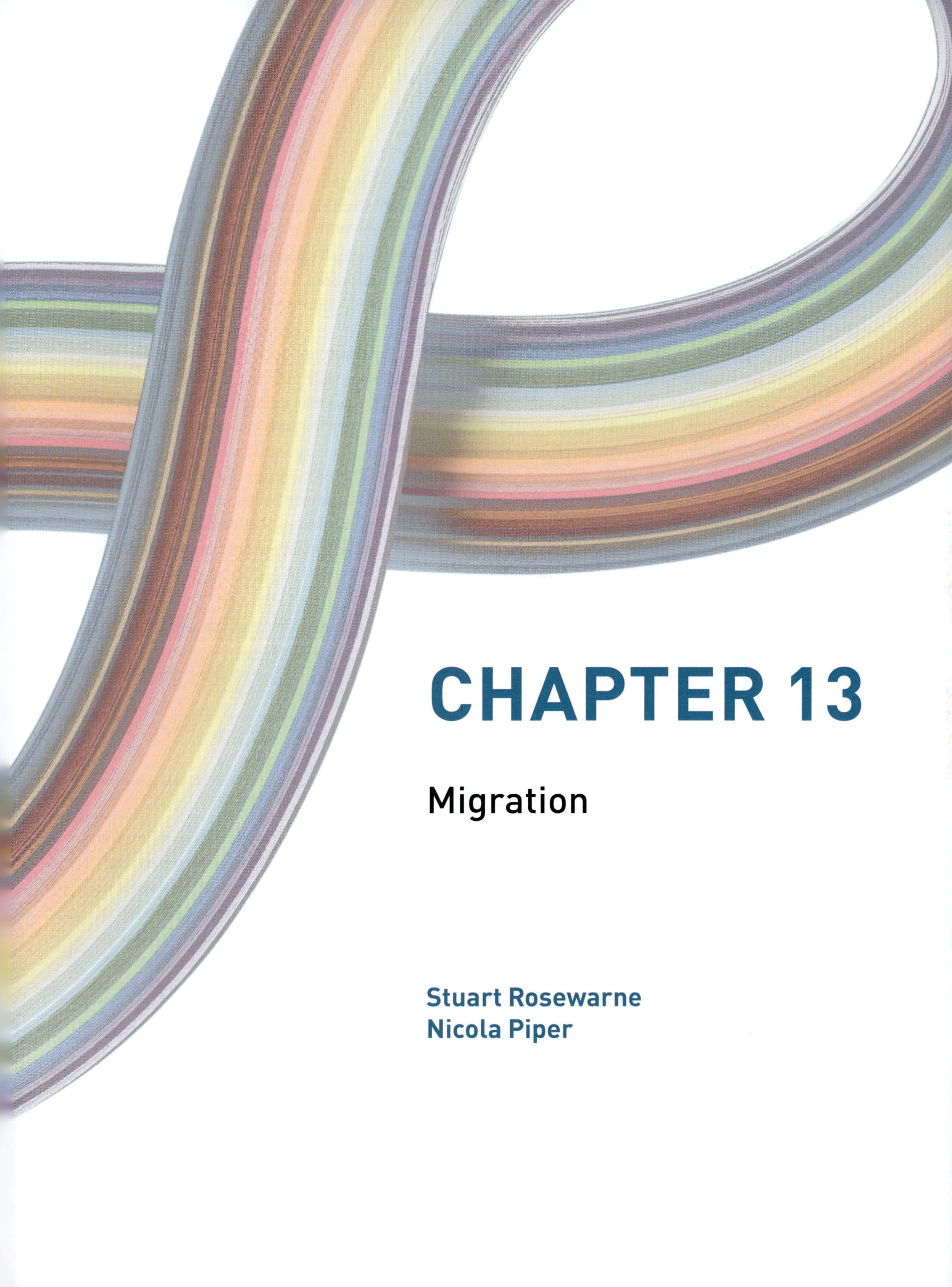

CHAPTER 13

Migration

Stuart Rosewarne
Nicola Piper

13.1 Introduction

People's movement between places and localities—migration—has always been part of human history, and migration in its many guises—including labour migration—is a defining feature of our contemporary era of globalization. With the creation of nation-states and the transformation of migration into an 'international' phenomenon, it has also become subject to evolving regulation and policy frameworks, particularly in relation to who has the right to migrate, and the control of access to labour markets and employment (**see Section 12.2.2**).

In this chapter, we will explore the transition in the dominant policies and practices that have impelled the momentum in international migration as a defining feature of globalization. Our focus will be on the dynamics of the international migration centred on the income-rich economies of the world because these are destinations that account for two-thirds of global movement. This is not to overlook the growing significance of migration, and especially internal migration (within-country migration), within the African, Asian, and South American continents as well as in Russia and the former Soviet satellite states. The focal point of this story, however, is to develop an appreciation of the high-income states' more instrumentalist approach to governing migration, and its impact both on the profile of migration and the lives of migrants themselves.

> ### Key Concepts
>
> **International migration:** Refers to the movement of people across national borders.
>
> **Internal migration:** Refers to the movement of people within a country, such as between rural and urban areas, or across internal state boundaries.

Three particular concerns will frame our focus as we look at the dynamics of migration across the dominant origin and destination countries and the impact of state power in shaping patterns and experiences of migration. First, we will explore the attempts to restrict or govern mobility through the *securitization of borders*, associated with the introduction of tighter, more restrictive border controls. Reflecting the non-existing legal right to freedom of movement across borders globally, policies have been structured around the ideologies and politics of privileging some constituents over others. The distinction is typically made on intersecting criteria: sex, gender, race, and class (Ferguson and McNally 2015).

Second, we will look at the reorientation that has taken place in the way migration is governed in order to achieve *the maximization of its economic benefits*. Many Organization for Economic Co-operation and Development (OECD) destination countries, including the United States, Canada, Australia, the UK, have adopted selective practices based on cherry-picking 'preferred' migrants—prioritizing entrepreneurs and highly skilled and innovative workers. In contrast, limited duration visas are issued to seasonal workers, working holidaymakers, and international students, that channel them into low-skilled, precarious, and low-paid work. These developments reflect and underline the 'capital accumulation' imperative as the motif of the neoliberal economic order (**see Chapter 4**).

Our third focus will be the negative consequences of discriminatory migration policies on the part of states and employers, and the resulting endeavours to enhance *labour rights for migrant workers.*

Let's begin the story of international migration with a brief survey of current policy priorities (**see Section 13.2**), before exploring some dominant theories of migration (**see Section 13.3**).

13.2　The ascendancy of international migration

The International Labour Organization (ILO) estimates that international migration has been growing at a steady pace—by some 3 per cent each year on average over the 2013–19 period, with the number of people migrating for work averaging closer to 4 per cent over this period (ILO 2021*a*; UN 2021; IOM 2019*b*). According to the ILO, the overwhelming proportion of migrants, some 90 per cent, have migrated or are migrating for work. However, some caution is warranted in drawing too much from population data that, in some instances, are not much more than speculative (Bakewell 2009).

India, China, and Mexico are the dominant countries of origin and contribute disproportionately to the profile of the world's international migrants. The overwhelming majority migrate for work. Almost all professional, skilled, and innovative migrants seek work in high- and medium-income countries and work in a range of occupations. The destinations of migrants who are channelled into routine, low-skilled, and poorly paid work are more diverse (ILO 2021*a*; IOM 2019*b*; OECD 2021*a*). This suggests there are multiple migration stories to be told, and that one story does not fit all.

Looking at migration patterns from the perspective of OECD member states, this array of data begins to generate some common stories. Migration for work has become a dominant motive for some half of the total population of international migrants to Europe, North America, and Australia (ILO 2021*a*). The other most prominent destinations are the Gulf and the Arab states, which account for more than a third of all migrant workers (ILO 2021*a*). There are comparatively low rates of mobility in the African states, although this is changing: migration within the African continent is increasing, and substantially smaller though growing numbers are migrating globally. A similar development is unfolding among South American states.

The increasing international mobility of people has ignited widespread calls within destination countries (also known as host states) to cap movement. These calls intensified with the surge in migration that occurred over 2015–16, involving mostly refugees and asylum seekers fleeing civil war in Syria, women and children escaping violence and disorder in Central American states, and those seeking safe haven from ethnic conflict and hostilities in Africa. This period of time was declared a 'migration crisis'. While the overwhelming population of refugees reside in low-income countries, the 'crisis' has possibly become a watershed moment in the history of migration governance (Castles, de Haas, and Miller 2015).

There are three main categories of migration that provide the possibility of permanent residence in OECD states (OECD 2020). Foremost among these has been the issuing of visas to those who will contribute to the economic development of the host state; these are generally framed as residence and the right to work visas. A second important category is humanitarian visas, which grant residence to refugees and asylum seekers. A third involves family reunion visas, entailing the issuance of residence visas to the parents, siblings, and children of migrants-turned-citizens.

> ### Key Concepts
>
> **Residence and the right to work visas:** A visa category allowing people the right to live and reside in a place of destination, and the right to work on either a temporary or an ongoing basis.
>
> **Humanitarian visas:** A visa category allowing people entry to a country on humanitarian grounds, as refugees or asylum seekers.
>
> **Family reunion visas:** A visa category observing the human right to family life, allowing family members to migrate in order to be reunited with one another.

What have been the main characteristics of contemporary migration policy in the main OECD host states? First, keeping in mind these three categories, the migration policies of the leading destination countries have begun to place greater weight on issuing visas to those recruited for work, at the cost of a reduction in quotas for humanitarian visas (OECD 2018*b*). More stringent refugee quotas were reported prior to the surge in refugees in 2015–16, and tighter controls have since been reinstated (OECD 2017; IOM 2019*b*). Host country government commitments to family reunion have also come under pressure. Several destination countries now require those applying for family resettlement visas to meet the costs of maintenance, medical coverage, and social security and aim to limit the overall numbers of this category of migrants in the migration profile (OECD 2017).

Giving preference to categories of migrants based on their capacity to become productive members of the community highlights the economically instrumentalist approach to governance that has come to prevail among OECD country governments. This is evident in the issuing of visas for entrepreneurs and innovators who are granted visas on the condition that they invest a stipulated amount of capital in the host country. The instrumentalist approach is similarly evident in refugee placement. Prospective host countries have been selecting refugees with skills deemed most suitable for meeting workforce needs (Gonzales Benson and Taccolini Panaggio 2019).

It is also apparent in the relatively recent growth and numerically significant category of international students. The international education industry has become highly lucrative. Most student visas authorize some qualified rights to work during their studies which has resulted in students becoming an important source of labour. Visa extensions that enable students to gain post-graduation work experience in some industries have expanded this pool of limited-term visa holders (Raghuram and Sondhi 2021).

Second, reflecting this emphasis on market-driven processes, states have in ever greater numbers and in a variety of ways retreated from a direct role in migration governance. The management of migration has become in ever greater numbers and in a variety of ways marketized, with governments divesting themselves of responsibility in the conviction that private enterprise can deliver services more efficiently and cost-effectively (Lahav 1998). For example, airlines have come to be at the frontline of checking sojourners' documentation, and private corporations have been contracted to repatriate unauthorized migrants or to detain prospective asylum seekers who await the processing of their applications.

Third, this has complemented the development of migration management as a global business, involving a vast assortment of agencies. These range from the local entrepreneurial figure who helps organize the recruitment of workers by introducing the worker to the recruitment and/or placement agencies that navigate employment contracts and provide logistical support including financing, to the banks or foreign exchange agencies that assist in the remittance of migrants' income to their families in their home countries, through to the deployment agency in the destination country or corporate employment agencies that conduct searches, and manage selection and transfers (Jones and Sha 2020).

In all of these aspects of contemporary migration policy, the historical role that states assumed over migration governance, which was crucial to their standing in the global inter-state system, has been complemented if not replaced by private actors or enterprises. The management of movement has become a profit-generating system in which private enterprises lay claim to a share of the wealth that is generated across the global labour supply chain.

13.3 Theories of international migration

As students of international migration in the Global Political Economy (GPE), you are fortunate to have within your reach a plethora of interdisciplinary theories that inform the critical analysis of migration (Castles, de Haas, and Miller 2015; Wickramasinghe and Wimalaratana 2016; Boucher and Gest 2018). This choice is not unproblematic: the varied factors that impel international migration and the diverse patterns of migration indicate the need for caution in presuming that one theory can suffice in providing a framework for analysing international migration.

Let us start with one of the most prominent theories of migration: the neoclassical perspective. This theory focuses on the impulse of individual mobility—why people migrate—in terms of the force of 'push' and 'pull' factors. The efficacy of the neoclassical approach can be questioned, given that it is narrowly conceived and defined by rational individual behaviour: it lacks a framework for understanding migration as a phenomenon or process that is more than an aggregation of lots of individual decisions motivated primarily by a narrowly conceived personal economic agenda.

The neoclassical economic approach has over time been repackaged in the New Economics of Labour Migration (NELM) approach, presenting the decision to migrate as a family-based calculation of who should migrate to maximize the gains from mobility (Stark and Bloom 1985). NELM at least expands the representation of those involved in decision-making, but it can be argued that it does not escape the 'rationalist' limitations of the neoclassical economic perspective.

Migration scholars have also developed 'migration systems' and 'network' approaches to explain emerging patterns of movement and how they are sustained (de Haas 2010). They focus on how social networks define patterns of migration which form migration systems, documenting how people's decisions to migrate, and to where, are shaped by family and social networks of people who have already migrated. While migration systems theory may usefully answer questions about how migration is perpetuated, in general it does not explain why and how a system comes into being in the first place, nor does it provide an answer to the question of why initial migration moves may *not* lead to network migration and migration system formation.

An explanation as to why many cases of initial migration do not lead to the formation of a migration system that exhibits systematic and self-reinforcing growth is instead provided by scholars who point to the formal (legal) and informal (sociopolitical) regulatory frameworks designed with the intention to 'manage' migration—in other words, to attract those 'wanted' and block those deemed 'unwanted'. A vital characteristic of the highly restrictive, selective, and discriminatory way of regulating ('managing') the flow of people is its intersectionality: that is, systemic differences in the ability to migrate in the first place are based on gender, class, and race/ethnicity as three key markers of differentiation (Crenshaw 1991).

An intersectional approach also lends itself to the analysis of the different experiences of migration and its outcomes by different (sub)groups in relation to their modes of border crossing, their labour market positioning, the value of the work they do, and the barriers they face in accessing social services (Piper and Satterthwaite 2007). By deconstructing the concepts of 'migrant' and 'worker', an intersectional lens highlights hierarchy and inequality involved in migration.

In sum, while the systems-driven perspectives provide the basis for a richer and more complex appreciation of international migration, they tend to depict most migrant workers as powerless—as pawns in an all-encompassing global dynamic—and they downplay the capacity of migrants to exercise some say over the migration experience. We argue that there is a need for these perspectives to adopt a more systematic appreciation of the collective organization of migrant workers and to frame migrants as active agents in making their own lives and experiences, and in the making of migration as a phenomenon (Piper, Rosewarne, and Withers 2017).

So, we can see that the tendency to appeal to a general or all-encompassing theory of international migration is hazardous. Nor does having a choice of theories at hand necessarily overcome the tendency toward doctrinaire interpretations that downplay the complexity of migration as an evolving story. Here, echoing the points made in **Chapter 2** and **Chapter 3**, there is a logic in not being too analytically prescriptive or dogmatic by adopting one definitive theoretical method to explain a pattern of migration. An alternative is to focus on eliciting the broad trends that define international migration, and to consider which combination of theories allows us to understand them most clearly.

To this end, let's turn now to outlining these broad trends in international migration.

13.4 The unfolding momentum of international migration governance

The international mobility of people is emblematic of globalization. Yet, as much as we are receptive to the possibilities for travelling the world, be it as tourists, students, professionals, or workers, mobility necessarily confronts the state and its authority to sanction or frustrate incoming and outgoing movements of people. Mobility is not an unfettered right, and is often politically and socially contentious, as made abundantly clear by the hostile reception that greeted the surge in asylum seekers and refugees over the course of 2015–16, and by the everyday experiences of migrants in societies across the world.

The securitization of borders—the first theme we flagged in **Section 13.1**—has recently assumed renewed significance as people fleeing wars, violence, or environmental disasters have been confronted by emphatic 'not welcome' messages in Europe and the United States. In these cases, residents and conservative domestic political forces considered the surge a breach of the nation's borders and the integrity of the nation-state—and hence a 'border security' issue. High-income states have also sought to secure borders by projecting their authority beyond their borders—blocking and turning back would-be migrants and offering development assistance to origin and transit states that is contingent on them more forcefully checking movement. Singling out the unregulated flows of people linked to purported increases in 'economic migrants' added another layer to the waves of xenophobia (Simeone and Piper 2021).

The 'migration crisis' of 2015–16 reanimated debate on how best to establish some sense of order to the international movement of people.

13.4.1 Early roots

The introduction of regulations restricting migration was a critical feature in the construction of the nation-state in the late nineteenth and early twentieth centuries, particularly with respect to identity for those countries that were the most favoured migrant destinations: the United States, Canada, Australia, and New Zealand. Each had adopted measures proscribing the migration of Chinese people, and these restrictions were subsequently extended to Indians and then to more generic designations of Asians and others. The United States, for example, responded to mounting anti-migrant sentiments in the wake of the 'great Italian immigration' by passing the 1921 *Emergency Quota Act* that introduced restrictions on migration from southern Europe.

Three years later, the US government affirmed the decision to end its (qualified) open-door policy when it passed the *National Origins Act* (1924) to establish a passport system that permitted closer scrutiny and filtering of arrivals from non-preferred origins. Immigration processing was relocated from Ellis Island to New Jersey and Ellis Island was designated as a National Monument. The symbolism of the iconic Statue of Liberty welcoming arrivals to the 'New World' remained, although the reality of a liberal open-door migration policy was otherwise. The exclusions were instead extended. The USA passed the 1934 *Philippine Independence Act* declaring Filipinos as aliens. These tight migration controls were consolidated by each of the favoured destinations through the 1930s and remained in force until after the Second World War (Hollifield, Martin, and Orrenius 2014).

The one significant counter to this trend was the United States' experimentation with seasonal agricultural worker programmes. Established towards the end of the First World War as one of the first substantial seasonal migrant worker programmes, West Coast farmers were permitted to recruit low-paid Mexicans to work in the fields. The scheme was revitalized at the beginning of the Second World War as the so-called Bracero Program, and this set a precedent for institutionalizing labour market disadvantage for migrants recruited into seasonal agricultural work. It also established the use of migrant workers as a norm in US agriculture.

The institutionalization of a migration corridor also facilitated undocumented migration as an enduring feature of the industry. 'Migrant work' was, and still is, work that was characteristically poorly paid. The dirty, dangerous, and difficult or demeaning (the '3-Ds') occupations were typecast in terms of race, ethnicity, and gender, subjecting workers to exploitative and abusive conditions. The prevalence of undocumented workers created downward pressures on pay and conditions, locking in disadvantage for agricultural workers (Massey and Liang 1989).

Strengthening migration management, most effectively pursued by simply introducing tighter border controls, had become the dominant motif of international migration governance prior to the Second World War (Karatani 2005).

13.4.2 The Second World War and the liberal turn

The post-war migration story evolved into one marked by a more liberal approach to migration governance, linking mobility to national economic development (Fanning and Piper 2021). This was a crucial factor in advancing economic goals—the second theme introduced in **Section 13.1**—with the formulation of migration policies that supported the resettlement of displaced Europeans and their employment in the expanding industrial economies of North America and Australia. It also evolved into a migration system that sought to advance opportunities for those migrating to be free of discriminatory employment practices. The pursuit of labour rights—the third theme we mentioned in **Section 13.1**—became the third element in contemporary international migration governance.

The Second World War wrought a watershed in the general thrust of migration policy, although most barriers based on race persisted through to the last quarter of the twentieth century. Plans to resettle refugees and other displaced peoples were being formulated well before the end of the conflict (Long 2013). Refugee resettlement was organized, and the establishment of the United Nations (UN) in 1945 set in train an era of international cooperation that, while not universal, prefigured the adoption of more liberal approaches to migration (Karatani 2005).

Liberalization was underscored by several developments. The United States' mid-1930s New Deal sought to spearhead economic recovery by launching major infrastructure developments that were premised on an accord between the state, employers, and workers, creating what amounted to a 'social contract'. This was a contract that subscribed to improving employment standards and industrial protections, especially securing employment standards for citizens.

In Australia, establishing a social contract not dissimilar to the New Deal in the United States was the foundation of the Australian Labor government's post-war development plan, which was set in place with the Post-War Reconstruction Commission established in 1942 and which was charged to begin preparations for demobilizing returned servicemen (Jupp 2002). Similar but less ambitious programmes were launched in Canada. A common feature of these policies was that they drew on the post-war migration programmes, which brought a substantial skilled workforce that was complemented by rising refugee intakes (Walsh 2012).

Reconstruction in Europe also relied on the recruitment of migrants from southern Europe, North Africa, and the Mediterranean periphery (Castles and Kosack 1985). This was a bit of a balancing act that involved many of the leading destination or host states acceding in some measure to the claims for asylum, family reunion, and migration for work. A parallel development followed the post-war independence movements in Europe's colonies. The exodus from the colonies furthered the development impetus generated from migration. In Europe, this encompassed the migration of people from the various powers' former colonies who swelled the ranks of the working populations of Britain and France (Bleich 2005).

Migration became an essential feature of the rebooting of the economies over the course of the 1950s and 1960s. This was explicitly encapsulated in the nation-building exercise of 'populate or perish', as was the case of Australia. However, as a rich literature on post-Second World War immigration programmes documents, this was to the systematic disadvantage of migrant workers (Gordon 1995). Reflecting the shift in the political order with the elevation of an accord between capital and labour enunciated in the US New Deal, the ILO saw the opportunity to extend the reach of the social contract to lay some foundations that restricted the potential for migrant workers to be exploited in the countries of resettlement.

The ILO had been established as an organization under the post-First World War League of Nations. It survived the League's demise to become a division of the UN when it was formed in 1945, and the ILO elevated labour rights as the cause célèbre (Fanning and Piper 2021). The ILO sanctioned the right of all workers to organize, the adoption of fair labour standards which included restrictions on hours worked and minimum rates of remuneration, and the provision of comparable rights to support, such as unemployment insurance, that would proscribe discrimination in employment. The liberal migration agenda brought to the fore an international focus on the potential that awarding equal rights for migrant workers could have, by blocking employer efforts to erode established employment standards and protections in occupations and industries in which there was a high concentration of migrant workers.

However, the immediate post-Second World War liberal period was not without its contradictions. While not universal, there was relatively unfettered international migration for a time as the dominant demographic pattern boosted the economic recovery among OECD member states. This occurred without much insight into the effects of this recourse to labour migration. Policies to regulate the flow of labour to boost the capacity of the workforce to support re-industrialization programmes could be easily undermined. This was the case with the 'guest worker' programmes designed to recruit labour from southern Europe. Instead of temporary residence and employment, many such as was the case of Turkish workers in Germany resettled.

These programmes came to an end in the mid-1970s as the industrial economies began to falter. Rising unemployment and the fragile state of the industrial economies underwrote pressures to cut immigration and the reluctance of guest workers to return to their countries of origin, where there were fewer employment opportunities (Castles 1986).

Yet the liberal character of this period was not all that it seemed. The social contract did not extend to many migrant workers. There was mounting evidence that much migrant worker employment was being concentrated in emergent 'secondary' labour markets. Employment in the secondary labour market was characterized by the '3-D' occupations, low pay, few career advancement opportunities, and poorly regulated and exploitative working conditions. At the other end of this spectrum of work, in the 'primary' labour market, were the professional highly skilled occupations that were dominated by citizens or highly skilled migrant workers who could exercise some negotiating power (Edwards 1982).

It was in this context that the ILO turned to laying the foundations of labour rights for migrant workers. In 1950, the *Discrimination in Respect of Employment and Occupation* or *Discrimination (Employment and Occupation) Convention* (C111) was negotiated. It was designed to discourage discrimination in labour markets and workplaces disadvantaging migrant workers, although C111 did not come into force until a much later date because many countries, including the major labour migration receiving states in Europe, North America, and Australia, resisted and refused to ratify it. Other migrant worker-related conventions were designed to encourage governments to work against the institutionalization of the divisions within labour markets but faced a similar reception (Simeone and Piper 2018).

The widespread refusal to ratify the ILO Convention highlighted the pervasive force of discrimination and how this structured national labour markets, channelling migrant workers into categories of work that are customarily regarded as migrant worker occupations. This segmentation has continued to define labour markets through to the present (OECD 2020).

13.4.3 International labour market liberalization and the rise of temporary migration

Migration had proved to be an important factor in the booming economies of the 1950s and 1960s, albeit subject to restrictions on the origin of migrants. But beginning in the mid-1960s there emerged a conviction in the benefits of liberalizing and invigorating the economy through the adoption of more relaxed labour migration policies and an early prioritizing of labour migration over other migration categories. The US *Immigration Act* (1965) removed the bar on immigration quotas, which radically reorientated the centre of gravity to migration from Asia and Latin America (Hatton 2015). Changes in Canada's migration policy in 1962 and 1967 placed greater emphasis on skills and talent and removed restrictions based on race (Simons and Clancy 2017).

A similar recasting of migration policy in Australia commenced with a review in 1966 and a formal renunciation of one of the most overt discriminatory migration policies, the 'White Australia' policy, in 1973 (Jupp 2002). Similar policies had been adopted in North America, Japan, China, and in several European states through more surreptitious, though heavy-handed, border securitization programmes. However, Australia's policy to proscribe the entry of People of Colour was quite unique in that prospective migrants had to undergo a language test which could be conducted in any language of the migration official's choosing.

The abandonment of this policy was a clear signal that the liberalization of migration policy was ascendent. This became apparent with the policy emphasis on attracting professional and talented migrant workers. As was the case in both Canada and the United States, there was a shift in the origin of migrants to more diverse sources, and particularly from Asia.

These policy shifts heralded the more expansive reach of labour migration within the global political economy. A more critically significant transformation in the pattern of migration and the prioritization of labour migration followed the formation of the Organization of the Petroleum Exporting Countries (OPEC), a cartel arrangement purposely designed to win support from OPEC members to increase oil prices. This engendered a massive redistribution of the world's wealth, with the Gulf states as the principal beneficiaries. Awash with 'petrodollars', and with comparatively small populations, the Gulf states recruited migrant workers from across the spectrum of occupations to meet the labour needs of their expanding economies.

A quite distinctive pattern of migration took shape in the Gulf states in response to the significant boost in the states' wealth (Khalaf, AlShehabi, and Hanieh 2015). Three fundamental changes to the global migration story stood out. First, it entailed a radical reorientation in the geography of international migration. Large numbers of predominantly male workers were recruited from the Indian subcontinent and from North Africa and other Arab states to work in a range of skilled and low-skilled occupations. Second, women migrant workers emerged for the first time as a significant component of the international migrant workforce; the great majority were engaged as live-in domestic workers.

Third, as the older European industrial economies wrestled with restricting migration, a new model of labour migration was forged in the Gulf states. Workers were employed under the *kafala* system (**see Case Study 13.1**). Migrant workers were engaged in employment through a sponsor, an arrangement that locks workers into a contract with no right to terminate or prematurely end the arrangement, meaning they have no right to escape from an abusive employer (Khan and Harroff-Tavel 2011). The *kafala* system makes for a form of employment that is particularly exploitative, exposing workers to a wide range of abuses and vulnerabilities which have been extensively documented by human rights organizations. For workers who had borrowed to finance their passage to work, their employment could amount to forced labour.

Case Study 13.1: The *kafala* system and migrant worker exploitation

In the aftermath of the oil price hike, the cash-rich economies of the Gulf states set out on an unparalleled development trajectory that, given their small populations, resulted in the states of Bahrain, Kuwait, Oman, Qatar, Saudi Arabia, and the United Arab Emirates, as well as Jordan and Lebanon, recruiting large numbers of migrant workers. This reliance on migrants to work in construction and the service sectors, including in households, transformed the Gulf states into one of the most significant destinations for migrant workers, accounting for a third of the world's migrant workforce.

Many workers were employed under the *kafala* system, based on a local resident—normally the employer—sponsoring the foreign worker. The *kafala* system establishes a marked power imbalance between workers and employers, with workers contractually bound to sponsors with no right to sever employment contracts, switch employers, or depart to escape mistreatment. Workers are vulnerable and often subject to exploitation, low wages, poor working conditions, endemic racial discrimination, and gender-based violence. This is compounded by the lack of effective industrial protections to safeguard workers from abuse.

The *kafala* system has been the object of forensic investigation and criticism. It faces lobbying for change by human rights groups and unions, and sustained pressure from the International Trade Union Confederation (ITUC) and the International Wood Workers and Construction Union. Qatar has been a particular focus of lobbying as the host of the 2022 football World Cup and because of its construction boom (Photo 13.1). The ILO and the ITUC have pressured FIFA, football's global governing body, to call the system to account and improve employment conditions.

Photo 13.1 The construction site of a football stadium in Doha, Qatar

Source: © iStock/Cylonphoto.

Qatar has made some cosmetic reforms to the *kafala* system, as have other Gulf States, but these have had little positive effect on migrant construction workers' employment conditions. The sponsorship system remains widespread and continues to contribute to the exploitation and vulnerability of migrant workers in the Gulf (OECD 2019).

Questions

1 What opportunities are there for countries of origin to address labour market violations in the countries in which their nationals work?
2 What other strategies could be used to improve employment conditions for migrant workers, and by whom?

The liberalization of restrictions on international labour migration was proffered as a panacea for 'underdevelopment' in low-income countries and the reluctance of citizens in medium- and high-income states to work in low-paid and precarious occupations. The problem is that measures which support labour migration could undermine the role of the nation-state in determining who is allowed to reside within its territory. Accordingly, the World Bank came to advocate temporary migration—using temporary visas—as a solution to this threat. This has become one of the key justifications for normalizing temporary labour migration.

Drawing on conventional economic theory, the World Bank's (1995) *World Development Report: Workers in an Integrating World* made a case for accommodating temporary labour migration as a means of increasing the material well-being of migrants' origin states as well as high-income states. The theory posits that economies should specialize in activities that make effective use of their natural endowments—capital, land, natural resources, and labour—conditional on their full employment. In contexts where there are high rates of unemployment or underemployment, as in many low-income countries, mobilizing and relocating labour to countries experiencing labour shortages is held to generate net global economic benefits.

Temporary labour migration has proved an appealing strategy for fostering development in low-income countries. The migration of citizens for work on a temporary basis can be a reliable source for income flows as workers unable to resettle and with family responsibilities are generally bound to 'remit' their overseas earnings to their families in their home countries. Apart from supporting families and communities, the remittances, especially as foreign exchange, can strengthen the international trading positions of workers' countries of origin. With the magnitude of remittances now exceeding international development assistance and foreign investment in most labour export countries, labour migration programmes have created a dependency on the export of labour as a means for families to meet their material needs and for the state to underwrite its fiscal well-being (Withers 2019).

Temporary migration programmes are also represented as a win-win because temporariness restricts the threat that low-income countries will lose forever their skilled workers to the Global North—the so-called 'brain drain' phenomenon—while the employment experience provides opportunities for upskilling.

> **Key Concepts**
>
> **Remittances:** The money from their earnings which migrant workers send 'home' to their families in another country.
>
> **Brain drain:** The negative impact on 'source' countries of large-scale emigration of educated citizens.

Hence the Gulf states, in engaging migrant workers on limited-term contracts, set the style for practices of temporariness that have become the norm in other destinations and a global phenomenon (ILO 2021*a*; Dauvergne and Marsden 2014; OECD 2020). Many OECD states have introduced an array of visa categories to attract temporary migrant workers to work in mostly low-skilled and low-paid occupations or industries that local workers are resistant to working in. Among the most significant are Working Holiday Maker programmes, international student visas that permit paid employment, and Seasonal Worker programmes (OECD 2019).

While professional and skilled migrant workers are generally more likely to have the option of linking employment contracts to permanent residence applications, the options for the great majority of low-skilled temporary migrant workers are limited. Fixed-duration employment generally does not prevent migrant workers from signing onto new contracts, but temporariness denies any recognition of continuity of service, which can impact social security entitlements and rights to apply for permanent residence. Temporariness also impacts the ability of migrant workers to contest untoward employment practices and to exercise their employment and industrial rights (**see Section 12.2.2**). Many host states ban temporary migrant workers' right to organize (Piper, Rosewarne, and Withers 2017).

13.4.4 **The 'feminization' of migration**

As we mentioned in **Section 13.4.3**, a critical development associated with the Gulf states and intra-Asian migration more broadly was that, for the first time, women migrant workers emerged as a significant component of the international migrant workforce.

A growing number of low-income states encourage women to migrate on a temporary basis as a counter to their low participation rates in the national labour market. The prospect of earning income can be empowering. An additional positive, according to many policymakers and researchers, albeit reflecting a gendered ascription, is that this can magnify women's contribution to development. This argument is made on the assumption that women will likely save and remit a greater share of their income as responsible family members than their male counterparts and will therefore have a greater impact on improving familial health and well-being, education, and housing.

The enthusiasm with which the promotion of women's participation in the global labour market has been proselytized, especially by the World Bank, has prompted more countries to support women's participation in this global market. However, the competition for work with workers from other sources can result in a 'race to the bottom' to lower remuneration and employment conditions.

Entrenched sex-typing of global work has resulted in the overwhelming proportion of women being engaged as domestic workers and care workers. It is extensively documented that migrant domestic workers undertake work that is devalued and experience greater vulnerability as live-in domestic workers; long and unregulated hours; and severe impositions on their personal space, human rights, and employment rights—where these do exist. Many others engage in domestic work as undocumented workers to avoid the cost and time required to apply for work permits which also makes for vulnerability. Migrant domestic work epitomizes how the intersection of class, race/ethnicity, and gender creates a hierarchy between migrant and non-migrant women as well as between different nationalities working within this sector (Lan 2006).

However, the global and collective advocacy efforts that resulted in the adoption of international labour standards for domestic workers—the ILO's *Domestic Workers Convention, 2011 (No. 189)*—illustrate the possibility of agency (**see Case Study 13.2**).

Case Study 13.2: The Domestic Workers Convention

A distinguishing feature of contemporary international labour migration has been the scale of women migrating independently to seek employment. Women account for a little less than half the global migrant workforce, and while they are employed across the occupation spectrum,

Photo 13.2 **A poster produced by the IDWF for the International Domestic Workers Day 2022, to honour the work and resilience of domestic workers**

Source: IDWF.

(Continued)

most work as household domestic labour. Many are engaged on a live-in basis. With the work being undertaken behind closed doors, migrant domestic workers are in an extremely vulnerable position.

Moreover, historically domestic work was not regarded as work that warranted regulation. As a result, the work has not been covered by employment or industrial regulations. Working in the isolation of the household, domestic workers could not easily challenge their situation. The limited contact these workers have with their peers contrasts with other workplaces, in which work characteristically involves interacting with other workers and so provides opportunities for collective action or organizing in trade unions.

Yet, against the odds, migrant women workers have been organizing domestic worker unions, often with the support of faith-based institutions, civil society organizations, and traditional unions to lobby governments to regulate conditions of employment (Photo 13.2). Just as significantly, domestic workers formed an international network with the support of civil society organizations such as Women in Informal Employment: Globalizing and Organizing (WIEGO) and peak union bodies such as the ITUC and the International Union of Food, Agricultural, Hotel, Restaurant, Catering, Tobacco and Allied Workers' Associations (IUF).

Domestic workers pursued their struggle to win employment recognition and employment rights to the ILO and won the support of representatives of states, employers, and trade unions for the *Domestic Workers Convention* (C189), which was adopted in 2011. The Convention came into force in 2013, after a successful grassroots campaign by domestic workers to lobby states to ratify it.

The formation of the International Domestic Workers Federation, with the continued support of the IUF and the ITUC, has advanced efforts to improve the working conditions of domestic workers.

Watch the video on the online resources to take your understanding of this case study further.

Questions

1 What kinds of vulnerabilities are experienced by migrant domestic workers? Why?
2 What does the case of the *Domestic Worker Convention* tell us about the possibilities for effective collective mobilization among migrant workers in other sectors? Or are domestic workers unique?

13.5 **The struggle for labour rights**

We have seen that temporary visas have become a key to reconciling migration governance, formalizing the authority to exercise the securitization of borders and maximizing the economic benefits of the qualified liberalization of border controls (**see Section 13.4.3**). The geographically extensive recourse to temporary migrant workers and the multiple forms that temporariness can take has become the dark side of the global political economy. The total number of temporary migrant workers now exceeds the number issued with permanent visas (OECD 2020).

So, what can be done? Efforts to address the exploitative conditions experienced by migrant workers confront the challenge of the absence of an international institution with the authority to advocate and enforce minimum employment standards. This contrasts with the presence of other institutions, such as the World Trade Organization (WTO), the World Bank, the International Monetary Fund (IMF), and the Bank for International Settlements (BIS), which have the power to remove obstacles impeding free trade in commodities and the circulation of capital and money (**see Chapter 5** and **Chapter 6**).

Certainly, the ILO and the UN have sought to set some minimum standards and rights for migrants by formulating international conventions. These include conventions for migrant workers, such as the UN's *International Convention on the Protection of the Rights of All Migrant Workers and Members of Their Families* and the ILO's *Convention Concerning Migration for Employment* (C97) and *Domestic Workers Convention* (C189). Other examples include UN conventions for refugees, such as *The Universal Declaration of Human Rights* (1948) and the *1951 Refugee Convention*. But these conventions are not binding on member states. There is no international legal instrument that compels host states to set minimum employment conditions and rights for migrant workers.

Those states whose citizens make up the bulk of the pool of low- and semi-skilled temporary migrant workers are hamstrung by the territorial limits of their ability to secure the most basic of labour rights for migrant workers. Some states have negotiated bilateral agreements with host states to agree on minimum conditions of employment, but these have been largely unsuccessful in upholding rights. Similarly, efforts to negotiate multilateral agreements, often with the support of the ILO, the International Organization for Migration (IOM), and UN Women, have generally proved futile (Hennebry and Hari 2021).

A state's commitment to combating exploitative practices can be compromised even in those instances in which it does have authority to act, such as with recruitment processes. An economic development strategy based on transforming citizens into migrant workers to become export earners can compromise efforts to set minimum conditions. In the final instance, state bans on recruiting workers to work in destinations where their citizens are being subjected to a pattern of severe maltreatment are not necessarily effective because the necessity to work can drive workers to ignore such bans, as has occurred on a seemingly regular basis with some Gulf states.

The story, however, is not entirely bleak. There are some signs within the international community of a more determined resolve to advance labour rights. The surge in migration that occurred over 2015–16 with the mobilization of refugees and asylum seekers and the flow of so-called 'economic migrants' to Europe and the United States brought such worrying displays of xenophobia that it forced a response to defend the liberal economic order along with its advocacy of human and labour rights.

The UN launched a forum to negotiate the formulation of both the *Compact for Safe, Orderly and Regular Migration* (2018)—also known as the *Global Compact for Migration*— and the *Global Compact on Refugees* (2018). The *Global Compact for Migration* reiterates the global commitment to enhancing labour rights as a foundation of international migration. Drawing on established principles, the Compact's ambition is framed as an 'action plan'. Member states are responsible for implementing the plan, with periodic implementation reviews by regions, backed up by a 'capacity-building mechanism' and the work of the UN Migration Network (IOM 2020).

The convening of the international forum—which involved member states, the key international economic organizations, the ILO, the IOM, the ITUC, and other social movement organizations—and the endorsement of the *Global Compact for Migration* may very well prove the beginning of a new pattern of migration governance. New cooperative organizational arrangements are being forged and appear to be successfully injecting renewed momentum into a collective purpose. 'Global partnerships' that bring together key international organizations, including the ILO and the IOM, and the decision to charge the ILO and the World Bank with oversight for advancing social protection as a universal right are creating fresh possibilities for advancing the rights and protections of migrant workers.

13.6 Conclusion

Migration has become a pervasive feature of the global economy, underpinning the evolution of labour markets and the nature of work and employment across the world (**see Chapter 12**). Labour 'export' has developed into an industry in its own right, but on a marked spectrum: at one end, the creation of a low-cost global labour force that is treated as a commodity, and at the other, the creation of a 'global talent' pool from which high- and medium-income industries can draw their professional and skilled workforce (OECD 2016).

In the contemporary Global Political Economy, the freedom of labour is highly circumscribed, in contrast with the freedom that underpins the circulation of capital and money and the trade in goods and services (**see Chapter 4**, **Chapter 5**, and **Chapter 6**). This restriction on the freedom of labour rests on nation-states exercising border controls, or border securitization, which enables the right to check unfettered mobility. These border controls serve two crucial economic functions. First, they underpin the ability of host countries to cherry-pick the 'best and the brightest' migrants to contribute to the development of the economy. Second, border controls establish the means to limit migrant workers' residence rights, creating a class of workers who—because of these restrictions—will be low-paid and subject to more intensive work patterns and a range of abuses. These patterns are crucial for sustaining the viability of a range of industries and adding momentum to the economy more generally.

The downside to global labour migration is that state institutions have demonstrated comparatively little resolve in securing employment rights and protections for migrant work forces. The response of the UN to the mounting evidence of anti-migrant sentiments following the 2015–16 surge in people movement has aroused a new determination to promote migrant workers' labour rights. However, progress will rest on challenging deep-seated economic and social inequalities as well as the economic imperatives that shape the global political economy.

Key Points

- Migration is a defining feature of contemporary globalization, but movements of people are much more restricted than movements of goods, money, or services.

- The securitization of national borders by many OECD governments has enabled the restriction of rights to migrate and privileged certain groups of migrants over others.
- Labour migration has come to be privileged over other forms of migration, but often involves temporary work visas and significant vulnerability for migrant workers.
- The global movement to protect migrants' labour rights has had generally limited impact, but with some notable successes and continued momentum.
- Migration continues to be politically and socially contentious in many parts of the world, adding to the vulnerability of many migrant workers.

Further Reading

Boucher, A., and Gest, J. (2018), *Crossroads: Comparative Immigration Regimes in a World of Demographic Change* (Cambridge: Cambridge University Press). A comparative analysis of different 'regimes' governing immigration in light of evolving migration patterns.

Castles, S., de Haas, H., and Miller, M. J. (2020), *The Age of Migration: International Population Movements in the Modern World* (London: Palgrave Macmillan). A classic and very readable introduction to international migration.

International Organization for Migration (2000–present), *World Migration Report* (Paris: IOM). An annual report offering a valuable global snapshot of migration patterns and issues.

Phillips, N. (2011) (ed.), *Migration in the Global Political Economy* (Boulder, CO: Lynne Rienner). A collection approaching migration from a GPE perspective, with chapters on a range of different dimensions of global migration.

Wickramasinghe, A. I. I. N., and Wimalaratana, W. (2016), 'International Migration and Migration Theories', *Social Affairs: A Journal for the Social Sciences*, 1(5): 13–32. A useful overview of theories of migration.

Chapter 13 Roundtable discussion

To what extent should states be open to migration?

Roundtable 13.1
Opening contribution **Stuart Rosewarne and Nicola Piper**

In 1971 an article was published entitled 'The Civil Right We Are Not Ready For: The Right of Free Movement of People', in which the author, Roger Nett, paints the following scenario: 'At some future point in world civilization, it may well be discovered that the right to free and open movement of people on the surface of the earth is fundamental to the structure of human opportunity and is therefore basic in the same sense as is free religion, speech, and the franchise' (Nett 1971: 218).

In the world as we know it, where free movement across borders has been hampered by increasingly selective and restrictive controls—ranging historically from the 1882 Chinese Exclusion Act of the United States to the White Australia policy and the EU Free Movement space excluding so-called 'third country nationals' ('Fortress Europe')—Nett's scenario still seems utopian. The position taken by political philosopher Joseph Carens (1987)—making a strong case for 'open borders' on the basis that borders are inherently unjust—is treated as extreme and, needless to say, remains a minority view.

The case for 'open borders' and the right of mobility, especially with limitations, can be approached from one of two perspectives: that of a global system of nation-states determined to secure their political integrity (Hollifield, Martin, and Orrenius 2014) or that of an internationalist argument seeking to advance human rights as a global development cause (Pecoud and de Guchteneire 2006).

It will not take you long to identify which of these has dominated much political discourse in recent times, most obviously in the populist politics that defined Brexit in the UK and the presidencies of Donald Trump in the United States, Viktor Orbán in Hungary, and others. It has been manifest in the incitement of xenophobic sentiment among voting publics, with arguments about foreigners invading 'their' country and the notion that advantages are earned rather than passively received through a 'birth lottery'.

The complex arguments to explain why the right to free migration has not attracted more support within the nation-state context can be clustered under three thematic headings:

Stability: Supporters of citizens' rights to social and economic security contend that welfare should be a universal right (human rights argument), while extending the right to migrants is seen as encouraging 'welfare scrounging' with migrants seen as becoming a significant drain on the nation's budget (economic argument). From a different perspective, uncontrolled migration or targeted recruitment of foreign labour may break up solidarity and cohesion among the working class, which in turn may weaken public support for, and at worst result in the dismantlement of, the welfare state (Freeman 1986).

Security: Border control is typically constructed as a counter-trafficking or smuggling measure, and thus a broader function of crime prevention. Yet, as critical voices would point out, restrictive immigration policies have also been argued to *cause* precisely these problems. Increasingly sophisticated border control mechanisms feed the need for semi-professional assistance in the crossing of heavily guarded borders. The gradual and pervasive commercialization of such assistance can easily lead to abuse, fraud, or greed (Pianezzi and Grossi 2018).

Identity: Supporting integration can lay the foundations for migrants to make a productive and diverse contribution to the nation. Successful integration can enrich the nation culturally, economically, and politically, especially in an increasingly interconnected world. At the opposite end of the spectrum are those who consider the idea of bestowing rights to non-citizens, especially when they entered in an unauthorized manner or engage in activities that their visa or work permits do not allow for, as 'counter-hegemonic' (Basok 2009). The large-scale immigration of the culturally and linguistically diverse 'other' is viewed as culturally disruptive.

What these three arguments have in common is that they are typically used to justify restrictions on international mobility, with economic justifications tending to overshadow the human rights approach. As a result, the much heralded 'triple win' solution of migration is skewed in favour of employers and governments, leaving many migrants empty-handed.

Within this nation-state frame, a different approach contrasts the developmental promise of labour migration for countries of origin versus its potential costs. One emphasis regards migration as a pathway 'out of poverty', most frequently expressed in terms of migrants remitting income to finance development (the 'migration–development nexus') (**see Section 13.4.3**). A counter to this points to the potential of migration as an impoverishing process ('migration into poverty') when migrants become indebted to meet the costs of migrating and are recruited into exploitative and precarious employment. These patterns are epitomized by South Asian domestic and construction workers bound for the Gulf countries on short-term contracts, without rights and access to justice (Foley and Piper 2021; **see Case Study 13.1**).

Although the scholarly and policy debate on international migration has resulted in greater appreciation of its globally interconnected nature, awareness of interconnectivity did not lead to an open debate on responsibility. This may change in the wake of the adoption of the *Global Compact for Safe, Orderly and Regular Migration* in December 2018, premised on the principle that migration is a shared responsibility in the international community. It reflects the ethos of the *2030 Agenda for Sustainable Development* of 'leaving no one behind'.

This challenge to prevailing orthodoxy requires a 180-degree change in thinking about migration and migrants' rights. If migration is a shared responsibility, what does this mean for countries of origin, transit, and destination? How should they work together to ensure that migration is safe, orderly, and regular?

Roundtable 13.2
Response **Jorge Tigno**

The question posed by Stuart Rosewarne and Nicola Piper in the opening contribution places the nation-state squarely at the centre of the migration discourse (**see Roundtable 13.1**). Doing so, however, only shows part of the full picture.

Migration cannot be seen in isolation from deeply embedded psycho-social factors. Family decisions, societal values, and community networks play a heavy role in one's desire to move. The role of the nation-state is often overshadowed by global events such as wars, natural disasters, and pandemics that also heavily impact the direction and extent of such population flows. Forced migration is the usual effect. Finally, there are economic and demographic forces that can attract people to seek greener pastures elsewhere. In a highly globalized, thoroughly interdependent, and complex world system, states would find it difficult (if not impossible) to effectively enforce restrictive immigration and emigration regulations.

Moreover, migration is heavily mediated and conditioned by a complex set of technological, social, commercial, and other institutional infrastructures (Xiang and Lindquist 2014). Their interplay can both facilitate and hinder migration, thus posing an even bigger challenge to any state in the long run.

Can and should states control migration? The simple answer is no, states cannot and should not control the movements of people. It may be politically expedient in the short-term for states to erect barriers to in-migration, but such measures reveal much ignorance about how the real world works in the long term. The argument about protecting borders and ensuring social cohesion harks back to a Westphalian epoch that has passed its 'best before' date. Even if one grants that state sovereignty continues to be the hallmark of the international landscape, states that wish to isolate their populations from the rest of the world are invariably seen more as pariahs than trendsetters.

Admittedly, for many source countries, migrants are a vital development resource. Large migrant-sending countries like the Philippines and India rely heavily on the billions of dollars in income that are sent each year by their respective overseas migrants to their families back home—that is, on remittances from migrant workers (**see Section 13.4.3**). Migrants in the Philippines are hailed as 'modern-day heroes' because of this (Encinas-Franco 2013). On the receiving end, Singapore, Malaysia, Hong Kong, Thailand, and many others that employ foreign workforces would no doubt be unable to experience the growth and prosperity that they have enjoyed since the 1980s and 1990s without the contributions of such an indispensable resource.

While migrants and migration bring a whole slew of problems with them, states alone are in no position to solve them all. Whether it's about solving the problem of global warming or solving the Covid-19 pandemic or addressing the migration question, states offer no silver bullets. National governments must face the reality that they need to also work together with non-state stakeholders.

Rosewarne and Piper raise the issue of states' willingness to share the responsibility of establishing a humane, free, and open global migration regime (**see Roundtable 13.1**). An intergovernmental perspective needs to be combined with a multilateral/multistakeholder approach to effectively manage migration, promote its developmental outcomes, and reduce its ill effects. Intergovernmental and multilateral initiatives such as the *Global Compact for Safe, Orderly and Regular Migration* (GCM) and the *Global Forum on Migration and Development* are major steps in the right direction, although there is still much room for improvement in them.

The same may be said about the 2007 Association of Southeast Asian Nations (ASEAN) Declaration on the Protection and Promotion of the Rights of Migrant Workers as well as the subsequent 2017 ASEAN Consensus on the Protection and Promotion of the Rights of

Migrant Workers. Both ASEAN edicts are hailed as noteworthy steps towards recognizing and uplifting the rights and welfare of migrant workers in the region, yet fall short of decisively addressing the specific and enduring issue of undocumented migration.

Multilateral initiatives, while strong on rhetoric and normative capacity, remain weak and non-binding as well as unable to recognize the proverbial 'elephant in the room'—namely, the continued resistance of governments in the Gulf to abandon their infamous *kafala* system (**see Case Study 13.1**). But this does not mean that multilateral initiatives ought to be abandoned altogether. They do serve to fill in gaps in the hard law on migration governance and can potentially and incrementally produce positive developments (see Höflinger 2020 on GCM).

At the end of the day, the free and open movement of people will remain a utopian idea from the vantage point of a global system that puts nation-states front and centre in the quest for a response to the migration question. As long as the nation-state system continues to dominate, an internationalist perspective that promotes the view that all migrants are human beings is going to be seen as a fruitless pipedream. We are still a long way from having a global citizenry. Indeed, since the 2010s, we have seen some major setbacks in this regard with Brexit in the UK and the abandonment of the multicultural agenda in places like Australia and the United States, among others. In not a few cases, internationalism has been replaced by populist nationalism and nationalist protectionism that regard migrants as invaders, interlopers, and competitors.

In the final analysis, we are still light years away from institutionalizing a free migration regime. Ironically, migration is not that different from international trade (**see Chapter 6**). Both involve movement across national boundaries—of goods and capital in the former and people in the latter. In an ideal world, if international trade is good for the economy, so should be free migration. The real world, however, is far from ideal and states are the likely culprit.

Roundtable 13.3
Response **Ariadna Estévez**

Stuart Rosewarne and Nicola Piper ask whether states can and should seek to control emigration and immigration (**see Roundtable 13.1**). The case for the right to mobility and open borders, they argue, can be seen either from the point of view of national interest, which endorses migration control, or from the internationalist perspective on human rights, which supports the right to migrate both outward and inward.

My straight answer is that borders should not exist, and all human beings should be able to cross borders and find a new home while seeking new opportunities, finding love, fleeing conflict, and pursuing happiness and hope. But a world with open borders is impossible because private and state interests need borders and the illegalization of migration to reproduce the economic and international status quo.

Private power produces migration through development projects, extractive industries, and other businesses that harm the environment. As soon as many such corporate activities start, contamination, criminal and sexual violence, poverty, deprivation, and lack of resources become widespread. Life eventually becomes impossible because gangs and criminals kill, extort, and rape hundreds in the community, including children; food and air become poisonous or scarce; and jobs and opportunities simply disappear.

In this context, people have no option: fleeing is their only chance of survival. However, emigrating legally becomes difficult because people have always lacked resources which would confer such rights: education, language skills, bank accounts, and work experience.

Take the case of Venezuela. In 2014, Venezuela approved the Law of Foreign Investment, which allows for international exploitation of gold, coltan, and other minerals in the Orinoco Mining Arc, which used to be an Indigenous and protected land. The Venezuelan government favours Canadian, Chinese, and Russian corporations over American corporations, which have been excluded. In 2016, the Venezuelan government set up its own military-run company called Anonymous Military Company of Mining, Oil and Gas Industries to become another investor. Illegal mining is also extensive, and Colombian and Venezuelan criminal groups use terror for these purposes (Ruiz 2018).

With this combination of authoritarian and militarized state politics, criminal violence, and resource exploitation, it is hardly surprising that there are 3.6 million Venezuelans displaced abroad.

But look at this from another angle: it seems hardly a coincidence that although there are twice as many Syrian refugees (6.6 million), the UN High Commissioner for Refugees singles out Venezuela in its report as if it was the most critical refugee situation in the world. Yet singling out Venezuela has no empirical justification; it can only be political.

Second, public power regulates migration through its international institutions and legal regimes, making the legal means of migrating impossible and turning migrants into commodities in the smuggling and trafficking industries, which move them along dangerous geographies. Those who survive and reach a country where they can finally apply for asylum must face Kafka-esque procedures in the migration regime.

Nicholas De Genova (2010) claims that since 9/11, there have been international efforts and cooperation to externalize border control—seeking to keep migrants off borders, chasing them, illegalizing them, and ultimately expelling and deporting them. I call this the necropolitical apparatus of forced migration, which produces migration through a series of laws and policies aimed at depopulating geographies rich in natural resources using criminal, state, and gender violence. Survivors flee, seeking refuge in rich countries. As a necropolitical technology, the legal category of asylum in human rights and humanitarian law becomes a legitimate way to exclude all those who fail to conform to its core definition.

An example of these controls is the legal instruments adopted by the UN, known as the Marrakech Pacts. As a result of the consultation process and adoption of the 2030 Agenda for Sustainable Development in 2015, the UN General Assembly embraced the New York Declaration which 'invite[s] the private sector and civil society, including refugee and migrant organizations, to participate in multi-stakeholder alliances to support efforts to implement the commitments we are making today' (Asamblea General de las Naciones Unidas 2016, Preamble, Para. 15).

You can see how the Declaration shifts the regime's focus from state responsibility to the cooperation of non-state actors. But also, while emphasizing the UN commitment to human rights, the Declaration calls for a policy designed to prevent refugees from fleeing to or seeking asylum in rich countries to 'ease pressure on host countries; enhance refugee self-reliance; expand access to third-country solutions; [and] support conditions in countries of origin for return'. While the Declaration was allegedly intended to tackle the shortcomings of hardcore refugee laws, it called on governments and civil society to work together to prevent refugees from reaching rich countries rather than doing anything to save lives.

In turn, the Declaration legitimized the so-called 'safe third country' treaties, which allow rich countries to use border and neighbour countries of the Global South as massive, open-air detention centres that eventually become tools for management technologies within the necropolitical apparatus of forced migration.

The *Global Compact for Safe, Orderly and Regular Migration* and the *Global Compact on Refugees*, both adopted in December 2018, reinforced this trend in international law (**see Section 13.5**). The goal of these non-binding instruments is to prevent asylum seekers and migrants from reaching the West. Countries of the Global South are requested to receive migrants; in exchange, rich countries and the private sector invest in services and infrastructure. There is no indication of how responsibility for the economic, political, and ethnic roots of international displacement—such as climate change, development, and crime—will be shared. Rich countries will only accept refugees and undocumented migrants through 'legal' and limited means such as family reunification, student scholarships, or humanitarian visas.

States should *and could* support an open borders policy for migration. But, for all these reasons, they won't.

Roundtable 13.4
Response **Oliver Bakewell**

There is no straightforward answer to the question of how open states should be to migration, as the opening discussion by Stuart Rosewarne and Nicola Piper illustrates (**see Roundtable 13.1**). They present it as a debate between two competing perspectives: the world of nation-states maintaining their security or a world of global justice providing equal opportunity for all. This looks compelling if we are thinking about migration from poor to wealthier regions of the world, as the pros and cons of migration control are so clearly tied up with concerns about development and global justice. As they note, arguments about stability, security, and identity are deployed primarily to make the case for more control of migration.

However, things look a bit different if we think more broadly about international migration in many directions across the world.

Rosewarne and Piper are certainly right to observe that we remain far from the vision of free movement described by Roger Nett (1971). However, from a global perspective, many more people can move more freely across the world today than in previous periods of history (although this freedom of movement was, at least temporarily, significantly impacted by Covid-19-related restrictions). Certainly, since the 1990s, there has been a trend towards ever more selective migration policy that has restricted the movement of the poorest and least educated. Nonetheless, overall, for much of the world's population, including many unskilled migrants, immigration controls have been eased.

In most regions too, emigration (exit) controls have been largely eliminated (de Haas, Natter, and Vezzoli 2018). The idea that states should have the right to prevent their citizens from taking up opportunities for jobs, education, falling in love, or going on adventures in other countries is the hallmark of a repressive state. Attempts to confine people's work to the service of the nation usually fail. The record of control of emigration on any grounds is poor.

There are still conditions in which states attempt to control the exit of their populations. The Covid-19 pandemic showed how these can be quickly resurrected in the face of a national emergency. Nonetheless, those who possess the 'right' passport can travel much of the world relatively freely and they expect to do so, even if they will not offer that right to others. While a country such as the UK demands that others jump through hoops to secure a visa to enter the country, its own citizens can enter 130 countries in the world either with no visa or a visa granted on arrival.

In thinking through these questions about migration control, we have to consider two related aspects of the issue which stimulate different arguments. First, there is the question of whether states can and should control the movement of people across their borders. The arguments on security will loom large here. Insofar as travellers may represent a threat to the security of the state, it is hard to avoid the idea that states should attempt to monitor movement, at least to the extent of being aware of who is coming and going. (Whether these travellers should be exposed to any greater surveillance than citizens who may equally pose a threat is an open question.)

This inevitably brings discrimination as those from some destinations may be perceived as a greater threat than others. One of the curious effects of the Covid-19 pandemic is that it has upturned the longstanding calculus of threat. No longer is this automatically associated with those from the poorest or most unstable countries; instead, it has been transformed into the one with the highest infection rate or most virulent variant. Moreover, the pandemic has illustrated the importance of border control. Ironically in the UK, it was a xenophobic, Conservative government which kept the borders open in early 2020 to the dismay of many on the liberal left who called for much tighter controls. There were also surprising levels of acceptance of tight controls of outward mobility through 2020–21, with most UK citizens not allowed to leave the country over some months.

The second question arises from the fact that migration goes beyond crossing borders: it is also about people's ability to re-establish their lives in new places. Should states control this process of settlement? As Rosewarne and Piper suggest, the argument is complicated. The politics are toxic and the points of debate that they raise will have different validity depending on the setting. In some contexts, where there are very delicate internal political balances, the arrival of those seen as outsiders may create new and dangerous challenges. In others, such as the arguments about the settlement of refugees in Europe, these are a thin veil for racism and nativism.

What about movement between two wealthy, stable states? If citizens of country A, who have perhaps always voted for lower taxation and enjoyed higher incomes, become unemployed and lose access to employer-provided health insurance, should they be able to move to country B, and become automatically eligible for welfare and healthcare, for which the citizens of that country have paid through higher taxes? We have not only an economic discussion here but also a moral one: should migration enable people to evade the consequences of their (albeit limited) democratic choices? And it is also a political one: who should have the right to vote and make decisions about how the polity is governed? Again, if anyone can arrive, vote, shape decisions, and then leave, it does create a problem for democracy.

The point is not to argue against migration. However, it does mean there need to be some clear mechanisms for enabling people to move, settle, and become incorporated into the full membership of the polity. Likewise, there needs to be some mechanism to enable people to leave.

Maybe this is not so much a question of control as one of regulation, in the sense of having a clear, transparent, non-discriminatory way of enabling transfers of membership from one polity to another.

Over to you ...

1 In the Chapter 13 Roundtable we have seen an interesting debate about what kinds of controls on migration should be imposed by governments—if any at all. Where do you stand? Can you see a case for open borders? Or do you agree that even while there is more movement across borders than ever, we need some way of regulating membership of polities and the benefits that citizenship confers?

2 Stuart Rosewarne and Nicola Piper draw attention to the ways in which restrictive border policies designed by governments can actually worsen the problems of trafficking and smuggling, and the abuse of migrants (**see Chapter 13**). **Chapter 11** discusses these issues in detail as well. How and why does this occur, and do you think that less restrictive border controls would have the opposite effect?

3 What does it mean to say that migration is a 'shared responsibility' among the world's states? What would look different if this shared responsibility was recognized and acted on?

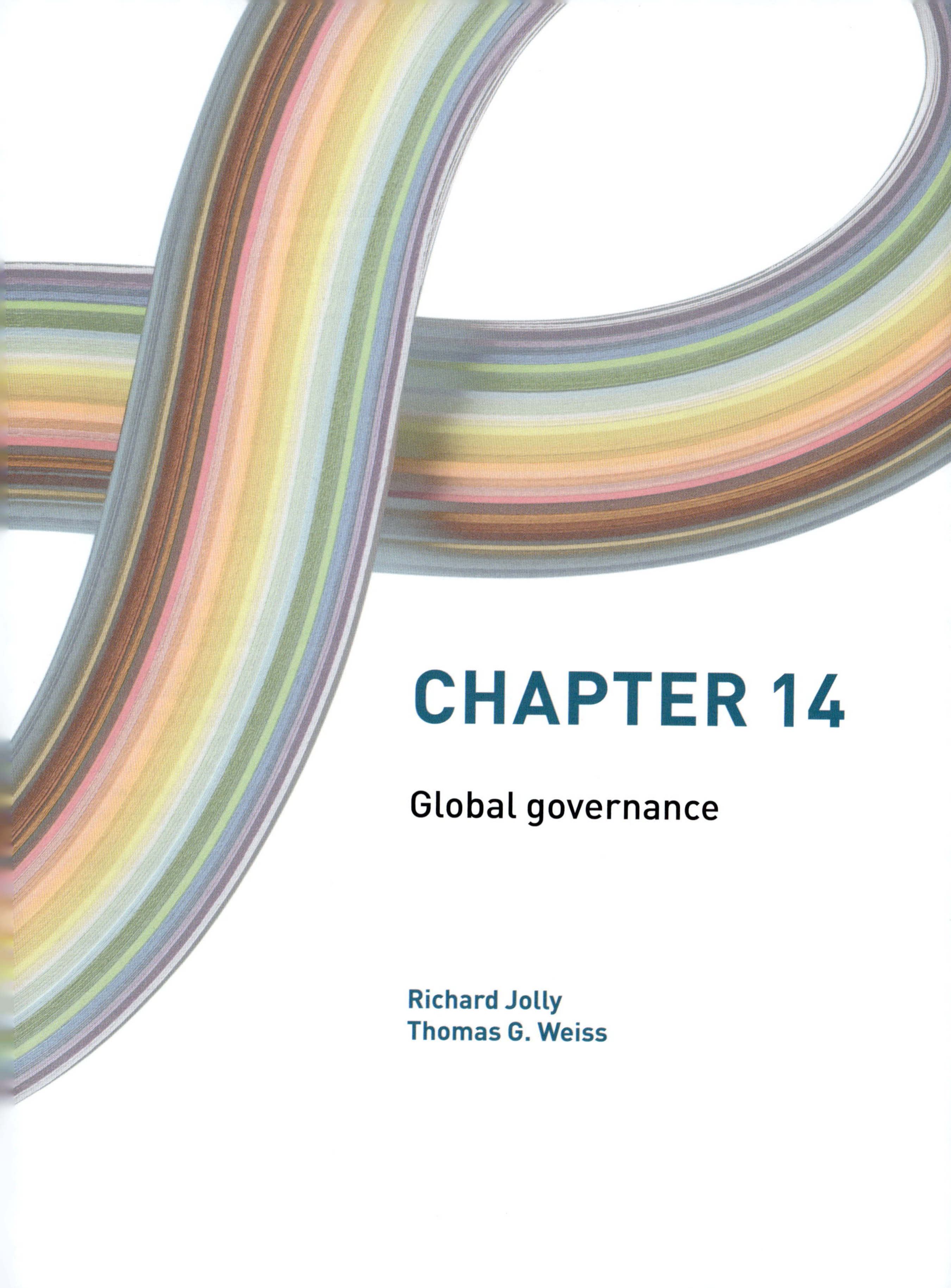

CHAPTER 14

Global governance

Richard Jolly
Thomas G. Weiss

14.1 Introduction

The late twentieth and early twenty-first centuries brought dramatic changes in international connectivity. The Internet linked people in webs of interactions. With increasingly connected societies and economies, the concept of 'global governance' emerged in the 1990s to respond to risks arising across country borders, including disruptions in international trade (**see Chapter 6**) and international finance (**see Chapter 5**).

> **Key Concepts**
>
> **Global governance:** Collective efforts to identify, understand, and address worldwide problems that go beyond the individual, problem-solving capabilities of any state, however powerful.
>
> **International trade:** The exchange of goods and services among two or more countries.
>
> **International finance:** The study of monetary interactions among two or more countries.
>
> **Three United Nations:** Member states (First), secretariats (Second), and non-state actors (Third).

With the establishment of the Bretton Woods institutions in 1944 (that is, the International Monetary Fund [IMF] and the World Bank), and the United Nations (UN) in 1945, governments were broadly supportive of institutionalized cooperation across national borders, which continued following decolonization. The number and influence of non-state actors also grew, operating alongside traditional intergovernmental organizations (IGOs). In particular, the concept of 'three United Nations' captured supportive non-governmental organizations (NGOs) and other non-state actors, which became known as the 'Third UN'. They played key roles in pressuring the 'First UN' of member states and the 'Second UN' of staff members (Weiss, Carayannis, and Jolly 2009; Carayannis and Weiss 2021*b*). Politically, right-wing nationalism also grew, with its proponents often rejecting globalization as well as the UN. However, this did not stop businesses, foundations, and civil society organizations (CSOs) from extending global ideational and operational links.

An analytical boom occurred among scholars and policy analysts about how best to understand and navigate these trends. Whatever the perspective, no one disputed the growing intensity in global interactions and their ensuing economic and political interdependencies. However, the proliferation of non-state actors in arenas that once were exclusive to states and IGOs means that studying the topic of global governance requires some intellectual stretching for those trained in the more 'state-centric' perspectives of inter*national* relations (IR), inter*national* law, inter*national* organization, or some parts of inter*national* political economy (IPE) (**see Chapter 3**). This intellectual stretching can be exciting and rewarding— helping us to understand how the world works and how the global political economy (GPE) is shaped by a multiplicity of actors and processes that reach beyond states and their borders.

We begin this chapter with a discussion of 'global governance', the term now used widely to analyse the international system (**see Section 14.2**). We then examine six gaps in global governance (**see Section 14.3**), followed by three illustrations of current issues in global governance— and the gaps therein—to help you understand international responses (both weak and strong) to communicable diseases, economic instability, and child welfare (**see Section 14.4**). Two case studies detail the challenging issues of climate change (**see Case Study 14.1**) and of poverty and inequality (**see Case Study 14.2**). The conclusion suggests how to close gaps (**see Section 14.5**).

Giving urgency to this discussion is the Covid-19 pandemic, which gripped the world in the early 2020s, and the accompanying spectre of global economic threats, including the erasure of decades of development progress. The lapses in international cooperation to manage the Covid-19 pandemic and the pressing need for a robust multilateral system are more obvious than ever, but so are the hostile geopolitical realities in the age of new nationalisms.

14.2 What does 'global governance' mean?

World government is a decidedly old-fashioned idea, although it briefly attracted interest in the interwar period and the years immediately before and after the UN's founding (Weiss 2009). No overarching global authority exists, and analytical conversations have since shifted away from the UN and other IGOs to the idea of 'global governance'. This term became familiar after 1995 when the Commission on Global Governance (1995) published *Our Global Neighbourhood* and the academic journal *Global Governance* first appeared. For scholars, the term has 'near-celebrity status' (Barnett and Duvall 2004: 1). The fact that new titles featuring the term 'global governance' recently outnumbered those about 'peace' or 'international cooperation' is telling (Zürn 2018: 263).

Global governance involves collective efforts to identify, understand, and address worldwide problems that go beyond the individual capabilities of any state, however powerful. Thomas G. Weiss and Rorden Wilkinson (2019) aim at 'rethinking global governance' because the term encompasses such a large *variety* of international arrangements. Some are formal, taking the shape of hard rules (laws and treaties) and institutions (with buildings and personnel). Others are informal (for example, practices and guidelines) or temporary (such as coalitions of the willing). The term also includes a wide variety of actors, from governments and IGOs to NGOs, businesses, and civil society.

Depending on political will, global collective action can be good, bad, or non-existent. There is no guaranteed success, but collective international interests can be articulated, collective international rights and obligations established, collective international differences mediated, and collective international actions mobilized.

States remain the most important actors and the foundation of the international system. Their inputs are essential for national, regional, and global problem-solving. By definition and constitutional arrangements, state sovereignty provides the basis for all IGOs. However, sovereigns must pool and coordinate efforts to tackle what former UN Secretary-General Kofi Annan called 'problems without passports' (2002: 30–31). In the nineteenth century, this led states to establish the Universal Postal Union and International Telegraph (now Telecommunications) Union—long before the UN system came into being.

Global problems rarely lend themselves to market solutions, in part because individual countries lack incentives or capacities to provide them. Global problems instead require international agreement and the political will to act, which only sometimes can be mobilized. Moreover, negotiating who pays for what raises collective action problems and is inapplicable to the poorest countries. Some transboundary problems can be solved regionally without worldwide participation. But truly global problems require global engagement if universal solutions are to be achieved. Other chapters in this textbook explore a range of challenges in the global political economy that require such action. But global cooperation takes time to build, and there are other challenges with acute consequences that demand effective or rapid action. Pandemics and climate change are two such examples that immediately come to mind.

A significant difference exists between national and international governance. In national contexts, we have governance *plus* government. For example, Egypt or the UK normally exert authority and enforce laws, which entails mobilizing the government *plus* additional mechanisms of governance. In international contexts, however, we have governance *minus* government. Here, there is no authority comparable to a state or government that can ensure compliance with collective decisions. Global governance thus reflects a lack of capacity in the international system to provide government-like services. In other words, it emerges from the *absence* of world government, as epitomized by one of the first major academic overviews on the subject: *Governance without Government* (Rosenau and Czempiel 1992).

Since the 1970s, deficiencies in patterns of national development fostered recognition of emerging global problems that required better coordination. The UN thus organized a series of global conferences on the environment, population, women, human rights, cities and urban settlements, technology, and disarmament. All concluded with proposals for international action to complement national follow-up. This interest in strengthening broader areas of global governance arose at a time when non-state actors (both civil society and markets) were growing in number, reach, and impact. The UN, World Bank, and IMF were no longer alone on the world stage.

This panoply of actors, public and private, operating at global, regional, national, and local levels are now integral to solutions, but they constitute a 'crazy quilt' of authority (Rosenau 1999: 293). This constantly shifting patchwork of institutional elements varies across problems, sectors, and time. Governments remain in the international system's driver seat, but non-state actors often pressure them to adapt and take on new responsibilities.

Today's world order is also in flux, pithily captured as a relatively declining West and an emerging rest of the world (Acharya 2014*a*). But dominant features from the twentieth century remain. We cannot fully appreciate the shape of contemporary global governance without reference to what came earlier. It is not merely a post-Cold War phenomenon. While not carrying the same label, there have been other 'systems of global governance', including empires and colonialism, that brought an ever-expanding 'human web' (McNeill and McNeill 2003).

The global governance of our era, however, mostly began after the Second World War, although architectural sketches were available earlier. Despite alterations since 1945, its overall shape remains familiar, and the term 'transformation' is over-used. For example, exchange rates and financial markets have evolved, but dominant power relations remain. There have been seismic changes—for instance, the demise of the Soviet Union and the 'rise' of China and other emerging economies—but they have not transformed world order. Nor have the end of the Bretton Woods system of fixed exchange rates in 1971 and the transition from the General Agreement on Tariffs and Trade (GATT) to the World Trade Organization (WTO) in 1995, important as these moments were for global economic governance. Continuity is, therefore, a more dominant trait in contemporary global governance than transformative change.

A further analytical shortcoming has been emphasis on the richest parts of the world at the expense of ignoring 'everyday global governance' (Weiss and Wilkinson 2018). Put differently, the focus is too often on the global 'governors' rather than on the globally 'governed'. Most practice and scholarship on global governance originates in the Western Hemisphere, but the vast majority of people who experience these ideas and actions—more than 80 per cent of the globe's population—reside in the Global South. The shortcomings of ignoring the latter are more evident still when we turn our attention to our understanding of the most vulnerable groups—such as women, children, the elderly, or Indigenous peoples.

Gazing from the top down impedes an appreciation of the impact of global governance on everyday lives. We thus need to cast our analytical nets wide enough to understand global governance from the ground up.

14.3　Global governance: filling gaps

During the three-quarters of a century after the Second World War, much progress was made in constructing the intergovernmental pillars of global governance. A crucial element was the UN system, even if it is at times viewed as more marginal than the Bretton Woods institutions, which are in practice, but not formally, part of the UN system. The UN fostered international legal agreements, including early adoption of the Genocide Convention and the Universal Declaration of Human Rights in 1948. Political independence for over 100 former colonies then occurred in the UN's first two decades, in accord with resolutions and political pressure from these countries in UN forums.

Key Concept: Bretton Woods institutions

The World Bank (and its subsidiaries) and the International Monetary Fund (IMF).

States created other multilateral institutions, both as part of the UN and independently, which helped shape the global political economy today—institutions like the European Union (EU), the World Trade Organization (WTO), the United Nations Conference on Trade and Development (UNCTAD), regional development banks, and many others.

The operations of this rules-based international system were imperfect and inconsistent. In particular, poorer countries faced a highly uneven playing field in bilateral negotiations and in global and regional gatherings. Nevertheless, the system was broadly progressive, partially effective, and certainly an improvement over earlier world orders.

It also proved relatively durable, despite recent setbacks from US unilateralism and attacks on the legal, political, moral, and financial foundations of the UN and other IGOs. Amidst the spread of nationalist populisms, further setbacks have been faced in global governance from stagnant and even decreased contributions to IGO budgets. Philanthropies, corporations, and civil society organizations have filled some shortfalls. But their resources are insufficient, and they lack the legitimacy of the UN's universal membership.

Beyond issues of money and funding, current geopolitics circumscribe the task of improving global economic governance. This requires filling long-standing and current 'gaps'. We adapt Thomas G. Weiss and Ramesh Thakur's (2010) framework to address what Thomas Kuhn calls 'pockets of apparent disorder' between existing global problems and available solutions (1970: 42). The metaphor is apt: the gaps can be cavernous (a mountain gap) or modest (a gap on a train platform). But they can and should be bridged or reduced.

Our task is to overcome or at least compensate for six key weaknesses in the global political economy: knowledge; norms; policies; institutions; leadership; and compliance.

14.3.1 Knowledge gaps

Filling knowledge gaps and generating timely information to guide action is a critical first step. If politicians, pundits, and people recognize the existence of a problem and agree on its dimensions, they can take steps to address it. However, staff and donor preferences influence global governance research. Advocacy without evidence is ideology, a danger that has become worse in an era of 'alternative facts'. What is the best strategy to combat climate change, for instance, if there are still serious political disputes about its severity and causes (Photo 14.1) (**see Case Study 14.1**)? How can we tackle development if there is no agreement on the merits of top-down versus bottom-up approaches or the merits of aid and technical assistance versus self-sufficiency? Can we get beyond ideology when applying information, data, experience, and science?

Case Study 14.1: Combating climate change

In 1972 in Stockholm, the UN convened the first global gathering on the human environment. In 1983, the UN Secretary-General set up a World Commission on Environment and Development chaired by Norway's prime minister Gro Harlem Brundtland. After its 1987 report, the World Meteorological Organization and the United Nations Environment Programme created the Intergovernmental Panel on Climate Change (IPCC) to analyse this existential threat. Climate change is now squarely on the public policy agenda, including the 2015 Paris Agreement, because of work by this group of some 2,000 world-class scientists from over 150 countries.

Almost 180 governments, over 100 heads of state, and some 24,000 NGO representatives attended the Earth Summit in 1992, which adopted Agenda 21—a non-binding agreement that detailed a comprehensive agenda for the human environment. This led to two conventions to protect biodiversity and to combat desertification. Over the next three decades, the evidence of rising temperatures and negotiations about climate change grew in tandem. In Japan in 1997, the Kyoto Protocol set out worldwide cuts in emissions by 2012 of about 5 per cent (relative to 1990 levels), with specific reduction targets for each developed country. Nevertheless, developing countries—including China, South Korea, Mexico, India, and other emerging economies— were allowed to continue increasing emissions. 'Common but differentiated responsibilities' are

Photo 14.1 **A youth march for climate change in London**

Source: © Ink Spot/Shutterstock.

arguably logical for poor countries, but their use by what were to become two of the three largest producers of greenhouse gases (China and India) led to opposition from the second largest, the United States.

In the twenty-first century, many countries reneged on their environmental targets, which led to conferences in Copenhagen in 2012 and Paris in 2015. The Copenhagen conference agreed to new targets for developing and developed countries, but once again many (especially the largest emitters of greenhouse gases) ignored their targets. Thus, the Paris deliberations pursued a different approach, which began with reports from the IPCC and other non-state actors that showed actions lagging dramatically behind what was essential. In Paris, after years of unsuccessful efforts to agree on legally binding targets, each country identified modest voluntary pledges, or 'nationally determined contributions', which 195 countries and the EU agreed to follow.

Most countries accept the science and the need for global action; many have begun to implement commitments, while others have fallen short. Some countries, including Brazil under President Jair Bolsonaro and the United States under President Donald Trump denied the evidence. Following the election of Joe Biden, the United States announced its intention to re-join the Paris Agreement and a number of other climate-friendly initiatives (**see Section 9.3.1**). Even so, assessments indicated that the planned cuts were insufficient to keep global warming below 2° C by 2050, let alone the preferable target of 1.5° C to reduce the extreme annual weather disasters—heatwaves, droughts, floods, and storms. All seven of the warmest years on record were the seven preceding the Glasgow Conference of Parties 26 in November 2021—with nineteen of the twenty warmest years registered since 2000.

(Continued)

The flagrant disregard for the global commons has led to widespread protests by scientists, political groups, and ordinary citizens. In late 2019, some 80 million children went on strike to demonstrate the need for greater action, following the lead by a then-16-year-old Swedish activist, Greta Thunberg. The generation today in school and universities will suffer the consequences of the failure to act.

Watch the video on the online resources to take your understanding of this case study further.

Questions

1 What is the likelihood that youth pleas will wake up governments?
2 How important was the Third UN's IPCC?

Recognizing the knowledge and experiences of non-Western actors is another challenge, especially when the United States and United Kingdom dominate English-language academic markets worldwide. In response, calls have been growing for more globally inclusive forms of knowledge production. These ideas build on contributions from institutions and individuals in the former Third World and beyond, from Paulo Freire (1970) to Samir Amin et al. (1978) at the Council for the Development of Social Science Research in Africa (CODESRIA) (see also Berthelot 2004; Jolly et al. 2004). One example is efforts towards 'decolonizing' knowledge and the curriculum to restore the knowledge, experiences, and agency of non-Western actors (Mbembe 2016; Kessi, Marks, and Ramugondo 2021). Another is efforts towards a more globally inclusive field of international relations or 'global IR' (Acharya 2014*b*; Acharya and Buzan 2007). This textbook is animated by similar goals (**see Chapter 1**).

Addressing knowledge gaps is likely to involve not only universities and research institutes, but also think tanks worldwide. Think tanks have seen their numbers rise dramatically since the turn of the twenty-first century, coinciding with the growth of the knowledge economy and a greater demand (and reliance) on intellectual and social capital. By one estimate, over half of think tanks globally are located in North America and Europe, but with Asia now registering the fastest growth (Carayannis and Weiss 2021*b*: 130–48). Whose ideas matter? Evidence-based policymaking has raised the political stakes of who within the Third UN gets to inform First UN and Second UN thinking—leading to outcries about the 'influence' of alternative voices from emerging powers (Carayannis and Weiss 2021*a*: 10).

'Knowledge networks' (Stone 2005; Stein et al 2001) are thus increasingly pertinent for global governance; physical location is less relevant than previously because they operate internationally and influence policymakers. They have, for instance, become central in the UN system (Dumitriu 2016). But no matter how well-founded the research and evidence, differences will remain. Countries are affected in different ways by global problems and, accordingly, give them different weights. In many areas, richer countries dominate research networks and the global media, leaving poorer countries without voice. Often little or no consensus exists about the nature, causes, or magnitude of problems. For many issues, evidence may or may not be persuasive enough to overcome ideologies, hardened long before data were available. Such issues as population growth in the 1970s or global warming in the 1990s appeared suddenly as priority agenda items. More recently, climate change denial and fake news have exacerbated knowledge gaps.

14.3.2 Normative gaps

Norms matter because people—ordinary citizens, as well as politicians and officials—care what others think and usually want to act in accordance with accepted norms. Approval and shaming can be effective regulators of social behaviour.

How do international norms emerge, diffuse, consolidate, and become internalized by international society? Martha Finnemore and Kathryn Sikkink (1998) offer a three-stage lifecycle of norms that, although criticized as too mechanical, is helpful: the emergence of a norm; sufficient agreement among major actors to reach a tipping point; and internalization, when behaviour becomes routine. Despite widespread criticism of Western predominance, research suggests that the Global South can be and has been a source of global norms (Helleiner et al. 2014; Weiss and Roy 2017; Acharya and Plesch 2020; Ayoob 2020).

Organizations with universal membership in the UN system are forums where states seek consensus about norms for worldwide application, whether led by UN staff or pressure from NGOs. Over the years, the UN has formulated many human rights conventions that have been adopted and ratified by many countries. Norms and standards have also emerged for problems ranging from drug-trafficking to money laundering, terrorism, and pandemics (**see Chapter 8** and **Chapter 11**).

Non-state actors also play a key role that should be strengthened and encouraged. They are often faster and more flexible than governments in drawing on research, advocacy, and learning. Civil society often identifies normative gaps and weaknesses and can press for mitigating measures. Recall our earlier mention of the Third UN (**see Section 14.1**), which often confronts the other two UNs of member states and secretariats. This dynamic encourages the pursuit of justice championed by non-state actors—including scholars, consultants, think tanks, NGOs, the private sector, and the media.

At the same time, not all non-state actors are progressive, globally minded, and altruistic. Internationalists and cosmopolitans must beware of counterproductive actions by non-state actors with vested interests—for example, of fossil-fuel producers lobbying against reducing carbon footprints or corporations emphasizing profits over poverty alleviation. Much has been made of the ugly elements of local civil society in atrocities in Rwanda, Myanmar, and Sudan. Other examples include government lobbyists working for unsavoury corporate patrons—for instance, the National Rifle Association (NRA) for gun manufacturers, and others for tobacco companies (**see Case Study 8.1**). In such cases, knowledge and research can also be influenced or funded to emphasize profits over human well-being or security.

14.3.3 Policy gaps

Policy covers principles and goals, along with agreed programmes of action. The UN's seventeen Sustainable Development Goals (SDGs) (Photo 14.2), with 169 targets, represent priority policies for combating climate change, alleviating poverty and inequality, and addressing other twenty-first century problems. These reflect the five 'P's' of human-focused progress: people, planet, prosperity, peace, and partnership (**see Case Study 14.2**).

Identifying agents (who is responsible?) and purposive actions (what works?) is essential for sound policies. States usually distinguish domestic from external policies. Both may

Case Study 14.2: The Sustainable Development Goals (SDGs)

Poverty reduction was a priority for the UN's First Development Decade, which was followed by further goals and initiatives in three subsequent development decades. The governments of many donor and developing countries, along with many NGOs, pressed for poverty reduction as a priority. However, poverty was a secondary issue for the international financial institutions in their dealings with much of Africa and Latin America in the 1980s and 1990s.

In 2000, as part of the UN's Millennium Declaration, poverty reduction re-emerged as a global objective in the Millennium Development Goals (MDGs). Considerable progress occurred, with extreme poverty reduced by more than half from 1990 to just over 700 million in 2015 (**see Section 10.5**). Other goals also registered gains, including reduced child mortality, expanded education (especially for girls), and increased access to clean water and sanitation (UNDP 2017).

Photo 14.2 **Sustainable Development Goals**

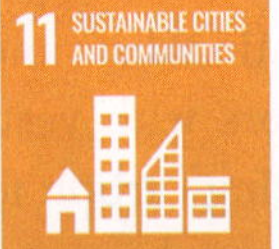

Racial inequalities became more visible with the emergence of a global 'Black Lives Matter' movement in 2020, but income inequalities in the Global North and Global South were obvious long before 'Occupy Wall Street' in 2011 (**see Chapter 10**). Oxfam reported that over the previous four decades, inequalities in income had soared so that by 2018 the world's 2,159 billionaires possessed more wealth than the bottom 4.6 billion people (Oxfam 2020: 1).

In 2015, at the endpoint of the MDGs, all three UNs formulated a new round of objectives: the SDGs. Over three years, development experts and NGOs pressed governments to go beyond what they would have agreed on their own (Weiss and Browne 2021). The goals and targets were to guide the UN system, member states, regions, and local communities for the 2030 Development Agenda.

These SDG objectives are universal—for industrialized, emerging, and poor countries—and cover people, prosperity, planet, peace, and partnership. All must be 'sustainable' in promoting development 'that meets the needs of the present without compromising the ability of future generations to meet their own needs' (UN 1987, 2022).

The goals cannot be fully or even adequately achieved without progress on the others. The first seven concern basic needs: health, food and nutrition, education, healthy lives, and access to clean water, basic sanitation, and energy. The next four goals focus on prosperity: growth and employment with decent work and gender equality along with cities and settlements that are safe, resilient, and sustainable. The following four focus on the planet and relate to consumption and production patterns alongside action to combat climate change and protect oceans, terrestrial eco-systems, and biodiversity. The final two goals promote peaceful and inclusive societies and stronger partnerships.

Four SDG-related priorities, detailed in other chapters, are compelling for all countries. The first regards climate change (**see Chapter 9**). In 2019 the IPCC reported that increases in global temperature must be kept below 1.5° C, with many countries in sub-Saharan Africa and South Asia already experiencing high temperatures and severe consequences for people's lives and agricultural production (IPCC 2019). Too many countries, especially some of the richest, are in denial.

The second priority relates to reducing inequalities within and among countries (**see Chapter 10**). Inequalities have soared along with the power and influence of the richest 1 and 0.1 per cent. Reducing their leverage is politically challenging because governments, democratic or dictatorial, depend on support from the rich and influential. However, reducing inequalities and redirecting wealth towards priority global actions are prerequisites for realizing the SDGs.

The third priority concerns changing the structures of national production and consumption (**see Chapter 7** and **Chapter 9**). Major investments in green technologies are required, along with reductions in fossil-fuel production and consumption. Some countries have national green investment plans, and some forward-looking cities and companies have launched green initiatives.

The fourth priority is hard-hitting SDG monitoring. Governments should be independently monitored by UN organizations and civil society, with additional media scrutiny. Coordinated pressure is essential to generate and maintain political support for action.

Questions

1 How important is goal setting in addressing issues like poverty or climate change?

2 Is 'sustainable development' an oxymoron?

> **Key Concept: sustainable development**
>
> The idea that human societies must grow, live, and meet their needs without compromising the ability of future generations to meet their needs.

be broken down sequentially into phases in the policy process: formulation, adoption, and implementation. Action may embrace three approaches: regulation (for example, of services for transport and postal rates); support from public resources (for example, for humanitarian relief and training); and redress of social inequality and poverty (such as services for vulnerable children; **see Section 14.4.3**).

The scale of many global challenges also requires funding and strong support for country-by-country implementation. The real challenge is reaching consensus across states: a fraught undertaking, given their vast diversity of contexts and interests. Sometimes, coordinated *regional* action can be a stepping-stone towards global action—but it can also be the opposite. The on-again-off-again policy formulation accompanying the Paris Agreement on climate change highlights the difficulty of framing effective planetary policies and action when decisions are made in the capitals of 193 UN member states (**see Section 9.3.1**).

14.3.4 Institutional gaps

To be more than ad hoc and idiosyncratic, policy must be located and implemented within organizations with sufficient financial resources and personnel for action—and not merely in headquarters or capitals. Institutional weaknesses can inhibit effective action even when knowledge, norms, and policies exist. It is important to recall two meanings of 'institutions': as formal, organizational entities; and as regimes or recurring and stable patterns of behaviour around which actor expectations converge. The former, with their buildings and personnel, are easier to grasp than the latter, but both are important.

Institutional gaps may not be obvious because of disparities in organizational capacities and because, by design, no IGO holds supranational authority. Their sovereign member states remain the ultimate decision-makers. For instance, the secretariats of the Organization for Economic Co-operation and Development (OECD) and the EU are well resourced and thus can outperform 'equivalent' organizations with less staff and resources, like the South Centre or the Gulf Cooperation Council. Moreover, even powerful IGOs like the Security Council or the World Bank that possess authority may still have budgets that are massively incommensurate with the transboundary problems on their agendas. In fact, substantial parts of many IGOs still remain on drawing boards with only a small prototype to deal with gargantuan problems.

Big budgets do not guarantee success, either internationally or nationally. Nonetheless, inadequate financial resources help explain minimal progress, whether it be for gender inclusion to improve life for half the world's population or for human rights protection presently financed with less than 4 per cent of the UN's already meagre regular budget. Climate change is an existential threat but, in comparison, the United Nations Environment Programme (UNEP)'s budget and staffing are risible (**see Section 9.3.1**).

At the same time, there are IGOs that deal well with an issue, usually because they address specific problems and have well-embedded norms, adequate funding, and consensus among member states. While UN-bashing is a favourite pastime, such organizations as the International Atomic Energy Agency (IAEA) and the United Nations Refugee Agency (UNHCR) make a difference.

There are also IGOs that fall between those that work and those so weak as to constitute a virtual void. How successful has the World Health Organization (WHO) been in dealing with SARS, HIV/AIDS, Ebola, or Covid-19? Its core budget was slashed for several years prior to the beginning of the Covid-19 pandemic and is overly dependent on mobilizing extra-budgetary resources when a crisis arises (**see Chapter 8**). Containing pandemics is an obvious threat for which knowledge, norms, and policies are proliferating. Yet, very large institutional gaps in finance and authority remain.

14.3.5 Leadership gaps

Even a well-funded institution may stumble with poor leadership. In contrast, a weaker institution can punch above its weight with inspired leadership. A case in point is the UN's performance and visibility under Secretaries-General Dag Hammarskjöld and Kofi Annan versus some of their predecessors and successors. Management is not the same thing as leadership; both are essential but seldom found in the same person.

While leadership is essential for all, UN organizations are especially prone to leadership gaps. Especially consequential are pressures from major and minor powers as well as geographic regions to have 'their' representatives at the top. In fact, pressures for placement of nationals exist at every level. Senior positions are 'reserved' for designated nationalities, sometimes in a fixed rotation, even if those nominated may lack professional experience, training, or even familiarity with multilateral diplomacy and the purported values of the international civil service. Many governments want neither robust IGOs nor strong executive heads. The Security Council's group of five permanent members (the P-5) are not, for instance, the only member states that prefer a secretary to a general.

What can be done? The UN system has taken some steps, including modestly more transparent election processes for the UN's top job and for those of the International Labour Organization (ILO) and the UN Educational, Scientific and Cultural Organization (UNESCO). Rather than opting for recycled diplomats, the appointment for senior posts of experienced people from within is desirable, as is making promotions a more professional process. Another advance would be to ask governments to offer several candidates for 'nominated' posts, resulting in some organizational choice. Greater professionalism and higher standards are desirable not only for posts at headquarters, but also at country and regional levels.

Ultimately, strong leadership and efficient management within all IGOs are prerequisites for better global governance. In general, filling leadership gaps requires more resistance to government pressures and less tolerance for interference. It also requires more insistence on staff adhering to the values of the UN Charter and rules, more willingness to dismiss underperforming individuals, and open appointments processes with competing candidates. An option to be considered is limiting to a single five- or seven-year term the posts of UN secretary-general and other heads of the system's organizations. This would help limit the tendency to give concessions and 'promise posts' when seeking re-election.

14.3.6 Compliance gaps

We save the most striking gap for last: compliance. In a world of sovereign states, there is no international capacity to force a country or party to comply with policies, recommendations, or decisions. Compliance has three facets: implementation, monitoring, and enforcement. Recalcitrant or fragile countries may be unwilling or unable to implement agreed international policy. Even when a treaty is in effect with elements of a working regime in place, there is often inadequate political will to ensure follow-up or implementation. Who in the global governance system has the authority, responsibility, and capacity to monitor commitments and obligations to enforce compliance?

In **Section 14.2**, we indicated that with sufficient political determination, major powers can agree and mobilize resources to act globally. The elimination of smallpox is a dramatic example. There have also been major reductions in such other communicable diseases such as guinea-worm, polio, and measles. When pressure is mobilized and richer countries are willing to push, global action can and does happen. Other examples include the expansion of education; greater access to water and sanitation; economic stability and steady growth from 1945 to 1971; reduction of child deaths from 1980 to the present; and reduction of poverty and other targets in the Millennium Development Goals (MDGs) from 2000 to 2015. However, these result from voluntary compliance, not enforcement.

Non-compliance in many cases arises from the lack of interest among key players in enforcement, especially from richer and more powerful states. Poorer countries can be more easily pressured, as with failures to alleviate debt in the 1980s when international support was tied to stringent conditions by international financial institutions (IFIs) (**see Chapter 4**). In international trade and finance, the WTO had a moderately effective enforcement mechanism until it was undermined by great power (especially US) unilateralism. While undoubtedly a step forward in comparison with the GATT (**see Chapter 6**), the settlement of international trade disputes nevertheless largely remains a bilateral affair—handled between one country and another, rather than multilaterally.

In short, no international capability exists to enforce the treaty obligations of signatory states to the Genocide Convention, nor to consensus accords such as the Paris Agreement on climate change or the SDGs. Things get even more difficult when it comes to non-state actors operating outside international legal jurisdiction. The available mechanisms of contemporary global governance typically are unable to ensure a modicum of compliance even when knowledge, norms, policies, institutions, and leadership are present.

14.4 Contemporary global economic governance: three illustrations

Traditionally, global economic governance has focused on international trade, investment, and finance, along with IFIs and the WTO. However, this focus is too narrow. Let's look at three illustrations from other arenas that illustrate aspects of today's global economic governance.

14.4.1 Health threats and the WHO

The Covid-19 pandemic hit the world at the start of 2020, beginning in Wuhan, China, before spreading across Asia, then Europe, and ultimately around the world (**see Chapter 8 Roundtable**). The immediate and longer-term consequences for the global economy were evident in falling stock markets, rising unemployment, and serious falls in the gross domestic product (GDP) of countries across the globe. Years of progress in development evaporated (Guterres 2021: 6–21).

The WHO is a UN specialized agency that declared the pandemic in March 2020. However, one of the striking features was the predominance of national action. International coordination was absent, feeble, or rejected, with little support for poorer countries and the weakest health systems. The WHO's regular budget had for some years reached barely 20 per cent of the secretariat's requests. For over a decade, several wealthy countries turned away from priorities determined internationally. They reduced obligatory financial support in favour of earmarked funding that matched their national priorities.

The Covid-19 pandemic's economic consequences have been larger than previous post-war economic disruptions. As of 2021, the total cost was estimated as a short-term loss of some 10–20 per cent of GDP in many countries, with medium- and longer-term losses totalling trillions of dollars.

NGOs offered help. For example, the International Chamber of Commerce signed an agreement with the WHO ensuring the latest and most accurate information was available for 45,000 businesses worldwide, and its members helped prevent transmission and worked closely with WHO field offices. The World Economic Forum declared a Covid Action Platform with the support of some 200 global corporate leaders, who pledged medical supplies, protective equipment, and support for vaccine research. The Gates Foundation had long warned about the need for preventive action against new viruses, with the foundation's international funding for health programmes now rivalling the WHO's.

The inadequate international preparation before and response after this disaster is a striking contrast to the 2 per cent or more of gross national product (GNP) that most industrialized countries devote annually to national military expenditures. Spending on military security vastly exceeds resources and preparations provided against threats to human insecurities. While military preparedness is a traditional national priority, why is there nothing comparable for the insecurity from global pandemics or other threats? The potential benefits would be considerable, especially preventing poorer countries with inadequate health systems from suffering from and—for richer country interests—spreading communicable diseases.

Still reeling from Covid-19, we should examine success stories in weighing costs versus benefits. Smallpox was eradicated between 1966 and 1977 in a WHO-led effort. Until then, smallpox had killed two million people annually. The total cost of eradication was $300 million, of which the WHO component was $100 million—at the time the cost of a single fighter bomber.

14.4.2 Financial instability and the international financial institutions

IMF and World Bank operations, along with other international initiatives like the Marshall Plan, enabled the Western countries to experience unprecedented rates of steady growth and high employment from 1945 to 1971. After this, the United States devalued its currency and moved away from a fixed dollar–gold exchange rate, effectively weakening international monetary arrangements (**see Chapter 5**).

Many developing countries had also enjoyed rapid economic growth in the post-independence boom of the 1950s and 1960s. In 1961, US President John F. Kennedy proposed at the UN that the next ten years should be a 'Development Decade', with a target for GDP growth in developing countries of 5 per cent by 1970. Over sixty countries achieved the target, although the IFIs never adopted this target or its accompanying goal of 0.7 per cent of GNP dedicated for official development assistance.

The IFIs continue to oversee the world economy by providing investment and loans to member states in debt with balance-of-payments difficulties (**see Section 5.2.3**). The World Bank also provides concessional loans to poorer countries and grants in priority areas like poverty reduction and climate change. Yet, their programming has been criticized, especially by CSOs and international NGOs like Oxfam and Save the Children. Many, including the *Bretton Woods Observer*, have been outspoken in calling for debt relief, less free-market dogmatism, and greater action on climate change and poverty reduction.

In response, IFI research divisions have broadened their attention to include poverty and inequality, but their operations have broadened to a lesser degree. Moreover, the voting shares among member countries (dominated by the West) have changed far less than would be expected given changes in the world economy, especially the growing weight of China, India, and Brazil (**see Chapter 13**).

The sharpest shift away from the dominance of the IFIs came after the Asian financial crisis of 1997–98 (**see Section 5.3.1**). The region's countries declared that never again would they be so dependent on the Washington-based institutions. They created a series of regional and bilateral arrangements, including agreements among their central banks. China later took further initiatives, extending the operations of its own banking system and in 2013 setting up the Asian Infrastructure Investment Bank (**see Section 5.2.3**). China has also extended massive volumes of aid to Africa, allegedly without Western-type conditions attached, but linked to Chinese trade and investment. In 2013, China launched the Belt and Road Initiative, through which it has invested in countries along the route to Europe, throughout Southeast Asia, and elsewhere.

Nevertheless, control of international finance is beyond the capacity of even the richest countries. Thus, the World Bank and the IMF continue their operations, although at a diminishing scale compared with foreign direct investment (FDI), remittances (the money that migrants send to their home countries), and Chinese overseas funding. Support by the Bretton Woods institutions for poorer countries remains essential, but they require borrowing countries to adopt stringent free-market policies, balance government budgets, and open their economies to foreign investment and trade. In the 1980s and 1990s, these policies were termed 'the Washington consensus' and justified cuts in education, health, and social services. Research subsequently demonstrated these policies to be counterproductive (**see Section 4.5**). The two decades before 2000 resulted in economic stagnation in Latin America and declines in per capita income in much of sub-Saharan Africa.

The UN has typically adopted and promoted different approaches and policies. The UN development system consists of over thirty special funds, programmes, and agencies working worldwide on such key human needs as food, gender equality, nutrition, and education. It also supports national efforts in such vital areas as statistics, weather forecasting, civil aviation, shipping, and the environment. Humanitarian relief in war and post-conflict situations is another major UN activity.

The hybrid nature of today's global economic governance is illustrated by the UN Global Compact (UNGC), which emerged in 2000 shortly before the Millennium Summit. A voluntary initiative to promote the adoption of human rights, labour, and environmental principles, the UNGC relies on accountability, transparency, and the enlightened self-interests of companies, labour, and civil society. The twentieth century's empty rhetoric gave way to twenty-first-century solutions. Corporate social responsibility for some 70,000 transnational corporations (TNCs), as well as ten times that number of subsidiaries and millions of suppliers, is essential for effective and progressive global economic governance (**see Section 7.4**). The harshest critics lament 'blue wash' in embracing for-profit organizations, but the UN has demonstrated a twenty-first-century flexibility to mobilize business.

14.4.3 Child welfare, development, and UNICEF

The UN Children's Fund (UNICEF) began in 1946 to provide emergency relief for children after the Second World War, but it soon adopted a broader agenda of promoting good health and nutrition, quality education, and community support for children in developing countries (Jolly 2014). Country programmes involve a six-month in-country process to define priorities for children over the age of five. UNICEF support is determined not as a separate contribution, but as a complement to what the government and others provide. Some 80 per cent of UNICEF staff work in the field.

In the 1980s and 1990s, UNICEF adopted a goal-oriented approach, focusing on priority actions to reduce child mortality. This included reaching 80 per cent coverage of growth monitoring, oral rehydration, breastfeeding, and immunization against the five most lethal diseases (tuberculosis, diphtheria, whooping cough, tetanus, and measles). Continuing support also increased access to safe water, basic sanitation, and good hygiene—as well as to education and other child-focused activities. Despite the economic setbacks in most of

Africa and Latin America in the 1980s and 1990s, child deaths fell from about 15 to about 12 million a year and continued to drop to about 5 million by 2020. UNICEF also worked in 1990 to define education goals towards 2000 with UNESCO, the World Bank, and many NGOs. Even though Save the Children and other international NGOs have worked to improve child welfare, only UNICEF had the size and legitimacy to set global goals.

As evidence mounted of the economic cutbacks from the Washington consensus in the 1980s, UNICEF challenged economic orthodoxy with the notion of 'Adjustment with a Human Face' (Cornia, Jolly, and Stewart 1987). This argued that it was counterproductive and illogical to neglect immediate human needs to protect a country's economic future. In 1989, the Convention on the Rights of the Child codified priorities for children, including greater support for poorer countries, which led in the following year to the World Summit for Children—the first such gathering of heads of state or government. This mobilized high-level attention to children's needs for the decade, in many ways setting the stage for the MDGs and the SDGs. The 1990s became a decade for such global conferences on key issues—for environment and development, social development, women, and population—illustrating how global economic governance required human and humane goals. These summits also involved greater participation by the Third UN.

Member states have treaty obligations to finance core budgets, and they also make voluntary contributions. UNICEF from its early days pioneered appeals to individuals and private sources, which now account for about a third of its annual budget. Some forty national committees in developed countries also raise funds, a model now used by such other intergovernmental organizations as UNHCR and UNESCO.

14.5 Conclusion

No state, no matter how powerful, can protect its citizens from global threats and instabilities on its own. Earlier, major powers could often address threats by erecting barriers—which are ineffective for many of today's life-threatening challenges. States and their governments remain crucial, but so too are other actors, principles, norms, networks, and mechanisms.

We have seen how states must collaborate with the multitude of other performers on the world's stage to make better use of the energy and resources of a wide range of non-state actors alongside universal, regional, and sub-regional IGOs—particularly those of the UN system. Problem-solving also needs to be blended with such mini-lateral forums as the Group of 20, the Islamic Conference, and the Group of 77. Similarly, innovative public–private partnerships are essential to mobilize civil society, business, philanthropies, and the media.

Over several decades, some transnational corporations (TNCs) and other non-state actors with burgeoning resources and influence have come to possess more problem-solving capabilities than many countries. They have become integral to comprehensive solutions promulgated and undertaken by global and regional IGOs, as well as member states. However, the limitations of non-state actors should be recognized. NGOs and TNCs cannot eliminate poverty, stop global warming, or halt mass murder on their own (**see Section 7.4**).

Often lost in the struggle to understand the indistinct mosaic of authority for global governance is that current IGOs have inadequate resources as well as incoherent policies and philosophies. At a minimum, the foundations for the UN system need to be reinforced. Collective imaginations and long-term vision have become feeble. The IMF is reviled for throwing its weight around but its resources—even after the 2008 infusion of $750 billion amid that global financial crisis—remain paltry and unambitious in comparison with original plans. In 1995, the celebrated development economist Hans Singer summarized: 'Today's [International Monetary] Fund is only 2 per cent of annual world imports. Perhaps the differences between [John Maynard] Keynes's originally proposed 50 per cent and the actual 2 per cent is a measure of the degree to which our vision of international economic management has shrunk' (H. Singer 1995: 19).

A much denser network of global governance institutions exists in the 2020s than in 1945, but the dearth of global public economic goods remains. In the aftermath of a global economic meltdown amid the Covid-19 pandemic, we are perplexed that anyone would dispute the need for more international cooperation and muscular IGOs. Yet, in the early 2020s, the onslaught on multilateralism—cooperation among three or more parties, especially states—was alarming. While the menace from the Covid-19 pandemic is short term, the threats to the planet and human civilization from climate change are far more dire.

Reaching global agreement about supportive action will require vision and creative innovation—above all, by you, the reader of this book. The younger generation will suffer most from contemporary failures to act, and has much to gain from more bold, focused, and effective international collaboration.

Key Points

- Global governance consists of collective efforts to identify, understand, and address worldwide problems and processes that go beyond the capacities of individual states.
- The UN's weaknesses have been partially complemented and supplemented by such non-state actors as NGOs, TNCs, and foundations.
- The question of how to improve global economic governance can be understood by addressing the main 'gaps' in the international system: knowledge, norms, policies, institutions, leadership, and compliance.
- The challenge of tackling such existential threats as climate change and poverty and inequality illustrates the need for a global governance perspective and collaboration.
- Addressing global governance problems requires more robust IGOs and international NGOs.

Further Reading

Acharya, A. (2016) (ed.), *Why Govern? Rethinking Demand and Progress in Global Governance* (Cambridge: Cambridge University Press). Interprets the unprecedented challenges facing the post-war system of international cooperation.

Adedeji, A. (1993) (ed.), *Africa within the World: Beyond Dispossession and Dependence* (London: Zed Books). Collection edited by a visible proponent of regional integration.

Avant, D. D., Finnemore, M., and Sell, S. K. (2010) (eds), *Who Governs the Globe?* (Cambridge: Cambridge University Press). Investigates the agents who do the governing.

Barnett, M., and Duvall, R. (2004) (eds), *Power in Global Governance* (Cambridge: Cambridge University Press). Collection that probes the 'power' of international organizations, a term typically applied to states and not to the organizations that they create.

Caglar, G., Prügl, E., and Zwingel, S. (2013) (eds), *Feminist Strategies in International Governance* (London: Routledge). Edited collection about the literature on the impact of feminist expertise and gender perspectives.

Johnson, T. (2017), *Organizational Progeny: Why Governments are Losing Control over the Proliferating Structures of Global Governance* (Oxford: Oxford University Press). Explores the influence of international officials on the origins and behaviour of intergovernmental organizations.

Weiss, T. G., and Thakur, R. (2010), *The UN and Global Governance: An Unfinished Journey* (Bloomington: Indiana University Press). Examines UN efforts to fill gaps in global governance.

Weiss, T. G., and Wilkinson, R. (2022) (eds), *Global Governance Futures* (London: Routledge). Critically examines the origins of the term 'global governance' and the prospects of various problems and solutions.

Chapter 14 Roundtable discussion

Has global economic governance failed over the last half-century?

Roundtable 14.1

Opening contribution **Richard Jolly and Thomas G. Weiss**

An answer to this question requires subjective judgement and two definitions—what do we mean by 'global economic governance' and what do we mean by 'failure'? As readers might suspect from two academics, the answer also will entail another qualifier: 'it depends!'

As we saw in **Section 14.2**, global governance involves collective efforts to identify, understand, and address worldwide problems—economic, social, and political—that go beyond the individual capabilities of any one state. A wide variety of actors are included—not only governments and intergovernmental organizations, but also non-governmental organizations, business, and civil society. States and their governments remain crucial, but so too are other formal and informal actors, principles, norms, networks, and mechanisms.

The term 'global governance' was coined in the early 1990s, but efforts to improve world order and the management of global problems predate that moment. The United Nations was created in 1945 and the International Monetary Fund (IMF) and the World Bank started operations in the same year. However, taking 1970 as a starting point is important because the international economic order of the early 2020s is distinctly different from that of a half-century earlier.

The 1970s were called the 'Second UN Development Decade', which began in 1971 when the United States abandoned the gold standard. The initial throes of decolonization were almost completed, and developing countries of what was then called the 'Third World' (now 'Global South') were clamouring through bodies like the Non-Aligned Movement and the Group of 77 for a fundamental levelling of the economic, trade, and financial playing fields. Five UN global conferences (on the human environment, food, population, urbanization, and technology) also signalled that interdependence was being recognized as central to world politics and global problem-solving.

The extent and pertinence of interdependence was disputed, but this essentially meant that the fortunes of countries—rich, poor, and otherwise—were inextricably tied together on many issues. Going-it-alone was not the best, nor even a plausible, problem-solving strategy because of the many challenges that did not respect national borders—a reality that former UN Secretary-General Kofi Annan called 'problems without passports' (2002: 30–31).

What are we to say if we fast forward to the early 2020s? We write amidst a global pandemic, along with an initial $10 trillion drop in global gross domestic project (GDP). We are at the end of a five-year period that registered four out of the five hottest years on record. We would have to say that global governance, in general, and global economic governance, in particular, have hardly been a roaring success.

But is that conclusion fair?

The last half-century certainly has been beneficial for many, although considerably less so than the initial quarter-century after 1945—the most stable ever in terms of economic growth. After 1970, growth became less stable and gaps in per capita income widened, sometimes considerably. From 1980, debt crises and ensuing structural adjustment policies promoted by the IMF and World Bank saddled Latin America with economic stagnation and most of sub-Saharan Africa with declining per capita incomes. After a regional financial crisis in the late 1990s, Asia turned its back on global institutions and shifted toward active and regionally focused policies while it created notable prosperity. Most importantly, China's soaring rate of economic growth, beginning in the 1980s, surpassed all historical precedents.

At the same time, no definition of success—or 'failure'—can ignore asking 'for whom?' What about those who have not been beneficiaries of growth and globalization? As we hear in **Chapter 10**, since 1980 and often continuing after 2000, income inequality has soared and poverty and unemployment have stubbornly remained—not everywhere, but especially in Africa, much of Latin America, and among many populations within many industrialized countries (especially in the United States and United Kingdom). Indeed, the Gini coefficient—a measure that provides a snapshot of inequality—worsened in many places. Of note were the dramatic levels of inequality in such emerging economies as South Africa (the worst) and Brazil (eighth worst). The Covid-19 pandemic has further wiped out several decades of successful development.

So, for those who emphasize economic growth and focus on the stock market, as well as those who have escaped poverty into the middle class, we could say that global economic governance has succeeded (albeit with major hiccups like the 2008–09 recession and the Covid-19 pandemic).

But for those who emphasize equality and justice, global economic governance clearly has failed since the 1970s, despite the many who have escaped poverty, gained education, and are leading longer lives. For those who cherish the environment, the market-incentive structure has also worked against sustainability and greater equality, both of which should stand at the top of global priorities.

There is nothing inevitable about any of this. We should recall and be buoyed by the experience of the quarter-century after 1945 when international action was strongly in support of widespread economic success, which represented considerable advances for many people in all parts of the world. It is hard to understand why anyone would seek to dismantle international cooperation, rather than call for more of it. Ultimately, citizens and voters will determine the values, narratives, and priorities that underpin global economic governance.

Roundtable 14.2
Response **Eka Ikpe**

Questioning the success or failure of global economic governance is pertinent and timely. In my response to this question I want to foreground the enduring hierarchies that shape the global political economy (GPE). These include the interrelated legacies of imperialism, longstanding geopolitical inequalities, and the dominance of ideological, intellectual, and policy approaches that affirm the status quo and can be inattentive to divergent perspectives from Global South contexts.

Richard Jolly and Thomas G. Weiss note that international cooperation should address contemporary challenges such as the global Covid-19 pandemic, climate change, and longstanding problems of global inequality and poverty (**see Roundtable 14.1**). I entirely agree. Yet the realities of the global pandemic and climate change show that some Global South populations face problems that are underpinned by a persistent core–periphery structure. This is despite notable shifts in the global political-economic order, including growing numbers of middle-income economies and China's economic expansion.

Some economies in parts of Africa and Asia are confronted by limited access to Covid-19 vaccines, while some of their Global North counterparts secure vaccines to cover their populations several times over (Wouters et al. 2021; Adepoju 2021). We see the disproportionate impact of climate change on those that pollute the least, exacerbated as waste-brokers in the Global North dump toxic waste in Global South contexts (Okafor-Yarwood and Adewumi 2020). While poverty is a global concern, the Covid-19 pandemic and climate change potentially reverse gains in poverty reduction in parts of Asia and Africa, including larger middle-income economies (World Bank 2020*a*).

These reflections draw to our attention the global inequality and divergence in socioeconomic conditions between different parts of the globe. These reverberate against the doubts expressed by critical thinkers Paul Baran (1957), Samir Amin (1974), and Jayati Ghosh (2019) about how the global economic system might serve harmoniously Global North and Global South constituencies and interests.

The structures of global economic governance in the key international financial institutions, the International Monetary Fund (IMF) and the World Bank, are of particular importance here. Power, agency, and influence in the functioning of these institutions have been longstanding concerns in relation to the knowledge and ideas that underpin their work, the space for critique and alternative discourses, and the voice of those in the Global South contexts within which they are most active. These are valid concerns when considering global economic governance as 'collective efforts to identify, understand, and address worldwide problems', to use Jolly and Weiss's phrase (**see Roundtable 14.1**).

'Identify(ing), understand(ing) . . . worldwide problems' immediately underlines the challenges of global inequality and links to the impacts of imperialism in global economic, political, and social systems. The legacy of European colonization has been distinctive in the way it locates certain Global South contexts as 'spaces of extraction' that continue to be characterized by technological dependence, neglect of domestic markets, and constrained industrial development, as is compellingly argued by Amin (1974) and Ake (1981). As a corollary to this, commodity dependence is at its highest in sub-Saharan Africa.

Global development policy as pursued by the World Bank and IMF has struggled and indeed *failed* to contend with this legacy due to their underpinning logic of privileging market fundamentalism and static comparative advantage as the ideal basis for the functioning of the global economy.

'Collective efforts to . . . address worldwide problems' call for reflections on who is part of the 'collective'. Let's take a pivotal example of how the global economic governance system ran roughshod over one of the most insightful advances in development thought, expressed in a collective vision at a critical juncture in Africa. Showcasing the wealth of knowledge and in-depth understandings of local realities, the *African Alternative Framework to Structural Adjustment Programmes for Socio-economic Recovery and Transformation* (AAF-SAP) centred on the particularities of economies and inter-country cooperation as well as the inter-dependencies between states and markets, environment, culture, politics, and local value creation and capture (United Nations Economic Commission for Africa 1990). While global economic governance within UN structures worked to privilege collective African thought (with African leadership), the international financial institutions barely engaged the AAF-SAP, despite the immense challenges wrought by the structural adjustment programmes (Mkandawire and Soludo 2003).

A final pertinent point concerns leadership representation. Over time—particularly within the United Nations—there have been shifts towards greater representation of Global South leaders. However, European and North American dominance continues in the leadership of the most critical and influential global economic governance institutions, the IMF and the World Bank. Following extensive efforts, 2021 saw the widely celebrated appointment of the World Trade Organization's (WTO) first female and African president, Ngozi Okonjo-Iweala.

Expanded representation in leadership is an important step in enabling 'collective efforts'. It is, of course, not a foregone conclusion that this leads to broader diversity and representation of ideas and approaches that challenge existing hierarchies. Indeed, Adebayo Adedeji and Leslie Sklair speak of coalitions between transnational elites that can maintain and deepen the disadvantages to the Global South in global economic governance (Adedeji 1994; Sprague 2009). But better leadership representation is undoubtedly vital in extending the space for critical ideas, policy, and practice to achieve progress for all.

As Jolly and Weiss note, the judgement on success or failure is far from straightforward and depends a great deal on which vantage point—and *whose* vantage point—we take as our starting point.

Roundtable 14.3
Response **Gabriele Koehler**

We need to look at global governance holistically—the governance of the economic, the social, the political, and the environmental—as situated in the UN system. Shocked by the horrors of colonialism, world wars, genocide, and political persecution, segments of the global polity convened in the 1940s to create the 'nations united' around a set of principles or norms, which culminated in the Universal Declaration of Human Rights and the Charter of the UN—as highlighted by Richard Jolly and Thomas G. Weiss in **Roundtable 14.1**.

Some of these norms are set out in resolutions which make recommendations—so-called soft law. Currently the best known of these is probably the UN's 2030 Agenda on Sustainable Development and its Sustainable Development Goals (SDGs), which actually commit to 'transform our world' (**see Case Study 14.2**). The Agenda now informs international, regional-level, and in-country policy discourse, as well as business language. In that respect, the Agenda has been successful in capturing imaginations, but SDG achievement is tracked only voluntarily, and countries are free to glamorize their achievements and ignore their failings.

The companion piece in the multilateral normative process is that of the binding norms, conceptualized and negotiated at the UN's Human Rights Council and the International Labour Organization (ILO), among other places, and resulting in conventions which, once ratified, are monitored pluri- or multilaterally. They can be claimed by civil society and citizens. Examples include the International Covenants on Economic, Social, and Cultural Rights and on Civil and Political Rights, the Convention on the Elimination of All Forms of Discrimination Against Women (CEDAW), and the Convention on the Rights of the Child (CRC), the Convention on the Rights of Migrants and their Families, and the ILO core conventions on the rights of workers. Most recently, the ILO adopted a convention prohibiting violence and sexual harassment at the workplace. The Paris Agreement on climate change, too, is binding.

Whether soft or binding, the universe of norms is where global governance has made great—and inspiring—strides at the ideational level, now comprising 560 multilateral agreements and 190 ILO conventions, monitored by a group of outspoken special rapporteurs who independently investigate human rights challenges. However, the UN is indeed multilateral—'many-sided'—and fraught with asymmetrical power hierarchies between the competing or even contradictory objectives of member states, the aspirations of the organization's staff and progressive civil society, and dominant business interests. And an increasing number of governments disregard its foundational norms, even those that are binding.

A considerable number of UN member states are not functioning democratically. CIVICUS (n.d., 2022), for example, rates fifty of the 197 countries and territories it observes as 'repressed' and another twenty-five as 'closed' with regard to respecting civil society and the freedoms of association, assembly, and expression. These countries hinder and oppress labour and civil society movements as well as independent media and investigative journalism, and persecute defenders of human rights. Climate-related commitments are systematically and continuously hollowed out and undermined. In some countries, human rights and climate activists are murdered with impunity. The UN has, in the majority of its member states, failed to anchor and claim the principles it stands for.

So, with Jolly and Weiss, one asks whether and 'for whom' global governance has worked or failed. Here, too, the assessment is damning: 1.3 billion people face multidimensional poverty. Close to 900 million people are projected to face not just food insecurity but hunger in the coming years. Five million young children continue to die every year of preventable diseases. 300,000 women die each year in childbirth. The Covid-19 pandemic has illustrated how many countries had dismantled their public health systems.

Global warming and the massive loss of biodiversity are threatening millions of lives—hollowing out livelihoods, increasing pressure on the care economy, and threatening health. The planet struggles with immense ecological imbalances. Inequities, measured in income or wealth Gini coefficients, or in education disparities, or in food waste, are exploding. Women and girl children, with compounded exclusions based on ethnicity, caste, location, sexual orientation, ability, and many others, are the worst affected by these inequities. For a majority of the planet's population, decent working conditions or even just minimalist social protection remain elusive. For half the world's population, child rights and gender justice are strangled.

Why is there this failure? I would argue it is because the UN's principles and norms are systemically undermined by the dominant global economic rationale. The global economy is profit driven: unfettered capitalism is no longer reined in by enlightened welfare states to balance the interest of citizens and residents versus economic elites (**see Chapter 4**). Large companies dominate global value chains (GVCs) as well as national policy decisions (**see Chapter 7**). Thus, there are too few brakes on a global race to the bottom—in terms of human rights, climate justice, incomes, and decent work.

There are myriad instances where governments and powerful private enterprises stall or even veto efforts for global justice—efforts led by progressive countries, supported by UN experts and civil society. Current examples include negotiations for a binding treaty on business and human rights which would require transnational corporations as well as smaller companies to comply with human rights, labour, and environmental standards in their GVCs. The campaigns to cancel debt—with reinforced urgency now in light of the Covid-19-recessions in many lower-income countries—remain unheeded, as are the initiatives requesting the WTO to waive intellectual property regulations so as to enable a wider range of countries to efficiently produce, and all countries to distribute, essential vaccines (**see Box 8.2**). The main polluting economies are downplaying the warnings on the imminent climate catastrophe, and they are reluctant to compensate the most vulnerable communities for the loss and damage their environmental behaviours create (**see Chapter 9**).

At this point in time, I would argue, global (economic) governance is failing. Or, as the UN Conference on Trade and Development put it at its founding: 'If privilege, extremes of wealth and poverty, and social injustice persist, then the goal of development is lost' (UNCTAD 1964: 3).

Whether global governance will succeed in the future depends on whether progressive forces in nation-states and civil society can recapture multilateralism and global governance for economic, social, political, gender, and climate justice.

Roundtable 14.4
Response Tana Johnson

As Richard Jolly and Thomas G. Weiss point out in **Roundtable 14.1**, answering the question of whether global economic governance has failed over the last half century requires a closer look at what constitutes global economic governance, and what constitutes success.

In the decades immediately following the Second World War, global economic governance centred on a small and relatively homogenous group of developed Western countries. Led by the United States, these countries designed and launched a system of major economic practices and institutions—such as the International Monetary Fund (IMF), the dollar-backed gold standard, the International Bank for Reconstruction and Development (World Bank), and the General Agreement on Tariffs and Trade (GATT).

But in the last half-century, that system experienced massive changes, including the abandonment of the gold standard, the promotion of free-market ideology, the ascendency of non-governmental actors such as corporations or civil society, the creation of the World Trade Organization (WTO), the rise of China, and the launch of the multistakeholder Sustainable Development Goals (SDGs). In short, the actors and tasks in global economic governance have dramatically increased.

The standards for success have increased, too. Global economic governance has never been easy, but today it is especially challenging. For example, protecting 'the world' from economic crises now means managing not fifty countries but approximately 200—each with its own vulnerabilities and resentments.

With both global economic governance and success being more complicated than in the early post-war era, then, my answer to this question rests on two paradoxes: failure may be success, and success can breed failure.

Paradox #1: Failure may be success

In the first paradox, what looks like failure might actually be success. For one thing, many global economic governors take up impossible goals, and therefore even if they fall short of an unachievable ideal, they may accomplish much. Major intergovernmental organizations, for example, trumpet astronomical aspirations. The IMF's mandate is to '*ensure stability in all macroeconomic and financial sectors affecting the international monetary system*' (IMF 2022). The World Bank's mission is to '*end extreme poverty and promote shared prosperity in a sustainable way*' (World Bank 2021*e*). The World Trade Organization's stated purpose is to '*open trade for the benefit of all*' (WTO 2021*b*). Stability, prosperity, and benefits will never be perfect—but movement toward those ideals is still a laudable achievement.

Indeed, although governments themselves often undermine and under-resource global economic governance, the past half-century exhibits many achievements. With a streak of relative peace and prosperity, average life expectancy soared from fifty-nine years in 1970 to about seventy-two years in 2018 (World Bank 2021*a*). The percentage of the world population living in poverty plummeted from 42 per cent in 1980 to about 9 per cent in 2017 (World Bank 2021*b*). Since the establishment of the World Bank's arm for no-interest loans in 1960, thirty-seven least-developed countries have grown prosperous enough to graduate from eligibility, without sliding back (International Development Association 2021).

Responsiveness to rising powers, terrorism, climate change, and other novel economic complications has led to new institutions such as the Group of 20 (G-20), the Financial Action Task Force (FATF), and the Global Environment Facility Trust Fund (GEF). Economic connectedness has permitted readier access to distant markets for consumers, workers, investors, and producers. Together, these signs of health, poverty reduction, development, responsiveness, and access are not perfect—but they are undoubtedly a feat.

Such achievements are easy to miss, however, because incremental progress grabs much less attention than a sudden setback does. Policymakers, scholars, and the public have been incensed that global economic governance did not stop the global financial crisis of 2008, nor the economic slowdown from the Covid-19 pandemic in the early 2020s. But what is hard to know is the counterfactual: without the existing system of global economic governance, would these calamities have been even more shattering? Moreover, have other menaces been entirely prevented, resulting in successes that are not even perceived?

Thus, for three reasons, failure may be success. Progress toward an impossible goal is still progress. Despite being undermined or under-resourced by governments, the system has produced some remarkable achievements. And the dangers that become full-blown crises are outnumbered by the dangers that are mitigated or prevented.

Paradox #2: Success can breed failure

Unfortunately, this heartening view is tempered by a second paradox: success can breed failure. As average life expectancy soared, so did the world's population, to nearly 8 billion people. As the percentage of the world population living in poverty plummeted, the environmental degradation associated with consumption skyrocketed. As more countries graduated to middle-income status, centres of economic power proliferated and became more heterogeneous, with the West losing ground to major developing countries such as China, India, and Brazil.

As global governance structures responded to new challenges by creating new institutions, institutional fragmentation increased. And as consumers, workers, investors, and producers found themselves connected economically, they also became connected socially—making it difficult to ignore the plights of faraway people.

All of this means that global economic governance faces severe challenges: delivering prosperity and dignity to an unprecedented world population; averting over-consumption and environmental devastation; coordinating antagonistic economic powers; harmonizing a fragmented institutional landscape; and taking responsibility for the welfare of all humanity.

There are reasons to regret how global economic governance has performed in the last half-century. But since failure may be success, and success can breed failure, the bigger worry is how global economic governance will fare in the *next* half-century.

Over to you . . .

1 All of the contributors to the **Chapter 14 Roundtable** echo Richard Jolly and Thomas G. Weiss's 'it depends' in answering the question—particularly in relation to which parts of the world you focus on, and whose vantage point you see from, as Eka Ikpe put it in **Roundtable 14.2**. What kinds of inequalities are revealed by the record of global governance on issues like poverty, climate change, and health? Do you think our systems of global governance merely reflect these inequalities, or are they part of their causes?

2 In **Roundtable 14.4**, Tana Johnson makes the intriguing argument that failure can be success, and success can be failure. Despite its problems, what do you think are the main arguments for international cooperation in addressing the big challenges facing the world today? Are you optimistic about the prospects for international cooperation? What will be the big tasks for global economic governance in the future?

3 How does your answer to the **Chapter 14 Roundtable** question change if you take a 'top-down' perspective compared with a 'bottom-up' one—in other words, if you focus on the global 'governors' or on the globally 'governed', as Jolly and Weiss put it in **Chapter 14**? Which perspective is reflected in the main theories of Global Political Economy that inform the study of global governance? How does this shape your view of their relevance and usefulness?

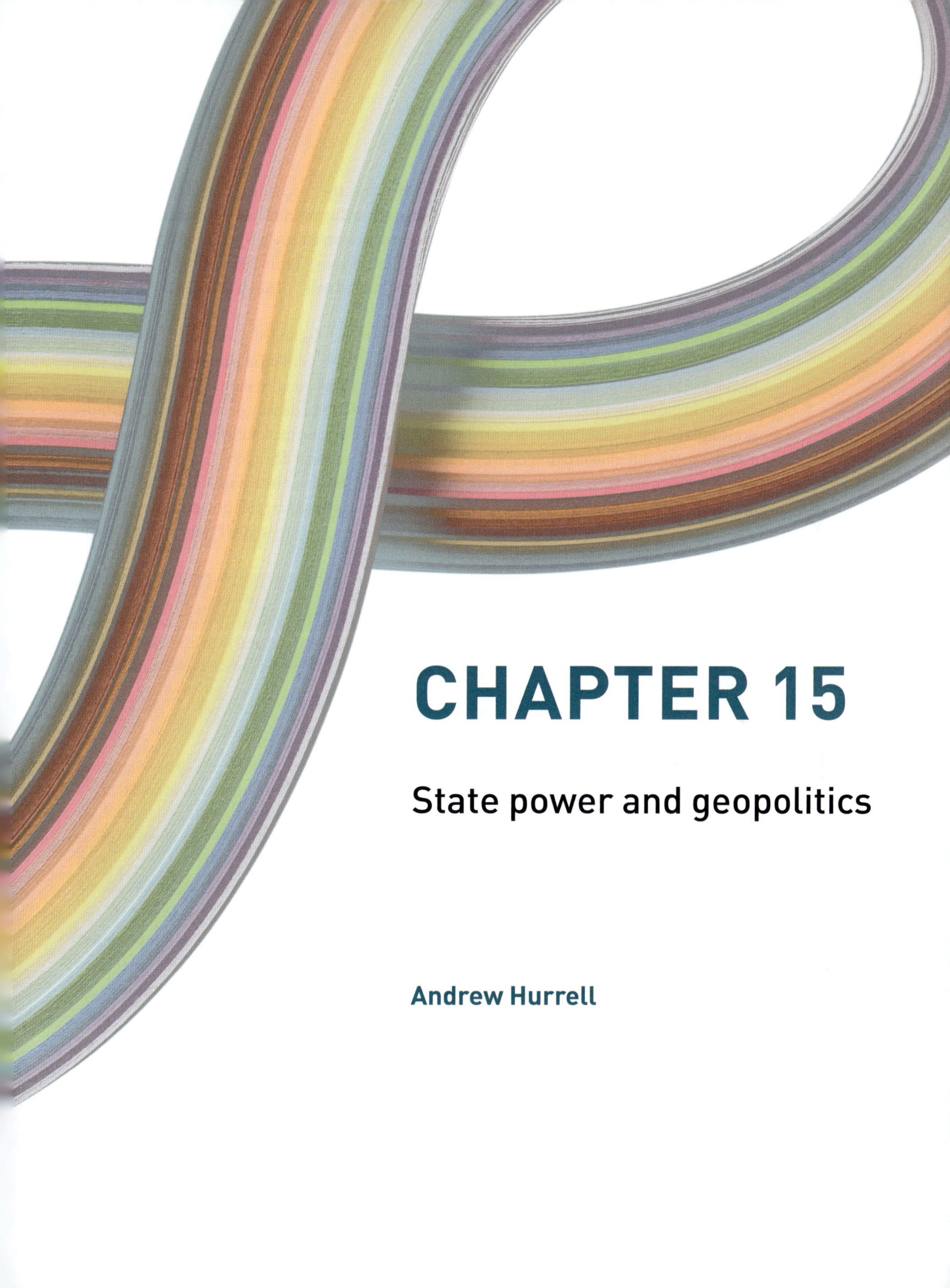

CHAPTER 15

State power and geopolitics

Andrew Hurrell

15.1 Introduction

The headlines are full of the return of geopolitics and the intensification of geoeconomic rivalry. 'The West tightens economic sanctions against Russia in response to the invasion of Ukraine'; 'Tackling the China threat with economic statecraft'; 'A US grand strategy for the digital economy'; 'The West imposes new sanctions on Iran'; 'From lightbulbs to 5G: China battles the West for control of vital technological standards'; 'The geopolitics of Europe's New Green Deal'. And so on and so on.

For much of the post-Cold War period, this kind of old-fashioned geopolitics appeared to have receded into the background. Liberals saw this as the result of the triumph of liberal values and of liberal capitalism as the only viable model for organizing economic life, the systemic changes instituted by globalization, and the increasing depth and density of international institutions and economic governance. The arrow of history was moving inexorably towards the success and the successful globalization of Western capitalist modernity. The global governance frame was replacing anarchy as the most important way of thinking about international relations. And, finally, the United States was able and willing to use both its hard and soft power to play the anchoring role as the (self-styled) indispensable nation of the (again self-styled) global liberal order.

> **Key Concepts**
>
> **Anarchy:** In everyday use 'anarchy' is used to describe disorder or even chaos. Within International Relations 'anarchy' is used to describe an international political system in which there is no central power or authority to enforce the law or protect individual states. In international life, if your security or vital interests are under threat, there is no one to call for help. Hence the system is said to be 'anarchical'.
>
> **Cold War:** Cold War is used in a historic sense to describe the rivalry between the United States and the Soviet Union in the period from 1946 to 1990. It was not a 'hot war' in that direct military conflict was avoided, although indirect militarized clashes were a common feature and nuclear weapons played a fundamental role. The term is also used generically to describe a situation of protracted rivalry and conflict that is neither peace nor war.

But it was not just liberals. One important strand of Marxist political economy argued that contemporary capitalism had come to operate primarily through transnational networks of power, integrated both by a unified transnational capitalist class and policed and constrained within the informal empire of the United States (Hardt and Negri 2001). Global capitalism was therefore no longer susceptible to the kinds of inter-imperialist rivalries and wars that had preoccupied earlier Marxist theorists from Lenin onwards.

The past few years have not been kind to such predictions. The reality of large-scale inter-state conflict and the potential for major power war have returned—most prominently between the West and Russia over Ukraine and between the United States and China—and regional tensions and conflicts have intensified in many parts of the world. And, as the headlines illustrate, there are many examples of how power and power politics have spilled over into the day-to-day functioning of the global economy—from challenges to what were apparently successful economic institutions such as the World Trade Organization (WTO); into the weaponization of trade and calls for national security controls on foreign investment; and into the operation of the world's leading high-tech firms and the increasingly important realms of the Internet and cybersecurity. The global Covid-19 pandemic provided a further example with calls for greater national resilience, the re-nationalization of global production chains, the closing of borders and the policing of travel, and the promotion of vaccine nationalism and national control over the development and production of medicines (**see Chapter 8**).

How can we make sense of these developments? How are state power and the changing character of global international society related to the global economy? In this chapter we will cover three dimensions in answering these questions, as a way of introducing you to thinking about the role of power and geopolitics in the global political economy (GPE).

The first answer begins by seeing the economic world and the political world as relatively separate and then concentrates on how changes in the global economy affect the nature and the effectiveness of the economic instruments available to governments as they pursue their foreign policy goals.

The second cluster of answers focuses instead on the ways in which politics and economics are necessarily bound together in the construction and evolution of economic institutions and economic orders and on the critical ways in which power operates within these orders.

The third cluster of answers accepts the need to think in terms of power operating within economic orders but this time with the causal arrow flowing from politics into the economy. From this perspective, the distinctive dynamics of the international political system are what drive the foreign economic policies of governments, shape many aspects of the states and societies that make up the global system, and help explain the character of the global economy and how it operates. (On geoeconomics and geopolitics, **see Case Study 15.1**.)

Case Study 15.1: What is geopolitics?

Geopolitics and geoeconomics have become increasingly common in describing developments taking place in the global economy. There are many aspects of economics in which geographical or spatial factors are important—as in the relationship between geography and patterns of trade or investment. But geoeconomics has come ever more to be used in close connection with politics, power, and conflict—and closely tied to geopolitics.

So, what is geopolitics? There are three broad approaches.

The first, as the name suggests, concentrates on the interplay between geography and politics—the ways in which objective geographical features shape or even determine the nature of international politics and the options available to individual states and their leaders. Thus, those concerned with military security and strategy have long been concerned with the role of rivers and mountains as natural borders, with the existence or absence of natural resources in whether a country is a satisfied or revisionist power, and with the role of physical communications in patterns of trade and migration.

The second connects politics with the changing character of the global. In 1904 Halford Mackinder suggested that a decisive turning point in human history had been reached when the

(Continued)

international political system became a 'closed political space' (Mackinder 1904). The world had become a whole or a single totality in which all politics, especially the relations of the major powers, necessarily become interconnected. Because the international political system is a closed space and because the competition between major states increasingly spread to all parts of the world (as in the idea of a 'world war'), then what happens in one part of the world will be 'geopolitically' connected to other parts.

For Mackinder in 1904 this worldwide competition was centred on the European colonial empires, now faced by the rise of the United States and Imperial Japan. During the Cold War, Henry Kissinger talked of the 'primacy of geopolitics' in a very similar way. Geopolitics for Kissinger was about the way in which political and economic developments in diverse parts of the world have the potential to connect with the central bipolar balance of power between the superpowers. And, as we think about the geopolitical impact of climate change this idea of a whole planet being connected in potentially destabilizing ways remains central. Hence, the melting of the Arctic ice cap does not just have ecological effects but potentially opens up new kinds of geopolitical relationships.

The third approach moves away from the idea that geography has an objective impact on politics. Instead, it focuses on the ways in which geographical features are represented or imagined or socially constructed. For critical geographers and for critical International Relations theorists, it is the politics of geography that matter most. In times of crisis or destabilizing change, people return to ideas of national community and to the mythologies of nationalism that associate the nation with particular geographical boundaries or with landscapes and territories that are seen to form part of the soul or intrinsic character of the nation. This has been very visible, for example, in the resurgence of geopolitical thought in recent Russian foreign policy. But examples can be found in many other places.

Questions

1 Does the 'geo' in 'geopolitics' or 'geoeconomics' add anything important to the study of GPE?
2 Does technological change mean the end of geography? Why have developments in digital and cyber technologies coincided with the 'return of geopolitics'?

15.2 Global Political Economy and economic statecraft

There is a long tradition of writing on 'economic statecraft', defined as the use of economic instruments to secure foreign policy goals and to promote and defend national interests (D. Baldwin 1985; Blackwill and Harris 2016). The writing on economic sanctions provides one of the clearest examples and addresses such questions as: Why do states choose to use economic sanctions? Under what conditions are economic sanctions more or less effective? Can different kinds of sanctions achieve better results (for example, sanctions that are targeted at particular individuals or state leaders)? To what extent do effective sanctions depend on legitimate authorization by the United Nations (UN) or other international bodies? Often the focus is on particular relationships, as, for example, in the case of the attempts by the United States and European countries to constrain Iranian nuclear choices or to impose severe costs on Russia (**see Case Study 15.2**).

Case Study 15.2: Do economic sanctions work?

Economic sanctions are one of the most common forms of economic statecraft. In 2022 the United States had thirty-five sanctions regimes in place, only ten of which were associated with UN Security Council (UNSC) Resolutions, and the European Union (EU) maintained forty-five sanctions regimes, nineteen of which had a UNSC mandate. The year 2022 saw the dramatic expansion of economic sanctions against Russia in response to the invasion of Ukraine (Photo 15.1). Economic sanctions are widely seen as powerful instruments—to force a change in foreign policy behaviour, to constrain proscribed activities, or to stigmatize those who are seen to have violated important international norms.

And yet there are many studies that show that trade and financial sanctions have a low success rate. And, when they do 'work', it is almost always in combination with a wide range of other factors. The role of international sanctions as one element in the end of apartheid in South Africa is a good example.

What are the reasons for this low success rate?

- External pressure can provide a way for governments to mobilize domestic support. Indeed, the more that sanctions hurt, the more the image of the external enemy can be fostered and exploited.
- Economic sanctions are a blunt instrument. Those who suffer are often the innocent and those who have nothing to do with the government or the leaders whose behaviour is the target.

Photo 15.1 Demonstrators protest against the Russian invasion of Ukraine and demand sanctions on Russia

Source: Vuk Valcic / Alamy Stock Photo.

(Continued)

- Sanctions are more likely to work if they include as many of the target's economic partners as possible and if they are endorsed by an international body, most notably the United Nations. UN sanctions can be made legally binding, which increases the difficulties for private economic actors.
- However, it is rarely the case that alternative partners for trade or for the sale of oil and natural resources cannot be found—either because the targeted state will have allies and supporters, or because of the overt or clandestine ways in which sanctions can be evaded or avoided.
- Because of these difficulties, governments have increasingly sought to develop targeted sanctions which impose costs on specific individuals or groups, or 'smart sanctions'. But powerful individuals are often the most able to secure and protect their own financial position and are also able to shift the costs onto the general population.

If sanctions have such a low success rate, then why are they so common? The answer is that we have to think not just about the costs and benefits of the sanctions but also about the costs of alternative options. Faced with perceived threats or behaviour that are seen to be unacceptable, the costs of doing nothing are often very high.

Alternatively, as in the case of Russia and Ukraine, direct military intervention carries a very high risk of escalation to larger-scale or even nuclear conflict. Economic sanctions are therefore seen as an unavoidable option. But to be successful, they can have their own tendency to escalate and expand. This means that they will only 'work' if the sanctioning societies are prepared to bear very heavy costs; expanding sanctions can come close to economic war, and the process of normalizing the global economy after the conflict becomes very difficult.

Watch the video on the online resources to take your understanding of this case study further.

Questions

1 What kinds of economic relations are most suited to effective sanctions?
2 Are sanctions legitimate if ordinary people suffer?

But sanctions have become a major feature of the broader politicization of economic transactions. In part this follows from the sheer increase in the number of cases of sanctions being used, especially unilateral sanctions imposed by the United States. But it also follows from the determination of Washington to use its extra-territorial legal powers over economic actors located outside the USA. Because of the size of the US economy and because so many global economic transactions must be cleared in US dollars via US banks, a far greater range of international economic actors have been brought into the sanctions net.

Conditionality provides a further example (**see Section 4.3.3**). Conditionality involves placing non-market conditions either on economic transactions and flows of aid, trade, investment, and technology, or on membership in economic institutions or trade groupings: you can only join this economic grouping if you accept these environmental or human rights conditions. Conditions might cover anything from domestic economic policy, to levels of arms spending, to the promotion of sustainable development or human rights and democratic governance. Conditionality is an important aspect of power in a globalizing system, not least because it usually has a consensual element and occupies the murky space between direct economic coercion and sanctions, on the one hand, and freely entered contractual arrangements, on the other.

Another traditional question concerns strategic assets. What parts of the economy, which resources, and which particular industries matter strategically, and why? In the world of nineteenth-century geopolitics, coal, iron, and steel were viewed as the sinews of war. For much of the twentieth century, oil was the quintessential strategic commodity and access to oil was one of the great drivers of geopolitical rivalry and intervention in regions where other economic interests were low—the Middle East most obviously. In the post-1945 period nuclear technology was seen as central to both long-term economic development and national security. In the twenty-first century, attention has shifted to artificial intelligence (AI), super-computing, quantum technologies, and the ability to foster and protect high-technology companies.

Political realists have long stressed the security importance of relative gains in how the global economy functions. We might all benefit from higher levels of economic exchange, but the crucial questions are, first, who gains how much? and, second, how does this unequal distribution of costs and benefits spill over into the world of security? Here, however, the focus is not on the overall security externalities of economic exchange, but rather on the externalities that are associated with particular assets and the factors that influence this calculation. Some believe that certain goods are intrinsically strategic and of potential military significance. Others argue that what matters is not just the ability to substitute a product or technology from another source, but the degree to which the national development of that product or technology can only be achieved on the back of a cumulative and long-term process of national research and industrial development.

Many of these questions are old. But the forms that they take change with economic and technological developments. Hence, some see 'weaponized interdependence' as being today far more closely connected with economic networks, the Internet, financial communications, and global supply chains (Farrell and Newman 2019). Another increasingly important aspect concerns the geopolitical implications of the infrastructures of globalization and the underlying patterns and structures of connectivity, how they have changed over time, and how they relate to different forms of power-political relations. Infrastructures can take many forms: from the physical infrastructures of travel and transport to the increasing importance of digital infrastructures. The securitization of infrastructures is therefore an increasingly important aspect of economic statecraft.

Key Concept: securitization

Securitization refers to the political process by which issues—here economic issues—come to be defined in terms of security and security threats; identifying the actors that are involved in the process of securitization; and being alert to whose interests are being served by treating issues as security issues. An issue becomes a security issue because a particular group (whether a state, an international organization, a company, or traditional or new media) has successfully forced it onto the security agenda, not because it is in some objective or natural sense important or threatening.

15.3 **Power within institutions and economic orders**

It is certainly possible to imagine how a market might emerge spontaneously by people coming together, trading and bartering, mixing, and moving. But all markets and all economies require political ordering and economic governance. Avinash Dixit suggests that:

> [E]conomic governance consists of the processes that support economic activity and economic transactions by protecting property rights, enforcing contracts, and taking collective action to provide appropriate physical and organizational infrastructure. These processes are carried out within institutions, formal and informal. (Dixit 2006)

Institutions have been central to the development of modern capitalist markets, especially as the range of policy goals expanded to include greater stability and equality. But the same is true of the new world of internet capitalism, where law is being enlisted to produce and accompany profound economic and sociotechnical shifts (J. Cohen 2019). The rules may be state-based; they may be created by private actors (think of the way in which Facebook seeks to regulate free speech); or, very often, they take a hybrid, public/private form (as is the case in many aspects of banking, securities, and insurance regulation) (Büthe and Mattli 2013).

The idea of the free market and of the invisible hand has exercised enormous rhetorical power, especially over the idea of a liberal market order. But what this has most often meant is that certain kinds of politics should be excluded from market operations. Hence, one of the leading figures of twentieth-century economic liberal thinking and one of the founding fathers of economic neoliberalism, Friedrich Hayek, believed that market orders had to be 'constituted' by an extremely strong set of laws and institutions, precisely to prevent unconstrained democratic politics both from disrupting efficient markets and from undermining individual freedom (Hayek [1960] 2006). This is extremely important for understanding the global neoliberalism of the post-Cold War world (**see Chapter 4**). This was certainly about economic and financial liberalization and free markets, but the deregulation of the economy domestically required the re-regulation at the level above the state—in the form of more far-reaching economic institutions and new forms of economic governance.

If political ordering and institutions are central to economic markets, including neoliberal economic globalization, then they naturally become central to our understanding of how power operates in the global political economy. Analysts of power distinguish between different levels, faces, or dimensions of power (Barnett and Duvall 2005). They often begin with relational power: the power to get someone to do something that they would not otherwise do. Many of the instruments of economic statecraft described in **Section 15.2** fall exactly into this category—using flows of trade, investment, or money as carrots and sticks to secure political objectives. And political realists have long stressed the kinds of power resources needed to become a major power and to exercise this form of power: size of population and territory, resource endowment, economic dynamism, military capabilities, and internal state strength and coherence.

But power is never simply relational. Institutions help project, cement, and stabilize power. They significantly affect the costs of rule, especially by reducing excessive reliance on direct and often risky and costly coercion, and by 'locking-in' preferred values and policies. This is the so-called second face of power: the power to set agendas, to 'decide what gets decided', and to mobilize bias. But power also has to do with the ideas, ideologies, and ways of thinking that animate those institutions.

Sometimes analysts look at particular sets of economic ideas, tracing, for example, the history and rise of economic neoliberalism from its roots in the 1930s to it becoming a widespread orthodoxy in the 1990s (**see Chapter 4**). Critical theorists seek to deconstruct the imagined geographies and taken-for-granted categories that shape how we think about the global economy. Examples include the categories of 'developed/underdeveloped' or 'First World' and 'Third World' (Doty 1996) or the ways in which the categories of 'emerging powers' and 'BRICS' became politically influential—created not by the states themselves but by Jim O'Neill at Goldman Sachs (J. O'Neill 2001). A wide variety of theoretical approaches have been adopted to unpack what is involved here, from constructivism, to neo-Gramscianism, to those drawing on the sociology of Pierre Bourdieu and Michel Foucault.

Such theories look beyond relational, institutional, and ideational power and often talk about constitutive power. Power cannot be reduced to the interactions of pre-given actors. It is also about the material and discursive conditions that make action possible and that constitute the subjects involved in global politics. Such approaches can sometimes sound abstract and overly structural. But they can have quite straightforward applications.

Consider, for example, the way in which the market-liberal economic orthodoxy of the 1980s and 1990s quite literally constituted finance ministries and central bankers as *the* central actors, both in the foreign economic policy of many developing countries and in most aspects of domestic economic management. Because of the way in which international and regional institutions operated, power shifted within governments: health and education policy came to be effectively controlled by finance ministers and central bankers, who in turn were often closely integrated into particular international and transnational networks. It also involved a discourse of development and of economic policy which delegitimized alternative values and voices. It became the only language in which economic issues could be discussed and it empowered those able or credentialized to speak that language—for example by having studied at particular universities.

So, we can think of functional institutions (in trade, finance, or investment); regional institutions (such as the EU or the Association of Southeast Asian Nations (ASEAN)); and global multilateral institutions (as with the International Monetary Fund (IMF) or World Bank). But individual institutions also come together to form economic orders: the formal rules, informal rules, and meta-rules that create stable expectations about behaviour in a particular economic domain (Drezner and McNamara 2013). Powerful states will always have more options: to determine which issues get negotiated via formal inter-state bodies and which are, for example, managed via market mechanisms; to influence both the rules of the bargaining game and what is allowed onto the agenda; to deploy a wide range of sticks and carrots in the bargaining process, including the threat of direct coercion; and, finally, to walk away from any institution that becomes too constraining.

Institutions are not just concerned with liberal purposes of solving common problems or promoting shared values. They also entrench power hierarchies and the interests of powerful states. The vast majority of weaker actors are increasingly 'rule takers' over a whole range of issues that affect all aspects of social, economic, and political life. But, as power shifts, they also become major sites of power competition and geopolitical rivalry.

15.4 The power of power politics

So far in this chapter we have considered economic statecraft (**see Section 15.2**) and some of the ways in which power operates in the global economy (**see Section 15.3**). But it still leaves open the question of the relative weight of economic factors and of economic structures in determining international political outcomes. Most economists, at the end of the day, believe that the economic story is the most important. Institutions, interest groups, and geopolitics might come in as part of that story. Sometimes they come in as positive factors, as with the role of strong and effective institutions in explanations of successful long-term economic growth. Sometimes they are clearly negative, as with war and geopolitics disrupting mutually beneficial economic exchange. But economics is where most of the work happens. Even if successful economic development does not always translate immediately into political power and military effectiveness, many will argue that all of the major shifts in the world's *military-power* balances have followed from alterations in the *productive* balances (Kennedy 1988).

Marxist economists are the most explicit. Yes, class conflict and the tensions that exist between the smooth development of economic and productive relations, on the one hand, and the rigidity of political structures, on the other, help us understand the contradictions of capitalism. And yes, we understand capitalism as a totality in which the social, the economic, the ecological, and the political are all related. But, in the final instance, it is capitalism that drives the system, and it is one level within the totality of capitalist social relations—the economy—that will be predominant.

An alternative view argues that the international political system has a distinctive dynamic and logic of its own, pressing states to act in particular ways and playing an often decisive influence over foreign economic policy, the character of globalization and global capitalism, and even the characteristics of the actors that make up the system. From this perspective there is something about the international—the coexistence of a multiplicity of separate polities—that cannot be reduced to something else, be it capitalism or some facet of domestic politics (Rosenberg 2016).

15.4.1 States and political realism

Such a view is most frequently found within the tradition of political realism. Realism starts with the assumption of anarchy. Unlike domestic politics, international politics is defined by the absence of a common sovereign or common power. Instead, we live in a self-help system in which each state must look after itself. There is no single government that has a monopoly on the legitimate use of force; international institutions are weak, and the sense of a global community is extremely fragile. Within this politically fragmented world some states are (and will always be) stronger than others, cooperation is difficult, and there is therefore a continual danger of the use of coercion or a resort to force. As John Mearsheimer put it: '[if] a state gets into trouble in the international system, it cannot dial 911 because there is nobody . . . to come to its rescue' (Mearsheimer 2002).

The analytical heartland of realism is therefore built around the role of anarchy, fear, the balance of power, and the national interest. The structural and systemic pressures generated by an anarchic political order shape the environment within which states, and indeed all economic actors, have to operate and make their decisions. It is from this position that realists are deeply suspicious of traditional liberal claims—that economic interdependence and trade are pacifying forces, that economic interdependence requires cooperative institutions, or that economic integration both empowers those groups domestically which have the greatest interest in a peaceful international order and creates transnational personal and social connections.

The claim made by this approach—and its influential variant, neorealism—is not that they offer determinate answers to causal questions, but rather that they tell us a few big and important things, above all about power and how shifting patterns of unequal and balanced power will affect the global political economy. Yet sometimes neorealism seems to concentrate so heavily on material power, war, and military security that the pervasive role of power in global politics is actually underplayed. How so?

In the first place, the importance of power is not limited to questions of military security. A power-inflected understanding of international society is not only concerned with states, anarchy, and military security. International Relations is concerned with the dilemmas of untamed power in all social settings that are characterized by weak institutions and deep value conflict. This view underscores the extent to which interdependence brings with it opportunities for conflict and for a concern with relative gains, along with the need to see relative gains in very broad terms, as the capacity of the strong to lay down the law to the weak and to structure the terms of international political and economic life in ways that reflect their particular interests, values, and ways of seeing the world—hence, its applicability to institutional analysis and political economy as well as security. Finally, it underscores the way in which challenges of shifting power go hand-in-hand with claims and assertions of cultural, national, or religious difference.

Second, the focus on states and state power does not mean that other aspects of the global economy are not important, nor that states are the only important or the all-dominant actors. Of course, as you see throughout this textbook, the global economy is made up of an enormously complex picture of all kinds of economic actors, networks, and varied forms of transnational connectivity and social exchange. However, state power very often *depends on* these other arenas: the existence of alternative governance options (market-based models, civil-society mechanisms); the capacity to shape social, political, and economic processes through which new international norms evolve; and the ability to navigate successfully within and across both global markets and global civil society.

And, still more importantly, we constantly need to ask how far what we see in these other domains may be related to what is happening in the world of states. To what extent was the emergence of economic openness or extensive transnational connections in a given period connected to the level and character of conflict or cooperation between the major powers, to the preferences of dominant actors, or to the distribution of political power? The answers will vary—although there is little to suggest that the movement towards or away from the centrality of states has been uniform or linear. But it is the question that is important, and too frequently neglected when—as in the 1890s, the 1970s, or the 1990s—so many people assumed that economic globalization was a one-way road that would inevitably constrain or erode the role of the state.

Third, material power is obviously and undeniably important to global politics and the global economy. How could it not be? However, neorealists have such a narrow and materialist view of power and such a reductionist view of institutions as simply reflective of state power that they are unable to appreciate the importance of norms and institutions to the stabilization and effectiveness of power. Power is, after all, a social attribute. A great deal of the struggle for political power is the quest for authoritative control that avoids costly and dangerous reliance on brute force and coercion.

To understand power in international relations we must place it side by side with other quintessentially social concepts such as prestige, authority, and legitimacy. And a great deal of what drives global politics has to do with the desire for status—status as rank and the perceived position of a state in the international pecking order (perceived both by oneself and by others), or status as membership within some desired grouping or institution. Status and recognition may have to do with a rising major power wanting equality of treatment from other major powers, whether Germany and Japan in the 1930s, the Soviet Union in the 1960s and 1970s, or China, India, and Russia in the 2020s. Or status may shape the foreign policy of declining powers, unable to adjust to their diminished role and to give up the presumptions of hegemony, as with Britain and the United States. Or it may have to do with the previously marginalized states and societies of the Global South seeking to redress their previous subordination and to build protection from alien domination.

> ### Key Concept: hegemony
>
> This is a concept used to describe a situation of unequal power. It is often used to describe unequal power that is neither exercised through formal empire and the direct control of foreign territories or peoples, nor understood as freely acknowledged leadership. Unlike direct or coercive subordination, hegemony is based on some degree of consent and on a constant, if usually unstable, process of negotiation between the strong and the weak.

Fourth, the modern international system of states has now become global. Globalization should not be seen only in contradistinction to the state. In part this follows from the deep connections between the drivers of globalization in particular periods and patterns of inter-national and inter-imperial politics. In part, and more fundamentally, the most ignored—or taken-for-granted—aspect of globalization has been the globalization of the nation-state. For the first time in human history there is a single global political system with a set of legal and political institutions, diplomatic practices, and accompanying ideologies that developed in Europe and then the wider Western world and which, in the traditional parlance, 'expanded' to form a global international society.

The way in which this story is now told has been extensively revised. There is now far greater emphasis on the agency of the non-Western world, on the role of hierarchy and coercion, on the density of encounters, connections, and contributions from those within but on the margin of a single global order, and on the processes of mutual interaction and constitution. Historians have increasingly sought to bring in the 'Rest' in order to explain the rise of the West. Nevertheless, the result remains that we live in a far more diverse world, with more participants, and with a far greater range of voices and views. Many of these participants come from parts of the world that played no part in the creation of the global economic order in which they are now playing a far more prominent role. Historical and cultural diversity and deep value pluralism erodes the utility of rationalist or economistic approaches to political economy that neglect culture and history.

Finally, there is the generative force of this now-global international. If you want as a society to resist external domination and to achieve meaningful self-determination, if you want to prosper in a highly competitive world, and if you want to secure a back-stop capacity for defence against the most serious threats to your security or identity, then you need to learn to play by the rules of the international political game. This is the sense in which some realists and international society theorists talk of new independent states or of post-revolutionary states being 'socialized' into the dynamics of international politics—under the whiplash of geopolitical necessity, as it is sometimes expressed.

But this is not just about patterns of foreign policy behaviour. It also shapes the character of a state and social organization, including their economic policy choices. After all, if the economic instruments described in **Section 15.2** are really important, you are not going to wait and see if they just happen to be there. You are going actively to seek to foster them by the development of industrial policies, state-led technological development (with geopolitics playing a crucial role in so many such developments from radar, to nuclear fission, to the Internet), and through educational and social policies.

15.4.2 **Power in GPE**

So what does all this mean for our understanding of Global Political Economy? It means that the study of Global Political Economy needs to pay close attention to the distribution of power and to the changing character of the international society. It is not the static distribution of power that matters most, but rather the dynamics of changes over time and the ways in which those changes are interpreted and understood from very different historical and cultural standpoints. Two patterns of power dominate: unequal or hegemonic power, on the one hand, and the balance of power, on the other.

If the international system is indeed conflict-prone and if cooperative institutions are likely to be fragile, then one 'solution' is to examine the potential role of leading states in stabilizing the global economy and in promoting a stable and cooperative economic order. This approach has often built on work in economic history that argues that it was the failure of the

United States to pick up the role of Britain in the nineteenth century international monetary order that led to the Great Depression in the 1930s. It was then the success of US power in the institution-building of the 1940s, followed by the challenges to those institutions in the 1970s and 1980s, that led to the development of so-called hegemonic stability theory, and a wide range of questions to do with how the preferences of dominant states have shaped the structure of world trade and the global political economy more broadly (Keohane 1984; Krasner 1976). With the unipolar moment following the end of the Cold War, the attention given to the links between US and Western power and economic globalization became stronger still.

But hegemony can matter in other ways. When looking at the nineteenth century, the question is not just about whether Britain was a global hegemon. It is also about broader imperial models of economic ordering. This was the central feature of the pre-1914 'liberal' global economy and of the intense wave of globalization which took place in this period. On one side, imperial powers sought colonial possessions as a means of exploiting gains from trade, applied metropolitan systems of law, property rights, and contract to their territories, and provided the physical infrastructure for the expansion of economic exchange. On the other side, there was the role played by collective political action by the colonial powers in defence of an open global economy. This included the collective coercive enforcement of debt (as against the Ottoman Empire); unequal treaties to enforce openness and low tariffs (as with China); the use of naval power to open markets (as in British policy towards Latin America); the collective suppression of piracy; the establishment of extra-territorial jurisdiction through consular, merchant, and admiralty courts scattered across the globe; and the upholding of the generally open system of migration and the mass movement of people, both within and across empires.

But this was also a period of intense geopolitical rivalry between and among the great powers. All of the major players were imperial nation-states and it is this combination of imperialism and nationalism that characterized the geopolitics of the period, driving the economic expansion of Europe and shaping this great wave of economic globalization, culminating in the First World War.

Even after the period of formal European empires, the continued structural inequalities between the developed and underdeveloped world continued to lie at the heart of how the global economy was structured. Formal empire lasted well into the post-1945 period and much historical work has shown how, even in the period of decolonization, policies and modes of thinking developed through empire were central both to relations with what came to be called the 'Third World' and to the design and operation of many economic international institutions. There is great continuity in theories and practices of economic development across the period from empire to decolonization.

How much inequality between North and South has changed is a matter of intense academic dispute. The diffusion of power away from Europe and the United States that was visible for much of the twentieth century seemed to have been reversed by the renewed dominance of the United States after the end of the Cold War. More recently, the rise of China, the development of regional and emerging powers and a broader diffusion of political agency, and the internal failings of the US-led so-called global liberal order have refocused attention on the idea of a post-Western world.

At a minimum, it seems clear that there is no longer a single axis of hierarchy or hegemony and certainly no longer one that places Western power as the sole centre. Instead, economic globalization has led both to the diffusion of power and agency, involving a shift in the balance of power toward China and toward Asia more generally, and to the reconstitution over time of new patterns of stratification and hierarchy, both within and across countries.

And, finally, inequality and different forms of hegemonic power remain central to understanding the forms and outcomes of economic development within particular geographical domains—the USA in Latin America, the Soviet Union in Eastern Europe, Britain and France in parts of Africa, China in Asia, and Russia in its self-described 'near abroad'. In thinking about the relationship between hegemony and the global political economy, great care needs to be taken to specify not just the extent of unequal power but also the functional or geographical domain to which it applies.

What, then, of the balance of power? With the partial and temporary exception of the 1940s, the United States was not a global hegemon after the Second World War. The United States was often challenged by the rise and recovery of other capitalist economies in Europe and Japan, by the Cold War conflict with the Soviet Union, and by the resistance of the Third World. The Cold War was an intensely conflictual balance of power in which geopolitics was intertwined with starkly conflicting ideologies of how modern societies and economies should be organized (Westad 2005). Economic integration between East and West was extremely low. It was an extremely dangerous period, both in terms of the imminent threat of nuclear conflict and, above all, for the millions who suffered as the superpowers fought out their rivalry across the Third World. But the balance of power and ideological conflict was also stabilizing for Western capitalism.

Capitalism across the Western industrialized world was characterized by an important degree of welfarism at home and a limited form of liberalization abroad: as much external liberalization abroad as was compatible with the priority given to social stability domestically. These developments followed from the need to save capitalism from the political and economic devastation caused by the Great Depression, and by the demands of organized labour and other social groups. But geopolitics was also crucial—an important example of the generative power of the international political system. Already in the period of the two World Wars, nationalist mobilization demanded a greater degree of welfare. And as the Cold War unfolded, capitalism was tamed not by the altruism of the capitalists but by the geopolitical and ideological competition with the Soviet Union.

The relationship between the balance of power and political economy has once more returned to the centre of academic and policy attention—with the increased rivalry between China and the United States, with Russia's war on Ukraine and associated conflict with the West, and with the attempts of many in Europe and the United States to see democracy vs authoritarianism as the central cleavage in global politics. The impact of these trends on the direction and character of economic globalization is the subject of the **Chapter 15 Roundtable**.

15.5 **Conclusion**

It is often argued that what makes political economy 'political' is its concern with power. As discussed in **Section 15.2**, this can involve understanding the ways in which foreign policy uses economic instruments for power-political ends. It can also mean understanding the ways in which power is central to the construction of both economic institutions and, more importantly, functional, regional, or global economic orders. But it also means seeing the international political system as something that needs to be understood in its own right and according to its distinctive logics and dynamics.

Such a view does not depend on some alleged deep-rooted human drive for power, as some realists have argued. Nor does it depend on some timeless and eternal logic of politics. The logics of state power and the territorial sources of power connected with state institutions as a distinctly modern phenomenon took shape in the course of the nineteenth century and, for the first time in human history, now constitute a global political order. Within this now-global system, diversity and difference remain basic features of our common humanity, and competition for power and contending conceptions of order create a strong tendency to encourage both sentiments of reasonable fear and apprehension, and still rational but far more dangerous sentiments about relative position, status, recognition, and resentment.

Sophisticated versions of Marxism have had to come to terms with the return of geopolitics and the revival of what they characterize as inter-imperialist rivalries. David Harvey, for example, sees 'imperialism as the outcome of tension between two sources of power. One is the territorial source of power lying in state organizations. The other is the capitalist logic of power, which is the control of money and assets, and the flow and circulation of capital' (Harvey 2003).

What of modern liberals? Dani Rodrik unpacks the paradox of globalization and of attempts to regulate globalization. The problem is that, as he puts it, 'global markets, states and democracy can't coexist' (Rodrik 2011: 200–01). This trilemma is undoubtedly important. But note what is missing: Rodrik sometimes shifts from talking about states to talking about nations and national self-determination, but there is little place for strong claims about identity, for the demands of resurgent nationalism, and for the argument that sovereignty matters because it enshrines, embodies, and protects some highly valued set of values that give meaning to a particular community. In contrast to what economists are likely to accept, this is the view that 'who we are' matters far more to many people than 'how much we get'—whether we are talking about Brexit in the United Kingdom or supporters of Donald Trump in the United States. And still more striking is the absence of any mention of power, conflict, and the renewed possibility of major war.

It is therefore very hard to make sense of the many spaces where geopolitics spills over into trade, foreign investment, the regulation of cyber technologies, and the ways in which distributional conflict and competition over substantive values trump any account built around actual or potential mutual interest. In short, Global Political Economy without a heavy emphasis on state power, geopolitics, and hegemony will be a stunted enquiry.

Key Points

- States use many forms of economic statecraft in pursuit of their foreign policy goals, including economic sanctions and different forms of conditionality.

- Strategic assets are parts of an economy that are seen as crucial to sovereignty and national power. In the twenty-first century, the nature of strategic assets is shifting and coming ever more to include AI, supercomputing, and quantum technologies.

- Markets depend on institutions and different forms of economic governance. Power and economic power operate at different levels: power exercised within a specific relationship; power through institutions; power via ideas and norms; and the power to constitute action and actors.

- Economics undoubtedly shapes international politics. But the international political system has a distinctive dynamic and logic of its own, pressing states to act in particular ways and having an often decisive influence over foreign economic policy, the character of globalization and global capitalism, and even the characteristics of the actors that make up the system.

- The global political economy continues to be shaped by geopolitical and military conflicts, both when these break out into the open (as between Russia and the West) and also by the likely protracted awkward and dangerous coexistence between the USA and China.

Further Reading

Baldwin, D. (1985), *Economic Statecraft* (Princeton, NJ: Princeton University Press). The classic modern study of economic statecraft, including economic power and economic coercion.

Barnett, M., and Duvall, R. (2005), *Power and Global Governance* (Cambridge: Cambridge University Press). Provides a clear exposition of the different faces or facets of power in International Relations.

Cohen, J. (2019), *Between Truth and Power: The Legal Construction of Informational Capitalism* (Oxford: Oxford University Press). Provides an analysis of how law and informational capitalism are deeply intertwined.

Drezner, D., and McNamara, K. (2013), 'International Political Economy: Global Financial Orders and the 2008 Financial Crisis', *Perspectives on Politics*, 11(1): 155–66. Using the financial crisis as a lens, this article unpacks how to think about an economic or financial 'order'.

Farrell, H., and Newman, A. (2019), 'Weaponized Interdependence: How Global Economic Networks Shape State Coercion', *International Security*, 44(1): 42–79. Examines the ways in which networked capitalism creates new spaces for weaponized interdependence.

Chapter 15 Roundtable discussion

Is the increasing geopolitical rivalry between the United States and China reshaping globalization?

Roundtable 15.1
Opening contribution **Andrew Hurrell**

Globalization has *always* been shaped by state power and geopolitics. What, then, does intensified geopolitical rivalry mean for globalization today?

First, as in previous periods, increased geopolitical rivalry is leading to the politicization and securitization of many aspects of the global economy—precisely of the kind illustrated by the headlines with which **Chapter 15** began. The line between 'normal economic exchange' and 'politically problematic economic exchange' is being redrawn. The instruments of economic statecraft are becoming once more central to the working of the global political economy. Both Covid-19 and the worsening of US–China relations had already intensified economic nationalism and economic rivalry. Economic sanctions against Russia since its invasion of Ukraine have taken this to a new level.

As happened in previous periods—such as the economic blockade against Germany in the First World War—it is far from easy to switch globalization back on once trade, investment, and other ties have been disrupted and so heavily politicized and securitized.

It is not difficult to imagine how intensified rivalry could continue to reshape both particular sets of economic ties and the broader management of the global economy. It is true that there are very important differences with the Cold War period: there is no straightforward ideological clash between two systems, nor can we see the rigid alliance systems of the Cold War (Christensen 2021). China's policy cannot be categorized simply in terms of revisionism (inevitably pressed, as realists would see it, to challenge core elements of the US-led post-Cold War order) or status quo (being socialized into the liberal global order by the obvious degree to which it is the liberal global order itself that has provided the very basis for China's rise).

Yet a military clash over Taiwan or the South China Sea would be highly disruptive. There are clear signs of deepening regulatory competition between the USA, the EU, and China over who will set the rules for economic globalization in the future. China has already begun to promote its own alternative institutional arrangements, as with the Asian Infrastructure Investment Bank (AIIB). And such developments could well intensify the already-existing trends towards a greater regionalization of the global economy, visible both in the general way in which the centre of gravity of global capitalism has shifted to Asia and the Indo-Pacific and in the conscious policy of China to pursue macro-regionalism in the form of the Belt and Road Initiative (Yan 2021).

Second, however, it is important not to exaggerate the role of geopolitics. There are many challenges to globalization that have little or nothing to do with US–China rivalry. The political backlash against what is characterized as neoliberal globalization and the desire to 'take back control' and reassert national sovereignty has many causes—the instabilities and inequalities of global capitalism, specific patterns of migration and people-movement, the undemocratic character of regional and global governance, and the many failures of the so-called global liberal order to deliver on its professed goals and values.

Equally, the diffusion of power away from the West and towards the Global South is a historical development that is far wider than just the rise of China. It is true that a geopolitically divided world will affect countries' foreign policy choices—for example in having to decide whether to 'choose sides' or to engage economically with one side or the other. But the countries of the Global South have been unwilling to take sides or to follow the USA and Europe, who seek to create a camp of liberal democratic states in opposition to authoritarian regimes.

Third, there are other forms of globalization whose consequences are difficult to escape. US–China rivalry is embedded in an increasingly complex system in which all states and societies face shared and potentially catastrophic global risks, from climate change, to pandemics, to rapid developments in artificial intelligence (AI). It is certainly true that many past predictions of the revolutionary impact of globalization proved to be exaggerated. Nevertheless, the move from the global to the planetary and the coming of all of humanity into a shared community of fate as a result of nuclear weapons, climate change, and perhaps now hard-to-control technologies around AI does represent a fundamental set of changes.

A major part of the complexity of the present and likely future Global Political Economy (GPE) has to do with the interaction of the 'old' and the 'new': of the impact of new technologies and of 'new' forms of scientific knowledge (on economics, on weapons systems, and on patterns of connectivity) on 'old' logics and dynamics, especially the dynamics of international political competition, geopolitical rivalry, nationalist self-assertion, and war. Even if gloomy realist predictions of inevitable major-power conflict prove wrong, all more elaborate forms of global governance will depend on stable understandings among the major states of the system. Spheres of influence, major-power arms control, and mutual geopolitical restraint may well have to sit side-by-side with the inevitability of complex and often intrusive forms of governance on climate change or global finance.

For much of the post-Cold War period, the 'global system' seemed stable—a combination of Western power and market-led and technologically driven globalization. However, the 2008 financial crisis, the gap between the liberal rhetoric of Western states and their often far from liberal behaviour, the Covid-19 pandemic, the continuing rise of China and the broader diffusion of power and political agency, and the Russian war against Ukraine have all made people more aware of the need to think about de-coupling, disintegration, and de-globalization.

But it has historically been precisely in previous periods of 'de-globalization' that crucial developments occurred which shaped the subsequent phase of globalization—think of the impact of the Great Depression on the industrialization of non-Western countries. And, while it is correct to think of globalization as a non-linear process, we should not think of the stops and starts as being on the same road leading to the same destination.

Roundtable 15.2
Response **Jue Wang**

Andrew Hurrell's opening statement underlines the complex impacts of the US–China rivalry on globalization (**see Roundtable 15.1**). On one hand, 'de-coupling' and 'greater regionalization' risk reversing globalization; on the other hand, China does not seek to overturn the 'US-led post-Cold War order' that facilitates globalization. Yet instead of focusing on the broader contextual factors of such complexity, as in Hurrell's discussion, I suggest it is also valuable to underline the dynamism of US–China rivalry itself. I want to argue that the power competition between the two countries does not reverse the (neo)liberal trend of globalization in the long run.

Let's start with what US–China rivalry is *not*. It is *not* a competition between two equal powers. The USA is superior in economic output, political influence, and governance capacity in global affairs.

Further, it is *neither* an exogenous factor *nor* a static condition of globalization. Instead, US–China rivalry reflects a dynamic power relationship between the world's largest and second largest economies. It specifically exhibits the process of China rising to challenge US hegemony, and the USA reacting with various tools ranging from defensive measures to hostile suppression. As Hurrell rightly points out, the rivalry is rooted in globalization, given that being integrated into the global economy enabled China to rise and rival the USA. And therefore, instead of being an exogenous variable shaping globalization, this rivalry evolves along with globalization.

Meanwhile, the power balance between the two countries varies over time. Sometimes China strongly challenges US dominance in the international economy. On other occasions, however, the tension between the two is alleviated through effective collaboration.

When the tension between the two countries rises, their rivalry undermines globalization. For instance, the 2018 US–China trade war jeopardized regional and global supply chains and caused turbulence in the international stock market. High tariffs were deployed in both countries on imports from the other country. Moreover, the US government not only tightened the screening of Chinese investment in the US high-tech sectors but also sanctioned Chinese tech companies. The USA dissuaded its Western allies from cooperating with China in high-tech, pushing China to turn to new partners. Consequently, China's engagement in the globalization of technological innovation has been severely hindered.

Further, as China's overseas development finance increases, the USA is wary about China's self-serving and state-led approach and its growing influence in the developing world. The Obama administration rejected the Asian Infrastructure Investment Bank (AIIB); the Biden administration proposed a Western alternative to China's Belt and Road Initiative. The USA also occasionally blocks China's overseas development projects. For instance, Washington opposed a World Bank project to connect Nauru to Guam—a regional hub and territory of the USA—with undersea cables, as the project included a bid from Huawei, a Chinese company (Barrett and Yew 2021).

US–China rivalry thus risks dividing the developing world into two camps that depend on finance from either China or the West. In a worse scenario, the rivalry may be a race to the bottom, as Scarlett Cornelissen suggests in **Roundtable 15.3**.

On the other hand, the dynamism of the power balance also depends on how each side handles the tension. Hurrell points out that China and the USA do not have fundamental or straightforward ideological clashes, which makes it easier to imagine them negotiating and compromising in order to de-escalate the tension. For instance, as the tension in trade and finance continues, both the USA and China have been making efforts to solve their disputes, despite the interruption caused by the rising nationalism in both countries, and especially China's swelling assertiveness and US political polarization.

In spite of these short-term disruptions, I would therefore suggest that US–China rivalry is unlikely to reverse globalization in the long run. Over time, US–China power competition will not fundamentally challenge the core elements of the (neo)liberal trend of globalization, nor its governance structure. China is indeed dissatisfied with the US- and Western-dominated policy focus and institutional structure of several liberal international institutions, especially the International Monetary Fund (IMF) and the World Bank. Beijing has accordingly advocated for reforms in the respective regimes in which these institutions are centred. But these reforms do not revoke the rules and norms of the liberal international economic regime, which have effectively facilitated globalization.

The most remarkable achievements of China's efforts toward IMF institutional reform were the 2010 voting share reform that made China the Fund's third-largest shareholder and the renminbi's entry into the Special Drawing Rights basket. Neither of these undermined US dominance in the IMF or the Fund's authority in international finance. In trade, although China's participation in regional trade institutions—such as the ASEAN–China Free Trade Agreement and Regional Comprehensive Economic Partnership—involves narrower issue coverage and lower levels of liberalization, it does not seriously challenge the principles of the World Trade Organization (WTO) and global trade regime (Sampson 2021).

To the contrary, on occasions when China did attempt to actually challenge the status quo, it was often not successful. For instance, China pushed the IMF to discipline the US dollar and to disconnect the international monetary system from US domestic interests following the 2008 financial crisis, but failed. China's attempt to be recognized at the WTO as a market economy, viewed by many as undermining the fair competition aims of the global trade regime, also failed.

Similarly, the China-led AIIB may be regarded as an alternative to the incumbent international development finance regime. Nevertheless, the AIIB replicates many features of the World Bank's institutional structure and project procedures. Further, although China's multilateral and bilateral development finance approaches encourage more involvement by state agencies, many of these agencies prioritize their commercial interests over the states' foreign policy goals.

So, the Chinese approach does not drastically challenge the status quo, nor does it fundamentally disrupt globalization. In fact, we could argue instead that the Chinese model presents merely a variation of the neoliberal business-centric and market-enabling rationale that prevails in globalization (Gonzalez-Vicente 2019).

Roundtable 15.3
Response Scarlett Cornelissen

In his opening contribution to the **Chapter 15 Roundtable**, Andrew Hurrell notes how intensifying geopolitical rivalry in the contemporary era has had important consequences for economic globalization (**see Roundtable 15.1**). What I think needs to be made more explicit are the structural underpinnings of this rivalry, which are often overlooked, as is the way this rivalry unevenly shapes political economic fortunes across the globe, and in particular in the Global South. I'll focus here on Africa.

Globalization is an interrelated process of flows—of commodities, ideas, people, data, intelligence, and of course, pathogens—as well as control (Harvey 1992; Middell and Naumann 2010). In the era of late globalization, and in the context of the rise of China and a number of other states from the Global South, these twin logics of flow and control have become of greater constitutive significance for the inter-state system. China's expansion has spearheaded new geographies of accumulation—new regional centres and sub-systems of production and consumption—but it has also entailed the development of alternative institutional regimes, including the BRICS grouping (Brazil, Russia, India, China, and South Africa), the New Development Bank, and the Asian Infrastructure Investment Bank.

These changes in the geographical, institutional, and ideological configurations of global capitalism trigger new geopolitical rivalries in the global political economy today. Hurrell correctly points out that globalization has its own dynamic. It is also important to point out that globalization takes on special significance in the context of geopolitics. Rather than only reshaping globalization, geopolitical competition between the major powers of the day is a function of the specific juncture of global capitalism and its contemporary form. But current major power conflict has been a race to the bottom, impacting multilateralism and global governance, and with some stark implications for the smaller and more peripheral members in the world system.

For the African continent, the changing geopolitical environment since the turn of the twenty-first century has had major repercussions on its political economy. Probably the most defining change has been in the form of Chinese capital. China's trade with the African continent rapidly surpassed that between Africa and traditional partners like the EU and the United States. Investment flows from China helped African mining, real estate, agricultural, and financial sectors grow. Large-scale commodity exports brought revenue and underpinned Africa's erstwhile 'rise'. And China has become the major financier and constructor of African infrastructure, changing the urban landscape across large parts of the continent (Oqubay and Lin 2019).

But there has been asymmetry and dependence in the economic relationship from the start. China casts a long shadow over Africa's political economy, while African states seemingly exercise little clout in this relationship. The new China-led financial institutions—and the envisaged Belt and Road Initiative—have drawn many African states more firmly into China's regime of accumulation, although the one-time promise of greater leverage for Africa through participation in an alternative, China-shaped global financial architecture (Qobo and Soko 2015) has not materialized. Instead, poor loan governance sees numerous African states facing a debt trap. In all, while in many ways Chinese capital has been transformative, it has not brought substantive improvement in terms of the continent's position in the world system.

This is because China's rise on the African continent is part of a wider geopolitical dynamic in which Africa simultaneously is an arena for big-power contesting for a stake in the continent's resource economies and infrastructure development agenda, and is incidental to the major forces of global realignment. Other states from the Global North and East have been responding to China's growing influence on the African continent. The increase in Africa development and investment promotion summits hosted by Asian and Western powers in recent years, and new channels of resource diplomacy, suggest a new geostrategic orientation to the continent. Rather than raise the continent's bargaining capacity, however, this sees it caught in the competing agendas of external players arranged along an East–West axis.

At the same time, the continent is largely cut off from the major shifts in global economic structures conditioned by US–China and broader geopolitical rivalry. Recent years have seen the formation of trade blocs across the Indo-Pacific and Atlantic worlds. Mega-trade blocs such as the Comprehensive and Progressive Agreement on Trans-Pacific Partnership, along with a number of smaller regional blocs, are likely to reshape global trade flows. While Africa launched its own continental bloc in 2021—the Africa Comprehensive Free Trade Area—it is unclear where Africa will position in the emerging global trade landscape and whether there will be more or less opportunity for the continent to participate in new global value chains—echoing the discussion in **Chapter 10**.

Furthermore, the spilling over of geopolitical rivalries into the science, technology, and research domains—and the spectre of global 'science blocs' with attendant knowledge and technology nationalism—also have implications for the continent's technology development needs and its longer-term post-Covid-19 recovery prospects. The fallouts from the global pandemic are likely to be prolonged on the African continent, marked by employment and livelihood loss, the expansion of poverty, and compounded food and human insecurity. Add to that the effects of climate change, generally affecting the most vulnerable more severely, and the challenges facing the continent are clear.

In an interdependent setting like the contemporary system, the risks of a global retreat into camps of 'haves' and 'have-nots' are large. Major power competition tends to reinforce this structural division.

In the process, major global commons issues are not addressed in a way that would ensure responsiveness to the concerns of the less powerful in the world system. Globalization has produced winners and losers over the past decades. It created new geographies of wealth, but it has also been associated with rising inequalities and deepening divisions. Intensified major power rivalry and the related tendency towards a descent into nationalism can create even more losers.

In reflecting on the nature of world order and the distribution of power, it is important to ask not only about what 'is', but also what 'ought to be' and why.

Roundtable 15.4
Response **Mustafa Kutlay**

The relative retreat of US hegemony and the parallel rise of China as an influential global player bring important questions to the fore concerning the future of the liberal international order and the evolution of state–market relations in the coming years. I argue that the impact of these shifts, and of increasing geopolitical rivalry, are significantly re-shaping globalization, and doing so in two major ways. First, the model of neoliberal globalization is becoming less popular in the face of major power transitions. Second, state capitalism is likely to emerge as an alternative political economy paradigm in different parts of the world.

It is clear that neoliberal globalization is facing significant challenges. Since the Global Financial Crisis of 2008, the orthodox policy compact has been questioned in different parts of the world. In his first major address to the US Congress, for instance, Joe Biden argued that 'trickle-down economics has never worked' and claimed, 'Wall Street did not build this country [United States]. The middle class built this country. And unions built the middle class' (Biden 2021).

At the same time, China has been experimenting with an alternative policy paradigm, dubbed 'state capitalism' (Kurlantzick 2016; Nölke et al. 2015). This model of state–market relations has two fundamental aspects. First, the state is considered a *market-maker* in the economy, not simply a regulatory actor providing a conducive institutional context for market activity. The state acts as an investor through various fiscal policy instruments, active industrial policy, and sovereign wealth funds. The idea is to implement certain competitive-advantage defying policies and support domestic companies in their quest for a larger market share in the world economy. This form of state capitalism does not reject globalization but envisions a more controlled integration of the world economy and global value chains. China, of course, is a prime example, with several state-controlled corporations making it into the *Fortune 500* list of companies.

Second, state capitalist models often rely on illiberal political regimes—mostly incompatible with liberal democracy. 'Strongmen' regimes, unconstrained by institutional checks and balance, appear as the predominant political governance type in most state capitalist economies. Therefore, state capitalism constitutes a challenge to both the liberal international order and neoliberal globalization as we know it (Nölke et al. 2015).

Although I agree with Andrew Hurrell and other contributors here that globalization is not likely to be reversed completely anytime soon, it may take a more controlled form, susceptible to conflict and more frequent disruptions, in the age of growing geopolitical rivalry between the United States and China. Furthermore, as Andrew Hurrell rightly points out, '[t]here are many challenges to globalization that have little or nothing to do with US–China rivalry' (**see Roundtable 15.1**). The widening income gap, wealth inequality, the inability of certain segments of societies to take advantage of globalization processes, and the growing power of a few large companies have all raised questions about the current version of globalization—all thrown into even sharper relief by the Covid-19 pandemic.

The upcoming period is likely to be a hybrid era in which competing political economy paradigms coexist and compete. With the Biden presidency in the United States, it has become clearer that the United States is likely to take a more determined stance in upholding the liberal international order—that is, liberal democracy, free market economy, and the rule-based international order. Meanwhile, China is likely to stick to state capitalism while not completely trying to overturn globalization. These competing political economy visions, along with hegemonic power transitions, seem likely to constitute the new ground in international political economy.

Like Scarlett Cornelissen (**see Roundtable 15.3**), I think there is a further important question to ask: What does this mean for developing countries in the Global South? The loosening of the neoliberal policy paradigm is an opportunity for states to implement more development-friendly and inclusive policies. Biden's administration seems attuned to the idea of the state playing an active role by creating 'good jobs', supporting the real economy, and implementing active distribution policies. The International Monetary Fund (IMF) similarly seems to have become more sensitive to the adverse impacts of neoliberal globalization (such as income inequality, the negative fallout of austerity policies, and the risks of social exclusion).

Only time will tell how these understandings will translate into actions—and to what extent, if at all. However, the apparent shift in the dominant economic discourse opens a window for states in the Global South to experiment with alternative development ideas beyond the neoliberal orthodoxy that has failed to deliver inclusive and sustainable development.

It is also promising to witness the 'democratization of globalization' process. The G7 grouping composed of advanced Western economies, for instance, was replaced by the G20, and the voting share of non-Western states increased in the World Bank and IMF. Of course, these and other governance reforms since the Global Financial Crisis of 2008 were not revolutionary. Nonetheless, they were an important step in the right direction to make global governance more pluralistic.

There is another side to the debate, though. The intensifying geopolitical and geoeconomic rivalry between the United States and China is likely to push states to take sides. At the same time, the democratic backlash in global politics is likely to create new uncertainties for those states. This creates new and complex challenges for developing countries in the Global South because liberal democracy is no longer the 'only game in town'.

Although globalization is unlikely to be reversed completely, it is likely to be more fragile and susceptible to disruptions in times of great power rivalry.

Over to you ...

1 Andrew Hurrell (**see Roundtable 15.1**) and Jue Wang (**see Roundtable 15.2**) both underline the important point that the contemporary rise of China was enabled by globalization, and Wang in particular makes the argument that we shouldn't get carried away with thinking that the character of China's political economy is really so different from the neoliberal model. Are we in danger of exaggerating a 'clash of globalizations' narrative when we talk about the impact of China's rise and the geopolitical rivalry between China and the United States?

2 In **Roundtable 15.3**, Scarlett Cornelissen talks powerfully about how intensified major power rivalry heightens the risk of a 'global retreat into camps of "haves" and "have-nots"'—an argument in different ways echoed by Mustafa Kutlay in **Roundtable 15.4**. What are the signs that this is happening, and what role does major power rivalry play in different parts of the world in creating this division?

3 What does the **Chapter 15 Roundtable** suggest to you about how well the major theories of GPE capture the evolving power structures of the contemporary global political economy? In what ways, if any, do new kinds of geopolitical rivalry and events like the Russian war in Ukraine challenge the dominant ways of thinking about GPE?

References

Abbott, K., and Snidal, D. (2009), 'Strengthening International Regulation Through Transnational New Governance: Overcoming the Orchestration Deficit', *Vanderbilt Journal of Transnational Law*, 42: 501–78.

Acharya, A. (2014a), *The End of American World Order* (Cambridge: Polity).

Acharya, A. (2014b), *Rethinking Power, Institutions and Ideas in World Politics: Whose IR?* (London: Routledge).

Acharya, A., and Buzan, B. (2007), 'Why Is There No Non-Western International Relations Theory? An Introduction', *International Relations of the Asia-Pacific*, 7(3): 287–312.

Acharya, A., and Plesch, D. (2020), 'The United Nations: Managing and Reshaping a World Order', *Global Governance*, 26(2): 221–35.

'Acta de Tarapacá' (Tarapacá Manifesto) (2020), http://www.chungara.cl/Vols/otros/acta_tarapaca.pdf, accessed 13 September 2022.

Adedeji, A. (1994), 'An Alternative for Africa', *Journal of Democracy*, 5(4): 119–32.

Adepoju, P. (2021), 'Africa Prepares for COVID-19 Vaccines', *Lancet Microbe*, 2(2).

Agarwala, N., and Chaudhary, R. D. (2021), 'Made in China 2025': Poised for Success? *India Quarterly*, 77(3): 424–61.

Aghion, P., and Bolton, P. (1997), 'A Theory of Trickle-Down Growth and Development', *Review of Economic Studies*, 64(2): 151–72.

Agnew, J. (2007), 'Know-Where: Geographies of Knowledge of World Politics', *International Political Sociology*, 1(2): 138–48.

Ake, C. (1981), *A Political Economy of Africa*, Vol. 4 (London: Longman).

Alesina A., and Rodrik, D. (1994), 'Distributive Politics and Economic Growth', *Quarterly Journal of Economics*, 109(2): 465–90.

Alford, M. (2016), 'Trans-scalar Embeddedness and Governance Deficits in Global Production Networks: Crisis in South African Fruit', *Geoforum*, 75: 52–63.

Alford, M. (2020), 'Antagonistic Governance in South African Fruit Global Production Networks: A Neo-Gramscian Perspective', *Global Networks*, 20(1): 42–64.

Alford, M., Barrientos, S., and Visser, M. (2017), 'Multi-scalar Labour Agency in Global Production Networks: Contestation and Crisis in South African Fruit', *Development and Change*, 48(4): 721–45.

Alford, M., Kothari, U., and Pottinger, L. (2019), 'Re-articulating Labour in Global Production Networks: The Case of Street Traders in Barcelona', *Environment and Planning D: Society and Space*, 37(6): 1081–99.

Alford, M., and Phillips, N. (2018), 'The Political Economy of State Governance in Global Production Networks: Change, Crisis and Contestation in the South African Fruit Sector', *Review of International Political Economy*, 25(1): 98–121.

Alkire, S. (2021), 'Progress in Eradicating Multidimensional Poverty: Evidence from the Global MPI', https://www.un.org/development/desa/dspd/wp-content/uploads/sites/22/2021/05/Alkire_paper.pdf, accessed 12 September 2022.

Alkire, S., and Foster, J. (2011), 'Counting and Multidimensional Poverty Measurement', *Journal of Public Economics*, 95(7–8): 476–87.

Allan, J. I. (2021), *The New Climate Activism* (Toronto: University of Toronto Press).

Almendral, A. (2020), 'Trapped by Pandemic, Ships' Crews Fight Exhaustion and Despair', *New York Times*, 9 September.

Alston, P. (2004), '"Core Labour Standards" and the Transformation of the International Labour Rights Regime', *European Journal of International Law*, 15(3): 457–521.

Altenburg, T., Chen, X., Lütkenhorst, W., Staritz, C., and Whitfield, L. (2020), 'Exporting Out of China or Out of Africa? Automation Versus Relocation in the Global Clothing Industry', Discussion Paper, No. 1/2020, Deutsches Institut für Entwicklungspolitik (DIE), Bonn.

Alvaredo, F., Chancel, L., Piketty, T., Saez, E., and Zucman, G. (2018), *World Inequality Report 2018* (Paris: World Inequality Lab).

Amadi, L. (2012), 'Africa, Beyond the New Dependency: A Political Economy', *African Journal of Political Science and International Relations*, 6(8): 191–203.

Amengual, M. (2010), 'Complementary Labor Regulation: The Uncoordinated Combination of

State and Private Regulators in the Dominican Republic', *World Development*, 38(3): 405–14.

Amengual, M., Distelhorst, G., and Tobin, D. (2020), 'Global Purchasing as Labor Regulation: The Missing Middle', *Industrial and Labor Relations Review*, 73(4): 817–40.

Amin, S. (1974), 'Accumulation and Development: A Theoretical Model', *Review of African Political Economy*, 1(1): 9–26.

Amin, S., Atta-Mills, C., Bujra, A., Hamid, G., and Mkandawire, T. (1978), 'Social Sciences and the Development Crisis in Africa: Problems and Prospects, A CODESRIA Working Paper', *Africa Development/Afrique et Développement*, 3(4): 23–45.

Andreas, P. (2010), 'The Politics of Measuring Illicit Flows and Policy Effectiveness', in **P. Andreas** and **K. Greenhill** (eds.), *Sex, Drugs, and Body Counts: The Politics of Numbers in Global Crime and Conflict* (Ithaca, NY: Cornell University Press), 23–45.

Andreas, P., and Nadelmann, E. (2006), *Policing the Globe: Criminalization and Crime Control in International Relations* (Oxford: Oxford University Press).

Annan, K. A. (2002), 'What Is the International Community? Problems without Passports', *Foreign Policy*, 132 (September/October): 30–31.

Anner, M. (2017), 'Monitoring Workers' Rights: The Limits of Voluntary Social Compliance Initiatives in Labor Repressive Regimes', *Global Policy*, 8: 56–65.

Anner, M. (2019), 'Predatory Purchasing Practices in Global Apparel Supply Chains and the Employment Relations Squeeze in the Indian Garment Export Industry', *International Labour Review*, 158(4): 705–27.

Anner, M. (2020), 'Squeezing Workers' Rights in Global Supply Chains: Purchasing Practices in the Bangladesh Garment Export Sector in Comparative Perspective', *Review of International Political Economy*, 27(2): 320–47.

Anner, M. (2022), 'Power Relations in Global Supply Chains and the Unequal Distribution of Costs during Crises: Abandoning Garment Suppliers and Workers during the COVID-19 Pandemic', *International Labour Review*, 161(1): 59–82.

Anner, M., and Bair, J. (2016), *The Bulk of the Iceberg: A Critique of the Stern Center's Report on Worker Safety in Bangladesh* (State College, PA: Center for Global Workers' Rights).

Anner, M., Bair, J., and Blasi, J. (2013), 'Towards Joint Liability in Global Supply Chains: Addressing the Root Causes of Labor Violations in International Subcontracting Networks', *Comparative Labor Law and Policy Journal*, 35(1), 1–43.

Archick, K. (2004), 'Cybercrime: The Council of Europe Convention', CRS Report for Congress, RS21208, 22 July.

Ariff, M. (2017), 'Islamic Banking in Malaysia: The Changing Landscape', *Institutions and Economies*, 9(2): 1–13.

Aronoff, K., Battistoni, A., Cohen, D. A., and Riofrancos, T. (2019), *A Planet to Win: Why We Need a Green New Deal* (Verso Books).

Asamblea General de las Naciones Unidas (2016), *Resolución aprobada por la Asamblea General el 19 de septiembre de 2016 [sin remisión previa a una Comisión Principal (A/71/L.1)] 70/1. Declaración de Nueva York para los Refugiados y los Migrantes.*

Atkinson, A. B. (2005), 'Is Rising Income Inequality Inevitable? A Critique of the Transatlantic Consensus', in *Wider Perspectives on Global Development*, Studies in Development Economics and Policy (London: Palgrave Macmillan).

Auld, G., Renckens, S., and Cashore, B. (2015), 'Transnational Private Governance between the Logics of Empowerment and Control', *Regulation & Governance*, 9(2): 108–24.

Autor, D. H., Dorn, D., and Hanson, G. H. (2013), 'The China Syndrome: Local Labor Market Effects of Import Competition in the United States', *American Economic Review*, 103(6): 2121–68.

Autor, D. H., Dorn, D., and Hanson, G. H. (2016), 'The China Shock: Learning from Labor-Market Adjustment to Large Changes in Trade', *Annual Review of Economics*, 8: 205–40.

Ayoob, M. (2020), 'The UN and North–South Relations in the Security Arena', *Global Governance*, 26(2): 251–61.

Azevedo, J. P., Inchauste, G., Olivieri, S., Saavedra, J., and Winkler, H. (2013), 'Is Labor Income Responsible for Poverty Reduction? A Decomposition Approach', Policy Research Working Paper No. 6414, The World Bank, Washington, DC.

Babic, M., Garcia-Bernardo, J., and Heemskerk, E. M. (2020), 'The Rise of Transnational State Capital: State-Led Foreign Investment in the 21st Century', *Review of International Political Economy*, 27(3): 433–75.

Bair, J. (2008), 'Analysing Global Economic Organization: Embedded Networks and Global Chains Compared', *Economy and Society*, 37(3): 339–64.

Bair, J. (2017), 'Contextualising Compliance: Hybrid Governance in Global Value Chains', *New Political Economy*, 22(2): 169–85.

Bair, J., Anner, M., and Blasi, J. (2020), 'The Political Economy of Private and Public Regulation in Post-Rana Plaza Bangladesh', *ILR Review*, 73(4): 969–94.

Bair, J., and Gereffi, G. (2001), 'Local Clusters in Global Chains: The Causes and Consequences of Export Dynamism in Torreon's Blue Jeans Industry', *World Development*, 29(11): 1885–903.

Bakewell, O. (2009), 'South–South Migration and Human Development: Reflections on African Experiences', MPRA Paper 19185, University Library of Munich, Germany.

Bakker, I. (2007), 'Social Reproduction and the Constitution of a Gendered Political Economy', *New Political Economy*, 12(4): 541–56.

Baldwin, D. (1985), *Economic Statecraft* (Princeton: Princeton University Press).

Baldwin, R. (2016), *The Great Convergence: Information Technology and the New Globalization* (Cambridge, MA: Belknap Press of Harvard University Press).

Ban, C. (2015), 'Austerity Versus Stimulus? Understanding Fiscal Policy Change at the International Monetary Fund Since the Great Recession', *Governance*, 28(2): 167–83.

Ban, C., Seabrooke, L., and Freitas, S. (2016), 'Grey Matter in Shadow Banking: International Organizations and Expert Strategies in Global Financial Governance', *Review of International Political Economy*, 23(6): 1001–33.

Baran, P., (1957), 'The Political Economy of Growth', *Monthly Review*.

Barbieri, P., Boffelli, A., and Elia, S., et al. (2020), 'What Can We Learn about Reshoring after Covid-19?' *Operations Management Research*, 13(3): 131–6.

Bardi, U. (2011), *The Limits to Growth Revisited* (New York: Springer).

Barnett, M., and Duvall, R. (2005) (eds.), *Power in Global Governance* (Cambridge: Cambridge University Press).

Barratt Brown, M. (2007), '"Fair Trade" with Africa', *Review of African Political Economy*, 34 (112): 267–77.

Barrett, J. and **Yew, L. T.** (2021), 'Exclusive Pacific Undersea Cable Project Sinks after U.S. Warns Against Chinese Bid', *Reuters*, 18 June, https://www.reuters.com/world/asia-pacific/exclusive-pacific-undersea-cable-project-sinks-after-us-warns-against-chinese-2021-06-18/, accessed 8 September 2022.

Barrientos, S. (2008), 'Contract Labour: The "Achilles Heel" of Corporate Codes in Commercial Value Chains', *Development and Change,* 39(6): 977–90.

Barrientos, S. (2013), '"Labour Chains": Analysing the Role of Labour Contractors in Global Production Networks', *Journal of Development Studies*, 49(8): 1058–71.

Barrientos, S. (2019), *Gender and Work in Global Value Chains: Capturing the Gains?* (Cambridge: Cambridge University Press).

Barrientos, S., Dolan, C., and Tallontire, A. (2003), 'A Gendered Value Chain Approach to Codes of Conduct in African Horticulture', *World Development*, 31(9): 1511–26.

Barrientos, S., Gereffi, G., and Rossi, A. (2011), 'Economic and Social Upgrading in Global Production Networks: A New Paradigm for a Changing World', *International Labour Review*, 150(3–4): 319–40.

Barrientos, S., Kabeer, N., and Hossain, N. (2004), 'The Gender Dimensions of Globalization of Production', *ILO Working Paper*, (17).

Barrientos, S., Knorringa, P., Evers, B., Visser, M., and Opondo, M. (2016), 'Shifting Regional Dynamics of Global Value Chains: Implications for Economic and Social Upgrading in African Horticulture', *Environment and Planning A*, 48(7).

Barrientos, S., and Kritzinger, A. (2004), 'Squaring the Circle: Global Production and the Informalisation of Work in South African Fruit Exports', *Journal of International Development*, 16(1): 81–92.

Barrientos, S., and Smith, S. (2007), 'Do Workers Benefit from Ethical Trade? Assessing Codes of Labour Practice in Global Production Systems', *Third World Quarterly*, 28(4): 713–29.

Barros, A. (2017), *Roots of Brazilian Relative Economic Backwardness* (Amsterdam: Elsevier).

Barry, J. (2012), *The Politics of Actually Existing Unsustainability: Human Flourishing in a Climate-Changed, Carbon Constrained World* (Oxford: Oxford University Press).

Bartley, T. (2010), 'Transnational Private Regulation in Practice: The Limits of Forest and Labor Standards Certification in Indonesia', *Business and Politics*, 12(3): 1–34.

Bartley, T. (2011), 'Transnational Governance as the Layering of Rules: Intersections of Public and Private Standards', *Theoretical Inquiries in Law*, 12(2): 517–42.

Bartley, T. (2018), *Rules Without Rights: Land, Labor, and Private Authority in the Global Economy* (Oxford: Oxford University Press).

Bartley, T. (2022), 'Power and the Practice of Transnational Private Regulation', *New Political Economy*, 27(2): 188–202.

Bartley, T., and Child, C. (2014), 'Shaming the Corporation: The Social Production of Targets and the Anti-sweatshop Movement', *American Sociological Review*, 79(4): 653–79.

Bartley, T., and Egels-Zanden, N. (2016), 'Beyond Decoupling: Unions and the Leveraging of Corporate Social Responsibility in Indonesia', *Socio-Economic Review*, 14(2): 231–55.

Basok, T. (2009), 'Counter-Hegemonic Human Rights Discourses and Migrant Rights Activism in the U.S. and Canada', *International Journal of Comparative Sociology*, 50(2): 179–201.

Basri, M. C. (2017), 'India and Indonesia: Lessons Learned from the 2013 Taper Tantrum', *Bulletin of Indonesian Economic Studies*, 53(2): 137–60.

Bastiaens, I., and Postnikov, E. (2020), 'Social Standards in Trade Agreements of Free Trade Preferences: An Empirical Investigation', *Review of International Organizations*, 15(4): 793–816.

Bayo, O. A. (2011), 'The Chinese in Africa: New Colonialism is Not a New Deal', *Pula: Botswana Journal of African Studies*, 25(2): 228–45.

Bazin, H. (1999), *The Eradication of Smallpox: Edward Jenner and The First and Only Eradication of a Human Infectious Disease* (Cambridge. MA: Academic Press).

BBC (2015), 'Will a Robot Take Your Job?', 11 September, https://www.bbc.com/news/technology-34066941, accessed 8 September 2022.

Bedford, K. (2019), *Bingo Capitalism: The Law and Political Economy of Everyday Gambling* (New York and Oxford: Oxford University Press).

Bergsten, F. C. (January 1996), 'Competitive Liberalization and Global Free Trade: A Vision for the Early 21st Century', PIIE Working Papers 96–15, https://www.piie.com/publications/working-papers/competitive-liberalization-and-global-free-trade-vision-early-21st.

Bergvall-Kåreborn, B., and Howcroft, D. (2014), 'Amazon Mechanical Turk and the Commodification of Labour', *New Technology, Work and Employment*, 29(3): 213–23.

Berliner, D., Greenleaf, A. R., Lake, M., and Noveck, J. (2015), 'Building Capacity, Building Rights? State Capacity and Labor Rights in Developing Countries', *World Development*, 72: 127–39.

Bernhardt, T., and Pollak, R. (2016), 'Economic and Social Upgrading Dynamics in Global Manufacturing Value Chains: A Comparative Analysis', *Environment and Planning A*, 48(7): 1220–43.

Bernstein, S. (2001), *The Compromise of Liberal Environmentalism* (New York: Columbia University Press).

Bernstein, W. J. (2009), *A Splendid Exchange: How Trade Shaped the World* (London: Atlantic Books).

Berthelot, Y. (2004) (ed.), *Unity and Diversity in Development Ideas* (Bloomington: Indiana University Press).

Bessell, S. (2020), 'The Individual Deprivation Measure: A Gender-Sensitive Approach to Multidimensional Poverty Measurement', in **M. Sawer, F. Jenkins, and K. Downing** (eds), *How Gender can Transform the Social Sciences: Innovation and Impact* (London: Palgrave Macmillan), 137–45.

Best, J. (2018), 'Technocratic Exceptionalism: Monetary Policy and the Fear of Democracy', *International Political Sociology*, 12: 326–45.

Best, J. (2020), 'The Quiet Failures of Early Neoliberalism: From Rational Expectations to Keynesianism in Reverse', *Review of International Studies*, 46: 594–612.

Best, J., and Paterson, M. (2010*a*) (eds), *Cultural Political Economy* (Abingdon: Routledge).

Best, J., and Paterson, M. (2010*b*), 'Introduction: Understanding Cultural Political Economy', in **J. Best** and **M. Paterson** (eds), *Cultural Political Economy* (New York: Routledge), 1–25.

Bewley-Taylor, D. (2001), *The United States and International Drug Control, 1909–1997* (London and New York: Continuum).

Bhagwati, J. (1958), 'Immiserizing Growth: A Geometrical Note, *Review of Economic Studies*, 25(3): 201–05.

Bhambra, G. K. (2021), 'Colonial Global Economy: Towards a Theoretical Reorientation of Political Economy', *Review of International Political Economy*, 28(2): 307–22.

Biden, J. (2021), 'Remarks as Prepared for Delivery by President Biden: Address to a Joint Session of Congress', The White House, Speeches and Remarks, 28 April.

Biermann, F., and Bauer, S. (2005) (eds), *A World Environment Organization* (Abingdon: Routledge).

Biermann, F., Pattberg, P., and van Asselt, H. (2009), 'The Fragmentation of Global Governance Architectures: A Framework for Analysis', *Global Environmental Politics*, 9(4): 14–40.

Birch, K. (2015), *We Have Never Been Neoliberal: A Manifesto for a Doomed Youth* (London: Zero).

Birdsall, N. (2006), 'The World is Not Flat: Inequality and Injustice in our Global Economy', UNU-WIDER Annual Lecture 9, United Nations University World Institute for Development Economics Research, Helsinki.

BIS (2019), *Triennial Central Bank Survey: Foreign Exchange Turnover in April 2019* (Basel: Bank for International Settlements).

Bisbee, J., Mosley, L., Pepinsky, T. B., and Rosendorff, B. P. (2020), 'Decompensating Domestically: The Political Economy of Anti-globalism', *Journal of European Public Policy*, 27(7): 1090–102.

Blackburn, R. (1997), *The Making of New World Slavery: From the Baroque to the Modern 1492–1800* (London: Verso).

Blackwill, R., and Harris, J. (2016), *War by Other Means: Geoeconomics and Statecraft* (Cambridge, MA: Harvard University Press).

Bland, A., and Kelly, A. (2020), 'Boohoo Booms as Leicester Garment Factories are Linked to Lockdown', *Guardian*, London, 4 July.

Bleich, E. (2005), 'The Legacies of History? Colonization and Immigrant Integration in Britain and France', *Theory and Society* 34(2): 171–e95.

Blyth, M. (ed.) (2009), *Routledge Handbook of International Political Economy: IPE as a Global Conversation* (Abingdon: Routledge).

Boddenberg, S., and Mortensen, N. H. (2020), 'Lithium Extraction for E-mobility Robs Chilean Communities of Water', *DW*, 23 January, https://p.dw.com/p/3VXDK, accessed 13 September 2022.

Boettke, P., Coyne, C., and Leeson, P. (2013), 'Comparative Historical Political Economy', *Journal of Institutional Economics*, 9(3): 285–301.

Bolwig, S., Ponte, S., Du Toit, A., Riisgaard, L., and Halberg, N. (2010), 'Integrating Poverty and Environmental Concerns into Value-Chain Analysis: A Conceptual Framework', *Development Policy Review*, 28(2): 173–94.

Bonacich, E., Alimahomed, S., and Wilson, J. B. (2008), 'The Racialization of Global Labor', *American Behavioral Scientist*, 52(3): 342–55.

Bonds, E., and Downey, L. (2012), '"Green" Technology and Ecologically Unequal Exchange: The Environmental and Social Consequences of Ecological Modernization in the World-System', *Journal of World-Systems Research*, 18(2): 167–86.

Bonizzi, B., Kaltenbrunner, A., and Michell, J. (2019), 'Monetary Sovereignty is a Spectrum: Modern Monetary Theory and Developing Countries', *Real-World Economics Review* 89: 46–61.

Bortz, P. G. and Kaltenbrunner, A. (2018) 'The International Dimension of Financialization in Developing and Emerging Economies', *Development and Change*, 49(2): 375–93.

Börzel, T. A., and Risse, T. (2010), 'Governance Without a State: Can It Work?' *Regulation & Governance* 4(2): 113–34.

Botezat, A., and Ramos, R. (2020), 'Physicians' Brain Drain: A Gravity Model of Migration Flows', *Globalization and Health* 16(7), https://doi.org/10.1186/s12992-019-0536-0, accessed 12 September 2022.

Boucher, A., and Gest, J. (2018), *Crossroads: Comparative Immigration Regimes in a World of Demographic Change* (Cambridge: Cambridge University Press).

Braithwaite, J. (2006), 'Responsive Regulation and Developing Economies', *World Development*, 34(5): 884–98.

Braithwaite, J., and Drahos, P. (2000), *Global Business Regulation* (Cambridge: Cambridge University Press).

Brassett, J., Elias, J., Rethel, L., and Richardson, B. (2021), 'International Political Economy', in **A. Atchison** (ed.), *Political Science is for Everybody* (Toronto: University of Toronto Press).

Brassett, J., and Rethel, L. (2015), 'Sexy Money: The Hetero-Normative Politics of Global Finance', *Review of International Studies* 41(3): 429–49.

Brinks, D., Dehm, J., Engle, K., and Taylor, K. (2021), 'Private Regulatory Initiatives and Beyond: Lessons and Reflections' in **D. Brinks, J. Dehm, K. Engle, and K. Taylor** (eds), *Power, Participation, and Private Regulatory Initiatives: Human Rights Under Supply Chain Capitalism* (Philadelphia: University of Pennsylvania Press), 258–69.

Brown, C. (2001), 'Our Side? Critical Theory and International Relations', in **R. W. Jones** (ed.), *Critical Theory and World Politics* (Boulder, CO: Lynne Rienner), 191–204.

Bruff, I., and Tansel, C. B. (2019), 'Authoritarian Neoliberalism: Trajectories of Knowledge Production and Praxis', *Globalizations,* 16: 233–44.

Brynjolfsson, E., and McAfee, A. (2014), *The Second Machine Age: Work, Progress, and Prosperity in a Time of Brilliant Technologies* (New York: W. W. Norton).

Buckley, C., (2020), 'China's Combative Nationalists See a World Turning Their Way', *New York Times*, 14 December, https://www.nytimes.com/2020/12/14/world/asia/china-nationalists-covid.html, accessed 9 September 2022.

Bullard, R. D. (2000), *Dumping in Dixie: Race, Class, And Environmental Quality*, 3rd edn (Boulder, CO: Westview Press).

Bureau for Food and Agricultural Policy (2012), *Farm Sectoral Determination: An Analysis of*

Agricultural Wages in South Africa (Pretoria: University of Pretoria).

Buthe, T. (2010), 'Private Regulation in the Global Economy', *Business and Politics*, 12(3).

Büthe, T., and Mattli, W. (2013), *The New Global Rulers: The Privatization of Regulation in the World Economy* (Princeton, NJ: Princeton University Press).

Cadbury, D. (2010), *Chocolate Wars: The 150-Year Rivalry Between the World's Greatest Chocolate Makers* (New York: PublicAffairs).

Cafruny, A., Talani, L., and Martin, G. (2016) (eds), *Palgrave Handbook of Critical International Political Economy* (London: Palgrave Macmillan).

Cambridge Bitcoin Electricity Consumption Index (n.d.), https://ccaf.io/cbeci/index, accessed 23 July 2022.

Carayannis, T., and Weiss, T. G. (2021*a*), 'The "Third" UN: Imagining Post-Covid-19 Multilateralism', *Global Policy*, 12(1): 5–14.

Carayannis, T., and Weiss, T. G. (2021*b*), *The 'Third' UN: How Knowledge Brokers Help the UN Think* (Oxford: Oxford University Press).

Carens, J. (1987), 'Aliens and Citizens: The Case for Open Borders', *The Review of Politics*, 49(2) (Spring): 251–73.

Carlson, L. (1952), *Queen of Inventions: How the Sewing Machine Changed the World* (Brookfield, CT: Millbrook Press).

Cashore, B. (2002), 'Legitimacy and the Privatization of Environmental Governance: How Non–state Market-Driven (NSMD) Governance Systems Gain Rule-Making Authority', *Governance*, 15(4): 503–29.

Castañeda-Navarrete, J., Hauge, J., and López-Gómez, C. (2021), 'COVID-19's Impacts on Global Value Chains, as Seen in the Apparel Industry', *Development Policy Review*, 39(6): 953–70.

Castles, S. (1986), 'The Guest-Worker in Western Europe: An Obituary', *International Migration Review*, 20(4): 761–78.

Castles, S., de Hass, H., and Miller, M. J. (2015), *The Age of Migration: International Population Movements in the Modern World* (London: Palgrave Macmillan).

Castles, S., and Kosack, G. (1985), *Immigrant Workers and Class Structures in Western Europe* (Oxford: Oxford University Press).

Cato, M. S. (2012), 'The Economist as Shaman: Revisioning Our Role for a Sustainable, Provisioning Economy', *Journal of Philosophical Economics*, 5(2): 64–83.

Cattaneo, O., Gereffi, G., and Staritz, C. (2010), 'Global Value Chains in a Post-crisis World: Resilience, Consolidation and Shifting End Markets', in **O. Cattaneo, G. Gereffi, and C. Staritz** (eds), *Global Value Chains in a Post-crisis World: A Development Perspective* (Washington, DC: World Bank), 3–20.

CBC News (2020), 'Black People, Minorities, Low-Income Earners at Higher Risk for COVID-19 Infection', *CBC News*, 18, November, https://www.cbc.ca/news/canada/kitchener-waterloo/public-health-data-Covid-19-community-impact-1.5805780, accessed 9 September 2022.

CDC (2021), *Risk for COVID-19 Infection, Hospitalization, and Death By Race/Ethnicity* (Washington, DC: Center for Disease Control and Prevention), https://www.cdc.gov/coronavirus/2019-ncov/covid-data/investigations-discovery/hospitalization-death-by-race-ethnicity.html, accessed 31 March 2021.

CEDLAS and The World Bank (2021), 'Socio-Economic Database for Latin America and the Caribbean', https://www.cedlas.econo.unlp.edu.ar/wp/en/estadisticas/sedlac/, accessed 31 July 2022.

Cerny, P. (1997), 'Paradoxes of the Competition State: The Dynamics of Political Globalization', *Government and Opposition*, 32(2): 251–74.

Chambers, R., and Yilmaz Vastardis, A. (2021), 'Human Rights Disclosure and Due Diligence Laws: The Role of Regulatory Oversight in Ensuring Corporate Accountability', *Chicago Journal of International Law*, 21(2): 323–66.

Chan, J., and Pun, N. (2010), 'Suicide as Protest for the New Generation of Chinese Migrant Workers: Foxconn, Global Capital, and the State', *Asia-Pacific Journal*, 37(2): 1–50.

Chancel, L., Piketty, T., Saez, E., and Zucman, G. (2021), *World Inequality Report 2022* (Paris: World Inequality Lab).

Chang, H. (2002), *Kicking Away the Ladder: Development Strategy in Historical Perspective* (New York: Anthem Press).

Chase-Dunn, C. (1989), *Global Formation: Structures of the World Economy* (New York: Basic Blackwell).

Chaudoin, S., and Milner, H. V. (2017), 'Science and the System: IPE and International Monetary Politics', *Review of International Political Economy*, 24(4): 681–98.

Chaudoin, S., Milner, H., and Pang, X. (2015), 'International Systems and Domestic Politics: Linking Complex Interactions with Empirical Models in International Relations', *International Organization*, 69(2) (Spring): 275–309.

Chile (Republic of) (2012), 'Advierten necesidad de activar nacionalización del Litio', 24 September, https://senado.cl/advierten-necesidad-de-activar-nacionalizacion-del-litio/senado/2012-09-24/114713.html, accessed 13 September 2022.

Christensen, T. J. (2021), 'There Will Be No New Cold War: The Limits of U.S.–PRC Strategic Competition," *Foreign Affairs*, March 22, 2021.

Christian, M. (2016), 'Kenya's Tourist Industry and Global Production Networks: Gender, Race and Inequality', *Global Networks*, 16(1): 25–44.

Chrysoloras, N., and Penna, K. (2013), 'Greece: Three Arrested in "Blood Strawberry", Farm Shooting', 19 April, www.equaltimes.org/greece-three-arrested-in-blood?lang=en#.Wt_eSYhuZPY, accessed 9 September 2022.

CIVICUS (n.d.), 'Ratings', https://monitor.civicus.org/Ratings/, accessed 11 September 2022.

CIVICUS (2022), 'Civic Space in Numbers', 22 June, https://monitor.civicus.org/quickfacts/, accessed 11 September 2022.

Clarke, T., and Boersma, M. (2017), 'The Governance of Global Value Chains: Unresolved Human Rights, Environmental and Ethical Dilemmas in the Apple Supply Chain', *Journal of Business Ethics*, 143(1): 111–31.

Clift, B. (2018), *The IMF and the Politics of Austerity in the Wake of the Global Financial Crisis* (Oxford: Oxford University Press).

Coe, N. M., Hess, M., Yeung, H. W. C., Dicken, P., and Henderson, J. (2004), '"Globalizing" Regional Development: A Global Production Networks Perspective', *Transactions of the Institute of British Geographers*, 29(4): 468–84.

Cohen, B. J. (2007), 'The Transatlantic Divide: Why are American and British IPE so Different?' *Review of International Political Economy*, 14(2): 197–219.

Cohen, B. J. (2008), *International Political Economy: An Intellectual History* (Princeton, NJ: Princeton University Press).

Cohen, B. J. (2009), 'The Multiple Traditions of American IPE', in **M. Blyth** (ed.), *Routledge Handbook of International Political Economy (IPE): IPE as a Global Conversation* (London: Routledge), 23–35.

Cohen, B. J. (2017), 'The IPE of Money Revisited', *Review of International Political Economy*, 24(4): 657–80.

Cohen, B. J. (2019), *Currency Statecraft: Monetary Rivalry and Geopolitical Ambition* (Chicago, IL: University of Chicago Press).

Cohen, B. J. (2022), *Rethinking International Political Economy* (Cheltenham: Edward Elgar).

Cohen, J. (2019), *Between Truth and Power: The Legal Construction of Informational Capitalism* (Oxford: Oxford University Press).

Collins, P. H. (1993), 'Toward a New Vision: Race, Class, and Gender as Categories of Analysis and Connection', *Race, Sex & Class,* 1: 25–45.

Commission on Global Governance (1995), *Our Global Neighbourhood* (Oxford: Oxford University Press).

Commission on Macroeconomics and Health (2001), *Macroeconomics and Health: Investing in Health for Economic Development* (Geneva: WHO), http://www1.worldbank.org/publicsector/pe/PEAMMarch2005/CMHReport.pdf, accessed 12 September 2022.

Conrad, P. (2007), *The Medicalization of Society: On the Transformation of Human Conditions into Treatable Disorders* (Baltimore, MD: Johns Hopkins University Press).

Cooper, F. (2001), 'What Is the Concept of Globalization Good for? An African Historian's Perspective', *African Affairs,* 100: 189–213.

Cooper, L. (2021), *Authoritarian Contagion: The Global Threat to Democracy* (Bristol: Bristol University Press).

Cooper, M. (2017), *Family Values: Between Neoliberalism and the New Social Conservatism* (New York: Zone Books).

Cornia, G. A. (2014) (ed.), *Falling Inequality in Latin America: Policy Changes and Lessons* (Oxford: Oxford University Press).

Cornia, A., Jolly, R., and Stewart, F. (1987), *Adjustment with a Human Face* (New York: UNICEF).

Coslovsky, S. V. (2011), 'Relational Regulation in the Brazilian Ministério Publico: The Organizational Basis of Regulatory Responsiveness', *Regulation & Governance*, 5(1): 70–89.

Coslovsky, S. V., and Locke, R. (2013), 'Parallel Paths to Enforcement: Private Compliance, Public Regulation, and Labor Standards in the Brazilian Sugar Sector', *Politics & Society*, 41(4): 497–526.

Cox, D. (2020), 'Health Tracking Could Mitigate Pandemic-Related Risks, But Will Employees See it as an Invasion of Their Privacy?' https://www.bbc.com/worklife/article/20201110-the-rise-of-employee-health-tracking, accessed 9 September 2022.

Cox, R. W. (1976), 'Labor and the Multinationals', *Foreign Affairs*, 54: 345–65.

Cox, R. W. (1981), 'Social Forces, States, and World Orders: Beyond International Relations Theory', *Millennium*, 10(2): 126–55.

CPHO (2021), *CPHO Sunday Edition: The Impact of COVID-19 on Racialized Communities* (Ottawa: Public Health Agency of Canada).

Crane, A., LeBaron, G., Phung, K., Behbahani, L., and Allain, J. (2021), 'Confronting the Business Models of Modern Slavery', *Journal of Management Inquiry*, 31(3): 264–85.

Crenshaw, K. (1991), 'Mapping the Margins: Intersectionality, Identity Politics, and Violence Against Women of Color', *Stanford Law Review* 43: 1241–99.

Cross, K. H., (2006), 'King Cotton, Developing Countries and the "Peace Clause": The WTO's US Cotton Subsidies Decision', *Journal of Economic Law*, 9(1): 149–95.

Da Silva, M. (2020), 'Making Sense of Visual Pollution: The Clean City Law in São Paulo, Brazil', in **T. Davis** and **A. Mah** (eds), *Toxic Truths* (Manchester University Press), 158–74.

Dahlin, E. (2019), 'Are Robots Stealing our Jobs?' *Socius*, 5: 1–14.

Datz, G. (2008), 'Governments as Market Players: State Innovation in the Global Economy', *Journal of International Affairs*, 62(1): 35–49.

Dauvergne, C., and Marsden, S. (2014), 'The Ideology of Temporary Labour Migration in the Post-Global Era', *Citizenship Studies*, 18(2): 224–42.

Dauvergne, P., and Lister, J. (2010), 'The Power of Big Box Retail in Global Environmental Governance: Bringing Commodity Chains Back Into IR', *Millennium*, 39(1): 145–60.

Dauvergne, P., and Lister, J. (2013), *Eco-business: A Big-Brand Takeover of Sustainability* (Cambridge, MA: MIT).

Davies, S. E., and Wenham, C. (2020), 'Why the COVID-19 Response Needs International Relations', *International Affairs*, (96)5: 1227–51.

Davis, M. (2017), *Late Victorian Holocausts: El Niño Famines and the Making of the Third World* (London and New York: Verso).

De Genova, N. (2010), 'The Deportation Regime: Sovereignty, Space, and the Freedom of Movement. Theoretical Overview', in **N. De Genova** and **N. Peutz** (eds), *The Deportation Regime: Sovereignty, Space, and the Freedom of Movement* (Durham, NC: Duke University Press).

De Goede, M. (2005), *Virtue, Faith and Fortune* (Minneapolis: University of Minnesota Press).

De Graaff, N., and Van Apeldoorn, B. (2021), 'The Transnationalist US Foreign-Policy Elite in Exile? A Comparative Network Analysis of the Trump Administration', *Global Networks*, 21(2): 238–64.

de Haan, A. (1998), 'Social Exclusion: An Alternative Concept for the Study of Deprivation', *IDS Bulletin*, 29(1): 10–19.

de Haas, H. (2010), 'The Internal Dynamics of Migration Processes: A Theoretical Inquiry', *Journal of Ethnic and Migration Studies*, 36: 1587–1617.

de Haas, H., Natter, K., and Vezzoli, S. (2018), 'Growing Restrictiveness or Changing Selection? The Nature and Evolution of Migration Policies', *International Migration Review,* 52(2): 324–67.

de Lacy-Vawdon, C., and Livingston, C. (2020), 'Defining the Commercial Determinants of Health: A Systematic Review', *BMC Public Health* 20, 1022, https://doi.org/10.1186/s12889-020-09126-1, accessed 12 September 2022.

De Marchi, V., and Alford, M. (2021), 'State Policies and Upgrading in Global Value Chains: A Systematic Literature Review', *Journal of International Business Policy*, 5(1): 88–111.

Dedeoglu S. (2010), 'Visible Hands—Invisible Women: Garment Production in Turkey', *Feminist Economics*, 16(4): 1–32.

Deininger, K., and Squire, L. (1998), 'New Ways of Looking at Old Issues: Inequality and Growth', *Journal of Development Economics*, 57: 259–87.

Del Rey, J. (2021), 'The Union Vote that Could Change Amazon Forever', *Recode,* 12 March, https://www.vox.com/recode/22311708/amazon-union-alabama-vote-explained, accessed 18 March 2021.

Delfanti, A. (2019), 'Machinic Dispossession and Augmented Despotism: Digital Work in an Amazon Warehouse', *New Media & Society*, 23(1): 39–55.

Delich, S., and Carter, A. O. (1994), 'Public Health Surveillance: Historical Origins, Methods and Evaluation', *Bulletin of the World Health Organization*, 72: 285–304.

De Marchi, V., Di Maria, E., Krishnan, A., and Ponte, S. (2019), 'Environmental Upgrading in Global Value Chains', in *Handbook on Global Value Chains* (Cheltenham: Edward Elgar), 310–23.

Dent, C. (2008), 'The Asian Development Bank and Developmental Regionalism in East Asia', *Third World Quarterly*, 29(4): 767–86.

Deva, S. (2021), 'The UN Guiding Principles' Orbit and Other Regulatory Regimes in the Business and Human Rights Universe: Managing the Interface', *Business and Human Rights Journal*, 6(2): 336–51.

Dicken, P., and Thrift, N. (1992), 'The Organization of Production and the Production of Organization: Why Business Enterprises Matter in the Study of Geographical Industrialization', *Transactions of the Institute of British Geographers*, 18(4): 279–91, https://doi.org/10.1177/030913259401800403

'Digital Taylorism' (2015), *Economist*, 12 September.

DinarStandard (2020), *The State of the Global Islamic Economy 2020–21* (Dubai: Refinitiv).

Dingel, J., and Neiman, B. (2020), 'How Many Jobs Can be Done at Home?' NBER Working Paper Working Paper 26948.

Diprose, R., Kurniawan, N., Macdonald, K., and Winanti, P. (2020), 'Regulating Sustainable Minerals in Electronics Supply Chains: Local Power Struggles and the "Hidden Costs" of Global Tin Supply Chain Governance', *Review of International Political Economy*: 1–26, https://doi.org/10.1080/09692290.2020.1814844

Dixit, A. (2006), 'Economic Governance', in *The New Palgrave Dictionary of Economics* (Basingstoke: Palgrave Macmillan).

Dollar, D., Kleineberg, T., and Kraay, A. (2013), 'Growth Still Is Good for the Poor', World Bank Policy Research Working Paper No. 6568, The World Bank, Washington, DC.

Dollar, D., and Kraay, A. (2002), 'Growth Is Good for the Poor', *Journal of Economic Growth*, 7: 195–225.

Domínguez-Villalobos, L., and Brown-Grossman, F. (2010), 'Trade Liberalization and Gender Wage Inequality in Mexico', *Feminist Economics*, 16(4): 53–79.

Donini, A. (2019), 'Social Suffering and Structural Violence: Nepali Workers in Qatar', in *The ILO @ 100*, 11: 178–99.

Dorling, D. (2013), *Unequal Health: The Scandal of Our Times* (Bristol: Policy Press).

Dorling, D. (2020), *Slowdown: The End of the Great Acceleration—and Why It's Good for the Planet, the Economy, and Our Lives* (New Haven, CT: Yale University Press).

Doty, R. L. (1996), *Imperial Encounters: The Politics of Representation in North–South Relations* (Minneapolis: University of Minnesota Press).

Dowie, M. (1996), *Losing Ground* (Cambridge, MA: MIT).

Drezner, D., and McNamara, K. (2013), 'International Political Economy: Global Financial Orders and the 2008 Financial Crisis', *Perspectives on Politics*, 11(1): 155–66.

Duanmu, J. L. (2014), 'A Race to Lower Standards? Labor Standards and Location Choice of Outward FDI from the BRIC Countries', *International Business Review*, 23(3): 620–34.

Dunaway, W. A. (2014), 'Bringing Commodity Chain Analysis Back to Its World-Systems Roots: Rediscovering Women's Work and Households', *Journal of World-Systems Research*, 20(1): 64–81, doi: https://doi.org/10.5195/jwsr.2014.576

Du Toit, A. (2004), 'Social Exclusion Discourse and Chronic Poverty: A South African Case Study', *Development and Change*, 35(5): 987–1010.

Dumitriu, P. (2016), *Knowledge Management in the United Nations System*, UN document JIU/REP/2016/10 (Geneva: Joint Inspection Unit).

Dyer-Witheford, N. (2015), *Cyber-Proletariat: Global Labour in the Digital Vortex* (London: Pluto).

Eagleton-Pierce, M. D. (2012), 'The Competing Kings of Cotton: (Re)framing the WTO African Cotton Initiative', *New Political Economy*, 17(3): 313–37.

Edward, E., and Sumner, A. (2019), *The End of Poverty: Inequality and Growth in a Global Perspective* (Basingstoke: Palgrave Macmillan).

Edwards, R. (1982), *Contested Terrain: The Transformation of the Workplace in the Twentieth Century* (New York: Basic Books).

Efrat, A. (2012), *Governing Guns, Preventing Plunder: International Cooperation against Illicit Trade* (New York: Oxford University Press).

Ehrlich, S. D. (2018), *The Politics of Fair Trade* (Oxford: Oxford University Press).

Eichengreen, B. (2016), *Hall of Mirrors: The Great Depression, the Great Recession, and the Uses-and Misuses-of History* (New York: Oxford University Press).

Ekins, P., and Voituriez, T. (2012), *Trade, Globalization and Sustainability Impact Assessment: A Critical Look at Methods and Outcomes* (Abingdon: Routledge).

Elder, S. D., and Dauvergne, P. (2015), 'Farming for Walmart: The Politics of Corporate Control and Responsibility in the Global South', *Journal of Peasant Studies*, 42(5): 1029–46.

Elias, J., and Roberts, A. (2016), 'Feminist Global Political Economies of the Everyday: From Bananas to Bingo', *Globalizations*, 13(6): 787–800.

Elias, J., Ma'ariyah, C., Suwarso, R., Rethel, L, and Tilley, L. (2018), *The Gendered Political Economy of Kampung Eviction and Resettlement in Jakarta: Final Project Report*, https://warwick.ac.uk/fac/soc/pais/research/researchcentres/ipe/jakarta/publications/final_project_report.pdf, accessed 12 September 2022.

Ellerbeck, A. (2021), 'The Energy 202: Advocates Want Biden to Use Trade Deals to Combat Climate Change', *Washington Post*, 20 January, https://www.washingtonpost.com/politics/2021/01/20/

energy-202-advocates-want-biden-use-trade-deals-combat-climate-change/, accessed 13 September 2022.

Elliott, L. (2018), 'Robots Will Take Our Jobs: We'd Better Plan Now, Before It's Too Late', *Guardian*, 1 February.

Elliott, L., and Schaedla, W. H. (2016) (eds), *Handbook of Transnational Environmental Crime* (Cheltenham: Edward Elgar).

eMarketer (2017), 'The Future of Retail: Nine Things to Watch for in the Coming Year'.

Encinas-Franco, J. (2013), 'The Language of Labor Export in Political Discourse: "Modern-day Heroism" and Constructions of Overseas Filipino Workers (OFWs)', *Philippine Political Science Journal*, 34(1): 97–112.

Eriksson, R., and Andersson, J. O. (2010), *Elements of Ecological Economics* (Oxford: Routledge).

Esbenshade, J. (2012), 'A Review of Private Regulation: Codes and Monitoring in the Apparel Industry', *Sociology Compass*, 6(7): 541–56.

Eurofound (2016), *European Quality of Life Survey 2016: Quality of Life, Quality of Public Services, and Quality of Society* (Luxembourg: Publications Office of the European Union).

European Parliament (2019), *Study: Misuse of Interpol's Red Notices and Impact on Human Rights—Recent Developments*, Brussels, EP/EXPO/B/COMMITTEE/FWC/2013-08/Lot8/22

Eurostat (2020), 'Glossary: Environmental Goods and Services Sector (EGSS)', https://ec.europa.eu/eurostat/statistics-explained/index.php/Glossary:Environmental_goods_and_services_sector_(EGSS), accessed 13 September 2022.

Ewert, J., and Du Toit, A. (2005), 'A Deepening Divide in the Countryside: Restructuring and Rural Livelihoods in the South African Wine Industry', *Journal of Southern African Studies*, 31(2): 315–32.

Falkner, R. (2012), 'Global Environmentalism and the Greening of International Society', *International Affairs*, 88(3): 503–22.

Falkner, R. (2016), 'The Paris Agreement and the New Logic of International Climate Politics', *International Affairs*, 92(5): 1107–25.

Fan, M.-F., Chiu, C.-M., and Mabon, L. (2022), 'Environmental Justice and the Politics of Pollution: The Case of the Formosa Ha Tinh Steel Pollution Incident in Vietnam', *EPE: Nature and Space*, 5(1): 189–206.

Fanning, C., and Piper, N. (2021), 'Global Labor Migration: Shifting Governance Regimes, Rights Deficits, and the Search for Order', *Labor: Studies in Working-Class History*, 18(1): 67–86.

Food and Agriculture Organization of the United Nations (FAO) (2020), *The State of the World's Forests: Forests, Biodiversity and People* (Rome: FAO and UNEP).

FAO (2021), *The State of Food Security and Nutrition in the World 2021* (Rome: FAO).

Farrands, C., and Worth, O. (2005), 'Critical Theory in Global Political Economy: Critique? Knowledge? Emancipation?', *Capital and Class*, 29(1): 43–61.

Farrell, H., and Newman, A. (2016), 'The New Interdependence Approach: Theoretical Development and Empirical Demonstration', *Review of International Political Economy*, 23(5): 713–36.

Farrell, H., and Newman, A. (2019), 'Weaponized Interdependence: How Global Economic Networks Shape State Coercion', *International Security*, 44(1): 42–79.

Fault Lines (2020), 'Pandemic in Chicago: Why Are More Black People Dying of COVID-19?', *Al Jazeera*, 21 November, https://www.aljazeera.com/features/2020/11/21/the-pandemic-in-chicago, accessed 12 September 2022.

Feedvisor (2019), 'The 2019 Amazon Consumer Behavior Report', 19 March, https://feedvisor.com/resources/amazon-trends/the-2019-amazon-consumer-behavior-report/, accessed 10 September 2022.

Feingold, D. A. (2010), 'Trafficking in Numbers: The Social Construction of Human Trafficking Data', in **P. Andreas** and **K. Greenhill** (eds), *Sex, Drugs, and Body Counts: The Politics of Numbers in Global Crime and Conflict* (Ithaca, NY: Cornell University Press), 46–74.

Felipe, J., Kumar, U., and Abdon, A. (2014), 'How Rich Countries Became Rich and Why Poor Countries Remain Poor: It's the Economic Structure … duh!' *Japan & the World Economy*, 29: 46–58.

Felipe, J., Mehta, A., and Rhee, C. (2018), 'Manufacturing Matters … But It's the Jobs that Count', *Cambridge Journal of Economics*, 43(1): 139–68.

Ferguson, J. (2005), 'Seeing Like an Oil Company: Space, Security, and Global Capital in Neoliberal Africa', *American Anthropologist*, 107: 377–82.

Ferguson, P. (2018), *Post-growth Politics: A Critical Theoretical and Policy Framework for Decarbonisation* (London: Springer).

Ferguson, S., and McNally, D. (2015), 'Precarious Migrants: Gender, Race and the Social Reproduction of a Global Working Class', *Socialist Register*, 51: 1–23.

Ferhani, A., and Rushton, S. (2020), 'The International Health Regulations, COVID-19, and Bordering Practices: Who Gets In, What Gets Out, and Who Gets Rescued?' *Contemporary Security Policy*, 41(3): 458–77.

Ferreira, F. H. G., Chen, S., Dabalen, A., et al. (2016), 'A Global Count of the Extreme Poor in 2012: Data Issues, Methodology and Initial Results', *Journal of Economic Inequality*, 14(2): 141–72.

Ferreira, F. H. G., and Ravallion, M. (2011), 'Poverty and Inequality: The Global Context', in **B. Nolan, W. Salverda, and T. M. Smeeding** (eds), *The Oxford Handbook of Economic Inequality* (Oxford: Oxford University Press), 599–636.

Findlay, R., and O'Rourke, K. H. (2009), *Power and Plenty* (Princeton, NJ: Princeton University Press).

Findley, M., Nielson, D., and Sharman, J. (2014), *Global Shell Games: Experiments in Transnational Relations, Crime, and Terrorism* (New York: Cambridge University Press).

Finnemore, M., and Sikkink, K. (1998), 'International Norm Dynamics and Political Change', *International Organization*, 52(4): 887–917.

Foley, J., and Piper, N. (2021), 'Returning Home Empty-Handed: Examining How COVID-19 Exacerbates the Non-payment of Temporary Migrant Workers' Wages', *Global Social Policy*, 21(3): 468–89.

Ford, M. (2015), *The Rise of the Robots. Technology and the Threat of Mass Unemployment* (London: Oneworld).

Foster, J. B., Clark, C., and York, R. (2010), *The Ecological Rift: Capitalism's War on the Earth* (New York: Monthly Review).

Foucault, M. (2004), *The Birth of Biopolitics: Lectures at the Collège de France, 1978–1979* (New York: Palgrave Macmillan).

Freeman, G. P. (1986), 'Migration and the Political Economy of the Welfare State', *Annals of the American Academy of Social and Political Sciences*, 485(1): 51–63.

Freeman, R. B. (2007), 'The Challenge of the Growing Globalization of Labor Markets to Economic and Social Policy', in **Eva Paus** (ed.), *Global Capitalism Unbound* (New York: Palgrave Macmillan), 23–39.

Freire, P. (1970), *Pedagogy of the Oppressed* (New York: Continuum).

Frey, C., and Osborne, M. (2015), *Technology at Work* (Oxford: Citi GPS).

Frey, C., and Osborne, M. (2017), 'The Future of Employment: How Susceptible Are Jobs to Computerisation?', *Technological Forecasting and Social Change*, 114: 254–80.

Friedrichs, J., and Kratochwil, F. (2009), 'On Acting and Knowing: How Pragmatism Can Advance International Relations Research and Methodology', *International Organization*, 63(4): 701–31.

Friends of the Earth Europe (2018), *Setting Course for Sustainable Trade: A New Trade Agenda that Serves People and the Environment*, https://www.foeeurope.org/sites/default/files/eu-us_trade_deal/2018/trade_alternatives_designreport_v6_ld.pdf, accessed 13 September 2022.

Friman, H. R. (2015), 'Behind the Curtain: Naming and Shaming in International Drug Control', in **H. R. Friman** (ed.), *The Politics of Leverage in International Relations: Name, Shame and Sanction* (Basingstoke: Palgrave Macmillan), 143–64.

Fröbel, F., Heinrichs, J., and Kreye, O. (1980), *The New International Division of Labour: Structural Unemployment in Industrialised Countries and Industrialisation in Developing Countries* (Cambridge: Cambridge University Press), 46.

Fuchs, D., Kalfagianni, A., and Arentsen, M. (2009), 'Retail Power, Private Standards, and Sustainability in the Global Food System', in **Arentsen, M. J., Falkner, R., and Kalfagianni, A.** (eds), *Corporate Power in Global Agrifood Governance* (Cambridge, MA: MIT), 29–59.

Fuchs, D., and Lederer, M. M. (2007), 'The Power of Business', *Business and Politics*, 9(3): 1–17.

Fung, A. (2003), 'Countervailing Power in Empowered Participatory Governance', in **A. Fung** and **E. O. Wright** (eds), *Deepening Democracy: Institutional Innovations in Empowered Participatory Governance* (London: Verso): 259–90.

Gabor, D. (2016), 'The (Impossible) Repo Trinity: The Political Economy of Repo Markets', *Review of International Political Economy*, 23(6): 967–1000.

Gago, V. (2017), *Neoliberalism from Below: Popular Pragmatics and Baroque Economies* (Durham, NC: Duke University Press).

Galea, S., and Vlahov, D. (2005), 'Urban Health: Evidence, Challenges, and Directions', *Annual Review of Public Health*, 26: 341–65.

Gamble, A. (2021), 'Making Sense of Populist Nationalism', *New Political Economy*, 26: 283–90.

Gamso, J., and Postnikov, E. (2022), 'Leveling-Up: Explaining the Depth of South–South Trade Agreements', *Review of International Political Economy*, 29(5): 1601–24, doi: 10.1080/09692290.2021.1939762

Garg, A. (2011), 'Pro-equity Effects of Ancillary Benefits of Climate Change Policies: A Case Study of Human Health Impacts of Outdoor Air Pollution in New Delhi', *World Development*, 39(6): 1002–25.

Garrett, G. (2010), 'G2 in G20: China, the United States and the World after the Global Financial Crisis', *Global Policy*, 1(1): 29–39.

GATT (The General Agreement on Tariffs and Trade) (1947), https://www.wto.org/english/docs_e/legal_e/gatt47_01_e.htm, accessed 11 September 2022.

GATT (The General Agreement on Tariffs and Trade) (1994), https://www.wto.org/english/docs_e/legal_e/06-gatt_e.htm, accessed 11 September 2022.

Geneva Declaration on Armed Violence and Development (2015), *Global Burden of Armed Violence*, Geneva Declaration Secretariat.

Gereffi, G. (1994), 'The Organization of Buyer-Driven Global Commodity Chains: How US Retailers Shape Overseas Production Networks', in **G. Gereffi** and **M. Korzeniewicz** (eds), *Commodity Chains and Global Capitalism* (Westport: Greenwood Press), 95–122.

Gereffi, G. (2014), 'Global Value Chains in a Post-Washington Consensus World', *Review of International Political Economy*, 21(1): 9–37.

Gereffi, G. (2020), 'What Does the COVID-19 Pandemic Teach Us about Global Value Chains? The Case of Medical Supplies', *Journal of International Business Policy*, 3(3): 287–301.

Gereffi, G., and Frederick, S. (2010), *The Global Apparel Value Chain, Trade and the Crisis: Challenges and Opportunities for Developing Countries* (World Bank).

Gereffi, G., and Lee, J. (2012), 'Why the World Suddenly Cares about Global Supply Chains', *Journal of Supply Chain Management*, 48(3): 24–32.

Gereffi, G., and Lee, J. (2016), 'Economic and Social Upgrading in Global Value Chains and Industrial Clusters: Why Governance Matters', *Journal of Business Ethics*, 133(1): 25–38.

Gereffi, G., and Mayer, F. (2006), 'Globalization and the Demand for Governance', in **G. Gereffi** (ed.), *The New Offshoring of Jobs and Global Development* (Geneva: International Labour Organization), 39–58.

Gerschenkron, A. (1962), *Economic Backwardness in Historical Perspective: A Book of Essays* (Cambridge, MA: Belknap Press of Harvard University Press).

Ghosh, J. (2019), 'A Brave New World, or the Same Old Story with New Characters?' *Development and Change*, 50(2): 379–93.

Gibbon, P., Bair, J., and Ponte, S. (2008), 'Governing Global Value Chains: An Introduction', *Economy and Society*, 37(3): 315–38.

Gibbon, P., and Ponte, S. (2005), *Trading Down: Africa, Value Chains, and the Global Economy* (Philadelphia: Temple University Press).

Gill, S. (1991), *American Hegemony and the Trilateral Commission* (Cambridge: Cambridge University Press).

Gill, S. (2002), 'Constitutionalizing Inequality and the Clash of Globalizations', *International Studies Review*, 4: 47–66.

Global Trade Alert, https://www.globaltradealert.org, accessed 10 September 2022.

Godley, A. (2006), 'Selling the Sewing Machine Around the World: Singer's International Marketing Strategies, 1850–1920', *Enterprise & Society* 7(2): 266–314.

Godziewski, C. (2020), 'Is "Health in All Policies" Everybody's Responsibility? Discourses of Multistakeholderism and the Lifestyle Drift Phenomenon', *Critical Policy Studies*, 15(2): 229–46.

Goga, S., and Paelo, A. (2019), 'Issues in the Regulation and Policy Surrounding E-Commerce in South Africa', Working Paper 2019/6, (Johannesburg: CCRED).

Goldstein, J. S. (2011), *Winning the War on War: The Decline of Armed Conflict Worldwide* (New York: Dutton).

Golgeci, I., Yildiz, H. E., and Andersson, U. R. (2020), 'The Rising Tensions between Efficiency and Resilience in Global Value Chains in the Post-COVID-19 World', *Transnational Corporations Journal*, 27(2): 127–41.

Gonzales Benson, O., and Taccolini Panaggio, A. (2019), '"Work Is Worship" in Refugee Policy: Diminution, Deindividualization, and Valuation in Policy Implementation', *Social Service Review* 93(1): 26–54.

Gonzalez-Vicente, R. (2019), 'Make Development Great Again? Accumulation Regimes, Spaces of Sovereign Exception and the Elite Development Paradigm of China's Belt and Road Initiative', *Business and Politics*, 21(4): 487–513.

Goodhart, C., Gabor, D., Vestergaard, J., and Erturk, I. (2014), *Central Banking at a Crossroads: Europe and Beyond* (London: Anthem).

Gordon, I. (1995), 'Migration in a Segmented Labour Market', *Transactions of the Institute of British Geographers*, 20(2): 139–55.

Gostin, L. O. (2008), 'The International Migration and Recruitment of Nurses: Human Rights and Global Justice', *Journal of the American Medical Association*, 299(15): 1827–29.

Government Accountability Office (2006), *Human Trafficking: Better Data, Strategy, and Reporting Needed to Enhance U.S. Antitrafficking Efforts Abroad*, GAO-06–825 (July).

Grabel, I. (2018), *When Things Don't Fall Apart: Global Financial Governance and Developmental Finance in an Age of Productive Incoherence* (Cambridge, MA and London: MIT).

Grabs, J., and Ponte, S. (2019), 'The Evolution of Power in the Global Coffee Value Chain and Production Network', *Journal of Economic Geography*, 19(4): 803–28.

Grant, J., and Taylor, I. (2004), 'Global Governance and Conflict Diamonds: The Kimberley Process and the Quest for Clean Gems', *Round Table*, 93(375): 385–401.

Gresser, C., and Tickell, S. (2002), *Mugged: Poverty in Your Coffee Cup* (Oxfam).

Grieco, J. (2019), 'The Schools of Thought Problem in International Relations', *International Studies Review*, 21(3): 424–46.

Griffin, P. (2019) 'The Everyday Practices of Global Finance: Gender and Regulatory Politics of "Diversity"', *International Affairs*, 95: 1215–33.

Griffiths, M. (1999), *Fifty Key Thinkers in International Relations* (New York: Routledge).

Grimes, W. W. (2009), *Currency and Contest in East Asia: The Great Power Politics of Financial Regionalism* (Ithaca, NY and London: Cornell University Press).

Grineski, S. E., and Juárez-Carrillo, P. M. (2012), 'Environmental Injustice in the US–Mexico Border Region', in **M. Lusk, K. Staudt, and E. Moya** (eds), *Social Justice in the U.S.–Mexico Border Region* (Dordrecht: Springer), 179–98.

Grossman, G. M., and Krueger, A. B. (1991), Environmental Impacts of the North American Free Trade Agreement', NBER Working Paper 3914, National Bureau of Economic Research, Cambridge, MA.

Grossman, G. M., and Krueger, A. B. (1994), 'Economic Growth and the Environment', NBER Working Papers 4634, National Bureau of Economic Research, https://www.nber.org/papers/w4634, accessed 13 September 2022.

Guarin, A., and Knorringa, P. (2014), '"New" Middle Class Consumers in Rising Powers: Responsible Consumption and Private Standards', *Oxford Development Studies*, 42(2), 151–71.

Gunawardana, S. J. (2016), '"To Finish, We Must Finish": Everyday Practices of Depletion in Sri Lankan Export-Processing Zones', *Globalizations*, 13(6): 861–75.

Gunder, F. A. (1966), *The Development of Underdevelopment* (New York: Monthly Review).

Gundermann, H., and Göbel, B. (2018), 'Comunidades Indígenas: Empresas del Litio y sus Relaciones en el Salar de Atacama', *Chungará*, 50(3): 471–86.

Guterres, A. (2021), *Report of the Secretary-General on the Work of the Organization*, UN document A/76/1, https://news.un.org/pages/durban-20-sketches/wp-content/uploads/sites/22/2022/04/2109745-e-arwo-2021-final-15-sept-web-pages-m-1.pdf accessed 10 September 2022.

Haines, F. and **Macdonald, K.** (2020), 'Nonjudicial Business Regulation and Community Access to Remedy', *Regulation & Governance*, 14(4): 840–60.

Hale, T., and Held, D. (eds) (2011), *Handbook of Transnational Governance* (Cambridge:Polity).

Hall, P. A. (1993), 'Policy Paradigms, Social-Learning, and the State: The Case of Economic Policy-Making in Britain', *Comparative Politics*, 25: 275–96.

Hamilton, C. (2010), 'Consumerism, Self-Creation and Prospects for a New Ecological Consciousness', *Journal of Cleaner Production*, 18: 571–75.

Hannah, E., Roberts, A., and Trommer, S. (2018), 'Gendering Global Trade Governance through Canada–UK Trade Relations', Knowledge synthesis grant: Final report, www.kings.uwo.ca/kings/assets/File/academics/polisci/bios/hannah/KSG-Final-Report.pdf, accessed 10 September 2022.

Hannah, E., Roberts, A., and Trommer, S. (2021), 'Towards a Feminist Global Trade Politics', *Globalizations*, 18(1): 70–85.

Hannah, E., Roberts, A., and Trommer, S. (2022*a*), 'Canada's Feminist Trade Policy', in **D. Carment, J. Paltiel, and L. MacDonald** (eds), *Canada and Great Power Competition: Canada Among Nations 2021* (Palgrave Macmillan).

Hannah, E., Roberts, A., and Trommer, S. (2022*b*), 'Feminist Interventions in Trade Governance', in **M. Sawer, L. A. Banaszak, J. True,** and **J. Kantola** (eds), *Handbook of Feminist Governance* (Cheltenham: Edward Elgar).

Hannah, E., Roberts, A., and Trommer, S. (2022*c*), 'Gender in Global Trade: Transforming or Reproducing the Orthodoxy?', *Review of International Political Economy*, 29(4): 1368–93.

Harcourt, W., and Nelson, I. L. (2015), 'Introduction: Are We "Green" Yet? And the Violence of Asking Such a Question', in **W. Harcourt and I. L. Nelson** (eds), *Practicing Feminist Political Ecologies* (London: Zed Books), 1–26.

Hardt, M., and Negri, A. (2001), *Empire* (Cambridge, MA: Harvard University Press).

Harlen, C. M. (1999), 'A Reappraisal of Classical Economic Nationalism and Economic Liberalism', *International Studies Quarterly*, 43(4): 733–44.

Harriss-White, B. (2006), 'Poverty and Capitalism', *Economic and Political Weekly*, pp. 1241–46.

Hart K. (1973), 'Informal Income Opportunities and Urban Employment in Ghana', *Journal of Modern African Studies*, 11(3): 61–89.

Harvey, D. (1990), *The Condition of Postmodernity: An Enquiry into the Origins of Cultural Change* (Oxford: Blackwell).

Harvey, D. (1992), *The Condition of Postmodernity: An Enquiry into the Origins of Cultural Change* (Hoboken, NJ: Wiley).

Harvey, D. (2003), *The New Imperialism* (New York: Oxford University Press).

Hatton, T. J. (2015), 'Migration Out of Europe', in **J. Wright** (ed.), *International Encyclopedia of the Social & Behavioral Sciences*, 2nd edn (Elsevier), 457–61.

Hawken, P., Lovins, A. B., and Lovins, L. H. (1999), *Natural Capitalism: The Next Industrial Revolution* (London: Earthscan).

Hay, C., and Rosamond B. (2002), 'Globalization, European Integration and the Discursive Construction of Economic Imperatives', *Journal of European Public Policy,* 9: 147–67.

Hayek, F. ([1960] 2006), *The Constitution of Liberty* (London: Routledge Classics).

Held, D., McGrew, A., Goldblatt, D., and Perraton, J. (1999), *Global Transformations: Politics, Economics and Culture* (Stanford, CA: Stanford University Press).

Helleiner, E. (2002), 'Economic Nationalism as a Challenge to Economic Liberalism? Lessons from the 19th Century', *International Studies Quarterly*, 46(3): 307–29.

Helleiner, E. (2010), 'A Bretton Woods Moment? The 2007–08 Financial Crisis and the Future of Bretton Woods', *International Affairs*, 86(3): 619–36.

Helleiner, E. (2014*a*), *Forgotten Foundations of Bretton Woods: International Development and the Making of the Postwar Order* (Ithaca, NY and London: Cornell University Press).

Helleiner, E. (2014*b*). *The Status Quo Crisis: Global Financial Governance after the 2008 Meltdown* (Oxford: Oxford University Press).

Helleiner, E. (2020), 'Globalizing the Historical Roots of IPE', in **E. Vivares** (ed.), *The Routledge Handbook to Global Political Economy* (New York: Routledge), 43–57.

Helleiner, E. (2021), 'The Diversity of Economic Nationalism', *New Political Economy*, 26(2): 229–38.

Helleiner, E., Finnemore, M., Jurkovich, M., Sikkink, K., and Acharya, A. (2014), 'Principles from the Periphery: The Neglected Southern Sources of Global Norms', *Global Governance* 20(3): 359–481.

Hannebery, J., and Hari, H. C. (2021), 'On Gendered Structures and Outcomes of Interstate Bilateral Labour Agreements as Migration Governance Instruments', in **C. Mora** and **N. Piper** (eds), *The Palgrave Handbook of Gender and Migration* (Palgrave Macmillan), 287–301.

Henriksen, L. F., and Seabrooke, L. (2016), 'Transnational Organizing: Issue Professionals in Environmental Sustainability Networks', *Organization*, 23(5): 722–41.

Henwood, D. (1995), 'Clinton's Trade Policy', in **F. Rosen** and **D. McFadyen** (eds), *Free Trade and Economic Restructuring in Latin America* (New York: Monthly Review Press), 27–38.

Hernández, D. (2015), 'Sacrifice Along the Energy Continuum: A Call for Energy Justice', *Environmental Justice*, 8(4): 151–56.

Hess, M., and Yeung, H. W. C. (2006), 'Whither Global Production Networks in Economic Geography? Past, Present and Future', *Environment and Planning A*, 38(7): 1193–204. https://doi.org/10.1068/a38463

Hickel, J. (2020), *Less is More: How De-growth Will Save the World* (London: Penguin Random House).

Hickey, S., and du Toit, A. (2007), 'Adverse Incorporation, Social Exclusion and Chronic Poverty', Chronic Poverty Research Centre Working Papers series, no. 81, University of Manchester.

Hirst, P., and **Thompson, G.** (1996), *Globalization in Question: The International Economy and the Possibilities of Governance.* (Cambridge: Polity).

HIV.gov (2021), 'PEPFAR', https://www.hiv.gov/federal-response/pepfar-global-aids/pepfar, accessed 12 September 2022.

Ho, P. S-W. (2010), *Rethinking Trade and Commercial Policy Theories: Development Perspectives.* (Cheltenham: Edward Elgar).

Hobson, J. M. (2013), 'Part 2 – Reconstructing the Non-Eurocentric Foundations of IPE: From Eurocentric "Open Economy Politics" to Inter-Civilizational Political Economy', *Review of International Political Economy*, 20(5): 1055–81.

Hobson, J. M. (2021), *Multicultural Origins of the Global Economy: Beyond the Western-Centric Frontier* (New York: Cambridge University Press).

Hobson, J. M., and Seabrooke, L. (2007) (eds), *Everyday Politics of the World Economy* (Cambridge: Cambridge University Press).

Hobson, J. M., and Seabrooke, L. (2009), 'Everyday International Political Economy', in **M. Blyth** (ed.), *Routledge Handbook of International Political Economy (IPE): IPE as a Global Conversation* (London: Routledge), 290–306.

Hoda, A., and Gulati, A. (2008), *WTO Negotiations on Agriculture and Developing Countries* (Washington, DC: IFPRI).

Höflinger, T. (2020), 'Non-binding and Therefore Irrelevant? The Global Compact for Migration', *International Journal: Canada's Journal of Global Policy Analysis*, 75(4): 662–72.

Hofmann, H., Schleper, M. C., and Blome, C. (2018), 'Conflict Minerals and Supply Chain Due Diligence: An Exploratory Study of Multi-tier Supply Chains', *Journal of Business Ethics*, 147(1): 115–41.

Hollifield, J. F., Martin, P. L., and Orrenius, P. M. (2014), *Controlling Immigration: A Global Perspective* (Stanford, CA: Stanford University Press).

Hook, G. D., and TAKEDA, H. (2007), '"Self-Responsibility" and the Nature of the Japanese State: Risk through the Looking Glass', *Journal of Japanese Studies*, 33(1): 93–123.

Hoopes, S., Abrahamson, A., Anglin, A., Connelly, C., Holdsworth, M., and Treglia, D. (2020), *ALICE in New York: A Financial Hardship Study* (Morristown, NJ: United Way of Northern New Jersey).

Hopewell, K. (2015), 'Multilateral Trade Governance as Social Field: Global Civil Society and the WTO', *Review of International Political Economy*, 22(6): 1128–58.

Hopewell, K. (2020), *Clash of Powers: US–China Rivalry in Global Trade Governance* (Cambridge: Cambridge University Press).

Hopkins, T. K., and Wallerstein, I. (1986), 'Commodity Chains in the World Economy Prior to 1800', *Review* (Fernand Braudel Center), 10(1): 157–70.

Hornborg, A., and Martínez-Alier, J. (2016), 'Ecologically Unequal Exchange and Ecological Debt', *Journal of Political Ecology*, 23: 328–491.

Horner, R. (2017), 'Beyond Facilitator? State Roles in Global Value Chains and Global Production Networks', *Geography Compass*, 11(2), e12307.

Horner, R., and Nadvi, K. (2018), 'Global Value Chains and the Rise of the Global South: Unpacking Twenty-First Century Polycentric Trade', *Global Networks*, 18(2): 207–37.

Huber, Machteld, Knottnerus, J. A., Green, L., et al. (2011), 'Health: How Should We Define It?' *British Medical Journal*, 343: 235–37.

Humphrey, J., and Schmitz, H. (2002), 'How Does Insertion in Global Value Chains Affect Upgrading in Industrial Clusters? *Regional Studies*, 36(9): 1017–27.

Hund, K., La Porta, D., Fabregas, T. P., Laing, T., and Drexhage, J. (2020), *Minerals for Climate Action: The Mineral Intensity of the Clean Energy Transition* (Washington, DC: World Bank), http://pubdocs.worldbank.org/en/961711588875536384/Minerals-for-Climate-Action-The-Mineral-Intensity-of-the-Clean-Energy-Transition.pdf, accessed 13 September 2022.

Huws, U. (2014), *Labor in the Global Digital Economy* (New York: Monthly Review).

IEA (International Energy Agency) (2016), *Energy Efficiency Market Report 2016*, https://www.iea.org/reports/energy-efficiency-2016, accessed 13 September 2022.

IEA (2018), 'Jawaharlal Nehru National Solar Mission (Phase I, II and III)', https://www.iea.org/policies/4916-jawaharlal-nehru-national-solar-mission-phase-i-ii-and-iii

IEA (2020), *Energy Efficiency 2020* (Paris: IEA), https://www.iea.org/reports/energy-efficiency-2020, accessed 13 September 2022.

IHME (2019), 'Global Burden of Disease', http://www.healthdata.org/gbd/2019, accessed 12 September 2022.

IISD (International Institute for Sustainable Development) and UNEP (United Nations Environment Programme) (2014), *Trade and Green Economy: A Handbook* (Geneva: IISD).

ILO (International Labour Organization) (1972), *Employment, Incomes and Equality: A Strategy for Increasing Productive Employment in Kenya* (Geneva: International Labour Organization).

ILO (2015), *World Employment Social Outlook: The Changing Nature of Jobs* (Geneva: International Labour Organization).

ILO (2016), *ASEAN in Transformation: How Technology is Changing Jobs and Enterprises.* (Geneva: International Labour Organization).

ILO (2018*a*), *Global Wage Report 2018/19: What Lies Behind Gender Pay Gaps* (Geneva: ILO), https://www.ilo.org/global/publications/books/WCMS_650553/lang—en/index.htm, accessed 14 September 2022.

ILO (2018*b*), 'The Impact of Technology on the Quality and Quantity of Jobs', Issue Brief 6, Prepared for the 2nd Meeting of the Global Commission on the Future of Work, 15–17 February (Geneva: International Labour Organization).

ILO (2019), 'The Working Poor or How a Job Is No Guarantee of Decent Living Conditions', ILOSTAT Spotlight on Work Statistics, no. 6, April (Geneva: International Labour Organization).

ILO (2021*a*), *ILO Global Estimates on International Migrant Workers: Results and Methodology*, 30 June (Geneva: Labour Migration Branch, Department of Statistics).

ILO (2021*b*), *ILO Monitor: COVID-19 and the World of Work*, 7th edn (Geneva: International Labour Organization).

IMF (International Monetary Fund) (2019), *World Economic Outlook Database* (version October 2019).

IMF (2021*a*), *Global Financial Stability Report: October 2021* (Washington, DC: IMF).

IMF (2021*b*), *World Economic Outlook: October 2021* (Washington, DC: IMF).

IMF (2022), 'About the IMF', https://www.imf.org/en/About, accessed 10 September 2022.

International Cotton Advisory Committee (ICAC), (2020), 'Production and Trade Policies Affecting the Cotton Industry' (Washington DC: ICAC).

International Development Association (2021), 'IDA Graduates', https://ida.worldbank.org/about/ida-graduates, accessed 10 September 2022.

IOM (International Organization for Migration) (2019*a*), 'International Migration Law: Glossary on Migration', no. 34, IOM, UN Migration, https://publications.iom.int/system/files/pdf/iml_34_glossary.pdf, accessed 10 September 2022.

IOM (2019*b*), *World Migration Report 2019* (Paris: IOM).

IOM (2020), *World Migration Report 2020* (Paris: IOM).

IPCC (2019), 'Special Report: Global Warming of 1.5C', https://www.ipcc.ch/sr15/, accessed 10 September 2022.

Issac, G., and Menon, T. (2017), 'When Good Intentions Are Not Enough: Revisiting the US–India Solar Panels WTO Dispute', *OIDA International Journal of Sustainable Development*, 10(2): 37–44.

Ivanova, M. (2010), 'UNEP in Global Environmental Governance: Design, Leadership, Location', *Global Environmental Politics*, 10(1): 30–1.

Jackson, B. (2012), 'The Think-Tank Archipelago: Thatcherism and Neo-Liberalism', in **B. Jackson** and **R. Saunders** (eds), *Making Thatcher's Britain* (Cambridge: Cambridge University Press).

Jackson, T. (2021), *Post Growth: Life after Capitalism* (Cambridge: Polity).

Jaffe, S., and Chen, M. (2020), 'Work in the Time of Coronavirus: Belabored Stories', *Dissent 67* (Summer): 138.

James, S., Pagliari, S., and Young, K. L. (2021), 'The Internationalization of European Financial Networks: A Quantitative Text Analysis of EU Consultation Responses', *Review of International Political Economy*, 28(4): 898–925.

Jameson, F. (1994), *The Seeds of Time* (New York: Columbia University Press).

Javid, S. (2020), 'Using the Response and Experience of Selected Countries to COVID-19 as Case Studies, How Can Democratic Industrialised States Better Prepare for the Next Pandemic?', The Mossavar-Rahmani Center for Business and Government, Senior Fellows Research Meeting, December, https://www.hks.harvard.edu/sites/default/files/centers/mrcbg/programs/senior.fellows/20-21/Sajid%20Javid.pdf, accessed 10 September 2022.

Jinnah, S., and Lindsay, A. (2016), 'Diffusion through Issue Linkage: Environmental Norms in US Trade Agreements', *Global Environmental Politics*, 16(3): 41–61.

Jinnah, S., and Morin, J.-F. (2020), *Greening through Trade: How American Trade Policy Is Linked to Environmental Protection Abroad* (Cambridge, MA: MIT).

Johnson, J. (2016), *Priests of Prosperity: How Central Bankers Transformed the Post-Communist World* (Ithaca, NY: Cornell University Press).

Johnson, S. (2021), *Extra Life: A Short History of Living Longer* (New York: Riverhead).

'Jokowi Eyes to End Extreme Poverty by 2024' (2021), *Tempo.co*, 5 January, https://en.tempo.co/read/1420311/jokowi-eyes-to-end-extreme-poverty-by-2024, accessed 12 September 2022.

Jolliffe, D., and Prydz, E. B. (2016), 'Estimating International Poverty Lines from Comparable National Thresholds', *Journal of Economic Inequality*, 14(2): 185–98.

Jolly, R. (2014), *UNICEF, Global Governance that Works* (London: Routledge).

Jolly, R., Emmerij, L., Ghai, D., and Lapeyre, F. (2004), *UN Contributions to Development Thinking and Practice* (Bloomington: Indiana University Press).

Jones, K., and Sha, S. (2020), *Mediated Migration: A Literature Review of Migration Intermediaries*, MIDEQ Working Paper, Coventry University, London.

Jones, L. and Hameiri, S. (2022), 'COVID-19 and the Failure of the Neoliberal Regulatory State', *Review of International Political Economy* 29(4), 1027–52.

Jupp, J. (2002), *From White Australia to Woomera: The Story of Australian Immigration* (Cambridge: Cambridge University Press).

Juska, A. (2010), '"Profits to the Danes, For Us—Hog Stench?" The Campaign against Danish Swine CAFOs in Rural Lithuania', *Journal of Rural Studies*, 26(3): 250–59.

Kacowicz, A., Lacovsky, E., Sasson, K., and Wajner, D. (2021), *The Unintended Consequences of Peace: Peaceful Borders and Illicit Transnational Flows* (New York: Cambridge University Press).

Kagawa, S., Suh, S., and Hubacek, K. et al. (2015), 'CO_2 Emission Clusters within Global Supply Chain Networks: Implications for Climate Change Mitigation', *Global Environmental Change*, 35: 486–96.

Kaika, D., and Zervas, E. (2013), 'The Environmental Kuznets Curve (EKC) Theory. Part B: Critical issues', *Energy Policy*, 62: 1403–11.

Kaos, Jr, J., and Zainal, F. (2020), 'National Poverty Line Revised', *The Star*, 11 July, https://www.thestar.com.my/news/nation/2020/07/11/national-poverty-line-revised, accessed 12 September 2022.

Kaplinsky, R. (2000), 'Globalisation and Unequalisation: What Can Be Learned from Value Chain Analysis?' *Journal of Development Studies*, 37(2): 117–46.

Kaplinsky, R. (2004), 'Spreading the Gains from Globalization: What Can Be Learned from Value-Chain Analysis?' *Problems of Economic Transition*, 47(2): 74–115.

Kaplinsky, R. (2005), *Globalization, Poverty and Inequality* (Cambridge: Polity).

Kaplinsky, R. (2013), *Globalization, Poverty and Inequality: Between a Rock and a Hard Place* (John Wiley).

Kaplinsky, R. (2019), 'Rents and Inequality in Global Value Chains', in **R. Kaplinsky, S. Ponte, G. Gereffi**, and **G. Raj-Reichert** (eds), *Handbook on Global Value Chains* (Cheltenham: Edward Elgar), 153–68.

Kaplinsky, R., Morris, M., and Readman, J. (2002), 'The Globalization of Product Markets and Immiserizing Growth: Lessons from the South African Furniture Industry', *World Development*, 30(7): 1159–77.

Karatani, R. (2005), 'How History Separated Refugee and Migrant Regimes: In Search of Their Institutional Origins', *International Journal of Refugee Law* 17(3): 517–41.

Karni, A., and Rogers, K. (2021), 'Timing Is Everything, Biden Says, and "Politics Is the Art of the Possible"', *New York Times*, 5 April, https://www.nytimes.com/2021/03/25/us/politics/biden-white-house-press-conference.html, accessed 10 September 2022.

Katada, S. N. (2009), 'Political Economy of East Asian Integration and Cooperation', Asian Development Bank Institute (ADBI) Working Paper.

Katz, C. (2019), 'Piling Up: How China's Ban on Importing Waste Has Stalled Global Recycling', *Yale Environment 360*, 7 March, https://e360.yale.edu/features/piling-up-how-chinas-ban-on-importing-waste-has-stalled-global-recycling, accessed 13 September 2022.

Katzenstein, P. (2005), *A World of Regions: Asia and Europe in the American Imperium* (Ithaca, NY: Cornell University Press).

Katz-Rosene, R., and Paterson, M. (2018), *Thinking Ecologically about the Global Political Economy* (London: Routledge).

Kelley, J. (2017), *Scorecard Diplomacy: Grading States to Influence Their Reputation and Behavior* (New York: Cambridge University Press).

Kennedy, P. (1988), *The Rise and Fall of Great Powers* (New York: Random House).

Keohane, R. O. (1984), *After Hegemony. Cooperation and Discord in the World Political Economy* (Princeton, NJ: Princeton University Press).

Kessi, S., Marks, Z., and Ramugondo, E. (2021), 'Decolonizing Knowledge Within and Beyond the Classroom', *Critical African Studies*, 13(1): 1–9.

Keynes, J. M. (1933), 'National Self-Sufficiency', *Yale Review*, 22: 755–69.

Khalaf, A., AlShehabi, O., and Hanieh, A. (eds) (2015), *Transit States: Labour, Migration and Citizenship in the Gulf* (London: Pluto).

Khan, A., and Harroff-Tavel, H. (2011), 'Reforming the Kafala: Challenges and Opportunities in Moving Forward', *Asian and Pacific Migration Journal*, 20 (3–4): 293–313.

Kickbusch, I., Allen, L., and Franz, C. (2016), 'The Commercial Determinants of Health', *Lancet Global Health*, 4(12): E895–96.

Kim, S. Y. (2011), *Power and Governance of Global Trade: From the GATT to the WTO.* (Ithaca, NY: Cornell University Press).

Kinder, M., and Stateler, L. (2021), 'Essential Workers Comprise about Half of all Workers in Low-Paid Occupations: They Deserve a $15 Minimum Wage', 5 February, The Brookings Institution, Washington, DC, https://www.brookings.edu/blog/the-avenue/2021/02/05/essential-workers-deserve-minimum-wage-increase/, accessed 10 September 2022.

Kindleberger, C. P. (1973), *The World in Depression, 1929–1939* (London: Allen Lane).

Kindleberger, C. P., and Aliber, R. Z. ([1978] 2005), *Manias, Panics, and Crashes: A History of Financial Crises*, 5th edn (Basingstoke: Palgrave Macmillan).

Kirk, J. M. (2015), *Healthcare Without Borders: Understanding Cuban Medical Internationalism* (Gainesville: University Press of Florida).

Kissinger, G. M., Herold, M., and De Sy, V. (2012), *Drivers of Deforestation and Forest Degradation: A Synthesis Report for REDD+ Policymakers* (Lexeme Consulting).

Koch, I. L. (2018), *Personalizing the State: An Anthropology of Law, Politics, and Welfare in Austerity Britain* (Oxford: Oxford University Press).

Koenig-Archibugi, M., and Macdonald, K. (2013), 'Accountability-by-Proxy in Transnational Non-state Governance', *Governance: An International Journal of Policy, Administration, and Institutions*, 26(3): 499–522.

Kornbluth, J. (2013) (dir.) (film), *Inequality for All* (United States of America: RADiUS).

Kraay, A. (2006), 'When Is Growth Pro-Poor? Evidence from a Panel of Countries', *Journal of Development Economics*, 80: 198–227.

Krasner, S. (1976), 'State Power and the Structure of World Trade', *World Politics*, 28(3): 317–47.

Krauss, J .E., and Barrientos, S. (2021), 'Fairtrade and Beyond: Shifting Dynamics in Cocoa Sustainability Production Networks', *Geoforum*, 120: 186–97.

Krippner, G. R. (2011), *Capitalizing on Crisis: The Political Origins of the Rise of Finance* (Cambridge, MA: Harvard University Press).

Kuhn, T. S. (1970), *The Structure of Scientific Revolutions*, 2nd edn (Chicago, IL: University of Chicago Press).

Kumar, A. (2020), *Monopsony Capitalism: Power and Production in the Twilight of the Sweatshop Age* (Cambridge: Cambridge University Press).

Kumarankandath, A. (2015), 'WTO Rules Against India's Domestic Content Requirements in Solar Power', *Down to Earth*, 2 September, https://www.downtoearth.org.in/news/energy/wto-rules-against-india-s-domestic-content-requirements-in-solar-power-50977, accessed 13 September 2022.

Kunz, R., Maisenbacher, J., and Paudel, L. N. (2021), 'The Financialization of Remittances: Governing through Emotions', *Review of International Political Economy*, 28(6): 1607–31.

Kurlantzick, J. (2016), *State Capitalism: How the Return of Statism Is Transforming the World* (Oxford and New York: Oxford University Press).

Kuznets, S. (1955), 'Economic Growth and Income Inequality', *American Economic Review*, 45(1): 1–28.

Kvangraven, I. H. (2021), 'Beyond the Stereotype: Restating the Relevance of the Dependency Research Programme', *Development and Change* 52(1): 76–112.

Lahav, G. (1998), 'Immigration and the State: The Devolution and Privatisation of Immigration Control in the EU', *Journal of Ethnic and Migration Studies*, 24(4): 675–94.

Lake, D. A. (1993), 'Leadership, Hegemony, and the International Economy: Naked Emperor or Tattered Monarch with Potential?' *International Studies Quarterly*, 37(4): 459–89.

Lake, D. A. (2006), 'International Political Economy: A Maturing Interdiscipline', in **B. Weingast** and **D. Wittman** (eds), *Oxford Handbook of Political Economy* (New York: Oxford University Press), 757–77.

Lake, D. A. (2009), 'Open Economy Politics: A Critical Review', *Review of International Organizations*, 4(3): 219–44.

Lan, P. (2006), *Global Cinderellas: Migrant Domestics and Newly Rich Employers in Taiwan.* (Durham, NC and London: Duke University Press).

Langford, N. J. (2019), 'The Governance of Social Standards in Emerging Markets: An Exploration of Actors and Interests Shaping Trustea as a Southern Multi-stakeholder Iinitiative', *Geoforum*, 104: 81–91.

Langley, P. (2008), *The Everyday Life of Global Finance: Saving and Borrowing in Anglo-America* (Oxford: Oxford University Press).

Lardy, N. R. (2019), *The State Strikes Back: The End of Economic Reform in China?* (Washington, DC: Peterson Institute for International Economics).

Lauber, K., Rutter, H., and Gilmore, A. B. (2021), 'Big Food and the World Health Organization: A Qualitative Study of Industry Attempts to Influence Global-Level Non-communicable Disease Policy', *BMJ Global Health*, 6:e005216.

LeBaron, G. (2014), 'Reconceptualizing Debt Bondage: Debt as a Class-Based Form of Labor Discipline', *Critical Sociology*, 40(5): 763–80.

LeBaron, G., Howard, N., Thibos, C., and Kyritsis, P. (2018), *Confronting Root Causes: Forced Labour in Global Supply Chains* (OpenDemocracy and University of Sheffield).

Lee, K. (2010), 'How Do We Move Forward on the Social Determinants of Health: The Global Governance Challenges', *Critical Public Health*, 20(1): 5–14.

Leiva, M. (2019), 'Cámara de Diputados rechaza articulado que planteaba expropiación del litio', *La Tercera*, https://www.latercera.com/pulso/noticia/camara-diputados-rechaza-articulado-planteaba-expropiacion-del-litio/835350/, accessed 13 September 2022.

Levy, D. L., and Newell, P. J. (2002), 'Business Strategy and International Environmental Governance: Toward a Neo-Gramscian Synthesis', *Global Environmental Politics* 2(4): 84–101.

Levy, D. L., and Prakash, A. (2003), 'Bargains Old and New: Multinational Corporations in Global Governance', *Business and Politics*, 5(2): 131–50.

Lin, J. Y., and Wang, Y. (2012), 'China's Integration with the World: Development as a Process of Learning and Industrial Upgrading', World Bank Policy Review Working Paper, no. 4799, (Washington, DC: World Bank).

Liu, A. B. (2020), *Tea War: A History of Capitalism in China and India* (New Haven, CT: Yale University Press).

Locke, R. (2013), *The Promise and Limits of Private Power: Promoting Labor Standards in a Global Economy* (Cambridge: Cambridge University Press).

Lockwood, E. (2021), 'The International Political Economy of Global Inequality', *Review of International Political Economy*, 28(2): 421–45.

Long, K. (2013), 'When Refugees Stopped Being Migrants: Movement, Labour and Humanitarian Protection', *Migration Studies* 1(1): 4–26.

Lustig, N., López-Calva, L. F., and Ortiz-Juarez, E. (2013), 'Declining Inequality in Latin America in the 2000s: The Cases of Argentina, Brazil, and Mexico', *World Development*, 44(C): 129–41.

Lustig, N., López-Calva, L. F., and Ortiz-Juarez, E. (2016), 'Deconstructing the Decline in Inequality in Latin America', in **K. Basu** and **J. Stiglitz** (eds), *Inequality and Growth: Patterns and Policy. Volume II: Regions and Regularities* (New York: Palgrave Macmillan).

Macartney, H. (2009), 'Variegated Neo-liberalism: Transnationally Oriented Fractions of Capital in EU Financial Market Integration', *Review of International Studies*, 35(2): 451–80.

Macdonald, K. (2007), 'Globalising Justice within Coffee Supply Chains? Fair Trade, Starbucks and the Transformation of Supply Chain Governance', *Third World Quarterly*, 28(4): 793–812.

Macdonald, K. (2012), 'Global Production: An Overview', in **R. Pettman** (ed.), *Handbook on International Political Economy* (Singapore: World Scientific), 57–71.

MacDonald, K. (2014), *The Politics of Global Supply Chains* (Cambridge: Polity).

MacDonald, K., and Balaton-Chrimes, S. (2016), 'The Complaints System of the Roundtable on Sustainable Palm Oil (RSPO)', Corporate Accountability Research, Non-Judicial Redress Mechanisms Report Series 15, https://ssrn.com/abstract=2880049, accessed 10 September 2022.

Mackinder, H. J. (1904), 'The Geographical Pivot of History', *Geographical Journal*, 23(4): 421–37.

Madrid, R. L. (1992), *Overexposed. US Banks Confront the Third World Debt Crisis* (Boulder, CO: Westview Press).

Malets, O. (2015), 'When Transnational Standards Hit the Ground: Domestic Regulations, Compliance Assessment and Forest Certification in Russia', *Journal of Environmental Policy & Planning* 17(3): 332–59.

Maniates, M. (2001), 'Individualisation: Plant a Tree, Buy a Bike, Save the World?' *Global Environmental Politics*, 1(3): 31–52.

Maniates, M. (2002), 'In Search of Consumptive Resistance: The Voluntary Simplicity Movement', in **T. Princen, M. Maniates, and K. Conca** (eds), *Confronting Consumption* (Cambridge, MA: MIT).

Mann, M. (2012), *The Sources of Social Power: Volume 4: Globalizations, 1945–2011* (Cambridge: Cambridge University Press).

Mares, R. (2017), 'Legalizing Human Rights Due Diligence and the Separation of Entities Principle', in **S. Deva** and **D. Bilchitz** (eds), *Building a Treaty on Business and Human Rights: Context and Contours* (Cambridge: Cambridge University Press), 266–96.

Markowitz, E., and Shariff, A. (2012), 'Climate Change and Moral Judgement', *Nature Climate Change*, 2: 243–47.

Marmot, M. (2015), *The Health Gap: The Challenge of an Unequal World* (London: Bloomsbury).

Marshall, S. (2004), 'Developing Countries Face Double Burden of Disease', *Bulletin of the World Health Organization*, 82(7): 556.

Marten, R., and Hawkins, B. (2018), 'Stop the Toasts: The Global Fund's Disturbing New Partnership', *Lancet*, 391(10122): 735–36.

Martin, A., and McLaughlin, S. (2021), 'COVID Response: The Primary Dealer Credit Facility', Federal Reserve Bank of New York Staff Report No. 981.

Marx, K., and Engels, F. (1848), *The Communist Manifesto*.

Mason, P. (2015), *Postcapitalism: A Guide to Our Future* (London: Allen Lane).

Massey, D. S., and Liang, Z. (1989), 'The Long-Term Consequences of a Temporary Worker Program: The US Bracero Experience', *Population Research and Policy Review* 8(3): 199–226.

Matejova, M., Parker, S., and Dauvergne, P. (2018), 'The Politics of Repressing Environmentalists as Agents of Foreign Influence', *Australian Journal of International Affairs*, 72(2): 145–62.

Mattli, W. (2018), *Darkness by Design: The Hidden Power in Global Capital Markets* (Princeton, NJ: Princeton University Press).

Mauad, A., and Betsill, M. (2019), 'A Changing Role in Global Climate Governance: São Paulo Mixing Its Climate and International Policies', *Revista Brasileira de Política Internacional*, 62(2) (17 October): e009, https://doi.org/10.1590/0034-7329201900209, accessed 13 September 2022.

Mayer, F., and Gereffi, G. (2010), 'Regulation and Economic Globalization: Prospects and Limits of Private Governance', *Business and Politics*, 12(3): 1–25.

Mayer, F., and Gereffi, G. (2019), 'International Development Organizations and Global Value Chains', in **Stefano Ponte, Gary Gereffi, and Gale Raj-Reichert** (eds), *Handbook on Global Value Chains* (Cheltenham: Edward Elgar).

Mayer, F., and Phillips, N. (2017), 'Outsourcing Governance: States and the Politics of a "Global Value Chain World"', *New Political Economy*, 22(2): 134–52.

Mbembe, A. J. (2016), 'Decolonizing the University: New Directions', *Arts and Humanities in Higher Education*, 15(1): 29–45.

McBarnet, D. J., Voiculescu, A., and Campbell, T. (eds) (2007), *The New Corporate Accountability: Corporate Social Responsibility and the Law.*(Cambridge University Press).

McCarthy, L., Soundararajan, V., and Taylor, S. (2021), 'The Hegemony of Men in Global Value Chains: Why It Matters for Labour Governance', *Human Relations*, 74(12): 2051–74.

McCoy, A. (2003), *The Politics of Heroin: CIA Complicity in the Global Heroin Trade* (New York: Lawrence Hill).

McDermott, C. L., Irland, L. C., and Pacheco, P. (2015), 'Forest Certification and Legality Initiatives in the Brazilian Amazon: Lessons for Effective and Equitable Forest Governance', *Forest Policy and Economics*, 50: 134–42.

McNamara, K. R. (2002), 'Rational Fictions: Central Bank Independence and the Social Logic of Delegation', *West European Politics*, 25: 47–76.

McNamara, K. R., and Newman A. L. (2020), 'The Big Reveal: COVID-19 and Globalization's Great Transformations', *International Organization*, 74: E59–E77.

McNeill, J. R., and McNeill, W. H. (2003), *The Human Web: A Bird's-Eye View of World History* (New York: W. W. Norton).

Meagher, K. (2019), 'Working in Chains: African Informal Workers and Global Value Chains', *Agrarian South: Journal of Political Economy*, 8(1–2): 64–92.

Mearsheimer, J. (2002), 'The False Promise of International Institutions', *International Security*, 19(3): 5–49.

Mellor, M. (2006), 'Ecofeminist Political Economy', *International Journal of Green Economics*, 1(1–2): 139–50.

Mellor, M. (2017), 'Ecofeminist Political Economy: A Green and Feminist Agenda', in **S. McGregor** (ed.), *Routledge Handbook of Gender and Environment* (London: Routledge), 86–100.

Merrill Lynch (2021), 'Capital Market Outlook', 13 December.

Mezzadri, A. (2016), 'Class, Gender and the Sweatshop: On the Nexus between Labour Commodification and Exploitation', *Third World Quarterly*, 37(10): 1877–1900.

Mezzadri, A. (2017), *The Sweatshop Regime: Labouring Bodies, Exploitation, and Garments 'Made in India'* (Cambridge: Cambridge University Press).

Mikler, J. (2018), *The Political Power of Global Corporations* (Oxford: John Wiley).

Middell, M., and Naumann, K. (2010), 'Global History and the Spatial Turn: From the Impact of Area Studies to the Study of Critical Junctures of Globalization', *Journal of Global History*, 5(1): 149–70.

Migration Data Portal (2022), 'Labour Migration', https://www.migrationdataportal.org/themes/labour-migration, accessed 10 September 2022.

Milanovic, B. (2005), *Worlds Apart* (Princeton, NJ: Princeton University Press).

Milanovic, B. (2016), *Global Inequality: A New Approach for the Age of Globalization* (Cambridge, MA: Belknap Press of Harvard University Press).

Milberg, W. (2008), 'Shifting Sources and Uses of Profits: Sustaining US Financialization with Global Value Chains', *Economy and Society*, 37(3): 420–51.

Milberg, W., and Winkler, D. (2013), *Outsourcing Economics: Global Value Chains in Capitalist Development* (Cambridge: Cambridge University Press).

Mill, J. S. (1909), *Principles of Political Economy, with Some of Their Applications to Social Philosophy* (London: Longmans, Green & Co.)

Milstein, E., and Wessel, D. (2021), 'What Did the Fed Do in Response to the Covid-19 Crisis?', Brookings Institution, 17 December.

Minsky, H. ([1986] 2008), *Stabilizing an Unstable Economy* (New York: McGraw-Hill).

Mitchell, A. D., and Studdert, D. M. (2012), 'Plain Packaging of Tobacco Products in Australia: A Novel Regulation Faces Legal Challenge', *Journal of the American Medical Association*, 307(3): 261–62.

Mkandawire, P. T., and Soludo, C. C. (2003) (eds), *African Voices on Structural Adjustment: A Companion to Our Continent, Our Future* (Lawrenceville, NJ: Africa World Press).

Montgomerie, J. (2019), *Should We Abolish Household Debts?* (Cambridge: Polity).

Montoya-Aguirre, M., Ortiz-Juarez, E., and Santiago, A. (2021), *Protecting Women's Livelihoods in Times of Pandemic: Temporary Basic Income and the Road to Gender Equality* (New York: United Nations Development Programme).

Moolakkattu, J. (2009), 'Robert W. Cox and Critical Theory of International Relations', *International Studies*, 46(4): 439–56.

Moon, Suerie, Sridhar, D., Pate, M. A., et al. (2015), 'Will Ebola Change the Game? Ten Essential Reforms Before the Next Pandemic: The Report of the Harvard-LSHTM Independent Panel on the Global Response to Ebola', *Lancet* 386(10009): 2204–21.

Moore, J. (2003), '"The Modern World-System" as Environmental History? Ecology and the Rise of Capitalism', *Theory and Society*, 32(3): 307–77.

Moore, J. (2015), *Capitalism in the Web of Life: Ecology and the Accumulation of Capital* (London: Verso).

Moore, S. (2012), 'Something in the Air: The Forgotten Crisis of Britain's Poor Air Quality' (London: Policy Exchange), https://policyexchange.org.uk/wp-content/uploads/2016/09/something-in-the-air-1.pdf, accessed 13 September 2022.

Moran, N. (2017), 'The First Twenty Cases Under GATT Article XX: Tuna or Shrimp Dear?', in **G. Adinolfi, F. Baetens, J. Caiado, A. Lupone, and A. Micara** (eds), *International Economic Law: Contemporary Issues* (Cham: Springer), 3–22.

Morand, S., and Lajaunie, C. (2021), 'Outbreaks of Vector-Borne and Zoonotic Diseases Are Associated With Changes in Forest Cover and Oil Palm Expansion at Global Scale', *Frontiers in Veterinary Science*, 8:661063.

Morin, J.-F., Dür, A., and Lechner, L. (2018), 'Mapping the Trade and Environment Nexus: Insights from a New Data Set', *Global Environmental Politics*, 18(1): 122–39.

Moschella, M. (2013), 'Designing the Financial Stability Board: A Theoretical Investigation of Mandate, Discretion, and Membership', *Journal of International Relations and Development* 16: 380–405.

Moschella, M. (2015), 'The Institutional Roots of Incremental Ideational Change: The IMF and Capital Controls After the Global Financial Crisis', *British Journal of Politics and International Relations*, 17: 442–60.

Moschella, M., and Tsingou, E. (2013) (eds), *Great Expectations, Slow Transformations: Incremental Change in Post-crisis Regulation* (Colchester: ECPR Press).

Mosley, L. (2017), 'Workers' Rights in Global Value Chains: Possibilities for Protection and for Peril', *New Political Economy*, 22(2): 153–68.

Mosley, L. (2021), 'Race and Identity in the Study of International Political Economy', *Global Perspectives*, 2(1): 1–2.

Mudambi, R. (2008), 'Location, Control and Innovation in Knowledge-Intensive Industries', *Journal of Economic Geography*, 8(5): 699–725.

Mudge, S. L. (2008), 'What Is Neo-Liberalism?', *Socio-Economic Review*, 6: 703–31.

Mudge, S. L. (2018), *Leftism Reinvented: Western Parties from Socialism to Neoliberalism* (Cambridge, MA: Harvard University Press).

Murphy, C., and Nelson, D. (2001), 'International Political Economy: A Tale of Two Heterodoxies', *British Journal of Politics and International Relations*, 3(3): 393–412.

Nadvi, K., and Raj-Reichert, G. (2015), 'Governing Health and Safety at Lower Tiers of the Computer Industry Global Value Chain', *Regulation & Governance*, 9(3): 243–58.

Naím, M. (2005), *Illicit: How Smugglers, Traffickers, and Copycats are Hijacking the Global Economy* (New York: Doubleday).

Nakamura, A. (2020), *Shingata conona to hinkon joshi* (COVID-19 and Young Women in Poverty) (Tokyo: Takarajimasha).

Nance, M. T. (2018), 'The Regime that FATF Built: An Introduction to the Financial Action Task Force', *Crime, Law and Social Change*, 69: 109–29.

Narayan, D., Chambers, R., Shah, M. K., and Petesch, P. (1999), *Voices of the Poor: Crying Out for Change* (Washington, DC: World Bank).

Nasdaq (2020), 'UK Online Shopping and E-Commerce Statistics for 2017', https://www.nasdaq.com/articles/uk-online-shopping-and-e-commerce-statistics-2017-2017-03-14, accessed 10 September 2022.

Nathan, D., and Kalpana, V. (2007), *Issues in the Analysis of Global Value Chains and Their Impact on Employment and Incomes in India* (Geneva: International Institute for Labour Studies).

Nathan, D., Tewari, M. and **Sarkar, S.** (2016) (eds), *Labour in Global Value Chains in Asia* (Cambridge: Cambridge University Press).

Naughton, B. (2015), 'China and the Two Crises', in **T. J. Pempel** and **K. Tsunekawa** (eds), *Two Crises, Different Outcomes: East Asia and Global Finance* (Ithaca, NY: Cornell University Press), 110–34.

Nayak, R., and Padhye, R. (2017) (eds), *Automation in Garment Manufacturing* (Duxford: Woodhead).

Neely, M. T. (2020), 'Essential and Expendable: Gendered Labor in the Coronavirus Crisis', Stanford Clayman Institute for Gender Research, Stanford, CA, 3 June, https://gender.stanford.edu/news-publications/gender-news/essential-and-expendable-gendered-labor-coronavirus-crisis, accessed 10 September 2022.

Neilson, J., and Pritchard, B. (2010), 'Fairness and Ethicality in Their Place: The Regional Dynamics of Fair Trade and Ethical Sourcing Agendas in the Plantation Districts of South India', *Environment and Planning A*, 42: 1833–51.

Neilson, J., Pritchard, B., and Yeung, H. W. C. (2014), 'Global Value Chains and Global Production Networks in the Changing International Political Economy: An Introduction', *Review of International Political Economy*, 21(1): 1–8.

Nett, R. (1971), 'The Civil Right We Are Not Ready For: The Right of Free Movement of People', *Ethics*, 8(3): 212–27.

Newell, P. (2005), 'Race, Class and the Global Politics of Environmental Inequality', *Global Environmental Politics*, 5(3): 70–94.

Ngai, P., and Smith, C. (2007), 'Putting Transnational Labour Process in Its Place: The Dormitory Labour Regime in Post-socialist China', *Work, Employment and Society*, 21(1): 27–45.

NHS Sheffield Clinical Commissioning Group (2012), 'NHS Sheffield CCG's Contribution to Reducing Health Inequalities in Sheffield', https://www.sheffieldccg.nhs.uk/Downloads/Equality%20and%20diversity/NHS%20Sheffield%20CCG%20contribution%20to%20reducing%20health%20inequalities.pdf, accessed 12 September 2022.

Nike (n.d.), http://manufacturingmap.nikeinc.com/, accessed 3 March 2021.

Nölke, A., ten Brink, T., Claar, S., and May, C. (2015), 'Domestic Structures, Foreign Economic Policies and Global Economic Order: Implications from the Rise of Large Emerging Economies', *European Journal of International Relations*, 21(3): 538–67.

North, P. (2005), 'Scaling Alternative Economic Practices? Some Lessons from Alternative Currencies', *Transactions of the Institute of British Geographers*, 30(2): 221–33.

Nussbaum, M. (2000), *Women and Human Development: The Capabilities Approach* (Cambridge: Cambridge University Press).

O'Neill, J. (2001), *Building Better Global Economic BRICs*, Global Economics Paper No. 66, November (London and New York: Goldman Sachs), http://www.goldmansachs.com/our-thinking/archive/archive-pdfs/build-better-brics.pdf, accessed 10 September 2022.

O'Neill, K. (2017), *The Environment and International Relations*, 2nd edn (Cambridge: Cambridge University Press).

Oatley, T. (2011), 'The Reductionist Gamble: Open Economy Politics in the Global Economy', *International Organization*, 65(2): 311–41.

Oatley, T. (2021), 'Regaining Relevance: IPE and a Changing Global Political Economy', *Cambridge Review of International Affairs*, 34(2): 318–27.

OCMAL (El Observatorio de Conflictos Mineros de América Latina) (2020), 'Tribunal Internacional de los Derechos de la Naturaleza dictamina moratoria para la minería del litio en Atacama', 21 January, https://www.ocmal.org/tribunal-internacional-de-los-derechos-de-la-naturaleza-dictamina-moratoria-para-la-mineria-del-litio-en-atacama/, accessed 13 September 2022.

OEC (n.d.), https://oec.world, accessed 22 July 2022.

OECD (Organization for Economic Co-operation and Development) (2016), *International Migration Outlook 2015* (Paris: OECD).

OECD (2017), *International Migration Outlook 2016* (Paris: OECD).

OECD (2018a), *Governance Frameworks to Counter Illicit Trade* (Paris: OECD).

OECD (2018b), *International Migration Outlook 2017* (Paris: OECD).

OECD (2019), *International Migration Outlook 2018* (Paris: OECD).

OECD (2020), *International Migration Outlook 2019* (Paris: OECD).

OECD (2021*a*), *International Migration Outlook 2020* (Paris: OECD).

OECD (2021*b*), 'OECD Income Distribution Database (IDD)', https://www.oecd.org/social/income-distribution-database.htm, accessed 14 September 2022.

Ohmae, K. (1995), *The End of the Nation-State: the Rise of Regional Economies* (New York: Simon & Schuster).

Okafor-Yarwood, I., and Adewumi, I. J. (2020), 'Toxic Waste Dumping in the Global South as a Form of Environmental Racism: Evidence from the Gulf of Guinea', *African Studies*, 79(3): 285–304.

Olivetti, C., and Petrongolo, B. (2008), 'Unequal Pay or Unequal Employment? A Cross-Country Analysis of Gender Gaps', *Journal of Labor Economics*, 26(4): 621–54.

Ollila, E. (2005), 'Global Health Priorities: Priorities of the Wealthy?', *Globalization and Health* 1, 6, https://doi.org/10.1186/1744-8603-1-6, accessed 12 September 2022.

ONS (Office of National Statistics, UK) (2019), 'The Decoupling of Economic Growth from Carbon Emissions: UK Evidence', https://www.ons.gov.uk/economy/nationalaccounts/uksectoraccounts/compendium/economicreview/october2019/thedecouplingofeconomicgrowthfromcarbonemissionsukevidence, accessed 13 September 2022.

Ontario (2009), 'Green Energy and Green Economy Act, 2009, S.O. 2009, c. 12 - Bill 150', https://www.ontario.ca/laws/statute/s09012, accessed 13 September 2022.

OPHI (Oxford Poverty and Human Development Initiative) (2022). Indonesia Country Briefing, Oxford Poverty and Human Development Initiative, University of Oxford.

Oqubay, A., and Lin, J. (2019), 'Preface', in **A. Oqubay** and **J. Lin** (eds), *China–Africa and an Economic Transformation* (Oxford: Oxford University Press).

Overeem, P., Theuws, M., and Heyl, D. (2021), *Spinning Around Workers' Rights: International Companies Linked to Forced Labour in Tamil Nadu Spinning Mills* (SOMO and Arisa).

Oxfam (2002), *Rigged Rules and Double Standards: Trade, Globalisation, and the Fight against Poverty* (Oxford: Oxfam).

Oxfam (2013), *Labour Rights in Unilever's Supply Chain: From Compliance Towards Good Practice* (Oxford: Oxfam International).

Oxfam (2020), *Levelling Up: How Wealth Taxes Can Reduce Inequalities*, Policy and Practice Presented to the World Economic Forum, 20 January.

Oxfam (2022), 'WTO Agrees a Deal on Patents for COVID Vaccines: But Campaigners Say This is Absolutely Not the Broad Intellectual Property Waiver the World Desperately Needs', 17 June, https://www.oxfam.org/en/press-releases/wto-agrees-deal-patents-covid-vaccines-campaigners-say-absolutely-not-broad, accessed 12 September 2022.

Oxford Economics (2019), *How Robots Change the World: What Automation Really Means for Jobs and Productivity* (Oxford: Oxford Economics).

Packard, R. M. (2016), *A History of Global Health: Interventions Into the Lives of Other Peoples* (Baltimore, MD: Johns Hopkins University Press).

Pagliari, S., and Wilf, M. (2021), 'Regulatory Novelty after Financial Crises: Evidence from International Banking and Securities Standards, 1975–2016', *Regulation & Governance*, 15(3): 933–51.

Pagliari, S., and Young, K. L. (2014), 'Leveraged Interests: Financial Industry Power and the Role of Private Sector Coalitions', *Review of International Political Economy*, 21(3): 575–610.

Palpacuer, F., and Smith, A. (eds) (2021), *Rethinking Value Chains: Tackling the Challenges of Global Capitalism* (Bristol: Policy Press).

Parker, L. (2018), 'China's Ban on Trash Imports Shifts Waste Crisis to Southeast Asia', *National Geographic*, 16 November, https://www.nationalgeographic.com/environment/2018/11/china-ban-plastic-trash-imports-shifts-waste-crisis-southeast-asia-malaysia/, accessed 13 September 2022.

Partzsch, L. (2020), *Alternatives to Multilateralism: New Forms of Social and Environmental Governance* (Cambridge, MA: MIT).

Partzsch, L., and Vlaskamp, M. C. (2016), 'Mandatory Due Diligence for "Conflict Minerals" and Illegally Logged Timber: Emergence and Cascade of a New Norm on Foreign Accountability', *Extractive Industries and Society*, 3(4): 978–86.

Patel, R., and Moore, J. W. (2017), *A History of the World in Seven Cheap Things: Guide to Capitalism, Nature, and the Future of the Planet* (Oakland: University of California Press).

Pauwelyn, J. (2020), 'Export Restrictions in Times of Pandemic: Options and Limits Under International Trade Agreements', *Journal of World Trade*, 54(5): 727–47.

Payne, A., and Phillips, N. (2014) (eds), *Handbook of the International Political Economy of Governance* (Cheltenham: Edward Elgar).

Pearse, G. (2012), *Greenwash: Big Brands and Carbon Scams* (Collingwood, VIC: Black Inc.).

Pearson, R. (2007), 'Beyond Women Workers: Gendering CSR', *Third World Quarterly*, 28(4): 731–49.

Pecoud, A., and de Guchteneire, P. (2006), 'International Migration, Border Controls and Human Rights: Assessing the Relevance of a Right to Mobility', *Journal of Borderlands Studies*, 21(1): 69–86.

People's Health Movement (2018), *The Struggle for Health Is the Struggle for a More Equitable, Just and Caring World*, Declaration of the Fourth People's Health Assembly.

Perez-Aleman, P. (2013), 'Regulation in the Process of Building Capabilities: Strengthening Competitiveness While Improving Food Safety and Environmental Sustainability in Nicaragua', *Politics & Society*, 41(4): 589–620.

Perry, J., and Nölke, A. (2006), 'The Political Economy of International Accounting Standards', *Review of International Political Economy* 13(4): 559–86.

Peterson, V. S. (2005), 'How (the Meaning of) Gender Matters in Political Economy', *New Political Economy* 10(4): 499–521.

Petrova, M. (2018), 'We Traced what It Takes to Make an iPhone, from Its Initial Design to the Components and Raw Materials Needed to Make it a Reality', CNBC, 14 December 2018, available at: www.cnbc.com/2018/12/13/inside-apple-iphone-where-parts-and-materials-come-from.html (last accessed February 2021).

Petry, J., Fichtner, J., and Heemskerk, E. (2021), 'Steering Capital: The Growing Private Authority of Index Providers in the Age of Passive Asset Management', *Review of International Political Economy*, 28(1): 152–76.

Pevehouse, J. C., and Seabrooke, L. (2022) (eds), *The Oxford Handbook of International Political Economy* (Oxford: Oxford University Press).

Phillips, N. (2011), 'Informality, Global Production Networks and the Dynamics of "Adverse Incorporation"', *Global Networks*, 11(3): 380–97.

Phillips, N. (2013), 'Unfree Labour and Adverse Incorporation in the Global Economy: Comparative Perspectives from Brazil and India', *Economy and Society*, 42(2): 171–96.

Phillips, N. (2016), 'Labour in Global Production: Reflections on Coxian Insights in a World of Global Value Chains', *Globalizations*, 13(5): 594–607.

Phillips, N. (2017), 'Power and Inequality in the Global Political Economy', *International Affairs*, 93(2): 429–44.

Phillips, N., and Sakamoto, L. (2012), 'Global Production Networks, Chronic Poverty and "Slave Labour" in Brazil', *Studies in Comparative International Development*, 47(3): 287–315.

Pianezzi, D., and Grossi, G. (2018), 'Corruption in Migration Management: A Network Perspective', *International Review of Administrative Sciences*, 86(1): 152–68.

Pickett, K., and Wilkinson, R. (2010), *The Spirit Level* (Harlow: Penguin).

Piketty, T. (2014), *Capital in the Twenty-First Century*, trans. Arthur Goldhammer (Cambridge, MA: Harvard University Press).

Piper, N., Rosewarne, S., and Withers, M. (2017), 'Migrant Precarity in Asia: "Networks of Labour Activism" for a Rights-Based Governance of Migration', *Development and Change*, 48(5): 1089–1110.

Piper, N., and Satterthwaite, M. (2007), 'The Rights of Migrant Women', in **R. Cholewinski, R. Perruchoud, and E. Macdonald** (eds), *International Migration Law: Developing Paradigms and Key Challenges* (The Hague: T.M.C. Asser), 237–54.

Plumwood, V. (2002), *Environmental Culture: The Ecological Crisis of Reason* (Oxford: Routledge).

Polanyi, K. (1944), *The Great Transformation: The Political and Economic Origins of Our Time* (Boston, NJ: Beacon).

Pollard, J., and Samers, M. (2007), 'Islamic Banking and Finance: Postcolonial Political Economy and the Decentring of Economic Geography', *Transactions of the Institute of British Geographers*, 32(3): 313–30.

Ponte, S. (2020), 'The Hidden Costs of Environmental Upgrading in Global Value Chains', *Review of International Political Economy*, available at: https://doi.org/10.1080/09692290.2020.1816199, pp. 1–26.

Ponte, S., Gereffi, G., and Raj-Reichert, G. (2019) (eds), *Handbook on Global Value Chains*, (Cheltenham: Edward Elgar).

Porritt, J. (2007), *Capitalism As If the World Matters* (New York: Earthscan).

Posen, A. S. (2021), 'The Price of Nostalgia: America's Self-Defeating Economic Retreat', *Foreign Affairs*, 100(3): 28–43.

Posthuma, A., and Rossi, A. (2017), 'Coordinated Governance in Global Value Chains: Supranational Dynamics and the Role of the International Labour Organization', *New Political Economy*, 22(2): 186–202.

Povoledo, E. (2008), 'Ancient Vase Comes Home to a Hero's Welcome', *New York Times*, 19 January.

Prasad, M. (2006), *The Politics of Free Markets: The Rise of Neoliberal Economic Policies in Britain,*

France, Germany and the United States (Chicago, IL: University of Chicago Press).

Prebisch, R. (1959), 'Commercial Policy in the Underdeveloped Countries (from the point of view of Latin America)', *American Economic Review,* 49(2): 251–73.

Prell, C., and Feng, K. (2015), 'Unequal Carbon Exchanges: The Environmental and Economic Impacts of Iconic U.S. Consumption Items', *Journal of Industrial Ecology,* 20(3): 537–46.

Qobo, M., and Soko, M. (2015), 'The Rise of Emerging Powers in the Global Development Finance Architecture: The Case of the BRICS and the New Development Bank', *South African Journal of International Affairs,* 22(3): 277–88.

Quaglia, L. (2019), 'The Politics of State Compliance with International "Soft Law" in Finance', *Governance,* 32(1): 45–62.

Quah, D. (1996), 'Twin Peaks: Growth and Convergence in Models of Distribution Dynamics', *Economic Journal,* 106(437): 1045–55.

Ragavan, S., and Vanni, A. (2021), *Intellectual Property Law and Access to Medicines: TRIPS Agreement, Health, and Pharmaceuticals* (Abingdon: Routledge).

Ragayah, H. M. Z. (2008), 'Income Inequality in Malaysia', *Asian Economic Policy Review,* 3(1): 114–32.

Raghuram, P., and Sondhi, G. (2021), 'Gender and International Student Migration', in **C. Mora** and **N. Piper** (eds), *Palgrave Handbook on Gender and Migration* (Palgrave Macmillan), 221–36.

Rai, S., Hoskyns, C., and Thomas, D. (2014), 'Depletion: The Cost of Social Reproduction', *International Feminist Journal of Politics,* 16(3): 407–29.

Rankin, Katherine N. (2001), 'Governing Development: Neoliberalism, Microcredit, and Rational Economic Woman', *Economy and Society,* 30(1): 18–37.

Rappeport, A., and Smialek, J. (2021), 'A K-Shaped Recovery: This Time on a Global Scale', *New York Times,* 6 April.

Rauber, P. (2018), 'Environmental Casualties of Trump's Trade War', 6 September, https://www. sierraclub.org/sierra/environmental-casualties-trump-s-trade-war, accessed 13 September 2022.

Raustiala, K. (1999), 'Liberalization and International Narcotics Trafficking', *NYU Journal of International Law and Politics,* 32: 89–145.

Ravallion, M. (1997), 'Can High-Inequality Developing Countries Escape Absolute Poverty?' *Economics Letters,* 56(1): 51–57.

Ravallion, M. (1998), 'Does Aggregation Hide the Harmful Effects of Inequality on Growth?' *Economic Letters,* 61(1): 73–77.

Rawls, J. (1971), *A Theory of Justice* (Cambridge, MA: Harvard University Press).

Ravenhill, J. (2008), 'In Search of the Missing Middle', *Review of International Political Economy,* 15(1): 18–29.

Raworth, K. (2017), *Doughnut Economics* (White River, VT: Chelsea Green).

Raworth, K., and Kidder, T. (2009), 'Mimicking "Lean" in Global Value Chains: It's the Workers Who Get Leaned On', in **J. Bair** (ed.), *Frontiers of Commodity Chain Research* (Stanford, CA: Stanford University Press), 165–89.

Retail Information Systems (RIS) (2020), 'Top 100 Retailers 2020', 29/06/2020, available at: https://risnews.com/top-100-retailers-2020

Rethel, L. (2011), 'Whose Legitimacy? Islamic Finance and the Global Financial Order', *Review of International Political Economy,* 18(1): 75–98.

Rethel, L., and Sinclair, T. J. (2012), *The Problem with Banks* (London: Zed Books).

Reuters (2017), 'The Philip Morris Files', https://www.reuters.com/investigates/section/pmi/, accessed 12 September 2022.

Rixen, T. (2013), 'Why Reregulation After the Crisis is Feeble: Shadow Banking, Offshore Financial Centers, and Jurisdictional Competition', *Regulation and Governance,* 7(4): 435–59.

Roberts, A., Trommer, S., and Hannah, E. (2019), 'Gender Impacts of Trade and Investment Agreements', Policy briefing prepared for the UK Women's Budget Group, September, https://wbg.org.uk/analysis/uk-policy-briefings/gender-impacts-of-trade-and-investment-agreements/, accessed 10 September 2022.

Roberts, C., Armijo, L. E., and Katada, S. N. (2018), *The BRICS and Collective Financial Statecraft* (New York: Oxford University Press).

Robinson, P. K. (2009), 'Responsible Retailing: Regulating Fair and Ethical Trade', *Journal of International Development,* 21(7): 1015–26.

Robinson, W. I. (2014), *Global Capitalism and the Crisis of Humanity* (New York: Cambridge University Press).

Robles Aguilar, G., and Sumner, A. (2019), 'Who Are the World's Poor? A New Profile of Global Multidimensional Poverty', CGD Working Paper No. 499, Center for Global Development, Washington, DC.

Rodríguez-Garavito, C. A. (2005), 'Global Governance and Labor Rights: Codes of Conduct and Anti-sweatshop Struggles in Global Apparel Factories in Mexico and Guatemala', *Politics & Society*, 33(2): 203–33.

Rodríguez-Garavito, C. A. (2017) (ed.), *Business and Human Rights: Beyond the End of the Beginning* (Cambridge: Cambridge University Press).

Rodrik, D. (2011), *The Globalization Paradox* (Oxford: Oxford University Press).

Rodrik, D. (2019), 'Many Forms of Populism', *VoxEU.Org*, 29 October, https://voxeu.org/article/many-forms-populism, accessed 10 September 2022.

Roemer, J. E. (1998), *Equality of Opportunity* (Cambridge, MA: Harvard University Press).

Roemer-Mahler, A. (2013), 'Business Conflict and Global Politics: The Pharmaceutical Industry and the Global Protection of Intellectual Property Rights', *Review of International Political Economy*, 20(1): 121–52.

Romero Toledo, H., Videla, A., and Gutiérrez, F. (2017), 'Explorando conflictos entre comunidades indígenas y la industria minera en Chile: las transformaciones socioambientales de la región de Tarapacá y el caso de Lagunillas', *Estudios atacameños*, 55: 231–50.

Rose, N. (1996), 'The Death of the Social? Re-figuring the Territory of Government', *Economy and Society*, 25: 327–56.

Rosenau, J. N. (1999), 'Toward an Ontology for Global Governance', in **M. Hewson** and **T. J. Sinclair** (eds), *Approaches to Global Governance Theory* (Albany: State University of New York).

Rosenau, J. N., and Czempiel, E.-O. (1992) (eds), *Governance without Government* (Cambridge: Cambridge University Press).

Rosenberg, J. (2016), 'International Relations and the Prison of Political Science', *International Relations*, 30(2): 127–53.

Roser, M., and Ortiz-Ospina, E. (2016), *Our World in Data: Income Inequality*, October, https://ourworldindata.org/income-inequality, accessed 10 September 2022.

Rossi, A. (2013), 'Does Economic Upgrading Lead to Social Upgrading in Global Production Networks? Evidence from Morocco', *World Development*, 46: 223–33.

Rossi, A. (2019), 'Social Upgrading', in **S. Ponte, G. Gereffi, and G. Raj-Reichert** (eds), *Handbook on Global Value Chains* (Cheltenham: Edward Elgar).

Ruckert, A., MacDonald L., and Proulx, K. R. (2017), 'Post-neoliberalism in Latin America: A Conceptual Review', *Third World Quarterly*, 38: 1583–1602.

Ruggie, J. G. (1982), 'International Regimes, Transactions, and Change: Embedded Liberalism in the Postwar Economic Order', *International Organization*, 36(2): 379–415.

Ruggie, J. G. (1999), 'What Makes the World Hang Together? Neo-utilitarianism and the Social Constructivist Challenge', in **P. Katzenstein, R. Keohane, and S. Krasner** (eds), *Exploration and Contestation in the Study of World Politics* (Cambridge, MA: MIT), 215–45.

Ruggie, J. G. (2014), 'Global Governance and "New Governance Theory": Lessons from Business and Human Rights', *Global Governance: A Review of Multilateralism and International Organizations*, 20(1): 5–17.

Ruiz, F. J. (2018), 'El Arco Minero del Orinoco: Diversificación del extractivismo y nuevos regímenes biopolíticos', Nueva Sociedad.

Rushton, S. (2020), 'The Growing Global Movement to End Outdoor Advertising', 11 August, http://www.ipsnews.net/2020/08/growing-global-movement-end-outdoor-advertising/, accessed 13 September 2022.

Saloojee, Y., and Dagli, E. (2000), 'Tobacco Industry Tactics for Resisting Public Policy on Health', *Bulletin of the World Health Organization*, 78(7): 902–10.

Sampson, M. (2021), 'The Evolution of China's Regional Trade Agreements: Power Dynamics and the Future of the Asia-Pacific', *Pacific Review*, 34(2): 259–89.

Samuelson, R. J. (2017), 'Will Robots Steal All Our Jobs?', *Washington Post*, 10 May, https://www.washingtonpost.com/opinions/will-robots-steal-all-our-jobs/2017/05/10/0a567a66-35a0-11e7-b412-62beef8121f7_story.html, accessed 10 September 2022.

Sandal, N. A. (2019), 'The Politics of Regime Mainstreaming: Knowledge Production and the Institutionalization of Islamic Finance', *Politics and Religion*, 12(4): 606–28.

Sarfaty, G. A. (2015), 'Shining Light on Global Supply Chains', *Harvard International Law Journal*, 56(2): 419–63.

Sassen, S. (1996), *Losing Control? Sovereignty in the Age of Globalization* (New York: Columbia University Press).

Schauenberg, T. (2019), 'After China's Import Ban, Where to with the World's Waste?', *DW*, 5 April, https://www.dw.com/en/after-chinas-import-ban-where-to-with-the-worlds-waste/a-48213871, accessed 13 September 2022.

Schell, O. (2011), 'How Walmart is Changing America', *Atlantic*, December 2011. Available at: www.theatlantic.com/magazine/archive/2011/12/how-walmart-is-changing-china/308709/ (last accessed February 2021).

Schrank, A., and Piore, M. (2018), *Root Cause Regulation: Protecting Work and Workers in the Twenty-First Century* (Cambridge, MA: Harvard University Press).

Scott, J. (2017), 'The Future of Agricultural Trade Governance in the World Trade Organization', *International Affairs*, 93(5): 1167–84.

Scott, J., and Wilkinson, R. (2011), 'The Poverty of the Doha Round and the Least Developed Countries', *Third World Quarterly*, 32(4): 611–27.

Scuffham, M. (2021), 'Wall Street Banks Set to Profit Again when Fed Withdraws Pandemic Stimulus', *Reuters*, 18 October, https://www.reuters.com/business/wall-street-banks-set-profit-again-when-fed-withdraws-pandemic-stimulus-2021-10-15/, accessed 11 September 2022.

Seabrooke, L. (2006), *The Social Sources of Financial Power* (Ithaca, NY and London: Cornell University Press).

Seabrooke, L., and Tsingou, E. (2021), 'Revolving Doors in International Financial Governance', *Global Networks*, 21(2): 294–319.

Seabrooke, L., and Young, K. L. (2017), 'The Networks and Niches of International Political Economy', *Review of International Political Economy*, 24(2): 288–331.

Selwyn, B. (2015), 'Twenty-First-Century International Political Economy: A Class-Relational Perspective', *European Journal of International Relations*, 21(3): 513–37.

Selwyn, B. (2019), 'Poverty Chains and Global Capitalism', *Competition & Change*, 23(1): 71–97.

Selwyn, B., Musiolek, B., and Ijarja, A. (2020), 'Making a Global Poverty Chain: Export Footwear Production and Gendered Labor Exploitation in Eastern and Central Europe', *Review of International Political Economy*, 27(2) 377–403.

Semuels, A. (2020), 'Millions of Americans Have Lost Jobs in the Pandemic: And Robots and AI Are Replacing Them Faster Than Ever', *Time*, 6 August, https://time.com/5876604/machines-jobs-coronavirus/, accessed 11 September 2022.

Sen, A. K. (1991), *Money and Value: On the Ethics and Economics of Finance* [Denaro e Valore: Etica ed Economia della Finanza] (Rome: Bank of Italy).

Sen, A. K. (1992), *Inequality Reexamined* (Cambridge, MA: Harvard University Press).

Sen, A. K. (1999), *Development as Freedom* (New York: Oxford University Press).

Seric, A., and Winkler, D. (2020), 'COVID-19 Could Spur Automation and Reverse Globalization: To Some Extent', *VoxEU.org*, https://voxeu.org/article/covid-19-could-spur-automation-and-reverse-globalisation-some-extent, accessed 11 September 2022.

Shafaeddin, M. (2000), 'What Did Frederick List Actually Say? Some Clarifications on the Infant Industry Argument', UNCTAD Discussion Paper 149, July, unctad.org/en/docs/dp_149.en.pdf, accessed 11 September 2022.

Shaffer, P., Kanbur, R., and Sandbrook, R. (eds) (2019), *Immiserizing Growth: When Growth Fails the Poor* (Oxford: Oxford University Press).

Shaw, D. J. (2011), *The World's Largest Humanitarian Agency: The Transformation of the UN World Food Programme and of Food Aid* (London: Palgrave Macmillan).

Sherman III, J. F. (2021), 'Irresponsible Exit: Exercising Force Majeure Provisions in Procurement Contracts', *Business and Human Rights Journal*, 6(1): 127–34.

Shields, S., Bruff, I., and Macartney, H. (2011), *Critical International Political Economy: Dialogue, Debate and Dissensus* (London: Palgrave Macmillan).

Shih, S. (1996), *Me-Too Is Not My Style: Challenge Difficulties, Break Through Bottlenecks, Create Values* (Taipei: Acer Foundation).

Shilliam, R. (2018*a*), 'Class Is Race: Brexit and the Popular Will', *International Political Sociology*, 12(1): 6–10.

Shilliam, R. (2018*b*), *Race and the Undeserving Poor: From Abolition to Brexit* (London: Agenda).

Shilliam, R. (2021), 'Enoch Powell: Britain's First Neoliberal Politician', *New Political Economy*, 26: 239–49.

Short, J. L., and Toffel, M. W. (2021), 'Manage the Suppliers That Could Harm Your Brand', *Harvard Business Review*, 99(2): 108–16.

Siciliano, G., Del Bene, D., Scheidel, A., Liu, J., and Urban, F. (2019), 'Environmental Justice and Chinese Dam-Building in the Global South', *Current Opinion in Environmental Sustainability*, 37: 20–27.

Sil, R., and Katzenstein, P. (2010), *Beyond Paradigms: Analytical Eclecticism in the Study of World Politics* (London: Palgrave Macmillan).

Siles-Brügge, G. (2014), 'Explaining the Resilience of Free Trade: The Smoot–Hawley Myth and the Crisis', *Review of International Political Economy*, 21(3): 535–75.

Simeone, L. M., and Piper, N. (2018), 'Making Rights in Times of Crisis: Civil Society and the Migrant Workers' Convention', in **A. Desmond** (ed.), *Shining New Light on the UN Migrant Workers Convention* (Pretoria: PULP), 45–71.

Simeone, L. M., and Piper, N. (2021), 'From Rights to Risk: Labour Migration and the Securitization of Justice', in **L. Weber** and **C. Tazreiter** (eds), *Handbook of Migration and Global Justice* (Cheltenham: Edward Elgar), 222–40.

Simone, A. (2004), 'People as Infrastructure: Intersecting Fragments in Johannesburg', *Public Culture*, 16(3): 407–29.

Simons, P., and Clancy, C. (2017), 'On Point: Fifty Years Ago, Canada Changed Its Immigration rules and in Doing so Changed the Face of this Country', *Edmonton Journal*, 29 June, https://edmontonjournal.com/news/insight/on-point-fifty-years-ago-canada-changed-its-immigration-rules-and-in-doing-so-changed-the-face-of-this-country, accessed 11 September 2022.

Sinclair, T. J. (2005), *The New Masters of Capital. American Bond Rating Agencies and the Politics of Creditworthiness* (Ithaca, NY: Cornell University Press).

Sinclair, T. J., and Thomas, K. P. (2001) (eds), *Structure and Agency in International Capital Mobility* (Basingstoke: Palgrave).

Singer, D. A. (2004), 'Capital Rules: The Domestic Politics of International Regulatory Harmonization', *International Organization*, 58(3): 531–65.

Singer, H. (1995), 'An Historical Perspective', in **M. ul Haq, R. Jolly, P, Streeten, and K. Haq** (eds), *The UN and the Bretton Woods Institutions: New Challenges for the Twenty-First Century* (London: Palgrave Macmillan).

Singh, J. P. (2016), *Sweet Talk: Paternalism and Collective Action in North–South Trade Negotiations* (Stanford, CA: Stanford University Press).

Singh, J. P. (2021), 'Race, Culture and Economics: An Example from North–South Trade Relations', *Review of International Political Economy*, 28(2): 323–35.

Singh, S. (2013), *Globalization & Money: A Global South Perspective* (Lanham and Plymouth: Rowman & Littlefield).

Slobodian, Q. (2018), *Globalists: The End of Empire and the Birth of Neoliberalism* (Cambridge, MA: Harvard University Press).

Smith, A. (1776), *On the Wealth of Nations* (London: W. Strahan and T. Cadell).

Smith, A. (1789), *An Inquiry into the Nature and Causes of the Wealth of Nations*, 5th edn.

Smith, C. (2021), 'US Inflation Hits Fastest Annual Pace Since 1982', *Financial Times*, 10 December, https://www.ft.com/content/f355feab-e9f0-4dfc-bcd7-1759983dfb16, accessed 19 July 2022.

Spencer, D. A. (2017), 'Work in and Beyond the Second Machine Age: The Politics of Production and Digital Technologies', *Work, Employment and Society*, 31: 142–52.

Spencer, D. A. (2018), 'Fear and Hope in an Age of Mass Automation: Debating the Future of Work', *New Technology, Work and Employment*, 33(1): 1–12.

Sprague, J. (2009), 'Transnational Capitalist Class in the Global Financial Crisis: A Discussion with Leslie Sklair', *Globalizations*, 6(4): 499–507.

Srnicek, N., and Williams, A. (2015), *Inventing the Future: Postcapitalism and a World without Work* (London: Verso).

Stark, S., and Bloom, D. E. (1985), 'The New Economics of Labor Migration', *American Economic Review*, 75(2): 173–78.

Statista (2020), 'E-commerce Share of Total Global Retail Sales from 2015 to 2023', https://www.statista.com/statistics/534123/e-commerce-share-of-retail-sales-worldwide/, accessed March 2021.

Statista (2021*a*), 'Advertising Media Owners Revenue Worldwide from 2012 to 2024', https://www.statista.com/statistics/236943/global-advertising-spending/

Statista (2021*b*), 'Number of Smartphones Sold to End Users Worldwide from 2007 to 2021', https://www.statista.com/statistics/263437/global-smartphone-sales-to-end-users-since-2007/, accessed 13 September 2022.

Steffen, W., Broadgate, W., Deutsch, L., Gaffney, O., and Ludwig, C. (2015), 'The Trajectory of the Anthropocene: The Great Acceleration', *Anthropocene Review*, 2(1): 81–98.

Stein, J. G., Stren, R., Fitzgibbon, J., and MacLean, M. (2001), *Networks of Knowledge: Collaborative Innovation in International Learning* (Toronto: University of Toronto Press).

Stephenson, J., Newman, K., and Mayhew, S. (2010), 'Population Dynamics and Climate Change: What Are the Links?' *Journal of Public Health*, 32(2): 150–56.

Stevenson, H. (2017), *Global Environmental Politics: Problems, Policy and Practice* (Cambridge: Cambridge University Press).

Stevenson, H. (2021), 'Reforming Global Environmental Governance in an Age of Bullshit', *Globalizations*, 18(1): 86–102.

Stewart, H. (2011), 'Robin Hood Tax: 1,000 Economists Urge G20 to Accept Tobin Tax',

Guardian, 13 April, https://www.theguardian.com/business/2011/apr/13/robin-hood-tax-economists-letter, accessed 12 September 2022.

Stone, D. (2005), *Global Knowledge Networks and International Development* (London: Routledge).

Stone, D. (2019), *Making Global Policy* (Cambridge: Cambridge University Press).

Strange, S. (1984), 'Preface', in **S. Strange** (ed.), *Paths to International Political Economy* (London: George Allen & Unwin), ix–xi.

Strange, S. (1986), *Casino Capitalism* (Oxford and New York: Basil Blackwell).

Strange, S. (1991), 'An Eclectic Approach', in **C. Murphy** and **R. Tooze** (eds), *The New International Political Economy* (Boulder, CO: Lynne Rienner), 33–49.

Stringer, C., and Michailova, S. (2018), 'Why Modern Slavery Thrives in Multinational Corporations' Global Value Chains', *Multinational Business Review*, 26(3): 194–206.

Stuart E., Samman, E., and Hunt, A. (2018), 'Informal is the New Normal', Working paper 530, Overseas Development Institute, London.

Sturgeon, T. J., and Kawakami, M. (2011), 'Global Value Chains in the Electronics Industry: Characteristics, Crisis, and Upgrading Opportunities for Firms from Developing Countries', *International Journal of Technological Learning, Innovation and Development*, 4(1–3): 120–47.

Suckling, J., and Lee, J. (2015), 'Redefining Scope: The True Environmental Impact of Smartphones?' *International Journal of Life Cycle Assessment*, 20(8): 1181–6.

Summan, A., Stacey, N., Birckmayer, J., Blecher, E., Chaloupka, F. J., and Laxminarayan, R. (2020), 'The Potential Global Gains in Health and Revenue from Increased Taxation of Tobacco, Alcohol and Sugar-Sweetened Beverages: A Modelling Analysis', *BMJ Global Health*, 5:e002143.

Sumner, A. (2021), *Deindustrialisation, Distribution and Development* (Oxford: Oxford University Press).

Sumner, A., Ortiz-Juarez, E., and Hoy, C. (2020), *Precarity and the Pandemic: COVID-19 and Poverty Incidence, Intensity, and Severity in Developing Countries*, UNU-WIDER Working Paper No. 77 (Helsinki: United Nations University World Institute for Development Economics Research).

Sun, Y. (1922), *The International Development of China* (New York: G. P. Putnam).

Sweeney, M. (2017), 'Amazon Paid Just £15m in Tax on European revenues of £19.5bn', *Guardian*, 10 August.

Szirmai, A. (2012), 'Industrialisation as an Engine of Growth in Developing Countries, 1950–2005', *Structural Change and Economic Dynamics*, 23(4): 406–20.

TAKEDA, H. (2008), 'Structural Reform of the Family and the Neoliberalisation of Everyday Life in Japan', *New Political Economy*, 13: 153–72.

TAKEDA, H. (2009), 'The Governing of Family Meals in the UK and Japan', in **P. Jackson** (ed.) *Changing Families, Changing Food* (Basingstoke: Palgrave Macmillan), 165–84.

Tansel, C. B. (2017), 'Authoritarian Neoliberalism: Towards a New Research Agenda', in **C. B. Tansel** (ed.), *States of Discipline: Authoritarian Neoliberalism and the Contested Reproduction of Capitalist Order* (London: Rowman & Littlefield International), 1–28.

Tejani, S., and Kucera, D. (2021), 'Defeminization, Structural Transformation and Technological Upgrading in Manufacturing', *Development and Change*, 52(3): 533–73.

The Care Collective (2020), *The Care Manifesto: The Politics of Interdependence* (London: Verso).

The Lancet (2009), 'Sexual and Reproductive Health and Climate Change', *The Lancet*, 374 (19 September): 949.

Thrift, N., Tickell, A., Woolgar, S., and Rupp, W. (2014), *Globalization in Practice* (Oxford: Oxford University Press).

Thun, E. (2008), 'The Globalization of Production', in John Ravenhill (ed.), *Global Political Economy*, 2 (Oxford: Oxford University Press), 346–72.

Tilley, L., and Shilliam, R. (2018), 'Raced Markets: An Introduction', *New Political Economy*, 23: 534–43.

Tilly, C. (1984), *Big Structures, Large Processes, Huge Comparisons* (New York: Russell Sage Foundation).

Tognotti, E. (2013), 'Lessons from the History of Quarantine, from Plague to Influenza A', *Emerging Infectious Disease*, 19(2): 254–59.

Tooker, L. (2017), *Ordinary Democracy: Reading Resistances to Debt after the Global Financial Crisis with Stanley Cavell's Ordinary Language Philosophy*, PhD thesis, University of Warwick.

Tooze, A. (2018), *Crashed: How a Decade of Financial Crises Changed the World* (New York: Viking).

Tooze, A. (2020), 'How Coronavirus Almost Brought Down the Global Financial System', *Guardian*, 16 April.

Tooze, R. (1985), 'International Political Economy', in **S. Smith** (ed.), *International Relations: British and American Perspectives* (Oxford: Basic Blackwell), 108–25.

Trommer, S. (2020), 'Global Trade and Production', in **J. Ravenhill** (ed.), *Global Political Economy*, 6th edn (Oxford: Oxford University Press).

Tsingou, E. (2015), 'Club Governance and the Making of Global Financial Rules', *Review of International Political Economy*, 22(2): 225–56.

Tukker, A., Bulavskaya, T., Giljum, S., et al. (2016), 'Environmental and Resource Footprints in a Global Context: Europe's Structural Deficit in Resource Endowments', *Global Environmental Change*, 40: 171–81.

UN (United Nations) (1948), 'Universal Declaration of Human Rights', https://www.un.org/en/about-us/universal-declaration-of-human-rights, accessed 14 September 2022.

UN (1987), *Report of the World Commission on Environment and Development: Our Common Future* [The Brundtland Report] (Oslo: UN), 20 March, https://sustainabledevelopment.un.org/content/documents/5987our-common-future.pdf, accessed 12 September 2022.

UN (1992), *United Nations Framework Convention on Climate Change*, https://unfccc.int/files/essential_background/background_publications_htmlpdf/application/pdf/conveng.pdf, accessed 13 September 2022.

UN (2015), *Transforming Our World: The 2030 Agenda for Sustainable Development*, https://sdgs.un.org/2030agenda, accessed 13 September 2022.

UN (2019), *World Population Prospects 2019: Highlights* (New York: United Nations, Department of Economic and Social Affairs, Population Division).

UN (2020*a*), 'Trafficking in Women and Girls: Report of the Secretary General', A/75/289, 7 August.

UN (2020*b*), *World Social Report: Inequality in a Rapidly Changing World* (New York: United Nations).

UN (2021), 'Migrant Worker Numbers Rise by Five Million: ILO', 30 June.

UN (2022), 'Sustainable Development Goals: Knowledge Platform', https://sustainabledevelopment.un.org/?menu=1300, accessed 11 September 2022.

UN Department of Economic and Social Affairs, Statistics Division (2021), 'SDG Indicators', https://unstats.un.org/sdgs/indicators/indicators-list/, 12 September 2022.

UN System Coordination Task Team on the Implementation of the UN System Common Position on Drug-related Matters (2019), 'What We Have Learned over the Last Ten Years: A Summary of Knowledge Acquired and Produced by the UN System on Drug-related Matters', March.

UNAIDS (2000), *Report on the Global HIV/AIDS Epidemic* (Geneva: UNAIDS), https://www.unaids.org/sites/default/files/media_asset/2000_gr_en_0.pdf, accessed 12 September 2022.

UNAIDS (2021), 'Press Release: Forty Years on and New UNAIDS Report Gives Evidence That We Can End AIDS', 3 June, https://www.unaids.org/en/resources/presscentre/pressreleaseandstatementarchive/2021/june/20210603_global-commitments-local-action, accessed 12 September 2022.

UNCTAD (United Nations Conference on Trade and Development) (1964), 'Proceedings of the United Nations Conference on Trade and Development', Geneva, https://unctad.org/system/files/official-document/econf46d141vol1_en.pdf, accessed 11 September 2022.

UNCTAD (2013), *Global Value Chains and Development: Investment and Value Added Trade in the Global Economy* (Geneva: United Nations Conference on Trade and Development).

UNCTAD (2017), *Trade and Gender Toolbox: How Will the Economic Partnership Agreement between the European Union and the East African Community Affect Kenyan Women?* (Geneva: United Nations).

UNDP (2017), *The Millennium Development Goals Final Report 2015,* https://www.undp.org/content/undp/en/home/librarypage/mdg/the-millennium-development-goals-report-2015.html, accessed 11 September 2022.

UNIDO (2018), *Global Value Chains and Industrial Development: Lessons from China, South-East and South Asia* (Vienna: United Nations Industrial Development Organization).

Unilever (2020), *A Living Wage*, https://www.unilever.com/planet-and-society/raise-living-standards/a-living-wage/, accessed 11 September 2022.

UNITAID (2013), 'French Levy on Airline Tickets Raises More than One Billion Euros for World's Poor since 2006', 25 January, https://unitaid.org/news-blog/french-levy-on-airline-tickets-raises-more-than-one-billion-euros-for-worlds-poor-since-2006/#en, 12 September 2022.

United Nations Economic Commission for Africa (1990), 'African Alternative Framework to Structural Adjustment Programmes for Socio-economic Recovery and Transformation (AAF-SAP)' (Addis Ababa), https://repository.uneca.org/handle/10855/5670, accessed 11 September 2022.

UNODC (UN Office on Drugs and Crime), (2020*a*), 'World Drug Report: Booklet 2: Drug Use and Health Consequences', Vienna.

UNODC (2020*b*), 'World Drug Report: Booklet 3: Drug Supply', Vienna.

UNODC (2020*c*), *World Wildlife Crime Report 2020: Trafficking in Protected Species* (Vienna: UN Office on Drugs and Crime).

UNU-WIDER (2022), *World Income Inequality Database*, https://www.wider.unu.edu/project/world-income-inequality-database-wiid, accessed 14 September 2022.

US Congress (2019), 'H.Res.109: Recognizing the Duty of the Federal Government to Create a Green New Deal', https://www.congress.gov/bill/116th-congress/house-resolution/109/text, accessed 13 September 2022.

US Department of State (2020), *Trafficking in Persons Report*.

US Department of State (2021), *Trafficking in Persons Report*.

Utting, P. (2008), 'The Struggle for Corporate Accountability', *Development and Change*, 39(6): 959–75.

Vaidyanathan, R. (2020), 'Indian Factory Workers Supplying Major Brands Allege Routine Exploitation', *BBC*, 17 November, https://www.bbc.co.uk/news/world-asia-54960346, accessed 11 September 2022.

Van Biesebroeck, J., and Sturgeon, T. J. (2010), *Effects of the Crisis on the Automotive Industry in Developing Countries: A Global Value Chain Perspective* (Washington DC: World Bank).

Van der Pijl, K. (2007), *Nomads, Empires, States: Modes of Foreign Relations and Political Economy, Volume I* (London: Pluto).

van der Ven, H. (2018), 'Gatekeeper Power: Understanding the Influence of Lead Firms over Transnational Sustainability Standards', *Review of International Political Economy*, 25(5): 624–46.

Van der Zee, B., Levitt, T., and McSweeney, E. (2020), '"Chaotic and Crazy": Meat Plants Around the World Struggle with Virus Outbreaks', *Guardian*, 11 May. https://www.theguardian.com/environment/2020/may/11/chaotic-and-crazy-meat-plants-around-the-world-struggle-with-virus-outbreaks, accessed 12 September 2022.

van Rooij, B., Stern, R. E., and Fürst, K. (2016), 'The Authoritarian Logic of Regulatory Pluralism: Understanding China's New Environmental Actors', *Regulation & Governance*, 10(1): 3–13.

Van Schendel, W., and Abraham, I. (2005) (eds), *Illicit Flows and Criminal Things: States, Borders, and the Other Side of Globalization* (Bloomington: Indiana University Press).

Visser, M. (2016), 'Going Nowhere Fast? Changed Working Conditions on Western Cape Fruit and Wine Farms: A State of Knowledge Review', Working Paper 41, PLAAS, University of the Western Cape, South Africa.

Wacjman, J. (2010), 'Feminist Theories of Technology', *Cambridge Journal of Economics*, 34(1): 143–52.

Wade, R. (1990), *Governing the Market* (Princeton, NJ: Princeton University Press).

Wallerstein, I. (1974), *The Modern World-System*, vol. 1 (New York: Academic Press).

Walsh, J. (2012), 'Mass Migration and the Mass Society: Fordism, Immigration Policy and the Post-war Long Boom in Canada and Australia, 1947–1970', *Journal of Historical Sociology*, 25(3): 352–85.

Waltz, K. (1959), *Man, the State, and War* (New York: Columbia University Press).

Wan, M., (2010), 'The Great Recession and China's Policy Toward Asian Regionalism', *Asian Survey*, 50(3): 520–38.

Wapner, P., and Willoughby, J. (2005), 'The Irony of Environmentalism: The Ecological Futility but Political Necessity of Lifestyle Change', *Ethics & International Affairs*, 19(3): 77–89.

Warde, I. (2010), *Islamic Finance in the Global Economy*, 2nd rev. edn (Edinburgh: Edinburgh University Press).

Waring, M. (1988), *If Women Counted: A New Feminist Economics* (London: Macmillan).

Waylen, G. (2006), 'You Still Don't Understand: Why Troubled Engagements Continue between Feminists and (Critical) IPE', *Review of International Studies*, 32(1): 145–64.

WCED (World Commission on Environment and Development) (1987), *Report of the World Commission on Environment and Development: Our Common Future*, www.un-documents.net/our-common-future.pdf, accessed 13 September 2022.

Webb, C. (2017), 'Between Precarity and Paternalism: Farm Workers and Trade Unions in South Africa's Western Cape Province', *Global Labour Journal*, 8(1): 49–64.

Weber, H. (2015), 'Is IPE Just "Boring", or Committed to Problematic Meta-theoretical Assumptions? A Critical Engagement with the Politics of Method', *Contexto Internacional*, 37(3): 913–44.

Weber, I. M. (2018), 'China and Neoliberalism: Moving Beyond the China Is/Is Not Neoliberal Dichotomy', in **D. Cahill, M. Cooper, and M. Konings** (eds), *The Sage Handbook of Neoliberalism* (London: Sage), 219–33.

Weise, K., and Scheiber, N. (2022), 'Amazon Workers on Staten Island Vote to Unionize in Landmark Win for Labor', *New York Times*, 1 April, https://www.nytimes.com/2022/04/01/technology/amazon-union-staten-island.html, accessed 11 September 2022.

Weiss, T. G. (2009), 'What Happened to the Idea of World Government?' *International Studies Quarterly*, 53(2): 253–71.

Weiss, T. G., and Browne, S. (2021) (eds), *Routledge Handbook on the UN and Development* (London: Routledge).

Weiss, T. G., Carayannis, T., and Jolly, R. (2009), 'The "Third" United Nations', *Global Governance*, 15(2): 123–42.

Weiss, T. G., and Roy, P. (2017) (eds), *The UN and the Global South, 1945 and 2015: Past as Prelude?* (London: Routledge).

Weiss, T. G., and Thakur, R. (2010), *Global Governance and the UN: An Unfinished Journey* (Bloomington: Indiana University Press).

Weiss, T. G., and Wilkinson, R. (2018), 'The Globally Governed: Everyday Global Governance', *Global Governance*, 24(2): 193–210.

Weiss, T. G., and Wilkinson, R. (2019), *Rethinking Global Governance* (Cambridge: Polity).

Wellner, G., and Rothman, T. (2020), 'Feminist AI: Can We Expect Our AI Systems to Become Feminist?' *Philosophy & Technology*, 33(2): 191–205.

Werner, M., and Bair, J. (2019), 'Global Value Chains and Uneven Development: A Disarticulations Perspective', in **S. Ponte, G. Gereffi, and G. Raj-Reichert** (eds), *Handbook on Global Value Chains* (Cheltenham: Edward Elgar).

West, R., and Marteau, T. (2013), 'Commentary on Casswell (2013): The Commercial Determinants of Health', *Addiction*, 108(4): 686–87.

Westad, A. (2005), *The Global Cold War* (Cambridge: Cambridge University Press).

White, C., and Nafilyan, V. (2020), 'Coronavirus (COVID-19) Related Deaths by Ethnic Group, England and Wales: 2 March 2020 to 15 May 2020', Office for National Statistics, London, UK, https://www.ons.gov.uk/peoplepopulationandcommunity/birthsdeathsandmarriages/deaths/articles/coronaviruscovid19relateddeathsbyethnicgroupenglandandwales/2march2020to15may2020, accessed 11 September 2022.

White, R., and Pink, G. (2017), 'Responding to Organised Environmental Crimes: Collaborative Approaches and Capacity Building', *South African Crime Quarterly*, 60: 37–44.

WHO (World Health Organization) (n.d.*a*), 'The Global Health Observatory', https://www.who.int/data/gho, accessed 12 September 2022.

WHO (n.d.*b*), 'Health Workforce', https://www.who.int/health-topics/health-workforce#tab=tab_1, accessed 12 September 2022.

WHO (1946), 'Constitution of the World Health Organization', http://apps.who.int/gb/bd/PDF/bd47/EN/constitution-en.pdf?ua=1, accessed 12 September 2022.

WHO (2003), 'WHO Framework Convention on Tobacco Control', https://fctc.who.int/who-fctc/overview, accessed 12 September 2022.

WHO (2008), *Closing the Gap in a Generation: Health Equity Through Action on the Social Determinants of Health—Final Report of the Commission on Social Determinants of Health* (Geneva: WHO), https://www.who.int/publications/i/item/WHO-IER-CSDH-08.1, accessed 12 September 2022.

WHO (2013), 'The Helsinki Statement on Health in All Policies 2013'.

WHO (2017), *Ten Years in Public Health, 2007–2017* (Geneva: WHO), http://apps.who.int/iris/bitstream/handle/10665/255355/9789241512442-eng.pdf;jsessionid=7A7AE3851DDAEE9CB70B16C2AAFBC8C2?sequence=1, accessed 12 September 2022.

WHO (2020), 'The Top 10 Causes of Death', 9 December, https://www.who.int/news-room/fact-sheets/detail/the-top-10-causes-of-death, accessed 12 September 2022.

Wickramasinghe, A. I. I. N., and Wimalaratana, W. (2016), 'International Migration and Migration Theories', *Social Affairs: A Journal for the Social Sciences*, 1(5): 13–32.

Wiedmann, T., and Lenzen, M. (2018), 'Environmental and Social Footprints of International Trade', *Nature Geoscience*, 11: 314–21.

Wight, C. (2019), 'Bringing the Outside In: The Limits of Theoretical Fragmentation and Pluralism in IR Theory', *Politics*, 39(1): 64–81.

Wilkinson, R. (2014), *What's Wrong with the WTO and How to Fix It* (John Wiley).

Williams, E. (1944), *Capitalism and Slavery* (Chapel Hill: University of North Carolina Press).

Williamson, J. (2002), *Did the Washington Consensus Fail?* Peterson Institute for International Affairs, https://www.piie.com/commentary/

speeches-papers/did-washington-consensus-fail, accessed 11 September 2022.

Williamson, P. (2021), 'De-Globalisation and Decoupling: Post-COVID-19 Myths Versus Realities', *Management and Organization Review*, 17(1): 29–34.

Willis, M. M., and Schor, J. B. (2012), 'Does Changing a Light Bulb Lead to Changing the World? Political Action and the Conscious Consumer', *Annals of the American Academy of Political and Social Science*, 644(1): 160–90.

Winecoff, W. K. (2017), 'How Did International Political Economy Become Reductionist? A Historiography of the Discipline', in **W. R. Thompson** (ed.), *Oxford Research Encyclopedia of Politics* (Oxford: Oxford University Press), 1–31.

Withers, M. (2019), *Sri Lanka's Remittance Economy: A Multiscalar Analysis of Migration-Underdevelopment* (London and New York: Routledge).

Wolf, M. (2005), *Why Globalization Works* (New Haven, CT: Yale University Press).

World Bank (1995), *World Development Report: Workers in an Integrating World* (New York).

World Bank (2013), *Measuring the Real Size of the World Economy: The Framework, Methodology, and Results of the International Comparison Program—ICP* (Washington, DC: World Bank).

World Bank (2018), *Stagnant Poverty Reduction in Latin America* (Washington, DC: World Bank).

World Bank (2020a), *Poverty and Shared Prosperity 2020: Reversals of Fortune* (Washington, DC: World Bank)

World Bank (2020b), *World Development Report 2020: Trading for Development in the Age of Global Value Chains* (Washington, DC: World Bank).

World Bank (2021a), 'Data: Life Expectancy at Birth, Total (Years)', https://data.worldbank.org/indicator/SP.DYN.LE00.IN, accessed 11 September 2022.

World Bank (2021b), 'Data: Poverty', https://data.worldbank.org/topic/poverty, accessed 11 September 2022.

World Bank (2021c), *International Debt Statistics 2022* (Washington, DC: World Bank).

World Bank (2021d), 'PovcalNet', March update, http://iresearch.worldbank.org/PovcalNet/povOnDemand.aspx.

World Bank (2021e), 'Who We Are', https://www.worldbank.org/en/who-we-are, accessed 11 September 2022.

World Bank (2022), 'World Development Indicators', https://databank.worldbank.org/source/world-development-indicators, accessed 12 September 2022.

World Bank, Equity Lab for Latin America (2021), https://www.worldbank.org/en/topic/poverty/lac-equity-lab1/ethnicity/ethnicity-poverty, accessed 31 July 2022.

World Inequality Database (n.d.), https://wid.world/, accessed 14 September 2022.

Worstall, T. (2016), 'India Loses WTO Solar Appeal Against US—As It Should: Next, India's WTO Solar Case Against US', *Forbes*, 17 September, https://www.forbes.com/sites/timworstall/2016/09/17/india-loses-wto-solar-appeal-against-us-as-it-should-next-indias-wto-solar-case-against-us/?sh=42214d217674, accessed 13 September 2022.

Wouters, O. J., McKee, M., and Luyten, J. (2020), 'Estimated Research and Development Investment Needed to Bring a New Medicine to Market, 2009–2018', *Journal of the American Medical Association*, 323(9): 844–53.

Wouters, O. J., Shadlen, K. C., Salcher-Konrad, M., et al. (2021), 'Challenges in Ensuring Global Access to COVID-19 Vaccines: Production, Affordability, Allocation, and Deployment', *The Lancet*, 397 (10278): 1023–34.

Wright, C., and Rwabizambuga, A. (2006), 'Institutional Pressures, Corporate Reputation, and Voluntary Codes of Conduct: An Examination of the Equator Principles', *Business and Society Review*, 111(1): 89–117.

Wright, L. (2019), 'No More Silence: Companies Must Address Caste in Their Global Supply Chains', 25 September 2019, Ethical Trade Initiative, London, available at: www.ethicaltrade.org/blog/no-more-silence-companies-must-address-caste-their-global-supply-chains

WTO (World Trade Organization) (n.d.a), 'India etc. Versus US: "Shrimp-Turtle"', https://www.wto.org/english/tratop_e/envir_e/edis08_e.htm, accessed 13 September 2022.

WTO (n.d.b), 'WTO Rules and Environmental Policies: GATT Exceptions', https://www.wto.org/english/tratop_e/envir_e/envt_rules_exceptions_e.htm, accessed 13 September 2022.

WTO (2000), 'WTO Negotiations: Agriculture and Developing Countries', Speech, Paris, 6 December, http://www.wto.org/english/news_e/spmm_e/spmm47_e.htm, accessed 11 September 2022.

WTO (2013), *World Trade Report* (Geneva: World Trade Organization).

WTO (2021a), *Evolution of Trade Under the WTO: Handy Statistics* (Geneva: World Trade

Organization), https://www.wto.org/english/res_e/statis_e/trade_evolution_e/evolution_trade_wto_e.htm, accessed 11 September 2022.

WTO (2021*b*), 'Overview', https://www.wto.org/english/thewto_e/whatis_e/wto_dg_stat_e.htm, accessed 11 September 2022.

WTO (2022), 'Current Status of Disputes'. Available from www.wto.org/english/tratop_e/dispu_e/dispu_current_status_e.htm, accessed 28 December 2022.

WTO Trade Monitoring Database, https://tmdb.wto.org/en/explore#page=1&members=&g20=0&measure_type=&measureclass=r&after_dt=2008-10-01&before_dt=2019-10-31&affected_members=&product_chapters=

Wullweber, J. (2019), 'Monism vs. Pluralism, the Global Financial Crisis, and the Methodological Struggle in the Field of International Political Economy', *Competition and Change*, 23(3): 287–311.

Xiang, B., and Lindquist, J. (2014), 'Migration Infrastructure', *International Migration Review*, 48(1): 122–48.

Yan, X. (2021), 'Becoming Strong: The New Chinese Foreign Policy', *Foreign Affairs*, July/August.

Young, K. L. (2021), 'Progress, Pluralism and Science: Moving from Alienated to Engaged Pluralism', *Review of International Political Economy*, 28(2): 406–20.

Young, K. L., Goldman, S., O'Connor, B., and Chuluun, T. (2021), 'How White is the Global Elite? An Analysis of Race, Gender and Network Structure', *Global Networks*, 21(2): 365–92.

Yu, X., and Ngai, P. (2011), 'Walmartization, Corporate Social Responsibility, and the Labor Standards of Toy Factories in South China', in **A. Chan** (ed.), *Walmart in China* (Cornell University Press), 54–70.

Yusuf, A. A. (2021), 'Time to Revisit Our Standard of Deprivation', Center of Sustainable Development Goals Studies, Universitas Padjadjaran.

Zürn, M. (2018), *A Theory of Global Governance: Authority, Legitimacy, and Contestation* (Oxford: Oxford University Press).